The German Dictatorship

The German Dictatorship

THE ORIGINS, STRUCTURE, AND EFFECTS OF NATIONAL SOCIALISM

Karl Dietrich Bracher

Translated from the German by Jean Steinberg
With an Introduction by Peter Gay

HOLT, RINEHART AND WINSTON
New York   Chicago   San Francisco   Atlanta
Dallas   Montreal   Toronto   London   Sydney

Published in the United States of America in 1970
by Praeger Publishers, Inc.

1 038 10

Originally published in Germany by Verlag Kiepenheuer & Witsch
under the title *Die deutsche Diktatur: Entstehung, Struktur,
Folgen des Nationalsozialismus.* © 1969 by Verlag Kiepenheuer
& Witsch Köln Berlin

© 1970 by Praeger Publishers, Inc.

Library of Congress Catalog Card Number: 70–95662

Printed in the United States of America

For Christian and Susanne

Introduction

Peter Gay

For those over forty, the Nazi nightmare remains a brooding omni-presence, a decisive experience. It has prompted disparate attempts to come to terms with a world capable of such organized sadism, such cowardice and cruelty: flight into hedonism as the only refuge from such a world, return to religion as the only salvation in such a world, reaffirmation of Enlightenment values—defiant in the face of so much unpalatable evidence—as the only rational method of triumphing over such a world. But whatever their reponse might be, all those who have the Nazi experience in their bones share one characteristic: they take it with deadly seriousness. And in consequence they rage at the facile abuse of the terrible words of the 1940's that disfigure so much of our discourse today. They resent casual use of the name Auschwitz—which should be sacred to us, and used sparingly, always recalling those who were there or in other, similar hells; the employment of the ominous word "genocide"; the obscene Soviet propaganda campaign that likens Zionism to Nazism. Such trivializing of the awesome is itself evidence that the world is a beastly place—impatient with precision, anxious to set memories aside, callous, heartlessly forgetful. To those over forty, the Nazi nightmare, terrible and oppressive as it is, remains a memory to be, in some special sense, cherished—that is, to be kept inviolate, intact, remembered as the tragic but indispensable counterpoint of a saner, humane view of the world and even of our time.

Those under forty—and, of course, particularly those under twenty —are haunted by no such ghosts. The Nazi dictatorship is mere history to them. In their indiscriminate indictment of modern society, they tend to treat the Nazi crimes as no less reprehensible, certainly, but also as no more reprehensible than the bombing of Dresden or the war in Vietnam. They see no incongruity in wearing Iron Crosses as sheer baubles, or in making easy references to concentration camps. And, in their ignorance and vast goodwill, they are likely to suspect that their

elders' obsessive harping on Hitler and on the extermination camps is
a form of self-absorbed self-pity, or, worse, a sly evasion of the evils
that beset *them*. Not for the first time, and, doubtless, not for the last,
innocence and experience confront one another in baffled incompre-
hension.

Karl Dietrich Bracher's *The German Dictatorship,* the first serious
comprehensive history of the Nazi phenomenon, is a gift to both the
old and the young. Is it too much to hope that it may even come to
serve as a bridge—slender but sturdy—between them? Not surprisingly,
in their effort to grasp the Nazi experience, those over forty have
easily been victimized by simplifying myths. They have adopted the
hostile myth of the "bad German," which holds that Nazism is a pure
and typically German phenomenon, or the apologetic myth of "mass
politics," which holds that Nazism is a twentieth-century disease quite
uncharacteristic of the nation of poets and thinkers and in fact
smuggled into Germany through the twin evils of modern technology
and mass democracy. Karl Dietrich Bracher has no truck with these,
or other, myths; he rejects the easy comfort of simplistic explanations.
With a grip as firm on nineteenth-century and European history as it
is on twentieth-century and German history, he is committed to the
"multicausal character of historical-political processes." A good deal
has been written on both sides of the question of professionalism:
here, I think, in the firm rejection of easy answers, is one advantage
the professional is likely to have over the amateur historian. It is significant, and one of the central virtues of this book, that nearly one
half of it is given over to the period before 1933. *The German Dictatorship* is a synthesis, and a masterly one, and more than other works of
history, a historical synthesis makes judgments by its mode of selection.
It reveals much by what it leaves out, by what it includes, and by what
it chooses to emphasize. Professor Bracher is perfectly ready to devote
some pages to the European background of the rise of Nazism; he
recognizes the universal tendencies that make democratic societies and
parliamentary regimes vulnerable in our time. But he seeks to explain,
never to obscure or apologize: German society, German history, German
styles of thinking made Germany particularly susceptible to the Nazi
bacillus. This is the meaning of the allocation of space governing his
long opening chapters. Nor does Professor Bracher, as a true historian,
neglect the immediate circumstances preceding and surrounding the
Nazi seizure of power. For some years now, in his path-breaking studies
on the collapse of the Weimar Republic and the early years of the Nazi
rule, he has insisted that the end of Weimar was not inevitable; the
Republic was sickly from the beginning, crowded with ineffectual
friends and implacable enemies, but to read the Third Reich into the
events of 1918 to 1920 is to practice impermissible hindsight. In true
synthetic fashion, *The German Dictatorship* offers a difficult but wholly
successful amalgam of long-range and short-range history, structural
and narrative history, intellectual, sociological, economic, and political

history. With its obvious, authoritative control over a vast array of material, the book debunks myths with its very sobriety.

This is the service the book can perform for those for whom Nazism remains a living, hideous reality. And for the young? Here, too, its tone is bound to make its point: It will gain a hearing with its unwillingness to shout amidst the clamor. Perhaps the most sensational aspect of *The German Dictatorship* is its refusal to be sensational. This, I think, is the best way, perhaps the only way, of serving the young: to relieve their ignorance by offering them not panaceas, not quick generalizations, but the truth.

The craft of history has two tasks to perform: to tell the truth about the past insofar as it lies in fallible men to tell the truth; and to give passing events a lasting memorial, mortal men, immortality. The two tasks may be distinct, but they are related, for if the historian tries to perform his second task without the most scrupulous attention to the first, he has failed in them both. In fulfilling this double task, *The German Dictatorship* is an impressive achievement. Quietly, never raising his voice, but with an intensity that is palpable just beneath the surface, Professor Bracher discusses the murderers and the victims; his section on the mass murder of the Jews is terrible in its authority. And, intent on remembering without distorting, he finds room for the resistance to Hitler, pathetic, scattered, often belated, though, as he reminds us, for some exceptional Germans resistance was persistent, faithful, self-sacrificial. Even here, where the temptation must have been almost irresistible, Karl Dietrich Bracher keeps his voice down and lets the men and the events testify for themselves.

But this is not all. Professor Bracher is a historian, and it is as a historian that he has written this masterly analysis. But he is also a German and a democrat, and it is in this latter role that he closes his book with a chapter on the reappearance of extreme right-wing groups and ideas in the Bonn Republic. "The German dictatorship has failed," he writes, "but German democracy has not yet been secured." He has written *The German Dictatorship,* as he notes in the Preface, in the hope that a portrait of the Nazi dictatorship that is free of illusions may help to check the dangers that threaten German democracy today. Whether this hope is realized or not, he has written a most remarkable book.

Preface

This book attempts to enlarge upon a series of detailed special studies by the author and at the same time to provide a comprehensive treatment of National Socialism—its presuppositions, rule, and aftereffects. It further deals with the problem of the authoritarian concept of the state and politics which in the nineteenth and twentieth centuries blocked the development of parliamentary and democratic structures and behavior and ultimately made the German dictatorship possible. The critical analysis and interpretation of German political life spans the years from the capitulation of bourgeois liberalism before the monarchic *Obrigkeitsstaat* and the unresisting collapse of the Weimar Republic to the latent threats to the Federal Republic.

The German tendency for dictatorship, which ultimately found realization in a ruling system of unprecedented seductive and destructive power, reflects organizational structural problems of the modern state and of bourgeois society in the transition to the democratic era characteristic of all European countries. But it is a tendency which was given unique sharpness and had unique consequences because of the special conditions and problems surrounding the process of nation-building and socio-economic modernization in Germany—a process which in the past has led to serious dislocations of political life and social behavior.

In examining this problem, the author has tried to combine historical description and systematic analysis. The discussion of the sociopolitical and ideological presuppositions is followed by a history of National Socialism beginning before Hitler and World War I—its organization and tactics under the Weimar Republic and its victory in a revolution *sui generis*. The Third Reich is presented in all its complex domestic, foreign, social, and intellectual aspects; persecution and resistance are discussed in the context of the totalitarian regime. The final chapter discusses the problem of the survival of radical Right tendencies in the Federal Republic. National Socialism is not dead, nor has the fascist era come to a final close. Many of its presuppositions are still with us in this era of global modernization; the developing countries of the Third World have brought new problems.

This work attempts to understand the multiplicity of conditions and causes, the multicausal nature of historico-political processes. This involves the rejection of single-tracked, ultimately ideological formulas and interpretations in favor of an integrating approach. Any attempt to reduce the subject to individual aspects would ignore its complexity, regardless of the important contributions of economic, sociological, intellectual, or institutional interpretations. This applies to the controversial application of a comprehensive theory of totalitarianism as well as to a broad concept of fascism—both generalizations which must not be permitted to distort the specifics and the concrete manifestations of the various related systems. However, such an approach raises questions of historical interpretation which in turn lead into the realm of the social sciences and call for an analysis of the German political structure and system that goes beyond mere description.

Two stimulating visits, one at the Center for Advanced Study in the Behavioral Sciences at Stanford and one at the Institute for Advanced Study at Princeton, gave the author the welcome opportunity to write this work in stimulating proximity to American and European colleagues from various disciplines. The book is dedicated to the hope that a sober picture of the German dictatorship may help avoid both old and new dangers, primarily the traditional authoritarian concept of the state, but also a radical utopianism—both expressions of intolerance and conceit, and, moreover, profoundly unpolitical modes of behavior.

K. D. BRACHER

Bonn
July, 1970

Contents

The German Dictatorship

I

The Preconditions

PROBLEMS OF INTERPRETATION

Although many studies have been devoted to the phenomenon of National Socialism, the controversy surrounding the subject continues. A number of detailed, critical analyses, beginning with Konrad Heiden's probing accounts, offer a comprehensive picture of Hitler's rule in Germany and Europe. In addition to the studies of totalitarianism and the key figure of Adolf Hitler published outside Germany after Hitler's rise to power, there exist numerous special studies dealing with specific aspects of Hitler's rule. A more recent attempt at a comprehensive treatment even became a world-wide best seller.[1]

Inherent in all these studies is the question of how a dictatorial regime of such dimensions could come to power so quickly and with so little or no resistance in a country with Germany's traditions and cultural heritage. But while the studies generally agree on how National Socialism developed and how it was structured, there is little agreement on its roots. Most treat the antecedents and rise of National Socialism superficially and summarily, as a logical end product of German historical development, the result of the intellectual, social, and political climate of nineteenth- and twentieth-century German life. This sort of shorthand, which seems to underlie Shirer's book also, is based on stereotypes about the preconditions of the National Socialist "movement." Yet, the question does remain why Germany, which after a century-long battle for democratic government had constructed, in the Weimar Republic, a seemingly perfect constitutional

---

[1] William L. Shirer, *The Rise and Fall of the Third Reich* (New York, 1960). For the best introduction to the problems and course of German history during the nineteenth and twentieth centuries, see Hajo Holborn, *A History of Modern Germany*, Vol. III: *1840–1945* (New York, 1969).

structure, capitulated unresistingly and within so short a period before so primitive a dictatorship as Hitler's. A study of the Nazi
takeover, or even of the Weimar Republic, cannot in itself furnish the
explanation for the "German catastrophe" of 1933.

The more remote antecedents and broad preconditions of National
Socialism are generally treated from the point of view of two overlapping yet diametrically opposed theses. The one sees the idea of
the German Reich and nation as the root of National Socialism, and
goes back to the Reformation and even to the Middle Ages in attempting to prove that a long tradition of nationalism, imperialism, and
authoritarian rule helped to shape the German political character.
Typical examples of this school of thought are the studies by the
French scholar Edmond Vermeil, as well as various books by British
and American authors who subscribe to this thesis.[2] The other school
emphatically maintains that National Socialism, like modern totalitarianism as a whole, is a twentieth-century phenomenon,[3] one of the
dictatorial movements which sprang up and came to power in many
countries and which, accordingly, must be viewed against the background of the intellectual, social, and political climate of Europe in an
era of world wars. Even though the spokesmen for this viewpoint
stress the special supranational conditions of our century, they do
not dismiss historical factors. They simply put the main emphasis on
the common European roots of the totalitarian trend. The real cause,
they maintain, is the revolutionary ferment that began at the end of
the eighteenth century, the growing class antagonism in the industrial
age, the loss of individuality and the collectivization of man, the complexity of the economic structure, and capitalism's proneness to crisis.
Ascribing the rise of dictatorial-authoritarian mass movements and
the capitulation of the free individual before the total state to these
supranational factors permits the conclusion that neither an individual
nor a people can be held fully responsible for the consequences of such
capitulation. Some have even gone so far as to claim that Germany, in
particular, was not prepared for the events that led to the triumph of
National Socialism.[4] They see the Hitler regime as a misfortune that,
given similar conditions, can befall any people; the catastrophe of 1918
and the severity of the economic crises of 1923 and 1930—and not a
specifically German predilection for dictatorship and power politics—
are held responsible for the political crisis and revolution in Germany,
as they are for the earlier upheavals in Russia and Italy. The dictator-

[2] Edmond Vermeil, *L'Allemagne, Essai d'explication* (Paris, 1945), and
Doctrinaires de la révolution allemande (Paris, 1938). Rohan Butler, *The
Roots of National Socialism* (London, 1941; New York, 1968).

[3] Gerhard Leibholz, "Das Phänomen des totalen Staates," in *Strukturprobleme der modernen Demokratie* (Karlsruhe, 1958), p. 225.

[4] Especially Gerhard Ritter, "The Historical Foundations of the Rise of
Socialism," in *The Third Reich, A Study Published under the Auspices of
the International Council for Philosophy and Humanistic Studies with the
Assistance of UNESCO* (New York, 1955), pp. 38 ff.

ships which defeated democracy in Spain and Portugal, in Poland and the Balkans, are also to be seen in this context.

Most existing analyses of National Socialism fall into the framework of these two theses.[5] The one extreme is given expression by Vermeil:

> At various periods in their history, particularly in the nineteenth century, the Germans have believed with a desperate conviction, born either of their internal divisions and weaknesses or, on the contrary, of the idea of a sovereign and invincible power, that they have a divine mission, that Germany has been singled out by Providence. . . . This irrational and fervent faith is the outcome of a historical development which, throughout the centuries, gives the German imagination, with its combination of fanatical nationalism and preoccupation with internal cohesion, precedents which it can never forget and on which it builds up limitless aspirations.[6]

Vermeil bases his interpretation of all of German history since the Teutonic invasion on this concept. In his view, the Germanization of the Reich idea, the rise of the Hanseatic League, and the expansion of Prussia were the first milestones; German mysticism and the Reformation were particularly distinctive forms of an early sense of uniqueness and mission; and, lastly, the conflict between German and Western political thought since the beginning of the nineteenth century, as well as German Romanticism, was the final stage on the road to doom. The degeneration of the German national idea since the Bismarckian era through imperialism and anti-Semitism is held to be the inevitable consequence of this development. Finally, the Weimar Republic is seen primarily as a preparation for the Third Reich:

> Hitler would never have established the totalitarian dictatorship he did establish in January, 1933, if his Party, so to speak under the mantle of the Weimar Republic, had not revived the essential themes of Pan-Germanic imperialism, reinforcing them with an extremely powerful propaganda machine, and if, on the other hand, the Schachts, von Seeckts, and Stresemanns had not reorganized industry and the banking system, the army and foreign policy. This dual effort is the really significant feature of the Weimar episode, and throws a revealing light not only on the past but also on the future of the German Reich.[7]

Gerhard Ritter, a leading German historian, has defended the opposite thesis, not without a note of apology:

[5] For an exemplary presentation of the different viewpoints, see *The Third Reich, op. cit.*

[6] Edmond Vermeil, "The Origin, Nature, and Development of German Nationalist Ideology in the 19th and 20th Centuries," in *ibid.*, pp. 6 ff.

[7] *Ibid.*, p. 111.

The Germans themselves were more surprised than anyone else by the rapid rise of the National-Socialist Party to a position in which over-all power in the state was at its disposal. Up to 1930 the vast majority of educated Germans thought Hitler's disciples to be a group of loud-mouthed extremists and super-patriots without any practical importance. . . . All agreed, however . . . that it must be regarded as the result of the effervescence of troubled times—all agreed not to take its leaders and its programme seriously. . . . There is no doubt that the majority of educated Germans—that part of the nation which was consciously aware of its historical traditions—was very distrustful of the Hitler propaganda, which assured them that his movement was continuing and fulfilling the best traditions and hopes of German history; very many felt at the time of Hitler's victory that his political system was foreign to them.

True, Ritter says, there have been excesses in the German past. "But was all this peculiar to Germany? It is surprising how many expressions of nationalist ambitions, of militarist mentality, of racial pride, and anti-democratic criticism are to be found in the literature of ideas, especially political literature, of any European country." [8]

There has been no dearth of studies attempting to weigh these contradictory notions critically against each other, among them one by the French historian Jacques Droz. In a comprehensive discussion, he reduces the problem of German guilt to three main arguments:

1. The teachings of Luther helped to make the Germans servile and subservient to the state.

2. Prussian militarism inculcated them with a love of armies and the wish to prove their superiority in this realm for the purpose of conquest.

3. The quest for power, intensified by Germany's astonishing progress during the Industrial Revolution, as well as by the pressure of its growing population, culminated in a policy of expansionism.

Droz, subjecting these postulates to sober examination, arrives at these conclusions:

1. Lutheranism cannot be held responsible for the political passivity of the broad masses, for while other nations in the era of religious wars rebelled against established authority, Lutheranism flourished under the rule of like-minded benevolent princes. Apart from that, however, acts of political courage were no rarer in Germany than elsewhere. It is, therefore, unfair to speak of a "spirit of servility" in connection with Lutheranism. On the other hand, it cannot be denied that the Protestant church, particularly in the nineteenth century, supported conservative trends and thus helped to inhibit progress.

2. The Prussian tradition must not be equated with a spirit of conquest and aggression. The only wars fought by Frederick the Great were Cabinet wars, and Bismarck, too, considered war only as a political tool. Still, the military aristocracy was held in high esteem,

[8] Ritter, *op. cit.*, pp. 381 ff.

and, consequently, military training and preparedness were given greater emphasis in Germany than elsewhere.

3. Pan-German organizations and ideas were never as influential in Germany as they are reputed to have been. But, on the other hand, the power ambitions of heavy industry and its role in the rise of Hitler cannot be disputed.[9]

In addition to such interpretations, we have the socio-economic school of thought, advanced most consistently in Marxist-oriented literature. Yet, the Communists have generally presented this point of view in so partisan and polemical a fashion that scholarly research tends to ignore this approach. Among the exceptions to the one-sidedness of the Marxist treatment is the work of the Hungarian philosopher and sociologist Georg Lukács. Yet Lukács is not so much concerned with socio-economic analysis as with a broad examination of the antirational and irrational ideologies of the nineteenth and twentieth centuries, which he sees as the roots of National Socialism.[10] The most important attempt at a socio-economic interpretation is to be found in the pioneering study of the German-American social scientist Franz Neumann.[11] He maintains that the origin, rise, and rule of National Socialism did not constitute a social and political revolution but simply manifested an extreme crisis of capitalism, and that the Third Reich, in effect, was the political system of a "totalitarian monopoly capitalism." It is Neumann's contention that the old ruling class continued at the helm after 1933, that the social structure remained unchanged, and that National Socialism was, in fact, a mass movement of the middle class pitted against the mass movement of the workers, a counterrevolution in the service, and a tool, of the capitalist system. Such an interpretation runs the risk of misjudging the revolutionary component of National Socialism, which cannot be dismissed as being simply reactionary. Rather, from the very outset, and particularly as it developed into the SS state, National Socialism aimed at a transformation of state and society. Neumann himself ultimately conceded that Hitler's seizure of power was impelled by the breaking through of vital noneconomic factors.

THE EUROPEAN BACKGROUND

Past research has made clear that an examination of the roots of National Socialism must be conducted simultaneously on two levels: the German and the over-all European. To date, not enough attention has been paid to this dual aspect. Most discussions treat either the Ger-

[9] Jacques Droz, "Les historiens français devant l'histoire allemande," in *Europa: Erbe und Aufgabe* (Wiesbaden, 1956), pp. 265 f.

[10] Georg Lukácz, *Die Zerstörung der Vernunft* (rev. ed.; Neuwied, 1962).

[11] Franz L. Neumann, *Behemoth: The Structure and Practice of National Socialism, 1933–1944* (2d rev. ed.; New York, 1944).

man or the European aspect of the early history of National Socialism.
The comparative study of the German, Italian, and French types of
fascism, which has helped Ernst Nolte to develop a typology of fascism on the European plane, is a step in the right direction.[12] But
Nolte's work is primarily an intellectual history of the three movements. Their political and social roots should not be neglected, and
similar phenomena in other countries (Spain and the Balkans, for example) deserve closer attention. Once such broader studies are undertaken, the sweepingly polemical concept of "fascism" could be broadened
to include the far more deep-rooted and widespread phenomenon of the
revolt against liberal democracy in many parts of Europe.

Ever since the end of the eighteenth century, Europe has been in the
throes of far-reaching structural changes of state, society, and economy. It is not unreasonable to maintain that the political, social, and
intellectual repercussions of this process ushered in an era of revolutions, or even an era of revolution. That is to say, we are dealing with
a single, interrelated process that dates from the storming of the Bastille and proceeds to the communist, fascist, and even the African and
Asian revolutions of our time. This modern concept of revolution ex-
amines the pattern of social upheavals beginning with the liberal
emancipation movement of the bourgeoisie during the rise of capitalism, followed by the socialist demand for equal rights, and, finally,
the power aspirations of the rapidly growing masses of the "fourth
estate" in the industrial age. After the Glorious Revolution, in the
age of the great philosophers of the Enlightenment, Europe was
caught up in a wave of unprecedented political passion which, filled
with revolutionary fervor, burst through the narrow framework of
absolutist rule and traditional order.

In France, this movement marked the beginning of a broad democratization, an extension of political activity to all areas of public life.
It spelled the birth of the age of popular movements and ideologies.
The paths of modern democracy and modern dictatorship began to
draw close to each other during the French Revolution. At that time,
the typical postulates of a new, all-embracing state and social order
which marked the victorious progress of democracy as well as of its
dictatorial-totalitarian counterpart made their first appearance: the
socialization and politicization of all citizens; majority rule and the
mobilization of the people through elections and ideological propaganda; the intensification of communal and civic awareness through
the new idea of a militant, exclusive nationalism, accompanied by a
militaristic extension of the idea of national defense via popular armies
into universal military training and arming; and, in dialectic contradiction to this last postulate, the imperialist claim of a universal mission. In sum, this development might be called the assertion of the

---

[12] Ernst Nolte, *The Three Faces of Fascism* (New York, 1966). See also
Eugen Weber, *Action Française* (Stanford, 1962) and *The Varieties of Fascism* (Princeton, 1964); and Francis L. Carsten, *The Reichswehr and Politics, 1918 to 1933* (Oxford, 1966) and *The Rise of Fascism* (Berkeley, 1967).

rule of the autonomous individual within the state yet at the same time a manifestation of the threat posed to him by this modern, all-encompassing state. These factors have prompted historians like J. L. Talmon to look for a close link between democracy and totalitarian dictatorship.[13] The phenomenon of the Communist "people's democracies," with their pseudo-democratic legitimization of a totalitarian new order, seem to bear this out as convincingly as the pseudo-democratic claims of National Socialism, which also resorted to elections and plebiscites and perfected the mobilization and politicization of the population.

According to this view, the totalitarian movements are the children of the age of democracy, having grown out of and being part of the problems and distortions of popular democracy; in this way, they differ from the prerevolutionary and predemocratic autocracy of absolutism. The political awakening of the populace is the decisive factor in this development. Since then, the face of dictatorship has also changed. It employs different methods and enhances its chances of winning universal, total control by utilizing, manipulating, and distorting the dynamic ideas of freedom and brotherhood of the democratic movement; it lays claim to the will and the sovereignty of the people as the basis for political rule; it proclaims itself the executor of history, of historical necessity; it stresses the higher legitimacy of its rule and clothes its seizure of power in pseudo-legal garb; it hides and intensifies dictatorial rule behind the screen of pseudo-democratically, pseudo-plebiscitarian–controlled elections and mass meetings, of acclamation and propaganda; it poses as the true, total democracy which will, if necessary, force happiness on its citizens. The absolutism of Rousseau's *volonté générale* apparently furnishes the justification for democracy and dictatorship alike.[14]

To be sure, modern dictatorship differs from absolutism insofar as it calls for the extinction of the individual. It forces him into mass organizations and commits him to a political creed which becomes a "political religion," a binding religious surrogate. This exaltation of the political rests on the absoluteness of a political myth: in the case of Fascism, the myth is of an imperial past; in the case of Communism, of a socialist-utopian future; and in the case of National Socialism, of racial superiority. Yet, despite the validity of this analysis, it is nonetheless inconclusive. National Socialism and its precursors essentially saw themselves as the great historical countermovements to the French Revolution and all it brought in its wake, as movements

[13] Jacob L. Talmon, *The Origins of Totalitarian Democracy* (New York, 1961).

[14] For a broad discussion of Rousseau, see Iring Fetscher, *Rousseaus politische Philosophie* (Neuwied, 1960); Alfred Cobban, *Rousseau and the Modern State* (London and Hamden, Conn., 1964); Otto Vossler, *Rousseaus Freiheitslehre* (Göttingen, 1963); Roger D. Masters, *The Political Philosophy of Rousseau* (Princeton, 1968); and, especially, John W. Chapman, *Rousseau—Totalitarian or Liberal?* (New York, 1956).

against liberalism and libertarian democracy, against individual and human rights, against Western civilization and international socialism. Its affinity for reactionary conservatism shaped both the aims and ideas of its adherents and, ultimately, helped it come to victory. The eradication of liberalism and individualism was the primary self-appointed goal of the National Socialist revolution. Thus, Goebbels, speaking in 1933, stated emphatically: "The year 1789 is hereby eradicated from history." [15] The intellectual forerunners on whom National Socialism drew in the development of its Weltanschauung were primarily ideologists fervently opposed to the ideas of democratic revolution, human rights, freedom, and equality.

This ideological "anti" front was forged by a combination of four tendencies: a new, essentially imperialistic nationalism; a conservative-authoritarian glorification of the all-powerful state; a nationalistic-statist abberration of socialism seeking to combine social romanticism and state socialism; and, finally, a *völkisch* * community ideology based on race, which, beginning as simple xenophobia, turned into a radical, biological anti-Semitism which ultimately became the major tenet of National Socialism. At the root of all these factors lie common European tendencies originating in the age of revolution. To see Fascism and National Socialism only as the final stage of a reactionary counterrevolution and to deny their revolutionary content is a fallacious simplification of these complicated relationships. The wellsprings of the Fascist and National Socialist ideologies were nourished by both revolutionary and reactionary sources: national imperialism as well as etatism, popular socialism as well as racism. The various movements which later were subsumed under the Italian concept of Fascism differed insofar as they acquired heterogeneous national forms and absorbed the basic tendencies in different degrees. In the case of Italian Fascism, a national-imperialist concept of the state formed the core of the totalitarian ideology; National Socialism ultimately subordinated everything to a *völkisch* racism and, consequently, arrived at a substantially different form of total rule than did Italy, with its Fascist state ideology.

The ideas of the national state and of nationalism did not develop along parallel lines, a fact which makes for a further distinction. The nationalist principle came to the fore at the turn of the eighteenth century on two levels simultaneously: the politics of the French Revolution, which led to the exaggerated imperialism of Napoleon, and the romantic conception of national cultures and peoples which, each in their own way, play a role in history. The distinction proved to be

---

[15] Radio Address, April 1, 1933, in Joseph Goebbels, *Revolution der Deutschen* (Oldenburg, 1933), p. 155. The French campaign of 1940 was celebrated as a victory over "discarded ideals" and the "subhuman revolution" of 1789; see *Schwarzes Korps*, August 22, 1940.

* There is no English equivalent for this term. It is a combination of ethnocentric, racial, and national. See especially George Mosse, *The Crisis of German Ideology* (New York, 1964), pp. 4 ff.—TRANSLATOR'S NOTE.

of signal importance. In central and eastern Europe, the French–
West European idea of the nation-state as a historical-political structural principle was pitted against the principle of the cultural and
ethnic nation, as developed primarily by German philosophers and
writers, disciples of Herder, Fichte, and Hegel. By "nation" they understood a community of people which, regardless of historical-national
boundaries, was united by language, culture, and descent, and now
aspired to full sovereignty within the old supranational empires.
This idea of the prestatist, ethnically determined nation originally (in
Herder's case) was still part of a universal humanistic and humanitarian idea. The ethnic nation became the ultimate political goal only
after revolutionary upheavals had brought on the collapse of supranational states and after the movement for democratic social emancipation fused with the national movements.

Now, every people discovered its own heroic history, its own special
characteristics and mission. In mid-nineteenth century, the belief in a
cultural mission was supplemented by arguments for an ethnic-
völkisch foundation of national life; this alone was held to be a valid
basis of statehood and was destined to become the accepted state myth.
The nation, by being endowed with the highest moral if not pseudo-
religious values, became the ultimate yardstick of all political life; it
replaced or destroyed all encroaching geographical, cultural, historical,
religious, social, or economic ties. Yet, at the same time, the supranational liberal and democratic movements, and, later, international
socialism, continued their successful course. But by mobilizing and
politicizing the masses and attacking existing governmental structures, they helped to prepare the ground for the enthusiastic catchphrases of a type of nationalism which was more appealing than the
intellectual, rational arguments of liberal democracy and socialism,
either because of its emotional, irrational intensity or because it successfully adapted and utilized those arguments.

None of this, however, precluded an alliance between nationalism
and conservative restorational efforts. Revolutionary as the appeal of
nationalism might be, it was still committed to the idea of reforging
an allegedly lost unity of the people. A conservative historical myth
was created, given currency, and made the spur and legitimization of
the national movement. Moreover, the old order was dying a slow and
painful death. The equating of "people" with "nation" led to insoluble
problems in the establishment of national boundaries in the ethnically
mixed areas of central and eastern Europe, and the assimilation of
national minorities frequently was accompanied by the brutal exercise
of power, which in turn gave rise to profound disaffection among
those so oppressed. This held true particularly in Austria-Hungary,
the multinational empire composed of Germans, Czechs, Slovaks, Hun-
garians, Romanians, Serbs, Croats, Slovenes, Italians, and others. The
ideas which Hitler acquired in Vienna in his youth were colored by the
fanatical intensity generated by this situation. And Italian Fascism,
as personified by Gabriele d'Annunzio, the poet and organizer of the

coup of Fiume in 1919, also was impelled by a nationalist "irreden-
tism." *Völkisch* anti-Semitism was yet another by-product of a
nationally, socially determined desire for unity against "hostile"
minorities, a desire that helped to feed the fires of nationalist pug-
nacity.

Thus, the newly stirring national feelings that had played so vital a
role in the emancipation of the people and the emergence of democracy
stood in constant danger of turning into dictatorship and destruction.
Examples of such a critical turn were present in Europe at the end of
the nineteenth century. We find it in the anti-Semitic climate that
prevailed in France—in the publicistic writings of Maurice Barrès
and Charles Maurras, in the disputes over the Dreyfus Affair, and in
the activities of the Action Française. In Italy, the course taken by
revolutionary liberalism is exemplified by the transformation of the
great liberal-democratic republican and prophet of national unity,
Guiseppe Mazzini (1805–72), who ultimately became the spokesman
for the idea of an imperialist, power-state nationalism, which, by its
evocation of the glories of ancient Rome, presaged the imperial pretensions of Fascism. Even more startling was the transformation of the
influential historian and publicist Heinrich von Treitschke from Saxonian liberal and anti-Bismarckian to the ideologist of a Prusso-
German power state with a national-imperialist mission. The
ideologists of the British colonial empire also gave evidence of this
relationship between liberalism, nationalism, and imperialism, and,
even in the polyethnic United States, a nationalist sense of mission
found expression in the idea of manifest destiny, a nationalist-
imperialistic aberration of the democratic idea.

This nineteenth-century transformation of nationalism into radical
imperialism played a major part in the forward thrust of the antidemocratic movements that culminated in Fascism and National
Socialism. Political tensions increased; the era of limited Cabinet
wars fought by mercenaries and professional soldiers came to an end,
while the state, with its national credentials, highly centralized and
bureaucratized, made ever greater power claims, both internally
and externally. Social problems multiplied along with rapid economic and
technical growth; the pressures generated found a psychological outlet
in a heightened national and imperial power consciousness. This diversion of the inner dynamic to external factors has been labeled "social
imperialism." The expanding population was to be settled in newly
acquired land; geopolitical arguments were to be heard everywhere, in
the United States and England as well as on the Continent. They found
their way into Germany around the time of World War I, largely
through the writings of the Swedish political scientist Rudolf Kjellen.
With increasing frequency, the ideology of a nationally based socialism
was being pitted against the Marxist doctrine of the class struggle,
the dictatorship of the proletariat, and the contention that the basic
transformation of the political and social structure held the key to

the solution of all problems everywhere. International revolutionary socialism found itself face to face with the national-revolutionary idea of an all-inclusive people's community (*Volksgemeinschaft*). Socialization within the framework of the national state was the vague program which was to reconcile socialism with the national state and serve that state.

The turn of the century saw the idea of a "national socialism" begin to take root in Europe. Though initially confined to small groups in Austria and Germany, it also was to be found in the France of Maurice Barrès, where, at the beginning of the twentieth century, the Action Française sought to promote a socialist-nationalist movement and win over the workers.[16] Internal unity rather than class struggle, vigilance against outside forces rather than internationalism, were the tenets of this defensive ideology, which hoped to build an alliance between the conservative elite and a middle class threatened by a growing proletariat. Despite the great differences between classical socialism and the fascist-nationalist movements, there nonetheless were defections from one to the other, as demonstrated by the careers of former socialists like Georges Sorel and Mussolini.

Modern anti-Semitism, destined to become the most important component of National Socialism, was another by-product of this process of political and social change and the ideologies growing out of it. Throughout most of Europe, racism became intertwined with nationalism. Xenophobia served as a distraction from foreign and domestic problems. A turning point was reached in the latter half of the nineteenth century, when the previously religiously motivated hatred of Jews changed into sociopolitical and biological anti-Semitism. In Germany, this brand of anti-Semitism was successfully propagated by the publicistic writings of Wilhelm Marr [17] and the philosopher Eugen Düring,[18] who, using pseudo-scientific arguments, spread the ideas and contentions of a new, biologically founded anti-Semitism and demanded special laws for and even the deportation of Jews.

This campaign paralleled the emergence of Social Darwinism. Basing itself on Darwin's theories of evolution and natural selection, Social Darwinism proclaimed the "fight for survival" and "survival of the fittest" as the motive forces of all life, individual and national. Historical development and the fate of nations were nothing more than biological facts: just as in the case of natural selection, the fight for survival, the triumph of one nation over another, were determined by the quality and progress of the nation and race.

---

[16] Eugen Weber, *op. cit.*, pp. 69 ff.

[17] With the significant title *Der Sieg des Judentums über das Germanentum, vom nichtkonfessionellen Standpunkt betrachtet, Vae victis! (The Victory of Jewry over the Germans, Seen from a Nonsectarian Point of View; 1873)*.

[18] *Die Judenfrage als Rassen-, Sitten- und Kulturfrage (The Jewish Question as a Racial, Moral, and Cultural Problem; 1881)*.

The second half of the nineteenth century has been called the Darwinian age.[19] Otto Ammon, Georges Vacher de Lapouge, Madison Grant, and the great sociologist Ludwig Gumplowicz, in his early writings, all sought to apply biological considerations to sociohistorical developments.[20] While Gumplowicz ultimately discarded this line of inquiry, one of his students, Ludwig Woltmann, developed an extreme form of Social Darwinism which later was incorporated into the ideology of National Socialism.[21]

The underlying idea was that, in the course of a ruthless competition and battle, a "natural" selection takes place which prevents or offsets aberrations and makes for a proper balance between population and available resources. In society, education and penal law serve as the instruments of this process of selection; according to the immutable laws of heredity, the unfit cannot be educated and therefore must be eliminated. Ammon was among the first to attempt to classify the fit and unfit according to physical characteristics. He maintained that the measurements of the skull or the length of the nose were related to the innate abilities of a people or a race in the fight for survival. The teachings of Social Darwinism were in contradiction to the egalitarian belief in an open, mobile society and the educability of man—the basis of the democratic idea of state and society. The humanitarian idea of evolution was replaced by the concept of the planned "breeding" of an elite and the proscription of intermarriage. Consequently, Ammon criticized any interference with the "natural" process of selection through the protection of the weaker, less fit individual at the expense of the stronger and healthier. The future of nations, in their ceaseless struggle for survival, depended on their adherence to this law of nature.

Such teachings continued to pour forth in vulgar elaboration. They helped shape the racial-biological, pseudo-scientific theories of National Socialism and culminated in the breeding and extermination policies of the Third Reich. Like racial anti-Semitism, these ideas were an expression of a profoundly pessimistic view of the world. Vacher de Lapouge believed that inherent in the struggle for survival was the danger of a decimation of the fittest: in war, which occupies a central place in Social Darwinism, the bravest die while the cowards survive; in democracy, the mass threatens to overwhelm the noblest. Christian morality and law also tend to be debilitating: committed as they are to compassion and the protection of the weak, they are obstacles to the "natural" fight for survival, and, by passing laws of

---

[19] Werner Stark, "Natural and Social Selection," in M. Banton (ed.), *Darwinism and the Study of Society* (London, 1961), pp. 49ff. On the spread of Social Darwinism in America, see Richard Hofstadter, *Social Darwinism in American Thought* (rev. ed.; Boston, 1955).

[20] Ammon, *Die Gesellschaftsordnung und ihre natürlichen Grundlagen* (Jena, 1895); Lapouge, *Les sélections sociales* (Paris, 1896); Grant, *The Passing of the Great Race* (New York, 1920); Gumplowicz, *Rasse und Staat* (Vienna, 1875) and *Der Rassenkampf* (Innsbruck, 1883).

[21] Ludwig Woltmann, *Politische Anthropologie* (Jena, 1903).

monogamy, they bar the unrestricted propagation of the strong. The capitalist economy has a like effect: it favors the "unproductive" businessman and speculator instead of the "honest workingman," who begets his children under far less favorable conditions. This tends to lower the birth rate of the best of the nation or encourages a mixing of the best and lesser groups, as can be seen in the marriages for money of the European aristocracy. The flight of rural populations and emigration to other lands cap this disastrous process: here, too, the strong and venturesome die off in cities and foreign countries, while the weaker remain behind and reproduce.

These theories had one common theme: a declaration of war on all those moral values stressing compassion, tolerance, and the protection and welfare of the individual. The pseudo-scientific theories applying the laws of nature to society opened the way to "eugenics" and breeding, to the relentless pursuit of racial policies and their consequence— the idea of planned extermination, which had been brewing in the mind of Hitler and his contemporaries since the early years of the century. Neither Darwin himself, who never dreamed that his discoveries would be so abused, nor the vast majority of social thinkers of his time, highly critical of the application of biological principles to social processes, can be held responsible. Social Darwinism remained a sectarian philosophy; seeing man only as a biological and not a thinking, moral being, it misjudged the nature of historical and social forces, the binding values of civilization, as well as the basic difference between biological and social selection. The most prominent of the Social Darwinists, Gumplowicz, later modified his ideas. Starting from the principle that man against man was the "natural" basis of all historical and social development, he arrived at the conclusion that the civilizing process had profound effects on this barbaric condition, that social life and peaceful cooperation could surmount the biological laws of war and heredity. In place of the concept of race, he substituted the idea of nations built on foundations of tradition and culture.

Thus, Social Darwinism underwent a major modification, although it had no effect on the spread of numerous vulgar biological theories at the turn of the century. The pseudo-scientific character of theories which equated man and beast as well as nation and race, and which, in contradiction to historical experience, saw the mixing of races as a sign of degeneracy, contributed to their popular appeal.

Already then, these ideas showed a remarkable affinity for anti-democratic ideologies. Equality and freedom, liberalism, democracy, and internationalism were equated with the "unnatural" evils of pacifism and miscegenation. The first major ideologists of racial theory, the French Count Gobineau and the Englishman Houston Stewart Chamberlain, a son-in-law of Richard Wagner who opted for German nationality, were violent, conservative-aristocratic enemies of democracy. Gobineau's three-volume *Essai sur l'inégalité des races humaines* (*Essay on the Inequality of the Races of Man;* 1853–55) predates Darwin. Significantly, he dedicated this work to the King of Hanover who had invalidated the Hanoverian constitution and against whom the protest of the Göttingen Seven* was directed. In this work, Gobineau proclaims the superiority of the white race—of which the Germans, as a subdivision of the Aryans, were a part—to Negroes and Semites, and the virtually totalitarian concept of the primacy of race over the individual and nation. And Chamberlain's widely read *Grundlagen des 19. Jahrhunderts (Foundations of the 19th Century;* 1899) sees all of Western history since the Greeks in terms of a race struggle: Only the Aryans, among them the Germans, are held capable of a "creative culture"; their intermingling with "inferior" races would lead to decline, just as the Roman Empire disintegrated in racial chaos. Chamberlain's correspondence with the widow of Richard Wagner also dwelled on anti-Semitism and the idea of a Jewish international conspiracy and world ruin.[22]

All of this was still nothing more than an experimentation with ideas. In the case of Gobineau, and even of Chamberlain, the ideas were part of a quasi-religious cultural philosophy with markedly conservative Christian overtones. A number of other publicists of that era, as, for example, Leon Daudet and Edouard Drumont[23] in France, and Paul de Lagarde and Julius Langbehn in Germany, used anti-Semitism to advance a pseudo-scientific sectarianism and to express a cultural pessimism, initially without broader political implications. But whereas France survived the Dreyfus Affair and, later, withstood the anti-Semitic nationalism of radical ideologists, Lagarde and Langbehn and, especially, the more persuasive Chamberlain, found a devoted following among the German middle class. Emperor William II was one of Chamberlain's devoted readers and corresponded with him. Alfred Rosenberg, the chief ideologist of National Socialism, based his nonsensical *Mythus des 20. Jahrhunderts (Myth of the 20th Century;* 1930) largely on Chamberlain, who let himself be celebrated as the prophetic "seer of National Socialism" before ending his life in Wagnerian Bayreuth in 1927. Even as mere theories, these books and brochures were weapons in the hands of the demagogues, and, after World War I, their effect in Germany and Austria was quite different from that in the rest of Europe.

THE PROBLEM OF GERMAN STATEHOOD

Why did these nationalist, anti-Semitic tendencies, present in all of Europe and not of exclusively German origin, spread so rapidly throughout German intellectual, social, and political life, and, ultimately, take such detrimental forms? It is not enough simply to cite

* Upon his ascension to the Hanoverian throne in 1837, Ernest Augustus, Duke of Cumberland, invalidated the constitution promulgated in 1833. Seven eminent professors at the University of Göttingen protested and lost their chairs; two who published the letter of protest were banished.—TRANSLATOR'S NOTE.

[22] *Cosima Wagner und Houston Stewart Chamberlain im Briefwechsel, 1888–1908* (Leipzig, 1934), pp. 604 ff., 641 ff.

[23] In *La France Juive* (2 vols.; Paris, 1885–86).

personages and writings of the past, for similar lists can be compiled for other countries. The extreme forms and consequences of the nationalist, etatist, pseudo-socialist, racist ideologies of central Europe were due, above all, to the special political and social history of the German states in the nineteenth and twentieth centuries, which left Germany with weaker powers of resistance than other countries. The problem of the national state was particularly difficult, and the failure of the democratic movement and liberalism in the face of both conservative and socialist pressures helped lay the groundwork for a union of the national idea with social-imperialist and racist philosophies of force. The catastrophe of World War I pushed these ideologies and catchphrases into a vacuum and permitted them to become the motive force of a militant political movement. It was this combination of circumstances that shattered the feeble powers of resistance of both the elite and the mass of the German people, and, ultimately, also of the democrats and socialists.

The specific political conditions in which National Socialism took shape might be divided into four phases. The first phase involves the special position and attitude of the Germans toward the French Revolution and its consequences. The second is marked by the failure of the revolution of 1848 and its aftermath, Bismarck's conservative-national revolution from above. In the third phase, the internal governmental problems of the German Empire and its drive to become a world power, which culminated in World War I, created the immediate conditions for the beginning and growth of National Socialism per se. And in the last stage, the deep disappointment over the defeat of 1918 turned the crisis-ridden postwar history of the Weimar Republic into a stepping-stone for Hitler's dictatorship.

1. After the old empire dissolved into a series of loosely linked territorial states, Germany's geographical situation in the center of Europe and its special position of leadership during the Medieval Empire prevented the development of the type of centrally governed state based on historic and national factors found in other Western nations. Unlike France, some of the eighteenth-century German states tended toward a moderate form of enlightened absolutism which seemed to allow for the organic transition to a modern state without a revolutionary rupture. But, under the impact of the Terror and the aggressive expansionism of the French Revolution and Napoleon, the initial enthusiasm for the principles of the Revolution gave way to profound disillusionment. Romantic-mystical feelings about a unique national consciousness sprang up, beliefs about a special attitude of the Germans toward the West and its revolutionary and political philosophies. Typical of this development is the rapid transition from a European, humanistic, cosmopolitan orientation to a national idea of the German cultural mission, as propounded by Fichte in particular. The wars of liberation against Napoleon emphasized the national interests and, ultimately, helped restorational efforts triumph over internal reform and revolution.

2. The historical consequences, which became apparent after the failure of the bourgeois-liberal revolution of 1848, were the alienation

and isolation of German political thought from West European trends. The German sense of uniqueness increasingly was combined with anti-Western sentiments, and the strong liberal movement more and more was swayed by ideas of freedom and unity based on foreign-policy considerations sacrificing the ideals of internal freedom and constitutionalism. The failure of 1848 also was more than simply the result of a series of unhappy circumstances. It was brought on by the ambivalence of German liberalism, which found itself squeezed between an unfulfilled desire for a national state and authoritarian government structures. Leonard Krieger's *The German Idea of Freedom* (1957) analyzes acutely how, even among the majority of liberals, the idea of freedom was overwhelmed by the idea of the state as a force above society assuring unity and efficiency, power and protection, and standing above the parties. In the age of Romanticism, this concept of the state, which originally sought to insure the rights of the citizen in society but which ultimately benefited defensive, conservative forces, came to dominate the legal and political thinking of the people. By accepting the primacy of external unity over internal freedom, the democratic, constitutional, and reform movements once again became subjugated to the power of the nobility, the military, and the bureaucracy. Bismarck, as the head of the Prussian authoritarian state, the main pillar and symbol of the reactionary order, succeeded in imposing the longed-for German national state, the "Second Reich," in a revolution from above.

It was an authoritarian surrogate solution for the liberal-democratic national state fought for in 1848. But, in fulfilling the apparent desire for unity, it succeeded astonishingly quickly in integrating the bourgeois-liberal emancipation movement into the structure of a pseudo-constitutional, semi-absolute feudal, military, bureaucratic state. The German bourgeoisie capitulated before Bismarck's dictum that the great issues of the day were settled not by speeches and majority decision but by iron and blood. At the same time, they feared the demands being made by an emergent socialist movement and the possible effects of a more thoroughgoing democratization. The failure of the Liberals, which in 1863 induced Lassalle to found the German Workers League, served to radicalize the socialists, who thereafter subordinated their liberal, social aims to a revolutionary ideology, though Marxism—contrary to general belief—never fully gained the upper hand in the German Social Democratic Party (Sozialdemokratische Partei Deutschlands, or SPD).[24] Influenced by Bismarck's success, the bourgeoisie went along with the vulgar, cynical contention that power, not justice and morality, is what matters in *Realpolitik*. Thomas Mann aptly captured these predominant authoritarian ideas of order and prestige in an ironic sobriquet that sums up the German

---

[24] Susanne Miller, *Das Problem der Freiheit im Sozialismus* (Frankfurt/Main, 1964), pp. 80 ff. An early basic work on this subject is Gustav Mayer, *Die Trennung der proletarischen von der bürgerlichen Demokratie in Deutschland 1863–1870* (Leipzig, 1911).

ideal: "General Doctor von Staat." [25] Power and submissiveness were the two poles of this flawed position. At the turn of the century, the historian Theodor Mommsen, himself a long-time National Liberal and an admirer of Bismarck, came in his old age to the bitter conclusion that "the injury done by the Bismarck era is infinitely greater than its benefits. The gains in power were values which the next world-historical storm might destroy, but the subjugation (*Knechtung*) of the German personality, of the German mind (*Geist*), was a misfortune (*Verhängnis*) which cannot be undone." [26]

3. From the very beginning, Bismarck's Reich was beset by great tensions and encumbered by structural defects which the luster of the founding years could not obscure. These tensions and defects hampered the development of a workable parliamentary system and of responsible political parties. The decline of the Liberals, who, in the 1870's, still commanded an absolute majority in the Reich and in Prussia, was particularly catastrophic. At the same time, the military-bureaucratic power state blocked the participation of the growing class of workers and their Social Democratic and trade-union organizations. The Prussian three-class suffrage system which prevailed until 1918 was characteristic of this policy; under it (as of 1893), the votes of 3.5 per cent, 12 per cent, and 84.5 per cent of the electorate, respectively, had equal weight.* However, the election of the Reichstag by absolute majority was also inequitable; it was based in part on an obsolete apportionment of election districts which, by failing to make allowances for population movements away from the country to the cities, favored conservative-rural candidates. There existed a great discrepancy between the changed social order and the political structure; the profound social changes wrought by the Industrial Revolution were not adequately heeded.

After the fall of Bismarck, there was a growing tendency to neutralize this problem by diverting the pressures created by special interest groups to the outside in the sense of a "social imperialism" designed and used to substitute expansionism for domestic democratization. Seen from the vantage point of foreign policy, the new unified Germany was a "belated nation." [27] Conservatives and Liberals shared the belief that Germany had to catch up with the national and foreign leads of the world powers, and that, as an aspiring major power, it had a natural right to hegemony over central Europe and to a share in the colonial, economic, and political penetration and apportionment of the world. In this context, the alliance between the feudal nobility and bourgeois capitalism, the foundation stone of the Second Reich,

---

[25] Cf. Helga Grebing, *Der Nationalsozialismus* (Munich, 1959), p. 92.

[26] Hans Kohn, *The Mind of Germany: The Education of a Nation* (New York, 1960), p. 188.

* Under the Prussian system of restricted franchise, the electorate was divided into three, numerically unequal, categories based on the amount of taxes paid.—TRANSLATOR'S NOTE.

[27] Helmuth Plessner, *Die verspätete Nation* (Stuttgart, 1959).

proved to be fatal, for it pitted German foreign policy in the era of imperialism simultaneously against two powerful adversaries, in the east and the west.

The social and economic factors responsible for this international isolation of German imperialism and for the events leading up to World War I were recognized quite clearly.[28] The political ambitions of the landowning Junkers collided with Russian interests, and those of heavy industry collided with the British. The fact that the objectives of both groups were pursued simultaneously, since the diverse interests could not be accommodated in a single, balanced foreign policy, was responsible for a foreign policy of "not-only-but-also," which ultimately brought Germany the much-bewailed "world of enemies" and lent support to the wild expansionist dreams of the war years. Sensible alternatives to this trend did, of course, exist, but the profound discrepancy between the political and social institutions impeded all efforts to solve the foreign-policy dilemma or any attempt to institute vital domestic reforms. Hitler conformed to this pattern after the Weimar Republic failed to win its battle against radical revisionism, which in effect sought to annul the outcome of the lost war. He attempted to solve the problems by force, substituting a European-imperial expansionism for the former colonial-political one.

The events of 1890, culminating in Bismarck's resignation, marked a decisive turning point in this respect as well. Bismarck had been able to balance the imperialist tendencies through a prudent policy of equilibrium, of mutual security and a careful equalization of interests. (This did not, however, prevent the Bismarck cult of later years from extolling him as a nationalist and an imperialist.) After Bismarck's retirement, the idea of the national-imperialist power state found its most extreme expression in the Pan-German movement of 1893. This trend, which combined historical and cultural arguments with economic and, later, racial ones, championed the gathering up of all Germans into one ethnic-national, united Reich. Rapid expansion was to make Germany a major world power alongside, or possibly against, England, France, and Russia. True, the Pan-German League encompassed only a small minority, though a highly vocal and influential one. At the beginning of this century, the League had about 20,000 members, and at the outbreak of World War I, between 30,000 and 40,000, of whom about one-third were engaged in academic professions; the League also maintained close contact with the Gobineau Society, founded by Professor Schemann in 1894. The turn to radical anti-Semitism came about after the replacement, in 1908, of the League's founder, Professor Ernst Hasse, by Counsellor of Justice Heinrich Class, a pupil of Treitschke's and a confirmed anti-Semite. Now, even

[28] See especially Eckart Kehr, *Der Primat der Innenpolitik* (Berlin, 1965) and George W. F. Hallgarten, *Imperialismus vor 1914* (2 vols.; Munich, 1963); also Helmut Böhme, *Deutschlands Weg zur Grossmacht* (Cologne, 1966); Fritz Fischer, *Griff nach der Weltmacht* (Düsseldorf, 1961).

assimilated Jews were denied membership; the organization played the role of "national opposition" against all moderate forces in the country, including Chancellor Bernhard von Bülow and his Foreign Minister, Alfred von Kiderlen-Wächter, and, later, against Theobald von Bethmann-Hollweg as well. These radical ideas corresponded to the imperial, hegemonic aspirations attendant on the expansion of the economy. The alliance of Pan-Germans and National Liberals, as personified by Krupp executive Alfred Hugenberg, typified this development. The imperial aspirations and considerations of military policy culminated in plans and aims for World War I that have since come to light. German hegemonic claims, even in the sublimated form of the idea of "Mitteleuropa," with its subdued proposals for German dominance,[29] were bound to strike Germany's neighbors as imperialist threats.

4. The situation of the Weimar Republic was the product of Germany's unequivocal defeat and its truncation at Versailles. However, the opposition to this treaty, the nonacceptance of defeat, lent special fervor to the idea of a national power state at the expense of the new democratic order. Efforts for a peaceful policy of reconstruction and understanding in Europe were further undermined by mistrust of the Western powers, the weakness of the League of Nations, and the isolationism of the United States. But, above all, these efforts were being pressured by a nationalist revisionism that affected large segments of the population between 1918 and 1923, and, once again, after the economic debacle of 1929. The foreign policy of Weimar, vacillating between East and West, resistance and compliance, cooperation and revision, was incapable of putting a brake on this dynamic.

The foreign-policy program of National Socialism reflected the ambivalence of the situation. In its day-to-day political life, National Socialism posed as the most fervent exponent of the anti-Versailles forces; in its ideology, it reached back to an older idea of the special German position in Europe and developed the doctrine of the cultural and racial supremacy of a future "Germanic empire of the German nation" (as a new form of the medieval Holy Roman Empire of the German nation). The personality and ideas of Hitler infused this nationalist-imperialist hegemony claim with the specifically Austrian nationalist ideology of a Greater Germany, and this was superimposed on the Prusso-German components of the philosophy of expansionism. Under cover of a cleverly manipulated strategy of treaty revision, which fooled many both inside and outside Germany, Hitler from the very outset fixed his sights on one unchanging goal: to round off the territory of the national state, and to expand Germany's *Lebensraum* far beyond the "racial core" of the German people. Hitler's basic idea was to break open the expansionist principle of the national state through the imperial principle of the primacy of the biologically and racially "superior," with the thrust directed against the racially "inferior" Slavs

[29] Cf. Henry Cord Meyer, *"Mitteleuropa" in German Thought and Action 1815–1945* (The Hague, 1955).

in the east, and, domestically, against the Jews, "World Enemy Number One."

The question of the role of German militarism in these causal factors has remained controversial. If by militarism one means military aggression, then the question is not crucial. Yet, it cannot be denied that the example and tradition of a predominantly military state like Prussia exerted a profound influence on the social and power structure of the Bismarckian Reich. The Army was held up as the training ground of the nation (*"Schule der Nation"*) ; a reserve commission enhanced the social standing of a civilian. Military considerations also determined the political ideas of large segments of the population. The war-directed ideology of National Socialism was able to build on this foundation; Hitler found it far less difficult than Mussolini to mobilize the people and win the Army. However, in contemplating the role of Prussian militaristic thinking, Hitler's *völkisch* ideas of Austro–Greater German origin must not be ignored. Thus, Hitler's expansionist drive was also directed against the Rump-German–Prussian idea of Bismarck's Reich, which, by excluding Austria-Hungary, excluded a large segment of the German nation.

It is therefore not surprising that the true forerunners of the National Socialist German Workers' Party (Nationalsozialistische Deutsche Arbeiterpartei, or NSDAP) at the turn of the century originated in Austria and Bohemia, areas in which the anti-Slav and anti-Semitic nationalism of a social *völkisch* as well as Christian national character had been strong for decades. It is also not surprising that Hitler's party was founded in Munich, a city which, like Vienna, favored the ideologies of obscure sects adhering to a fanciful Germanic mysticism and the Catholic–Greater German rather than Protestant-Prussian concept of statehood. In the leadership of the National Socialists, South Germans, Austrians, and ethnic Germans outnumbered Prussians. Yet were it not for the military-political and etatist tradition of Prussia, the ideas and life of the German people under the Empire and the Weimar Republic would not have been militarized, nor would the total state have solidified its power. The union of nationalism and militarism in World War I had a deep effect on Hitler, and its survival in the battle against the Weimar Republic and in the alliance of the reactionary nationalists and the National Socialist revolutionaries made possible the events of 1933.

The German and *Völkisch* Sense of Special Destiny

The special historical burdens and ferments of the idea of the German state and nationhood were given their most extreme expression in the National Socialist ideology. At the same time, it is true that the National Socialist Weltanschauung, unlike Marxism and Communism, did not derive from any consistent philosophy or theory. It was a conglomerate of ideas and precepts, of concepts, hopes, and emotions, welded together by a radical political movement in a time of crisis.

This brings us to the central question of necessity and choice in Germany's acceptance of National Socialism. Germany did not have to take the road to the Third Reich. The fact that it chose that road while others did not was due to the specific nature of the antidemocratic trend in Germany as well as to the special conditions under which the rise of National Socialism in Weimar took place. The ultimate cause, however, was the deep schism between German and Western political thought, and the emergence of a special German sense of destiny with anti-Western overtones.

In this sense—not in the sense of a doubtful "ancestor's gallery" of National Socialism—the genesis of National Socialism does, indeed, point back to the beginning of the nineteenth century. The national reaction to the Napoleonic perversion of the French Revolution is embodied in Fichte's famous *Addresses to the German Nation* (1807–08), a widely read book which was to play a vital role.[30] Fichte's basic contention was that Germany was selected for a special mission for mankind, which set it apart from the hitherto much admired and imitated French. A battle against undue Western influence (*Überfremdung*) had to be fought, because the "German spirit" was innately superior, and destined to become the guiding light of all Germanic peoples, if not of all mankind. In his Fifth Address, Fichte advanced the notion that the Germans are the only people capable of profound, original thought; other peoples, by contrast, are capable only of a superficial, childish understanding of the classical culture of Antiquity. In phrases foreshadowing the comparison of Western civilization and German culture by such ideologists as Oswald Spengler, this special destiny is invoked:

> The German spirit, however, will open up new battles and introduce light and day in their abysses and throw out massifs of ideas on which the future age will build its homes. The foreign genius will be like a lovely sylph, which in gentle flight hovers above the flowers sprouting from its own soil and settles on them without bending them and drinks their refreshing dew, or like a bee which skillfully collects the nectar from the rare flowers and deposits it in dainty order in evenly constructed cells; the German spirit, however, is like an eagle which forcefully lifts up his great body and with strong, practiced wings pushes down the air so as to lift himself nearer to the sun, which enraptures him.

Expressed here, though without the destructive sense of exclusivity of future polemics, is the idea of the superiority of German culture, extremely profound and imbued with the idea of a universal mission, set against the superficial, imitative civilization of others. This idea was still lacking in political concretion, but the dismissal of Western political thought as "merely rational," and the polemic against the rationalist constitutional state, had major political-philosophical con-

[30] Cf. Friedrich C. Sell, *Die Tragödie des deutschen Liberalismus* (Stuttgart, 1953), pp. 59 ff.

sequences. And, while the Germans, philosophically speaking, were praised as an "archetypal people," compared to whom others were "second-rate" and "stale," the idea of the "alien" and the "foreigner" was invested with a derogatory meaning (Seventh Address). This change in political thought was the result of what was then happening in the country. The occupation and division of Germany, the profound foreign influences, the belated forming of the nation, all these made for an ambivalent self-concept, in which dissatisfaction with the state of the nation was mixed with overcompensation for this special state of affairs.

This concept of the nation gave rise to an idea which went far beyond Herder's ideals, i.e., that the individual was unimportant as compared to the nation, for which, if need be, he had to sacrifice himself. The nation alone mattered in the changing destiny of states. Fichte saw it as the "bearer and pledge of earthly eternity," and, because of this, it went "far beyond the state in the ordinary sense of the word—beyond the social order" (Eighth Address). Thus was established the basis for a *völkisch* ideology unlike the etatist doctrine of Fascism, one which was to become the governing principle of the National Socialist Weltanschauung. Both postulates—Germany's special mission and the pre-eminence of the nation—were taken up by Romanticism and given historical or pseudo-historical underpinnings. They combined with the idea that the national community was fundamentally different from an administrative union in the sense of the classical social compact, that it was an elemental, natural "organic community" spanning generations, differing basically from a mechanically built "society." The later distinctions between community and society, formulated by Ferdinand Tönnies in his work of that name (*Gemeinschaft und Gesellschaft;* 1887), had their beginnings here.

The years to come saw the development and honing of two important ideas which, in embryonic form, were inherent in this concept of the national community: one was that of the superiority of an antiliberal, anti-enlightened German political tradition, and the other, that of protecting the uniqueness of German culture from alien influence and of exercising the sovereignty deriving from the Reich idea of the Middle Ages. Symptomatic of this thinking, which apparently legitimized the transformation to the conservative, authoritarian, antiliberal, and anti-enlightened political ideas of the post-1848 era, were the ideas of the Romantic political philosopher Adam Müller. Müller, mixing fact and fiction, had been talking and writing about the insoluble, ineradicable ties of man to the state since 1805. His contention that the more profound German spirit would prevail over the absorption of the statehood idea by the individualistic liberalism propounded by the Enlightenment, and that this spirit would ultimately dominate our hemisphere, was still meant in the sense of an intellectual penetration of Europe by the "middle land" Germany, and not in the sense of political subjugation. Yet at the same time, implicit in this contention was the belief that mankind stood to gain not by eternal peace, world govern-

ment, and leagues of nations patterned on the ideals of the Enlightenment and Kant, but rather by the separation of one nation from the
other, and even by war, for these would strengthen the national and
communal spirit of the people. The glorification of the national state
was the ideal held up against that "wishy-washy" world citizenship
which the precursors of National Socialism were to call the main misfortune of the Germans. Above all, however, stress was laid on the
special, higher, universal mission of the Germans. "The great confed-
eration of European nations will one day be a reality and, as sure as I
am alive, will fly the German flag, for everything that is great, everything that is thorough, everything that is enduring in European institutions is German—that is what I have held on to, when all my hopes
were dashed." [31]

The fight against the West, which turned into a fight against "Western" liberalism in Germany, remained the battle cry well after the
Napoleonic wars. It served patriotic publicists like Ernst Moritz Arndt
as justification for a German national feeling that demanded unconditional, unique, and almost religious dedication. The precipitous
retreat of liberal trends before a political, quasi-*völkisch* idea of freedom, the rejection of universalism and of a humanitarian interpretation of freedom, for which Arndt was celebrated as the "rouser of
Germandom," found its strongest expression in the effective activities
and writings of *"Turnvater"* Friedrich Ludwig Jahn.[32] The glorification of Prussia's natural superiority in one of Jahn's early programmatic works with the significant title *Deutsches Volkstum
(German Nationhood;* 1810) laid the groundwork for the evolution of
a German-*völkisch* theory on which three movements of major ideological, social, and political impact based themselves. This idea furnished
the ideological foundation for the Free Corps of the Napoleonic wars,
which was to reappear in 1918 in perverted form. Similarly, the year
1811 saw the formation of the gymnastic groups (*Turnvereine*),
whose ideas of nationhood and patriotic-military training survived
ideologically in the later gymnastic societies. These groups derived
from the medieval tournaments; unlike ordinary sports clubs, they
hoped to revive the romantic idea of combat and to serve patriotic
renewal and "national education." Finally, the liberal element was
gradually overpowered by the nationalistic fervor of the student corporations of 1815. Jews were excluded, although still on "religious"
grounds; the guiding principle was education for loyalty, for national
feeling, for discipline and submission to the *völkisch*-national community, all of which were contrasted to the "mere" personal freedom
of the West. Jahn understood the "democratization" he proclaimed as
the inclusion of all citizens into the national community; that is why
he supported a people's army and the elimination of class differences.

The essence of these early manifestations of a *völkisch* ideology

[31] Adam Müller, *Die Elemente der Staatskunst* (Vienna and Leipzig,
1922), I, 48.
[32] Kohn, *op. cit.*, pp. 81–98 *passim;* cf. Sell *op. cit.*, pp. 61 ff.

was the conviction that nationhood took precedence over statehood and that Germany was to become a national state: "nation" and "Germandom" had priority. Only by remembering their ancient nationhood could the German people regain their dominant political position as the largest nation in Europe, which the Thirty Years' War and the defection of the Netherlands and Switzerland had destroyed. In addition to these countries and Austria, Jahn also included Denmark in the future Greater Germany, whose new capital, "Teutonia," he hoped to build in the center of the new country on the Elbe. (This Pan-Germanic fantasy resembled Hitler's plans for a capital city to be named "Germania.") Jahn's ideas were based on a concept of nationhood which, unlike Herder's, was expressed in terms of the superiority and uniqueness of the Germans and attuned to an idea which was to gain fatal significance, i.e., *racial purity* as the basis of historical national grandeur. Jahn was the architect of portions of the later master plan. The decline of Rome, according to him, was the consequence of racial mixing; he insisted on the basic difference of nations, and this difference ruled out world government, a universal language, and a universal religion; he put national life and nationhood, the source of all life and creativity, above individual rights and the idea of universalism and one mankind; he naturally opposed mixed marriages and alien, particularly Western, influences on language, culture, and political thought—the cause of Germany's misfortune. This national-*völkisch* ideology was disseminated in the new movements on which Jahn exerted such influence, and hence his early designs and visions are more than mere intellectual and historical curiosities. The education of the future was to be based on a popularized national history, on a language cleansed of all foreign words, on physical labor and military sports, on the glorification of national symbols and heroes; the goal was a true "people's democracy" in which all participated. Its precondition was a new "war on one's own hook," which, unlike 1813, when Germany remained split into numerous principalities, was to weld the people together forever: here, the blood-and-iron slogans of Bismarck's time were anticipated.

These ideas served also to stimulate a cultural anti-Semitism that continued to gain ground at the universities. As early as the mid-nineteenth century, such influential and widely read publicists as Wolfgang Menzel became its spokesmen. For Menzel, a member of a student corporation and ardent gymnast who in the course of his anti-Western campaign also attacked Goethe's individualism and estheticism, the Germanic-Christian Middle Ages rather than classical literature represented a cultural acme. In his *Deutsche Mythologie* (*On German Mythology*), he even went so far, in an anti-Christian–Germanomanic turn of phrase, as to call Odin the personification of that driving power of the German people "which made the German people supreme in world history," through which Christendom was truly ennobled.[33] History, he held, was a series of plots to weaken the

[33] Kohn, *op. cit.*, pp. 96–97.

German people; Goethe, a man without understanding of the German sense of uniqueness, was part of this series. Menzel's critique ended in that plaintive lament about the undeserved fate of the Germans and the envy of their neighbors which in later years was employed to justify the National Socialist philosophy of violence. Indeed, the National Socialists claimed that they led the German people from historical aberration back on the right track. Characteristically, in 1938, a book entitled *Die Deutschen als Volk für andere (The Germans as a People for Others)* deplored the "Siegfried fate" of the good-natured Germans who always worked for others and got nothing in return—including their role in the building of the United States.[34] In a similar vein, Goebbels described the Germans as the "drudges of the world," on "whose willing backs are piled the burdens of an entire continent." [35] And Hitler himself joined the chorus in a speech delivered at Potsdam on March 21, 1933, the Day of National Upheaval:

> The German, collapsing into himself, divided in spirit, disunited in his purpose and thus powerless to act, becomes enfeebled in his own existence. He dreams about justice in the heavens and loses ground on earth. But the more nation and Reich were shattered and the safeguards of national life weakened, the more he tried at all times to turn necessity into virtue. . . . Ultimately, the only road remaining open to the German people was the inward road. As the nation of the bards, poets, and thinkers, they then dreamed of a world in which the others lived. And only after being battered unmercifully by privation and misery, there grew up the longing, perhaps out of the arts, for a renewal, for a new Reich, and thus for a new life.[36]

This was only one of the themes of the older German national idea; it was not one typical of nineteenth-century German political thought. There still existed powerful counterforces in both the liberal and conservative camps, and, above all, in the emerging socialist movement. The possibility of a democratic development in Germany remained. Not until later was this possibility ruled out. The events of 1870, 1914, 1918, and 1933 were decisive crossroads. Because of them, one cannot speak of the inevitability of Germany's course. But the German middle class was undoubtedly receptive toward a radicalization of national and *völkisch* ideas, which had their beginnings in the failure of 1848, and, even more so, after 1866 and 1870. During the enthusiasm over military victories and national unification, a Machiavellian adoration of the state was gaining ground, abetted by some Hegelians as well as by a preoccupation with historical inevitability. The ultimate broadening of the national-*völkisch* ideology at the close of the last century must be seen within the framework of the Second Reich and against the background of the failure of the democratic movement in

[34] Emil Quentin, *Die Deutschen als Volk für andere* (Berlin and Leipzig, 1938), pp. 26, 55, 80, 121, 129.
[35] *Völkischer Beobachter*, February 28, 1933.
[36] *Verhandlungen des Reichstags*, CDLVII, 6.

1848 and 1870, even though the ideology itself may have predated these events.

THE TRANSITION TO NATIONAL-IMPERIALIST IDEOLOGY

As a result of the widening gulf between Western and German political thought, and in line with the diminution of humanitarianism and natural law in a country without a well-founded political tradition, the German intelligentsia and bourgeoisie—the professors and teachers, the writers, civil servants, soldiers, and industrialists—were more readily seduced by the siren calls of antidemocratic, anti-individualist, and irrational ideologies than were their counterparts in other countries. In the mood prevailing in the Second Reich, Treitschke was able to proclaim effectively that the individual ought to sacrifice himself for the greater community of which he was a link, and that therefore he did not have the right to resist the authority of the state, even if it were held to be "immoral." [37] Such reasoning might well lead to the conclusion that man was a mere object and tool of the political power of the state and the nation. Race theoreticians and social hygienists were able to connect this with their demand for the official breeding of "superior" beings and the extermination of "inferiors." From this it was only a step to the total submission of the individual to the state, the nation, and the race principle.

The hectic neo-German nationalism of the Second Reich, in which the old Prussian ideas of discipline and obedience were distorted and exaggerated, furnished fertile ground for all such concepts. Student organizations, led by the anti-Semitic League of German Students,[38] patriotic clubs, military and nationalistic groups, as well as the conservative, nationally oriented Protestant churches, all helped to disseminate them. Grandiose ideas about national and imperial prestige covered over and compensated for the inferiority complexes of a belatedly unified nation, and steered a social discontent intensified by economic crisis, *Kulturkampf,** and the Anti-Socialist Law † into widening anti-Semitic channels. At the same time, a cynical disdain for international law and international agreements was actively promoted. Pitted against such allegedly cowardly and sentimental notions was the superiority of war as the renewer of life, in which battle was the highest law.

It is generally believed that these tendencies found their strongest exponent in Friedrich Nietzsche. But, in fact, Nietzsche himself was severely critical of the Second Reich as well as of Germanomania

[37] Heinrich von Treitschke, *Politik* (Leipzig, 1899), I, 100 ff.

[38] See Hellmuth von Gerlach's autobiography, *Von rechts nach links* (Zurich, 1937), pp. 108 ff.

* The conflict between the state and the Conservative Liberal Parties, on the one hand, and the Catholic Center Party, on the other.—TRANSLATOR'S NOTE.

† A special law passed in 1878 that outlawed the SPD, prohibiting it from holding meetings and banning its publications.—TRANSLATOR'S NOTE.

and anti-Semitism. He believed assimilation and the mixing of races to be "the source of great cultures," and he feared that the military and economic successes of the Second Reich would result in the corruption, even the "extirpation of the German spirit in favor of the 'German Reich.' " [39] At the same time, he passionately objected to the generally accepted identification of spirit with power, which, in his eyes, was tantamount to the submission of the spirit to power: "Coming to power costs dearly, power stupefies. . . . 'Germany above all,' I fear that this spelled the end of German philosophy." But Nietzsche's impassioned, brutalized catchphrases about the will to power, superman, the blond German beast, and the triumph of the strong over the weak, however deeply rooted they may have been in a radical individualism, lent themselves to any distortion. Nietzsche was promoted to the "prompter of ideas" of fascism.[40] His misinterpretation by his sister and by his disciples, and his later misuse by National Socialism have been amply documented. He himself stated emphatically that his *Will to Power* was nothing more than a book of ideas. "It belongs to those who take pleasure in thinking, nothing more. . . . The fact that it is written in German is at the very least inopportune. I wish I had written it in French, so that it would not seem to support some sort of German imperial aspirations," he wrote in the introduction. But in its popularized form, Nietzsche's heroic elitist philosophy, however paradoxical its formulations and however many arguments it furnished to all sides, was as effective as the antirational power and elitist philosophies of Georges Sorel and Vilfredo Pareto, which so influenced Mussolini and Italian Fascism. And finally, Oswald Spengler, who considered himself the true heir of the misunderstood Nietzsche, told his vast readership that man was a predator. Spengler kept aloof from National Socialism not for reasons of ideology but because of his disdain for the "masses."

There was still another specifically Germanic element in German nationalism. This essentially insubstantial nationalist ideology of power and community sought to justify itself historically by calling upon a unique Germanic-pagan prehistory whose heroic tradition was broken by Roman and Christian influences. The German was bound to the nation, whether he wished or not, by an inescapable fateful heritage, not by the exercise of free choice and vote. This belief, too, unlike the Western concept of nation, was only a step away from the blood-and-soil ideology of National Socialism. None of these factors was instrumental in shaping national policy before 1914, while a liberal and humanistic tradition still survived; nonetheless, they were widespread ideas and sentiments. The Germanization cult of the Wagner

[39] Friedrich Nietzsche, *Erste unzeitgemässe Betrachtung* (1873); cf. Theodor Schieder, *"Nietzsche und Bismarck,"* in *Historische Zeitschrift*, No. 196 (1963), pp. 322 ff.

[40] Thus, Thomas Mann, "Nietzsches Philosophie im Lichte unserer Erfahrung, in *Schriften und Reden zur Literatur, Kunst und Philosophie* (Frankfurt/Main, 1968), III, 41.

operas, which appealed also to Hitler, and the huge, frequently sectarian fanatical Wagner following played a significant role. True, Hitler
looked toward this only for confirmation of his ambitions and dreams,
and Wagner's fanatical disciples—just as Nietzsche's—are responsible
for his fatal influence. But Wagner himself offered them ample en-
couragement.[41]

The fact that Wagner started out as a liberal revolutionary and participant in the Dresden uprising of 1848 and that he spent the years
between 1849 and 1860 in exile is evidence of the close connection
between liberalism, nationalism, and traditionalist *völkisch* ideology.
But early in his career, Wagner invoked the myths of a grandiose Germanic past to do battle against an "unheroic" civilization; by creating
the "total work of art" of his enormously effective operas, and, finally,
through the Bayreuth Festival, he sought to create national symbols
in which the romantic invocation of a barbaric-heroic past played a
major role. Wagner's writings are even clearer evidence of this transformation to an anti-civilatory, myth-making nationalism which early
allied itself with anti-Semitism: building on Christian-religious foundations, he voiced criticism of the cultural and economic role of
the Jews. In numerous confused essays, Wagner attempted to develop
the Germanic-national myth which was to furnish intellectual justification for Germany's power and missionary claims. He developed the
idea of salvation through a leader, likened Christ to Siegfried and
Barbarossa, and, for a while, believed he had found the dreamed-of
ruler in his eccentric patron, Ludwig II of Bavaria, whose brilliant,
inspired herald he wished to be.

Wagner's store of political ideas included a hatred of Jews, which
Cosima Wagner later continued to nurture from Bayreuth; paralleling
the fatal role played by Nietzsche's sister, Elisabeth Förster, she
succeeded in building a direct bridge to National Socialism. The influence of Gobineau, whom Wagner had met in Rome in 1876, becomes
particularly apparent in one of Wagner's major essays, *Das Judentum
in der Musik* (*World Jewry in Music;* 1869), which seemed to fulfill the
prophetic words Tocqueville wrote in a critical letter to Gobineau: "I
think that your book is fated to return to France from abroad, especially from Germany. Alone in Europe, the Germans possess the particular talent of becoming impassioned with what they take as abstract
truths, without considering their practical consequences." Tocqueville's prophesy was turned into fact by the National Socialists, after
Chamberlain had produced a melange of the race mystique of Wagner,
Gobineau, and the new anti-Semites; Alfred Rosenberg took it over,
and Hitler and Himmler drew the logical conclusions. Wagner's anti-
Semitism was still of a purely theoretical nature. His immediate
circle included many Jews who were his fervent champions. Yet, this
did not prevent him from saying "I consider the Jewish race the sworn

[41] See George H. Windell, "Hitler, National Socialism and Richard Wagner," in *Journal of Central European Affairs*, No. 27 (1962–63), pp. 479 ff.

enemy of man and all that is noble in him. That we Germans in particular will be ruined by them is beyond dispute." In theory, Wagner, despite his debt to international, and particularly French, influences, insisted on the uniqueness and exclusivity of the Germans: "I prefer the worst German book to the best French." In 1870, he demanded the razing of Paris as a symbolic act of deliverance of the world from evil; he opposed the imposition of a "Franco-Jewish democracy" on the "misunderstood and damaged German national spirit"; he called for the de-Jewification of Christianity, for the deportation of Jews to Palestine, and he held forth against mixed marriages and assimilation. This is yet another example of the profound difference between him and Nietzsche, the European moralist, who, after an initial spurt of enthusiasm, bitterly fought Wagner, calling him an expression of the crisis and sickness of Europe.

What is significant is that these radical notions combined with the political ideas being espoused by conservative political theorists and historians, in sharp contradiction to Western-liberal political and historical thought. The conservative political thinkers saw the state not only as an instrument for promoting the general welfare but also as an end in itself. In this belief, one shared by Hegel, Ranke, and Ranke's disciples, the uniquely German idea of nation and community plays a central role, noticeably so in the basic contention that considerations of foreign policy and power politics take precedence over domestic policy, reform, and the constitutional state. This conviction, shared by historians, philosophers, legal scholars, and poets, reached its apex in the fervent anti-Western proclamations of German scholars and writers in World War I; [42] in appropriately popularized form it dominated the educational system and public life. Symptomatic of this attitude was the basic tenor of a widely read book, *Der deutsche Gedanke in der Welt* (*The German Idea in the World;* 1912), by the National Liberal Baltic German Paul Rohrbach, which had as its epigram Emmanuel Geibel's sloganeering verse *"Am deutschen Wesen wird die Welt genesen"* ("The German spirit shall cure the world").[43]

Typical of the interaction of etatistic, nationalist, and *völkisch* tendencies and conservatism in this era of power intoxication were the works of Paul de Lagarde (real name Paul Bötticher, 1827–91), Professor of Oriental Languages at the University of Göttingen.[44] His *Deutsche Schriften (German Writings;* 2 vols., 1878–81) reached a wide readership. In them may be found almost all later *völkisch*-nationalist arguments: the purification of the genuine Germanic spirit through the elimination of everything "alien" borrowed from other cultures— Roman law, the ideals of the Enlightenment, urbanization, parliamen-

---

[42] Hermann Lübbe, *Politische Philosophie in Deutschland* (Basel and Stuttgart, 1963), pp. 173 ff.

[43] Numerous other examples up to and including William Ἱι are cited by Kohn, *op. cit.*, pp. 262 ff.

[44] See Fritz Stern, *The Politics of Cultural Despair* (Berkeley, 1961), pp. 3 ff.

tarianism, French democratic egalitarianism; the creation of an
aristocratic elite to replace the un-Germanic "Celtic egalitarianism";
opposition even to Bismarck and the bureaucratic, new-fangled dilu-
tion of the German state idea. Lagarde believed that a national church
able to transform the entire nation into one religious community
would help forge the desired internal unity. This new church was to
be based on a "pure" Christianity devoid of any Jewish traces. Both
Lagarde and Chamberlain thought this preferable to a Germanomani-
acal Wotan cult. While domestic affairs were to be governed by religious principles, foreign relations were to follow the lines of a
nationalist imperialism which was to create a Greater Germany, including the entire Habsburg Empire in eastern and southeastern
Europe; and war with Russia, in defiance of Bismarck's policies, was
to open up new land for Germany by moving Russia "some fifty miles
toward Asia" and settling German beggars and peasants on the Black
Sea and in Asia Minor. This approach was the first clear expression of
the philosophy of social imperialism and *Lebensraum*.

More radical still were the ideas of the "conservative Germanophiles"
formulated a decade later by Julius Langbehn (1851–1907), a writer
from Schleswig-Holstein. His anonymously published *Rembrandt als
Erzieher: von einem Deutschen veröffentlicht (Rembrandt as Educator: By a German)*, which went through thirteen printings in 1890,
the year of its publication, and, by 1904, had gone through ninety, continued to exert great influence even after 1918. The book was a plea for
irrationalism, with Rembrandt its chosen symbol. The idea of race was
made the determining factor in all human events, transcending even
the nation: the "power of the blood" was all important; inherited
characteristics superseded acquired traits; an elite state based on race
rose above the egalitarian "mishmash" of democracy. Langbehn singled
out the "Germanic–Low German race," in which he included Holland
and England, as particularly desirable. This was a rather anti-Prussian concept directed against Bismarck and William II. The book even
attacked the "intoxicating" effect of Wagner and the influence of
French and Jewish music on him.

Numerous writers and artists joined in the *völkisch*-racist culture
critique. Denunciations of capitalism and cosmopolitanism as "neo-
German" and Jewish were rampant in books and periodicals in the
early days of this century. Of course, these ideas were still a far cry
from the culture critique of the National Socialists. This was an elitist
conception which, looking to the past, rejected industrial mass society
along with modern technology and organization—those essential components of modern totalitarianism. The basic tendency of this school
of thought was anti-Western and opposed to the international rights of
man. Its significance lay in the fact that it did away with moral inhibitions and promoted a sense of uniqueness.

The spread of these tendencies and slogans, which National Socialism
fell back on so eclectically, was helped by the unrest over the social,
economic, and cultural changes which the new Reich was unable to

deflect. Efforts, partly regressive and partly progressive, were made to solve these problems through nationalistic isolation and power-political expansion. By advocating an imperialist solution to the social problem in a "national social" state, liberals like Friedrich Naumann and Max Weber at one time fell in with this trend.[45] They hoped to win the support of the workers for the national state, whereby reforms and expansion, which were to make this state a reality, went hand in hand. Thus, Naumann, around·the turn of the century, prompted by Christian, liberal, and social motives, yet with his sights fixed on the national state, developed the concept of a "national-social" movement and of a popular monarchy (*Volkskaisertum*). His championing of parliamentary democracy and his opposition to the Wilhelminian authoritarian state must be seen in this context: both had as their objective the national mobilization and unification of the population, including the workers, within the framework and in the service of the national-imperial state. The susceptibility toward a policy of imperialist wars among the "liberal" bourgeoisie and intelligentsia—though strong opposition also came from that quarter—must be understood against this background.[46]

The wealth of theories, plans, and efforts which, in the course of World War I, produced elaborate *"Lebensraum* philosophies" marked a peak in the development of the Germanic sense of uniqueness, expressed in the anti-Western memorandums and war declamations of a great many German professors, and even, toward the end of the war, in Thomas Mann's *Reflections of a Nonpolitical Man.* The influential economist Werner Sombart published a classic anti-Western manifesto, *Händler und Helden (Traders and Heroes;* 1915), in which he drew comparisons between Western trader nations and the heroic Germans. Sombart's attempts to offer economic and sociopolitical proofs were matched by the idealistic-philosophical and metaphysical arguments of others, the wellsprings of the Nazi ideology, which adopted, vulgarized, and brutally perfected these notions, under the special conditions created by the defeat of 1918 and the permanent crisis of the Weimar Republic. The slogans of a war ideology pitted culture and Reich against Western civilization and formal democracy, poets against literati, soul against society, freedom against mere suffrage, spirituality against politics, genius against intellect, war as an end in itself against internationalism and pacifism, metaphysical profundity and mystique against shallow rationalism, a soldier's ethos against technical and material superiority, a disciplined authoritarian state against parliamentary and party rule.

This unbroken ideology now clashed with the reality of 1918 and the climate of revolution, with a harsh peace and a half-hearted turn toward a democracy made to look contemptible—an "un-German"

---

[45] See, particularly, Wolfgang Mommsen, *Max Weber und die deutsche Politik 1890–1920* (Tübingen, 1959).

[46] E.g., Anneliese Thimme, *Hans Delbrück als Kritiker der wilhelminischen Epoche* (Düsseldorf, 1955).

Western import that was intertwined with the stab-in-the-back legend. National Socialism, a product of the prewar and war ideologies, had its beginning in this setting. By crudely simplifying these ideas, it made them serviceable in the organization of a mass movement. Thus, the decisive bridge is not so much the spread of the prefascist philosophers and their pseudo-scientific theories, but rather the specifically German phenomenon of their ready acceptance in a concrete political and social situation.

The Role of Anti-Semitism

Modern anti-Semitism is also closely related to the rise of nationalism and the Industrial Revolution. Even before 1870 and the outbreak of the Franco-Prussian War, during the apparently successful emancipation era, a Jewish stereotype gained currency which, predating racist embellishments, became part of the new, artificially stimulated German national consciousness. While modern racism à la Gobineau was directed against all "Semites," in practice it concentrated on the Jews. Against them, it was possible to mobilize the religious, social, economic, and psychological forces that furnished an ideological impetus. The hatred of Jews in the Middle Ages had taken similar forms. Jews then were relegated to certain roles and functions, for the Church prohibition against the collection of interest limited Christian trade and money transactions. On the other hand, Jews were denied the right to own real property. At the same time, they were made the scapegoats in times of crisis and mass hysteria. The Crucifixion remained their unexpiated guilt. Set apart by their religious rituals, they lived in the isolation of the ghettos and Jewish quarters, frequently officially designated as an alien minority. Proscription of mixed marriages, high taxes, a variety of negative "special rights", discriminatory employment practices, and periodic waves of persecution were their lot, exacerbated by the special position of a handful of envied Court Jews and their finance policies.

With the improvement of living conditions, many of those who had fled to eastern Europe returned to Germany, and anti-Jewish feelings flared up anew. The slow emancipation of the Enlightenment, which after the eighteenth century gradually extended ideals of tolerance and humanitarianism to Jews as well, simultaneously gave fresh impetus to the motives of anti-Semitism. The removal of existing barriers stimulated the rapid rise of the hitherto repressed. The argument that the Jews, because of their specialization and disproportionate representation in economic and cultural life, controlled certain aspects of life became the prime factor in the spread of anti-Jewish feelings. A new version of the "anti" myths gained currency. Though clothed in pseudo-scientific garb, it retained its basic irrational character, and the hideous "ritual murder" stories even were revived. These ideas, coupled with nationalism and a growing anticapitalism, culminated in the myth of a secret Jewish plot for world domination which was simultaneously part of the internationalism of the Freemasons. This combination of primitive patchwork history and racist naturalism sought to make the history of man subject to unchanging, profoundly unhistorical biological laws.

The most important instrument in this attempt was the invention and falsification of historical "evidence," of which the Protocols of Zion became the most outstanding example. The Protocols, a horror tale imported from Russia about purported secret plans for Jewish world domination, were to play a significant role in National Socialist ideology as well. Allegedly the minutes of a secret meeting of Jewish leaders held in Berne in 1897, the Protocols served as the pretext for the bloody pogroms loosened in Czarist Russia to sidetrack movements for political and agrarian reform. They were read by Hitler in his youth and were disseminated in both England and the United States: Henry Ford was one of those who were helping to spread these myths as late as the 1920's. In fact, however, this so-called document was an out-and-out forgery, a copy of an attack on Napoleon III by Maurice Joly, a French lawyer sentenced to prison in 1865. Joly has Montesquieu confront Machiavelli; the target of his invention was Napoleon's despotic rule. This harmless pamphlet was invested with an anti-Semitic twist around the turn of the century and published in Russia in 1903 as a "document." Its obscure origins were not revealed, and no amount of objective rebuttals could put a stop to its dissemination.[47] The myth of a world conspiracy to "rationalize" fears of crisis, xenophobia, and social conflicts, and such absurd "documents" as the Protocols took on a dreadful importance in the plans for the annihilation of the Jews. These arguments continue to embellish racist literature, and, though repeatedly given the lie, they apparently are indestructible so long as prejudice and race hatred survive.

The anti-Semites saw assimilation not as a solution to a national problem but as an existential threat. Jewish participation in liberal and socialist causes, those mainstays of emancipation, and their ready adjustment to the social scene, were suspect. The fact that the Jewish political philosopher Friedrich Julius Stahl was one of the leading theorists of Prussian conservatism meant nothing in the face of the stereotype of the Jews as decadent literati, exploitative businessmen, rootless revolutionaries, and conspirators. This concept of the Jew was nourished by social resentments even before the formulation of the extremist ideas of a biological anti-Semitism. The Jews were identified with the problems of progress and modernization in general. The growing pains of modern society furnished an ideal soil for the development of a totalitarian friend-foe ideology in need of a scapegoat. This held true particularly for countries like Germany and Austria-Hungary, primarily for these five reasons: (1) As a result of the persecutions in Russia and Poland and the improved conditions in Central Europe, there was an increase of Jewish immigration;

[47] Cf. the definitive study by Norman Cohn, *Warrant for Genocide* (London, 1966).

(2) at the same time, strong tensions between social and political development persisted; (3) the minority problems were acute in countries that had become national states only recently; (4) anti-Semitism was a welcome distraction from the serious economic and social problems of the early years of the Second Reich; (5) anti-Semitism was a manifestation of a rejection of the "West," with which the Jews were identified, even though they may have come from the East, because the Enlightenment and democracy were essential preconditions for their acceptance and progress.

This was the political and social setting in which the stereotype of "the" Jew evolved and gained currency. The image of the "typical" Jew found in popular literature, even by such liberal authors as Gustav Freytag *(Soll und Haben [Debit and Credit]*; 1855) and Wilhelm Raabe *(Der Hungerpastor [The Hunger Pastor]*; 1862), was not at all racially conditioned, a fact which later made it possible for many a good German who did not accept racist doctrines passively to accept Nazi anti-Semitism. Even in the preracist stereotype, the Jew was thought to be incapable of creativity and spirituality. He was the embodiment of everything negative which, under the heading "civilization," was counterposed to the higher value of true "culture." This discord between the inner "soul" as the basis of culture and superficial "intellect" as the embodiment of civilization spelled the end of culture, according to the widely accepted ideas of Chamberlain and Spengler. The growing conflict between the reality of an industrial urban world and the poetic glorification of rural virtues, of the simple life, of irrational life forces, was linked to the repellent figure of the urban, commercial Jew.

So long as this idea was confined to the religious sphere, a gradual assimilation of the Jews into and their ultimate acceptance by the German nation seemed possible as the ideas of the Enlightenment spread. But when the optimism of the Enlightenment began to give way to an irrational *völkisch* nationalism, the idea of the eternally "demoralizing" role of the Jew began to take root. His assimilation seemed impossible; his character was unalterably negative. The religious difference became a moral one; the image of the secularized Jew was based on a mythical-deterministic concept, a combination of reaction and impotence, hatred and fear. The quintessence of this type of anti-Semitism was the fear of the dark world of the ghetto and of the conspiratorial workings of "international Jewry" as told of in pamphlets and novels since the turn of the century, a fantastic mixture of falsified and misunderstood Jewish works and stereotyped invention. The influx of Jews from the ghettos of the East furnished daily proof and arguments for the fear and hatred of the unknown. At the same time, their presence was held responsible for the problems and difficulties which changing social and economic conditions wrought in the lives of a people in an industrial society brought up on preindustrial social ideals. According to Wilhelm Marr, Bismarck's Reich was practically a "New Palestine," which in all vital respects was under Jewish alien domination. The right-wing anti-Bismarck opposition was a mainstay of this early wave of the 1870's and 1880's, when conservative Protestant and antiliberal Catholic forces forged a temporary alliance.

With the rise of the socialist movement and the onset of the economic crisis of 1873, these anti-Semitic excursions gained the support of Bismarck and of right-wing Liberals, who felt threatened from two sides. This trend reached its height in the era of the Anti-Socialist Law (1878–90). Anti-Semitism was now officially encouraged, or at least tolerated, in opposition to liberalism and socialism. Equating the Jewish world conspiracy with international socialism and later communism was merely another step in the forward march and purpose of modern anti-Semitism—i.e., to close the gap that had opened up between the romantic self-image and the reality of modern life after the old corporate-agrarian order had collapsed. All Germans had to be made aware that the fate of the nation and the people was at stake. The threats posed by the problems of emigration and urbanization, displacement and modern life, commercialization and proletarization, internationalization and secularization, all these were ascribed to the presence and activities of the Jews. It was in line with this trend that literary critics called Heinrich Heine superficial and disdainful of all "genuine" values, a rootless, shameless skeptic, a soulless intellectual —in short, the quintessence of the Jewish "threat" to German culture.

The rise of biological anthropology, the science of man as the product of heredity, also worked to change the Jewish stereotype from the religious, moral, and cultural to the racist-biological. Henceforth, the character and role of the Jew were held to be immutable. All persons of Jewish descent, in the East and West, Germans and non-Germans, were alike, and neither assimilation nor individual characteristics could alter this racially preordained fact. This process of depersonalization eliminated the individual and created the preconditions for the coldly impersonal, detached planning of mass disenfranchisement and, ultimately, for extermination. If the Jew was merely a species, and, according to Governor Hans Frank's later proclamations in occupied Poland, nothing more than vermin, then the road to the quasi-bureaucratic, unemotional "carrying through" (*Durchführung*) of the annihilation exemplified by Adolf Eichmann was clear.

Of course, even in Germany this logical final conclusion was never as widely accepted as the religious, social, and cultural nineteenth-century image of the Jew. It was limited to small circles of sectarian race theorists, and after World War I, given voice in some minor literary works, such as Nathaniel Jünger's *Volk in Gefahr* (*Nation in Danger;* 1921), Werner Jansen's *Die Kinder Israel'* (*The Children of Israel;* 1927), Arthur Dinter's *Sünde wider das Blut* (*Sin Against the Blood;* 1918), but also in a play by Carl Hauptmann (the brother of Gerhart) entitled *Ismael Friedmann* (1913). In them, religious and cultural differences became differences of blood. The mixing of different bloods is disastrous, thus said the atavistic thesis propounded in countless pamphlets and pseudo-scientific journals, foremost among them, after 1923, *Der Stürmer* (*The Attacker*) of Julius Streicher, the man who later plastered the streets and squares of the Third Reich with posters proclaiming *"Die Juden sind unser Unglück"* ("The Jews are our misfortune").

Anti-Semitism as a separate movement or as part of an increasingly popular race theory generally flared up in times of economic and political crisis. That was true in France up to the Dreyfus Affair, and it was true particularly during the German and Austrian economic crisis of 1873. Wilhelm Marr's pamphlet of that year had gone through twelve printings by 1879.

It was the time of the first serious economic depression of the new industrial-capitalist society. Then and later, as, for example, in Gobineau's pessimistic exercise, anti-Semitism primarily saw itself as a "defensive combat" and "anti" movement, a position taken also by Otto von Glogau in a series of articles that appeared in the widely read periodical *Die Gartenlaube* (*The Bower*) in 1874. Von Glogau emphasized his point by charging that the economic and social problems of the middle class were due to Jewish-inspired market and financial manipulations. "Jewish high finance" came to epitomize the stereotype of the Jew, and its allegedly negative role was contrasted with "German" industry and agriculture, those "true" workers and producers. Later, the engineer and amateur economist Gottfried Feder was to employ ideas such as these to document his thesis that the "yoke of high finance" was the root of all evil, an idea that made a deep impression on the young Hitler and probably determined the course of his early political career and the vaguely "socialist" content of his ideology. The *Gartenlaube* series also spoke of a conspiracy of shadowy, elusive financial and economic forces, which were equated with Jewish efforts for influence and domination and held responsible for all ills and problems in an increasingly complex economic and political setting. The personal mishaps of von Glogau possibly played a role as well: He apparently had lost his fortune in stock speculations.

The political and social groups that rallied to the growing movement were not of a uniform cast. A Christian-social orientation was one of the early aspects. But, after 1875, the *Kreuzzeitung* (*The Cross*), a Conservative paper, from time to time joined in the campaign. Tactical partisan considerations probably were responsible for their polemics against the "Jewish" domination of the National Liberal party, one of Bismarck's mainstays at the time, but, nonetheless, they helped to disseminate and lend respectability to anti-Semitism. Even the leading Berlin Catholic Center paper, *Germania,* at one time opened its columns to this propaganda, and the *Kulturkampf* played a part as well: The Catholics in their fight against the Liberals also resorted to the argument of Jewish domination, and, in 1874, the anti-Bismarckian Catholic Constantin Frantz published his book *Der Nationalliberalismus und die Judenherrschaft* (*National Liberalism and Jewish Rule*).

While these factions actively engaged in anti-Semitism only sporadically, the major themes and theses of the anti-Semitic propaganda, whether biologically founded or not, continued unswervingly. The standard anti-Jewish myth continued to base itself on three assertions: (1) that the Jews were the mainstays and beneficiaries of exploitative capitalism; (2) that they were the mainstays of Marxian socialism and internationalism, and, consequently, the main enemy of any "national-social" movement; (3) that everything they did was in the service of a world-wide conspiracy against either national interests (the prebiological argumentation) or Aryans (the racist version).

The reasons for the intensification and stepping-up of anti-Semitic propaganda in the Germany of the 1870's and '80's, a campaign in which so eminent a figure as Treitschke also joined, were complex, and it is therefore instructive to examine the social and professional backgrounds of the men who, with varying degrees of success, used these arguments to further their political careers.[48] Most of them came from urban areas, were alienated from the Christian churches, and were members of the steadily growing semi-educated lower middle class. The majority were Protestants and nationalists, with an above-average though frequently incomplete education. Many had tried their hand at various jobs, were hard-pressed economically, had sought their fortune in foreign countries, and had come into conflict with the law. Without means to carry on their political activity, they were like fanatical, persuasive, "idealistic" sectarians who dedicated their lives to a cause, and therefore they found some admirers. They owed their careers and their influence to social and professional frustration and anti-intellectualism.

The propagandists of radical anti-Semitism were primarily industrial and commercial employees, lower civil servants and small businessmen, teachers and students, but, above all, they were sectarians with highly personal philosophies of life, followers of reform movements, food faddists, vegetarians, and nature worshipers. They saw themselves as the main victims of Jewish emancipation. Their fanatical, pseudo-religious theories of world salvation did not admit the possibility that conversion and assimilation could solve the "Jewish problem." Thus, they went beyond the traditional national-Christian anti-Semitism which had paved the way for them. Instead of the optimistic Christian-social assimilation idea which Court Chaplain Adolf Stoecker continued to propagate, they propounded the pessimistic racial anti-Semitism of Marr, which frequently served also as an expression of their personal and professional frustrations. Regardless of how splintered and insignificant their grouplets, their noisy agitation radically pointed the way to future developments. One of the leaders

---

[48] See, above all, Paul Massing, *Rehearsal for Destruction* (New York, 1949); Alexander Bein, "Der jüdische Parasit," *Vierteljahrshefte für Zeitgeschichte*, No. 13 (1965), pp. 121 ff. On the socio-economic factors, see Hans Rosenberg, *Grosse Depression und Bismarck-Zeit* (Berlin, 1967), pp. 88 ff. On Treitschke, see Walter Boehlich (ed.), *Der Berliner Antisemitismusstreit* (Frankfurt/Main, 1965).

of this agitation was the elementary school principal Hermann Ahlwardt of Berlin, the author of *Der Verzweiflungskampf der arischen
Völker mit dem Judentum* (*The Desperate Battle of the Aryan Peoples
and Jewry;* 1890). Both the title and tone of this book are reminiscent
of Marr's work. Its pseudo-scientific "documentation," with its countless footnotes and appendixes, was meant to emphasize its serious
character. Ahlwardt (1846–1914), a worker's son from a Pomeranian
village, had gotten into debt, for which he blamed Jewish machina-
tions, and this lay at the bottom of his obsessive anti-Semitism. His
dismissal, in 1890, from his post for embezzlement of school funds
only intensified his mania. In 1892, he "exposed" an alleged armaments
swindle by the Leipzig firm of Löwe, whose "Jewish guns" he said
were acts of national sabotage. His prison sentence did not stop his
agitation. He had in the meantime been elected to the Reichstag and
thus enjoyed immunity.

The organizational growth of the anti-Semitic groups went through
several stages. In 1879, Marr founded the not very successful League
of Anti-Semites (Bund der Antisemiten); a year later, the Social
Reich Party (Soziale Reichspartei) and the German Reform Party
(Deutsche Reformpartei) came into being. None of them had a mass
base, but each hoped to become the integrating mass party of all
classes and political and social groups, with anti-Semitism as the unifying factor, which, they said, was *the* prime national and political
issue. Other attempts to form parties followed, and the unsuccessful
founders generally disappeared from the scene after a while, some
emigrating to foreign countries. In 1881, Max Liebermann von Son-
nenberg, a former officer, and Bernhard Förster, Nietzsche's brother-
in-law, founded the German People's League (Deutscher Volksverein).
Förster emigrated to Paraguay in 1886, where, in 1889, he committed
suicide after the failure of the experimental New Germania community.

In the meantime, the German Anti-Semitic League (Deutsche antisemitische Vereinigung) had been formed, and, taking a firm position
against the assimilation movement of the Stoecker anti-Semites, called
for special anti-Jewish laws. The League based its demand for special legislation on such contemporary measures as the American laws
against Chinese immigration.[49] One of the founders of the League was
Theodor Fritsch, the author of the *Handbuch der Judenfrage* (*Hand-
book of the Jewish Question*), who continued to write up to the Nazi
era. His publishing house, the Hammer Verlag (Leipzig) and the
journal *Hammer* became centers of anti-Semitic propaganda. Then, in
1887, the folklorist Otto Boeckel published his pamphlet *Die Juden—die
Könige unserer Zeit* (*The Jews—The Kings of Our Time*), a title
probably copied from antidemocratic slogans of French monarchists.
In 1887, Boeckel, then aged twenty-six, became the first independent
anti-Semite to be elected to the Reichstag. He won election in a con-

[49] Kurt Wawrzinek, *Die Entstehung der deutschen Antisemitenparteien
(1873–1980)* (Berlin, 1927), p. 44.

servative stronghold near Marburg by telling the impoverished rural population about the exploitative role of the "Jewish middleman" and by his demand for complete "Jewish freedom" (*"Judenfreiheit"*)—that is, freedom from Jews. His paper, *Reichsherold*, had a pronouncedly progressive, anticlerical, anticapitalist tenor. It propounded near-radical democratic ideas, but its major tenet was the demand for a complete separation of Germans, the natural rulers, and Jews, who were to be treated as mere guests but not assimilated. The ideas and methods of this "progressive" anti-Semitism differed sharply from the conservative model; Stoecker deplored its "social-democratic" character. Boeckel himself soon broke with the League because he thought it overly conservative. The conflict between small and large landholders played a vital role in his defection. After losing his seat in 1903, he disappeared from public view and died poor and embittered in 1923.

Other organizational efforts followed a similar pattern. In 1889, Liebermann, further to the Right, had founded the German Social Anti-Semitic Party (Deutschsoziale antisemitische Partei) in Bochum, which cooperated with Boeckel's newly founded Anti-Semitic People's Party (Antisemitische Volkspartei) in the Reichstag elections of 1890, and succeeded in winning five seats—four for Boeckel's group, one for Liebermann's. In the final elections, they even won over some National Liberal as well as a handful of Socialist voters. The next Reichstag elections proved to be the high mark for this first wave of a radical political anti-Semitism which temporarily was able to loosen the Conservative grip. Two-thirds of the approximately 400,000 votes cast for anti-Semitic groups went to the radicals, who apparently had gained some strength because of the scandal surrounding Ahlwardt. The sentencing of Ahlwardt, like the trials of Nazis in the days of the Weimar Republic, intensified the effectiveness of the propaganda campaign, a clear indication of the revolutionary character of the movement. There were men at work here who had nothing to lose, and quite a few were inclined to believe their agitation and to find confirmation of the thesis that the little man was persecuted by the big capitalists and by the legal system in their pay—just as the peasants lost their court fights against the "Jewish usurers" who were better versed in the complicated mechanism of modern administration and justice. A direct line also leads from this denunciation of an "aloof" system of justice to the *völkisch*-racist judicial reforms of the National Socialists.

Indeed, the convicted Ahlwardt, just as Boeckel before him, won the election against a Conservative candidate in a rural district near Berlin. He had neither organization nor funds, but he traveled tirelessly through the countryside to preach his anti-Semitic, anti-aristocratic gospel to the peasants. His campaign was directed against "Jews and Junkers," against the racially marked "parasites," the "predatory beasts" and "contaminators." He used socialist arguments to indict the economic "exploiters" who were abusing a notoriously blind "Germanic" trustfulness. His contention that were it not for Jews, only half of all existing laws would be necessary held particular appeal.

That art and artistic sensibilities were connected with race was another one of his arguments. His solution and goal was the complete
segregation of the races. With the support of some Conservatives, the
anti-Semites in 1895 indeed introduced a resolution by Ahlwardt to
stop the admission of Jews into the country. The parliamentary vote
on this, however, showed up the limits of the noisy movement. The
motion was rejected by 167 votes to 51. This defeat in effect put an
abrupt halt to further advances. The movement failed to score concrete gains; decline seemed inevitable, and the complete disappearance
from the scene only a matter of time.

In the meantime, it had become obvious that the effort of Stoecker
and his supporters to mobilize a "moderate" anti-Semitism behind the
Conservative cause was not only hopeless but also dangerous. It is
reminiscent of the later union of expediency between Conservatives and
National Socialists and of the fatal illusion of the Conservatives that
they could control and make use of the radicalism of the Nazis. The
ambivalence inherent in such an alliance manifested itself at the very
outset. The radical anti-Semites of the 1890's needed the Conservatives,
as Hitler did later. In the final analysis, they were the only possible
allies on the broad platform of national and imperial power politics.
When they were in opposition, the Conservatives for their part always
fell back on the radical anti-Semites: in the "Liberal" period of Bismarck's rule (1875–78), during Caprivi's Chancellorship (1890–94),
and during the Weimar Republic. At those times, they hoped to use
the radicals to manipulate the petty bourgeoisie. In the long run, this
strategy was bound to prove fatal: It kept the anti-Semitic undercur-
rent alive, made its radical methods acceptable and respectable, and
thus made possible the revitalization and success of a more determined,
purposeful radical movement. The fact that Germany did not go
through the moral turmoil of a Dreyfus trial only contributed to the
unbroken though devious continuation of anti-Semitism.

The most important anti-Semitic organization within the conservative camp was the Christian Social Party (Christlich-soziale Partei), founded by Stoecker in 1878. Initially, until 1881, calling itself a
"workers' party," it sought to lead the lower social classes back into
the fold of the conservative-Christian authoritarian state. The defeat of Marxian socialism through social reforms was Stoecker's
avowed goal. The son of a sergeant and prison guard, Stoecker had
risen socially and found himself torn between a desire for status in the
upper class (in his position as Court chaplain) and his efforts to
solve pressing social problems (as chief of the Berlin Municipal Mission Society). His sociopolitical aims became intermingled with an
effective anti-Semitic propaganda which, spreading rapidly, became
the focal point of a mass movement with pseudo-democratic methods.
The dawning recognition that democratization was a phenomenon of
the times was countered by the effort to pose a right-wing mass movement against the ascendant Left.

The attempt failed. Stoecker was unable to gain a foothold among the workers, though he had some success with the middle class. Their hatred of the Social Democrats was matched by their distrust of "Jewish" capital, which Stoecker hoped to make the basis of his Christian, national, social mass party. But the essential feature of the campaign was the dissemination of the socio-economic, nationlist catchphrases of anti-Semitism among conservatives. This was a job in which many groups and organizations cooperated, not the least of them student groups such as the League of German Students (Verein deutscher Studenten) founded in 1881. Among the documents of this time of ferment were the anti-Semitic petitions (with 250,000 signatures) addressed to the Kaiser demanding the liberation of the German people from alien Jewish rule through rigid regulations and the exclusion of Jews from public employment. The Reichstag elections of 1881 were also marked by violent anti-Semitic campaigns. Stoecker himself was a member of the Reichstag from 1881 to 1908. Whereas his policies dominated in the 1880's, the radical racist groups prevailed in the 1890's. The anti-Semitic groups held a total of sixteen seats in 1893, and thirteen in 1898. Clearly, the trend was downward. In 1903, they held eleven seats; by 1912, the number had declined to seven, yet they remained an influential latent force when tactics dictated collaboration with the Conservatives, who furnished both funds and respectability. The radicals became demagogic auxiliaries, and the Conservatives themselves incorporated anti-Semitic slogans in their platforms, as in the so-called Tivoli Program of the Berlin party congress of 1892. The agrarian interest groups (the Farmers' League [Bund der Landwirte]) and the German National League of Commercial Employees (Deutschnationaler Handlungsgehilfenverband) organized in 1893, became stanch backers of this course. The individual splinter groups now were replaced by the institutionalization of anti-Semitism within the framework of an anti-Marxist, nationalistic, traditionalist ideology. The year 1893, the year of transition, also saw the founding of the Pan-German League (Alldeutscher Verband), which was conceived of as the vanguard in the fight against the continuing influx of "eastern Jews," the electoral victories of the SPD in the Reichstag elections of 1893, and the policies of Bismarck's successor, Caprivi.

Events in Austria followed a similar course. There that peculiarly *völkisch* element symptomatic of Hitler and of the early manifestations of National Socialism was even more pronounced. The stock-market crash of 1873 in Vienna, like the crisis of the German founding years, ushered in the anti-Semitic movement. Moreover, in Austria, the economic and social factors were supplemented by the special problem of the assertion of German national feelings in a multinational state in which the balance of power had shifted to the disadvantage of the German-speaking Austrians after the Prusso-Austrian war of 1866 and with the increasing nationalism of the non-German populations. As a result, Austria also witnessed the introduction of a Christian-social German ideology, the formation of Pan-German organizations, and the incorporation of scattered workers' organizations into one national anti-Marxist movement. By 1901, the Pan-Germans held twenty-one seats in the Austrian parliament. The pioneer of this trend was a large landowner named Georg Ritter von Schönerer, an effective speaker and demagogue who exercised great influence on the young Hitler. He first appeared on the public scene in the 1870's as a radical democrat with a program of social reforms patterned on Bismarck's, calling for universal suffrage, wage and labor reforms, and the right to strike. But his demands for an equitable distribution of income and property and his aggressive anticapitalism were subordinated to a passionate nationalism and anti-internationalism. *Anschluss* to Bismarck's Reich, the fight against "foreign domination," the movement "away from Rome," and anticlericalism supported by German and Swiss Protestants (the Gustav-Adolf League), and, finally, an out-and-out racial anti-Semitism even stronger than his anti-Slavism—these formed the basis of Schönerer's creed. His criterion was race, not religion, and consequently he rejected all proposals for assimilation. The widely quoted dictum *"Religion ist einerlei, in der Rasse liegt die Schweinerei"* ("Religion is nothing, race makes for the filth") [50] testifies to the level of his argumentation. The Jews, because of their "racial peculiarities," were responsible for all evils: corruption and freedom of the press, unnational liberalism, and the social misery of capitalism. Schönerer predicted that the guilt of the Jews would one day be settled "on their bodies"; his radical declaration of war on the Jews culminated in a demand for special anti-Jewish laws. Austrian anti-Semites in the parliament went so far as to ask that a reward be paid to anyone who murdered a Jew and that the property of the victim be awarded to the murderer.

After his electoral victory in 1901, Schönerer gradually dropped the socialist points of his program and edged closer to a conservative-bourgeois Pan-Germanism. However, another precursor of German national anti-Semitism, a man of petty-bourgeois origins, Karl Lueger, made an even greater impression on the young Hitler, who called him "the mightiest mayor of all times." Lueger came out of the Catholic social-reform movement, which called for an "organic" social order and was opposed to the rule of finance and capitalism, the alleged province of Jews. This stance was a reversion to the economic and social ideas of the Middle Ages, when anti-Semitism was based on similar notions. The removal of Jews from public life and all vital professions, and even the promulgation of a special law for the handling of that troublesome minority were among the major tenets of Lueger, a popular mayor of Vienna wielding considerable influence. (His movement, which flowed directly into the early phases of National Socialism, will be discussed in the next chapter.) The anti-Semitic campaign in Austria did in fact experience some setbacks after the turn of the century.

[50] Cf. Massing, *op. cit.*, p. 241; Gerlach, *op. cit.*, pp. 112 ff.; Andrew G. Whiteside, *Austrian National Socialism Before 1918* (The Hague, 1962), p. 65; Peter Pulzer, *The Rise of Political Antisemitism in Germany and Austria* (New York, 1964), pp. 148 ff.

Its history continued to be marked by internal fights and splits. Lueger softened his stand, and Schönerer's influence, because of his away-from-Rome campaign (which, incidentally, Hitler later was to label a tactical mistake), remained limited.[51]

But it would be fallacious to maintain that the years preceding World War I saw a deceleration and decline of the anti-Semitic hate movement. The fact of the matter is that anti-Semitic emotions intensified and were fostered by an underground movement of fervent, militant sects which nurtured a *völkisch* anti-Semitism like a secret science. During his Viennese years, Hitler apparently found inspiration in their literature. And they were effective in Germany as well. One of these sects, the Germanic Order, founded in Munich in 1913 and reorganized as the Thule Society in 1918, became the godfather of the Hitler party and put a permanent stamp on the early phase of the movement."

In retrospect, it is undoubtedly correct to say that the anti-Semitic precursors of National Socialism did not stand a chance of political success before World War I. They were splinter groups, divided in their objectives, not least in their ideas about the role of the Jew. They had no influence whatsoever on the legislative process and were unable either to push through anti-Jewish laws or to check Jewish emancipation and assimilation, despite the volume of their agitation between 1873 and the turn of the century. This lack of effectiveness had a number of causes. In the eyes of the dominant conservative group, socialism, not "Jewish" capitalism, was the main enemy; economic well-being served to allay the fears of the middle class and eased the adjustment to industrial society; the energies of domestic rebelliousness were channeled into active support of a policy of imperialist and economic expansion. And, even though the ruling conservative groups from time to time utilized anti-Semitism for their own purposes, thereby opening up the way for its implantation and growth, they did not make many concessions to it in political practice. Prior to Hitler's emergence, outbreaks of anti-Semitic violence were rare in Germany, unlike eastern Europe. Of course, anti-Semitism was ever present, waiting for fresh opportunities, particularly in times of political and economic crisis. It flared up with great intensity in 1873–95, 1918–23, 1930–33, but its influence on political life and the terrible realization of its barbaric goals became possible only after it had become part of an antidemocratic mass movement.

A LOOK AHEAD TOWARD 1933

This brings us to the question of what special circumstances made possible the rise of National Socialism. The answer must be sought in the combination of the shortcomings of German policy from the early

---

[51] For the best analysis of the personalities of Schönerer and Lueger, see Carl E. Schorske, "Politics in a New Key," *Journal of Modern History,* XXXIX (1967), 346 ff., 355 ff.

nineteenth century on and the fatal roots and crisis-ridden history of the Weimar Republic. The democracy of 1918 was held responsible for the aftereffects of defeat suffered in the war. The new government became the scapegoat and hate-object of the forces of restoration and reaction in state and society, as well as of the revolutionary dictatorial movements gathered in the militant Free Corps,* in *völkisch*–anti-Semitic sects, and in paramilitary outfits. The "Red specter" of Communist revolution did the rest to make Army and bureaucracy, middle class and business, susceptible to these sentiments. The democratic forces extended to their enemies the tolerance of a liberal legal system. They were also confronted with the desire for authority nurtured by an authoritarian bureaucratic state, and this created serious organizational problems in the Republic.

The conflict between authoritarian tradition and the new democracy had a number of consequences: a nonfunctioning of parliamentary government; agitation for a Presidential system as a sort of ersatz empire and quasi dictatorship; the splintering and lack of cooperation of ideologically and politically rigid parties; the rise of antidemocratic movements which, being in opposition to the government, limited the maneuverability of the political coalitions; the militarization of the nongovernmental sector by militant groups; the spread of a terrorist power philosophy which propounded a barbaric friend-foe principle as opposed to the democratic idea of compromise; the radicalization of the economically and socially threatened urban and rural middle classes; the susceptibility of the bureaucracy and judiciary to hierarchical-authoritarian ideas of order; and, finally, the Army's suspicious attitude toward the democratic Republic.

It was against this background that National Socialism took shape as a new type of integrating force. Being a specifically German manifestation of European antidemocratism, it was completely attuned to the German situation and even less of an export article than Italian Fascism. This is yet another example of the limits of the conception of a universal fascism. The nationalist foundation makes for profound differences from country to country. Nor is there any monocausal explanation, whether it be based on economic, political, or ideological premises. National Socialism, like Hitler, was the product of World War I, but it was given its shape and force by those basic problems of modern German history which marked the painful road of the democratic movement. Among these were the fragility of the democratic tradition and the powerful remnants of authoritarian governmental and social institutions before and after 1848; the susceptibility to nationalistic, imperialistic ideas, a product of the belated and never fully realized creation of a German national state; the problems arising out of the unexpected defeat and the resultant stab-in-the-back legend, and the widespread disgruntlement over the Versailles peace; the perma-

---

* Volunteer defense units organized by former imperial officers, and owing allegiance to these officers.—TRANSLATOR'S NOTE.

nent crisis of a republic which never won the full support of the majority of the people; the explosive consequences of the Depression on this highly industrialized, socially and religiously divided state with its feudalistic, traditionalistic remnants; and, finally, the middle class's fear of proletarization and Communism, and the added resentment and panic of a rural population threatened by the spread of modern technology. It should, therefore, not come as a surprise that National Socialism scored its greatest electoral successes first in rural Bavaria and then in the rural provinces of Schleswig-Holstein and Lower Saxony.

Among the special factors of the early days of National Socialism was the tremendously important part played by the spectacular rise and near-religious veneration of a Führer. The organizational structure and activities of this new type of movement were based completely on the leader principle. In the center stood the figure of Adolf Hitler. In terms of social psychology, he represented the disenfranchised little man eager to compensate for his feelings of inferiority through militancy and political radicalism. His Austrian birth, educational and professional failure, and the redeeming experience of the male camaraderie of the war shaped his own life as well as the ideology of National Socialism.

National Socialism was based on a nationalistic, racist, oversimplified Social Darwinism popularized in the writings of radical sectarians. Yet at the same time, through an eclectic mixture of doctrinaire and political programs, it sought to appeal to all parts of the population. The early slogans of National Socialism, by their championship of expansionist social imperialism and by their submission to nationalist dictatorial rule, were intended to divert the middle class and the working class from domestic troubles. The "national community" was proclaimed as the panacea for the cure of economic and political ills, in place of the pluralism of democracy and the class society. Militaristic and racist doctrines were the instruments used to woo and win over the population. An aggressive nationalism appealing to the traditional German sense of uniqueness and the vision of a unified Greater Germany were used in the campaign against the Versailles treaty. The next step was a demand for the expansion of the national and ethnic boundaries, for *Lebensraum* in the East for the allegedly superior German and Germanic peoples.

In addition to the Führer cult, which appealed to the authoritarian desire for order, the social and biological version of anti-Semitism became one of the early fanatical fixtures of Hitler's program. This issue lent itself to the concept of the absolute enemy which every totalitarian movement has to have in order to direct and deflect the aggressiveness it has mobilized. Above all, National Socialist ideology and political strategy were based on the right of the stronger, as propounded by Social Darwinism. The exaltation of "action" as the highest ideal, above reason and intellect, defined the basically irrational nature of National Socialism. Its ultimate purpose was the acquisition of unlimited power through oppression inside the country and expansion outside. The history of the Third Reich reveals that National Socialism followed Hitler's early plans, despite its offhand dismissal by the social critics of the time. The history of National Socialism, in effect, is the history of its fatal underestimation.

This is true also of Hitler's victory of 1933. The Third Reich came into being as a result of a series of effective deceptive maneuvers. Without them, Hitler probably could not have come to power. His, he said, was a "legal revolution." By combining these two contradictory concepts, the National Socialists paid homage to the popular desire for legality as well as the wish for complete change in a period of grave economic ills. After the failure of his putsch of 1923, as well as the reactionary Kapp Putsch of 1920,* which manifested the distaste of the bourgeoisie and civil service for overt coups and revolutions, Hitler confined himself to pseudo-legal tactics. Instead of attempting a putsch against the Republic, he made use of the possibilities offered by the emergency provisions of the Weimar Constitution to abrogate it. The road of a Presidential dictatorship had always been a favored recommendation of conservative opponents of parliamentary democracy, and, after 1930, it was actively supported by the authoritarian, monarchic President of Germany, Field Marshal Hindenburg. It was he who helped the National Socialist Party shed the shackles of a minority party that never had won much more than a third of the popular vote in any election. The special powers granting the President the right to dissolve the Reichstag and appoint a Chancellor made possible the legal dictatorship of the President. It was exercise of these prerogatives, not the voice of a majority government, which brought Hitler to power.

The successful imposition of autocratic rule was augmented by the appeal for a "national revolution." As far as Hitler was concerned, the alliance with rightist parties, industrial circles, agrarian interests, and the military was merely one of expediency. When a serious party crisis threatened at the end of 1932, he did make major concessions to the champions of a "national concentration" of the Right assembled by von Papen, Hindenburg's confidant. But even if as Chancellor he accepted a majority of Conservative ministers, he nonetheless insisted on the right to exercise the dictatorial Presidential powers. Disguising the power claims of the National Socialists as the call for a Christian-national resurgence had the desired effect in the Government as well as among the public, and did not interfere with the ruthless oppressive measures Hitler pushed through with the help of those "legal" dictatorial powers in February, 1933. Hitler's allies had initially overestimated their own power, and later they tried to steer the revolution into orderly channels. But by their cooperation they first made possible the pseudo-legality of that revolution. For similar reasons, the opposition of the middle class capitulated before the Enabling Act, and the civil

* This attempt by an antirepublican military coalition under Wolfgang Kapp and General von Lüttwitz to overthrow the Government failed after only four days.—TRANSLATOR'S NOTE.

service cooperated in the legalization of the Nazi revolution. The Left also let itself be duped. For too long it remained almost paralyzed in the face of the novel situation of a "legal" and "national" revolution.

In the final analysis, Hitler came to power as a result of a series of avoidable errors. He was neither elected freely by a majority of the German people nor were there compelling reasons for the capitulation of the Republic. However, in the end, the democratic forces were in the minority vis-à-vis the totalitarian, dictatorial parties of the National Socialists and the Communists. And in this situation a large portion of Germany's top echelons went over to Hitler after 1933. The susceptibility of the middle class had historical as well as immediate reasons. As confusing as the history of Hitler's takeover may be, the preconditions of National Socialism also do not lend themselves to simple explanations. A number of not too clearly defined factors and elements played a part, forces of a dark underground of German and European social and national conditions. The fatal emergence of Hitler is closely linked to a main current of German events in the nineteenth and twentieth centuries, even if National Socialism cannot be equated with German history. Looking back after 1945, Friedrich Meinecke put the problem of the antecedents of National Socialism and its links to German thought and attitudes thus:

One can always object that the power-state and Machiavellism were not confined to Germany, that they were more often preached but not more strongly practiced by us Germans. This view is quite true. Specifically German, however, was the frankness and nakedness of the German power-state and Machiavellism, its hard and deliberate formulation as a principle of conduct, and the pleasure taken in its reckless consequences. Specifically German also was the tendency to elevate something primarily practical into a universal world-view theory. It was a serious thing for the future that these ideas about power-state and Machiavellism, at first expressed merely as theories, might become practical weapons in the hands of ruling authorities. The German power-state idea, whose history began with Hegel, was to find in Hitler its worst and most fatal application and extension.[52]

[52] *The German Catastrophe: Reflections and Recollections* (Cambridge, Mass., 1950), pp. 14–15.

II

The Origins of the National Socialist Movement

The groundwork for the political movements which may be considered the immediate precursors of National Socialism was laid around the turn of the century. Although the national-social and Christian-social *völkisch* and anti-Semitic groups that emerged in the 1870's had proved small and rather unstable, their noisy propaganda had penetrated the political thinking of wider circles. It had also had its effects on the large rightist parties, the Conservatives and National Liberals, in whom nationalism and Germanomania, adulation of the state and imperial claims, were nurtured as part of a bourgeois ideology. World War I magnified these tendencies and spread them. This general background and the specific antecedents of radical extremist movements combined to form the preconditions and origins of National Socialism.

The German Workers' Party (Deutsche Arbeiter Partei, or DAP), which Hitler encountered in Munich in 1919, was certainly nothing new. Though its formation and growth were closely connected with the recent military defeat and the revolutionary climate of 1918–19, it could not have come into being except for the intellectual, social, and political growth of Austro-German *völkisch* nationalism. It was one of the numerous sectarian "anti" movements—anti-Semitic, anti-Western, anti-Slav—that accompanied Germany on the road to the twentieth century. Like Hitler himself, these movements must be seen within the context of the nationalistic and socio-economic conflicts of Austria-Hungary, a multinational state in decline. It was there that the most prominent forerunners of National Socialism made their first appearance. The earliest area of such activities was the German-Czech border region of Bohemia and Moravia. There the nationality conflict, conducted with increasing antagonism by both sides, was exacerbated and covered over by the social conflicts arising out of industrialization. The Czech problem had not been solved by the institution of the dual monarchy in 1867. By the turn of century, it had become increasingly acute.

While German dominance-claims, Czech nationalism, and political and social dynamics clashed with increasing severity, Austria resounded with the national-*völkisch* slogans of Schönerer and Lueger. Lueger, with the help of the Catholic trade unions, had succeeded in making his Christian Social Party the strongest political party after the Social Democratic Party, formed at about the same time. As the party of the Catholic lower middle class, the Christian Socialists opposed liberalism and capitalism, which they considered the repository of un-Christian materialism, excessive individualism, and, above all, disproportionate Jewish influence. Religious as well as socioeconomic factors were responsible for the anti-Semitism of the Christian Social Party. In this, it resembled the Christian-social movement of Court Chaplain Stoecker of Berlin, though Stoecker's group had a Protestant cast and, being considerably smaller, was merely a temporary phenomenon, for Germany's Catholic "socialism" was absorbed largely by the Center Party (Zentrumspartei). In the face of the dual threat posed by socialism and capitalism, the Christian Social Party succeeded in attracting workers, shopkeepers, and white-collar workers with national-social and anti-Semitic catchphrases. Splinter groups such as the German Anti-Semitic People's Party (Deutschantisemitische Bürgerpartei) of Vienna (1911) combined anti-Semitic with *völkisch*-national slogans.

These nationalistic tendencies also began to make inroads among the working class.[1] The Social Democratic trade unions, themselves rent by the German-Czech conflict and the defection of Czech unions, were being challenged by splinter groups propagating a socialism free from internationalism; the proclaimed purpose of these "national socialists" was the achievement of an egalitarian, anticapitalist, anticlerical new social order, and the elimination of all non-Germanic, Slavic, and Jewish influence. These splinter groups, a force between the Christian Socialists and the Social Democrats, attempted to win the German workers of the multinational state for a "community" run along nationalist, socialist lines. The fight for national emancipation, particularly by the Czechs, accelerated this development. Soon after the turn of the century, and spurred by the disappointment over Schönerer's defection to the bourgeoisie, a new party, the German

---

[1] For a discussion of this topic, see Otto Bauer, *Die Nationalitätenfrage und die österreichische Sozialdemokratie*, (2d ed.; Vienna, 1924). Hans Mommsen, *Die Sozialdemokratie und die Nationalitätenfrage im habsburgischen Vielvölkerstaat* (Vienna, 1963).

Workers' Party (Deutsche Arbeiterpartei), was formed in the recently industrialized regions of Bohemia and Moravia; it called for an ethnically based opposition to the "alien domination" of the Czechs.[2] The party specifically opposed the influx of Czech workers from the countryside, who, though despised for their lower standard of living, nonetheless constituted unwelcome competition and during labor conflicts, such as the great strike of 1900, furnished most of the strikebreakers. This competition was a threat which the supranational socialism of Austro-Marxist vintage was unable to ward off; it practically cried out for a national German socialist organization.

The socialist dilemma in the face of the nationality problem was indeed one of the essential prerequisites of the early brand of National Socialism. It would, therefore, be a mistake to say that this early version was nothing more than a manifestation of agrarian and petty-bourgeois reaction to modernization and industrialization. The nationalist (anti-Czech) and anti-Semitic (anticapitalist) content of this new type of "socialism" grew out of the feeling that the socialist concept of class consciousness failed to take into account the national prestige feelings of the German workers. One school of thought maintains that the Social Democrats therefore bear some of the blame, for in their preoccupation with the class struggle they failed to consider national feelings and needs. It was a problem of major importance which continued to be debated in the post-1933 emigration and inside the SPD after 1945. The Czech Social Democrats, on the other hand, were able to absorb the nationalist forces more successfully and bring them into their broad framework. The problems of the national boundaries and of acclimatization had already given rise to a "national socialism" in German Bohemia prior to 1900, and the socio-economic rivalry was quickly transformed into the *völkisch*-ideological realm and radicalized politically. It began with the split of the Bohemian unions, followed by the formation of independent Czech unions. In 1898, a Czech national socialist party was organized, and, in 1904, the German Workers' Party (DAP) was founded in Trautenau (Bohemia).[3] Its main base was nationalist German workers' organizations headquartered in Linz, the city in which just about then the young Hitler was ending his unsuccessful school career.

From a sociological point of view, the new party might be considered a workers' party, even though the impoverished lower middle class and shopkeepers formed a part. Not a few of its members had come from the ranks of the Social Democrats, as did those of the rival Czech party, which for its part called for the national unity of all Czechs, regardless of class. The first DAP program of Trautenau—a mixture of socialist, anticapitalist, anticlerical, and antifeudal ideas interspersed with anti-Marxist, *völkisch* catchphrases—reflected both the

[2] Andrew G. Whiteside, *Austrian National Socialism Before 1918* (The Hague, 1962), pp. 37 ff.

[3] *Ibid.*, pp. 72 ff. Cf. the basic work of J. W. Brügel, *Tschechen und Deutsche, 1918–1938* (Munich, 1967).

party's proletarian origins and its specifically German Bohemian character. It was born of the conviction that the Marxist idea of international solidarity played into the hands of the Czechs. That is why, in the words of its program, this "libertarian national party, which with all its strength was dedicated to fighting reaction, feudal, clerical, and capitalist special privileges, and alien national influences" was formed. Its proclaimed aim was "the economic and political mobilization of the German working people" in defense of the "interests of the broad masses." At that time, "libertarian," "socialist," and "democratic" ideas still played a major role. However, its followers soon began to call themselves simply "national socialists." Their basic contention was that the interests of the "Germanic" nation transcended those of individual and class. But their positions on political and social issues, property rights and form of government, national sovereignty and individual rights, and political and economic equality were far more ambiguous. Democratic and authoritarian approaches overlapped; at times, the party seemed to veer toward the right, at others, toward the left. Its direction was determined largely by the background and personality of its leaders.

The founders and early supporters of the DAP were laborers, apprentices, and unionists from small mining and textile enterprises, as well as from the railroads, where, ever since their nationalization (1877), the problem of language had created antagonisms between German- and non–German-speaking railroad officials. The early organizers of the DAP included the apprentice bookbinder Ludwig Vogel of Brüx and the laborer Franz Stein of Eger, who, as the founder of the German National Workers' League (Deutschnationaler Arbeiterbund; 1893) and the later League of German Workers Germania (Bund deutscher Arbeiter Germania), had been in close contact with Schönerer's organizations; in 1899, Stein had organized a national workers' congress in Eger. Twenty years before Hitler, this congress drew up a 25-point program that called for granting workers equal rights with all other "national comrades" (*Volksgenossen*), nationalization of large enterprises, mines, and railroads, and the protection of skilled workers against the influx of unskilled (Czech) workers. The basic tenor still was that of the radical-democratic "people's community" of a socialist cast. However, one of the founding members, the twenty-two-year-old foreman Hans Knirsch, amidst shouts of "*Heil!*," proposed that the congress send greetings to Schönerer. Knirsch had come to Eger from Linz; from 1918 until his death in 1933, he headed the Sudeten German National Socialist Party (Sudetendeutsche nationalsozialistische Partei); he was succeeded by Konrad Henlein. Another early member of the Sudeten German nucleus of the DAP was Ferdinand Burschowsky, a printer from Hohenstadt (Moravia). He wrote for and was the publisher of a nationalist monthly, *Der deutsche Gehilfe* (*The German Apprentice*), renamed *Der deutsche Arbeiter* (*The German Worker*) in 1898.

All these men held fast to the idea that Czech influx into the Sudeten

German cities was the primary cause of all social ills and that the synthesis of nationalism and socialism, in their most radical sense, was the only hope for betterment. This simple belief that social and national problems were identical and, even more, that antisocialist capitalism must be opposed, ultimately led to a split with the Schönerer movement and the formation of a separate party. In effect, of course, little was accomplished beyond political speechifying and demands for the division of Bohemia and for preferential treatment of German workers by German-Bohemian industries. Moreover, the confusing multiplicity of organizations, fusions, splits, and rivalries among the Christian-national, social, and Pan-German parties did not exactly help the DAP. In 1907, it was able to mobilize only a few thousand votes in all of Bohemia.

Its fortunes improved only after a civil servant from Reichenberg, Dr. Walter Riehl, joined the party. A former Social Democrat whose grandfather had been a Radical Democratic deputy in Germany's first elected National Assembly at Frankfurt's St. Paul's Church in 1848, Riehl proved to be the sort of effective publicist, speaker, and organizer the party needed. As late as 1908, Riehl still thought of himself as a revisionist socialist; he had dreams of transforming the Social Democrats into national socialists. Writing in the *Reichenberger Zeitung,* he exhorted Bohemia's German workers to be "class-conscious as well as national-conscious socialists." The Social Democrats, he held, had to become a national socialist party. Impelled by the German-Czech nationality struggle, Riehl began to work for the DAP a year later. His first priority was to broaden the influence of the party among the German middle class and to mobilize public opinion against "alien" Czech influences. The creation of a movement encompassing all classes for national liberation and social justice was the cause to which he now devoted himself wholeheartedly, particularly after being discharged from his civil service post in 1910 for his political activities. He organized socialist youth groups, became a discussion speaker at mass meetings which frequently disintegrated into brawls, and engaged in far-flung publicistic ventures. In the elections of 1911, the DAP outpolled the Pan-Germans, though the total number of votes was still small (26,000) and the forces of this movement still divided.

The party then devoted itself to developing its ideology and program and to winning broader support. This effort became the special province of Rudolf Jung, a railroad engineer who joined the DAP in 1910. Jung was a native of Iglau, a town rent by national antagonisms, particularly between the German and Czech railroad workers. Later, railroad workers were also to play a significant role in the founding of Anton Drexler's National Socialist Party in Munich in 1919. Discharged by the railroad because of his political activity, Jung in 1910 was put on the party payroll and devoted himself to theoretical work. Together with Riehl, he drafted the Iglau party program (1913), which contained a more detailed comparison of international Marxism and national socialism and a more pointed attack on capitalism, Social

Democracy, alien peoples, and Jews. In contrast to the programs of bourgeois extremists, anti-Semitism here ranked in importance after anti-Slav, anticlerical, and anticapitalist slogans.

The concrete objectives of the "movement" (this was the first time it so designated itself) were, however, no less vague than before. Its program called for "positive creative reform" through "socialization of the monopolies" and the "abolition of unearned increment," and for "war on finance capital." Instead of international class struggle (an act of national suicide), a "people's community" to fight "alien influences" was to come into being. One looks in vain for concrete details about the "reform," let alone for a genuine theory of state and society. The only clearly stated issues were the "anti" positions and the resentments underlying them. The substance was thoroughly irrational— an appeal to hatred and wishful thinking.

In its eclecticism and opportunism, the last prewar program of the DAP was typical of the National Socialist approach to political theory. The most varied, even contradictory, positions were set forth and artificially combined with one another, without regard to their historico-political context. Emotional appeal was the prime criterion; consistency and logic lagged behind. This held true even more for the new program Jung drafted for the next party congress, held in Vienna in August, 1918. During the war, the DAP had propagated a militant patriotism but had not been particularly active politically, despite the availability of Jung, who was exempted from military service. Then, in the summer of 1918, the party took the final step toward becoming the party of all classes. It adopted a new official name, German National Socialist Workers' Party (Deutsche Nationalsozialistische Arbeiterpartei, or DNSAP), and stated specifically that the term "workers" no longer was to be considered a designation of class but, rather, the honorific of all who worked.

In the midst of the defeat of Germany and Austria, doubly difficult for the Bohemian central group of the party, for it now was cut off from its own state, Jung finally completed his long-planned "theoretical work," published in Aussig in 1919 under the title *Der Nationale Sozialismus, sein Werdegang und seine Ziele* (*National Socialism, Its Development and Its Goals*). The introduction stated that the book was to play the same role for national socialism as *Das Kapital* did for Marxian socialism. Written in the bombastic style of vague banalities, it set forth the stereotyped ideas of the *völkisch* movement, though, here, in conjunction with socialist goals. Its point of departure was a lament over the destruction of German culture by foreign influences: modern civilization and "mammonism," wage labor and finance capital, liberal democracy and Marxism. Behind this process, Jung saw the forces of international Jewry seeking world domination, forces which dominated capitalism and liberal democracy as well as Marxian socialism. Once again, the point of departure, the "anti" position, was clearly defined. Yet, the concrete picture of the new national socialism remained the same vague conglomerate of emotional slogans, though spelled out in greater detail and encompassing concepts which were later incorporated into the ideology and program of the Hitler movement: the idea of "common good before individual good," the primacy of nation over individual and class, the evasion of the burning problems of modern industrial society through an appeal to romantic ideas of a militaristic or imperialistic social order.

Nonetheless, this irrational, power-oriented ideology was not without a revolutionary kernel. By no means was it merely an expression of reactionary tendencies; it had its roots in the working class, and only gradually, as the Hitler movement grew, did its influence spread to the peasantry, the middle class, and the military. The revolutionary ingredient remained the dominant element in its appeal to the masses and its demand for a sweeping "renewal" of state and society. It played a role in the virulent opposition to everything "foreign to the nation"— the "subhuman" Czechs and Jews—in the *völkisch* rationalization of national and social resentments, in the sovereignty claims of the "nobler" German race. Accordingly, the solution lay not in accommodation, not in a conservative stabilization of the status quo or the restoration of preindustrial society, but in forcible expulsion, in the acquisition of *Lebensraum,* in the abolition of foreign competition and the protection of the German "worker" of all classes in a strong and united "people's community" free from internal division. Jung's philosophy still bore the traces of the multinational problems of the Sudeten Germans, who wanted socialism but felt a greater kinship with their own bourgeoisie than with the Czech proletariat. The minority problem, together with the lost war, was a founding stone of National Socialism.

Of course, no inspired mass leader had as yet emerged; the small "movement" was still nothing more than a regional phenomenon latching on to specific conditions and issues, such as the pressures of immigration, competition, labor, and social insecurity. Its concrete impact on the growth and resurgence of *völkisch* and National Socialist groups after 1918 is hard to estimate. But it is likely that Hitler had come into contact with this movement during his Vienna years, if not still earlier in Linz. When the demand for self-determination for German Bohemia, a demand supported by every party, was frustrated by the Treaty of St. Germain of 1919, the party organization split up: Jung and Knirsch stayed in Czechoslovakia, and Riehl took over the Austro-German branch, which began to concentrate on demands for union with Germany. As early as 1920, a joint conference with Hitler's new, Munich-based National Socialist German Workers' Party (NSDAP) was held in Salzburg; Hitler himself delivered speeches in Linz and Vienna. For a while, Riehl's Vienna headquarters coordinated these activities, but, after 1923, Hitler took charge, and the Austrian National Socialists became subordinate to the stronger German organization—a logical consequence of the program for union with Germany. At a meeting held in Salzburg in 1923, Riehl was forced to resign, and in a plenary session in Munich in 1926, Hitler, heading the reorganized NSDAP, became the dictatorial leader of both the German and Austrian parties. His 25-point program became binding on all.

Thus, the early history of Austrian National Socialism is intertwined with the development of the Hitler movement in Germany. The emergence of Hitler, and the special conditions in postwar Germany in which National Socialism was organized, made for a situation in which a small sect soon found itself able to become a political power. Familiarity with that early Austrian history is essential to an understanding of the German phenomenon of National Socialism as well. This holds true even more so for Hitler himself, who, growing up between Austria and Germany, took in the most extreme manifestations of *völkisch* radicalism and hurled its slogans into the tumultuous political scene of postwar Germany.

ADOLF HITLER

The triumph of National Socialism over the Weimar Republic and its realization in the Third Reich are so closely connected with the life of Adolf Hitler that one tends to equate the two. National Socialism has also been called "Hitlerism" and "nothing other than the projection of the will of the man Adolf Hitler into the realm of ideas and words," coming into existence with Hitler and also disappearing with him.[4] And the rise, triumph, and defeat of National Socialism undoubtedly cannot be divorced from Hitler. But National Socialism is more than the gigantic mistake of misguided followers, the product solely of the demonic powers of one individual. Some of the intellectual and political currents which fed National Socialism and made possible the emergence of a man like Hitler have already been mentioned. His life must be seen against the background of *fin-de-siècle* Austria, and his political rise falls within the framework of postwar Germany and Europe, burdened by grave intellectual and social problems.

Neither Hitler himself nor his closest collaborators, such as National Socialism's chief ideologist, Alfred Rosenberg, or the guiding spirit of Jewish extermination, Reinhard Heydrich, measured up to the prerequisites of the biological postulates of National Socialism: race and ancestry. Official data about Hitler were confined to scant information about his date of birth, scarcely detailed enough for that "small Aryan pass" which he later demanded of all his subjects. Whatever facts about his background have been unearthed give the lie to his story of the harsh early life of an ambitious genius frustrated by circumstances. Still more interesting are the many questions that remain unanswered,[5] beginning with the name and ancestry of the Austrian customs official Alois Hitler; Adolf Hitler, the fourth child

---

[4] Helmuth Heiber, *Adolf Hitler* (Berlin, 1960), p. 157.

[5] See, particularly, the special studies by Franz Jetzinger (*Hitler's Jugend* [Zurich, 1956]) and Werner Maser (*Die Frühgeschichte der NSDAP* [Frankfurt/Main, 1965]).

of Alois' third marriage, was born on April 20, 1889, in the border town of Braunau am Inn. The name "Hitler" is possibly of Czech origin; the family originally came from the Waldviertel, an Austrian border region near Bohemia. But even this much is not certain, for Alois Hitler, the illegitimate son of a servant girl by the name of Maria Anna Schicklgruber, did not change his name to Hitler until 1876, when he was forty. The identity of Alois' father is not known; Maria Schicklgruber presumably had brought the child with her from the city where she had worked, and, five years after her return, at the age of forty-seven, had married a miller's helper by the name of Georg Hiedler. Almost thirty years after her and Hiedler's deaths, Alois Schicklgruber, with the help of a stepuncle and a gullible village priest, had his birth "legitimized," a step he believed essential to his career and one his step-uncle thought he owed his ambitious ward.

Thus, neither Adolf nor Alois could rightfully claim the name of Hitler. Later rumors and speculations, reaching the top echelons of National Socialism,[6] thought it highly probable that Hitler had a Jewish grandfather and ascribed the radicalization of anti-Semitism to Hitler's pathological eagerness to repress this fact. However, no conclusive evidence has thus far been turned up. Recent findings indicate that the name of Grandmother Schicklgruber's last employer in Graz was Frankenberger—by no means invariably a Jewish name—and his son might possibly have fathered her child.

Such digressions are as sensational as they are questionable and pointless, for, though well-meaning, they are rooted in racist superstitions. Hitler's early years and development, particularly his Vienna period, offer ample explanation for his intellectual and psychological development. He grew up in the secure household of a minor civil servant, by no means as impoverished a home as later legend had it. The nice house of his birth, the family property, and his father's pension would indicate that Hitler's years of poverty were the result of his own failure. The father, contrary to his son's later claims, was not a chronic alcoholic, but, rather, a comparatively progressive man with a good job; the mother devoted herself to the care of her home and children. The only thing that seemed to be lacking was a sensible education. The note of self-pity struck by Hitler in making the sad fate of his early years responsible for his failures, culminating in the moving story of the young orphan who finally had to leave home to earn his living, is as contrived as it is untrue.

In 1892, the family moved from Braunau to Passau (Bavaria) and in 1894, to Linz (Austria). Alois Hitler retired a year later, and for a while ran a farm in the Traun valley; in 1898, he purchased a house in Leonding near Linz. Thus, the symbolic significance which Hitler in *Mein Kampf* ascribed to his being born in Braunau, where in 1812 a patriotic bookdealer by the name of Palm was executed for anti-

---

[6] Thus, particularly, Hans Frank, *Im Angesicht des Galgens* (Munich, 1953), pp. 330. f.

Napoleonic activities, also has little foundation, for Hitler spent part of his formative years in the Bavarian border town of Passau and the rest in Linz, the capital city of Upper Austria. His school career in Linz (he had to repeat his fifth year and was transferred to another school in his ninth) was a fiasco; Hitler was not only labeled indolent, but his performance in mathematics and shorthand as well as in German was considered unsatisfactory—a judgment borne out by his later style. Contrary to his claims in *Mein Kampf*, his grades in geography and history were only passing; his only above-average marks were in drawing and gymnastics. One of his teachers called him lopsidedly talented, uncontrolled, high-handed, dogmatic, ill-tempered, lacking in perseverance, and despotic.

After the death of his father (1903), his mother afforded the high-school dropout two-and-a-half years of idleness (1905–7), which he spent daydreaming, occasionally drawing, and going to the theater. At this time, the sixteen-year-old began to manifest some of the traits that marked the later political fanatic and demagogue: utter self-involvement to the point of hysterical self-pity, a mania for untrammeled speechifying and equally grandiose and uncontrolled plan-making, combined with listlessness and an inability to concentrate, let alone work productively. The serious lung disease which Hitler invoked to explain the way he lived is pure invention. A sentence in *Mein Kampf* about the end of his school career is most revealing: "Suddenly I was helped by an illness." The life he led after failing at school was exactly the sort of life that appealed to him. The irresponsible lack of restraint of his Vienna years may be seen as a direct consequence of his two years of idleness. It is simply not true that financial need was responsible for his life in Vienna. Even after the death of his overindulgent mother in late 1907, Adolf and his sister, Paula, were financially secure.

The Hitler myth has it that the seventeen-year-old, forced to earn his living, had to go to that decadent metropolis, Vienna. The fact is that in 1906, his mother treated him to a trip to Vienna, where he passed the time sightseeing and going to the theater, particularly to his beloved Wagner operas. The next year was spent in the protected setting of his mother's house. Neither school nor work was allowed to interrupt his routine. The only "work" he did was occasional drawings, and his grandiose plans for the rebuilding of Linz foreshadowed the extravagant ideas of the master builder of the Third Reich. These youthful fantasies re-emerged in the "monumental" designs he prepared after his entry into Linz in 1938. The pre-Vienna period of this "work-shy dreamer" already contained the seeds of the type of life and thoughts which have come to light in studies of Hitler's early years. An episode of 1906 is typical: He had an idea for a large-scale research project, complete with housekeeper and cook, which was to afford him and his musician friend August Kubizek the necessary leisure and comfort for the study of "German art" and the formation of a circle of "art lovers," said project to be realized through the purchase of a winning lottery ticket. According to his friend, "Adolf Hitler could plan and look into the future so beautifully that I could have listened to him forever." [7] Equally typical is the violence with which he reacted to the news that he had won neither the first nor any of the other lottery prizes: It was the fault of the "entire social order." This episode offers an almost uncanny preview of the later Hitler.

It is pointless to speculate about possible breakdowns suffered during his adolescence, Oedipal complexes, unrequited love, etc. Understandably enough, the relatives of the young man of leisure who refused to entertain any idea about simply "working for a living" began to pressure him to learn a trade. Having failed in his efforts to gain admission to the Vienna Academy of Art (September, 1907), he gave no thought to the possibility of any other profession. He stayed on in Vienna, living the comfortable life of the "art student," without telling his ailing mother the truth. After his mother's death, he still was not under any immediate financial pressure; there was a substantial inheritance in addition to his orphan's allowance, which he continued to collect until his twenty-third year under the pretext of being enrolled at the Vienna Academy. Later, he also inherited a fairly substantial sum from an aunt. All these facts underscore the dishonesty of the piteous note struck in his autobiography.

The nineteen-year-old Hitler floundering in Vienna did not, contrary to the self-image of *Mein Kampf*, have any definite political orientation. His "nationalism" was in line with the national German tendencies prevalent in Linz, and his knowledge of history, in which he allegedly excelled at school, was limited. As late as the 1930's, his history instructor, Leopold Pötsch, of whom he speaks highly in *Mein Kampf*, did not want to be part of this myth. As to the "Jewish problem," Hitler also had little knowledge and no firm opinions. His family doctor was Jewish, and Hitler used to send him hand-painted postcards from Vienna. He also accepted money gifts from him, yet in 1938, after the *Anschluss*, the doctor was driven into exile. Against these facts we have Hitler's contention that while in Linz he had already learned "to understand and comprehend the meaning of history" and that the Austrian nationality conflict had taught him that the meaning of history was to be found in the battle for the "nation" (*Volkstum*) and in the victory of "*völkisch* nationalism" *(Mein Kampf,* pp. 8 ff.). Yet, some of the basic traits and thoughts which took shape during his five-and-a-half years in Vienna were, according to Kubizek, his patient audience, already to be found in the endless speeches and grandiose plans of his Linzer days. The experiences of Vienna, Munich, and World War I lent them substance and embellished them with the up-to-date content and impulses which so profoundly were to shape Hitler the political man.

He was driven to Vienna not by "need and harsh reality" but by the

[7] August Kubizek, *Adolf Hitler—mein Jugendfreund* (Graz, 1953); see also Jetzinger, *op. cit.,* pp. 166 ff.

desire to escape work, the need to learn a trade, and the wish to continue the life-style of the "future artist," a pose which he was unable to maintain any longer under the watchful eyes of his relatives in Linz. He kept on urging his friend Kubizek to join him in Vienna. In the ensuing months, he was an almost daily visitor to the opera, went sightseeing, developed grandiose plans for a musical drama and for all sorts of building projects, while Kubizek, who had been as unaware of his friend's academic failure as the family, enrolled in the Vienna Conservatory. Hitler, as he proudly stated, was supreme master of his time. The harsh life of the "common laborer" who had to earn his "crust of bread" is one of the heart-rending myths of his autobiography. Between 1909 and 1913, the unsuccessful art student and self-designated "artist" and "writer" was introduced to the political ideas and currents that were to furnish the decisive concepts and stimuli for his later career. The political and social conflicts and emotions in the Vienna of that era offered material and food for a radical critique of society, and the unbridgable gap between Hitler's wants, ambitions, and fantasies and naked reality made him accept and enlarge on this critique. It was the same impulse that later, in crisis-ridden postwar Germany, drove so large a segment of the lower middle class, its feelings of superiority threatened, into the arms of the radical-Right doctrine of salvation—a sociopolitical flight into an irrational political creed thriving on hatred and fear and demanding to be saved from conflict through the institution of a total "new order."

The rejection of Hitler's second application for admission to the Art Academy in the fall of 1908 seems to have been a turning point in his life. He broke off his friendship with Kubizek and became submerged in the shadowy world of public shelters (1908–9) and homes for men (1910–13), though the allowance and the gifts from relatives continued. Moreover, the "hard labor" referred to in *Mein Kampf* should have brought him additional funds. During this period, Hitler discovered the political and social slogans then in vogue, an encounter reminiscent of his earlier introduction to art. Contrary to his testimony, Hitler had read few books and had not really concerned himself with the political and social problems of his environment. A chance reading of books, occasional pamphlets, and generalizations based on subjective impressions combined to form the distorted political picture which, in almost pristine form, became the "Weltanschauung" that dominated Hitler's future life and work.

The only work he did was an occasional copying of picture postcards which his fellow inmates of the men's home sold for him. He spent most of his time piecing together his Weltanschauung from obscure sources. Its essence was extreme nationalism and a radical racial anti-Semitism. The literature which stimulated Hitler's interest in politics forms the subject of a comprehensive study.[8] Among his reading

---

[8] Wilfried Daim, *Der Mann, der Hitler die Ideen gab* (Munich, 1958). On the religious background, see Friedrich Heer, *Der Glaube des Adolf Hitler* (Munich, 1968).

matter was a periodical with the resounding name of *Ostara*, the German goddess of spring, a publication which, from 1905 on, was widely sold in the tobacco kiosks of Vienna. It gave voice to the eccentric and bloodthirsty race mythology of Adolf Lanz (1874–1954), an ex-monk who called himself Lanz von Liebenfels. His program called for the founding of a male order of blue-eyed, blond "Aryans." His headquarters were in a castle in Lower Austria which he had bought with the help of industrialist patrons. There Lanz hoisted the swastika banner in 1906 as the symbol of the Aryan movement. This pathological founding father of an "Aryan" hero cult was the author of *Theozoology* (1901), a work offering a particularly abstruse mixture of an extreme, pseudo-religious racism. Apparently, Hitler got in touch with Lanz personally in 1909, asking for copies of *Ostara* that were missing from his own collection. Lanz's views, and similarly fantastic notions from the "European underground," which later were to make their way into the Ludendorff movement, helped to shape Hitler's political ideology. Lanz's works disseminated the crass exaggerations of the Social Darwinist theory of survival, the superman and superrace theory, the dogma of race conflict, and the breeding and extermination theories of the future SS state. The scheme was simple: a blond, heroic race of "Arioheroes" was engaged in battle with inferior mixed races whose annihilation was deemed a historico-political necessity; "race defilement" was not to be tolerated, and the master race was to multiply with the help of "race hygiene," polygamy, and breeding stations; sterilization, debilitating forced labor, and systematic liquidation were to offer a final solution.

Such pamphlets were fatal reading for an unstable youth with few ideas of his own, even though, as Hitler himself confessed, his middle class, liberal background initially led him to rebel against these teachings. This literature took on great significance against the background of impressions received by a footloose youth on the lowest rung of the social ladder in the capital city of a multinational monarchy. Hitler's acquaintance with Marxist socialism also was not the product of close study, as he claimed, but of obscure subjective impressions marked by the sort of class and cultural snobbery which was still part of him and which he now directed toward social and political issues. A passage in *Mein Kampf* (p. 25), precisely because of its exaggeration, throws interesting light on its author and the substance of his Weltanschauung: "At that time I read ceaselessly and very thoroughly." (He never is specific about his reading matter; his "books," according to his own account of the genesis of his anti-Semitism [p. 59], are polemical pamphlets bought "for a few pennies.") The passage continues: "What free time I had left from my work was spent on my studies. In a few years I thus created for myself the basis of the knowledge on which I still feed. During that time I formed a picture of the world and an ideology which has become the granite foundation of my deeds. I only had to add a little more knowledge to that which I had acquired at that time; I did not have to revise anything."

Who else can say this of his impressions at the age of twenty? This passage is more revealing of the level of his Viennese "studies" (mostly, endless debates between the idle smart aleck and his fellow inmates at the shelter) and of the substance of the later National Socialist ideology than the most probing analysis. What Hitler "learned" in Vienna, and subsequently elevated to the status of a "constructive ideology," was that monomaniacal, obsessive, unseeing yet effective method of political argumentation which led from the evenings in the men's shelter of Vienna to the endless monologues of the demagogue.

In addition to inventing the story of the day laborer who while on the job had his eyes opened to Marxism and its Jewish "backers," Hitler also makes mention of the anti-Semitic movement of the Austro-Pan-German nationalist von Schönerer. The actual impact of this antimonarchist, anti-Marxist social movement, the Austrian version of a decidedly national "German socialism," is hard to assess, but its nationalist, *völkisch* battle cries undoubtedly are among the roots of National Socialism. They furnished the young Hitler with a political framework for his personal and social resentments against a society in which his adolescent daydreams and wants found neither response nor expression.

The substance of the ideas which Hitler made into the "granite foundation" of his future policies has been paraphrased repeatedly. It is nothing more than a sweeping rejection of and opposition to tolerance and cosmopolitanism, democracy and parliamentarianism, Marxism and Jewry, which, in primitive equation, were called the primary evils of the world. Even then, however, the core, probably the only "genuine" fanatically held and realized conviction of his entire life, was anti-Semitism and race mania. An enormously oversimplified scheme of good and evil, transplanted to the biological and racial sphere, was made to serve as the master key to the history of political thought. Hitler's fanatical hatred of the Jews defies all rational explanation; it cannot be measured by political and pragmatic gauges. The fact that an entire nation followed him and furnished a legion of executioners does demonstrate, however, that we are confronted not merely with the inexplicable dynamics of one man, but with a terrible disease of modern nationalism, whose desire for exclusivity and war against everything "alien" constitutes one of the root causes of anti-Semitism.

The psychopathic features of Hitler's Weltanschauung were discernible even then: the social envy of the failure and the discrepancy between his exalted vision of personal prestige and the poverty of the unemployed man who held ordinary work in disdain both played a role. The much-abused Nietzsche once called anti-Semitism the ideology of the "those who feel cheated." Unconfirmed rumor has it that Hitler arrived at the "awareness" that the creative person—and he, being a painter, belonged to this category—gets cheated by the sly, worldly, aggressive Jewish trader after he himself had had an unpleasant experience with a Jewish art dealer. Such personal resentments may have contributed to the rationalization of his perverse anti-Semitism.

At about that time, Hitler had also become a "fanatical nationalist." At its highest pitch, nationalist ideology appeals to mass insanity, assuming the force of a collective psychosis in which the annihilation of the enemy spells one's own success and salvation. The anti-Semitic atmosphere of the Vienna of that time provided Hitler's new eclectic philosophy with the firm base on which militant nationalism could develop to its most extreme form and be carried to the point of absurdity. The Jews are the cause of all misfortune; ruthless battle against them holds the key to national if not universal salvation: This precept formed the base of Hitler's later nationalism and imperialism, which ultimately combined forcible expansion beyond the national boundaries with the missionary zeal of a German war on "world Jewry." After Hitler became Chancellor, he confided to intimates that he had been compelled to resort to nationalism because of "the conditions of the times," but that he had always been convinced that "we have to get rid of this false conception" of democracy and liberalism and in its place "set up . . . the conception of race, which has not yet been politically used up." [9]

The "studies" and "harsh lessons" of his Vienna years, which Hitler said were the foundation of his entire career, thus provided the immature youth with the kind of banal, limited semi-education which is among the most dangerous impulses for the destructive forces of our time. Just as he failed to persevere in school and work, this rambling autodidact failed to gain real insight into the problems of the time. His tirelessly fundamental, global "debates" with Marxism and democracy, despite their manic repetition, also never went beyond generalities and platitudes. In *Mein Kampf*, he describes the method of reading and studying through which he acquired his pseudo-education: He always knew how to separate the wheat from the chaff and to extract the true content of everything. In this way, he gathered a store of semi-information which he put to good use; his was a "pigeon-hole mind" (Heiber), lacking the ability to see things in their context. But, at the same time, he satisfied his adolescent "striving for self-worth" (Daim) and also developed a set of ideas of whose simplicity he was to furnish proof. When, in 1924, Hitler proudly told a Munich court that by the time he left Vienna he had become "an absolute anti-Semite, a mortal enemy of the entire Marxist philosophy, Pan-German in my political convictions," he was probably telling the truth (*Mein Kampf*, pp. 130 ff.).

In May, 1913, a year later than stated in *Mein Kampf*, Hitler suddenly turned up in Munich, after more than five years of obscurity. The reasons for his abrupt departure from Vienna are not clear. One might think he was telling the truth when he said that he was prompted by a dislike for the Habsburg Empire and a yearning for the

[9] Hermann Rauschning, *Hitler Speaks: A Series of Political Conversations with Adolf Hitler on His Real Aims* (London, 1939), p. 229.

Bavarian art capital, were it not for the recent revelation of an embarrassing episode. It seems that this future ideologist of combat, the "military genius," had evaded military service in 1909–10, just as he had evaded all other duties, quite unlike those reviled "homeless" Marxists and Jews. Like all of Hitler's major "decisions"—leaving school, moving to Vienna, going to war, entering politics, again going to war, and, finally, his egocentric fall—the road to Munich was also an escape route, this time from military service. This is attested to also by the fact that the then twenty-four-year-old Hitler, who, in fact, remained a citizen of Austria until 1925, called himself "stateless." When arrested and extradited to Salzburg at the request of Austria, he fawningly told the court about his sad life, and, in fact, his poor physical condition saved him from punishment and conscription. Hitler's long letter of explanation (January, 1914) to the Linz authorities hints at the legend of later years. When he writes, "I have never known the lovely word 'youth,' " it almost reads like a "draft for *Mein Kampf*" (Jetzinger). This shameful affair, the documents of which became the object of a feverish search after Hitler's invasion of Austria, testifies to his dishonesty and cowardice and to the mendacity of a Weltanschauung whose rigorous precepts were valid only for others.

He fared no better in Munich than he had in Vienna. The sale of his bad paintings brought in little. The future looked no rosier in Germany. The outbreak of World War I almost seemed like salvation. A rare photograph of that time shows Hitler, wearing a dashing artist's hat, among the masses at the Odeonsplatz cheering the news that war had been declared. Carried away by the popular enthusiasm, he felt liberated from his unproductive, unsuccessful life. As a volunteer not expected to act or decide independently, freed from the purposeless existence of the occasional painter and coffeehouse habitué incapable of establishing personal relationships, he now found himself subject to a discipline which, unlike the disreputable camaraderie of the Vienna shelter, also satisfied his dreams of national and social grandeur. Hitler later justified and glorified the fact that he served in the German Army rather than that of his homeland by denouncing the Habsburg Empire, however inconsistent this may have seemed with his critical attitude toward Wilhelminian Germany. The fact that once more he found himself in a male community indelibly affected his future life and ideas. "Destiny," which he liked to invoke, had pointed the way: "To me, those times were like a deliverance from the vexing emotions of my youth . . . so that, overcome by passionate enthusiasm, I fell to my knees and thanked heaven out of an overflowing heart" (*Mein Kampf*, p. 177). The war seemed to put an end to all problems of daily life in a society in which he had not been able to find his way and which, in typically egocentric fashion, he held responsible for his failure. This, not the dramatically stilted phrase of 1918 ("I, however, decided to become a politician"), was the decisive turning point; war as the transmutation of all values, battle as the father of all things, was the dominant force of Hitler's future life. Hence, the eagerly sought for prolongation of the war beyond the peace agreement into the crises and civil-war atmosphere of the Weimar Republic became the basis of Hitler's activities.

Little worth mentioning happened to Hitler during the war years. Though as a courier he remained a mere corporal, he did have occasion to distinguish himself. He remained a loner, nonsmoker, teetotaler, and lover of sweets, a model patriot and tireless polemicist against Jews, Marxists, and defeatists; he had little in common with the ordinary soldier. The pronounced ascetic-heroic "idealism," the bent toward the undeviatingly radical, the rejection of "ordinary" and erotic pleasures, the feeling of superiority and the sacrificing of personal interests for a "higher ideal"—all these were already hinted at in his monologues and schemes in Linz. Later, Hitler permitted these tendencies to be magnified into an effective myth of a demigod free from ordinary human needs and failings. This, too, was, in effect, an escape, an "escape into legend" (Heiden).

It was the discipline of war and the "front-line acquaintance" with the clear and simple military hierarchy of order and values which were to shape Hitler's sense of values and turn this unstable dreamer unable to come to terms with the bourgeois world of work and order into the rigid fanatic with incredibly oversimplified ideas of war and order. This military male order was the model for the future armed party organizations, for the ideal of a "national community" ready for battle, and for the leader idea; it was elevated to the guiding principle of the political, social, and intellectual life of the country. Therefore Germany's defeat, news of which reached Hitler in the field hospital of Pasewalk, where he was being treated for gas poisoning, not only touched his patriotic feelings but affected his very existence: He was faced with the prospect of returning to his miserable prewar existence. The war simply could not be over, and if, as Hitler was convinced, it had been lost because of defeatism on the home front and the Jewish-Marxist "stab in the back," then this conviction had to be validated by continuing the fight at home. This "national" necessity took on existential significance for Hitler. Ever since those liberating days of 1914, the private and now "professional" life of Hitler, a man with little education and no personal ties, had been based on perpetuating the state of war. It was this which lay at the root of the fanatical energy with which Hitler turned the war into his motivating principle. That is how he looked at politics as a career—as a means for gaining power which would make possible a new war, this one, however, fought according to his ideas until final victory was won.

Hitler's turn to politics also was not the logical outcome of his own decision and resolution, as the legend of *Mein Kampf* would have it. It, too, was an escape from regular work; once again, having returned to Munich, he let events force a decision on him, one, however, to which he held fast. But, initially, Hitler did little to translate into fact his alleged decision of November 9, 1918, "to get into politics." Fearing civilian life, he clung to the security of military service and witnessed, from his barracks, the brief turmoil of the Munich *Räterepublik* (April, 1919). Only later was he given the opportunity, for the first time in his life, to exercise a political function. His "nationalistic" zeal in the service of a commission engaged in ferreting out revolutionary elements among the troops persuaded his superiors to make him an "information officer" responsible for the nationalist education and control of his comrades. Since this assignment involved contact with rightist groups, he found himself, in September, 1919, as an observer at a meeting of one of the numerous new small right-wing parties, the German Workers' Party, in a Munich beer hall.

This chance happening was to make history and decide Hitler's career. Drexler's group of sectarians and beer-hall politicians gathered at this meeting to listen to a speech by the engineer Feder about the abolition of capitalism and the rule of finance capital; the speech was not very impressive. But Hitler felt at home in this uncritical assemblage, and so when informed some time later of his admission into the party, though he himself had never applied, he accepted. He became Party Comrade No. 55, and, simultaneously, the seventh member of the executive committee. Hitler may have been incapable of taking the initiative, let alone of founding a political party, but, once a decision had been made without his active help, he zealously threw himself into the new role of politician. In view of the disarmament provisions of the Versailles Treaty, his days in the rump army were probably numbered anyway; now he found the framework which might possibly combine the ideas of his Vienna days with a wartime order, offering him a chance to use his modicum of "learning" to secure his existence and to compensate for his fear of the demands of a civilian life in which he had failed.

PROBLEMS OF THE REVOLUTION AND THE REPUBLIC

For the countries and peoples of Europe, the year 1918 possesses a significance far greater than the history of World War I would indicate. Not only did international power relationships change fundamentally within the space of a few months, not only did new states come into being and boundaries shift, with far-reaching consequences, but the internal structure of the countries of Europe was disrupted, bringing with it revolutionary changes in state and social systems. The upheaval of domestic and foreign relations ranged from the Bolshevik October Revolution in Russia to the installation of democratic regimes throughout Europe.

Thus, the outcome of World War I was both celebrated and attacked as a triumph of democracy. While the Europe of 1914 could claim only three democratic republics and seventeen monarchies, after the end of the war there were as many republics as monarchies—thirteen. The trend toward democracy, with or without a monarchical superstructure, seemed unstoppable. But appearances were deceptive: only a few years later, the trend was clearly reversed. The crisis of democracy was inherent in its very triumph. Twenty years later, even before Hitler's war had overturned its last bastions, democracy had survived in only nine European countries—six monarchies and three republics. The seeds of authoritarian and dictatorial rule had already been planted in the early days of most of the postwar democracies. Hence, the events of 1918 should be viewed in the context of four main points: (1) The year 1918 saw the end of a war of hitherto unprecedented intensity and scope; (2) the most obvious consequence of that war was the internal collapse of authoritarian rule in Russia, Austria-Hungary, and Germany; (3) these regimes were replaced by democratically constituted national governments; (4) the unsolved problems of the postwar order, in turn, gave birth to new types of authoritarian and dictatorial revolutionary movements and regimes, some of which were radical-democratic-revolutionary (the Soviet Union), yet most of which were antidemocratic-nationalist. The outcome of World War I prepared the way for a wave of democratization and simultaneously planted the seeds for countermovements which within a short time were to overwhelm all the new democracies except Finland and Czechoslovakia: that is, in Russia and the Baltic states, in Hungary, Poland, and the Balkan countries, in Italy, Germany, and Austria, and in Spain and Portugal. Even the old, established democracies—England and, more particularly, France—showed signs of crisis.

Among these states, Germany occupied both an examplary and unique position. The precipitous changes of conditions in Germany accurately reflected the general problems of that period. Yet at the same time, the German transformation from monarchical authoritarian state to democratic republic shows some highly individual traits. The reasons are historical. The German national state had been imposed from above in 1871; Bismarck's Reich rose up from the ruins of the abortive attempt of 1848 to incorporate Prussia and Austria into a single national democracy. The Second Reich labored under the burden of three major problems, upon which, ultimately, it foundered: the never fully achieved national state, the discrepancy between economic and national renewal and a deficient democratization, and the international problems arising from Germany's desire for great-power status. The road to war was paved with more than merely a series of unfortunate incidents; it was the result of the failure to master the national and imperial problem, and simultaneously also a consequence of the internal weakness of a Bismarckian system without Bismarck, ruled by a swaggering emperor and populated by a "nonpolitical" citizenry which had capitulated before the successful policies of the "Iron Chancellor."

The burdens and conduct of the war turned this flawed structure into the quasi-military dictatorship of Hindenburg and Ludendorff. Only their failure was able to weaken the authoritarian system in the fall of 1918 and open the way for the long-stifled efforts for parliamentary and democratic reforms. The parliamentary parties of the Center and the Left had been preparing for this eventuality in joint meetings since 1917. But only military collapse and revolution made possible the breakthrough to a new constitutional system eager to utilize the principles and experiences of modern democratic constitutionalism.

The result was the "Weimar Constitution," adopted by a large majority of the German National Assembly meeting in the National Theater of Weimar on July 31, 1919. However, the implementation of the new Constitution was beset by problems, and soon it became apparent that even the most carefully drafted law could not accord with political reality if public awareness and internal developments failed to keep pace with efforts to democratize the government, or even opposed such efforts. These problems were inherent in the events of the year 1918. Three factors were destined to have a deleterious effect on the structure and vitality of a democratic German republic: the sudden confrontation of an ill-prepared population with the actuality of military defeat; the alliance of the new political leadership with the old army; and the resultant ending of the revolution before it had a chance to effect a more profound remodeling of the sociopolitical power structure. Once again, efforts to develop democratic approaches out of the cleansing process and conscious experience of a successful revolution misfired. The desire for immediate restoration of order and stability proved stronger, even though this entailed a rejection of vital aspects of democratization and a return to obsolete ideas and practices.

Under the parliamentary democratic constitution born in the wake of defeat and "unfinished revolution," the basic problems of the Bismarckian Reich lived on. True, the Reich had failed to pass the test of war. And it is also true that the parliamentarization of 1918 was not as complete an innovation as might appear at first glance. Even before the outbreak of the war, parliamentary majorities had been formed, which, though they did not form governments, nonetheless influenced official policy. After the outbreak of the war, the Reichstag first knuckled under to the Emperor, and, later, to the military high command. However, the Reichstag's growing awareness of its own importance was expressed by its passage of a peace resolution in July, 1917, and also in its role in the change of government in October, 1917. It was fatal, however, that in so vital a political decision as the Brest-Litovsk Treaty (March, 1918), the military high command should have had the decisive voice. At the end of September, 1918, on the threshold of defeat, Ludendorff finally dropped his slogan of a victorious peace and called for negotiations, thereby opening up the way for parliamentarization.

Thus, parliamentary rule was ushered in by a last dictatorial act of the military high command—and by military defeat. From the very outset this cast a shadow over the founding of German democracy. That which parliament and political parties had been unable to bring about was once again introduced from above and given impetus by the outbreak of the revolution. To be sure, the time was ripe, and preparations were well advanced. Ten days before the outbreak of the revolution, the transition to a parliamentary system of government had been practically completed. But it came too late to stem the revolutionary tide, which also tore down the monarchy when William II hesitated about abdicating. The Princes' League of 1871 was no longer viable; the German monarchs fell unresistingly. Even if the Social Democratic leadership had been so inclined, and even if the Emperor and his advisers had been more skillful tacticians and the Crown Prince more able, it is unlikely that the monarchy could have been saved. Moreover, in a parliamentary monarchy the position of the other German royal houses, with their equally anachronistic sovereignty claims, would have posed an insoluble problem. Hence, the road to republicanism was not an unhappy accident resulting from the precipitate actions of Scheidemann, as some history texts maintain to this day. When the Republic was proclaimed by Scheidemann on the afternoon of November 9, 1918, it had already become an accomplished fact in Bavaria and other provinces; its recognition was, in fact, an effort to gain control over the spreading revolutionary tendencies.

It was a time of the most diverse ideas about the nature of the future state and social order. These ideas cannot be reduced to the simple formula of democracy versus Bolshevism. The activities of the radical Left were soon opposed by the reactionary and radical-Right dictatorial ideas of the Free Corps and combat groups. Between these extremes, various democratic ideas, ranging from the radical-democratic soviet state to the Christian or conservative corporate state, strove to assert themselves. In terms of constitutional law, Friedrich Ebert's assumption of the Chancellorship on November 9, 1918, undoubtedly was a revolutionary breakthrough. The Council of People's Delegates was a transitional government whose constitutionality was not readily definable. Since this government was under the leadership of the strongest party (SPD), it could claim to embody the implementation of parliamentary democracy. Yet at the same time, it was a government installed by revolution. The Council of People's Delegates might be seen as the expression of political and social revolution as long as it had the support both of the SPD and the leftist Independent Social Democratic Party (Unabhängige Sozialdemokratische Partei Deutschlands, or USPD).

It soon became apparent, however, particularly after the resignation of the USPD (December 29), that the Council of People's Delegates was concerned less with changing the existing order than with checking a radical democratic and radical Left continuation and spread of the revolution. In December, 1918, the Social Democrats were still able to push through a parliamentary solution, a compromise between the old and the new, even in the workers' and soldiers' councils, the representatives of the revolution. This preliminary decision against a soviet democracy was won through an alliance of expediency between the SPD and the old rulers of the military and civil service. This cooperation between the moderate Left and the middle class helped to stabilize the parliamentary republic. But by taking a position against an overrated radical Left, the Social Democrats found themselves dependent on the Army, the Free Corps, and the civil-service bureaucracy, which promptly put rigid limits on the further democratization of state and society.

The importance and need for this alliance of expediency remains a moot point, but it undeniably hampered the development of a democratic governmental apparatus and made possible the questionable role of the Reichswehr as a "state within a state." And it was fatal of Friedrich Ebert and his SPD colleagues, particularly Defense Minister Gustav Noske, to think that "order" could be restored only with the help of antirevolutionary and overtly antidemocratic forces. As a result, they were unable to prevent the sort of violence which culminated first in the brutal murder in January, 1919, of the Spartacist leaders Karl Liebknecht and Rosa Luxemburg by these forces, and later (1921–22) in the murder of democratic ministers (Mathias Erzberger and Walter Rathenau) by nationalists. This was the setting in which the radical Right countermovement had its beginnings. Soon it was directed not only against the revolution, but against the democratic Republic itself. The political career of Corporal Adolf Hitler, stationed in Munich, also had its beginnings in this antirevolutionary atmosphere.

The seeds of deep division and lasting danger to the Republic were thus sown in the closing days of 1918. It should have been evident that the enemy stood at the Right: the Kapp Putsch and the political assassinations, the murders of Erzberger and Rathenau and the Hitler Putsch, and, finally, the wrecking of democracy by the alliance of Conservatives and the radical Right make this clear. The question arises whether the energetic actions of 1918, influenced by the widespread fear of revolution and the overrated "Bolshevik threat" (both prevalent among the Social Democratic leadership), were, in fact, the only alternative to dictatorship. At any rate, by fixing their sights on the danger from the Left, then and later (in 1923 and after 1930), they overlooked the danger of a dictatorship of the Right.

The revolution of 1918 ended in compromise before it really got under way. The desire for continuity found expression in the cooperation of the middle class and the Social Democrats. However, the vast majority of the middle class was still under the sway of authoritarian ideas. There was a lack of civil consciousness; it had begun to wither away after 1848. Respect for the existing power structure was matched by a lack of imagination about the new order. The revolution remained unfinished. The old power structure survived within the new framework; the social, economic, and bureaucratic balance of power was preserved with only minor changes. The bankruptcy of the old forces, though obvious, was not followed by any real reorientation and restructuring. Instead, the democrats put themselves into the hands of the military and the old civil servants, who knew how to exploit this cooperation without themselves changing. The inviolability of the professional civil service and respect for its "well-earned" rights was the price the new rulers willingly paid for this cooperation. After some disputes, the workers' and soldiers' councils were relegated to a handful of supervisory functions, and after the convocation of the National Assembly they were stripped of all functions.

As a result of this continuity of administration, which, in the emergency situation of the winter of 1918–19, may have appeared essential, the relationships between the military and democracy and the civil service and democracy never were clarified, and a precedent was set for the almost uninterrupted perpetuation of authoritarian elements. Throughout the life of the Weimar Republic, this tradition was constantly buttressed by the formation of "above-party" specialists' Cabinets, along with the dominance of civil service and military influences on the Presidential government. Consequently, the civil service and Army survived the change of government of 1933; in fact, it was their cooperation that enabled the National Socialist dictatorship to govern. One may call it the blindness of the Social Democrats or possibly a tragedy that the same forces whose help the SPD enlisted in 1918–19 to save Germany at the cost of a democratic revolution were able to topple the democratic Republic.

That the founding of the Weimar Republic took place amid a confusion of cooperating and opposing revolutionary, reform, and traditionalist efforts and forces also was made evident in the history of the political parties and electoral results. The year 1918 meant neither an absolute rupture nor a complete regrouping of the political forces; rather, the extent to which the tendencies of the prewar and war years lived on despite the revolution is well-nigh astonishing, even though the military defeat and the internal changes naturally also altered the complexion of the political parties. Of the four major political groups, only the Social Democrats and the Center Party kept their names; the "conservative" and "liberal" name tags vanished. The former liberal-Left, "free-thinking," "progressive" groups around Friedrich Naumann founded the new German Democratic Party (Deutsche Demokratische Partei, or DDP), while the majority of the National Liberals around Gustav Stresemann, after meandering between the Democrats and the conservative Nationalists, finally decided to form their own party, the German People's Party (Deutsche Volkspartei, or DVP). The former conservative parties, who as the main enemies of parliamentarization and republicanism were hit hardest by the collapse of the monarchy, reorganized as an obviously rightist party under the name of German National People's Party (Deutschnationale Volkspartei, or DNVP). The Center Party, in contemplating a new name—Christian People's Party (Christliche Volkspartei)—also sought to burst through its traditional religious framework and exchange its minority status for the majority position of an all-encompassing Christian party. That, of course, happened only after Hitler, with the founding of the CDU. After World War I, the party not only reverted to its old name but very soon, with the defection of the Bavarian People's Party (Bayerische Volkspartei, or BVP), lost a major regional organization which, despite all organizational and sociopolitical similarities, often followed an independent course. This independence was demonstrated most glaringly during the Presidential elections of 1925, when the BVP voted against the Catholic Center candidate, Wilhelm Marx, and in so doing helped Hindenburg, the Protestant candidate of the Prussian conservative Right, to victory.

Yet all these reorganizations—and the early elections also bear this out—were comparatively superficial changes without any real influence on the political composition of the population. Immediately after the revolution, the dominant trend seemed to be toward the Left, a tendency which had already manifested itself before and during the war. It was part of the total picture of a shift toward the democratic, parliamentary groups of the Left and Center which had begun at the turn of the century. But within a few months this tendency was displaced by a regressive movement that restored old power relations and at times, particularly in the final stages of the Republic, even gave way to a pronounced electoral trend toward the Right. This was not altered by the fact that the SPD split of 1916, which saw its left wing form the USPD, had deepened, and that with the formation of the Communist Party (Kommunistische Partei Deutschlands, or KPD) in 1919 a radical Left movement bitterly opposed to the SPD introduced a brand-new political element into the existing scene.

On the whole, the parties as well as the voters who sustained them displayed well-nigh amazing staying power, even under the changed constitutional as well as material conditions of the parliamentary Republic. The population remained divided into four major camps: conservative, liberal, Catholic, and socialist, except now the attitudes toward the new state were reversed. As early as 1919, Naumann pointed out that the party system which had come into being during the monarchy did not meet the needs of a democratic, parliamentary system of government. This system, and also the survival of many of the old institutions, set limits on the extent of the changes of the 1918 revolution. Thus the Weimar period has been interpreted as a gradual fading away of the Wilhelminian era rather than a new beginning. On the other hand, the parties and electoral contests of 1918–19 certainly refuted the frequently voiced contention that the development toward a moderate democracy was accidental and haphazard and did not express the will of the majority, which, according to some, did not want any revolutionary change, or, according to others, wanted a much more purposeful radical political and social revolution.

Yet the majority decision of the workers' and soldiers' councils of mid-December, 1918, to elect a constitutional National Assembly was, in fact, tantamount to a vote for parliamentary democracy and simultaneously for the status quo. Two weeks earlier, the revolutionary government had introduced proportional representation and, along with this, granted women the vote and lowered the voting age to twenty. Critical opinion held this provision responsible for the trend toward radicalization and the division of the electorate. However, at that time, majority elections would undoubtedly have given the Left an absolute majority in the National Assembly, which would have prevented the formation of a moderate center and might even have led to civil war. For these reasons also, the "bourgeois" parties supported the traditional socialist demand for proportional representation. Nor can women's suffrage be held responsible for the radicalization.

In the first election of January 19, 1919, the left-wing parties surprisingly enough did not win the expected majority. The disappointment of the USPD, which polled 7.6 per cent of all votes, was particularly great; its strength and that of the entire radical Left had obviously been vastly overrated. The SPD, on the other hand (with almost 38 per cent of the votes) continued its upswing and emerged as by far the strongest party. But the grand total of Socialist votes was still far below a majority, and they had to work together with the parties of the Center, a fact which was to play a decisive role in the future of the Republic. To be sure, the NSDAP never was able to equal the votes of the Left of that time; when Hitler seized power, the total National Socialist vote, even together with the votes of the German National Party, was considerably below that of the Socialists of 1919. But, whereas the Socialists accepted a democratic coalition, Hitler misrepresented the election results and claimed total power on the basis of the decision of the National Socialist voters. This is a fact also worth remembering when confronted either with efforts to establish the legality of Hitler's takeover on the basis of electoral trends or with conclusions that Hitler was "the consequence of democracy." [10]

However small the vote in January, 1919, for the radical Left course of a soviet republic (the appeal of the newly founded KPD to abstain from voting also was ignored), the success of the antirepublican rightist parties also was modest (10.3 per cent). The following of the DVP (4.4 per cent), which continued to champion a monarchy against the Republic, also was weak. The Democrats, however, scored a substantial victory (18.6 per cent). By winning the contest for the liberal bourgeoisie, they demonstrated the support of this portion of the electorate for a democratic, parliamentary republic. If the 19.7 per cent of the Center votes are added, we find that the three parties of the so-called Weimar Coalition (SPD, DDP, Center), which formed the first parliamentarily elected government, received an undisputed three-quarter majority (76.2 per cent).

Contrary to later myths, it can therefore be recorded that the overwhelming majority of German voters had consciously decided in favor of a parliamentary republic, though only a year later (June, 1920), the pendulum swung back. It would seem that the election results of January, 1919, had merely covered over a difficult psychological situation or, rather, under the influence of the changed situation, only quieted it temporarily by catering to the desire for peace and order. However, that the new order had been approved by a clear popular majority is

[10] Thus, Winfried Martini, *Das Ende aller Sicherheit* (Stuttgart, 1954), pp. 94 ff.

beyond dispute. This was underscored by the first state elections held at that time. The Bavarian Left revolutionary government of Kurt Eisner was resoundingly defeated by moderate forces, and the Prussian elections also paralleled the results of the National Assembly. Thus, radicalism, restorational aims, and separatism were all rejected in these first elections, and the preservation of the parliamentary republic seemed a distinct possibility.

Three major events influenced public opinion during the truly critical year between the elections of the National Assembly and the first Reichstag elections: (1) the drafting of the Weimar Constitution, which furnished the Republic with an institutional framework; (2) the imposition of the Versailles Treaty, which put a heavy burden on that Republic; (3) the efforts of monarchist circles, culminating in the Kapp Putsch of March, 1920, to reverse developments and to restore prerepublican conditions with the help of a military dictatorship.

Though the Republic ultimately succeeded in weathering the threats of the early years, the Kapp Putsch nonetheless had an indelible effect on the political climate. It came about not only because of the whim of a segment of the military but also because of the profound internal problems of the new state. This was made evident by the election, in June, 1920, of the first regular Reichstag in place of the National Assembly. Contrary to the hopes of the governing parties, which, now that the Putsch had been quashed, expected a favorable vote, the opposition scored major gains over the Weimar Coalition. In this first Reichstag, the National Assembly Coalition majority of 76 per cent shrank to a 47 per cent minority. Only 11 million voters instead of the 19 million of January, 1919, now came out in support of the original pillars of the Weimar Republic, while their opponents almost doubled their vote, from 7.7 to 14.4 million, with the Right going from 5.6 to 9.1 million, and the radical Left from 2.1 to 5.3. The middle-of-the-road supporters of the Constitution were now faced by a right- and left-wing opposition which seemed to rule out the normal interplay between government and opposition.

Thus, after eighteen months of statehood, and barely ten months after the promulgation of a constitution, the founders and supporters of the new state had turned into a minority, never again to achieve a Reichstag majority. This fact not only puts the Kapp Putsch and the political dangers connected with it into the proper perspective, but it may also have played a decisive role in the critical years up to 1923, and later in the beginning and development of the final crisis after 1929. Stable democratic government was in jeopardy throughout the life of the Weimar Republic. The country was governed either by unpopular minority cabinets, by internally weak Grand Coalitions, or finally, by extraparliamentary authoritarian Presidential Cabinets. Most of the twenty Cabinets of the Republic lasted only for brief periods; eight and a half months was the average life-span; the longest period, twenty-one months, was granted to the trouble-ridden

Grand Coalition of 1928, whose defeat ushered in the last, great governmental crisis.

The significance of the elections of June, 1920, becomes even more apparent if one analyzes the votes cast for the various parties. The most important result was the well-nigh catastrophic loss suffered by the DDP. They lost almost half of their Reichstag seats and ceased to be the main pillar of a strong liberal-bourgeois center. Here the shift to the Right was quite apparent, for on the whole the Democratic losses meant gains for the DVP and the DNVP, both of which were critical of and hostile to the Republic. The People's Party almost tripled the number of its Reichstag seats over 1919 (from 22 to 62), overtaking the Democrats. It won back the many voters who had been National Liberals during the monarchy and who, out of fear of the revolution, had temporarily veered to the Left; but after the disappointment over Versailles and after overcoming their fear of the revolution, they returned to the right-wing camp. In the years to come, these voters went even further to the Right. From that time on, both liberal parties continued to lose ground. The shrinkage of the bourgeois-liberal middle contributed to the structural weakness of the Republic and its ultimate atomization between radical extremes. If the DDP was, in fact, "the single reliable support of German republicanism for those who were neither Socialist nor Catholic" (Eyck), then as early as 1920 the majority of this portion of the population—encompassing the leaders in education, government, the civil service, business, and the professions—had begun to turn its back on, or even had already turned against, the Republic. For at that time, a substantial segment went over to the avowedly antirepublican DNVP, which went from 42 to 65 seats and which was to remain the strongest middle-class party. It was a trend that reached its height in 1924, when the German National Party equaled the strength of the SPD. The parliamentary political consequences of this development expressed a deep division in German political life. A young state beset by domestic and foreign problems cannot survive if its constitutional core not only is not supported, but quite obviously is even rejected by a large portion of its intellectual, economic, and social elite.

The situation was made even more critical by the heavy defeat suffered by that other mainstay of the Republic, democratic socialism. Between 1919 and 1920, the SPD lost more than one-third of its seats (from 165 to 102), while the extreme Left quadrupled (the USPD, from 22 to 84; the KPD, from 0 initially, to 4 seats). Here, too, the economic crisis and the Kapp Putsch played a part, though to opposite effect. The seeds of a parliamentary radicalization and crisis were being planted, a crisis which ten years hence was to be revived in the plebiscitary elections of September, 1930, and which ultimately prevented the democracy from functioning.

Only the third pillar of the state, political Catholicism, retained its stability. As a "third force," the Center Party, which took an ambiguous position toward the Republic, remained the crystallization point of all coalition politics. Until the ouster of Heinrich Brüning in 1932 and the installation of the authoritarian caretaker regime of the backsliding Center politician Franz von Papen, the Center Party, playing the role of intermediary between Left and Right, between constitutional parties and constitutional opposition, was represented in every Weimar Cabinet. As the reigning government party, it furnished the Chancellor of nine such governments as well as a number of Cabinet ministers in eighteen of the twenty governments.

The first Center Chancellor was appointed in the summer of 1920. Since the SPD believed that it had suffered defeat at the polls because of its having been in power, it was willing to enter into a coalition only with the USPD, in order to deprive this Left competitor of its easy opposition perch. Finally, the SPD, though the largest democratic party, also went into opposition. It was essentially the same escape from power as that of ten years hence, when the SPD, by toppling its own Chancellor, Hermann Müller, not only destroyed the last majority government of the Republic and cleared the way for the authoritarian experimentation of Brüning, von Papen, and Schleicher but also, by hesitating to participate in a national government, even though it was still the strongest party, indirectly and unwillingly contributed to the defeat of democracy.

Despite the numerous differences between the situations of 1920 and 1930, the reasons for this position were in many ways similar. And they most certainly were based on political miscalculation, namely the fear that participation in an unpopular government might lose them popular support. At work also was the fact that the SPD's leaders, functionaries, and long-time members simply could not break with the tradition of opposition and hence accepted the compromise structure of Weimar only halfheartedly. The transition to a political sense of responsibility was slow; not many were able to emulate Ebert and overcome the traditional and ideological party limitations, a step more easily taken on the state level, particularly in Prussia, which from 1920 to 1932 was governed by the Social Democrats Otto Braun and Carl Severing. The SPD missed the promising opportunity to break through the barrier of a class party and become a popular majority party, not least because it hesitated in this new situation. Democratic socialism in Germany, unlike in Scandinavia, remained imprisoned in the 30 per cent fortress. And, in contradiction to the propaganda sneers spread by Hitler and others about "fourteen years of SPD rule," this strongest party in fact furnished the Chancellor in only three of those fourteen years and in only four of the twenty governments, and its ministers sat in only eight of the twenty Cabinets.

All subsequent efforts to form Cabinets suffered from the SPD's withdrawal. While the SPD stayed away from the government, the middle-of-the-road parties tended to bring the right wing into their governments: at first the DVP, which until Stresemann's death remained capable of cooperating; then, from time to time, the German National Party; and, ultimately, the Conservatives around Count

Westarp, who resisted Hugenberg's radical course. The era of the middle-class bloc governments tending toward the Right which began in 1920 generally was one of minority Cabinets—a problematical situation which, except for brief interludes of either Social Democractic or German National participation in government, set the tone for future policy. No parliamentary government could be formed without the acquiescence of the SPD, yet the logical consequence—Social Democratic participation in government—was not drawn. The parties had only a very limited talent for coalition and compromise, and the inhibitions on both sides were too great, due both to the traditional misgivings of the middle-class parties and to the immutable oppositional tendencies and feeble power drive of the SPD, which lacked full understanding of its role as the strongest party in a parliamentary democracy. The Cabinet crises which plagued the German Republic throughout its life were the direct consequence of the nature of German political parties, their unwillingness to form coalitions and to compromise, their rigid ideological stance, their preoccupation with prestige, and their authoritarian tradition.

This was the price paid for the partly forced, partly voluntary rejection of parliament and parties during the monarchy, a policy whose negative aspects were pinpointed very clearly by Max Weber at the end of World War I. In his *Parlament und Regierung im neugeordneten Deutschland (Parliament and Government in Reorganized Germany,* p. 75), he insisted that the absence of a two-party system was not the main obstacle: "Far more important is another difficulty: parliamentary government is possible only if the largest parties of the parliament are in principle *on the whole ready* to take over the responsible conduct of the business of state. And that certainly has not been the case up to now." Now, with the promulgation of a parliamentary constitution, this disinclination to exercise responsibility manifested itself even more strongly, because its political effects were now more immediate. A predisposition toward supraparliamentary, bureaucratic political administration remained the guiding principle of political debate and of criticism directed against the parliamentary multiparty state as well as of the attitude and inner insecurity of the parties. The fateful history of the implementation and misapplication of emergency legislation (Article 48), intended by its drafters to protect the Republic, could not have come about without this basic mood, without this helplessness in the face of a grave crisis of the party state which steadily grew more acute.

The effects of this historically rooted dilemma proved doubly detrimental in the years to come, when vast problems, both domestic and foreign, called for clear, energetic political measures and consequently for a firm, secure majority government. On the foreign front, negotiations over reparations and a possible revision of the Versailles Treaty had gotten under way, and on the domestic front, the growing economic crisis and inflation, the occupation of the Ruhr, and the attendant left- and right-wing coups of 1923 were to put a heavy burden on the fledgling Republic.

As a federation of states, the Weimar Republic naturally also had to deal with the political problems of the state legislatures. Most of these proved to possess considerable stability; to a large degree they were for a time able to weather the Nazi takeover. On the whole, the results of the state elections of 1919 (particularly those of Prussia) paralleled the National Assembly elections. But upon closer examination, significant regional differences emerge. In Bavaria, the second-largest state, the BVP, though showing a decline over the prewar years, retained its dominance over the Social Democrats in the election of January 12, 1919 (36 per cent against 32 per cent), and later also outpolled the NSDAP until the death of the Republic, a fact which underscores the special position of this state. In Saxony, on the other hand, the Socialists won an absolute majority on February 2, 1919, a victory which was to play a role in the crisis in which Saxony found itself in 1923. The fact that the Democratic Party emerged with its strength intact in Württemberg (January 12, 1919) and held on to it longer than in most other sections of the country must be taken into consideration in analyses of the different political factors of the member states of the Republic. In Württemberg's predominantly Catholic neighbor Baden, on the other hand, the Center Party preserved its position as the strongest party (January 5, 1919), even against the Social Democrats. Aside from Saxony, the Socialists won a temporary majority only in Brunswick in the first state elections of 1919. In Thuringia, on the other hand, which had elected a rightist government quite early and in 1930 became the first state to install a Nazi minister (Wilhelm Frick), the Socialists suffered a major defeat in 1919; the German National Party emerged as the strongest party in the state legislature. However, despite regional differences, subsequent state elections on the whole followed the pattern of national elections. The swing of 1920, with the large gains made by the Right and the setbacks suffered by the forces of moderation, also made itself felt in the coalition and governmental crises in the individual states and their legislatures. The Catholic electorate remained stable, most obviously so in Bavaria; however, the Catholic Bavarian People's Party, which in the state elections of 1920 succeeded in strengthening its already powerful position, leaned toward the Right, showing a monarchic-conservative bent and a receptivity to antidemocratic activities.

THE BEGINNINGS OF THE NSDAP

The Munich of 1919, the city in which the real history of National Socialism began when Hitler joined the DAP, offered exceptionally fertile soil for the development of right-wing extremism. After the assassination of Kurt Eisner, the Prime Minister of the Bavarian revolutionary government, and after the bloody suppression of the Munich

Räterepublik (accomplished with the help of counterrevolutionary and antidemocratic forces), the political pressures brought to bear by military and paramilitary groups in Munich was greater than anywhere else in Germany. Feeling threatened by the Versailles Treaty provisions for the reduction of the Army, numerous officers and professional soldiers grown unaccustomed to civilian life turned to what they called "politics." Their service in the transitional forces afforded them leisure for speeches, discussions, and for nationalistic indoctrination; military-political groups formed around Free Corps officers like Colonel Ritter von Epp, who won renown for his crushing of the *Räterepublik*, and Major Ernst Röhm, who, as chief of staff of the Munich City Commandant, worked for the promotion of "national" associations. Secret weapons caches proliferated, and a far-flung conspiracy of right-wing and militarist extremists came into being. Countless radical groups and grouplets, in which the military had its liaison men and informers, were organized, flourished, and dissolved again.

The *völkisch* Pan-German Thule Society mentioned earlier constituted an important focal point.[11] As the front organization of the prewar Germanic Order, it enjoyed a measure of prominence; its contacts reached into broad circles of Munich society, and its club rooms in the fashionable Hotel Vierjahreszeiten served as a gathering place for other "national clubs." The Thule Society had its own paper, the anticlerical, anti-Semitic *Münchener Beobachter* (*Munich Observer*) founded in 1868 (after 1900, it was published by the Franz Eher Verlag). Its leading figure was a nationalist adventurer going by the name of Rudolf Count von Sebottendorff, a man of rather obscure provenance. His reminiscences, with the significant title *Bevor Hitler kam* (*Before Hitler Came;* 1933), in which he stresses the role played by the Thule Society in the birth of National Socialism, seem to contradict Hitler's claim to parentage; Hitler had never acknowledged any "precursors," let alone competitors; at best, he tolerated a handful of prominent prophets.

Sebottendorff (whose real name presumably was Rudolf Glauer), the son of a Silesian railway engineer, had apparently been convicted for fraud in 1909; he turned up in 1913 with a newly acquired title of nobility (which he owed to his adoption by an Austrian) as well as a brand-new Turkish passport. After his political venture in Bavaria (1917–19), he disappeared in Istanbul; he then spent some time in Mexico and the United States, only to reappear in Munich in 1933 with the hope of reactivating the Thule Society. His subsequent fate remains unknown; he may possibly have been eliminated by the National Socialists as an embarrassing witness out of the past. According to his own testimony, Sebottendorff was influenced by such *völkisch* pioneers as Fritsch, Guido von List, Lanz von Liebenfels, and Baron von Wittgenberg—the same Austro-German sectarian proponents of Germano-

[11] On the Thule Society, see Reginald H. Phelps, "Before Hitler Came," *Journal of Modern History,* XXXV (1963), 245 ff. Cf. Allan Mitchell, *Revolution in Bavaria 1918–1919* (Princeton, 1965), pp. 110 ff.

manic, anti-Semitic, somewhat occult theories whose writings presumably also influenced the young Hitler in Vienna. Closely connected with these tendencies was the founding in Leipzig in 1912 of the Germanic (Thule) Order, which was in contact with Fritsch's anti-Semitic Hammer League (Hammerbund, founded in 1910) as well as with the Pan-German League and the German National Association of Commercial Employees. The members of the Order had to be of "Aryan blood" and pledge themselves to fight against Jews, avenge treason, and eradicate all enemies. The admission procedure involved an absurd ritual: filling out a form indicating the degree of hairiness of various parts of the body and, as proof of "Aryan" descent, putting a footprint on a separate piece of paper. The Order's organization and terminology was reminiscent of the Freemasons, except that the purpose and aims of the Germanic Lodge were diametrically opposed. As in many other groups of this type, Germanic runes and swastikas were used as symbols.

At first the war was somewhat of a deterrent to this type of activity; persons and groupings continued to alternate in confusing succession. A turning point was reached around Christmas of 1917, when Sebottendorff took over leadership in Bavaria and unleashed an intensive anti-Semitic and antiliberal propaganda campaign with anti-Jewish leaflets. In August, 1918, the Germanic Order re-formed as the Thule Society at a meeting at the Hotel Vierjahreszeiten, where Sebottendorff had leased the rooms of the Naval Officers' Club; on October 24, 1918, the Society held a joint meeting with the Pan-Germans, at which the possibility of a right-wing coup as proposed by the nationalist publisher J. F. Lehmann was discussed. The Thule Society responded to the revolution and the Bavarian governmental crisis with exhortations against "Jewry" and new plans for a coup; surveillance and arrests temporarily forced them to adopt the cover name "Study Group of German Antiquity," which was entered in the Munich organization register in March, 1919. At the same time, they were engaged in organizing a "combat league" (*Kampfbund*), which sought to unify the Free Corps for a march on Munich and which participated in an abortive putsch on Palm Sunday (April 13) of 1919; however, the group was very small. While Sebottendorff was courting the Free Corps in Bamberg, the seat of the Bavarian government-in-exile, supporters of the *Räterepublik* occupied the rooms of the Society in Munich on April 26 and arrested seven of its members, including the secretary, Countess Heila Westarp; they were shot four days later, probably in reprisal for the murder of Communists in nearby Starnberg.

Whatever one's opinion about the questionable details of the executions—and on this matter there was disagreement among the members of the revolutionary government—they stirred up far greater public indignation than all the past murders of Communists and Socialists committed by the Free Corps and combat leagues, beginning with the assassination of Rosa Luxemburg and Karl Liebknecht. The lamentable "hostage murder of Munich," blown up by propaganda and embellished with gruesome details, furnished another effective platform for a radical anti-Semitic campaign which now was assured a sympathetic hearing by the people of Munich. The vicious retaliation of the Free Corps and the reprisals against Communists and left-wing Socialists were followed by a violent anti-Jewish campaign against the deposed "racially alien government," in which portions of the BVP and the Church joined in. The *Räterepublik* was reviled as a Jewish undertaking, and the fact that the actual terrorists were not Jews, but that one of the victims was, proved of little consequence amid this atmosphere. Leaflets distributed by newly organized propaganda centers of the radical Right, such as the "Committee for Popular Enlightenment" (whose name may have furnished the inspiration for Goebbels' later propaganda ministry), depicted the doubtlessly unpopular short-lived revolutionary government as a pogrom against the German people staged by Jews, a phase in the Jewish conspiracy for world domination. The propaganda resorted to ancient, oft-repeated diatribes, but now there was the added bonus of widespread popular resentment against the *Räte* experiment and the bloody events surrounding it. It was a climate of opinion favoring the development of National Socialism, and Hitler's career as an agitator may be said to have begun here. In this, too, the Thule Society played a key role. On May 31, 1919, the *Münchener Beobachter* published the twelve points of Sebottendorff's "political program"; his new tack was that typical combination of anti-Semitic and anticapitalist catchwords which was to become the hallmark of the National Socialist program.

As the center of old and new *völkisch* prophets, the Thule Society gave many of the future ideologists of National Socialism their first public platform. Gathered here were Alfred Rosenberg, Hans Frank, Gottfried Feder, Dietrich Eckart, who in December, 1918, had begun to publish the anti-Semitic journal *Auf gut deutsch* (*In Plain Language*), as well as a *völkisch* Catholic priest, Father Bernhard Stempfle, who helped Hitler in the writing of *Mein Kampf*. (As a reward, he was among those murdered in the purge of June 30, 1934.) The Thule Society's *Münchener Beobachter* proved of invaluable help by publishing a stream of anti-Semitic "documentary evidence" and acting as a clearing house for the innumerable *völkisch*-radical Right events in and around Munich. But the Society and the influential tools at its disposal served not only as a platform for numerous nationalist splinter groups, with links to such organizations as the Pan-German *Völkisch* Defense and Offense League (Deutschvölkischer Schutz- und Trutzbund) or the Munich branch of the Ostara League, but also as the organizer of *völkisch* workers' clubs fighting the Left. One such effort was the Political Workers' Circle founded by the sportswriter Karl Harrer (1890–1926) in the fall of 1918. In December, 1918, Harrer introduced his collaborators, a railroad mechanic in the Munich municipal works, Anton Drexler (1884–1942), and his colleague Michael Lotter to the Thule Society. Drexler in turn, together with twenty-five railroad workers from his shop, founded the new German Workers' Party

(DAP) at a conference at the Fürstenfelder Hof on January 2–5, 1919. The party's early history was marked by a nationalism with anti-Semitic and socialist overtones. The DAP thus differed from the Thule Society which, with its racial theories and elitism, continued to be a small, conspiratorial prestige organization. Hitler himself later spoke with derisive scorn of "*völkisch* sleepwalkers" and "itinerant preachers." This difference in organization and propaganda played an important role from the very outset: The National Socialists, going beyond an exclusive doctrinaire sect without a mass basis and without the prospect of political power, sought to become a strategic, broadly based mass party. But at the same time, the anti-Communist, anti-Semitic excitement stirred up in the aftermath of the *Räterepublik* offered an opportunity for the full incorporation of the racist arguments into the socialist-nationalist ideology of the party.

Like other groups hatched in the womb of the Thule Society, the DAP enjoyed the benevolent approval of militaristic circles. As a delegate and functionary of the defense and political propaganda program of the Munich Military Group Commando, Adolf Hitler had also come into contact with the new party. He was an avid reader of the *Münchener Beobachter,* though his offer to become a contributor had been turned down. On September 12, 1919, he, as mentioned earlier, went to one of the weekly DAP meetings in the Sterneckerbräu beer hall; these meetings were generally attended by anywhere from ten to forty followers. Inspired by a speech by Feder about the abolition of capitalism, Hitler apparently effectively rebutted an alleged proponent of Bavarian separatism, and after returning home read a pamphlet entitled *Mein politisches Erwachen (My Political Awakening)* given him by Drexler. Soon thereafter, he let himself be recruited as "propaganda chairman" (*Werbeobmann*) of the party.[12] This proved a stroke of luck: before the feared discharge into civilian life in March, 1920, he had managed to find an outlet for his newly discovered agitational talents. It is significant that Hitler had never been a member of any of the numerous *völkisch* sects. He won his spurs and acquired the propaganda tools for his political rise not among racist theorists but in the concrete situation of local and national issues, particularly in the fight against "Versailles," however deeply rooted the anti-Semitism that ultimately determined his policies.

In line with his unbridled ambition to dominate, Hitler came to believe that by taking this road into politics, he could establish his claim to unlimited power. Having at long last found an outlet for his long-frus-

---

[12] On this, Reginald Phelps, "Hitler and the DAP," *American Historical Review,* LXVIII (1963), 976 ff.; and "Anton Drexler, der Gründer der NSDAP," *Deutsche Rundschau,* LXXXVII (1961), 1136 ff.; Ernst Deuerlein, "Hitlers Eintritt in die Politik und die Reichswehr," *Vierteljahrshefte für Zeitgeschichte (VfZG),* No. 7 (1959), pp. 206 ff.; Werner Maser, *Die Frühgeschichte der NSDAP* (Frankfurt/Main, 1965); Dietrich Orlow, "The Organizational History and Structure of the NSDAP 1919–1923," *Journal of Modern History,* XXXVII (1965), 208 ff.; and *The History of the Nazi Party: 1918–1933* (Pittsburg, 1969), pp. 14 ff.

trated gigantomania, Hitler, in the narrow circle of this small party, developed organizational and speaking talents which within a short span of time carved out a special place for his party among the radical Right sectarians of Munich. The self-designated "artist" now called himself "writer"; in the unattainable, dreamed-of middle-class scale of values, these two professions ranked equally, regardless of the meagerness of his writings and the inadequacy of his stylistic gifts. But above all he was a speaker: after a brief apprenticeship as propaganda chairman of the party, he became aware of this essential talent. The skills acquired in his debates in the men's home at Vienna and while delivering the patriotic monologues of the war years were now put to the test and perfected in activities which gave him an intoxicating feeling of power.

To be sure, the DAP was a small, unpretentious starting point. Yet this very fact made Hitler's position less competitive, and the support given him, a useful and presumably harmless propagandist and "drummer" for the "national" cause, by influential military and social circles was, accordingly, indulgent. His closer collaborators—Ernst Röhm, Alfred Rosenberg, Dietrich Eckart, Rudolf Hess—came from various groups amid the welter of *völkisch* organizations. But Hitler's primary concern—the reorganization and broadening of the DAP through the recruitment of ex-soldiers and Free Corps members grown unaccustomed to civilian life—soon brought him into conflict with the old leadership. There began the trek from the small politicking debating society to the political combat organization which came on the scene with noisy mass agitation. A month after joining the party, on October 16, 1919, Hitler was one of the speakers at a meeting in the Hofbräuhaus before an audience of a hundred. Soon he was also invited to speak before *völkisch* groups outside of Munich, as, for example, in May, 1920, when he addressed a rally of the German *Völkisch* Defense and Offense League in Stuttgart.

The first real mass meeting, held on February 24, 1920, at Munich's Hofbräuhaus, proved to be a milestone. By then, Hitler had begun to make a name for himself as the party's foremost propaganda speaker.[13] The nominal main speaker, a physician, had been furnished by another *völkisch* group, but it was Hitler who played the leading role in the organization of this meeting and who announced the two major events: the new "25-point" party program, and the change of name to National Socialist German Workers' Party—a name which betrayed the Austrian influence and at the same time was intended to differentiate the German Workers' Party from the socialist parties. Its "socialism" was meant to combat Bolshevism among the working class in an attempt to win the support of the Reichswehr and politically influential social circles. The same holds true for the claim that Hitler was a

[13] Phelps, "Hitler als Parteiredner im Jahre 1920," *VfZG*, No. 11 (1963), pp. 289 ff.

"good Catholic" [14] acceptable to the traditional establishment of Catholic Bavaria.

The mass meetings were the true beginnings of the "Hitler movement," the consolidation of Hitler's dictatorial position within the party and beyond its confines. Moreover, Drexler, the party's founder and nominal chairman, held an outside job and therefore could not devote as much time either to the party or to his career as propagandist as his indefatigable colleague Hitler, who, as a jobless politician, had nothing to lose and much to gain. Hitler attended almost every important meeting, turned up at the Kapp Putsch in Berlin (together with Eckart), and, in the summer and fall of 1920, went to conferences of the Austrian National Socialists.

The new program, which replaced the guidelines which Drexler had laid down at the DAP's founding in January, 1919, had been compiled by Drexler in December, 1919, from a jumble of *völkisch* ideological sources and edited by Hitler. Appended to this program was a specific reference to "breaking the shackles of finance capital," Feder's pet theory which had strongly impressed Hitler, though it was an old idea found in the programs of many national-social reform movements. The other parts of the program also were hardly new; German, Austrian, and Bohemian proponents of anticapitalist, nationalist-imperialist, anti-Semitic movements were resorted to in its compilation. The individual points were phrased like slogans; they lent themselves to the concise, sensational dissemination of the "anti" position on which the party thrived, while its positive goals remained as vague as the programs of its precursors. But two of its new and basic features clearly betrayed Hitler's influence: the radical revisionism with its militant stance against Versailles and the outcome of the war in general, and the emphasis on the "unalterable" nature of the program, reminiscent of Hitler's rigid insistence on the "granite foundation" of his youthful "Weltanschauung."

Hitler's address at the Hofbräuhaus meeting was typical of those uninhibited, forceful diatribes against Marxists and democrats, "November criminals" and Jews, Versailles and the "world of enemies" encircling Germany with which the "unknown frontline soldier" was beginning to stir up public enthusiasm and violent hostility in Munich. In addition to its negative slogans, the new program contained a confused collection of high-flown postulates and promises for all. Its quintessence was the unification of the nation under a "national socialism" which, unlike the Marxist class struggle, promised to abolish the injustices of capitalism by uniting the workers and all other classes in one mighty, unified, powerful "people's community." Ideologically speaking, it was a woolly, eclectic mixture of political, social, racist, national-imperialist wishful thinking of the type which after the nine-

[14] Thus, in a letter from Rudolf Hess to von Kahr (May 17, 1921), quoted in Maser, *op. cit.*, p. 289.

teenth century, and more particularly since the unexpected catastrophe of the war, had inspired the "national Right," ranging from disappointed Conservatives and Pan-Germans to the national-revolutionary adventurists of the Free Corps. The Army, which in many parts of the new Republic served only reluctantly, also was in full sympathy, particularly in Bavaria. Thus, the organization's new star speaker was given a double opportunity to prove his effectiveness and promote his career: he could offer a despairing population torn by war and revolution and victimized economically by mounting inflation a simple explanation for their misery (Jews, Marxists, Versailles, and democrats), and in Munich, a city caught in the ferment of revolution and separatism, reaction and monarchism, he could form a "cell of national order" drawing from all walks of life, thereby attracting notice and gaining the support of Munich's not overly democratic military guardians of order.

There can be no doubt that Hitler, unlike many of his gullible cohorts, had little feeling for the program of "national socialism," except for its intense anti-Semitic nationalism. To him, it was little more than an effective, persuasive propaganda weapon for mobilizing and manipulating the masses. Once it had brought him to power, it became pure decoration: "unalterable," yet unrealized in its demands for nationalization and expropriation, for land reform and "breaking the shackles of finance capital." Yet it nonetheless fulfilled its role as backdrop and pseudo-theory, against which the future dictator could unfold his rhetorical and dramatic talents. After only a few months in his new role, Hitler began to be received in the salons of influential members of the *völkisch* literary, economic, social, and military establishment. Here was manifested for the first time that fatal belief of his intellectual, social, and economic superiors that they could make use of the energies and talents of the "mass drummer" and that, having served their purposes, he could be tamed and fitted into their scheme of things. This delusion figured in the putsch of 1923, in the undertakings of von Papen and Schleicher at the end of the Weimar Republic, in the formation of the Hitler Cabinet in 1933 with Hindenburg, Hugenberg, and heavy industry, and finally, also in the appeasement policies of the Western powers and the Soviet Union (1939); it proved to be the most important pacemaker in Hitler's forward march, for despite all his energy and luck, he would probably never have crashed the gates of power without outside help; he would have remained a would-be tyrant, just as he always remained a would-be artist.

Even though the NSDAP kept aloof from *völkisch* sects, it saw itself not merely as just another political party, but as a truly unique "movement" above the usual "political" organizations. "Party politics" was and remained a term of disdain in the National Socialist vocabulary. But it was not only in this respect that the NSDAP was tied to the antidemocratic and antiliberal groups outside the traditional party system; it also developed the structure of a male-oriented revolutionary order and elitist movement seeking mass support yet not considering the masses sufficiently knowledgeable politically to share in the decision-making process. The minor role assigned to women was typical of this, and even more so the resolution adopted by the first general membership meeting, including the handful of women present, in January, 1921: "A woman can never be admitted into the leadership of the party and into the executive committee." [15]

Of greater initial importance than ideology was the development of a strong organizational structure through which the party hoped to be able to extricate itself from the jungle of competing organizations. In this, the introduction of an all-encompassing symbolism proved highly effective. In their appeal to irrational emotions, the *völkisch* groups had developed a rich store of frequently scurrilous signs and symbols, and the new party made more definitive, purposeful, and cohesive use of them than its competitors. To begin with, there was the sign of the swastika, which as sun circle or sun wheel was to be found in many ancient cultures (including "non-Aryan" ones in Central America), but which, since the turn of the century, through a characteristic misunderstanding and misapplication of newly developed scientific theories, had been adopted by *völkisch* sects as the symbol of "Aryan" anti-Semitic revival movements. That the literary circle around Stefan George with its elitist ideology contributed to this symbolism, even though well-known Jewish writers and intellectuals belonged to it, is one of the tragedies of the early history of National Socialism. Lanz von Liebenfels, the Germanic Order, and the Thule Society all used the swastika as a symbol. One of the party's members, a dentist by the name of Friedrich Krohn, in May, 1919, wrote a memorandum about the swastika as the symbol of national-socialist groups. And he was probably the first to use it in its later form—against a black-white-and-red background—at the founding meeting of the Starnberg party local, where it was draped around the speaker's lectern. In *Mein Kampf*, Hitler inaccurately claims the invention for himself, though doubtlessly he was instrumental in the decision to make the swastika the official party emblem. He obviously recognized quite early the importance of symbolism and its unifying potential force for a young, aggressive party as well as for a future mass party, and then systematically nurtured and exploited it.

No other party was so astutely aware of the unifying force of symbols in mass demonstrations and as an expression of solidarity. In the early years there was a confusion of symbols. The brown shirt did not come into general use until 1924, via Rossbach's Free Corps; before that time the party units wore windbreakers and ski caps. The use of a ceremonial standard in 1922–23 obviously was taken from the Italian Fascists. But the Heil salute, then of course still without the attribute "Hitler," already came into use in 1920, having originated with Austrian *völkisch* groups. And the mandatory wearing of badges and uni-

[15] Georg Franz-Willing, *Die Hitler-Bewegung* (Hamburg and Berlin, 1962), pp. 80 ff.

forms, as well as the glittering abundance of symbols at meetings, undeniably added to the "movement's" appeal and its much-touted feeling of community, even though the pseudo-military trappings and pseudo-religious idolization of symbols more and more repelled its opponents.

The earliest collaborators of Hitler contributed materially to this rapid transformation of the insignificant Drexler group into an organizationally and ideologically taut party, which as early as 1920 stood out among the groups of the radical Right and by the end of that year boasted a membership of 3,000.[16] Ernst Röhm (1887–1934), who joined the DAP in November, 1919, at the latest, is first among these. The son of a railroad employee and himself an active officer, Röhm told the story of his life as a *völkisch* monarchist and mercenary soldier in his autobiography, eloquently entitled *Die Geschichte eines Hochverräters (The Story of a Traitor; 1928)*. To commit "treason" against a despised Republic that also threatened his military career seemed to him a self-evident duty. He played a most important role as the right hand of the Free Corps General von Epp and as the first promoter of the political career of Corporal Hitler. By introducing the unknown Hitler, a man without a past and without contacts, to "patriotic" officers and politicians, Röhm furnished the springboard for Hitler's entry into politics. He lent active support to radical right-wing armed organizations (*Wehrverbände*), giving fully of his talents as a military organizer, adventurer, and conspirator, and it was he who built the party troops, the Sturmabteilung (SA), into an instrument of fear and terror. Yet for these very reasons, he again and again came into conflict with Hitler, a conflict which in 1925 resulted in a five-year-long estrangement, some of which Röhm spent as a military instructor in Bolivia. After being called back in 1930 to head the SA, new conflicts arose, ending with his execution in 1934. In fact, Röhm was the only one Hitler truly respected, the only one with whom he was on familiar *"du"* terms; but he also was a rival whose idea of a powerful fighting organization parallel to the party again and again ran up against Hitler's idea of total party control.

Hitler's early encounter with Dietrich Eckart (1868–1923) was equally important. A lawyer's son from Neumarkt in Bavaria, Eckart had tried his hand at writing in Berlin where, apparently out of pique over his literary failure, he became an anti-Semite and finally landed in the DAP via the Thule Society. His intellectual influence on Hitler (he was Hitler's first educated and socially adept acquaintance) apparently was quite considerable, even given the assumption that Hitler came out of the war with firm basic ideas. It was due to Eckart's military and social connections that the NSDAP was able to acquire the *Münchener Beobachter* in December, 1920, which, renamed *Völkischer Beobachter*, became the official party paper. Eckart was its first publisher until his premature death, doubtlessly hastened by his im-

---

[16] Wolfgang Schäfer, *NSDAP* (Hanover, 1956), p. 7.

moderate drinking. As the author of the National Socialist slogan *"Deutschland erwache"* ("Germany, Awaken"), which he immortalized in a bloodthirsty civil war song, he entered into National Socialist heroic literature. Hitler acknowledged Eckart (who, incidentally, introduced him to his favorite retreat, Berchtesgaden) as the spiritual cofounder of National Socialism. Given Hitler's blatant egocentricity, his dedication of *Mein Kampf* to Eckart must be seen as an extraordinary recognition of this influence, even though he does not spell it out in any detail. One might say that Röhm and Eckart "made" Hitler. At any rate, Hitler's political career is unthinkable without these two midwives.

Hitler was provided with the economic formula for the anticapitalist and anti-Semitic explanation of the world by the speaker of the first DAP meeting he attended, the engineer Gottfried Feder (1883–1941). This son of a civil servant from Würzburg had dabbled in the study of fiscal affairs; now he simplified the sweeping polemic against finance capital by reducing it to the monocausal assertion that the working class was kept in bondage by a class of financial speculators, who in turn were dominated by Jews. It was an essentially reactionary idea directed against all of modern economic development, harking back to almost medieval social and economic theories. Its slogan was "Break the shackles of finance capital," the root, so Feder believed, of all evil, all economic and social crises of our times. That National Socialism succeeded in incorporating into itself a petty-bourgeois movement fighting modern economic and social development was in no small measure possible because of slogans such as these. In 1918, Feder had unsuccessfully approached the Bavarian revolutionary government with his reform ideas, which simultaneously he had sought to spread in pamphlets. He then found a haven in the DAP and the program of the NSDAP, which he reached via the Thule Society and the indoctrination program of the Army, where Hitler first heard and was impressed by him. He founded a sect to propagate his *idée fixe*, the League for Breaking the Shackles of High Finance. But Feder also played a rather significant role in .the early days of the party as a liaison man to certain economic groups, particularly to the threatened middle class, which was receptive to his ideas. To be sure, his sectarian notions influenced neither the planning nor the practice of National Socialist policy. The implementation of Feder's ideas, to which he devoted himself briefly as State Secretary in 1933, was of course out of the question. They remained nothing more than a propaganda weapon, a reform façade of a government which considered and used economic policy only as a means for accruing power and for aggressive expansion. In 1934, Feder was sent off to the Technological Institute of Berlin, a harmless professor.

The picture of the role played by Alfred Rosenberg (1893–1946) is also inconsistent. The first in a long series of ethnic German (*Auslandsdeutsche*) party officials, he was born in the then Russian city of Riga. War and revolution interrupted his architectural studies; he came to Munich, where he met Eckart, and through him found his way into the DAP. In 1921, the *Völkische Beobachter* offered him the platform from which to proclaim a Weltanschauung pieced together out of personal resentments and pseudo-scientific readings—a mixture of Chamberlain, Langbehn, Lagarde, and others, its edge sharpened by an ethnic German, Baltic brand of *völkisch* anti-Semitism, anti-Slavism, and radical anti-Communism, paired for the first time with an anti-Christian concept of history. Although his major work, *Der Mythus des 20. Jahrhunderts (The Myth of the Twentieth Century)* was not published until 1930, Rosenberg was the only leading National Socialist who, from the very beginning, sought to systematize the National Socialist "Weltanschauung." His actual influence on the course of the party, however, remained slight. Hitler was not really influenced by Rosenberg's writings; he himself said that he had not even read the *Mythus*. Throughout his life, Rosenberg remained a subservient acolyte of Hitler's, even though the unscrupulous utilization and violation of his "idea" distressed him, particularly the Hitler-Stalin Pact of 1939 and the party's Russian policy. But it suited Hitler's tactics, as the situation demanded, either to invoke Rosenberg and make him into the ideological high priest of the party, or to keep him at a distance and dismiss his theories as expressions of personal opinion, as he did specifically in his dispute with the Catholic Church.

Another Baltic German, Max Erwin von Scheubner-Richter (1884–1923), attracted attention in the early days as an astute contact man. He was brought into the party in 1920 by Rosenberg, who knew him from Riga. Scheubner-Richter was widely traveled, spoke many languages, and had served in various diplomatic posts during the war. A participant in the Kapp Putsch, he established the important contact between the Hitler movement and Ludendorff, and was also invaluable in opening doors to industry, monarchist circles, and the Church. An unusual man in the circle of limited, radical right-wing fanatics around Hitler, Scheubner-Richter, of all people, was the only leading National Socialist killed during the abortive putsch at the Feldherrnhalle.

The youngest of the founding fathers, Hermann Esser (b. 1900), Hitler's devoted propaganda planner, was a highly controversial figure even within the party. The son of a railway official, Esser had joined the SPD in 1919 but at the same time handled press relations for the "education" department of the Army's Munich sector, where he met Hitler and Feder. He became an effective propaganda speaker at party meetings and rose rapidly to the editorship of the *Völkische Beobachter*. He made up for his instability and questionable character by his unconditional loyalty to Hitler, who, after gaining control of the party, made him propaganda chief. Long before Goebbels came on the scene, this unscrupulous fanatic found the lowest common denominator in anti-Semitic, antidemocratic propaganda. Only a man like Streicher, who at the time still headed his own anti-Semitic outfit in Nuremberg, was comparable to Esser in this respect.

Even so meager a survey as this gives a hint about the personalities of the earliest leaders around Hitler. They were a mixture of Bavarian and ethnic German radicals, mostly the sons of the lower middle class, between the ages of twenty and thirty-five. As to the general membership, ex-soldiers and Free Corps members joined at an increasing rate, while the working-class element diminished. At the same time, many unemployed found their way into the party, which either made them paid propagandists or fighting troops or got them jobs through its network of *völkisch* contacts. This membership composition explains the drive for revolutionary action which exploded in 1923. But equally important is the fact that Hitler, within a remarkably short span of time, was able to gain control of the party apparatus and also outmaneuver the rival groups of the radical Right.

THE RISE OF HITLER

Despite his extraordinary drive, Hitler in 1920 had not yet gained complete control of the expanding party. Though as an indispensible propagandist he enjoyed great prestige and was able to influence the structure and activities of the party, he still had not penetrated into its innermost councils when, in the summer of 1921, he prepared for his grand coup, by ousting Drexler as chairman, assuming near-dictatorial power, and making himself largely independent of the executive committee. This turn of events becomes comprehensible if one studies the tactics he employed. He was determined to outdo all rival parties in activity and forcefulness. By turning sharply against bourgeois-romantic sectarian groups and their pseudo-democratic organizational tactics, he sought to cash in on the trend of the times toward a "strong man," toward the remaking of the shattered postwar world by a "dictatorship of order." More than any of the other party functionaries, Hitler knew how to make himself indispensible by working without letup, pushing the more sedate Drexler, hobbled by his job, into the background. When it came to a test of strength, it became obvious that most of the party executives, though sympathetic to Drexler—and even Drexler himself—felt that that they could not dispense with the driving force of Hitler. It was a demonstration of the tactics which Hitler was to apply successfully again and again, as for example during the final party dispute with Gregor Strasser in December, 1932.

On July 11, 1921, Hitler in a dramatic gesture announced his resignation from the NSDAP, and at the same time just as dramatically made known his conditions for rejoining: absolute primacy for the Munich party local and its program over all other National Socialist local groups which had sprung up in and outside Bavaria; the expulsion of a number of undesirable individuals and groups, particularly one local in Augsburg which was critical of his power aspirations and had proposed fusion with the German Socialist Party (Deutschsozialistische Partei, or DSP), a similarly oriented party, with future headquarters in Berlin. Hitler called for pursuing a radical course and keeping aloof from any nationalist groups inclining toward compromise. The ultimatum he laid down for his leadership gave unmistakable hints of what the future held in store. Among his specific demands were the election of a new executive committee within a week, the conferral on him of the "post of first chairman with dictatorial powers," and the continuance in perpetuity of Munich as the "seat of the movement." He furthermore insisted on the expulsion of any member who attempted to change the name of the party or its program. Also, he ruled out union with rival groups; only unconditional affiliation on their part was acceptable, and any negotiations on that were to be conducted by him "exclusively." [17]

It soon became apparent that this strategy was bound to be successful, for Hitler had made himself indispensible to the life and work of the party. Again Eckart became the liaison man who persuaded the party leadership, including Drexler, to capitulate to Hitler's demands with some minor reservations. However, in the next few days new problems arose which almost led to a split, when the Hitler wing, acting on its own, called a special membership meeting to seal its victory. A countercampaign was launched within the party, and handbills were distributed casting doubt on Hitler's and his friend Esser's integrity, asking embarrassing questions about the source of their "income," castigating the maintenance of a private Hitler army (made up of unemployed), and calling for the founding of a National Socialist organization without Hitler. But once again Drexler, at the urging of Eckart, gave in at the last moment. The extraordinary membership meeting of July 29, 1921, attended by only 550 members, and chaired by Esser, ended in a rhetorical victory for Hitler. The assemblage voted to make Drexler honorary chairman and to revise the statutes so as to reorganize the party, involving pseudo-elections to the executive council but in fact instituting dictatorial leadership with an "action committee" under Hitler. Hitler's men moved into the key positions.

This was the beginning of the myth of the "Leader" Hitler, at first consciously promoted by Eckart in the *Völkische Beobachter* and already hinting at the mystical idealization typical of the future. Rudolf Hess, a student of the Munich geopolitician Karl Haushofer, furnished the first example of these panegyrics. Hitler's proud assertion that he had won the "position of first chairman with dictatorial powers" made the "leader principle" into the central organizational principle of the party. As the "leader of the NSDAP," as he now called himself, Hitler demanded not only unlimited control over the party hierarchy but increasingly also the unconditional loyalty and almost pseudo-religious allegiance of the membership. This type of leader principle was in line with the widespread craving for security, order, authority, and hero worship unfulfilled since the overthrow of the monarchy.

---

[17] Konrad Heiden, *Hitler—A Biography* (New York, 1963), p. 108; Maser, *op. cit.*, p. 232; Franz-Willing, *op. cit.*, pp. 110 f.

The victory of the Hitler wing brought immediate major changes in the leadership and structure of the party. Max Amann, Hitler's former sergeant, became its new secretary general; the number of secretariat employees was increased to thirteen. This was the beginning of Amann's career as the party's press secretary who ultimately administered the far-flung newspaper empire of the Third Reich.[18] Eckart's position as editor in chief of the *Völkische Beobachter* also took on new importance, and the propaganda and recruitment sections of the party were expanded. But most important of all, Hitler was successful in forming a party troop—the SA—organized along military lines; initially appearing in the guise of a sports group, it soon emerged as a powerful party army in street and indoor brawls. Hitler, in the stilted, bureaucratic prose of *Mein Kampf* (pp. 658 f.), oversimplifies his first major triumph, of course without detailing the problems that accompanied his rise to party dictator or the vital role played by Eckart. He writes: "The attempt of a group of *völkisch* dreamers supported by the then chairman of the party to take over the leadership led to the collapse of this minor intrigue, and a general membership meeting unanimously handed over the entire leadership of the movement to me. At the same time new statutes were adopted giving the first chairman of the movement full responsibility, wiping out decisions of the executive, and in their place introducing a system of a division of tasks which has proved to be most beneficial. On August 1, 1921, I took over this internal reorganization of the movement."

Thus the party formally became the instrument of Hitler's policies. But the setting up of a party army, the greater role of propaganda, the expansion of the party organization, and the coordination of its work through dictatorial "bulletins" were not the only factors responsible for the now almost total leadership position of Hitler. Equally significant was the fact that in this period in 1921–22, he succeeded in inducing other radical-Right groups to submit to or become part of his Munich party local. Among the most important of these was the German Socialist Party (DSP), founded in Hanover in 1919. Unlike the DAP-NSDAP, the DSP had locals throughout most of Germany. But it also had an active membership in Munich which the Thule Society and the *Münchener Beobachter* initially had supported as strongly as they did the DAP. Its socialist-reformist character was well-defined; the land-reform program developed by the agricultural expert Adolf Damaschke at the beginning of the century formed a vital part of its political propaganda. And later the "German Socialist" wing, particularly the group around the Strasser brothers, Otto and Gregor, which took the "socialist" aspect of the movement rather more seriously than Hitler, played a role in the NSDAP, until

[18] For a characterization of Amann, cf. Albert Krebs, *Tendenzen und Gestalten der NSDAP* (Stuttgart, 1959), pp. 195 ff. On the *Völkische Beobachter* and the National Socialist press, see Oron Hale, *The Captive Press in the Third Reich* (Princeton, 1964), pp. 15 ff.

the defection of Otto Strasser (1930) and the submission (1932) and, finally, the murder of Gregor (1934) sealed the victory of the opportunists around Hitler.

The North German DSP leader, Alfred Brunner (1871–1936), fought against Hitler's claim to undisputed leadership of the radical Right, and in 1921 sought to gain control of the NSDAP via its Augsburg local; Brunner in no uncertain terms criticized the "party papacy" of the self-styled "leader" in Munich. But the great weakness of the DSP lay in its loose organization throughout Germany, which in the long run was no match for the tightly organized, dictatorially controlled Munich NSDAP. During 1922, the DSP capitulated, and in December it dissolved and voted to join the NSDAP.[19] This development was given a major boost by the fact that the DSP's Nuremberg group, led by the radical anti-Semitic elementary school teacher Streicher, after some bitter battles went over to Hitler. The Streicher group with its paper, *Der Deutschsozialist,* formed a particularly important part of the DSP. Streicher's going over to the rising Hitler party put an end to the long-drawn-out dispute over the highly criticized Hitler cult of the Munich National Socialists. Hitler valued Streicher's role so highly that he supported this extraordinarily vulgar anti-Semitic agitator against all attacks and, by appointing him Gauleiter (district leader) of Nuremberg-Franconia, ultimately made him the official host of the Nuremberg party congresses.

During this period Hitler also consolidated his undisputed leadership in Austria. As mentioned earlier, Hitler was one of the main speakers at the Salzburg congress, a subcommittee of the "National Socialist Parties of Greater Germany." The practical work of this committee included a speaker exchange, which in 1921 brought Hitler back to Linz, Drexler to Czechoslovakia, and Riehl, Jung, and Knirsch to Munich. By June, 1922, when another German-Austrian party congress was convened in Vienna, Hitler's control of the strongest party local was firmly established. He appeared at the head of a large delegation and delivered the warmly applauded keynote address. It was his first return to Vienna; the second, sixteen years later, sealed the *Anschluss* and the "coordination" (*Gleichschaltung*) of his homeland.

Munich remained the power center of the party, but the "movement" spread; its impressive symbols—swastika, Heil salutes, and fantastic uniforms—were seen throughout Germany and Austria. In addition to the Army, influential economic and social circles lent Hitler a helping hand. General Hans von Seeckt and Hugo Stinnes * showed an interest in Hitler.[20] Contributions by big industrialists—Thyssen, Kirdorf, Brosig—began to pour in, and Mrs. Bruckmann,

---

[19] Maser, *op. cit.,* p. 233.

* Seeckt was chief of the German Army command; Stinnes was a major industrialist and DVP Reichstag member.

[20] See Wolfgang F. W. Hallgarten, *Hitler, Reichswehr und Industrie* (Frankfurt/Main, 1955), p. 89 and *passim.*

the wife of a publisher, and the piano builder Bechstein opened their salons to Hitler. The niche which Hitler had carved out for himself with his drive could of course not alter the fact of his being the leader of a comparatively small radical Munich-based party, even though his hectic campaign, featuring rallies in beer halls, circus tents, and public squares, was obviously highly successful. But the breakthrough to a mass movement was not made until a new wave of domestic unrest broke out in the wake of the Ruhr occupation and the 1923 inflation.

The main strength of the NSDAP, unlike the other parties—except those of the Left—lay in its organizational structure, which had grown more elaborate and concentrated. This held true particularly for the growing SA, which, though posing as the athletic and defense arm of the party, had from the very outset sported a military air. Hitler himself had filled it with ex-soldiers, and even more came in from the Free Corps, which were in the process of dissolution, particularly the Oberland and Epp Corps and the Ehrhardt Brigade. It was no mere coincidence that in the early days meetings frequently were held in the vicinity of military barracks. These "political soldiers" acted as guards at meetings and simultaneously as body guards. Hitler justified the building of a party army by saying that "terror can be broken only by terror." By applying military civil-war tactics in the political sphere, he made the use of force an important component of his strategy. It is true that National Socialist meetings were often disrupted by the Left, but in view of the aggressive National Socialist propaganda, this was not surprising.

Gradually, the improvised defense troops turned into a more cohesive organization. The pseudo-military cast the party had assumed with Hitler's emergence appealed to the young people of military age who could not be absorbed by the new 100,000-man army. In August, 1921, when the new era of the leader principle began, the Gymnastics and Sports Division of the NSDAP became a formal entity under the command of the Free Corps naval officer Lieutenant Johann Ulrich Klintzsch of the Ehrhardt Brigade. The August 14, 1921, issue of the *Völkische Beobachter* appealed "to our German youth" "to bring together our young party members into an iron organization whose strength would be available to the entire movement as a battering ram. It should be the bearer of the military ideals of a free people. It should furnish protection for the work to be done by the leaders."

This set forth a dual and at the same time conflicting purpose, carrying within itself the seeds of the recurrent differences within the SA and between the SA and the party hierarchy. To what extent was the SA simply an instrument of the party, to what extent was it an avant garde, and to what extent was it an independent combat group, a political free corps with sovereign powers? These questions were not resolved by Hitler, who, although he considered the SA subordinate to the party, also needed it; he avoided taking a stand until after the takeover, in the murders of June 30, 1934. The dichotomous position of the SA was probably unavoidable. It was rooted in the necessity to win and hold the support of the military, which saw its role largely as self-sufficient. This was the position of Röhm as well of the famous Free Corps officer Captain Ehrhardt, whose brigade did in fact furnish many of the training officers and recruits of the new organization; and the Reichswehr, particularly in the crisis-ridden year of 1923, was more interested in the military-political aspects of that enterprise than in its party-political role. After a series of victorious brawls at indoor meetings, Hitler in November, 1921, officially conferred the honorary designation *"Sturmabteilung"* on the troops.[21]

The alarming growth of the SA was due not only to the recruitment of stranded soldiers and unemployed workers. Young people in particular found it seductively adventurous to court danger by plastering stickers and painting slogans on buildings, to fight with opponents, to hold noisy parades and go on exciting cross-country van trips, to conduct membership drives, and to experience the intoxication of attending conspiratorial secret meetings and planning attacks. The Munich police, presided over by Ernst Pöhner, who played an equivocal role and finally openly sympathized with the National Socialists, acted only reluctantly. Generally speaking, the recruitment drives of the National Socialists were aimed at the youth. As early as February, 1921, Hess founded a National Socialist student organization at the University of Munich with its own SA troop. A year later, in May, 1922, Hitler ceremoniously baptized the "Youth League of the NSDAP" at the Bürgerbräu cellar. At the same time, the influx from the Free Corps continued; in December, 1922, the former Free Corps Rossbach, under the command of Lieutenant Edmund Heines, who later earned dubious fame as a particularly brutal SA group leader, joined the SA as a unit. Rossbach himself cooperated in this course.

The effectiveness of all this activity, which enabled Hitler's party to outstrip all other right-wing extremist groups, was further enhanced by Hitler's receptivity toward modern propaganda techniques. In his meetings and propaganda work, Hitler, discarding the traditional methods of the conservative, *völkisch* antidemocratic forces, utilized the new techniques to "absorb" large numbers of people. For example, he made the greatest possible use of motor vehicles. The SA, supplemented by special divisions, formed its own motorized unit, which, under the leadership of Major Adolf Hühnlein, formed the nucleus of the future National Socialist Motor Corps (Nationalsozialistisches Kraftfahrkorps, or NSKK); furthermore, "technical," "artillery," and "bicycle" squads were organized, as well as "equestrian" and "music" corps—a symbol of the blend of tradition and modernity. Initially organized in groups of one hundred, the SA later was divided into military companies. Most of these were under the Munich SA regimental commander Heinrich Bennecke, a history student who had come from the Ehrhardt Brigade. But at the same time, all com-

---

[21] Thilo Vogelsang, *Reichswehr, Staat und NSDAP* (Stuttgart, 1962), p. 35. See also Heinrich Bennecke, *Hitler und die SA* (Munich, 1962).

panies were personally responsible to Hitler. It was a private army of
the total "leader" who demanded unconditional loyalty, including
the readiness to die.

AGITATION AND ORGANIZATION

Everything Hitler said made it clear that to him, mass psychological
propaganda and a taut organization were the most vital presuppositions for political success. Intellectual and economic considerations
ranked second. The central portions of *Mein Kampf,* and obviously
those which interested Hitler most, are devoted to propaganda techniques and mass persuasion; compared to them, the political and
ideological portions are nothing but a collection of clichés and catchwords. Hitler doubtlessly owed his rise and the growth of the party
to this preoccupation and to his unquestionable genius for mass persuasion. Later, he was to find a most able assistant in Joseph Goebbels.
But in the beginning, he was pre-eminent in this area in his own
party as well as among other groups of the radical Right. It will not
do, however, to stress only his innate oratorical and propaganda
talents, to imbue them with an almost demoniacal quality, as some
are wont to do. Hitler himself made a point of saying how great a
debt he owed to the lessons he learned from the propaganda of World
War I. He maintained that the Allies, particularly the British, were
far superior to the Central Powers in this respect, and that their
victory was due largely to that superiority.

Questionable though this assertion may appear to a serious student
of the nationalistic mobilization of German public opinion in 1914–18,
it lends effective support to the stab-in-the-back myth and the wish for
a nonmilitary explanation for the defeat. As a matter of fact, exactly
the opposite is true: against a background of crisis and civil war, of
the psychosis of defeat, of revisionism, National Socialist propaganda
was effective precisely because it was a radical continuation and an
even more imbalanced exaggeration of the wartime propaganda. Its
arguments, insofar as they did not derive from prewar radicalism,
drew largely on the arsenal of war and enemy propaganda. At the
same time, Hitler's typical method—to reduce aggressive, emotional,
fragmentary ideas to simple slogans and catchwords, thereby assuring the widest possible dissemination and forcefulness—presupposed
the mass-propaganda technique in which lay the real strength of the
National Socialists.

The most effective tool was the elaborate rite of the mass meeting,
with all its emotional trappings, into which the major speech was
cleverly incorporated: high point and release from tension built up
almost to the breaking point by means of martial music and songs,
mass demonstrations and flags, radical slogans and the belated arrival
of the "leader." The feverish propaganda campaign with leaflets and
posters was not nearly so effective. Its purpose was to support the
oratorical demagoguery let loose by Hitler in meeting upon meeting

after October, 1919, and which, after 1920, became an accepted part of life in Munich. The main themes rolled forth in almost monotonous repetition: the fight against the peace treaties, Marxism, separatism, international capitalism, and the "November democracy," against the profiteers of the lost war and the "Jewish conspiracy" backing them. Anti-Semitism was an active ingredient from the very outset: propaganda posters invariably bore the legend "Jews not admitted." After 1921, the SA was the embodiment of the pseudo-military framework and the constant threat of terror; through it, the party was visible everywhere; even before the adoption of the official uniform in 1923, its parades, posters and leaflets, flags and armbands, were part of the daily life of Munich, giving an exaggerated picture of the movement's size.

Although the NSDAP of 1920, in its agitational fervor and in the resultant public notice it attracted, soon overtook the larger parties, it did not yet venture into electoral politics; all of its efforts were concentrated on agitation and organization. A popular election was too great a risk, and until the electoral success of 1930, this aspect of political work was minimized and stress laid on antiparliamentary methods and aims. The mass-meeting campaign was astonishingly effective; the meetings frequently drew audiences of more than a thousand, although many curious citizens of Munich came only because of the spectacle: the brutal "fun" and the brawls. Thus, on February 3, 1921, about sixty-five hundred people came to the Krone Circus to hear Hitler castigate the reparations conference, a surefire topic in vying for the support of "nationally thinking" persons, even those who might otherwise be put off by the radical slogans of the National Socialists.

The critical attention the opposition press showered on the National Socialists only added to the effectiveness of their campaigns. Hitler consciously tried to get into the papers day after day through aggressive, provocative tactics which did not shy away from making propaganda capital out of arrests and court trials. As early as 1920, the Munich-based party expanded its activities far beyond the borders of Bavaria. Local groups were formed in Stuttgart, Pforzheim, Hanover, and Halle. Borrowing a page from the Socialists, they tried to tie members to the party in their personal lives as well. Each member had to attend at least one of the weekly "conferences" a month. Outings and Wagner concerts, solstice and Christmas festivals, with their ideologically tinged Germanic rites, served to strengthen the bonds between the members, who regarded the party as their homeland and their surrogate religion. Here, too, anti-Semitism as the all-inclusive unifying, and interpretative principle took center stage.

The increasing political weight of the party became apparent in the course of 1922, when its propaganda openly threatened a coup in case the vacillating government and courts moved to outlaw the party and deport Hitler to Austria. The semimilitary displays staged at the party congresses, which also served to demonstrate the NSDAP's pre-eminence among the radical Right, became the favorite expression of this policy of intimidation. At first, these displays took place within the setting of "national" groups. But in October, 1922, Hitler appeared at the "German Day" in Coburg escorted by 800 SA men. Their martial demeanor dominated the *völkisch* military review, and they also proved this dominance in a number of victorious brawls. It was the time of Mussolini's March on Rome, an event which stimulated and set the example for the dawning era of the mass demonstrations and power struggles. The first "national" congress of the NSDAP, held in Munich's largest meeting hall on January 27–29, 1923, was the high point of this development. The German and Austrian leaders of the "movement" appeared at twelve mass meetings. Hitler himself was the main speaker at each of these, and at one staged with almost pseudo-religious symbolism at Munich's Marsfeld, he "dedicated" the first SA standards—imitations of the Fascist insignia. In the year 1923, he had arrived at the point at which he decided to set out on the road to power.

Even though the rapid ascent of the party was inextricably linked to Hitler's tireless, almost obsessive drive, it nonetheless could not have come about without outside support. This was obvious above all in two areas: in the intensive organizational drive of the "movement" and in the matter of party finances. The idea of a "movement" that aspires to be something more than a mere party, that wants to be all-encompassing, above "political" differences, was also held by other groups. But in steering clear of *völkisch* sectarians and theorizing "cowards," and in his determination to build an effective party organization, Hitler proved to be a realist. He always favored the party structure, despite his ideological "movement" talk, even though early in his career—in the aftermath of his professional failure—he had said that the *völkisch* movement could not become a "people's movement" and win over the "broad masses" to the "national cause" while it was controlled by "highly honorable yet fantastic-naïve academics, professors, and governmental, educational, and legal officials." [22]

His, of course, was a new type of party, with many of the characteristics of the tautly organized, militant socialist parties; in contrast to the loosely structured traditional middle-class, special-interest parties, its objective was an all-embracing organization with a pseudo-military nucleus and broad influence, appealing to all layers of the population. Even its basic anti-Communist position did not prevent it from welcoming all kinds of political converts and occasionally even from collaborating with the radical Left, as, for example, in its fight against the Republic in its final stages in 1930–32, and in the Stalin-Hitler Pact of 1939. Only *one* group—the Jews, regardless of their religious persuasion—was unremittingly and unconditionally barred from this "all-embracing party." Racist anti-Semitism was and remained the one basic principle to which Hitler subscribed deeply, blindly, and

[22] *Mitteilungsblatt* of January 7, 1922, in Franz-Willing, *op. cit.*, p. 170.

ruthlessly. Membership applications specifically stated that they were intended only for "German comrades"; they asked for a statement of "German (Aryan) descent," and only persons "without racially alien ancestors" were eligible.

After Hitler's usurpation of the dictatorial party leadership in July, 1921, the organizational structure became thoroughly authoritarian. Though the first edition of *Mein Kampf* still spoke of the "election of the leadership," it did lay stress on the "unconditional authority" and complete and sole responsibility of the top leadership. In later editions even this last concession to democratic procedure, at best nothing more than a tactical concession, was replaced by total dictatorial control. The leader principle and the military command structure did in fact form the essence of the National Socialist party organization. All attempts to change this, before and after the putsch of 1923, were systematically quashed by Hitler—even more systematically than similar moves were put down by Mussolini, who in 1943 did bow to his "Fascist Council." Characteristically, in the early days local groups were formed only if, aside from the requisite solvency, they had an acceptable leader willing to submit without qualms to the command structure of the party. Hitler was wary of fusion or genuine compromise with other groups, including the existing *völkisch* "working committees"; he invariably rejected them. Not growth at any price, but cohesion and subordination marked Hitler's ideal organization.

In fact, in early 1922, the party had only about 6,000 members, many fewer than its political activities and effectiveness would have led one to believe. There was a sizable influx of new members after each member was exhorted to recruit three new ones and one subscriber to the *Völkische Beobachter* every three months. Hitler devoted himself to developing public speakers and refining meeting techniques, the basic principle being that meetings were to be held in halls too small for the audience and that one-third were to be supporters. The remnants of the DSP gradually helped to swell the number of local groups in northern Germany, until the first wave of prohibitions in November, 1922, in Prussia and up to September, 1923, in Saxony, Thuringia, Hamburg, Hesse, and Brunswick put a stop to the party's growth. The fact that its membership multiplied almost tenfold (ca. 55,000) before the party was outlawed altogether in November, 1923, may be attributed to the profoundly disturbing events of 1923 which made possible Hitler's attempted takeover.

An important question remains: which social and economic forces were behind the young "movement," and how were its hectic activities and expanding organization financed? Initially, the movement suffered from a chronic shortage of funds. And its membership was so small and the resources of its leaders were so puny compared to the noise it made that, granting the much-vaunted "idealism" of its fanatical adherents, the question of outside financing remains a valid issue. A thesis advanced by Marxist polemicists in particular, namely that National Socialism was in fact the invention and creation of monopoly capitalism, is a gross oversimplification of its background and early history. The anticapitalist impulse was more than a mere pretext, and it took the militant fanaticism of the Hitler group to give the party the importance to attract wealthy backers. The smaller contributions of middle-class followers, admission charged at gatherings, collections, and membership dues paid rental and printing costs; the financial situation of the early leadership, including Hitler's, was modest.

On the other hand, it is clear that without the financial assistance first of the Thule Society and then of the Munich army and portions of the Free Corps, the rapid transition of the DAP into the Hitler party could not have taken place, nor could the new party have acquired the *Völkische Beobachter,* despite membership assessments and compulsory subscriptions. With the upswing in party activity after Hitler's "takeover" in the summer of 1921, outside contributions also increased considerably. As mentioned earlier, Eckart in particular had contacts with socially prominent and moneyed circles. One of his Berlin friends, Dr. Emil Gansser, established connections with the influential National Club of Berlin. As early as 1922, Hitler addressed this club composed of respectable industrialists, landowners, bankers, high-ranking officers, and university professors. The Pan-German League, presided over by Court Councillor Heinrich Class, a radical proponent of expansionism, was among the influential organizations that were beginning to open their doors to the successful demagogue. Röhm had contacts in the legal and also the illegal (Black) Reichswehr, and they proved a source of vehicles and weapons. Most of these were the same groups which all along had supported and sought to use the National Socialists. But now the National Socialists were much stronger and more effective; Drexler's party of railroad workers had become a party of the uprooted lower-middle and middle class and simultaneously a military organization of ideological fanatics and ex-soldiers.

As to the amount of the contributions from German and foreign sources—particularly from Switzerland, which Hitler himself visited— exact information is still difficult to come by. But these contributions were fairly sizable, particularly in 1923, after Scheubner-Richter and (through him) Ludendorff had called the attention of prominent monarchist and reactionary circles to Hitler's able opposition to the Left, Versailles, and the Republic. Wealthy Russian émigrés also seemed to have played a part in this. But the best-known examples of help extended are the financial assistance of industrialist Fritz Thyssen, and Hitler's social grooming by Mmes. Bechstein and Bruckmann. In addition to Bruckmann, the notorious right-wing Lehmann Verlag, Borsig-Berlin, Daimler, and the Bavarian Industrial League all rendered financial and organizational help at one time or another. The reasons for this early support varied from case to case, but Hitler's sensational ventures of 1922 and 1923 could not have been undertaken without it, despite the stress put on the early "socialist" history of National Socialism.

THE CRISIS OF BAVARIA AND THE REICH

Even after three years of arduous work, Hitler still was the leader of only *one* right-wing group among many, though his, because of the beer-hall and circus-tent meetings, the demonstrations and parades, was attracting more and more public notice and adherents. But Hitler's breakthrough into politics was possible only amid the confused and alarming events of 1923—the Ruhr occupation and abortive coups, economic crisis and inflation, governmental crises and conflicts between Bavaria and the Reich.

The assassination of Reich Ministers Erzberger (August 26, 1921) and Rathenau (June 22, 1922) added to the conspiratorial and hostile atmosphere in which the forces of the antidemocratic Right thrived. Countermeasures and a Presidential decree for the safeguarding of the Republic (August 29, 1921) were of little avail; a condition of latent civil war remained the hallmark of Germany's domestic scene even after the failure of the counterrevolutionary Kapp Putsch. The political and anti-Semitic threats that marked the hate campaigns of the extreme Right found their most visible fulfillment in the murder of Rathenau. The assassins, among them a twenty-five-year-old naval officer named Erwin Kern, were, like the murderers of Erzberger, members of Consul, a secret organization headed by Captain Ehrhardt. They were quickly traced to their hideout, Castle Saaleck near Kosen, where Kern was killed in a battle with the police while one of his accomplices, Hermann Fischer, committed suicide. The Nazis later erected a memorial at the site. From the testimony of the captured driver of the murder vehicle, the twenty-year-old Ernst Techow, and other participants during their trial at Leipzig, there emerged a picture of the nationalistic atmosphere of murder which has been described so cynically by Ernst von Salomon, one of the conspirators, in his postwar book *Der Fragebogen (The Questionnaire;* 1950).

The political motives behind these deeds were an expression of the demagogic indoctrination of the younger generation in particular, which equated Bolshevism, democracy, and Jewish world domination, and consequently believed that loyalty to the Weimar Republic was treason and opposition to it true patriotism. The murder of Rathenau on the heels of Erzberger's assassination created a great stir. There were protest demonstrations against the antirepublican Right and the defamatory propaganda campaigns responsible for the atmosphere in which these assassinations could take place. The Reichstag was the scene of violent attacks on the German National Party, and mass demonstrations were held in the streets; a twenty-four-hour general strike was followed by a demand for sterner measures against the enemies of the Republic. A formal law for the protection of the Republic was adopted on July 21, 1922, making the extolling or condoning of acts of violence and antirepublican activities a punishable offense, prohibiting meetings promoting such practices, and setting up a special State Court for the Protection of the Republic.

Three days after Rathenau's murder (June 25, 1922), there was a heated Reichstag debate in the course of which Chancellor Joseph Wirth ended his indictment with the words: "The enemy stands on the Right." The Law for the Protection of the Republic provided a tool against the crudest antirepublican excesses, though events the following year, and even more so post-1929 developments, proved how ineffective even such laws were in getting at the root of the evil when the judiciary, civil service, and Army, the country's most important executive agencies, did not pledge their loyalty to the Republic.[23]

In addition, Bavaria, a hotbed of right-wing extremism, again went its own way and refused to recognize the Law for the Protection of the Republic, which had been passed over the objections of the German National and Bavarian People's Parties. Bavaria, in violation of the Weimar Constitution, issued an edict limiting the jurisdiction of the Protective Law and asserting the authority of the Bavarian Special Courts, which ever since the demise of the Bavarian republic had been convened almost exclusively against the Left, not against Bavaria's flourishing radical Right. The trial in October, 1922, of Felix Fechenbach constituted a frightening example of this policy. Fechenbach, the secretary of Kurt Eisner, the assassinated Minister President of the Bavarian revolutionary government, was tried allegedly for high treason, but in fact for a violation of a press law. His sentence to eleven years in prison—a naked act of political revenge completely devoid of justice—testifies to the partiality of these Special Courts. Shortly thereafter, the participants in the Hitler Putsch either were freed or given ridiculously lenient sentences and soon pardoned. But it took four years of effort to have Fechenbach's sentence reviewed by a higher federal court; in 1933, a Nazi murder squad passed the final sentence in this case.

The confusion of the early days of the Weimar Republic reached a climax in 1923, when outside military and economic intervention coincided with serious and dangerous internal conflicts. It began with the French occupation of the Ruhr, followed by a Communist uprising in central Germany and attempted nationalist coups in northern Germany and Munich. Added to this there was the run away inflation, which was rapidly reaching catastrophic proportions. The shaky edifice of the Weimar Republic, erected in three years of laborious work, seemed near collapse. The restoration of the monarchy was being openly discussed, and there also loomed the possibility of either a military or Communist dictatorship. It is to the credit of the Reichswehr, and

[23] Basic to this, Gotthard Jasper, *Der Schutz der Republik* (Tübingen, 1963).

above all its commander in chief, Seeckt, that this did not come to pass. Seeckt's attitude was motivated not by concern for the fate of the Republic but rather by a preoccupation with far broader goals and with the special position of the Reichswehr. He needed a period of internal and foreign tranquility in which to strengthen the Reichswehr. But the result was that the Republic was saved, at least for the time being. This has to be said, regardless of any other charges that can be leveled against Seeckt.

Let us briefly reconstruct the general situation. For the first time since the end of 1922, the country, under the Government of Chancellor Wilhelm Cuno, the president of the Hamburg-America Line, had a so-called Cabinet of specialists made up of civil servants and various experts without overt (or formal) party ties. Like every other subsequent "non-party" Cabinet of this type, it leaned fairly strongly toward the Right and was close to the interests of high finance. The pending reparations negotiations loomed as a major issue. Cuno, pointing to the growing economic plight of Germany, asked for a four-year moratorium on reparations payments. Britain sought to mediate, but Poincaré, representing France, insisted that Germany meet its obligations and threatened military sanctions. At the Paris conference of January, 1923, Britain and France clashed; Britain withdrew its delegation, and Poincaré maintained that this action gave France a free hand to set the reparations conditions. A few days later, on January 11, French and Belgian troops marched into the Ruhr. The Cuno Government, supported by Ebert, promptly protested this violation of the Versailles Treaty, and announced—since Germany did not possess military means of defense—the passive resistance on the part of all political and economic offices of the Ruhr area. At the same time, the Government said that Germany would not make any reparations payments so long as the occupation continued. In turn, the Reparations Commission said that this was a breach of agreement, and the French and Belgian governments declared that their troops would stay in the Ruhr until Germany met its obligations. It became obvious in March, 1923, that a complete impasse had been reached.

German and French public opinion faced each other in almost warlike hostility. In France, Poincaré's interventionist policy was defended as strongly as was the call for passive resistance in Germany. The situation was reminiscent of the unanimous indignation over the Versailles Treaty in the summer of 1919. A very, very cold war began; passive resistance turned into open sabotage; in retaliation the French arrested union leaders and industrialists alike and shot saboteurs, as for example the Free Corps officer Albert Schlageter, who became the hero of both Nationalists and Communists. This conflict offered both the illegal, clandestine Free Corps and the radical Left the opportunity for renewed activity, and this soon turned against the Republic. The country was given no respite, neither by internal forces nor by the Allies. The battle for the Ruhr turned into a new focal point of antidemocratic nationalism, not without the help of Germany's former enemies.

This trend was given a boost when France and Belgium, ignorant of the existing psychological mood and against the vote of Britain, revived the old idea of separating the Rhineland from the rest of Germany. Autonomous Rhenish and Palatine republics were proclaimed in Aachen and Speyer and recognized by Paris and Brussels. These separatist movements were neither spontaneous nor widespread, and the action promptly rebounded, for it only served to strengthen the will for resistance and nationalism. These shortsighted tactics did not survive the occupation; moreover, they contributed to the spread of anti-republicanism. Also, the occupation itself proved highly uneconomical; it was unprofitable for the French economy and at the same time brought the passively resisting German economy to the brink of bankruptcy. The German currency fell disastrously, and the psychological effects of the inflation on a growing political radicalization are well known. The inflation brought impoverishment to large segments of the population, and then as well as six years later, during the world-wide economic depression, Nationalist and National Socialist agitators reaped the profits.

By August, 1923, it had become clear that passive resistance was too costly and could not continue. The Cuno Cabinet was replaced by a coalition government headed by Gustav Stresemann, the leader of the DVP. Stresemann, a wartime National Liberal deputy who had supported annexational demands and until almost the very end had opted for holding out, had since turned into a "common-sense republican" (*Vernunftrepublikaner*); his assumption of the Chancellorship cast him in the role of Republican statesman, and his conduct of foreign affairs earned him a leading position among European statesmen. This remarkable transformation was apparent from the very outset of his tenure. With realistic insight, he broke with the rigid, national-prestige policy of Cuno by terminating the passive resistance in the Ruhr so as to re-establish normal relations with the Western powers. It was a psychological sacrifice, but it lifted the catastrophic burden of what had become a futile test of strength. There began that careful and tenaciously pursued policy of *rapprochement* which the enemies of the Republic denounced as "fulfillment policy." This policy was dictated by the conviction that what Germany needed above all was a period of tranquility in order to win its campaign for a revision of the Versailles Treaty and improve its general situation. This meant that Stresemann—and also Seeckt, for reasons of his own—steered clear of all reactionary and revolutionary adventurers and made the safeguarding of the Republic the primary goal, even though he may never have altogether relinquished his basic belief in the monarchy. He combined his desire to strengthen and rehabilitate the Republic with efforts for a reconciliation with France and close German cooperation with the West. On this basis, he was able to establish a minimal working relationship with Seeckt, even though the latter saw this German dependence on the West as a violation of his Russian military plans, and though Stresemann in turn never ceased to be displeased with the Reichswehr for its high-handed, illegal military ventures and their adverse effects on his foreign policy.

Although the termination of the passive resistance was supported by the parties that formed Stresemann's Grand Coalition (SPD, Center, DDP, DVP), the extremist opposition—the Nationalists on the Right and the Communists on the Left—was strong. Being implacable enemies of the Republic, both parties in their own way sought to exploit the chaotic situation for their own purposes. Consequently they opposed the cessation of the battle of the Ruhr as a "betrayal" of, respectively, the national honor and the working class. At this juncture, beset by such extreme tension, Stresemann had to make certain of the Reichswehr. Initially he was by no means certain of its loyalty. Barred from intervention in the demilitarized zone, the Reichswehr had stood by and watched the Ruhr battle at parade rest. Seeckt was determined to intervene only if absolutely necessary. Furthermore, he did not approve of the fantastic plans for the creation of a "Ruhr Free Corps" put in circulation by men like Fritz Thyssen, for he had come to disapprove of the idea of militias. Also, he feared that such a course might lead to war not only with France but with Poland and Czechoslovakia as well, and he was not at all ready for such an eventuality. To be sure, during the early months of 1923, Seeckt had been brought into contact with Ludendorff as well as with Hitler. Mobilization preparations had been made and volunteers trained. Seeckt nursed the hope that the rift between England and France would deepen and the German military situation would ease. But now he saw the "Reich"—and this, not the Republic, was his Germany—threatened by internal disorder. His reason for supporting the Government was to prevent a civil war, and, above all, to protect the "unpolitical, nonpartisan" role—that is, the independence—of the Reichswehr. Even prior to this, he had confidently informed the Cabinet that he alone was in a position to stage a putsch, and that he would not do so. Now, in September, 1923, he refused to fulfill the wishes and demands of the extreme Right, which hoped to win him over for their old and new plans. Again and again he was offered dictatorial powers. But however strong the appeal of such an offer, he was sufficiently cautious not to join a Kapp Putsch–type gamble. This earned him the enmity of the Pan-Germans, and there were even plans afoot to assassinate him.

After September, however, almost simultaneously with the cessation of the Ruhr resistance, alarming news began to come out of Munich, the seat of the counterrevolutionary movement. Once again, the special position of Bavaria, which displayed aggressive independence and overtly opposed the Central Government in Berlin, made itself felt. Added to anti-Prussian tradition and monarchist activities were suspicions stemming from the very existence of a Social Democratic President and SPD representation in the Government. Bavaria remained in opposition to the Weimar Constitutional Government, not only as the center of an undisguised federalism, but also as the refuge of old Free Corps officers, putschists, and resentful generals like Ludendorff. After the Kapp Putsch, Bavaria's Socialist Hoffmann Government was followed by a series of right-wing Cabinets under Ritter von Kahr, Count Lerchenfeld, and Freiherr von Knilling, all of whom opposed the Republic, the Central Government, and Berlin.

The attitude of the Army in Bavaria was in line with this. Unlike the units in the rest of the country, the Bavarian Army displayed particularist tendencies, turning not only against the democratic Republic, but also against the central Army command under Seeckt. Above all, departing from the Seeckt line, it became markedly "politicized." There was Ritter von Epp, who in 1919 had entered Munich to "liberate" Bavaria from the revolutionary government, and as military commandant of Munich had turned toward the NSDAP; in 1933, he was to become the Reich Governor (*Reichsstatthalter*) of Bavaria. His General Staff officer Röhm openly stated in a memorandum dated August 13, 1922: "If everything accomplished thus far in Bavaria, Germany's last bastion, is not to be destroyed, an open break with Berlin must be made." And this officer not only was in charge of sizable arms and munitions stores and maintained important contacts with combat leagues, but also was an active National Socialist and SA leader. Then there was General Otto von Lossow, whose monarchist, right-wing sympathies were an open secret, and next to him, the likeminded police official Colonel Hans von Seisser. Furthermore, the Reichswehr kept in touch not only with numerous Free Corps and assorted right-wing groups, but also with the political plans of its former "education officer," Adolf Hitler, and the activities of his nascent party.

Hitler as well as von Epp and Röhm continued to hold military positions after working for the NSDAP and making its policy. The military leadership of Bavaria saw in the NSDAP program welcome support for their own plans insofar as the program called for opposition to Versailles and for the creation of a large national army. Even after the failure of the Kapp Putsch, cooperation between the subsequent right-wing governments, the Reichswehr, and Hitler's party continued. Pöhner, the former police president of Munich (1919–21), and one of his aides, Wilhelm Frick, proved particularly helpful to Hitler's growing party. At the same time, Hitler continued to gain greater self-confidence. He wanted to be more than a tool in the hands of monarchists and the military. He began to see himself as the leader of a future German dictatorship, just as he had replaced the leadership of his Munich party and become its absolute head. Informal cooperation with the Reichswehr, even a measure of rivalry, took the place of subservience. The SA was being built up in order to make the party independent of both the Army and the police. At first the Bavarian Reichswehr looked upon these activities benevolently (wel-

coming them as another link in the creation of a "viable defense"),
helped with the technical and tactical training of the SA, and in some
instances opened its weapons depots to them.

THE HITLER PUTSCH

The battle of the Ruhr gave Hitler his first great opportunity. Pursuing his own goals, he did not offer his assistance in the defensive
battle against foreign occupation. He did not want mere "equal standing" with other organizations, but hoped to exploit the existing confusion to consolidate his position in Bavaria, and from there to move
on to a nationwide rebellion against the Republican Central Government, carried out according to his dictates. The recurrent rumors of
substantial French financial assistance to the NSDAP in 1923 must be
understood in this context. No proof has been found, but oddly enough
Hitler himself never commented on this point, and his silence is not
necessarily to be construed as a denial. Be that as it may, Hitler's energies during these months, to which he devoted many pages in *Mein
Kampf,* were directed not against the occupation powers but rather
against the "government of November criminals" in Berlin. To be
sure, this did not find any response outside of Bavaria; contrary to
Hitler's expectations, the passive resistance movement set the political
tone in the rest of Germany. In the end, the NSDAP not only risked
political embarrassment, but found itself being proscribed in Prussia,
Saxony, Thuringia, Hamburg, Bremen, and Mecklenburg. Hitler's efforts thus remained confined to Bavaria, and there his was still only
one among many groups of the radical Right.

Within the radical Right, however, he did rise to a leading position.
After the success of his first Munich party congress in January, 1923,
he became the head of one of the two existing roof organizations of
Bavarian nationalists, the Working Group of Patriotic Combat Leagues
(Kampfbund), founded by Röhm with strong military support. Its more
radical political and anti-Semitic position set it apart from the League
of Patriotic Organizations (Vereinigte vaterländische Verbände, or
VVV) led by Kahr and a high-school teacher by the name of Hermann
Bauer. The VVV was a conglomerate of Pan-German, student, monarchist, officers' and veterans' organizations, while the more militant
Combat League fell under the increasing dominance of the National
Socialists, whose critical attitude toward the Bavarian right-wing
government was supported by a number of Free Corps brigades.[24]
The occupation of the Ruhr, the economic crisis, the example of the
Fascist power grab in Italy, and finally the victory of the Young Turks
under Kemal Pasha Ataturk seemed to improve the chances for overthrowing the government and lent impetus to the plans of the Kampfbund. A "fascist wave" was sweeping Europe, a countermovement to

---

[24] For a detailed discussion, see Ernst Deuerlein, *Der Hitler-Putsch*
(Stuttgart, 1962), pp. 58 ff., 697 ff.

the democratic, socialist, and communist trends of the early postwar years. The nationalist groups began to call for a "March on Berlin," for the overthrow of the "system" by force and its radical transformation.

This was the wave Hitler was riding, and it carried him to the top of the rival factions. Ludendorff was their symbol, Hitler their most militant drummer, the Bavarian military and influential civil servants their sympathetic assistants. In a misunderstanding resembling that of 1933, many of those who later became disillusioned believed that Hitler's activities were directed against Berlin and not against the "national" leadership in Bavaria. As a matter of fact, the Bavarian Government had watched his efforts with benevolence, its highest officials took part in his meetings, and their threats to outlaw the National Socialists went unfulfilled. The hope that radicalism could thus be kept under control played a role in this, and Hitler was repeatedly asked to refrain from staging a coup. However, this left him with the impression that determined action was needed to handle a hesitant government and civil service as well as the police and a sympathetic military, insofar as they were not already involved in his determined actions.

The dramatic events leading up to the Hitler Putsch were based on these presuppositions. Calls for a "national uprising" and a "second revolution," mass demonstrations and parades, became an integral part of life in Bavaria, whereas other German states outlawed the NSDAP, and the Supreme Court of the Reich, in a memorable opinion (March 15, 1923) that offered profound insight into the terrorist and usurpational activities of the National Socialists, upheld these prohibitions. In the spring of 1923, rumors of a putsch reached fever pitch; the expectations of the party faithful grew immeasurably, while the Bavarian Government, as well as the BVP, vacillated. This situation reached a climax in the counterdemonstrations staged by the radical Right in answer to the May Day demonstrations of the trade unions. In line with tried tactics, the pretext that vigilance was required to thwart an alleged putsch plan of the Left, thousands of marchers were brought to Munich from far and wide, turning the event into a triumph for Hitler. He delivered an aggressive, radical, rousing speech on the evening of May 1 in the overcrowded arena of the Krone Circus. In this civil-war atmosphere, the National Socialists apparently took command, and the putsch on which they would sweep their friends along became only a question of time.

Once again, matters stopped at mass demonstrations. But the exacerbation of the situation during the summer months, and finally the renewed tensions between Munich and Berlin that fall, prepared the way for the final push. Demonstrations followed demonstrations. The so-called German Days held on weekends throughout Bavaria proved particularly effective public displays of nationalist and National Socialist strength. The people flocked to the pseudo-military programs attended by local dignitaries, retired generals, and even Crown Prince

Ruprecht of Bavaria. These "lofty" spectacles were not only effective propaganda weapons, but Hitler also considered them as putsch rehearsals. The National Socialists, with their elite SA troop, their stanch radicalism, and their superior organization and leadership formed the avant garde, even though within the total spectrum of "patriotic" groups they were a minority. However, they enjoyed a distinct advantage over the divided, politically naïve, hair-splitting patriotic and adventuristic nationalist and monarchist groups.

On September 26, in the midst of this disturbed, emotional, confused atmosphere, von Knilling's Bavarian Government proclaimed a state of emergency, suspended all civil rights, and for the second time von Knilling appointed Ritter von Kahr State Commissioner (he had served in this capacity in 1920), making him de facto dictator. The Berlin Government promptly summoned its members into session under the chairmanship of Ebert. The main problem under discussion was the position of the Reichswehr. Seeckt made an effectively late appearance. There ensued a scene most characteristic and highly revelatory about the attitude of the Reichswehr toward the Republic. It has been frequently described, and although disagreement exists over some details, the facts have not been disputed.[25] In reply to a question of Ebert's about where the Reichswehr stood, Seeckt replied with the unruffled disdain of the Prussian officer for the political civilian: "The Reichswehr, Mr. President, stands behind me." This accorded with his concept of the Army and its independent, aloof attitude toward the Republic. The Republic had turned to the Reichswehr for assistance as a last resort, and with Seeckt's reply, the Government had to accept the fact that the Army was an independent state within the state. There could be no question that since Ebert was its constitutional commander in chief, the Army was subject to civilian control, that it was the military instrument of the Republic. Yet it opted for this Republic not because of any political order but by decision of its highest officer. That this could happen was not so much due to any dictatorial pretensions of Seeckt; it simply expressed the facts of the matter. Ebert as well as Stresemann accepted it in the awareness that the acute situation left them little choice.

As a result, on that very same day—September 26—a state of emergency was proclaimed in Germany by Presidential decree, in accord with Article 48 of the Weimar Constitution, that very same Article which, in an inversion of its intent, was to play such a fatal role in the death of the Republic. Simultaneously, all executive functions and powers were put into the hands of Defense Minister Otto Gessler. This, too, was simply a constitutional disguise of the fact that the highest powers in Germany now temporarily rested in the hands of Seeckt, as chief of the Reichswehr. This situation prevailed for almost half a year,

[25] Friedrich von Rabenau, *Seeckt: Aus seinem Leben 1918–1936* (Leipzig, 1940), p. 342. See also F. L. Carsten, *The Reichswehr and Politics: 1918 to 1933* (Oxford, 1966), pp. 166 ff.; and the detailed though somewhat apologetic Hans Meier-Welcker, *Seeckt* (Frankfurt/Main, 1967).

until February, 1924. Throughout this period, and until the state of emergency was lifted, the Reichswehr high command and its local commanders held practically all executive power. They also determined the economic measures necessitated by the fight against inflation and by the introduction of the new currency in November, 1923.

For the time being, the numerous groups of the radical Right in both Bavaria and Prussia continued to prepare their putsch; their planning, however, was very poor. The various groups and putsch centers were badly coordinated. Having failed to win over Seeckt's Reichswehr, they relied on the illegal Black Reichswehr, which combined Free Corps and student organizations. Once Seeckt had turned them down, however, all such undertakings were doomed. The first feelers were extended in northern Germany. Again, as in the case of the Kapp Putsch, Berlin was to be the site of a coup, this time involving the Black Reichswehr under Major Ernst Buchrucker. Either the planners were not quite certain of what Seeckt's final position would be, or they hoped to win over at least a portion of the Reichswehr as matters developed. Plans called for the coup to be staged on the night of September 29–30. At the same time, Bavarian right-wing organizations staged their "German Day" in Bayreuth, culminating with an emotional visit by Hitler to Cosima Wagner at her villa, Wahnfried. On September 27, a day after the state of emergency was proclaimed, Buchrucker learned through his Reichswehr contact (Colonel Fedor von Bock) that Seeckt was most displeased by the mobilization, let alone any action, of the Black Reichswehr. Thereupon, Buchrucker, on the night of September 29–30, launched a desperate scheme; with 500 men from his headquarters at Küstrin, he occupied some forts, and hoisted the black, white, and red flag, apparently in the hope of getting things started. Seeckt reacted promptly, laying siege to Buchrucker's strongholds and forcing his immediate capitulation. Buchrucker was tried and sentenced to ten years' imprisonment; his "work commandos"—i.e., the Black Reichswehr—were dissolved. After the general amnesty of 1927, he wrote his memoirs, *Im Schatten Seeckts* (*In the Shadow of Seeckt;* 1928), which offer a graphic account of that period.

By acting as he did, Seeckt seemed to justify the confidence placed in him by the political leadership, and at the same time he rid himself of a disturbing, most annoying problem—the Black Reichswehr. But on the heels of this crisis there was trouble with the Left in Saxony. Erich Zeigner, Saxony's Social Democratic Minister President, had won Communist support in the legislature by permitting the organization of a Red militia. When the nationwide state of emergency was proclaimed, the Saxonian Communists forced a reorganization of their Cabinet and took two of the posts, thereby putting pressure on the Government. On October 5, they issued a number of demands on the Reich Government, above all the recognition of the Red militia, and the democratization—that is, the reorganization—of the Reichswehr. Disorder spread throughout Saxony.

It goes without saying that Seeckt reacted to these demands, so diametrically opposed to his own ideas, much more sharply than to the
actions of the radical Right. The "nonpartisanship" of the Reichswehr
command always tended toward the Right rather than the Left. Of
course, the demonstrations of the Saxonian Communists were quite
openly directed against the Reich Government, reviled as reactionary,
and rumors about a Communist dictatorship were set in motion. The
Reich Government answered with a sharply worded ultimatum calling
for the restoration of order, the dissolution of the Red militia, and the
ouster of Saxony's Communist Cabinet ministers. When these demands
were not met, the local military commander, General Alfred Müller, at
the end of October, 1923, ordered the dissolution of the militia and
arrested not only the two Communist ministers but the Social Democratic Cabinet members as well. Rudolf Heinze, a DVP leader who had
sat in on the negotiations between the right-wing parties and Lüttwitz
before the Kapp Putsch, was appointed Reich Commissar in place of
Zeigner. At the same time, the Reichswehr took similar steps against
Communist takeover threats in Hamburg and Thuringia. The Army
acted with unmistakable firmness and effectiveness, and certainly with
far more severity than against the putschists of the radical Right. The
Social Democratic members of the Reich Government resigned in protest; Stresemann formed another Government without SPD participation.

The most difficult problem besetting the country, the antirepublican putsch movement in Bavaria, still had not been solved, another
demonstration of the disparity in the Government's, particularly the
Reichswehr's, treatment of the actions of the Left and of similar and
more dangerous actions of the Right. The Bavarian situation had
grown even more involved with the emergence of various centers of
political activity. There was Kahr, for one, whose authoritarian regime
protested against the state of emergency declared by the Central Government, and in this was supported by patriotic organizations. At the
same time, there was the more radical Kampfbund, over which Hitler
had gained political control on September 25, even though as far as
the outside world was concerned, Ludendorff, since the Kapp Putsch
a resident of Bavaria, was still the foremost figure.

The differences among right-wing groups obviously continued, and
the old, never-resolved conflict between the implacably antirepublican
military and the Seeckt faction broke out anew. Once again the Reichswehr was put to a severe psychological test. This was a different problem from its determined battle against the Left, in which the
deep-seated hatred of the revolutionary era could be drawn upon. Here
the opponents were old soldiers, ideologically friendly nationalists, Free
Corps officers, and a celebrated general and war hero like Ludendorff.
To complicate matters even more, General Otto von Lossow, the military commander of Bavaria, was working closely with Kahr. Like
Kahr, he looked on Hitler's rival efforts with a mixture of distrust and
disdain, yet at the same time the local Reichswehr had close contacts

with the NSDAP through some of its officers, particularly Major Röhm, and Hitler was gaining the sympathy of a growing number of younger officers and cadets of Munich's infantry training school. Thus, Lossow's position cast grave doubt, at least in Bavaria, on Seeckt's assurance that the Reichswehr stood behind him. The Reichswehr survived this episode without a permanent rift only because of the growing suspicion with which Kahr and Hitler, the leaders of the two putschist centers, regarded each other.

It is also of interest to note the care (compared to Saxony) with which this matter was handled in Berlin. To begin with, the retired hero of the war, Field Marshal Hindenburg, was persuaded to undermine Ludendorff's authority by sending a telegram to the Kampfbund cautioning against Bavarian separatism. Hitler and Ludendorff replied to this telegram by issuing a proclamation that they would march on Berlin and overthrow the Government, while Kahr in turn, so as not to lag behind the putschists, refused to obey Ebert and proclaimed himself sole authority in Bavaria. At the same time, the *Völkische Beobachter* unleashed a violent campaign against the Central Government, particularly against Seeckt and Gessler. Kahr and Lossow refused to carry out Seeckt's order to ban the paper, and Lossow failed to follow a subsequent order for the arrest of leading nationalists. When Ebert thereupon, with the concurrence of Seeckt and Gessler, fired Lossow on October 20 and appointed General Kress von Kressenstein in his stead, Kahr, in line with his declared independence from Berlin, appointed Lossow Commandant of the Bavarian Reichswehr. Colonel von Seisser, the head of the Bavarian State Police, supported Kahr. In reply, Seeckt issued a proclamation reminding the Bavarian Reichswehr of its oath and calling for strict obedience; on November 4, in an order of the day to the entire German Army, he discussed the Government's intervention in Saxony, Thuringia, and Hamburg, but significantly kept silent about the affair of the Black Reichswehr. The text in a nutshell, with the mandatory phraseological evasiveness, spelled out Seeckt's concept of the Reichswehr and its aims—internal peace and order. At the same time, however, marginal comments in a letter from Seeckt to Kahr contain Seeckt's famous words that as far as he was concerned, the Republic was no *"noli me tangere."* [26] And on November 8, when the Prussian Social Democratic Minister of the Interior, Carl Severing, asked Ebert to make sure that a scheduled array of the Bavarian Reichswehr division would not disturb the peace in Berlin, Seeckt repeated his laconic words of the Kapp Putsch: The Reichswehr does not fire on the Reichswehr.[27] And so the Reichswehr continued to be a questionable instrument of the state to which it owed its allegiance.

In the meantime it was becoming evident that the substantial differences between the monarchic particularism of Kahr and Lossow and

[26] Otto-Ernst Schüddekopf, *Das Heer und die Republik* (Hanover, 1955), p. 187.
[27] Carl Severing, *Mein Lebensweg* (Cologne, 1950), I, 447.

the revolutionary ideas of Hitler were not being resolved. While the first two dreamed of restoring the Bavarian monarchy and of the coronation of Prince Ruprecht, and also, inspired by Ataturk's dictatorship, spoke of turning the "center of order, Bavaria" into the "Ankara of Germany," Hitler, acting more and more independently, worked toward a German dictatorship—with or without a monarch. The idea of a march on Berlin, with Mussolini's theatrical but successful March on Rome as the great example, daily took on more concrete form.

And in fact, in mid-October the plans of the Kampfbund took on firm shape. An order of the German Fighting League for the Solidification of the "Border Protection" in the North, issued on October 16 and signed by its commander Colonel (ret.) Hermann Kriebel (of the Oberland Brigade), though in the guise of "police emergency assistance" against "Red" Thuringia, opened up the chance for offensive action, and above all provided the leverage for the mobilization of forces for a civil war. The word was passed that the march on Berlin was to begin on November 15. Amid the confusion of rumors, hopes, and ambitions, Hitler was busy consolidating his independent position and strengthening his leadership. Therefore, when word reached him that Kahr and Lossow were planning a political move for November 9, the fifth anniversary of the hated revolution, possibly without him and in conjunction with Seeckt, whom they still hoped to win over, he decided to forge ahead. However, if as in the past they decided to postpone matters, then it was imperative to prod them into action.

On October 23, Göring, as the head of the SA, announced the planned putsch and dictatorship at a military conference of National Socialist organizations and asked for a list of "personalities who will have to be eliminated [and] at least one will have to be shot immediately after the issuance of the proclamation [announcing the takeover] as an example." [28] The next day Lossow, at a meeting held at the Munich Defense Ministry with police and heads of patriotic organizations, came out in support of a march on Berlin and the "erection of the national dictatorship." However, the "possible march," he said, necessitated the "incorporation of all patriotic organizations into the Reichswehr or state police." "All of us have but one goal—to free Germany from Marxism, under the black, white, and red flag." Reactions to this appeal for unity were divided. Kriebel and the majority favored it, but the National Socialists did not participate in this conference. Hitler, for his part, was preparing a surprise coup to win the holders of power for his plans or force them, *nolens volens,* to go along with him once he got matters under way.

On November 6, amid the chaos of inflation and the Berlin-Munich conflict, the Kahr-Lossow-Seisser "triumvirate" and representatives of patriotic organizations held a meeting at which Kahr demanded their loyalty in his fight against Berlin, and Lossow, though warning against precipitate actions like the Kapp and Küstrin coups, promised

[28] Deuerlein, *op. cit.,* pp. 505 f.

to support the setting up of a central right-wing dictatorship if this held the promise of success. Both Kahr and Lossow opposed isolated action and separatism. The fact that Hitler had not been invited to this gathering may have been the catalyst prompting his decision to strike out. And other members of the Kampfbund nursing doubts about the will and ability of the Kahr group to carry out its plans also were determined to act. On November 7, Kriebel issued a declaration of war on the triumvirate. In vain Ludendorff, as late as the afternoon of November 8, tried to persuade the triumvirate to bring Hitler into their fold. Kahr refused. They were aware of Hitler's putsch plans but did not take them seriously. They knew him as an able propagandist but did not believe him capable of this sweeping and independent action against the holders of power.

The great opportunity came on November 8, with a "patriotic demonstration" in support of Kahr held in the crowded main room of the Bürgerbräu beer hall, attended by Cabinet members and other high officials, military leaders, and well-known economists, among them Professor of History Karl Alexander von Müller. In commemoration of the outbreak of the revolution five years earlier, Kahr read an address against "Marxism." Shortly before 9:00 P.M., Hitler, accompanied by an armed group of men led by SA chief Göring, broke into this gathering of Nationalist dignitaries. In a dramatic gesture he fired a shot into the ceiling to attract the attention of the assemblage—the opening shot of his attempted coup, which was to end ignominiously by noon of the following day.

Accounts of what followed are contradictory; propaganda and apologies serve to confuse the picture, and the subsequent Hitler trial also left many questions unanswered: it avoided exposing embarrassing ties and treated the participants gently. The main points, however, are clear. Hitler, waving his pistol, announced from the platform that the "national revolution" had begun, that the hall was occupied by heavily armed men, that the Bavarian Government had been overthrown, and that a provisional central government was being formed. He then asked Kahr, Lossow, and Seisser to accompany him to an adjoining room, where he informed them that Police President Pöhner had been appointed Minister President of Bavaria and invested with dictatorial powers, that Kahr had been made Regent of Bavaria, while he himself would head a new Reich government, while Ludendorff was to command the new "National Army" built around the Kampfbund (which would march on Berlin). Lossow would become Reich Defense Minister, and Seisser the new Reich Police Minister.

Meanwhile, Göring took charge of the meeting. He, too, began his speech with a pistol shot to the ceiling. Hitler hurried back into the hall and informed the initially critical and later jubilant assemblage of his new governmental appointments, while, in the next room, the Oberland leader (and veterinarian) Friedrich Weber sought to persuade the well-guarded triumvirate to acquiesce. Finally, Ludendorff appeared, amid shouts of *Heil!*, and announced his willingness to participate; he was followed by Pöhner. In view of this, the triumvirate capitulated and returned to the hall, now the scene of great fraternization. There were more speeches and the playing of the national anthem. After that, however, some of those present were put under arrest. Minister President von Knilling and a number of Bavarian Cabinet Ministers were led away by Rudolf Hess and his SA students. But Kahr, Lossow, and Seisser were permitted to leave the scene of the putsch on their own. Ludendorff guaranteed their word as officers. Then began that strange night in which the putschists failed to take advantage of their opportunity and instead left their rivals, whom they had caught unawares, free to gather their forces.

In the event, Hitler proved to be as poor a putschist as the organizers of the Kapp and Küstrin coups. Although a series of arbitrary acts against political opponents and anti-Semitic outbursts gave an inkling of what a successful National Socialist takeover would hold in store, the night passed and Hitler and the Kampfbund, assisted by the infantry training school under the ex-lieutenant and Free Corps man Rossbach, failed to consolidate the power they had proclaimed as theirs. They had relied on the proclamation that, in addition to Ludendorff, they had the triumvirate on their side, and thus they won the support of sympathizers in the state civil service and Army. But their calculation that Kahr and Lossow, themselves so deeply committed, could be swept along by a *fait accompli* proved to be wrong, even though some Kampfbund units were given arms by Munich Army depots and even though the energetic Major Röhm and some Free Corps men did occupy the local Army headquarters at 11:00 P.M. Ludendorff, Hitler, Kriebel, and other organizers of the putsch were gathered at the Army headquarters.

But when Pöhner and Frick, who apparently had prevented the state police from intervening at the Bürgerbräu, arrived at police headquarters, they were put under arrest by Lossow's men. And no real effort was made to occupy vital government and telegraph offices or railroad stations. The triumvirate was able to get to the barracks of a loyal regiment and mobilize military and police units. The Bavarian Government itself remained in hiding; a few Cabinet ministers went to Regensburg. During the night, a number of Kampfbund units were disarmed; the general confusion in the ranks of the Right now began to work against Hitler. Shortly before 3:00 A.M. the next morning, word went out to all radio stations in Germany that the triumvirate had been deceived and that it opposed the Hitler putsch. This announcement came rather late, and it is an open question whether Kahr and Lossow did not, despite their later explanations, vacillate for a while. Were they perhaps opposed only to Hitler's claim to leadership but not to the putsch itself? But at any rate, a major decision had been reached.

The morning of November 9 found Munich in a state of extreme agitation. Kahr had not been able to prevent the appearance of the morning papers carrying news about the putsch. The city was covered with posters proclaiming the start of the revolution. A proclamation by Kahr also had been posted and handed to the press. But the National Socialists had succeeded in arousing public opinion against Kahr, even though the putschists had met with little success in the rest of Bavaria and even though the man on the street and most of the participants were not at all clear about the alignments. While Army units were assembling shortly before noon to recapture the Defense Ministry, the putschists were conducting their now famous march through Munich, which ended at the Feldherrnhalle at about 1:00 P.M. At 2:00 P.M., Röhm surrendered at the Defense Ministry.

A long column of armed National Socialists and Kampfbund members (possibly around two thousand) headed by Hitler, Ludendorff, Göring, Kriebel, and Weber had managed to overpower the police guard at the Isar Bridge and then had marched through the inner city to the government offices. Sensation-hungry onlookers had gathered at the narrow passageway to the Feldherrnhalle; the state police tried to seal off the approaches, and disorders broke out. Who fired the first shot is still not clear. There were some casualties in the brief exchange of shots that followed, among them Scheubner-Richter, who had been marching next to Hitler. When the shooting began, the crowds scattered wildly; the whole affair took less than one minute. Ludendorff continued to march until he was arrested at the Odeonsplatz. Hitler, who apparently dislocated his shoulder when he threw himself on the ground, managed to escape ignobly in an SA ambulance amid the confusion, later metamorphosed into a heroic battle. Contrary to his dramatic promise in the Bürgerbräu cellar, November 9 did not find him either "in power or dead"; death was a fate he left to others. He took refuge in nearby Uffing, in a villa belonging to one of his early patrons, the art critic Ernst Hanfstaengl. And there, on the afternoon of November 11, he was arrested, clad in his pyjamas. Before being taken away, he dramatically had his Iron Cross pinned to his chest. At Landsberg prison, Count Arco, Eisner's assassin, was asked to vacate his room for Hitler, who at this juncture still "believed that he would be shot." [29]

This was the Bavarian triumvirate's revenge for having been taken by surprise. To be sure, Kahr and his friends did not stay in office very long after this, despite all their explanations and efforts to cover up what had happened. They had played a questionable double game, and the ill feelings aroused on both sides—republican as well as nationalist —were too strong. In mid-February, 1924, after a protracted tug of war and the stabilization of relations between Munich and Berlin, they had to go. Seeckt had been spared direct intervention; the unity of the Army had been preserved despite the Bavarian debacle, and the dilemma of its attitude toward the Republic temporarily solved, without Seeckt's having had to take too exposed a position against the nationalists and the military "comrades" in their camp. The fact that

[29] Police report quoted in *ibid.*, pp. 357 f.

no further coup attempts were made proved of help. The National Socialists and their allies remained surprisingly quiet.

The reverberations in Munich and Bavaria were, of course, felt for weeks. Munich University in particular became the scene of turbulent gatherings, such as a student meeting of November 12 in the presence of two rectors and some eminent professors, one of them Ferdinand Sauerbruch, the chief surgeon in whose clinic the wounded demonstrators of November 9 had been treated. The faculty, according to a police report, tried, "while recognizing the valid national goals of Hitler and his followers, and in part also condemning the government," to calm the radical mood, but it was unable to prevent a stormy demonstration in support of Hitler, culminating in an appeal by Captain Ehrhardt, for whom an arrest warrant was out in the rest of Germany.[30] The situation remained tense; similar meetings added to the turbulence. The "betrayal of the ninth of November" became a catchphrase of the radical Right. It was to play a major part in the trial of Hitler and in the sentences meted out. The murder of Kahr on June 30, 1934, was Hitler's belated but bloody revenge.

The megalomaniacal putsch attempt and its panic-stricken, unheroic failure are reminiscent of Hitler's daydreams of his Linz and Vienna years. But in two respects this latest venture had a decisive bearing on the future of National Socialism: It influenced the further course of the NSDAP, which now charted a new political strategy, and it altered the relationship between the Army and the NSDAP. Hitler had to recognize that his grandiose flop was due in no small measure to his failure to exploit the disgruntlement of the military leadership, and that he would not be able to win them over by precipitate action, despite all their sympathies for the "national drummer." The ninth of November had taught him the great lesson that the powers that be could not be overthrown, only undermined. The result was the adoption of that "policy of legality" which marked the second phase of the "fighting years," the tactic of winning power through the unremitting exploitation of the legal and pseudo-legal opportunities offered by a tolerant democratic framework, rather than through an overt *coup d'état*.

Of course, the "Leader" had also suffered a loss of personal prestige in this ignoble outcome. Ludendorff was the only one who refused to let the shots of the Bavarian police stop his march to the Feldherrnhalle. But as the irony of history would have it, and in a twist typical of that time, Hitler's chances to employ his oratorical gifts to win back the prestige he had dissipated in his abortive enterprise were now greater than ever. The leader of a party that stressed action rather than words paved his road to power primarily through his insistent use of words. The trial of the putschists gave Hitler the chance to turn the fiasco of the armed uprising into a triumphant personal defense

[30] Deuerlein, *op. cit.*, pp. 357 f.

and, at the same time, a political indictment of the Republic. The public forum he won was a vast one. Here Hitler was truly in his element, while Ludendorff remained far in the background.

The significance of the Hitler trial of February–March, 1924, cannot therefore be stressed too strongly. Germany's domestic situation was beginning to show signs of improvement. The inflation was halted, the Central Government gained a firmer foothold, and the search for a more rational solution to the reparations issue was showing progress in the deliberations of the Dawes Commission. There Stresemann, in his first meeting with the Western powers, set forth the idea of a security agreement, which ultimately took shape as the Locarno Treaty (1925). In the course of the domestic stabilization, Kahr's badly compromised authoritarian regime in Bavaria was replaced by a moderate government under Heinrich Held, the leader of the BVP; Kress, a supporter of Seeckt, replaced Lossow as military commander, and the rebellious infantry training school of Munich was transferred to Thuringia and sternly disciplined by Seeckt. This was the setting in which the treason trial against Hitler, Ludendorff, Pöhner, Röhm, Frick, and five others began on February 26, 1924, in the People's Court of Munich. Göring and other participants in the putsch had managed to get out of Germany with the help of friendly public officials. The matter seemed closed, but Hitler had learned to exploit every situation. Thus at the trial he did not proclaim his innocence, as the Kapp putschists had done; instead, he used the opportunity to great advantage, spelling out his program and the political intentions which had motivated him on November 9, 1923. His defense speeches, indictments of the "system" of the "November criminals" and "slaves of the dictate of Versailles," were widely publicized by the press throughout the country and moved him into the center of the "national revolution," hitherto a diffuse mixture of assorted ambitions and certainly no clear-cut master plan. At the same time, he sought to reforge his ties to the military leadership by exonerating the Reichswehr and assigning blame partly to Lossow and Kahr personally and partly to the "system" of the democratic Republic collectively.

In this Hitler was partially successful. To begin with, the court itself was by no means unresponsive to his arguments. And no wonder. In it sat men who only a little while back had sympathized with him, or at least with Kahr's plans. Thus the State Prosecutor, Stenglein, went so far as to preface his plea on March 21, 1924, with a paean to the nobility of Hitler's purpose:

Hitler came of a simple background; in the big war as a brave soldier he showed a German spirit, and afterward, beginning from scratch and working hard, he created a great party, the "National Socialist German Workers' Party," which is pledged to fighting international Marxism and Jewry, to settling accounts with the November criminals, and to disseminating the national idea among all layers of the population, in particular the workers. I am not called to pass judgment on his party program, but his honest endeavor to reawaken the belief in the German cause among an oppressed and disarmed people is most certainly to his credit. Here, helped by his unique oratorical gift, he has made a significant contribution. Even though the aggressive mood in the ranks of his followers led him into a one-sided position, it would nonetheless be unfair to call him a demagogue; against this charge he is protected by the sincerity of his beliefs and the unselfish dedication to his chosen task. His private life has always been clean, which deserves special approbation in view of the temptations which naturally came to him as a celebrated party leader. . . . Hitler is a highly gifted man who, coming out of a simple background, has, through serious and hard work, won for himself a respected place in public life. He dedicated himself to the ideas which inspired him to the point of self-sacrifice, and as a soldier he fulfilled his duty in the highest measure. He cannot be blamed for exploiting the position which he created for himself to his own purposes. [31]

But more was to come: By skillfully emphasizing Kahr's, Lossow's, and Seisser's coresponsibility, Hitler caused further embarrassment for the court. The involvement of high public officials and political leaders in the planning of the coup made for some courtroom taboos and softened the stand of both prosecutors and judges. Hitler put the major blame for the failure of the "national revolution" and at the same time for the danger of a divided Reichswehr on Lossow. His arguments revolved around the assurance that the actions of the NSDAP were in the best interests of the nation, particularly of the Reichswehr. Thus Hitler, having learned by experience that he could come to power only with the support of the Army, not by acting against it, began to woo the Army. He followed this policy consistently through January 30, 1933, and until June 30, 1934, the date of the full consolidation of his dictatorship.

As for the rest, Hitler knew how to transform his defense into a public demonstration in support of his act, to stray from the theme of the trial, and with national passion and prophecies of victory, to arouse the partisan audience to applause. The court, obviously impressed by the amount of public notice Hitler was attracting, tolerated this. Consequently Hitler was not given a severe sentence nor was he, still an Austrian subject, expelled from Germany. The Bavarian Minister of the Interior, Franz Schweyer, had been trying to have Hitler expelled since 1922, but he met with resistance from the Minister of Justice, Franz Gürtner, a German National who was to play a role in Hitler's premature amnesty and who, in 1933, was to become Hitler's own Minister of Justice. The sentencing by the court, in April, 1924, turned into a social event. Again, as often before in the course of the trial, the accused men were bedecked with flowers and nationalist symbols, while officers in full dress uniform demonstrated their sympathy,

[31] Bennecke, *op. cit.*, pp. 103 f.

if not with Hitler at least with Ludendorff. These were the sentences meted out: Röhm and Frick were acquitted, as was Ludendorff, and Hitler received the lowest possible sentence for high treason: five years' imprisonment, with the expressed probability of an early pardon.

An era of unrest had come to an end, but at the same time the seeds had been sown for future upheavals. Presently the state of emergency was lifted without Seeckt's having lived up to the dictatorial expectations of the Right, despite his many differences with Ebert and Stresemann. Seeckt was unwilling to do more than wait for the dictator to whom he might possibly have handed over his power. In letters written in November, 1923, the position which guided the General's conduct is made clear: vacillation between the wish for a dictatorship and the restraint of the soldier awaiting the appearance of the successful dictator. It was a position that would characterize the future attitude of the Reichswehr toward the Republic and its enemies.

III

The New Party in the "Era of Struggle"

For Bavaria, November 9, 1923, marked the end of an epoch. The retirement of the triumvirate meant that the postwar period, an era in which combat leagues and Army, reactionaries and radicals, had kept the country in a constant state of turmoil, was over. Attempts emanating from Bavaria to revolutionize the country "nationally" were as abortive as the contrary efforts of radical Left groups in central Germany. With the advent of the Hitler party, the Kampfbund dissolved, the other patriotic organizations diminished in importance, and the stabilization that marked the middle years of the Weimar Republic proceeded apace throughout the country, Bavaria included. The circumstances of the earlier crisis-ridden years, when the Reichswehr together with combat organizations and the radical Right determined Bavarian politics and, most important of all, made possible the rise of Hitler, did not recur. The road toward normalization was, of course, long. The reverberations of the putsch were felt throughout 1924, even though the center of radical Right activities was beginning to shift toward northern Bavaria (Franconia) and North Germany.

The Right managed to achieve one electoral victory in which the turmoil of the preceding years still played a role. Although the National Socialists, in the expectation of the imminent overthrow of the Government, had disdained participation in parliamentary life, they did come before the German electorate in 1924 under the label National Socialist Freedom Party (Nationalsozialistische Freiheitspartei); in Bavaria they went under the name of the *Völkisch* Bloc. The NSDAP itself had been outlawed in all of Germany after the Hitler putsch, as had its sister organization in North Germany, the German *Völkisch* Freedom Party (Deutschvölkische Freiheitspartei). But the result of

122

the Bavarian parliamentary elections of April 6, 1924—only five days after the end of the Hitler trial—gave an idea of the degree of radicalization, particularly in Munich, where the *Völkisch* Bloc received by far the biggest vote. In the rest of Bavaria it also showed remarkable strength, winning 17 per cent of all votes. The nationwide parliamentary elections of May 4 underscored this situation; the disorders of 1923 and the aftereffects of the inflation were belatedly reflected in the strength both of the radical Right and of the Communist groups. This presaged the "new course" which was to guide the reorganization of the NSDAP and its use of pseudo-democratic tactics. From an over-all perspective, the elections of May, 1924, were yet another step in the retreat of the democratic parties. On the whole, they must be seen as a triumph of the German National party, which, through an alliance with a handful of agrarian deputies, temporarily even became the strongest parliamentary delegation; on the other side of the aisle, the Communists profited from the losses of the SPD (DNVP, 106 seats; SPD, 100). The SPD's vacillation between participation in the Government and opposition was as responsible for its stunning defeat as the defection of many USPD adherents to the Communists. In their second venture into parliamentary politics, the Communists increased their delegation from seventeen to sixty-two members, thus nearly rivaling the strength of the Center Party (sixty-five seats). The middle-of-the-road liberal parties continued to decline; not only the Democrats, but also the DVP, which had made such a successful showing in the 1920 elections, lost seats. The trend of 1919 persisted: the electorate continued to desert the pillars of the Republic for the outer flanks, and the formation of a parliamentary majority remained problematical.

The trend manifested itself not only in the gains of the Communists, but also in the success of the radical Right, the *völkisch,* anti-Semitic, and National Socialist groups making their first foray into electoral politics. Despite the failure of their political undertakings, they won more Reichstag seats in their maiden appearance than the Democrats (thirty-two to the Democrats' twenty-eight), and in some areas more than 20 per cent of the votes cast. Leading off was Mecklenburg, with a healthy 20.8 per cent; next came Franconia, with 20.7 per cent; followed by Upper Bavaria and Swabia, with 17 per cent each; Lower Bavaria, 10.2 per cent; Thuringia, 9.9 per cent; and Merseburg, eastern Hanover, and East Prussia, all of which responded to the radical Right appeal. However, the success proved to be temporary. The next few years saw a shift in strength from Bavaria to those parts of northern Germany where Hitler, toward the end of the Republic, won his biggest and most critical electoral victories—Schleswig-Holstein, parts of Lower Saxony, Brandenburg, Lower Silesia, Saxony, and East Prussia.

The year 1924 ushered in a period of economic recovery and stabilization, and this was reflected in subsequent elections. Because the Reichstag elected in May of that year was unable to support a stable government, new elections were held in December, 1924; although the new Reichstag also found no satisfactory solution, the antirepublican trend of the previous election was halted. The left- and right-wing extremists suffered their first sizable setback after their initial rapid rise. The Communists lost one-third of their seats, the National Socialist groups more than one-half; for the next five years or so they remained an insignificant splinter group. Between April and December, 1924, their following in the Bavarian heartland declined by more than two-thirds (from 17 to 5 per cent), and, even after 1930, the National Socialist percentage in Bavaria, the place of its origin, remained below the national average.

To be sure, the clear-cut majorities of the Weimar National Assembly were never again achieved. The great losses of the radical Right and Left were not paralleled by the sort of meaningful gains of the moderate parties which would have facilitated the formation of a democratic government. The middle-of-the-road parties registered only minor gains, and the SPD only slightly larger ones. Hence, the German Nationals, although outpolled by the SPD, and only barely able to participate in coalitions, managed to strengthen their already strong position. Even the years of so-called stability were burdened by a series of embattled, internally unstable minority Cabinets.

The magnitude of the continuously precarious situation became apparent in the Presidential elections held after the sudden death of Friedrich Ebert in the spring of 1925. According to the Constitution, the new President was to be elected to a seven-year term in direct elections. This provision presupposed a politically mature electorate as well as outstanding men of strong republican convictions, neither of which was too much in evidence in the young state. And so the parties proceeded along their separate paths: the Social Democrats with the prominent Minister President of Prussia, Otto Braun; the Center with the Chancellor, Wilhelm Marx; and the Right with the Lord Mayor of Duisburg, Karl Jarres, who had links to the DVP. The Bavarians ran their own candidate (Heinrich Held), as did the Democrats (Willy Hellpach), the Communists (Ernst Thälmann), and the National Socialists (Ludendorff). The candidature of seven men obviously prevented any one of them from winning the required absolute majority in the first round: Jarres received 10.7 million votes; Braun, 7.8 million; Marx, a bare 4 million; and Ludendorff—a sign of the continuing decline of the radical Right—a mere 200,000.

The run-off election, in which an absolute majority was not required, saw the various parties reaching agreements on joint candidates. The republican parties put up the Center candidate, Marx, who thus seemed to be assured of victory. The Right responded with an unexpected and successful maneuver; abandoning Jarres and dashing the hopes of General von Seeckt, they brought the soldier-hero of World War I, the seventy-eight-year-old Field Marshal von Hindenburg, out from his retirement in Hanover. Hindenburg himself had said at first that he was unsuited for the presidency of a republic whose nature and principles were completely alien to his beliefs—not to mention his distaste for civilian, democratic politics, which he frankly admitted he knew nothing about. But his was a great and popular name, the only one holding out any hope of defeating a republican candidate.

It was typical of the outspokenly antirepublican, emotional character of the Hindenburg campaign that the man who succeeded in persuading Hindenburg to run was the archmonarchist Admiral von Tirpitz. Stresemann, whose party supported these efforts, was extremely perturbed that foreign reaction was predictably negative, even, according to his informants, "catastrophic." But he simply was unable to take a strong position.

Thus it came to pass that on April 26, 1925, Hindenburg was elected President of the Republic, though with only a narrow margin, not an absolute majority. Marx received 13.7 million votes against Hindenburg's 14.6 million. The narrow defeat of the republican candidate was aided by three factors. The Communist Party, by insisting on Thälmann's hopeless candidacy, split off some of the Socialist voters. Half of the Communist votes would have sealed Hindenburg's defeat. More important, however, and ultimately more decisive, was the fact that the Bavarian People's Party, the sister organization of the Center, out of narrow partisan interests came out in support of Hindenburg. The Catholic Bavarians preferred the Protestant, Prussian Field Marshal to their fellow Catholic and fellow party member Marx, primarily out of resentment over Marx's alliance with the Social Democrats. The million votes cast for the BVP in the first electoral round were significant, the more so as—and this is the third factor—the anti-Catholicism of a number of Liberal and Social Democratic voters counteracted their parties' support of Marx.

This triumph of the Right was to bear its obvious fruit only five years later. For the time being, the trend toward peace and quiet continued. The state elections in this period followed a similar pattern; at the same time (1926), a plebiscite initiated by the Left aimed at the expropriation of German princes failed to win a majority. The next Reichstag elections, in May, 1928, also gave no indication that the period of consolidation was about to end and that, within a short time, the signs of approaching catastrophe would multiply. On the contrary, the 1928 elections, in which the German Nationals lost one-third of their seats and the Social Democrats almost regained their 1919 strength, seemed to forecast the exact opposite. For the last time, a clear majority of the voters came out against the extremist parties, even reversing the shift toward the Right of 1920–24, and for the last time also, a majority coalition government, headed by the Social Democrat Hermann Müller, was formed after protracted negotiations. It remained in power for almost two years, longer than any of the other Cabinets. True, the fatal decline of the center parties continued, and the increase in the Communist vote—though the 10.6 per cent was still far below their 1924 strength of 12.6 per cent—were omens of things to come. But the biggest disappointment was suffered by the

National Socialists who, despite their noisy propaganda, received only 2.6 per cent of the votes, not even enough to form a parliamentary group (*Fraktion*). Only in Schleswig-Holstein (4 per cent), Weser-Ems (5.2 per cent), Hanover-Brunswick (4.4 per cent), Upper Bavaria–Swabia (6.2 per cent), and especially Franconia (8.1 per cent) were the National Socialists relatively successful; in the cities (Berlin, 1.4 per cent) and industrial regions (Ruhr, 1.35 per cent) they sustained enormous setbacks.

The general situation in this second period of the Weimar Republic also was to appear more favorable than ever before. Domestic crises and threats of overthrow seemed mastered; the economy was recovering and making steady progress. Though the country may not have had a large number of confirmed democrats, it seemed as though a gradual acclimatization to the Republic would, in the course of time, solidify and strengthen its political powers of resistance. This assumption was based on the premise that the situation would continue to improve and that time thus gained would automatically blunt the arguments of the enemies of the Republic. And initially this seemed indeed to be the case. The Stresemann era opened up prospects for fresh approaches to the reparations problem and for an early evacuation of the occupation forces in the Rhineland. A Franco-German *rapprochement* and the improvement of Germany's international position was effected. However—and this was cause for grave concern—throughout the 1924–28 Reichstag, the Social Democrats, the strongest single party, were in opposition; by leaving the Government to a weak middle-class bloc, they nurtured a fatal tendency toward minority Cabinets. Not the least reason for their policy was the hope of attracting voters more readily while in opposition, and also the fear of losing votes to their Communist rivals if they were to join the Government. Consequently, the Social Democrats, with their vast potential power, were deprived of the opportunity to exert political influence in their own Republic, and moreover at a time when a prerepublican Field Marshal rather than a Social Democrat presided over the Republic. This dilemma was assuaged somewhat by the fact that until the Papen Putsch in 1932, the Minister President of Prussia, the largest German state, was a Social Democrat, and that his party also sat in other state and municipal governments. But the parliamentary and general political and psychological situation on the national level remained unstable, even after the SPD became the senior partner of a Grand Coalition in 1928.

Mein Kampf AND NEW BEGINNINGS

The Hitler trial and the electoral gains in the spring of 1924 could not obscure the fact that after the abortive putsch the NSDAP, which on November 9, 1923, counted about 55,000 members,[1] was in a state of chaos. Differences among the leaders brought on conflicts and intra-

[1] Werner Maser, *Die Frühgeschichte der NSDAP* (Frankfurt/Main, 1965), p. 463.

mural fights; radical antiparliamentary groups around Rosenberg, Streicher, and Esser opposed the successful "liberation movement" of Ludendorff, Albrecht von Graefe (formerly of the German National Party), Gregor Strasser, and—-in Bavaria—Frick, Feder, and Röhm, all of whom had been elected to the Reichstag. Hitler certainly looked with distaste at the parliamentary road; since, as a non-German, he was ineligible to run, this meant yet another obstacle in his claim to leadership. Yet in fact this exclusion helped his campaign against the "system" and strengthened his special position in the party. For the time being, Hitler, in jail in Landsberg, refrained from taking sides in the party disputes. The future was to prove that this foot-dragging helped his divide-and-conquer strategy and facilitated his return to politics and to the leadership of a reorganized NSDAP.

Although Hitler was crippled by his detention, at the same time it relieved him of having to take a stand and of the responsibility for the consequences of his political disaster. Once again, as he stood at the end of a miscarried stage of his life, circumstances came to his aid. The trial itself, and even more so the subsequent confinement, presented him with the opportunity for a new beginning. And he did indeed manage brilliantly to turn the ignominious events of November 9 into a mysterious beacon of the "new German beginning" and an almost religious cult. "For us, the steps of the Feldherrnhalle are an altar," later sang the bard of the Hitler youth, Baldur von Schirach, the son of a Weimar theatrical producer and an American mother. After 1933, the memorial festivities at the Feldherrnhalle became a cult of glorification; the official publication *Gedenkhalle für die Gefallenen des Dritten Reiches* (*Memorial Hall for the Fallen of the Third Reich;* 1935) summed this up in a downright blasphemous sacramental slogan: "The blood they shed became the baptismal water of the Reich."

Just as the abortive putschist managed to turn the courtroom into a platform for his sweeping indictment of the "Jew Republic," so the execution of his sentence also helped him in every possible way. Instead of being deported as an unwelcome alien, as was planned in the fall of 1924, Hitler was given what was almost a vacation in Landsberg Castle, in the company of forty of his jailed followers. His detention there ended most prematurely in December, 1924, with his amnesty. The room in which Hitler daily presided over lunch was decorated with a swastika banner. On November 8, 1924, memorial festivities were held. The prison took on the air of a party headquarters, a first Brown House, with Hitler, dressed in leather shorts and Tyrolese blazer, receiving the tributes of his minions, and the letters, floral gifts, and expressions of sympathy of the outside world. These included birthday greetings from the aged Houston Stewart Chamberlain in Bayreuth, in which he called Hitler the "great simplifier" and closed with this sentence: "May God, who gave him to us, preserve him for many more years for the glory of the German Fatherland." [2]

Above all, the hitherto nonwriting "writer" now had the leisure and

[2] Walter Görlitz and Herbert A. Quint, *Hitler* (Stuttgart, 1952), p. 234.

means to acquire—as he himself said sardonically—a higher education at public expense. He read voraciously, and pursued the study of congenial theories, such as the geopolitics of Karl Haushofer, who at the instigation of his pupil Rudolf Hess visited Hitler more than once. In June, Hitler began work on his book, intended as a settling of accounts with the past and present and as a plan for the new, "legal" road to power and the glorious National Socialist future. He probably hoped to overshadow his comrades Rosenberg, Feder, and Eckart, both as writer and leader. In his sunny room, he dictated the first volume of *Mein Kampf* to his chauffeur, Emil Maurice, and to his devoted "secretary" and future deputy, Rudolf Hess, who had voluntarily returned from his Tyrolean refuge to Landsberg. The second volume was written two years later. As mentioned earlier, the requisite editorial work was performed by the ex-priest Bernhard Stempfle, whose confidential services were later rewarded by murder.

Whether looked at as a memoir or as a presentation of an ideological system, *Mein Kampf* lacks both form and substance. It is a tedious compilation of turgid discourses on repetitive themes, and despite great editorial effort, it retains the pretentious semi-educated style of his early letters. The ideas and fragments drawn from nationalist, racist, imperialist, and antidemocratic sources did not constitute its "substance." The book borrowed from the *Rassenkunde des deutschen Volkes* (*Race History of the German Nation;* 1922) by the anthropologist Hans F. K. Günther and his theories of "Nordification." Chamberlain, Fritsch, Spengler, Lagarde, Schopenhauer, Wagner, in addition to numerous obscure, pseudo-scientific works, are the sources which the author, naturally without direct citation or annotation, used and vulgarized. Hitler proved to be more than simply a reactionary. His "anti" positions were of a revolutionary nature: destruction of existing political and social structures and their supporting elites; profound disdain for civic order, for human and moral values, for Habsburg and Hohenzollern, for liberal and Marxist ideas. The middle class and middle-class values, bourgeois nationalism and capitalism, the professionals, the intelligentsia, and the upper class were dealt the sharpest rebuff. These were the groups that had to be uprooted and to accomplish this, the impoverished masses, and the young in particular, had to be mobilized.

Hitler broke new ground when discussing the realization and implementation of these ideas. In contrast to his theoretical forerunners, he had, with uncanny instinct, managed to put the practical aspects of the problem of power into the foreground; all "mere" theories hinged on this. It is undoubtedly true that ideological considerations—most particularly a barbaric anti-Semitism—which were more than merely a means for unification and mobilization against *the* enemy, entered into the origins and aims of this Weltanschauung. But within this framework, Hitler's pragmatism, his sure feeling for the practical and organizational aspects of the struggle for power, had become his real strength.

This also answers the question of how far National Socialism could have developed without Hitler. Despite the paucity of original political ideas in *Mein Kampf,* and even though the ideas and slogans of National Socialism predated Hitler, there can be no doubt that after the failure of 1923 as well as after the triumph of 1933, Hitler was the only one who could have brought these ideas to their terrible logical fruition in the Third Reich. This does not mean that he can be taxed with all responsibility for the German catastrophe, as is attempted only too frequently. Adolf Hitler was no mere accident, he was a "condition," above all, as Heiden said, a German condition. But none of his comrades showed a similar aptitude in combining ideology and practice, organization and manipulation. It is therefore no accident that *Mein Kampf* (particularly the second volume) is truly original only in those parts in which Hitler discusses his crude and effective methods of propaganda, organization, and mass psychology with cynical frankness. [3] One of the most effective methods, he said, was an appeal to the lowest aspirations and instincts, the constant repetition of one-track friend-foe catchphrases, the "rape" of the public—the "womanish masses"—through brutal exhortations to do battle. The quintessence of this strategy was the bestial philosophy of the "right of the stronger" in a world-wide racial war, culminating in a radical expansionism. For Germany, this meant reversing the outcome of the war by nullifying all provisions of the Versailles Treaty and planning a new eastward drive which could be skillfully combined with the drawing power of anti-Communism. Virulent hatred of Jews, a sweeping *Lebensraum* philosophy, and a Führer dictatorship were the three recurrent themes of this aggressive ideology. The half-baked ideas of the eternally adolescent charlatan and rootless wastrel of Vienna formed the core of this philosophy, now cast into the mold of a pretentious Weltanschauung and endowed with political effectiveness by the virtuosity of the born demagogue.

The farcical putsch and imprisonment had made Hitler into a martyr; the nameless man became known, and for many was the symbol of their blind quest for change. His first and only published book was bound to frighten off any sensible person; at first it sold poorly, but by 1933, it had sold almost 300,000 copies, and finally was disseminated by the millions as the bible of the Third Reich. There were many who, basking in a false feeling of superiority, refused to take it seriously. They failed to acquaint themselves with the candidly discussed violent plans for the future, plans that were to become such a terrible reality. And although Hitler's following did not include many readers, especially not of so huge a volume, it nonetheless earned the author substantial royalties. He soon became the owner of a big limousine, and later of a magnificent house at Obersalzberg, near Berchtesgaden; when he was in Munich, however, he donned the garb of the simple "labor leader" going forth into battle against the "bossocracy" of the

[3] Cf. Werner Maser, *Hitlers "Mein Kampf"* (Munich, 1966). On the political aims, see Eberhard Jäckel, *Hitlers Weltanschauung* (Tübingen, 1969).

Republic and living in a modest little apartment. The Munich party publishing house of Franz Eher, headed by Hitler's former company sergeant Max Amann, and the Brown House, were to form the propaganda and organizational mainstays of the party's resurgence.

Upon his release from prison on December 20, 1924, Hitler was put on four years' probation. He was now faced with the task of restructuring his party. Alfred Rosenberg, the Baltic race ideologist, had not been an effective keeper of the keys in his dealings with rival groups. After his return, Hitler resorted to the same divide-and-conquer tactics he was to apply so deftly when he seized power. By pitting possible rivals against one another, delegating responsibility, and tolerating overlapping, rival activities, he made himself into that indispensable, supreme arbiter who solves all problems, and surrounded his leadership with increasing prestige. Thus, he returned to politics as the savior of the "movement" from disintegration and division, elbowing aside all possible rivals, particularly Ludendorff and Röhm. He had learned *one* bitter lesson: the road to power did not lead via a putsch but via a more tedious and slow route of "legality." The defeat of democracy by pseudo-democratic means was the new course to which Hitler now devoted himself, even though voting one's opponents down would prove more laborious than shooting them down. The heralded "revolution" and the new German order would have to be the second step. It undoubtedly took a great deal of persuasion to win the activist leaders and adherents who stayed with him over to this approach. There were tactical squabbles and separatist trends, particularly in northern Germany, the province of the self-confident Strasser brothers, Gregor and Otto. In this conflict, the articulate journalist Joseph Goebbels played a prominent part. And the end of this period saw the cementing and organizational tightening of the party and its numerous auxiliaries, and their unconditional commitment to the religiously exalted, unlimited power position of the "Leader."

The republican camp, for its part, also failed to put any major obstacles in the path of Hitler's resurgence. Those who did not generally sympathize with the "national" image of the Hitler movement and did not ascribe its radicalism to the youthful fervor of this superpatriot nonetheless, in naïve adherence to principle, believed that democratic tolerance ought to be extended to the enemies of democracy. Moreover, the danger of revolution seemed to have abated with Hitler's turn toward legal means. Why then, make much ado about a party which was nothing more than a mere splinter group? For years, regional bans and economic well-being were to rob Hitler of his prime weapon—the mass meeting, through which, with theatrical flair and oratory, he disseminated the most banal ideas and promises. His technique was based on two presuppositions—the exclusion of "intellectuals," whom he hated with the passion of the failed "student," and the general lack of political understanding and sophistication of a population come of age in the authoritarian Wilhelminian state and which, after the shock of defeat and the crisis of the Republic, had not been able to arrive at a constructive relationship of mutual cooperation. And this factor had not changed in the years of waning radicalism. In the wings stood a new NSDAP, waiting for its main chance: a second national crisis.

THE STRUCTURE OF THE NEW PARTY

The world into which Hitler returned from Landsberg had changed. Dietrich Eckart and Scheubner-Richter, his patrons, were dead; Göring was in exile in Austria and later went to Sweden. The precarious postwar situation in Bavaria and in the Reich, so ripe for a coup, had given way to stability. The NSDAP was outlawed, as was the *Völkische Beobachter,* and its leadership was divided. Hitler's deputy, Rosenberg, had proved to be a hesitant theoretician, unequal to the practical demands of political life. But it was precisely this dismal situation within the party, which Hitler made no effort to alter while still in Landsberg, that offered him the chance to start anew as undisputed party dictator. For this very reason, he also was opposed to any fusion with other *völkisch* groups, particularly with those in northern Germany started by Ludendorff and Gregor Strasser after the 1924 elections and which, in August of that year, held their first congress in Weimar. As in the years 1920–23, Hitler maintained that such a union tended to sap rather than add to the strength of National Socialism. And again he succeeded in consolidating his own position. Subjugation, not compromise, was his method of cooperation, even though this meant that the party had to start all over again from scratch.

In the second volume of *Mein Kampf,* Hitler argued this basic approach in detail; he applied it in the reorganization of the NSDAP and he was to remain faithful to it in the years to come in all innerparty and external conflicts. [4] When, thanks to the magnanimity of Bavarian officialdom, Hitler stood godfather to the new party on February 27, 1925—once again at the Bürgerbräu in Munich—he kept sternly aloof from his then most important rivals, Ludendorff and Röhm, both of whom had gone their respective ways after the Hitler trial. His alienation from Ludendorff deepened after Ludendorff's defeat in the Presidential elections of March, 1925. Ludendorff, prodded by his second wife, the ambitious Mathilde von Kemnitz, organized an independent political, pseudo-religious sect, whose vague *völkisch* ideology posited a Germanic deity cult in opposition to the trinitarian "world conspiracy" of Jews, Catholics, and Freemasons. This apparent reversion to the fanciful notions of the Thule Society did not gibe with Hitler's political pragmatism. Ludendorff's Tannen-

[4] Jeremy Noakes, "Conflict and Development in the NSDAP 1924–1927," *Journal of Contemporary History,* I (October, 1966), 4 ff.; Dietrich Orlow, "The Conversion of Myth into Power: The NSDAP 1925–1926," *American Historical Review,* LXXII (1967), 906 ff.

berg League lived on, as a dissident sect, in a relationship of mutual distrust with the National Socialists until the death of the General in 1937, and was even outlawed in the Third Reich.

The second problem in the reorganization of the party was that of Röhm's position. This tough mercenary soldier promptly tried to revive the military force he had created in 1922 under the new name "Frontbann." He did in fact succeed in gathering a sizable number of former Free Corps and Army comrades. Hitler saw this as a threat to his newly established position. The abortive putsch had strengthened his determination to make himself completely independent of paramilitary organizations. The new legality strategy, so vital to his future plans, might well be endangered by a reversion to the practices of 1923. In a typical display of egocentricity, he furthermore claimed that activities such as these had delayed his release from prison—a more important consideration than any matter of principle—from October until December. The controversy that was being revived here under new labels was the old one over the role of the SA: in future, it was to be a political instrument and not Röhm's private organization. Hitler resisted all of Röhm's pleas, until the latter, disappointed, resigned his party posts in April, 1925; in 1928, he went to South America as a military adviser. Hitler recalled him only at the end of 1930 to organize the SA for the expected takeover. The era of politicizing military organizations had come to an end.

Hitler himself had given a demonstration of the new tack when, shortly after his return from prison, he paid a call on the Bavarian Minister President, Heinrich Held, pledging his loyalty and offering his services in the fight against Marxism. Through the intercession of Justice Minister Franz Gürtner, he managed to have the Bavarian prohibition of the party and the *Völkische Beobachter* rescinded. He gladly accepted the price he had to pay for this—the defection of a large number of *völkisch* Bavarian deputies (eighteen out of twenty-four) extremely critical of any compromise with the "Black" government. As a matter of fact, defections such as these served to accelerate the party's transformation into a Hitler party. The *Völkische Beobachter* of February 26, 1925, the first issue of the newly legalized paper, now appearing as a weekly, outlined the new course: the leadership of the new National Socialist party was concerned with organization and policy, not with personal or religious differences. In this vein, the founding meeting of early followers who had remained faithful turned into one long testimonial to the old and new "Leader." Drexler, who had been invited to chair the meeting, did not attend, nor did Strasser, Röhm, and Rosenberg. The new nucleus consisted of Amann, Streicher, Esser, Feder, and Frick. Again Hitler's oratory triumphed. Again he solemnly affirmed that if the battle should be lost, the swastika flag was to be his shroud. He was enthusiastically supported in his renewed claim to dictatorial leadership powers, and thus the hurdle to his second goal was also cleared—turning the party into a willing instrument of the legality strategy, which for the time being camouflaged the fight against democracy under the old anti-Semitic and anti-Marxist battle cries.

Initially, the new tactics did not pay off. Conditions had changed considerably since the early postwar years; the political atmosphere had calmed down and the radical Right was deeply divided. Hitler's personal success in the internal reorganization was followed by a long series of failures in the public activities of the party, beginning with the fact that subsequent to his re-emergence, Hitler was barred from making public appearances in Bavaria (March 9, 1925), and later in almost every other German state; his major weapon was thus blunted until 1927–28. The ever-present threat of probation and expulsion to Austria added to his problems. Also, the old financial sources had dried up almost completely. The Army could no longer be counted on, industrialists and social figures no longer thought him worthy of their support, and the contributions of self-sacrificing members were only a drop in the bucket. Hitler himself was able to live very well at Obersalzberg on his book royalties, fees for newspaper articles, and probably the party treasury as well. There he spent his period of enforced silence working on the second volume of *Mein Kampf,* and later (1928) writing a tract on National Socialist foreign policy, which for tactical reasons was never published.[5] Yet despite all these factors, he succeeded in turning the party into an unprecedentedly close-knit and effective body. Although to all effects and purposes Hitler was shut off from public life for three years, he devoted himself with even greater intensity than in the 1919–22 period to organizational tasks. The party membership continued to grow, even if not quite so rapidly as in the past. By the end of 1925, 27,000 of the 55,000 members of 1923 were once more in the party. In 1926, the number doubled; in 1927, it tripled; and by 1928, four times that number had been recruited. The under-thirty age group constituted a substantial portion. In 1928, the 100,000-strong NSDAP, unlike the putschist party of 1923, controlled tightly knit cadres in all parts of Germany which, with the approaching economic crisis, stood ready to branch out into a mass organization. In 1929, and certainly after the electoral gains of 1930, the membership increased rapidly; Hitler no longer had to fear any serious internal challenge to his absolute internal rule. This new party was his creature even more than its predecessor; he was responsible for organization, functionaries, and, once the speaking ban was lifted, influencing the "masses." Theodor Heuss aptly called this combination of leader principle and bureaucracy "bureaucratized romanticism."[6]

At first, of course, this new source of strength could not automatically be relied upon. Because the numerous regional organizations were attuned to different local conditions, coordination, particularly of northern Germany, presented Munich headquarters with a problem. As

---

[5] Gerhard Weinberg (ed.), *Hitlers zweites Buch* (Stuttgart, 1961).
[6] Theodor Heuss, *Hitlers Weg* (1932; rev. ed.; Stuttgart, 1968), pp. 118 ff.

early as 1925, there were once more 607 local groups, half of them in Bavaria and its adjacent regions (*Gaue*). But as the distance from Munich increased, organizational density, and consequently Hitler's influence as well, decreased markedly, bringing with it a growing tendency toward criticism of and independence from Munich. The *Völkische Beobachter*, still edited largely in Bavaria, and since March, 1925, once more a daily, was of limited effectiveness. Much tedious work was required to win over local leaders; frequently, their affiliation was preceded by protracted tugs of war with each other in the course of a conflict-ridden consolidation, and still more protracted efforts on their part to preserve a measure of independence.

Gregor Strasser was undoubtedly the most forceful figure of the new era. In 1924, Strasser gave evidence of his practical approach to politics by capitalizing on his privileges as a member of the Reichstag —free travel, parliamentary immunity, and the right to speak—to strengthen his position among the geographically remote North German groups. To Hitler, the powerful, outgoing personality of this ex-officer and pharmacist from Landshut, a gifted organizer and speaker who had the support of his brother, Otto, himself a skillful journalist and fellow fighter, must have appeared as a threat. Moreover, the Strassers were inclined to take the "socialist" program of the party rather seriously; they supported the idea of a fascist-corporate state and the nationalization of heavy industry and large landholdings. Hitler, on the other hand, both for strategic and ideological reasons, was wary of this sort of "national Bolshevik" opening toward the Left. He did not want to spoil his chances with the ruling elite; his anticapitalism was purely anti-Semitic and only allowed for attacks on Jewish "capitalists" (who in his view dominated everything), but not for union and syndicalist policies of his own. His 1930 and 1932 conflicts with the Strasser brothers and Gregor's murder in the bloodbath of 1934 were a logical consequence of this rivalry, the only remaining one after Röhm's retreat. But in March, 1925, it was Hitler who yielded, acknowledging Gregor Strasser's control in northern Germany, in order to be able to devote himself completely to the Bavarian headquarters. Of the twenty-three party regions only one, Munich–Upper Bavaria, was under Hitler's firm control; the others were torn by internal power struggles, job rivalries, ideological conflicts, and fights for control of the party press.

In this period, a new star arose amid the mediocrity of the old and new leadership: Joseph Goebbels, the future propaganda chief. The son of a Rhenish petty-bourgeois Catholic family, Goebbels was disqualified from war service because of a club foot. He studied German literature on a Catholic scholarship, and after graduating from Heidelberg, he found himself without a job. As the unsuccessful author of romantic, nationalistic novels, he was one of those later so reviled "littérateurs" and "unstable, rootless intellectuals." As late as 1924, he was still vainly applying for work at various "Jewish" newspapers, including the *Berliner Tageblatt*. This future enemy of "capitalism" also tried his hand at banking and worked as a floorman at the Cologne stock exchange. He was a man eager to grasp the opportunity to compensate for his feelings of inferiority in the propaganda service of a party offering an outlet for his rhetorical and journalistic gifts as well as for his vanity. He began his career at the side of Gregor Strasser, and after initial hesitation, he submitted to the Führer cult with all the emotionalism and extremism of which he was capable. With great intensity, he employed his literary and propagandistic skill to create and spread a pseudo-religious Hitler cult. In the course of this, he developed a keen sense for the effective utilization of modern propaganda methods: caustic journalism, cynical Reichstag speeches, and the use of broadcasting, then a still largely untapped medium.

A preliminary decision about the party's totalitarian structure and Strasser's future role in it was already reached in early 1926. In November, 1925, at a conference of twenty-five North German party leaders at Hanover, to which Feder, Hitler's representative, was admitted only reluctantly (and, at the time, against Goebbels' advice), Strasser supported the socialist demand for the expropriation of the aristocracy. This brought on a test of strength with Hitler, who dismissed this demand as a "Jewish swindle." Only Robert Ley and Feder opposed Strasser's proposal at Hanover; Goebbels reputedly went so far as to call for the expulsion of the "petty-bourgeois Adolf Hitler," who did not take socialism seriously. In February, 1926, Hitler answered with an impressively staged conference in Bamberg. There the Strasser group, not fully represented, was in the minority. After a five-hour oration by Hitler, Gregor Strasser agreed to a reconciliation with him. Goebbels, still hesitating, was won over completely by Hitler's flattery and a personal invitation to Munich in April, 1926.[7] This move strengthened not only the much-vaunted party unity but, above all, Hitler's authority. All future internal differences bearing on organizational matters were adjudicated by a party arbitration tribunal (Untersuchungs- und Schlichtungsausschuss [Uschla]) appointed by Hitler. Thus, the Leader held yet another control and purge instrument, one in which Martin Bormann's father-in-law, ex-Major Walter Buch, worked with devotion and in which the National Socialist supreme legal authority, Hans Frank, later earned his spurs.

So we find that Hitler was able, step by step, to establish the basic principle of his ascendancy and rule, to wit, that the Munich party local was the pillar of the National Socialist movement and consequently the one to furnish the leadership of the national party. This concept was endorsed by a general membership meeting at the Bürgerbräu on May 22, 1926, at which Hitler drew a sharp distinction between the NSDAP, a "workers' movement," and all other *völkisch* rivals. For tactical reasons, the ultimate goal was still camouflaged by pseudo-democratic electoral methods. In the second volume of *Mein Kampf*,

---

[7] Helmut Heiber (ed.), *The Early Goebbels Diaries, 1925–1926* (London, 1962; New York, 1963), Entry for April 13, 1926, pp. 76–79.

Hitler still speaks of "Germanic democracy." But in later editions, he talks of the principle of the "unconditional authority of the leader" instead of elections, which are mentioned only for "statutory reasons" —i.e., for maintaining a façade of legality. In any case, the Supreme Leader was specifically invested with the power to appoint and dismiss subleaders; the abolition of the election of regional leaders by the regional party groups further consolidated Hitler's position. The decision, in 1926, making the party program an "unalterable" document also was nothing but a move to solidify Hitler's authoritarian leadership structure and at the same time to ward off any individual attempt to invade the ideological sector, as had been the case in the Strasser episode.

The year 1926 was significant for the internal structure of the NSDAP in other respects as well, even if the party did not cause any great public stir. The National Theater in the city of Weimar, the cradle of German classicism and, seven years earlier, the birthplace of Germany's first democratic regime, was made into an arena for the party. This city was purposely chosen for a cynical demonstration of the "policy of legality." Moreover, Weimar was in Thuringia, one of the few states in which Hitler was allowed to speak. And there, in July, 1926, the first party congress of the new era was held. The Führer, clad in leather-belted field jacket, hunter's hat, and puttees, solemnly greeted 5,000 followers parading past him with the "Roman salute" imported from Austria and Fascist Italy. Through this display, the National Socialists hoped to call public notice to the re-emergence and unity of their party. Among the honorary guests were the Stahlhelm* commander Theodor Düsterberg and a son of the Kaiser, Prince August Wilhelm of Prussia, who soon left the Stahlhelm for the NSDAP and SA. Göring, with his connections among the aristocracy, had also succeeded in establishing contact with other princely houses, as for example, with the Prince of Schaumburg-Lippe. For strategic reasons, this "workers' party" kept open the door to the monarchy until the "Day of Potsdam" (March 21, 1933), when victory was theirs.

The year 1926 also saw the appointment of that highly enthusiastic convert, Dr. Goebbels, to the post of regional leader of "Red" Berlin, a city in which the party's prospects were particularly dim and its organization split by local rivalries.[8] Here the "Doctor" found adequate scope for the development of his agitational and journalistic talents. At the same time, he had the opportunity to prove his newly acquired loyalty to Hitler against the continuing divisive activities of the Strasser group, which had its own Berlin paper and counted among its own such old-time comrades as Rudolf Jung and the putschist Ernst Buchrucker. With the founding of his own paper, *Der Angriff* (*Attack*), in 1927, Goebbels inaugurated a new propaganda style, in which intellectual cunning and the mass appeal of tabloids were combined into

---

* Literally, Steelhelmet, a right-wing veterans' army.—TRANSLATOR'S NOTE.
[8] Martin Broszat, "Die Anfänge der Berliner NSDAP," *Vierteljahrshefte für Zeitgeschichte*, No. 8 (1960), pp. 8 ff.

an effective amalgam of slander and pathos. All protests of the Strasser camp against the unfair competition were rebuffed by Hitler's studied reserve. For the first time, the new NSDAP made its presence felt in Berlin as well.

The third significant development of that year was the appointment of a new SA chief. Hitler had let a year pass, in which he secured the consolidation of his party dictatorship, before naming Franz Pfeffer von Salomon, a retired army major, son of a high-ranking Prussian state servant, and Free Corps officer involved in political assassinations, the supreme leader of the reorganized SA in the late summer of 1926. [9] In the second volume of *Mein Kampf,* written during that period, Hitler spelled out in detail his ideas about the new role of a party army. The sweeping reorganization of the SA was helped by various factors: Many of its former leaders and organizers—for example, Göring, Hoffmann, Rossbach—had fled to Austria; Röhm had resigned; and in the years of illegality the organization had disintegrated. Hitler believed that the era of combat corps was over, that the debacle of 1923 was the result of the faulty coordination of political and military aims, and that the time for establishing the primacy of the new party over all military (auxiliary) groups had come. These stated beliefs guided the reorganization and for the time being also determined the outcome of the conflict with Röhm. It meant in effect that the SA would dissolve all ties to similar organizations outside the party (Röhm's "Frontbann" was such a group) and become solely an instrument of the Hitler-controlled party. This plan, to be sure, succeeded only up to a point. The leadership of the SA continued to be based on former Army and Free Corps officers; the seven top leaders in 1928 (Major Stennes, Major Dincklage, Lieutenant Colonel von Ulrich, Lieutenant Commander von Killinger, Major Schneidhuber, Lieutenant Lutze, Major Reschny of Vienna) all belonged to this category. Although the conflicts between SA leaders and political sub-lieutenants continued until the bloody "purge" of 1934, they no longer seriously threatened Hitler's dictatorial position in the party leadership and organization; conflicts in Berlin and Munich (May, 1927) or "revolts" like those of the Berlin SA officer Stennes (1930) were settled at the local level, and Hitler's absolute authority, which the SA also was wont to invoke, was never really in dispute, even in the so-called Röhm putsch of 1934.

This sharp line dividing it from all nonparty organizations was already drawn in the first "Basic Guidelines for the Reorganization of the NSDAP," published in the *Völkische Beobachter* of February 26, 1925. The SA was prevented from admitting "armed groups and organizations" as well as from acting independently; it was made subject to political controls and ordered to follow the strategy of legality; its sole troop functions were to be indoctrination, training, and maintaining order. If the SA men now wore the brown uniform Rossbach

[9] Heinrich Bennecke, *Hitler und die SA* (Munich, 1962), pp. 125 ff.

had introduced during their period of illegality in 1924, it seems that the adoption of the Brown Shirt as the official uniform was probably a matter of chance. Inspired by the example of the Fascist Black Shirts, the party had acquired a shipment of brown shirts originally destined for German troops in Africa.

It soon became apparent that the battle for the streets and the numerical show of strength were to be the essential functions of the SA in the new era. Provocative demonstrations, particularly in "Marxist" working-class quarters, were among the most effective means both of gaining public notice in the fight between sympathizers and opponents and of disturbing the so unwelcome peace of the Republic. This held true particularly in the Berlin region under Goebbels, who, through increasingly violent encounters with the combat organizations of the Left, tried to keep in the headlines. The Storm Troops, fearing renewed bans, had initially reorganized merely as a "sports division," and officially this precaution remained in force; in 1929, by order of the party, the SA was enjoined from physical attacks on political opponents, even from interfering with public meetings. But at the same time, the party sanctioned the "pitiless" defense against attacks and disturbances, thereby opening the door to the "defensive attack."

At the July, 1926, Weimar congress, Hitler ceremoniously installed eight new SA units (the first four had been installed at the 1923 congress at Munich); this action was also intended to demonstrate the party's aloofness from other combat organizations and the absorption of the SA by the party. Furthermore, Hitler thought the time had come to coordinate the growing local and regional troops, which attracted many younger men, through a central SA leadership. The appointment of Pfeffer, who had come to the regional Ruhr headquarters via the Free Corps and the Ruhr campaign, simultaneously paid heed to the long-standing demand for North German representation in the top echelons. The position of the new SA leadership was further enhanced by its control over the youth and student organizations and an elite "defense corps" (SS) set up in 1925–26 for special duties, in place of the old "Shocktroop Hitler." However, until the advent of Himmler (1929), the SS remained rather insignificant. Only under Himmler's leadership did the Black Shirts, with their death's-head insignia, take over the role of an elite troop sworn to Hitler, in contrast to the mass organization of the SA; in 1934, the SS emerged victorious from its conflict with the SA and became the all-important instrument of internal rule in the Third Reich.

Hand in hand with the expansion and tightening of the leadership and organizational structure, which in effect formed the framework for the rather surprising sudden transformation from cadre to mass party, went the creation of a departmentalized party bureaucracy. It, too, became two things simultaneously: a framework for the future mass party, with governmentlike "ministries" for the different departments, and the ruling instrument of the Leader, who, by following a policy of division of powers and patronage, consolidated his position still further. In 1926, a "Reich directorate," with a secretary (Hess), a treasurer (F. K. Schwarz), a secretary general (Philipp Bouhler), and a number of subcommittees, was formed. Initially, the Reich directorate had twenty-five employees and three automobiles. The apparatus grew quickly, giving a deceptive picture of the size of the party. Departments for foreign policy, press, industrial relations, agriculture, economy, interior, justice, science, and labor formed a miniature state apparatus. In addition, there came into being institutions to support genuinely National Socialist issues, such as "race and culture" and "propaganda," which began to play an increasingly important part in party affairs. In 1926, the groundwork was also laid for still more party auxiliaries, the so-called *Gliederungen* (formations). In addition to the Hitler Youth (Hitlerjugend, or HJ) and the NS German Student League (NS-Deutscher Studentenbund, or NSDStB) under Baldur von Schirach (who, as the eternal juvenile, took over the HJ in 1931, later advancing to Reich Youth Leader), there also was an NS Pupils' League (NS-Schülerbund) and the first professional units—the NS Teachers' League (NS-Lehrerbund), NS Law Officers' League (NS-Rechtswahrerbund), NS Physicians' League (NS-Ärztebund)—as well as an NS Women's League (NS-Frauenschaft), whose task it was to turn the party's thoroughly reactionary attitude toward the women's rights question into an asset and offer admiring female supporters limited participation in the male party. The idea of a women's SA, briefly considered in 1927, was dropped, however.

With institutions such as these, in part copied from the all-encompassing auxiliaries of the left-wing parties, the NSDAP moved toward the total "inclusion" of its supporters, toward that state within the state which Hitler demanded in *Mein Kampf* (p. 503) : The movement was to be so organized that not only would it "in itself contain the germ of the future state" but "also have it in readiness as the perfected embodiment of its own state." There came into being a shadow state which, with the "seizure of power," was able almost automatically to take over the reins of government: Reich and regional leaders supplied ministers and government leaders, SA and SS staffed the police, and the swastika symbol became the country's official insignia. Hitler used the expansion for the further solidification of his control over every leader and employee of the party. It was he who determined their remuneration, their eligibility for party office, the party's electoral candidates, and the personnel and finance policies of the regional offices.[10] The leadership of Munich was conclusive and total. Governmental surveillance of the new party, however loose, also contributed inadvertently to the organizational tightening of the party. It helped to turn its leaders into more experienced, better-versed, and at the same time ideologically more fanatical strategists. Thus, prohibitions of political parties were of doubtful value, though the

[10] Karl Wahl, *Es ist das deutsche Herz: Erlebnisse und Erkenntnisse eines deutschen Gauleiters* (Augsburg, 1954), p. 53; Hans Fabricius, *Geschichte der nationalsozialistischen Bewegung* (Berlin, 1937), p. 38.

speaking ban imposed on Hitler until 1927 (in Prussia, until September, 1928) did seriously impair his effectiveness. It just did not last long enough. While he was enjoined from speaking, his addresses were usually read aloud by the future Gauleiter (regional leader) of Munich, Adolf Wagner, who had not only the same first name but also the same vocal timbre and local inflection as Hitler. But this prohibition allowed Hitler to concentrate on closed party meetings. Furthermore, the vigilance called for to avoid further prohibitions stimulated and justified his championship of a policy of legality vis-à-vis rival policies within the party. The organizational centralization and discipline which enabled the party to absorb many new members and at the same time keep functioning despite all internal pressures could not have been achieved without the constant sense of outside threat and the resultant feeling of community. In *Mein Kampf*, Hitler called the winning over of people to the organization the first task of propaganda, and the winning over of people for propaganda the first task of the organization. This aptly sums up the development of the NSDAP in this period of waiting and cadre-formation, the function of the minor party in its early "years of struggle" (*Kampfzeit*).

That the next step, planned by Hitler apparently with an eye toward both the Fascist and the Bolshevik examples, would also be realized so quickly was, however, not to be expected: "The overthrow of the existing condition and the saturation of this condition with the new teaching" was the second task of propaganda, "while the second task of the organization was the fight for power in order to achieve the ultimate victory of the teaching." Circumstances undoubtedly turned out to be of unexpected help. Yet, it cannot be denied that the perseverance with which the goals were pursued during the first phase, which in effect coincided with Hitler's four-year probationary period, was responsible for the transition to the second phase, and in the critically decisive stage—after mid-1932—saved the NSDAP from the erosion and dissolution on which its enemies had banked. True, initially the party stagnated after this second period of development and consolidation. The breakthrough to a mass party was nowhere in sight. The financial situation was critical. The only bright spot was a new party congress in August, 1927, held in Nuremberg, the ancient Roman imperial city and the headquarters of the rabid Julius Streicher. It was the first of the series of grandiose national party congresses. Despite the smallness of the party, the congress was a far more elaborate affair than the previous year's meeting at Weimar. Nuremberg was intended to demonstrate the unity of the "movement" after the reorganization, and, simultaneously, the propagandistic display was to show the public the unbroken strength of the party and win it new support. SA and party formations by the thousands arrived in special trains. After a festive address by Hitler, twelve new SA units were dedicated, an overt demonstration of the nationwide spread of the Storm Troops. The National Socialist press, exaggerating somewhat, spoke of 30,000 SA men passing in review before Hitler and Pfeffer;

the *Völkische Beobachter* claimed that the railroads mentioned bringing in 100,000 participants; realistic estimates spoke of 15,000–20,-000.[11] Be that as it may, the effect of the congress on the inner cohesion and self-confidence of the party and its leaders was probably of greater significance than its outside impact.

Only months later, during the Reichstag elections of May, 1928, the NSDAP, despite all propaganda efforts, still found itself in the role of a splinter party, even though it ran nationwide candidates. This nationwide participation gave a deceptive picture of the inner strength and power of the organization with which, for the first time, the party ventured forth as a united "Hitler movement" (thus the official label), with candidates and supporters throughout Germany. In addition to Bavaria and Franconia, North German voters contributed considerably to the exceedingly modest vote (2.6 per cent). In the rural coastal region of Schleswig-Holstein, the NSDAP won as much as 18 per cent of the vote, while doing very poorly in the industrial areas and in Prussia east of the Elbe. The elections, to which Hitler agreed only after long hesitation, did not necessarily mean a decision for the parliamentary road to power. Rather, his ideas took as models the mass strikes during the revolution of 1918 and the Fascist street demonstrations which in 1922 led to Mussolini's legal summoning. Such a development would require neither electoral victory nor a putsch, but only massive organization and the SA to put constant pressure on the body politic.

Hitler, stateless since 1925, was barred from participation in any election. But he turned necessity into a virtue and exploited the restriction to emphasize his unique special position in the party as well as in political life as a whole. Göring, who had returned from Sweden at the end of 1927 and who, as a well-traveled man of the world, had, together with his Swedish wife, made fresh social contacts for the NSDAP, was elected to the Reichstag, as were Gregor Strasser, Frick, von Epp, Feder, and Goebbels. The twelve NSDAP deputies could not hope to exert any influence on parliamentary politics, but the party profited from the parliamentary privileges they enjoyed. Goebbels with cynical candor revealed the real meaning of the legality policy. Even before the elections, in an article entitled "What Do We Want in the Reichstag?" in *Der Angriff* of April 30, 1928, he had stated point-blank:

We go into the Reichstag in order to acquire the weapons of democracy from its arsenal. We become Reichstag deputies in order to paralyze the Weimar democracy with its own assistance. If democracy is stupid enough to give us free travel privileges and per diem allowances for this service, that is its affair. . . . We'll take any legal means to revolutionize the existing situation. If we succeed in putting sixty to seventy agitators of our party into the various

[11] Albert Krebs, *Tendenzen und Gestalten der NSDAP* (Stuttgart, 1959), p. 58.

parliaments in these elections, then in future the state itself will supply and finance our fighting machinery. . . . Mussolini also went into parliament, yet soon thereafter he marched into Rome with his Black Shirts. . . . One should not believe that parliamentarism is our Damascus. . . . We come as enemies! Like the wolf tearing into the flock of sheep, that is how we come. Now you are no longer among yourselves!

And after the election, Goebbels, in *Der Angriff* of May 28, 1928, again offered this interpretation of the legality tactic:

I am not a member of the Reichstag. I am a holder of immunity, a holder of travel privileges. . . . We were elected against the Reichstag, and we will carry out our mandate in the sense of those who furnished that mandate. . . . A holder of immunity has free admission into the Reichstag without having to pay amusement tax. He can, when Mr. Stresemann tells about Geneva, pose irrelevant questions, as for example whether it is a fact that Stresemann is a Freemason and married to a Jewess. He reviles the "system" and in return receives the gratitude of the Republic in the form of seven hundred and fifty marks monthly salary—for faithful service.

These samples of Goebbels' propaganda style probably also were intended as justification against the vocal critics of parliamentary participation in the Nazi camp. But the changed party was reorganized under changed conditions according to this recipe, and with its help sailed toward the "legal revolution."

IDEOLOGY AND PROPAGANDA

The literary movement which somewhat paradoxically has been labeled the "conservative revolution" remained a significant causal factor in the rise of National Socialism even after 1923. It was part of the broader area of the antidemocratic ideologies growing out of the reaction against the French Revolution and its aftermath. But it differed from reactionary conservatism in the radical consequences and visions of the future which its diverse spokesmen drew from the war experience and collapse. There are those who claim that this conservative revolution has been "misunderstood"; by that, they mean that only the misapplication of its ideas made it into the precursor and fellow traveler of National Socialist power politics. But there can be no denying that the writings that came out of this motley camp during the 1920's contained much of the explosive dynamite handled by the Free Corps and the youth movement, by radicalized student organizations and soldiers, and by political adventurers and intellectual worshipers of power. They were the sublimation of the antidemocratic wave of the postwar years. New, ambitious, historico-philosophical notions and cultural criticism took up some of the ideas of the prewar movements mentioned in Chapter I.

Once again, the main theme was the singularity and superiority of German nationalism, its anti-Western mission in the fight against the allegedly destructive influences of liberalism and capitalism, of race-mixing and emancipation, of international socialism as well as pacifism and democratization. Like the radical pioneers of the youth movement, the conservative revolutionaries proclaimed the replacement of the "bourgeois era" by a specifically German, Prussian-nationalist, conservative "socialism," based on organic rather than materialist thinking, on quality instead of quantity, on *völkisch* community rather than class and mass. The community forged in the "storms of steel" of the war, which overcame the harmful "ideas of 1789" through the "ideas of 1914," would overcome the Republic, the unworthy successor of the "Second Reich," through the definitive "Third Reich" of the future: the "Thousand-year Reich" toward which all of German history has aspired.

These romantic-irrational reveries, devoid of all concrete political reality, were in themselves extremely heterogeneous and unclear. But as antidemocratic ferment, such ideas proved effective among the semi-educated middle class as well as in the universities. Postwar Germany showed itself more receptive than ever before. Above all, there existed—as in German conservatism as a whole—no real defense against National Socialism, which understood how to utilize such dreams by absorbing them into its concrete organization and agitation techniques. The conservative revolution, which saw itself as an elite movement and looked with disdain on the "plebeian" petty-bourgeois movement of National Socialism, was in fact highly susceptible to this sort of manipulation. In the final phase, it split up into turncoats, accepters, and oppositionists who, sooner or later—but, in the final analysis, too late—found their way into the resistance. The resentments against the West were greatest among the so-called National Bolsheviks. Nationalists like Ernst Niekisch were fascinated by certain aspects of the Russian Revolution and saw the system of soviets as the model for a corporate order of "working" people, in place of parliamentarianism; out of Germany's position between East and West was to emerge a new, major power, freed from the shackles of Versailles and oriented toward the East. The basically utopian nature of their ideas manifested itself in constantly new, different interpretations and plans; its essential effect was to undermine the Republic and subsequently—directly or indirectly—to enhance the crude National Socialist "ideology," which became socially acceptable only after the flirtation with eminent writers and poets, among them the widely read Oswald Spengler, whose *Preussentum und Sozialismus* (*Prussianism and Socialism;* 1920) called "barbaric Caesarism" the wave of the future. In 1919, Arthur Moeller van den Bruck had programmatically demanded for Germany "the Right of the Young Nations" (against the West), and in his book *Das Dritte Reich* (*The Third Reich;* 1923) furnished the formula for the future Hitler Reich, though without grasping its reality. Ernst Jünger wrote of the war's steel bath, and in his *Die totale Mobilmachung (Total Mobilization;* 1931) and *Der Arbeiter (The Worker;* 1932) (in which he made the worker into a stylized soldier of technology), he fixed the heroic accents for what was to come. Edgar Jung, in his antirepublican *Die Herr-schaft der Minderwertigen (The Rule of the Inferior;* 1927), championed a corporate elite state, and Hans Grimm's bestseller, *Volk ohne Raum (Nation Without Space;* 1926) popularized the breakthrough of the *Lebensraum* idea into politics. The corporate state of fascist coinage had already been propagated by the Austrian Ottmar Spann in his book *Der Wahre Staat (The True State;* 1921), which strongly influenced Fascist and National Socialist theoreticians as well as the experiments of Dollfuss and Schuschnigg in pre-Hitler Austria. Carl Schmitt, Hans Freyer *(Revolution von rechts) (Revolution from the Right;* 1931), and the circle around the periodical *Die Tat* (Hans Zehrer, Ferdinand Fried, Giselher Wirsing), with their political and social fantasies, were among the many conscious or unconscious helpers who prepared the ground for National Socialism.

On the poetic and literary scene, the sectarian, pseudo-religious influence of Stefan George's political poetry was considerable; in his collection of poems *Das Neue Reich,* he who in 1933, embittered, died in his Swiss exile and whose disciples in part emigrated or (like Stauffenberg) later joined the resistance, sang paeans to the antidemocratic, elitist combat and leader ideology. It was a vast backdrop of exalted prophecies founded on a vague, irrational mysticism that became concrete only in their criticism of the West and in the arrogant vilification of the democratic present. But their exalted and exaggerated feelings and thoughts fell on fertile ground, however different and "lower" the intellectual world of the *völkisch* movements and the ideologies of the reorganized Hitler party.[12]

The National Socialist movement itself had three main roots. Ideologically, it rested on the duality of nationalism (toward the outside) and antiparliamentarianism (within). Economically it was rooted in that "middle-class panic" in which the fight against the decline of economic, social, and national prestige was easily transposed to the realm of chauvinism and imperialism. Psychologically, the "movement" profited in no small measure from the generation problem and the romantic protest mood of the youth. Above all, there loomed an ideology of unity, in which the heterogeneity of the social ties and interests of the ideology's supporters, the antagonisms of the petty-bourgeoisie, small landowners, dissatisfied intellectuals, and nationalist adventurers, were to be welded into a mystical community and the suppressed aggression turned toward the outside.[13]

The economic and social program pledged itself to the fight against

[12] On the "conservative revolution," see the works of Mohler, Kohn, Neurohr, Glum, von Klemperer, Sontheimer, and Schüddekopf (cited in the Bibliography).

[13] See K. D. Bracher, *Die Auflösung der Weimarer Republik* (5th ed.; Villingen, 1971), pp. 100 ff.

Marxism, yet at the same time its position on the problem of "capital-ism" combined rather glittering "socialist," nationalist–anti-Semitic, and purely emotional viewpoints. To be sure, initially a radical critical attitude, in which regional and social factors played a major role, predominated. Fantastic and contradictory ideas about profit-sharing were given currency and raised widespread hopes for the redistribution of profits reaped in war and inflation. Promises of socialist sharing in industry and higher wages for workers abounded; labor was to be up-graded; small businessmen were to be freed of the competition of big business; the mortgages and taxes of homeowners and farmers were to be abolished or reduced; and heavy industry was to be given a shot in the arm through the national "preparedness" program. There was something for everyone. However, the program closed with this sen-tence: "How the question of profit-sharing will be solved in the future National Socialist state is not under discussion here." [14] Not only the nature of the party structure, but also Hitler's tactical, opportunistic wooing of antilabor capitalists contributed to the effective though not overt defeat of the "anticapitalist" ideology of men like the Strassers and Feder. "Socialism" was reduced to a vague, verbal invocation of a na-tional, community-directed economic idea.

The party's official statements and publications on questions of prac-tical politics were as ambiguous and inherently contradictory as its demands for "breaking the shackles of high finance" or for the crea-tion of "etatist economic systems" modeled on Mussolini's experiments (as a quick solution of pressing social and national problems and the Jewish question), or its position on private property. The party's po-sitions were effective solely in their radical, negative analysis of exist-ing conditions and in the mobilization of old resentments. With the onset of a new economic crisis, the vague unease over the shortcomings of parliamentary democracy and the party system supporting it stimu-lated gropings for political solutions outside the boundaries of the existing order.

Pronouncements on the future National Socialist form of govern-ment also remained vague. Although the idea of "dictatorship" was not part of the party program, it nonetheless became the most telling argument against the despised parliamentary system. Generally, there was only a careful mention of a "temporary dictatorship," which would last until the new ideas could be implemented and had become part of a never clearly defined authoritarian-corporate order. Other voices, like that of Goebbels, were raised in support of "handing over politics to a political committee formed on the basis of the law of power and selec-tion. At any rate: No more democratic parliamentarianism!" (*Angriff*, August 6, 1928.) There was also talk of a parliament of es-tates to deal solely with economic policy; furthermore, Goebbels spoke of a senate—an upper house appointed for life by the dictator-chancellor,

[14] Gottfried Feder, *Das Programm der NSDAP und seine weltanschau-liche Grundgedanken* (Munich, 1932), p. 46.

who in turn would be elected by this upper house![15] This thinly veiled dictatorship was only one of many tangible plans; to what extent Goebbels, much less Hitler, considered any of this binding remained as unclear as the question about the form of government itself. For Hitler also succeeded in persuading monarchists, and ultimately the Crown Prince himself, to join in his game. For tactical reasons, the position on the controversial issue of federalism versus centralism remained no less vague. And with the pledge of a "positive Christianity," all tactically inconvenient consequences of a "National Socialist ideology" were evaded; the churches were mollified and religious conflicts prevented.

Programmatically both anticapitalist and antiproletarian, conservative and revolutionary, the NSDAP appealed to a middle class threatened by modern capitalism, fighting off proletarization, and hoping for "any kind" of change. Proletarianized classes sought to win back their lost prestige in the fight against a changing world, and—feeling pressed from all sides by both capitalism and Communism—they took refuge in a mixture of restorational and revolutionary daydreams which transcended the prosaic republican everyday existence. Of all social classes, this group was most receptive to the irrational ideologies by which National Socialism promised a new purpose to life and new national and social prestige. Above all, the "movement" knew how to make political capital out of the traditional anti-Semitism of the lower middle class. And with its vague slogans of "land reform" and its appeal to rural anti-Semitism, the NSDAP also knew how to latch on to the agricultural protest movement, which had begun to spread throughout northern Germany even before the onset of the great economic crisis. As a result, the party was able to register by far the greatest electoral gains after 1929 in Protestant agricultural regions (Schleswig-Holstein and Lower Saxony), while never succeeding in breaking the "Red" supremacy in the cities.

The youthful following, attracted by the romantic radicalism and emotional appeal of the "movement," became a significant factor. The NSDAP offered the youth movement, which had never been able to gain a firm foothold in the democratic parties, the most consistent acceptance of its leadership role: "National Socialism is the organized will of the youth" proclaimed the official slogan.[16] Whereas the war veterans were the party's early organizers and leaders—though many more joined the Stahlhelm—postwar youth, including significant numbers of university students, increasingly formed the core of the militant party adherents: in 1931, almost 40 per cent of the members were under thirty, compared with a bare 20 per cent in the SPD.[17] The National Socialists concentrated on the recruitment of these young people. Engage-

[15] Goebbels, *Der Nazi-Sozi, Fragen und Antworten für den National-sozialisten* (Munich, 1931), pp. 20 f.

[16] Otto Dietrich, *Mit Hitler in die Macht* (Munich, 1934), p. 135.

[17] Hans Gerth, "The Nazi Party, Its Leadership and Composition," *American Journal of Sociology*, XIV (1940), 530.

ment, application, and dedication to irrational forces rather than discussion and compromise were the values which this group made its gauge for the critique of liberalism, democratism, parliamentarianism, and a sober approach to the settlement of conflicts in domestic and foreign policy.

Youth was indignant over the difficult and frequently unfair conditions of life, the manifold limitations of the times. The "movement" provided them with an outlet for energies thwarted by unemployment and uncertainty over the future. The under-thirty group had no understanding of the historical background and political possibilities of the Weimar Republic. They protested against the seeming inertia of the politicians of the older generation, who had in fact failed in the task of political education. Only the extreme protest movement of the NSDAP—and the Communist Party—seemed to offer youth the chance of rapid advancement. "Make room, you old ones!" shouted Gregor Strasser.[18] The NSDAP was an organization which demanded the "complete man," which pronounced the "old ones" guilty, and which satisfied the need for a community, a "movement" that promised to defeat the "tepid present" and to replace the crisis-ridden bourgeois order with more determined leadership. Community: that meant "socialism"; action and leadership: that meant "nationalism." The "false enmity" of socialism and nationalism was to be destroyed; socialism was to be pried loose from "Marxist" internationalism, and nationalism from capitalism. The resounding synthesis of National Socialism promised salvation—through unquestioning obedience to the leader dictatorship —to the many inspired by a naïve view of freedom and utopian ideas. The community and leader idea of the youth movement, which above all had stressed the small entity, was perverted into a centralist-bureaucratic collective organization. Though the Hitler Youth adopted the terminology and style of the youth movement, its uniformed organization was not at all in accord with the individualism propounded by the youth movement.

Would the party be able to cloak the innate lie of the program and the dichotomy of its structure until it came to power? Were not its leaders part of a failed in-between generation which went into politics solely out of resentment and disappointment? Did not the whole program rest on negative "values" like anti-Semitism, antiparliamentarianism, unlimited nationalism, and imperialism, while the real political problems— republic versus monarchy, unitary versus federal state, socialism versus capitalism, revolution versus legality, land reform versus preservation of private property—were neither defined nor really thought through?

The incredible success of this conglomerate of ideas cannot be understood without considering the special position of National Socialist propaganda. Its astonishing effect was enhanced still more by the inspired handling of new techniques of opinion-making. But at the same

[18] "Macht Platz, ihr Alten" (article by Strasser written in May, 1927), in *Kampf um Deutschland* (Munich, 1932), pp. 171 ff. Also, Hermann Heller, *Europa und der Faschismus* (Berlin and Leipzig, 1931).

time, it was a truly religio-psychological phenomenon. Just as the concept of "belief" occupied a central place in the postulates and self-fulfillments of National Socialist policy, the "ideological" base of the movement and its aims formed the backbone of its argumentation. They removed themselves from the grasp of all rational criticism by the constant invocation of a biological mysticism: The "song of their blood" [19] was to endow the believers with the fanatical power to act. Whether one ascribes the effectiveness of such political religions to the situation of rootless masses in a secularized world needing something to believe in, or whether one sees it as the product of real political, economic, and social needs combined with wishful thinking in a postwar society beset by crisis, disappointments, and resentments—at any rate, in the early days of the NSDAP there already emerged exalted forms of leader worship which hinted at the bottomless Byzantinism of the Third Reich. To be sure, these manifestations were being used quite consciously in the manipulation, coordination, and metaphysical support of the movement's total leadership structure. Nevertheless, leader worship found a growing response in a democratic, free society, and it proved to be the most effective part of a propaganda which promised not only victory and greatness but also salvation and security. Long before 1933, a wealth of grotesque practices and religious fervor testified to the quasi-religious impact of the Leader propaganda, as, for example, obituaries in which the name of Hitler was invoked in place of the name of the Lord.

The Führer stood as the absolute unifying point in and above the movement. As sole authority, as the "charismatic leader" (in Max Weber's sense), as the acme of the hierarchic structure and focal point of all action and ideas, he directed the organization, course, and tactics of the entire movement down to the personnel policies of regional offices. The fact that the centralized, militarily structured machinery was split into numerous rival centers held together only by the figure of the Leader merely helped to strengthen the power position and manipulative scope of Hitler within as well as outside the party.

Hitler appeared as the exponent of a new sense of life, fulfilling the need for devotion, service, and subordination, as the one who alone could meet this need and transform it into liberating political deed. He was the incarnation of the "national community"; thanks to his intuition and his leadership talent, he was "invariably right"; he was the indisputable interpreter of the interests of the "people's community" whose emanation he claimed to be. Thus he was not bound by any rules of law, not even vis-à-vis his own followers. This sense of mission was greater still than the monarchic sense of legitimacy; even to a Hohenzollern prince like August Wilhelm, Hitler appeared as the "leader sent by God." [20] Thus all discussions on National Socialism centered on him. The party apparatus was also completely focused on him;

[19] Gregor Strasser, *op. cit.*, (Munich, 1932), p. 222.
[20] Speech delivered at Brunswick, *Berliner Tageblatt*, June 17, 1931.

his figure held together the organization's peculiar mixture of youth, military, and bureaucratic components. The autocratic party organization, through which the NSDAP accomplished its unique parliamentary ascendancy after 1929, subjugated all outside spontaneity to the will of the irreplaceable Leader. The abolition of the majority principle throttled all possibility of internal change, caucusing, and the democratic settlement of inner-party differences. Unquestioning discipline and a rigid command structure from top to bottom made for a submissive fatalism of both membership and bureaucracy which was given direction by the consummate exploitation of the pseudo-religious, mystical, providential role of the one and only Leader. The unity of the party guaranteed the unconditional execution of all orders to the point of abdication of all individual powers of judgment and decision. And with the help of this unity the new Weltanschauung was displayed before the people, in order to gain a sympathetic hearing, or at least attract public attention.

In this ideal type of totalitarian party, revising any decision, even a bad one, was ruled out so that the structure of absolute subordination could be preserved even in the face of obvious mistakes. Not only the slavish dependence of the lower echelons on their higher manipulators, but also the sharp differences in the treatment and compensation of party officials showed up the antidemocratic nature as well as the ruthless purposefulness of the party structure. Added to this were party purges à la Bolshevism and the closing of membership rolls à la Fascism—measures covered over by the intensification of the strategy of parliamentary legality when sudden favorable circumstances after 1929 aided the transition from revolutionary cadre party to evolutionary popular mass movement. Now the close-knit organization underwent a process of regimentation down to the smallest units, which in many respects resembled the machinery of the hostile Communist Party. The similarity was particularly obvious in the system of "street cells." This guaranteed control from above as well as —in case of prohibitions—the possibility of working illegally through decentralized, easily controlled small units. There were also the numerous auxiliaries designed to serve the "total encompassing" of man and his special professional and age interests: youth and women's leagues, the highly successful student organizations, the teachers', lawyers', and physicians' groups, and so on.

The main attribute of the "new party" was its military, not merely militant, character. This was revealed in its authoritarian command structure, in the authoritative tone of its statements, and in all its external forms, but above all it was revealed in the stress on drill in the SA and similar party defense and elite groups. It is difficult to gauge to what extent the military, aggressive façade of the party and its elite formations was merely psychological intimidation and to what extent it represented real power; at any rate, the generally rather harmless playing at soldier did have its effect on the public. As it happened, the activities of these groups developed a measure of autonomy whose revolutionary direction and leadership repeatedly came into conflict with the opportunistic legality strategy of the party. Despite the importance of the military groups to the party's ideological position, its political and psychological appeal, and its organizational structure, they nonetheless were kept firmly in check, to ward off the danger of furnishing the indecisive "pillars of the Republic" with ammunition for prohibition and harassment, thus clearing the road for the winning over of large segments of the population who supported a strong but not revolutionary nationalism, and anti-Communist but not socialist "socialism." Many an outsider who could not see a totalitarian mass party "taking power legally" saw this course as the end of Hitler's revolutionary future. Curzio Malaparte prophesied: "A would-be dictator—Hitler." [21] The departure of Otto Strasser's revolutionary socialists in the summer of 1930 seemed to signify most clearly and apparently for good the domesticization of the combatant revolutionary party. This pseudo-democratization, however, was just that; at the moment of taking power, the now useless democratic wraps were stripped off.

Under the shield of these tactics, the NSDAP became increasingly skillful in the use of modern techniques of mass propaganda; it learned to clothe its vague theories in terse and easily remembered phrases and slogans, to implant facts by suggestive repetition, to stir up irrational, subconscious emotions by means of simple symbolism, and to direct the dynamic of the movement toward pithy notions of the enemy. Added to this was the uninhibited use of denunciations and force, and all this on behalf of a systematic demagoguery which individuals might find repulsive but which won the masses once they had been stirred up. The party owed its growth to the application of commercial advertising techniques to political recruitment, which, violating the rules of good taste and acceptable levels of noise, began an assault on the collective subconscious. It also now became clear how important the period of apparent stagnation had been for the preparation of leaders within the framework of a still small, malleable party machinery and for the trying out and perfection of psycho-technical methods. At the moment of growing economic, social, and political crisis, the instruments were ready for offering up a melange of seemingly plausible stereotyped explanations, solutions, and cures, and simultaneously for holding them in check politically. And while the troubled individual may still have believed that he was given a choice and could influence the course of events, the reins holding him in passed via a disciplined party machinery into the hands of the one, omnipotent driver whose visions of power determined both direction and pace.

The simplicity and primitiveness of National Socialist ideas and programs, theses and revolutionary recipes, visions and power ideas that

[21] Curzio Malaparte, *Coup d'Etat, the Technique of Revolution* (New York, 1932), chap. viii, pp. 223–41.

might have repelled the unbiased bystander were helped along by the mastery of slogans and a vast propaganda effort skilled in the appeal to mass emotions and in the use of varied and unscrupulous means. The entire spectrum of political sophistry served as material and vehicle for influencing the people. Even ideas of political order, including the National Socialist idea of the "national community," were nothing more than way stations on the road to the total control and manipulation of all ideas and feelings. The realm of freedom, which competing philosophies—particularly in the political arena—hoped to expand by opening up new vistas of thought, feeling, and action, was systematically destroyed by the mechanical imposition of pieced-together idea fragments offered up in noisy emotional appeals.

Hitler himself outlined this process in his brutally consistent, unmistakable evaluation and analysis of modern political propaganda methods in *Mein Kampf* (pp. 375 ff.). The first commandment was "popular appeal," achieved by spreading monotonous slogans in all directions: from the malleable vagueness of the imagery and the flexibility and adaptability of the terminology to the total control of opinion and movement. When the NSDAP blossomed forth into a mass party, this approach proved as flexible as it needed to be: applicable to highly varied social and political levels, to heterogeneous emotions and ideas, to a whole universe of ideal images, loyalties, and reactions. The backbone of the National Socialist philosophy of power was that disdain of the "masses" on which all authoritarian and totalitarian movements since time immemorial have based themselves. This disdain motivated those passages of *Mein Kampf* (pp. 197 f.) in which Hitler, with unmistakable logic, sums up his ideas: "Every propaganda must be popular and adjust its intellectual level to the receptivity of the most limited person among those to whom it addresses itself. Thus, the greater the number of people appealed to, the lower the intellectual level must be. . . . the receptivity of the great mass is very limited, its understanding small, but its forgetfulness great. Based on these facts, all effective propaganda must limit itself to only a very few points and use these as slogans until even the last one can draw the desired conclusion."

Clearly, Hitler's strength was rooted in formal techniques, in the command of methods of manipulation. It overshadowed the banal message attuned to irrationally elaborate visions, which, repeated in endless variations and reduced to terse formulas, to justify the ruthless virtuosity of the formal-propagandistic means; yet the eclectic historical components of this message proved effective even with portions of the intelligentsia. Brutally "either-or," the propaganda appealed to the audience's primitive desire for simplification. Thus: "There are . . . only two possibilities: either the victory of the Aryan side or its annihilation and the victory of the Jews." [22] The propaganda tools were

[22] Speech by Hitler in Munich, April 12, 1922, quoted by Werner Siebarth, *Hitlers Wollen* (Munich, 1935), pp. 91 ff.

utilized in the most economical manner possible. Objectivity was wasteful; the suggestive power of the spoken word—the written form was much less forceful—stood in the forefront. "Fanaticism"—a key word of the Hitlerian terminology—the stirring up of mass hysteria, the development of a special style of mass meetings, these were the primary weapons; the press played an absolutely secondary role in the opinion-molding process of the masses.[23] In line with the Hitlerian concept of the mass, the systematic weakening of individual powers of resistance—analogous to the principles of military drill—was the first presupposition for the successful "integration" of divergent desires. Goebbels did not cease to celebrate the "great simplifier" and the "magical effect of his words," before which all resistance collapses.[24] Hitler himself interpreted this as the forcible rule of a "stronger will," which makes use of effective external as well as internal sedatives and intoxicants, even taking into account the diminution of the powers of mind and will in the evening. Only "the agitator" who possessed these abilities, Hitler declared, was "a great leader; his entire effect and power lie in the virtuosity with which he can move masses." [25]

Behind all this there was a ruthless drive for power which kept the followers at fever pitch: "We are avid for power, and we take it wherever we can get it. . . . Wherever we see a possibility to move in, we go! . . . Whoever has us clinging to his coattails can never get rid of us again." [26]

TOWARD A MIDDLE-CLASS MASS PARTY

The re-emergence and subsequent growth of the NSDAP cannot be understood without an examination of its connections with middle-class organizations. The party's changing relationship to the German National League of Commercial Employees (DHV) is a typical case in point. Pronouncedly right-wing, anti-Marxist, and anti-Semitic, this large organization offered numerous points of contact and made it easier for the NSDAP's "Left" wing to gain a foothold in industry and trade groups. In contrast to the class and special-interest parties, the NSDAP saw itself as a modern "collective party," and this facilitated its rapid development into a mass movement. But its essential base and its most important connections were above all among the petty-bourgeois, middle-class, and small landholding groups which had been hardest hit by the outcome of the war, the economic crisis, and the structural changes of modern society. The memoirs of Albert Krebs, a leader of the Hamburg NSDAP (1926–28) coming from the youth movement and Free Corps and also active in the DHV, who was expelled from the party by Hitler in May, 1932, offer valuable insights into the internal developments of that period.

[23] See Adolf Hitler, *Mein Kampf* (Munich, 1925–28), pp. 525 ff., 371.
[24] "Wenn Hitler spricht," *Der Angriff*, November 19, 1928.
[25] Hitler, *op. cit.*, pp. 530 ff., 650.
[26] Goebbels, in *Der Angriff*, December 1, 1929.

The relationship between the party and right-wing special-interest groups was marked by an alternation of cooperation and rivalry. Whereas Max Habermann, the leader of the DHV, accepted the growing cooperation only reluctantly, many of the younger DHV functionaries tended toward closer ties. But how the more pragmatic interests of the DHV, which had to enter into compromises with the "bourgeois" parties, were to be brought into accord with the absolutist demands of the rigidly antirepublican, antiparliamentarian NSDAP remained a constant problem. The conflict later flared up particularly in the attitude toward the Brüning Government; Habermann, who had connections with the People's Conservatives in the Brüning Cabinet, wished to support it, while the membership and functionaries of the DHV displayed pro–National Socialist tendencies. But all efforts to solve the dilemma by including the NSDAP in the Government were doomed from the very outset. The DHV remained stuck in its ambiguous position; in the end, without being able to exert any real influence on National Socialist policy, it substantially furthered and accelerated the drift of the middle-class white-collar workers to the NSDAP. Many a disenchanted bridge-builder ended up by breaking with Hitler or in belated opposition to the Third Reich; Habermann himself died in 1944 as a leading member of the resistance. But after 1929, many DHV functionaries followed the road into the NSDAP, strengthened the National Socialist Reichstag delegation, and gave the party the broad basis among white-collar workers which buttressed its claim of being a "party of all working people" and also helped in solving its precarious financial situation. The transition to a mass party was prepared and accelerated by such—even though only partial—unions with social special-interest organizations. To the degree to which its activism attracted organizations, the small cadre and "elite" party was able to stage its rapid transition to a "people's party" and its infiltration of various classes and spheres of influence of the Republic.

This connection was no less clearly in evidence in the sphere of agricultural organizations. Although initially the NSDAP, being a petty-bourgeois, semisocialist *ressentiment* movement, had practically no dealings with the peasantry and no agricultural policy, its anti-Semitic, anticapitalist pronouncements nonetheless contained elements of the criticism of the structural reorganization and urbanization of modern society prevalent in the early anti-Semitic movement of the 1880's and 1890's.[27] The combination of biological ideology and social and economic resentments eventuated in the slogan of "blood and soil," by which Walter Darré, the Argentine-born Nazi agrarian high priest, author of *Das Bauerntum als Lebensquell der nordischen Rasse* (*The Peasantry as the Life Source of the Nordic Race;* 1928) and *Neuadel aus Blut und Boden* (*New Nobility from Blood and Soil;* 1934), sought to move the peasantry, as the first estate in the pro-

---

[27] In agrarian Schleswig-Holstein, anti-Semitic candidates won more than 6 per cent of the votes in 1898.

jected National Socialist state, into the center of the racist rejuvenation creed of National Socialism. *Nährstand* and *Wehrstand* (peasantry and soldiery) were to be the pillars of the future new order.

These ideological declamations coincided with the persistent unrest of a peasantry faced with adjustment to the postwar world. This sense of unrest gave rise to a strong organized agrarian movement, especially in rural Schleswig-Holstein. There the economic and social causes of the agrarian protest movement were further augmented by traditional anti-Prussian sentiments magnified by the fact of Prussian Socialist rule. The SPD basically was considered an "urban" party. The farmers' organizations looked to the center and right-wing parties for support of their interests. Their conservative-romantic, anti-Semitic stand against modern capitalist society found expression in the slogan of the "Green Democracy," which was posited against the "Golden Democracy." Behind this loomed an antiliberal, middle-class ideology which was as much opposed to big capital and its factories and merchandise marts as to socialism and the feared decline to the status of laborers.

With this ideological turn, the farm movement came close to the social criticism of the Nazis; contacts between the two were merely a question of time and organizational links. The writings of Langbehn, himself a native of Schleswig-Holstein, undoubtedly influenced this ideological trend. The "soil-rooted" national community was pitted against the bureaucratic, capitalist, commercial modern state identified with the democratic Republic. To be sure, the truly conservative nature of this agrarian protest movement set it apart from the NSDAP's revolutionary, technological, organizational approach toward politics. The relationship between the farm organizations and National Socialism was based on misuse and manipulation rather than on genuine cooperation. Yet this did not prevent the peasant movement, in tactics and organizations so inferior to the National Socialists, from preparing, and to a large measure making possible, the National Socialist victory in Schleswig-Holstein. In January, 1928, there began a series of mass demonstrations and strikes against the crisis and indebtedness of the small farmers, which radical spokesmen turned into terrorist conflicts with the government. Even thought Hitler, in line with his legality course, steered clear of some of the violent actions, this movement clearly benefited the most radical of the right-wing parties.

The collapse of the revolts created a vacuum which the better organized and tactically superior NSDAP, revising its agrarian plank in the "unalterable" party program by watering down the unpopular "land reform" plank, proceeded to fill. It outmaneuvered the competing German Nationals, who anyway seemed too closely allied with a despised capitalism and too Prussia-oriented. Although in 1924 the DNVP had still garnered 33 per cent of the votes in Schleswig-Holstein, it suffered a devastating decline between 1928 (23 per cent) and 1930 (6 per cent), the sole beneficiary being the NSDAP (1928: 4 per cent; 1930: 27 per cent). While prior to 1924 the NSDAP had shown greater strength in the cities, it now dominated in the rural areas. The middle-class electorate of Schleswig-Holstein collapsed completely; in the elections of 1932, the middle-class parties (including the DNVP) were practically demolished between the 51 per cent of the National Socialists and the 37 per cent of the Left. This fact had major repercussions in other agricultural regions of Germany, even those with vastly different problems. Schleswig-Holstein became a milestone on the NSDAP's forward march toward a popular mass party.

The "agrarian" apparatus of the NSDAP, which Walter Darré built in the summer of 1930 in the wake of this trend, served the instrumentalization, not the reform and rescue, of agriculture. The internal discussion between Darré and Hitler dealt solely with the question of "how agriculture can be used in the present battle for the state." Darré, in a secret report to Hitler, named three goals: exploitation of the unrest and farm strikes against the "urbanized government of the Republic"; securing of the agricultural base and the "ideologic" winning over of the peasantry as the "life motor of the national organism and biological blood renewal source of the body politic"; and utilization of the peasants as the pillars of the new settlements in the "eastern regions" to be conquered from the Slavs.[28] In this sense, one can speak of an organizational agrarian policy-net being spread over the Reich. Agitation and propaganda in the countryside, infiltration and increased influence in farm organizations, the ousting of German National leadership, and the spurring on of rivalries between the various groups—these were the tactics that brought the National Socialist leadership early success in Lower Saxony as well, and after 1929 helped it roll up the largest electoral gains in all agrarian regions.

The NSDAP did not succeed in making like inroads among the workers and the trade unions. Despite all efforts of the "left" wing, the NSDAP claim to being a "socialist workers' party" remained a propaganda façade. Compared with the early days of the party and its (Bohemian) precursors, the newly formed NSDAP had, sociologically speaking, turned into a middle-class right-wing party without any ties to organized labor. This fact, however, was consciously glossed over by the claim that National Socialism was healing the class divisions between the middle class and the workers through the concept of the "national community." Hitler's slogan of "workers of brawn and brain" was the formula with which the NSDAP sought to cover over its failure in the battle against "Marxism," both before and after its transition to a mass party. The conversion of the organized socialist workers to "national socialism" was one of the early aims of National Socialism. But the workers did not come to their meetings; the membership of the NSDAP was composed of the lower middle class, of

[28] Nürnberger Dokumente (unpublished), NG-448.

merchants, artisans, white-collar workers, military adventurers, and youthful romantic activists.

Hitler's attitude toward the workers' question and his knowledge in this area were not very profound; the stories in *Mein Kampf* about his existential debate with Marxism are apparently pure legend. He saw socialism—as he informed the "socialists" in his party—as a "purely Jewish invention to pit the German people against one another." In another context, he said: "What is this socialism?! If the people have something to eat and their pleasures, then they have their socialism." [29] His agitation and propaganda with the help of clamorous mass meetings, martial parades, paramilitary organizations, and subordination proved to be ineffective when confronted with a population group with great organizations and traditions, with a sense of mission, and political and social power. But Hitler was skeptical of all conventional efforts of recruitment among special groups, let alone the formation of trade unions. His metier was and remained the general appeal to the (despised) "masses" and their collective emotions. The lasting conflict with the Strasser group was due in no small measure to Strasser's efforts to establish contact with the unions.

True, after 1928 the NSDAP discontinued its unsuccessful fight against the unions and came out of its isolation. This opening toward the Left was, however, handled very carefully, and even in the era of the mass party, it never scored comparable successes in the camp of labor. Under the slogan "Into the Factories" (*Hinein in die Betriebe,* or Hib), Gregor Strasser built a "National Socialist Factory Cell Organization" (Nationalsozialistische Betriebszellenorganisation, or NSBO) in Berlin, though until the spring of 1933 it remained a small splinter group in the labor camp, particularly since the working plants, more than any other sector, lacked the necessary National Socialist subleaders to form cells. The debate about the right tactics periodically flared up anew. The wish for genuine work among the trade unions (Strasser group) ran up against the purely propagandistic and utilitarian ideas of Goebbels (particularly in Berlin) and of Hitler himself, both of whom had little use for reform and were interested solely in revolutionizing the country. Yet, even in this respect, the party had become more receptive by the time the mass membership influx had begun. [30]

At any rate, the effort begun in 1928 to win over the growing mass of unemployed proved more successful. The centrally organized recruitment units of the National Socialist propaganda paper *Der Erwerbslose* (*The Unemployed*) would distribute leaflets in the unemployment-compensation offices, provoking counterpropaganda, brawls, and expulsion from the premises. But they did succeed in making some inroads into the working class from this side; after the onset of the

[29] Krebs, *op. cit.*, pp. 46, 143.

[30] See, especially, Hans Gerd Schumann, *Nationalsozialismus und Gewerkschaftsbewegung* (Hanover, 1958) and Reinhard Kühnl, *Die nationalsozialistische Linke 1925 bis 1930* (Meisenheim, 1966).

economic crisis, the unions and Left parties were in a most sensitive spot. These offices were also the place where young Communist activists, impelled by economic problems, not infrequently were induced to become SA mercenaries. The pragmatic leadership thought it could use them without regard to principle and without fear of infiltration from within. But as a rule the cells of the unemployed won only the driftwood—young unstable workers, down-and-out petty-bourgeois, or unemployed white-collar workers.

On the whole, the Hib campaign suffered from the dilemma of its anti-union approach of organizing both workers and employers in the NSBO. The Nazi community ideology was unable to gain a footing among the class-conscious workers; it succeeded in the German Labor Front (Deutsche Arbeitsfront, or DAF) with the smashing of the unions and political parties. Yet, here too an outpost had been set up —if not for the working class, at least, after the political takeover, for the taking of power in the industrial enterprises and for paralyzing resistance.

It was the rural and urban "middle class," in the broad sense of the term, which started and carried out the breakthrough of the NSDAP. The "panic of the middle class," which set in with the outbreak of the economic crisis, was sharpened by the fact that the middle class felt threatened not only economically but, more important, socially as well. The violent reaction which drove many of its members toward the radical Right arose out of a subjective feeling of crisis in a time of social upheaval in an industrial, democratic age. The power of the old middle class continued to decline within an expanding population; its nervous irritability and susceptibility to radical slogans was the result of this prestige loss as well as of economic plight. Out of a general desire for security after the catastrophe of the inflation, this group, after having for so long maintained an apolitical isolation from democracy, reacted in a markedly political fashion to the new crisis. And that was why it turned to the "new" party.[31]

The successful onslaught of National Socialism on the middle classes begun in 1929 was closely connected with the frequently invoked "anticapitalist sentiments" of these groups. What they wanted was not socialism but protection of the small property owners against the growing incursion of big capital; the middle classes, contrary to Marxist expectations, did not come over into the ideological realm of socialism. Generally, in times of crisis the hopeless elements in the middle class tend to listen to fascist slogans, while the working class, on the other hand, tends toward Communism. The conflict between ideas of property and socialization, fought out with particular sharpness in the mixed industrial-agrarian regions, brought a parting of the ways. National Socialist propaganda knew how to operate flexibly and attractively without ignoring the pro-union, anticapitalist sentiments of

---

[31] Cf. Theodor Geiger, *Die soziale Schichtung des deutschen Volkes* (Stuttgart, 1932), pp. 106 ff.; K. D. Bracher, *op. cit.*, chap. vi.

those middle-class workers toward whom the appeal of the "workers' party" was initially directed. The slogan of the dual fight of the "idealistic, national" people against the decadent "foreign powers" of both proletarian as well as capitalist materialism proclaimed the primacy of national "idealism" over economic materialism.

Growing pressure from both camps, from egalitarian socialism as well as powerful capitalist organizations, put great stress on the middle classes and threatened to split them into hopelessly disenfranchised heaps (*Interessenhaufen*). But here was a program which, in combination with the social-imperialist solution of the *Lebensraum* philosophy, promised to resolve the conflict between economic situation and social prestige in favor of the latter. In the final phase of the Republic, when it had become obvious that no inroads were being made into the working-class parties and their unions—aside from the unemployed—even when scoring major electoral victories, National Socialist mass propaganda was directed almost exclusively toward the middle classes. This concentration on a social group which unquestionably occupied a key position brought the loosely knit middle-of-the-road parties, with the exception of the Center, to the brink of disintegration. Moreover, the NSDAP mobilized many new voters and nonvoters, until it ran up against those sociologically conditioned limits which in 1932 put an end to its further expansion.

Thus, though the NSDAP failed to become the all-inclusive popular movement demanded by its ideology, it did nonetheless become the powerful party of the middle classes, and not only because of its broad economic promises. The heterogeneous, tense nature of middle-class economic thinking set natural limits to the unifying efforts on the economic-ideological plane. Therefore, contemporary socialist interpretations which saw the NSDAP in purely socio-economic terms as a reactionary middle-class and peasant movement considered only one side of the phenomenon and ultimately failed in the task of unmasking it ideologically and effectively halting its progress. What is important is that National Socialist propaganda, with its appeal to the "national idealism" of the middle classes, brought into play attractions and ties which promised an integration beyond the manifold immediate interests.

National Socialism's dynamics and appeal—like Fascism's—did not lie in a socially closed interest movement of the middle classes—that is, a class movement—but, on the contrary, in its emphasis on being a unifying movement of the most varied and antagonistic groups. The fact that it was able to develop this cohesive force across heterogeneous interests, considerations, and feelings is connected with the lack of fervor that accompanied the founding of the Republic in a time of military collapse and fear of a Left revolution.

The predominantly Social Democratic working class was unable, even in the democratic Republic, to rid itself of the charge of being anational, and since the Wilhelminian authoritarian state had not imbued them with a more profound patriotic tradition, the workers confined themselves to sober skepticism. Large segments of the middle classes, on the other hand, once more manifested an urge for the glorifying myth of the fatherland which the Republic, with its manifold international obligations, could not satisfy with sufficient splendor and pomp. National Socialism built on this dissatisfaction. With an eye toward the failure of its labor policy, it did away with earlier concessions to socialist economic ideas and concentrated on the anticapitalism of the lower and middle bourgeoisie. This turn did cause some internal conflicts, such as the splitting off of (Otto) Strasser's "socialist" wing in the summer of 1930. But at the same time, the National Socialist ideologues with their concept of nationalism went far beyond the traditionalist conservative patriotism of the bourgeois middle classes. They elevated a blood-based, profoundly unhistorical idea of nation to an all-encompassing absolute. The activist, revolutionary postwar youth were the pillar of this "nationalism." To them, the "national revolution" did not conjure up glorious memories of the empire or a renewal of "bourgeois" prestige in a leveled society but rather the triumph of the pursuit of unconditional power. For them the war, and not prewar Germany, was the conscious, determining experience and point of orientation. They held the key positions within the NSDAP; the victory of their blood romanticism over the historical patriotism of the bourgeoisie was an expression both of profound misunderstanding and social insecurity as well as of political-ideological confusion and weakness. The vote of the white-collar workers, the middle class, and the peasants for the NSDAP, the most radical opposition party and noisiest anti-Communist movement, primarily was a vote against the existing state, not a vote for the barely defined National Socialist state. The NSDAP supported these voters in their desperate two-front battle against capital and proletariat, so vital a part of fascist movements.

To be sure, every formulation of National Socialist aims, every concrete treatment of the special interests behind the ideological ideal, reawakened the many differences and tensions within the middle class; proposals acceptable to business were looked upon with mistrust by the higher wage earners favoring trade-union ideas. The antisocialist turn of the NSDAP brought with it the danger that the multiplicity of interest groups in its fold might seriously press for clear-cut positions. The question arose how long and in what form the multifarious middle classes could be kept together with nothing more than a propaganda program. In 1932, the limits of the movement and the first signs of its deterioration became apparent, and there were many who believed that with the expected economic upturn or with responsible participation in government, it would face dissolution. But then at the last moment came the leap to power which relieved the party of all democratic responsibility for its political course. In view of the new upturn in the international economic situation, it was seemingly able to fulfill a number of the promises so magnanimously scattered by its propaganda.

The fact that the crisis of the middle classes was not really being solved in the Third Reich through any "corporate new order" no longer mattered. As far as the middle class was concerned, the slogans had done their job in 1933. Using the political tools which it had won in a ruthless power grab, the NSDAP was able to replace the laborious tactics of mass appeal with the tight power-monopoly of the totalitarian governing party.

THE BREAKTHROUGH OF 1929

The NSDAP of 1928 was still a small though tightly knit party waiting for its chance. Thanks to Hitler's victory over rivals and individual efforts, it had kept to the road of legality and put all its expectations on a new radicalization of the political climate. Hitler himself was interested primarily in foreign and revisionist policies. They represented the best hope for breaking into the stabilized structure of the Republic and for changing the party and parliamentary situation in his favor. Just as in his (then unpublished) piece on National Socialist foreign policy (1928), the main attack of his propaganda and speeches, as for example at a leadership conference in Munich (September, 1928), was directed against Stresemann's international policy, making "fanatical nationalism"—the conscious and systematic undermining of faith in international understanding, the League of Nations, and world peace—the central means and aim of National Socialist policy. There was only one right in the world, and that was one's own strength. And, indeed, the new chance came with the renewed intensification of the debate on foreign policy and revision in the summer of 1929.

Stresemann's dogged pursuit of gradual revision had proved successful. That, however, did not prevent the German Nationals from greeting every step with sharp attacks on the "policy of fulfillment." The "too little" or "too late" with which they reviled every agreement and every forward move in turn impeded Franco-German *rapprochement* and reawakened old misgivings. At the very moment when Stresemann's efforts were heading toward a new partial success, the impatient nationalist resentments re-formed, for the first time since 1923, in a strong countermovement of German Nationals and National Socialists. After lengthy negotiations, a special commission headed by Owen D. Young had, in July, 1929, proposed new regulations of German reparations payments far more realistic than the provisions of the Dawes Plan though by no means in complete accord with German wishes. Stresemann nonetheless came out for acceptance, after having successfully linked the new proposal to the evacuation of Allied troops from the Rhineland, which in fact was completed in the summer of 1930, five years before the date specified.

But shortly before Stresemann's death (October 3, 1929), a truly tragic event in these circumstances, the right-wing opposition took advantage of the rekindling of the dispute over reparations to land a blow against the Republic itself. On July 9, 1929, German National and Stahlhelm leaders with great fanfare instituted a national committee for a plebiscite against the Young Plan, in which the National Socialists, with a sure instinct for the main chance, actively joined. The goal of the agitation was a law drafted by the National Socialist Reichstag Deputy Frick "against the enslavement of the German people," calling upon the Government to fight for the repeal of the war-guilt provision of the Versailles Treaty (Article 231) as well as the cessation of all reparations payments and the immediate evacuation of the occupied territories. In addition, every German minister or public official who had signed "tribute agreements" was to be tried for treason.

This radical and unrealistic move failed completely, but the wild campaign it unleashed, together with the farm unrest, presented the National Socialists with a second great opportunity for the mobilization of their propaganda and organizational apparatus. But above all, it took the NSDAP out of the isolation of a radical splinter-group and brought it, as the most militant fighting organization, within the frame of a socially influential, well-financed coalition of the antirepublican Right now being formed against the Weimar democracy. At the head of this "national opposition" stood Alfred Hugenberg, a wealthy and influential pigheaded Pan-German and narrow-minded reactionary. A former director of Krupp, he headed a large network of newspapers, a news agency, and the largest German film company (Ufa). He thus influenced a significant portion of the press and also controlled substantial sums contributed by industry to the parties of the Right. Hatred of Social Democracy and the democratic Republic was the motive force of his life and activities. After the electoral defeat of the German Nationalists in December, 1928, he forced out the more moderate leadership under Count Westarp and steered the DNVP toward the radical course which reached a first high point in the fight against the Young Plan. While a conservative wing left the party, and later on, beginning in 1930, supported the Brüning Government, Hugenberg decided for a fighting union with Hitler.

Through this alliance, the long-despised NSDAP gained new access to social respectability, finances, and influence; suddenly the party found itself with undreamed-of propaganda and organizational resources. The contacts with Fritz Thyssen were revived; a growing number of economic leaders began to show an interest in the NSDAP and in the propaganda talents of its leadership. Once more, Hitler moved into the position of the courted "drummer." And now he showed himself better able than in 1923 to handle the problems as well as the opportunities arising out of this role. He soon became the strongest and loudest member of the newly formed "national opposition." Again his self-confident, blinded partners believed they could use him for their objectives and then tame him. No one was able to match the venom and ruthlessness of National Socialist propaganda. The NSDAP did not share any of the inhibitions of its allies; more radical than the others, it turned the campaign into a vast indictment of the Government, the democratic parties, and the "system." By labeling the political leaders of the Grand Coalition traitors and reviling their efforts for revisions as "enslavement," the NSDAP more and more directed the fear of the threatening economic crisis into the channels of its radical revision and dictatorship propaganda. The wave of hatred, lies, and denunciation that swept the nation had its desired effect, even though the National Socialists obviously saw the fight against the Young Plan only as a means toward an end—the elimination of democracy. Toward this end, political intoxicants were brought into play—and financed for Hitler—which ultimately even the stolid German Nationals were not equal to. But Hugenberg remained stricken by blindness up to the very last, and with him many of his friends in the party and Stahlhelm, and particularly the future ally Franz von Papen.

The counterefforts of the state were weak, although it seemed as if the attack had been repulsed for the time being. The Müller Government, and Müller's successor after March, 1930, Brüning, sought to counter these campaigns with logical arguments, but they underestimated the power of emotional thinking and the growing influence of those who knew how to mobilize this force. The onslaught of the radical Right was, to be sure, apparently unsuccessful. They could barely muster the necessary 10 per cent signatures for the plebiscite against the Young Plan, and on November 30, 1929, the Reichstag rejected the radical draft law of the national opposition with a resounding majority of 318 to 82 votes. And the plebiscite that followed (December 22, 1929) was supported by only 13.8 per cent of the voters, far fewer than the votes the DNVP and NSDAP had won in the Reichstag elections of 1928 (18.4 per cent). In the Rhineland, where the plebiscite held particular meaning because of the connection between the Young Plan and the evacuation of the Rhineland, the percentage was between 2 and 5; the national opposition won its greatest victories in eastern Germany: Pomerania, 33 per cent; East Prussia, 26 per cent; Frankfurt/Oder, 24 per cent. But there still was no question of a "breakthrough." On the contrary, the dismay of moderate German Nationals took on more impassioned forms; Count Westarp now also resigned as the parliamentary whip of his party. However, this merely accelerated the radicalization of the Hugenberg party; above all, Hitler, as the stronger, more purposeful leader, with the best organized groups of the radical Right, moved more and more into the limelight. The importance of the campaign lay not in the plebiscite itself but in the chances it offered to National Socialist propaganda. Moreover, the result of the plebiscite once more gave the democrats that sense of false security which was responsible for the underestimation of the NSDAP and the weak defenses in the years to come.

Meanwhile, a second major development helped to solidify the newly won position of the NSDAP and to change it from a splinter party into a quickly growing popular movement: the beginning of the world economic crisis.

Growing unemployment, a sign of approaching crisis, set in at the end of 1928, and the New York Stock Market crash on Black Friday, October 24, 1929, only three weeks after Stresemann's death, added to the economic and even more so to the psychological effects of this development. Germany was particularly hard hit, since its economic recovery depended largely on short-term credits that were now being canceled. In addition, the psychological impact of the memories of the inflation had immediate political effects. Once more, Versailles and reparations were made responsible for the developing crisis, despite the fact that Britain and the wealthy United States were hit with equal force. The enemies of the Republic proclaimed triumphantly that they had been right in their agitation against Germany's "enslavement." Little heed was paid to more differentiated explanations. The fact that agriculture had been in a state of crisis since 1927 only accelerated the chain reaction of falling production, unemployment, and business failures, adding to the feeling of disaster.

One of the early consequences of the economic crisis was the weakening of the labor unions, one of the props of the democratic Republic. The unions lost influence and control over the rapidly growing number of unemployed. Their membership declined, their economic power dwindled, the weapon of the strike became blunted to the degree to which the idle labor force increased. The union-allied SPD, the largest political party of the Republic, was similarly affected; 1929 saw a resurgence of the tendency to stay out of the government, a feeling that was strengthened by the attitude of the bourgeois coalition partners, particularly the DVP, which after the death of Stresemann began to veer to the Right and away from the Socialist-controlled Government. But above all, in the camp of Hindenburg, who until now had apparently carried out his office in constitutional fashion, there now began the maturation of long-nurtured plans of right-wing publicists, political law specialists, and the military for an extraparliamentary Presidential government.

In the crisis of the winter of 1929–30, it became clear that even the period of "normalization" had supplied the democratic regime with only weak foundations. Once again the party system displayed serious functional disorders. In the political consciousness of the people, there again came to the fore the resentments against Versailles and the outcome of the war, the terrible memories of inflation and collapse. National Socialist propaganda latched on to this, and from the campaign against the Young Plan went over directly to a general attack on the Weimar "system." The Nazis, following a well-tried recipe, proceeded to put the blame for all complicated problems and pressing daily burdens on a few apparently simple causes: the "November criminals" and "system parties," the Marxists and internationalists, the economic profiteers, and behind them all, the Jews. The crisis was more than welcome to the National Socialist leaders, who in this respect found themselves in significant agreement with their hostile brothers on the other side, the Communists. Both saw the crisis as essential and inevitable, a consequence of the regime; both in their fashion held to a theory of impoverishment, according to which the solution lay in a catastrophe and the overthrow of the democratic Republic; both therefore worked energetically against all efforts to improve the situation. Consequently, National Socialist propaganda claimed that the German

Government was unworthy of credit and warned the outside world against granting the Republic any financial assistance. Again and again, the National Socialist leaders admitted with cynical candor that they welcomed the crisis and the further deterioration of the political and economic conditions, and that they would do anything in their power to speed it up. They liked nothing less than German successes on the question of revision and reparations, which after all they held responsible for all existing ills.

The general situation provided the radical critics with sufficient fuel: decline of tax receipts, the growing funds required by the unemployment insurance, intensification of partisan squabbles on how the deficit was to be met. The SPD came out for higher taxes, the DVP for the abolition of social welfare and for lowered wages. The resignation of the SPD Minister of Finance, Rudolf Hilferding, at the end of the year hinted at the collapse of the Grand Coalition and lent support to the tendency toward a return to bourgeois minority governments and withdrawal of the SPD from responsibility. The fight over social policy accompanying the intensification of the crisis and the split of the democratic parties furnished the anti-Marxist and anti-union propaganda of the NSDAP with added ammunition. Growing numbers of economic leaders and the bourgeois Right were sympathetic toward the militant mass agitation of the allegedly "social" but antisocialist Hitler movement; its "excesses" were tolerated with mild feelings of superiority as unfortunate by-products of a radical national idealism.

In the course of the year, an increasingly favorable set of circumstances favored the organizational and numerical expansion of the NSDAP; the era of stagnation and waiting was drawing to a close. The earliest visible breakthrough was accomplished among the students.[32] Here generational problems and activist enthusiasm for radical solutions, anti-Republican attitudes of many student organizations, and poor future prospects coalesced. Just as in the early postwar years universities and fraternities had been closely allied with the Free Corps and combat leagues and had supported the Black Reichswehr with its own fighting groups, so had nationalistic and radical Right ideas remained a vociferous element of university life. To stand outside and against the "system" was considered good form. The students tried to imitate and rival their predecessors of the early postwar years. They were helped in no small measure by the negative or aloof attitude of many of their professors who were unable to come to terms with the democracy. But more importantly, the traditionalist, socially exclusive structure of higher education, which kept large segments of the population from institutions of higher learning, helped conserve reactionary organizations or favored radical antidemocratic tendencies among stu-

[32] Wolfgang Zorn, "Student Politics in the Weimar Republic," *Journal of Contemporary History*, V (1970), 128 ff. *Nationalsozialismus und die deutsche Universität* (Berlin, 1966), pp. 24 ff., 127 ff., 156 ff., and *passim*. H. P. Bleuel and A. Klimert, *Deutsche Studenten auf dem Weg ins Dritte Reich* (Gütersloh, 1967).

dents. Professors and students felt themselves the victims of the social upheavals of the times, and their status and prestige threatened by democratic ideas of government and society. A large portion of the revived fraternities and corps organizations were anti-Semitic in theory and practice; the influence of the "old grads," with their Wilhelminian mentality, combined with the resentments produced by the crisis-ridden postwar years.

Only a small minority of free student groups were united in a Republican central organization. They faced the "German University Ring," a powerful union of nationalist, *völkisch*-oriented, and above all dueling fraternities. The Ring was an early affiliate of the "United Patriotic Organizations"; among its demands was "Greater German" expansion to Austria, Bohemia, and to ethnic German groups elsewhere, buttressing these demands with racist arguments in radical campaigns against the "Jewification" of the universities. As early as 1924, the Ring won a majority of student votes in numerous universities— e.g., Königsberg, Greifswald, Rostock, Kiel, Göttingen, Hanover, Jena, Darmstadt, Karlsruhe, Erlangen, and the Technical Institute of Munich. In the years to come, constant conflicts at the universities and with the higher-education authorities, strongly supported by the anti-Semitic position and activities of the student self-government organization (ASTA), kept this radicalism alive. Whereas Bavaria permitted this development to continue, the Prussian Ministry of Culture under C. A. Becker in 1927 finally sought to put a stop to it by limiting the self-government of ASTA and halting the discrimination against "non-Aryan" students. This action resulted in a further radicalization, increasing disorders, and a growing influence of National Socialist propaganda. Thus it came about that the ASTA elections of 1929, held before the general elections, let loose a National Socialist storm at the universities which pre-empted and accelerated developments. Meanwhile, the National Socialist student organization, in alliance with other right-wing groups which it skillfully used, gained considerable power. Ultimately it succeeded in hitching to its wagon not only the *völkisch*-nationalist student corporations and fraternities, but also the increasingly radicalized main organization of German students.

At first, the majority of nonorganized students remained politically indifferent, until the new rise of the national opposition, which found its greatest supporters among the students. The lack of contact of that segment of youth which aspired toward leadership in the democratic state manifested itself in a long series of scandals and unrest, which after 1928 assumed an increasingly nationalistic character and was directed primarily against politically and "racially" undesirable professors. The commemorative day that defined the political profile of the institutes of higher education was not Constitution Day, which never achieved symbolic force, but rather—in deference to the rigidly maintained Bismarck myth—the "Reich Founding Day," January 18. Governmental countermeasures remained too weak. Political education and training were sadly deficient. "Academic freedom" increasingly became a factor exploited for the benefit of antidemocratism, reaction, and extreme nationalism.

National Socialist student groups moved into the forefront everywhere, at first primarily at the cost of the German Nationals but soon also of the more moderate groups; only the small left-wing groups were able to hold on to their membership. In Leipzig, National Socialist representation had quintupled by 1930; in Greifswald, they were the strongest group; the Universities of Bonn, Munich, Würzburg, and Hamburg were the least infected.

The NSDAP achieved large-scale success by infiltrating and assimilating the student corporations even before its successes among the youth organizations. The activism of its followers was in effective contrast to the usual indifference of the moderate and politically uninterested students—a fact which here too lent the radical groups a superiority disproportionate to their numerical strength. The party press supported this activism with every means at its disposal—as, for example, by accusing the German National students of alliances with the SPD. Or they provoked the university administrations and in this way won over stirred-up students. The tolerance of the responsible authorities permitted the organs of student self-government to become arenas for noisy National Socialist undertakings—with the result that the ASTA elections turned into a vast triumph of the radical Right, even before the NSDAP breakthrough in the Reichstag elections of 1930. In 1929, the National Socialists won an absolute majority in the Universities of Erlangen and Greifswald; in 1930, Breslau, Berlin's Technical and Veterinary institutes, Giessen, Rostock, Jena, and Königsberg were added to this list; at other universities, they won almost 50 per cent. At the Technical Institute of Munich, things had gone so far that the student government in July, 1930, unanimously thanked the then Minister of Thuringia, Frick, for the appointment of Hans F. K. Günther to the chair of Racial Research at the University of Jena—made against the wishes of the University —and demanded the creation of similar chairs at all other universities. This trend continued and brought unusually large participation in university elections the next year (1931). The National Socialist student organization gained practically a majority of ASTA seats in numerous universities, with the technical colleges in the lead; the heaviest losses were suffered by the German National groups. The early disaffection of university students went hand in hand with the alienation of the youth movement; it signaled a psychological loss of power of democracy which probably mattered even more than the lasting mistrust of, and opposition to the "system" in the Army, the middle class, the civil service, and business.

At the moment in which Hitler, in alliance with Hugenberg, succeeded in his breakthrough into German public life, the NSDAP for the first time also demonstrated the rapidly growing strength of its organization in a great mass show. The Nuremberg party congress of August 3–4, 1929, brought together an unprecedented number of officials, followers, and SA formations from all parts of Germany. Carefully planned and organized with technical virtuosity—thirty-five special trains alone rolled into Nuremberg—the proceedings of the congress were fixed down to the smallest detail and units. Again twenty-four new SA units were sworn in, most of them from Schleswig-Holstein, Austria, and Bavaria. About 30,000 SA men, Hitler Youth, and finally the still small SS under its new leader, Himmler, marched through Nuremberg; a memorial celebration featuring Ritter von Epp and a Hitler oration were further high points. Influential economic leaders, such as the wealthy coal and iron magnate Emil Kirdorf, who had come to Nuremberg as an honorary guest, went away impressed. The rally marked the successful reconstruction of the party and SA and simultaneously the transition to the era of mass organization and mass demonstrations. By the end of 1929, the SA rivaled the manpower of the Reichswehr (100,000). With the greatly accelerated propaganda campaign in the fall of 1929, the NSDAP was once more able to make major inroads among the German electorate.

The plebiscite against the Young Plan had failed, but electoral statistics showed that this was essentially a defeat for the German Nationals. In the state elections held in this period, the NSDAP registered strong gains in Saxony, Thuringia, Mecklenburg, Baden, Lübeck, Brunswick, as well as in the Prussian municipal elections. On May 18, 1929, 5 per cent of Saxony's electorate voted for the Hitler party; a year later (June, 1930), 14.4 per cent did, and in September, 1930, their number had risen to 21.5 per cent. The parliamentary elections in Thuringia on December 8, 1929, had brought NSDAP gains from 4.6 per cent (1927) to 11.3 per cent. It was there that the NSDAP succeeded in becoming a member of a coalition government: incredibly enough, Wilhelm Frick, the putschist of 1923, was appointed Minister of the Interior of that small state; he promptly began to agitate for the hiring of National Socialists by the police, bringing on a conflict between the Central Government and Thuringia. In Coburg, the National Socialists even won a majority in the municipal government. Now the masses started streaming into the party. At the end of 1929, the membership stood at 178,000; by March of the next year, it had increased to 210,000. National Socialist propaganda held a lack of enthusiasm of the divided German Nationals responsible for the failure of the plebiscite. Hitler himself countered all internal criticism (particularly of the Strasser wing) of the alliance with the "reactionaries" around Hugenberg by pointing to these tactical successes; in the future, he never felt any scruples about breaking this "national" alliance whenever he felt strong enough. Thus finally, in June, 1933, he also destroyed the DNVP, after it had played out its fatal role in the seizure of power.

Long before the famous parliamentary elections of September, 1930, the successful course which within three years was to bring the splinter party to total power had begun.

IV

The Road to Power

Among the variety of factors which contributed to the accelerated rise of National Socialism after 1928, four in particular stand out:

1. The radicalization of the German National Party once Hugenberg gained control made it possible for Hitler to share in the social respectability, the political influence, and the financial resources of these circles and simultaneously to become part of a broad "National Opposition" to the Weimar Republic. His methods resembled those he had used in 1923 in his dealings with the patriotic organizations, only now he was determined not to let himself be outwitted by his confederates.

2. The economic crisis, bringing with it the collapse of small business and industry and rapidly rising unemployment, filled the middle class and peasantry with even greater panic than had the postwar inflation. Politically, this panic was expressed by attacks on Versailles and reparations; socially (particularly on the part of the petty bourgeoisie), it took the form of fear of proletarianization; and ideologically, it surfaced as fear of Communism. National Socialist propaganda —at once revisionist, social-anticapitalist, anti-Marxist, and anti-Communist—seemed to offer the simplest and most persuasive alternative.

3. New governmental crises after Stresemann's death smoothed the road toward an extraparliamentary quasi dictatorship, which weakened the influence of the democratic parties and organizations in favor of the President, the Army command, and bureaucratic rule, and prepared public opinion for dictatorial solutions. With the diminishing of democratic responsibility after the change of government of 1930 and, more particularly, of 1932, by which political life was reduced to government by emergency law, faith in democratic solutions evaporated. The resultant power vacuum offered wide openings for the radicalism of the Left and even more so for that of the Right.

4. Initially, the National Socialists patterned their technique for seizing power on the 1922 tactics of the Italian Fascists, although they

made more determined and successful use of modern means of mass communication through the unrivaled combination of force and persuasion, terror and propaganda, pseudo-legal measures and deception and violence. The National Socialists pitted the technique of the *fait accompli* and of quick, propagandistically inflated sham successes against the effectiveness of institutional and traditional safeguards. Once it has seized power, such a regime cannot really be overthrown from within, even if initially it holds only a minority of government positions, as was the case with the Fascists (1922) and the National Socialists (1933). The die is cast before the actual seizure of power; later on, the only possibility remaining is its overthrow by outside forces.

DEMOCRACY IN CRISIS

Political developments after 1929 were overshadowed by the psychological effects of the steady rise in unemployment. According to official figures—and these did not include unregistered unemployed and part-time workers—1.3 million employable workers were unemployed in September, 1929; one year later, this figure had risen to 3 million; in September, 1931, to 4.35 million; and in 1932, to 5.1 million. In the winter months of 1931–32 and 1932–33, unemployment exceeded 6 million. This meant, in effect, that one out of two German families was affected—the lower middle class and white-collar workers no less than the working class; the first two groups, moreover, felt threatened by the loss of social prestige and status. The trend toward the Left, which worked for the Communist Party, was matched by a rush to the Right, and the most radical of the right-wing parties reaped the greatest profits.

However, the objective conditions of the economic crisis do not by themselves explain why the economic crisis turned into a social and political crisis, and ultimately into a crisis of the democratic system. What is of greater significance is the fact that in Germany, in contrast to countries like England and the United States, which were experiencing equally great economic pressures, Government, political parties, interest groups, Army, and public-opinion leaders, in part gloating and in part helpless, saw the economic crisis as a crisis of the "system." The combination of political inexperience, lack of familiarity with the workings of parliamentary democracy, and powerful residues of authoritarianism proved fatal.

To be sure, the Depression offered the partially submerged destructive forces of an antidemocratic radicalism a major opening. But the political development that culminated in the overpowering of the Republic by National Socialism was by no means inevitable. In 1923, in similar circumstances but then under the aegis of Reich President Ebert, the onslaught of the radical enemy had been successfully repulsed. The fact that the crisis of 1929–33 took a different course cannot be explained by economic factors alone, nor can it be looked upon as a consequence of democracy, for Hitler after all did not come to power via a parliamentary majority. Under the prevailing conditions, the political activities of an influential group of critics and enemies of the Republic took on major importance. This of course holds true for Hitler and Hugenberg, but even more so for those who controlled the Government. Beginning with the well-intentioned though mistaken policies of Brüning, Germany became the stage on which a procession of ambitious and misguided men sought to make history, from Schleicher and Papen to Hindenburg (father and son) to the flexible Meissner,* who managed to survive all changes of government. Whereas the crisis of 1920–23, which had brought with it equally serious internal and even more serious external problems, was overcome without damage to the democratic order thanks to the balancing leadership of Ebert, the Reich Presidency now was in the hands of a glorified though militarily defeated and politically ill-qualified field marshal. Though initially loyal, Hindenburg was filled with profound distaste for civilian, let alone republican, politics. With the onset of this new crisis, he permitted his advisers to push him further along the road of authoritarian, extraparliamentary experiments.

The Presidential dictatorial powers—that is, the emergency powers granted by Article 48 of the Weimar Constitution—furnished the desired leverage. In drafting the far-reaching emergency powers of the President, the fathers of the Constitution had had in mind the protection of the Republic in times of crisis and had invoked them only in this sense. But the restrictions and controls set on these powers proved to be fatally inadequate. True, Article 48 stipulated that the Reichstag could order the repeal of such emergency measures, but the President, thanks to his power to dissolve parliament, held the stronger cards. And since he also had the power to appoint or dismiss the Chancellor and the Government without parliamentary approval, he could in effect govern without parliamentary restraints. In the Ebert era, the combination of these three Presidential powers served to protect the democratic order; but after 1930, in the hands of Hindenburg, they resulted first in the suspension of the Reichstag, then in the authoritarian experiments of Papen and Schleicher and in the abolition of democratic government in Prussia, and ultimately in the terrorist power grab of a minority government under Hitler.

Here, too, the importance of individuals is quite evident. To be sure, the transition from parliamentary democracy to one-party state began with the overthrow of the Grand Coalition in the spring of 1930—that is, with the failure of the two wings of the coalition to master the problems of political compromise. In fact, the influence of antagonistic special-interest groups vitally affected the various parties: on the one hand, the employer organizations, generally in the camp of the DVP and free from the restraints imposed by Stresemann,

* Otto Meissner was Hindenburg's State Secretary, a post he had held under Ebert as well and continued to hold under Hitler.—TRANSLATOR'S NOTE.

were mobilized by Hugenberg; on the other hand, the crisis-ridden trade unions pushed the SPD out of an unpopular Government and steered it into a still more unpopular course of acquiescence devoid of all possibility of exerting political leverage. But this governmental crisis assumed fatal significance only after the basic criticism of party democracy and parliamentarianism by specialists in public law and political writers was taken up by the Army command and Hindenburg's conservative advisers and transformed into concrete plans for the authoritarian restructuring of the Government, for the creation of a more rigid "above-party" Presidential government—one clearly oriented toward the Right.

These determined efforts, with all the dangers inherent in inadequate controls and the destruction of the democratic will, were aimed at further strengthening the growing executive power over the legislature. In the Brüning Government, which was to operate solely on the basis of Presidential emergency laws for two years, parliament was relegated to a largely negative role, and the domination of bureaucratic agencies was assured. The President and the Army pursued a course which, with the elimination of parliamentary authority, meant that the parliament's influence on public opinion also was waning; this in turn magnified the attraction of radical propaganda and accelerated the rise of extremist mass movements appealing to a wide range of interests and emotions and promising a social order based on class or one-man rule.

On this point, opinions still differ. Given the continuous coalition problems and constantly changing governments, many historians and political writers in Germany (probably a conservative majority) tend to accept or justify this authoritarian interlude as the inevitable consequence of a hopeless structural crisis of political democracy. However, let it be emphatically stated that the parliamentary alternative to the Presidential experiment was never seriously tried after 1929.[1] From that time on, Cabinets—supraparliamentary Hindenburg Governments—were appointed precipitately without consultation of the political parties. Parliament and parties were thus relieved of that responsibility for constructive cooperation, that pressure to work out compromises and form the workable majorities, which ultimately constitutes the foundation of their existence in a democracy. The easy way out, via Presidential rule, paralyzed their activity and their sense of responsibility. The economic and parliamentary crisis and the demand for the immediate authoritarian restructuring of the state supplied the agitation for antidemocratic reforms and dictatorship with its most obvious arguments. And finally, this agitation offered the National Socialists a welcome pretext for their strategy of achieving their totalitarian objective by pseudo-legal means. The road to extraparliamentary government was entered upon when, immediately after the

[1] On the controversy, see K. D. Bracher, *Deutschland zwischen Demokratie und Diktatur* (Berlin and Munich, 1964), pp. 33 ff.; *Nationalsozialistische Machtergreifung* (2d ed.; Cologne and Opladen, 1962), pp. 35 ff.; and *Von Weimar zu Hitler* (Cologne and Berlin, 1968), pp. 69 f.

resignation of the Müller Cabinet (March 27, 1930), and without consultation of parliament, Hindenburg appointed his Brüning Cabinet (March 30)—threatening that Presidential emergency power would replace parliamentary rule if the Reichstag should fail to go along. And shortly thereafter, in July, 1930, at the very moment of worsening crisis, Brüning dissolved parliament for its refusal to support him in his authoritarian rule by emergency law. Thus the Reichstag was reduced to the role of tolerative body; the election called with unseemly haste in September, 1930, turned out to be detrimental to the composition of parliament. The enormous increase in the number of National Socialist deputies (from 12 to 107) bore out the fatal error of Brüning's hasty move. (It would also seem to indicate that modern democracy cannot afford to ignore the findings of opinion and election research.) The factors that tended to exacerbate the crisis were quite obvious: the premature dissolution of a parliament opposed to government by emergency regulation but still not radicalized in a time of deepening economic crisis, seriously weakening the parties capable of cooperation; the fatal coexistence of semidictatorial government, of parliament set aside, and radicalization of the population; and finally the belief that the race with the domestic crisis could be won through successes in the realm of foreign policy. These factors intensified the crisis; they were not simply, as is frequently maintained, its natural consequence, let alone the only possible "political" antidote.

For now the Reichstag was indeed crippled, and the Presidential Cabinet, at no time a true representative of the popular will, more and more came to be considered a bureaucratic foreign body. The experience of Weimar makes highly questionable the widespread belief that a crisis situation demands a nonparliamentary cabinet of specialists. From 1930 on, the existence of an authoritarian Presidential government not subject to the will of the people merely served to increase the trend toward radicalism. Since Brüning rejected all efforts to form a broadly based government (in contrast to the practice in Britain during the economic crisis), public influence on politics through the democratic parties and parliament seemed even less likely than before. In their quest for manifesting their dissatisfaction, the crisis-ridden middle class and peasants turned to a National Socialist collective movement that promised all things to all men, while the impoverished mass of workers turned toward the Communist counterpart.

What is significant in this context is the reaction of the democratic state to the rapid rise of the totalitarian parties, which in the summer of 1932 had come to command a spurious majority of destructive opposition voices in the Reichstag. This threat could have been met in two ways: either by permitting a carefully contained National Socialist participation in a parliamentary government, thus limiting their chances of easy opposition, or by decisive action—political as well as legal—against their antidemocratic activities. In fact, however, nothing was done, even though the legalistic camouflage tactics of the Nazi leadership were unmistakably clear. However one may feel about the banning of parties in a democratic society, the antidemocratic, antiparliamentarian nature of the National Socialist movement was readily apparent both juridically and constitutionally. The failure of the judicial authorities, their partly resigned, partly hostile attitude toward the Republic, became strikingly apparent in the autumn of 1931, when the Attorney General refused to prosecute Nazi functionaries around Hitler's legal adviser Werner Best, who in the secret "Boxheim Documents" had set down elaborate plans for the terrorist regime after a Nazi coup—the shooting of enemies, the suppression of public life by Draconian measures, total party dictatorship.

This was the reality. The central and regional governments were in possession of plans, designs, and unmistakable documentary evidence, but they responded with only feeble controls and regional countermeasures. Effective defenses that would simultaneously have served to inform the population about the functioning and meaning of democracy were forever being tabled or postponed. The reasons lay in a lack of self-confidence rather than in a frivolous overestimation of their own power and means. That was true not only of the Brüning Cabinet but also of the democratically governed states. The effects of this paralysis on a rapidly eroding Republic, as well as the consequences of the authoritarian tendencies of the Brüning Government, revealed themselves with sudden force in the spring of 1932. Through a by no means coincidental chain of events, Brüning lost the support of the two main pillars of his semiparliamentary, semi-authoritarian policy: the President and the Army command. To what extent the various causal agents—Army leadership, agrarian interests, and individual ambitions—were involved in this fatal toppling of the Government remains an open question. When Hindenburg's seven-year term expired, Brüning even considered the restoration of the monarchy with Hindenburg as acting regent, but after unsuccessful negotiations with Hitler and Hugenberg, he finally came out for the re-election of the then eighty-four-year-old President. He was able to win the support of the parties of his tolerative majority, from the Social Democrats to those of the moderate Right, and thus, in April, 1932, score a clear-cut victory over the National Socialist power claim—his final victory. The fact that the Reichstag majority was, up to the very end, able to defeat all votes of no confidence against the Government may strike one as paradoxical, but in fact it testifies to the existence of parliamentary alternatives fallen into disuse. The threat to the Government came from its former pillars—the authoritarian critics of a parliamentary solution.

This was the situation when the acting Minister of the Interior, General Wilhelm Groener, outlawed the SA, a long-overdue blow against the NSDAP. Immediately the full extent of the growing impotence of the democratic forces and institutions was revealed. Hindenburg reacted by calling either for a simultaneous ban of the Republican defense corps Reichsbanner or for the rescission of the SA ban. In the end he let Groener go, when Schleicher hinted that the Brüning policies no longer enjoyed the support of the Army. With Groener, the Defense Minister from 1928 to 1932, fell one of the main supports of the Government; subsequently, with the help of the landholding circles around Hindenburg, Brüning himself fell, and with him the then still semidemocratic version of the Presidential system. Brüning's vacillation over the inclusion of the National Socialist potential in an authoritarian solution, and the accelerated pursuit of an antiparliamentary course, furnished the Army and the group around Hindenburg with the main impetus for the fatal overthrow of the Cabinet on May 30, 1932, a move accomplished without vote of parliament and parties, solely by Presidential dictum. Only six weeks after his re-election, Hindenburg, the epitome of "soldierly loyalty," brusquely disregarded the mandate of his democratic electorate and lent his support to a combination of forces which only weeks earlier had fought his candidacy.

The new Cabinet of the Center Party defector Franz von Papen was installed even more precipitately and heedlessly than its predecessor, and despite its clear-cut right-wing orientation was lauded in even stronger terms as a "national" government above the parties. Its aim was nothing less than the concretization of the authoritarian restructuring, now set in motion by considerably different methods than the Brüning experiment. While accepting the criticism of Brüning's emergency law and deflationary policies, one can still agree with Arnold Brecht when he says that rarely has a government erred with a cleaner conscience than that of Brüning.[2] The majority of the parliament that Brüning had sought to limit tolerated him to the end, while his original allies overthrew him. Not so Papen. He shelved his predecessor's tolerative approach to parliament in favor of a "New State" built on Hindenburg's prestige and on the "national forces," a move which finally was to bring the political and institutional fulfillment of the longed-for authoritarian solution. According to the testimony of men close to Papen, his goal was a corporate, aristocratic Presidential leadership state with an upper chamber appointed by Hindenburg and a pluralistic rather than universally elected lower chamber. Such a state, it was proclaimed, would ensure government by the "elite" instead of democratic parliamentary government by "inferiors." As far as can be gleaned from the vague ideological phrases of the champions of this New State, all powers of decision were to be vested in Hindenburg and his appointed leaders, while the parliamentary residues in the form of the two chambers were to be limited to advisory and proclamatory functions. Although such an authoritarian transformation of the Government, which also was meant to halt and block the totalitarian aspirations of National Socialism, was never realized, it nonetheless played a fatal role in the ill-conceived efforts to delimit and restrain the National Socialist revolution.

To begin with, Papen immediately set about to win Hitler's coopera-

[2] Arnold Brecht, *Prelude to Silence* (New York, 1944), p. 35.

tion. Toward this end, he made a series of concessions which meant a basic break with Brüning's moderate authoritarian course. The first concession was one the National Socialists found most pleasing: the dissolution of the Reichstag on June 4, 1932, that is, before it could meet and vote—undoubtedly negatively—on the course of the new government. This ended the era of emergency laws tolerated by parliament; the shutting-out of the Reichstag by repeated suspensions meant that the ensuing period of rule by emergency law was completely contrary to the democratic will. Unlike Brüning, Papen himself attended only one regular session of the newly elected Reichstag, in September, 1932, and he then prevented a devastating vote of no confidence (512 to 42) by again dissolving the Reichstag.

The second hasty concession to the courted NSDAP, the rescission of the SA ban on June 16, 1932, promptly brought Papen into conflict with those state governments which Groener had persuaded to issue a ban; since the deployment of police was a state function, the states also bore the main responsibility for the prevention of bloody street battles between the armed troops of the radical Right and Left. Now such battles resumed with unprecedented violence. This again pointed up the ineffectiveness of a government without any real popular base seeking to implement sweeping reactionary reforms. The difference between its methods and the strict legalism of the Brüning era was forcefully demonstrated by its third move. This one, however, was more than simply a concession to the NSDAP; instead, it was intrinsic to Papen's policies: the Prussian *coup d'état* of July 20, 1932. When the hope for National Socialist support of the Papen experiment turned out to be illusory, the New State found itself hopelessly blocked and isolated, even before its authoritarian postulates could be realized. Papen, fearing the outcome of the imminent Reichstag elections, and with the support of the President and the Army, sought by an act of force to break through the political isolation and, by taking over Prussia, to consolidate his authoritarian position in at least that state, three-fifths of Germany.

The demand for reform of the federal structure formed the background. And, in fact, the dualism of Reich and Prussia was a major structural deficiency of the Weimar Republic. The problem was made doubly acute by the questionable position of the Prussian coalition government under Otto Braun and Carl Severing; since the state elections of April, 1932, it had commanded only a parliamentary minority, and, in the absence of a government based on a constructive majority, merely exercised administrative functions. But the true political motive of Papen's move against the Government of Prussia, a move again based on Article 48 of the Constitution, was a last-ditch attempt to strengthen the political base of his hopelessly isolated regime by a display of authoritarian self-confidence which he hoped would be greeted with admiration, applause, or wholesome fear, and thus be instrumental in winning the respect and support of National Socialist circles.

The hasty and peaceful capitulation of the Prussian Government astonished even Papen himself; the only fight put up by the Government against its illegal deposition was to launch lengthy, politically ineffective court proceedings, a sign of the rapidly dwindling strength of the forces of democracy and of the imminence of their defeat at the hands of authoritarianism and subsequently of totalitarianism. However one may feel about the effectiveness of political strikes, this first 20th of July certainly encouraged the more ambitious plans of the National Socialists and the later policies of the Third Reich. The ensuing campaign to purge and reorganize the Prussian administrative apparatus gave a foretaste of the political coordination (*Gleichshaltung*) which seven months hence was to turn all political organs into obedient administrative pillars of an untrammeled ruling clique. But, like the other concessions aimed at realizing the goals of the agitation of the National Opposition against the existing system, this act of force also was unable to find the promised solution between democracy and dictatorship. The political stabilization of an authoritarian right-wing government of Papen's coinage was not achieved, and the result of the elections so lightheartedly set for July 31, 1932, only served to underscore the unpopularity of Papen's experiment.

The analysis of the election results shows with unmistakable clarity to what extent the period after Brüning's ouster was dominated by an unresolved, alternating blocking of the political party camps.[3] Three major groups met head on in the struggle for power, paralyzed their own freedom of movement, and at the same time proved unable to gain control over the existing power vacuum. First, there were the outmaneuvered democratic groups, which still represented a considerable power base, even though seemingly relegated to the role of negative resistance and robbed of all possibilities of constructive influence on the course of events. Second, the Nazi and Communist totalitarians now held 53 per cent of all Reichstag seats and thus were in a position to block the formation of any democratic government. But beyond such a purely negative cooperation, they of course could not form a coalition and thus they, too, stood helplessly outside the gates of power. And, third, Papen's authoritarian regime, despite all his self-confident declarations, was a minute minority, and it, too, remained immobilized. To be sure, the Papen Government was able to base its temporary executive powers on the President and the Army, on continuous suspension of parliament, and finally on plans for a coup. But the desired authoritarian solution did not stand the slightest chance against nine-tenths of the German electorate and against the opposition of both the democratic and the totalitarian forces.

The various groups undoubtedly tried with all their might to overcome this general paralysis, or at least exploit it for their own benefit.

---

[3] See the voting pattern analyses by Alfred Milatz, *Wähler und Wahlen in der Weimarer Republik* (Bonn, 1965), pp. 141 ff.; and K. D. Bracher, *Die Auflösung der Weimarer Republik* (5th ed.; Villingen, 1970), Part II, chap. x.

Three attempts in particular, all of them made in August, 1932, sought such a breakthrough. Influenced by the recent National Socialist electoral victory, Papen and Schleicher in early August made renewed efforts to persuade Hitler to join a government of their design. But since they, and particularly Hindenburg also, insisted on considerable assurances and offered Hitler nothing more than the Vice Chancellorship, the result was another falling-out with the National Socialists. They, of course, had seen through Papen's plan of taming the NSDAP by including it in the government, thereby blunting its popular appeal and at the same time exploiting its vote potential. For this reason, Papen was most displeased by a move initiated by the National Socialists a few days later. By negotiating with the Center leadership, Hitler temporarily managed to give the impression that he was interested in the formation of a regular parliamentary majority government, which automatically would have meant the end of the Papen interlude. In view of the unbridgeable differences of the two parties, this remained a purely tactical threat, the negative product of the discontent of all parties except the DNVP, which supported Papen. But it was sufficient to make Papen look forward with trepidation to the session of the newly elected Reichstag.

In order to forestall further surprises, Papen induced Hindenburg to issue a new dissolution decree even before the opening session of this Reichstag—a truly unique development in the history of parliamentarianism. This blanket authorization, in which Papen only needed to insert a date and vague justifications, clearly showed the extent to which parliamentary rule had been replaced by authoritarian government. At the same time, Hindenburg was tendered a plan for the long-term suspension of the hostile Reichstag. The Government was to use this interlude free of controls to institute the long-contemplated authoritarian constitutional reforms, in which the dictatorial powers of the President were to be interpreted quite broadly. When Papen managed to forestall the anticipated overwhelming vote of no confidence by the new Reichstag with the decree of dissolution he carried in his pocket, the time for reform via *coup d'état* seemed to have arrived. But now it was Hindenburg and the Army command who feared an explosion of the tense situation, the transition from cold to hot civil war, and who refused to support the moves of Papen and his Minister of the Interior, Wilhelm von Gayl.

The Reichstag elections of November 6, 1932—the fifth in the series of disruptive elections held that year—could neither change the existing situation nor offer any new solutions. To be sure, a marked decline of National Socialist votes seemed to put a clear limit on the number of votes Hitler could gather in free elections, and consequently ruined his plans for taking power via a parliamentary majority. When Hitler stuck to his demands, Hindenburg once more rebuffed him, and now the NSDAP found itself in serious trouble. The road to power seemed blocked by Hindenburg's rejection of a Presidential Cabinet under Hitler. The National Socialist leadership demanded governmental power; Strasser, in charge of organization, called for a coalition; the financial situation deteriorated; influential supporters threatened to desert. In addition, the worst of the economic crisis seemed over. Inherent in any economic recovery was the danger that the mass of voters would stream back to the traditional political organizations. The municipal elections of November and December, 1932, had borne this out.

In the opinion of Defense Minister General Schleicher, this situation, so alarming to the National Socialists, favored the chances of a renewed attempt to implement his plan for the taming and exploitation of the NSDAP, only now the plan was considerably altered. When Papen submitted his formal resignation, hoping thereby to prod Hindenburg into approving his authoritarian coup plans, Schleicher edged away from the Chancellor, whom he had supported up to then. He refused to assign troops to domestic duty in the setting-up of the planned dictatorship and won over other Cabinet members. After all his own intrigues and experiments, Schleicher at the last hour showed enough political realism to oppose the dangerous delusion of a reactionary autocracy of Papen's design. Instead, he held out to the battleweary President the possibility of a peaceful resolution of the crisis. He developed a plan for broadening the base of the Government by splitting the NSDAP and following a conciliatory course toward the other parties, including the SPD and the trade unions, designed to stem radicalism—if necessary by relinquishing unpopular authoritarian undertakings.

The result—after deliberate hesitation on the part of Hindenburg— was Schleicher's appointment to the Chancellorship on December 2, 1932. But there remained a residue of ill feeling in the palace of the Reich President which shortly brought on the last governmental crisis, and with the ouster of Schleicher together with his plan, rapidly demolished the carefully erected dams against a National Socialist seizure of power. Contrary to Schleicher's efforts to have Papen sent to Paris as Ambassador, the ex-Chancellor, enjoying Hindenburg's confidence, continued to play a vital role in the maneuvers around the Chancellery. And from him came the final initiative which made it possible for the NSDAP unexpectedly to break through the power vacuum into the decisive takeover phase at a time when the party was contending with serious internal problems.

NATIONAL SOCIALIST TACTICS BEFORE THE SEIZURE OF POWER

The economic and governmental crisis spurred the NSDAP to unprecedented, massive propaganda and organizational drives. As early as the summer of 1928, Hitler told a leadership conference in Munich that regional results of the Reichstag elections indicated that the party had to concentrate its efforts on the rural areas rather than the cities. The rural nationalistic protest mood constituted a huge electoral potential. The party regions were coordinated with electoral districts;

organizational efforts in rural areas were intensified; the transformation into a petty-bourgeois–rural mass movement was speeded up. By 1932, under Gregor Strasser's direction, the party had become a veritable microcosm of state and society. The rigid organizational structuring from above to below in every party region was the triumph of the "bureaucraticized romanticism" of the leader party.

At the turn of 1928, the success of this approach was evidenced by a rapid increase in membership. The party sought to spread out in every direction. Nationalism and anti-Marxism were the recipe by which the various interest groups could be outmaneuvered propagandistically and also used. This was demonstrated in the turn toward cooperation with other nationalist groups, the Stahlhelm and the German Nationals, culminating in the campaigns of autumn, 1929, and finally in the formation of the Harzburg Front (1931).

But above all, the NSDAP, in contrast to other parties, instituted a continuous voter recruitment drive, both during and between election campaigns. Toward this end, it set up intensive public-speaking courses at special NSDAP Speakers' Schools for the training of primitive yet forceful propaganda speakers for the many meetings being held in the countryside and small towns—more than two thousand between April, 1929, and May, 1930. The trainees memorized standardized texts and rehearsed answers in front of a mirror—techniques more in keeping with acting than politics. Similar training was also offered through correspondence courses. These efforts explain the frequency of meetings throughout Germany, despite the shortage of first-rate speakers. Although the political understanding and rhetorical gifts of these trainees were minimal, they did make possible an uninterrupted flow of activity down to the smallest village. Above the local speakers were the regional and national speakers, who appeared at more important occasions within the framework of carefully planned propaganda gatherings. Successful local agitation facilitated the mobilization of the population for mass meetings in regional capitals.

This mobilization was prepared through carefully organized poster and leaflet campaigns controlled from above, and reaching down via the regions to the local groups. Illustrated magazines and films augmented the drives; the image of the party was to be disseminated through all available mass media. The man in charge of propaganda at the Munich headquarters, Heinrich Himmler, earned his spurs in this organizational and planning drive from 1928 on, until his promotion to the head of the SS. In addition, Goebbels set up branch offices of his Reich Propaganda Office on all party levels. Generally speaking, Hitler or his adjutant, Hess, had the final say on all important posters and leaflets. The result of these efforts was a growing awareness of National Socialist presence on the part of the press and general public (for example, in Saxony, 1,300 Nazi meetings were held just before the state parliamentary elections of June, 1929); the pull of the successful party began to have its effect even before it scored any major electoral victories.

In these circumstances, the Nuremberg party congress of August, 1929, turned into a great public demonstration of the growth and prestige of the NSDAP. Its nationalist appeal was strengthened by staging the congress on the fifteenth anniversary of the declaration of World War I, an event celebrated in speeches and ceremonials. The German National heads of the Patriotic Corps (Rüdiger von der Goltz) and the Stahlhelm (Theodor Düsterberg) were honorary guests, and soon thereafter the supporters of other right-wing groups began to flock to that noisiest of parties. Another consequence of these tactics was the steady improvement of the party's financial situation. In the summer of 1929, the party still had financial problems, but now it began to profit from the influx of more affluent middle-class supporters and the growing interest of business leaders. Above all, the political unrest growing out of the nascent economic crisis began to have its effects.

While efforts in rural areas in 1929–30 were rewarded, the winning over of the urban and industrial population, whose interests were vastly different and whom the crisis affected differently, proved to be far more difficult. Workers and "capitalists," large entrepreneurs and small businessmen, merchants and consumers, confronted one another in bitter opposition. How were these conflicting groups to be united along the lines of the National Socialist ideology of unity in a movement dependent both on the money and influence of big business and on the votes of the lower middle class and employees, on both "capitalism" and "socialism"?

All the parties, not least among them the German Nationals, had run up against this problem. Hitler's attempt to solve the dilemma through the unscrupulous, opportunistic tactic of promising everything to everybody led to inner party crises and reverses. The pronounced anticapitalism of the early years had been badly battered, but the dedication to a socialism of national cast seemed to take on fresh importance in a time of economic and social crisis. That was true particularly of the renewed determination to make greater inroads into the working class. The well-known anticapitalist tendencies of a lower middle class and peasantry feeling threatened by modern economic developments and industrialization favored the "socialist" aspect of National Socialism. With the transition to a mass party and the deepening of the economic crisis, the old conflict entered into a new stage; it lasted until the bloody party purge of 1934.

But by the spring of 1930, a preliminary decision had already been reached. Otto Strasser had held to a willful radical course with his Berlin publishing house and papers. Repeatedly, and again in the spring of 1930, he had foiled Hitler's balancing strategy with his determined championship of an opening toward the Left, of trade unions and strikes, of far-reaching nationalization and an alliance with Russia. This jeopardized the profitable relationship of the NSDAP with newly won friends in industry and commerce. A dramatic meeting between Hitler and Otto Strasser on May 21–22 in the presence of Amann, Hess, and Gregor Strasser, who once more was moving close to Hitler's course, led to a complete rupture shortly afterward. Hitler failed with both inducements and threats to persuade this "left" deviationist; Otto Strasser issued his declaration of war in a pamphlet with the telling title *Ministersessel oder Revolution (Cabinet Seat or Revolution)*, in which Hitler was accused of betraying the basic revolutionary and socialist ideas of National Socialism. At the same time, it was an attack on the total leadership principle by which Hitler decreed that the party and his personal will were one and the same, and on his demand for complete acquiescence to the tactics he felt he had to pursue in his fight for power, regardless of ideology and convictions.[4]

Hitler's idea of socialism, then and later, was in complete accord with his feelings about the stupid, tractable, manipulable mass, whose needs could be satisfied with the classical method of *panem et circenses*. Anyone genuinely concerned about the people was in Hitler's eyes a socialist. The coming revolution was not meant for this popular mass but for a new elite of racially superior leaders. Their rule and victory over Jews and other "inferiors"—the true *völkisch*-racist revolution—remained the only genuine kernel of Hitler's ideology, regardless of the proclamations of National Socialist doctrine and propaganda; almost everything else was utilitarian, Machiavellian power politics. Hitler also looked at economic and social programs from this vantage point. The leader principle explained the superior position of business leaders; they had succeeded because of their abilities; socialization or codetermination would be nothing more than a return to democracy and popular rule. A strong state and the leader principle, not economic and social reform, were the ideas guiding Hitler's policies on capitalism and socialism, organizations and group interests, reform and revolution, in the ensuing fight for power. They proved to be successful.

The National Socialist Fighting League of Germany (Nationalsozialistische Kampfgemeinschaft Deutschlands, or NSKD) (founded by the radical National Socialists and the Black Front), in which Otto Strasser, after his expulsion by Goebbels from the Berlin party organization, gathered his forces for the building of German Socialism (*Aufbau des deutschen Sozialismus*, his book of 1932) could not stem the movement toward the NSDAP. Hitler even managed to ward off the serious conflict between the Berlin SA under Walter Stennes and the regional command under Goebbels, which was accused of inadequately supporting the SA and of favoring capitalist interests. After renewed conflicts with Pfeffer over the ranking of the SA on the Reichstag roster, Hitler had himself appointed Supreme Leader of the SA (OSAF) and made Röhm, who had returned from Bolivia, the new SA chief of staff.[5] Hitler overcame the conflict over the question of

---

[4] A dramatized account of this may be found in Otto Strasser, *Hitler und Ich* (Konstanz, 1948), pp. 122 ff.

[5] Heinrich Bennecke, *Hitler und die SA* (Munich, 1962), pp. 147 ff.

tactics in a democracy—a conflict brought on by the transition to a mass organization—by submerging the discrepancy between the strategy of legality and the seizure-of-power propaganda in the leader myth. Nonetheless, the SA crisis continued to smolder until the expulsion of the rebellious Stennes faction in April, 1931.

The election campaign of mid-1930, which was caused by Brüning's untimely suspension of the Reichstag, presented the National Socialists with a great propaganda opportunity. Once the NSDAP had secured the sympathies of the Right, it could well afford to be radical, but it could also stop leaning on the German Nationals, who clearly had emerged as the loser in party splits and in the anti-Young Plan campaign. The National Socialists, with their noisy and violent SA demonstrations, tireless propaganda forces, turbulent mass meetings, and interminable speeches, dominated public life more than any other party. Again, the pompously staged Hitler speeches proved to be highly effective. Now the party and its leader were everywhere; this no longer was the lark of the Munich days. In a deluge of public meetings, bridging the distances between the various "fronts" by airplane, literally descending from the heavens, Hitler and his first-rank speaker corps stirred up the people in town and country. They addressed themselves mainly to the supporters of the moderate and right-wing parties, who were easily outcriticized and outpromised. Instead of the politics of special interests and compromise, the NSDAP offered the collectivist slogans of a broad front of all classes against the democratic system, united in the fight against Versailles and the "November criminals"—the ready targets of these attacks. Not burdened by the monarchic, reactionary, special-interest heritage of the German Nationals, and superior to the left-wing radicalism of the Communists weighed down by class-struggle ideology, the National Socialists profited more than any other group from the first election to be held in this period of crisis. They proved the strongest magnet for a motley assemblage of dissatisfied, nonpolitical individuals, of activists and fearful men from all walks of life.

The elections of September 14, 1930, both bore out and accelerated this trend. Their most striking aspect was the unusually high participation (82 per cent, as compared to 76.6 per cent in 1928), proof of a strong popular urge to give vent to feelings which a government leaning primarily on the President, the Army, and emergency laws was unable to satisfy. The result was an NSDAP election victory whose magnitude surprised even its own leaders. It polled almost eight times as many votes as in 1928 (18.3 per cent, compared to 2.6 per cent); the number of parliamentary seats it won increased ninefold (from 12 to 107). Probably never before had a party registered such gains within a two-year period. It was a development of truly historic significance. The NSDAP emerged as the second-strongest party, following the SPD. The KPD was the only other party to chalk up any gains, though much smaller ones (from 10.6 per cent to 13.1 per cent); the Center was the only one to remain stable

(15 per cent). All the others suffered substantial losses. Hugenberg obviously had miscalculated. The DNVP vote declined by more than half (from 14.3 to 7 per cent). The Liberals were hardest hit; the DVP and the State Party (the former DDP) became mere splinter groups. Since the days of the National Assembly, they had declined steadily (from 23 per cent to 13 in 1928, to their lowest point, 8.5 per cent, in 1930). The middle class was veering toward the Right. The Left as a whole also suffered losses (from 42.2 to 38.2 per cent), the burden of which fell on the SPD, while the Communists, blindly complacent, announced: "The Communist Party was the only victor in the September elections." However, the NSDAP did not succeed in making substantial inroads into the Left. Its major gains came from the center and right-wing parties, including the DNVP, whose devastating defeat also thwarted Brüning's plans for a center-right coalition government.

The new Reichstag was marked by an invasion of parliamentary neophytes: 88 per cent of the National Socialist and 53 per cent of the Communist delegates were newcomers to a parliament with whose work they were unfamiliar and which they tried to obstruct with all their might. The propaganda demands of the National Socialist parliamentary delegation—for example, confiscation of the assets of "financial princes" and the prohibition of sexual intercourse between Jews and Aryans—may have seemed harmless so long as there were only twelve delegates, but now the delegation had parliamentary leverage. At the same time, the parliament experienced an invasion by youth, a group particularly well represented in the leadership corps of the radical parties. Political experience and constructive work in this "youngest" Reichstag, whose average age was forty-six (60 per cent of the National Socialist and Communist delegates, but only 10 per cent of the SPD's, were under forty), were replaced by uniforms and tumult. The social and occupational composition of the Nazi delegation also was of interest: sixteen had a commercial, handicraft, or industrial background; twenty-five were employees; thirteen were teachers; twelve, civil servants; fifteen, party functionaries; eight, ex-officers; twelve, farmers; one, a clergyman, and one, a pharmacist (Gregor Strasser). Two years later, the 230-man National Socialist delegation included fifty-five employees or workers, fifty farmers, forty-three from business, handicraft, and industry, twenty-nine party functionaries, twenty civil servants, twelve teachers, and nine ex-officers—a considerable increase of farmer delegates, though not of farmer members. Employees were most strongly represented, industrial workers the least. The state legislatures showed a similar pattern. In Thuringia, followed by Brunswick and other small states, the National Socialists were able to enter the government, or at least tip the scales between the bourgeois and socialist parties in the formation of cabinets.

And thus the premature elections which Brüning, despite the storm signals of the regional elections, risked in pursuit of his authoritarian course and in the hope of a more favorable constellation of forces, once and for all destroyed the chances for a broad coalition in this time of crisis. The weight of the radicalized new voters and of former nonvoters who now flocked to the polls to cast their ballots for the National Socialists obviously had been underestimated. Now the totalitarian parties—the National Socialists and the Communists— moved up into second and third place, respectively. Instead of the 13.5 per cent of 1928, they now commanded a destructive Reichstag minority of 32 per cent, and the old Weimar coalition (40 per cent instead of the 48.6 per cent of 1928) as well as the imposing Grand Coalition of 1928 (57 per cent) was reduced to a minority (of 47 per cent). The psychological and material effects of this major shift of forces were as significant as the blocking of the democratic mechanism. Opportunists began to flock around; a variety of special-interest groups sought to fall in line with the new power relations, and the Nazis almost automatically began to establish cross-connections and positions that facilitated the spread and consolidation of their movement. Instead of foundering in the transition to a mass movement, as many had expected, the recently insignificant party moved effortlessly into the areas opened up by a society in upheaval, a crumbling democratic order, a minority government by the grace of Hindenburg, and an Army vacillating between various authoritarian solutions.

Whereas a Presidential government tolerated by parliament was accepted as the lesser evil by the democratic parties, including the SPD, the NSDAP after its triumph was faced with some tactical problems. The enormous new following of "Septemberites," [6] which alone between September and the end of the year accounted for an increase in membership from 293,000 to 389,000,[7] had to be organized and controlled. A long road still lay ahead for the party. The mass of new adherents, who could scatter as quickly as they had after 1923, was extremely heterogeneous, held together only by an indiscriminate mood of protest. Two problems were uppermost. What countermeasures might be taken against them by the state or hostile parties if, in their role as a major parliamentary party, they pursued their tested tactic of combining a policy of legality with revolutionary aims? And what about the efforts to include the NSDAP in the government and tame it by giving it responsibility, to force it to work within the existing state and thus rob it of the facile propaganda opportunities inherent in a radical opposition, the basis of its most recent successes?

However, neither approach to the National Socialist threat—suppression or a role in the government—risky though these might have been, was seriously pursued. Patient tolerance and helplessness marked the official attitude. The NSDAP had obviously become too

[6] This is how Goebbels himself later described undesirable elements. See editorial by that title in *Der Angriff*, November 2, 1931.

[7] Wolfgang Schäfer, *NSDAP, Entwicklung und Struktur der Staatspartei des Dritten Reiches* (Hanover, 1956), p. 17.

big. Prohibition, it was feared, would only result in civil-warlike strife, and furthermore, neither a positivist public law nor the Army could be won over to such a measure. The idea that a militant democracy might deny its enemies the right to destroy the Republic by pseudo-legal means was not firmly enough implanted. To be sure, there existed defense organizations like the Reichsbanner Schwarz-Rot-Gold (supported by the parties of the old Weimar Coalition—SPD, Center, DDP), but their work was hampered by the supineness and increasing paralysis of the democratic parties, their hesitancy in the face of National Socialist aggression, and the two-front battle against the radical Right and Left. National Socialist propaganda unimpededly reiterated its unspeakable vilifications of the "system," of living as well as dead political figures, and it found a large and guillible audience. Socialists and Jews, they said, should be strung up on the highest gallows; the late Stresemann was excoriated for his "execrable activities," and regrets were voiced that this "betrayer of the people" could no longer be brought before the bars of justice. None of this, however, prevented the DVP (Stresemann's party) from entering into a coalition with the National Socialists in Thuringia.

To be sure, countermeasures were taken. Even before the election, the Prussian Government, by a decree of July 3, 1930, barred all civil servants from supporting Nazi and Communist organizations. The wearing of Brown Shirts in Prussia was also forbidden, and so the SA made do with white shirts. But the Central Government was not ready to take similar steps, and this duality largely canceled out the effects of regional measures. The courts also did not react to Prussian proposals and memorandums on the antistate activities of the NSDAP. In these circumstances, the disciplining of individual Nazi civil servants had no effect; as a matter of fact, it gave the propaganda machine welcome martyrs. The April, 1932, ban of the SA and SS also was bound to be futile because it had come too late. Regardless of one's attitude toward the feasibility and advisability of political bans, once the opportunity for interposition had been missed, the threat of countermeasures was bound to be ineffective. For many otherwise timid citizens, National Socialism had become rather a welcome, because nondangerous, adventure.

The subsequent course of the NSDAP was more than ever before attuned to catastrophe and misery; the greater the national crisis, the greater the propaganda successes. In line with this approach, the financial and economic effects of the September elections of 1930, which had brought panic on the financial market, were fully exploited by the Nazi propaganda machine. By predicting inflation, it accelerated the detrimental withdrawal of credits and savings. Reveling in its success and growth, the party proceeded in its efforts to install itself as a powerful state within the state. Hitler held press conferences to convince the outside world that he was the future ruler of Germany; he received foreign delegations and sent representatives to German diplomatic missions. The party apparatus began to assume the shape of an independent government apparatus, a countergovernment drafting policies ranging from social to military affairs, with the *Völkische Beobachter* as a quasi-official paper. By the end of 1931, every party region had more than a thousand employees. An efficient and meticulous treasurer (Franz Schwarz) was in charge of the party's financial affairs at Munich; with the help of contributions from the business sector, party finances had improved, until the decline of 1932 once more brought some anxious moments. All these moves obviously were overt preparations for a seizure of power by which the state was to be undermined and taken over. And in all this the legality strategy was consistently followed in all its ambiguity. When the Central Court of Leipzig, in October, 1930, conducted a trial against the formation of National Socialist cells within the Army, Hitler appeared before it and rendered an "oath of legality." He swore to refrain from any but constitutional methods in his quest for power. Yet at the same time, he left no doubt that once he had won his legal victory "heads would roll." [8]

Despite all tactical maneuvers, radical revisionism, which Hitler linked to the solution of all problems, remained the most important and effective propaganda thrust. In practice, the NSDAP had to realize that its goal was still far off. Talks with Brüning and Hindenburg did not seem to open up any opportunities for a role in the Government. The dangers inherent in the National Socialist demand for the Ministries of the Interior and Defense were patently obvious. The parliamentary activities of its huge Reichstag delegation were so clearly demagogic that the sympathies of the center and right-wing parties, as well as of wealthy backers, were strained. The proposals for the expropriation of the "bank and money-market princes" and "Eastern Jews," for the nationalization of commercial banks, for strict controls of mortgage, stock, and credit policies, quite obviously designed to get votes, only exacerbated the crisis situation. On the other hand, Brüning's rigorous deflationary course and his efforts to improve foreign relations were not designed to counteract the rapid deterioration of the situation and its domestic consequences. The noisy National Socialist Reichstag faction, in union with the Communists, had, back in October, 1930, succeeded in its main objective: the obstruction and paralysis of parliament. The tumultuous and inconsequential debates only seemed to bear out the popular propaganda against parliamentary democracy which maintained that the "gossip chamber" was completely unqualified to find a way out of the German crisis. In March, 1931, the National Socialists even considered briefly whether or not to form an independent Reichstag of the National Opposition in Weimar, under the chairmanship of their parliamentary chief, Frick. But in the end they believed the Government's threat to act against Thuringia.

[8] Otto-Ernst Schüddekopf, *Das Heer und die Republik* (Hanover, 1955), pp. 265 ff. See also Edouard Calic, *Ohne Maske: Hitler—Breiting Geheimgespräche 1931* (Frankfurt/Main, 1968).

The party's standard response to specific demands continued to be a mixture of ideology, Machiavellianism, and baseless demagoguery, yet this did not appear to lessen its impact. The belief of democrats and political experts that this young movement could be halted or won over or refuted by rational arguments proved overly optimistic in an atmosphere of intense national crisis. Even at this stage of parliamentary participation of the NSDAP—and also in the small states with NSDAP Cabinet members (Thuringia, Brunswick)—it became obvious that the problem could not be solved by giving the party responsibilities and duties. Neither defeats of Nazi propaganda proposals nor the party's repeated violations of tactical compromises and guarantees could halt its spread or destroy the illusions of the appeasers in the population, business groups, and the aristocracy. In fact it was late, perhaps too late, for rational discussions of programs, measures, and aims. The decisions that made an impact and overshadowed all efforts to rebut National Socialism were made not at this level but in brutal street battles and in mass meetings. Noise and violence were the means by which the fight for power was being conducted. (For example, noisemakers, stink bombs, and white mice were used by Goebbels to break up the film premiere of *All Quiet on the Western Front*.) Bloody fights and street brawls marked the debate with the opponents of the Left—the enemy incarnate. A minor civil war enveloped the country, at the cost of about three hundred lives in one year. The SA brought the growing number of unemployed workers into its ranks by offering pay, adventure, and the promise of victory. At the end of 1930, the National Socialists tried, at first in Thuringia and Brunswick, to have the Reichsbanner outlawed, even invoking the antimilitary provisions of the Versailles Treaty in this effort.

The helplessness of the Brüning Government and the regional elections of 1931 testified to the effectiveness of the Nazi strategy. The trend toward radicalism increased everywhere; in some places, the number of their votes was twice that of 1930. From different sides but with the same disastrous effects, Hitler, Hugenberg, and the Communists stormed the crumbling bastions of the democratic parties and governments. Prussia, still governed by the Weimar coalition under Social Democratic leadership, was a major objective. The attempt to topple this democratic stronghold through a plebiscite for the dissolution of the Prussian legislature found the hostile brothers of the radical Left and Right—NSDAP, DNVP, Stahlhelm, KPD, and even the DVP—on the same side. A total of 37 per cent of all eligible voters went to the polls on August 9, 1931, in support of the plebiscite. The fatal throttling of the moderate and democratic groups had gotten under way.

Yet there was still reason to believe that National Socialism would not be able to hold to its course, that it would founder on its own inner contradictions and on the impossibility of satisfying all its creditors, of doing justice to both the upper and the lower social classes. The antiparliamentary party found itself in an embarrassing position not only in parliament. A chain of bloody and violent acts endangered the legality fiction and in the eyes of many citizens put the National Socialists on a similar level as the feared Bolshevists—or what the Bolshevists were imagined to be. This congruence seemed to be borne out also by some interchanges between the radical Left and Right, as for example the defection to the KPD of Lieutenant Richard Scheringer, who at the Leipzig Reichswehr trial had been found guilty of Nazi activities. In March, 1931, the Central Government finally roused itself to more stringent countermeasures in an emergency decree against political excesses; the NSDAP responded merely with a not particularly popular demand for Hindenburg's resignation. At the same time, the party found itself publicly condemned by the Catholic Church for its ideology and cultural policies. Violence and racism, however, did not prevent the party from acquiring a growing following among Protestants; it even formed a separate National Socialist elite troop, the German Christians.

Hitler himself clung to his pose of the remote leader and arbiter outside and above everyday affairs, a tactic that allowed him to divorce himself from the risks inherent in his course. He still had to fear the consequences of possible official moves against a party dependent on the good will of the Right, of economic interests, and of the Army. Moreover, his expulsion from Germany as a stateless foreigner was a real possibility. He could not afford to repeat the mistakes of 1923. Army and Government had to be placated. This was done whenever a hitch developed in the legality course and the true intentions of the Nazi activists emerged too nakedly, as for example the renewed revolt of SA chieftain Stennes in April, 1931, who had pressed his demands for a violent seizure of power and a march on Berlin too hard and had refused to knuckle under to the evasionary tactics of Munich.

The problem of the SA did not abate after Röhm's reappearance. Since Hitler had become the supreme head of the SA after Pfeffer's departure, he could not dodge decisions about the relationship between party and SA as readily as in the past. The conflict over financing, as well as over the political functions and organizational status of the growing and increasingly confident party army, remained unresolved. The SA's claim to be the political soldiers of the entire party, and not simply the instrument of regional chiefs and functionaries, intensified the ambivalence of the party structure at a time of tactical and organizational difficulties created by the mass organization. This unsettling of the party structure did not make the controls and discipline dictated by the legality strategy any easier. This continuing dilemma undoubtedly was a contributory factor in Hitler's decision to build up an SS largely independent of the SA leadership as the more reliable instrument for the strengthening of his own position. Already in November, 1930, Hitler put the SS in charge of policy functions within the party and relieved the SA of its authority in this area. The future role of the SS in the transformation of the Third Reich from police state to SS state was becoming discernible. In return, Hitler tolerated the expectation that after his victory, the SA would play a major role in the building up of the Army. As the "reservoir of a future national army," it was to prepare itself for this task.

The bloody "solution" of 1934 is connected with the problems inherent in this extremely vague arrangement of party, SS, SA, and the military, for Hitler simultaneously was making every effort to establish good relations with the Army. One of the central precepts of the legality course—in deference to the memory of 1923—was to avoid conflict and rivalry with the military, or any act that might provoke calling out the Army against the party or SA. Now as later Hitler, in characteristic temporizing fashion, permitted two basically incompatible tendencies to coexist. In this he was helped by the inclination in the officer corps, including Schleicher and occasionally even Groener, to see the SA and the Stahlhelm as welcome helpers in their quest to strengthen the "defensive will" so long as the harsh provisions of Versailles prevailed—provided Hitler accepted the primacy of the Reichswehr and kept his impatient subordinates from violent actions and putsch attempts. And this the Leader did whenever the tacit agreement seemed in danger. The constant tensions between the Army and Republican politics, especially the traditional distrust of the military on the part of the SPD, which a youthful group around Reichstag Deputy Julius Leber vainly sought to win over to a more modern position, also made the Army more receptive toward the promilitary NSDAP. In 1931, Hitler's protestations of adherence to legality were rewarded with the revocation of a 1929 law barring the employment of NSDAP members in defense plants.

But the SA continued to be barred from legal military training and activity. Its main task was the staging of demonstrations, parades, and mass meetings. The Army command believed that the expulsion of Stennes—like the removal of Röhm in 1934—bore out their fatal delusion that Hitler was pursuing and was the guarantor of a course of moderation and cooperation, against the revolutionaries of his party. After all, at the height of the conflict, Stennes' followers had leveled the charge against Hitler "that the NSDAP had departed from the revolutionary course of true National Socialism, had followed the reactionary line of a coalition party and consequently had relinquished —purposely or accidentally—the pure ideal for which we are fighting." [9] And Schleicher himself assured the Army command time and again that the NSDAP was developing fealty to the state and under Hitler's influence could be made into a party capable of governance.

The National Socialist strategy manifested itself with particularly momentous consequences in the reorganization of the national opposition against Weimar, which made its public bow with great fanfare at a conference in Bad Harzburg in October, 1931. Even in these changed conditions, the occasion was reminiscent of the military re-

[9] Declaration of support for Stennes by Pomeranian SA chieftains, quoted by Bennecke, *op. cit.*, p. 165.

views that preceded Hitler's abortive putsch of 1923. To be sure, the Harzburg Front from the very outset was burdened by grave conflicts within the right-wing camp; Hugenberg and Hitler were as disunited as ever in their claim to leadership, and the rivals of the NSDAP pitted their greater economic and social influence against the party's obvious numerical superiority. But Harzburg was nonetheless another way station on the road to the destructive alliance between NSDAP–SA and DNVP–Stahlhelm—supported by aristocratic honoraries like the Crown Prince and ex-generals like the politicized Seeckt—which, after some friction between those unequal partners, finally formed the basis of the Hitler coalition. The breakthrough, in January, 1933, was in large measure effected through a revival of the Harzburg Front. Hitler's strategy had to survive three critical stages: the Presidential elections, the attempts to form a government in the summer of 1932, and finally the party crisis at the end of that year.

Hitler's decision to run for the Presidency was his first venture into electoral politics. His departure from his position of standing outside the Republic and his decision to compete in democratic elections for the highest office in the land meant a further broadening of his strategy of legality. It also meant that the National Socialists came out not only against Hindenburg but also against the nationally tinged alternative to Hindenburg, their Harzburg partners. The fact that Hitler received more than one-third of the total vote (36.8 per cent), while Düsterberg, the candidate of the German Nationals and the Stahlhelm, was badly beaten (6.8 per cent) demonstrated the superiority of the National Socialists over the Conservative–German National forces; only one year later, the illusions of the Hugenberg-Papen camp were to come to an ignominious end. At the same time, the Presidential elections led to another step in the tactics of legality: a contemptible move on the part of Brunswick made the stateless professional politician Hitler a pro forma government councillor. Ironically, his nominal job was to represent that minute state in Berlin. And so in February, 1932, Hitler finally became a German citizen, eligible to vote and to run for public office. Another plan that had been considered was to give him the chair of Political Pedagogy at the Technical University of Brunswick. Such were the convoluted ways and possibilities opened up by the legality strategy.

The waiting period following the temporary ban of the SA, the Papen interlude, and finally Schleicher's attempt to split the NSDAP put additional burdens on the National Socialist leadership. They failed to make the breakthrough in the large cities which might have brought them closer to an absolute majority. The dilemma of the legality strategy increased in proportion to the growth of the radical parties brought on by unemployment and general opposition to Presidential rule. It is entirely possible that Hitler ultimately would have foundered on this dilemma if in the early days of 1933 he had not, most unexpectedly, been presented with the chance of forming a government by a revived Harzburg Front. Numerous apologists maintain to this day that it was only proper that the leader of the strongest party be called upon to form a government. But there are at least two reasons why such a formalistic approach evades the core of the problem. First, there was never any doubt how this party leader and his chieftains, the sworn enemies of democracy, would use their power, and second, Hitler was determined to govern by extraparliamentary methods, by Presidential decree and suspension of parliament, and not with a democratic majority government. The argument that the legal summons of the leader of the strongest party was in line with democratic procedure, that it was in effect obligatory, must be measured against these factors. Moreover, the fact that throughout the life of the Weimar Republic, until 1932, the SPD, the strongest German party, was by no means invariably called upon to form the Government would seem to argue against the justification offered for the National Socialist takeover.

REFLECTION: THE "LEGAL REVOLUTION"

The victory of National Socialism, the alarmingly rapid triumphant march of an apparently irrevocable totalitarian system of government in Germany, was consolidated in less than two years, between January 30, 1933, and August, 1934. By the summer of 1933, totalitarian one-party rule had become a reality. A comparison of events in Germany with those which ten years earlier in Italy and fifteen years earlier in Russia had led to the installation of totalitarian systems points up many differences. Though the Bolshevik seizure of power was accomplished as rapidly, it was the result of a planned, armed *coup d'état*, and moreover, the revolutionary Soviet Government turned into a totalitarian dictatorship only after some years. And it took Italian Fascism, in appearance and aims more closely related to National Socialism, six years to overwhelm the opposition completely and establish its one-party dictatorship, and even then not in the same total, exclusive fashion as Hitler's Third Reich. Whereas Hitler, as Leader and Chancellor, formally retained all power in his hands, in Italy the King and monarchy, however insignificant their weight, continued their existence alongside and above Mussolini. To be sure, in all three cases we are dealing with the seizure of power by a violent minority. The methods they used had many similarities, and in many respects they even copied from each other; the Communist coup tactics undoubtedly served as an example in the planning of the Fascist seizure, and the Fascist example in turn played a role in the National Socialist takeover. Yet considerable differences remain.

If nothing else, the preconditions differed. In Russia, the revolution took place against the background of an absolutistic state and agrarian, feudal society of an "underdeveloped" country. In "semideveloped" Italy, parliamentary democracy was unable to cope with the explosive force of the transition to industrialism. Germany, on the other hand, was faced with the political and psychological problems of the unresolved defeat of 1918, and above all with internal structural crises of its already highly developed industrial mass society. These factors underlie all explanations of the unique course and success of the National Socialist seizure of power. Essential to any such attempt is the stress laid on the individual components of the development.

In addition to the ideological and sociological reflections according to which the totalitarian state was the product of an almost unstoppable series of historical and socio-economic causal factors, there is the political analysis which considers the immediate process of the seizure of power in the light of the special conditions of our time. Though taking account of historical and sociological factors, it nonetheless confines itself to the concrete, differentiated facts of the event itself. This type of analysis maintains that only an in-depth study of the specific development, of the special technique and tactics of the seizure of power, can avoid the pitfalls of erroneous generalizations and, out of the welter of historical and sociological determinism, sift and classify the causes.

The slogan of legal revolution offers the key to the character and development of the National Socialist power seizure. National Socialist propagandists, politicians, and constitutional experts all along emphasized that although Hitler's takeover was the beginning of a revolution that would profoundly affect all aspects of life, it was a completely legal, constitutional process. The paradoxical concept of a "legal revolution" artificially linked two contradictory axioms of political action and behavior. The significance of this legality tactic with revolutionary aspirations was in fact more than a mere propaganda gimmick and should not be underestimated. In examining specific components of the political process, we find that this tactic played a decisive role in surrounding this new type of totalitarian power seizure with its seductive aura of effectiveness and made all legal, political, or even intellectual resistance so difficult, and, in the opinion of many, well-nigh impossible.

This holds true of the earlier preconditions as well. The abortive putsch of 1923 had convinced Hitler that any direct attack on the existing order was doomed. Neither the Government nor the Army had been caught napping in 1923; the defenses of the democratic parties, including the unions, proved strong enough to withstand a putsch, despite all the internal and external problems of the Republic. Above all, the very respect for authority and bureaucracy which so strained the fabric of the Weimar Republic at the same time proved a considerable obstacle to all coup attempts. However great the sympathies for the critics and enemies of the Republic, it seems that holding fast to legality, legitimacy, and the values of law and order (if not freedom) were among the traditions of the authoritarian state in Germany. That is why the 1918 revolution did not spread, why the Kapp Putsch of 1920 failed, and why, despite all dictatorial aspirations of the Army and of Seeckt, the Republic survived in 1923.

These factors prescribed the road of the reorganized NSDAP after

Hitler's release from prison, a road to which he kept despite impatient revolutionaries in his party and the SA, despite the seeming weakness and hopelessness of his position in a parliamentary democracy. Yet at the same time, the German people's deeply rooted aversion to and mistrust of overt revolution opened up a new possibility to the tactician of legal revolution: the road via Presidential dictatorship.

A double defect of the Weimar Constitution made this possible. First, in the overwhelming opinion of scholars, the Constitution did not preclude the erosion and abrogation of its substance by constitutional means. This basically is what had been happening since 1930, and particularly after 1932; the process was completed in 1933 with the Reichstag fire decree and the Enabling Act. Hitler spelled out the possibility of the legal dismemberment of the Constitution in unmistakable terms in his legality oath at the 1930 Leipzig Reichswehr trial, when he told the court: "The Constitution only maps out the arena of battle, not the goal. We enter the legal agencies and in that way will make our party the determining factor. However, once we possess the constitutional power, we will mold the state into the shape we hold to be suitable." [10]

At that time the NSDAP was of course still far from playing a decisive role in parliament. And even at the moment of its greatest expansion, in the summer of 1932, it held little more than one-third of the parliamentary seats; the legal road via a majority party remained blocked to Hitler, particularly when the elections of November, 1932, showed a clear decline in National Socialist strength.

But here a second weakness of the Weimar constitutional and governmental system offered a way out of the seemingly insurmountable dilemma created by the legality strategy, namely the possibility of a Presidential government without and even against the will of parliament and of democratic public opinion. The gist of the growing body of literature on this theme is that the Presidential dictatorial powers under the famous-infamous Article 48 of the Weimar Constitution, intended specifically to protect the democratic order against radical efforts to overthrow it in the early postwar years, now, under a President with a different orientation, served diametrically opposite purposes. In the days of the Brüning Government (1930), and certainly during the authoritarian Papen and Schleicher Cabinets (1932), it became apparent that the possibility of an extra- let alone antiparliamentary government would inevitably paralyze parliament and parties. The ever-present possibility of invoking emergency powers offered a convenient escape-hatch from political responsibility, and at the same time prepared the population for the type of authoritarian ideas of government which were being bandied about with growing force by propagandists and in the universities. The catastrophic repercussions of the world-wide economic crisis, together with the public esteem

[10] Hitler before the Federal Court of Leipzig, September 25, 1930, in Schüddekopf, *op. cit.*, pp. 265 ff.

enjoyed by a President receptive to such authoritarian concepts, turned the possibility of throttling democracy by authoritarianism into reality. Out of the confusing welter of political and personal factors leading to Hitler's Chancellorship, one fact emerges clearly: in the course of the negotiations, Hitler adhered to the basic demand that as the head of a Presidential government he, too, must be granted the extraordinary dictatorial emergency powers. Hitler gained "legitimate" control of the Government not as the head of a parliamentary coalition, as a misleading apologia still suggests, but through this authoritarian loophole in the Weimar Constitution. On January 30, 1933, the new Chancellor found himself in a position to reap the fruit of his successful legality strategy—swearing formal allegiance to a Constitution which he immediately set about to destroy. With that, the real seizure of power got under way; now it was demonstrated how the tactic of gaining power by legal means could be brought into line with the strategy of revolution and blended with the technique of seizing power by overtaking, eliminating, and leveling all political, social, and intellectual safeguards and counterforces. To do this, another magic formula was needed to confuse the mind, deflect the opponents, and deceive or seduce Hitler's allies. The name of this magic formula was "national revolution."

This was the slogan under which the so-called legal revolution unfolded in the first seven weeks of Hitler's Presidential rule—up to the remolding of the basis of government through passage of the Enabling Act on March 23, 1933. Ever since the anti–Young Plan campaign, and particularly since the establishment of the Harzburg Front, Hitler had courted industry, the military, and large landholders to join in a national opposition of right-wing parties, but now no longer as a mere drummer and pioneer whom his conservative-national partners could discard. In this, too, he had learned the lesson of 1923 well. In the years that followed, the alliance with the reactionary Right served merely as a political tool in the battle against the Republic. Wherever this alliance was put to the test, it fell apart, as during the Presidential elections of 1932, when Hitler on his own tried to run against Hindenburg and Düsterberg. But at the end of 1932, once his conservative partners—the German Nationals with Papen and Hugenberg, the Stahlhelm and its industrial and agrarian backers—indicated their willingness to accept a government under National Socialist direction, Hitler readily accepted Papen's offer to revive the alliance. The result was the reappearance of the Harzburg Front, at the very moment when the NSDAP faced grave internal problems, when the economy stood on the brink of recovery, and when the Schleicher Government was about to institute determined countermeasures.

It became apparent during the formation of the new Government that the National Socialists, in making their power claims by donning the programmatic garb of the "above-party" national revolution, also acquired an unrivaled ideological framework for the constitutional implementation of their legal revolution. The Government was composed of only three National Socialists and eight conservatives, who in addition to the Vice Chancellorship held such important Ministries as Defense, Economics, and Foreign Affairs; moreover, the conservatives felt confident of the President and the Army. To all appearances, this was surely a coalition Cabinet capable of containing National Socialist ambitions: "We have engaged him [Hitler]," Vice Chancellor Papen, the initiator of the Government, stated triumphantly, in view of his own firm ties to Hindenburg.[11] And he told a conservative critic, Ewald von Kleist-Schmenzin, who later joined the resistance: "What do you want? I have Hindenburg's confidence. Within two months we will have pushed Hitler so far into a corner that he'll squeak." [12] In fact, however, it was not the National Socialists but their self-assured partners who were roped in. Even before the swearing-in of this "Government of the national concentration" on January 30, the dominating power of Chancellor Hitler, who in contrast to his partners knew what he wanted, became apparent: When, in opposition to Hugenberg, he was able to win his fight to have the Reichstag dissolved once again, the non–National Socialist front in the Cabinet was already broken. This breakthrough was to be repeated time and again in Cabinet sessions. No resistance on this level ever materialized, even though the National Socialists took over the majority of ministry posts only at a much later date.

This, however, was not only a consequence of the delusions and opportunism with which the German Nationals entered into the alliance, confident of their prestige and their influence in economic life, society, and Army. It was a consequence as well of the unequal distribution of power in the Government and in the political arena as a whole, all external appearances to the contrary. As it turned out, possession of the Chancellorship and of the Interior Ministries in the Reich and in Prussia (posts held by Frick and Göring, respectively), was all that was needed to turn the national revolution into a National Socialist takeover. Reich Defense Minister Blomberg's ready susceptibility to the blandishments of the National Socialists and their promises to rearm the military was yet another contributing factor. A series of emergency laws based on the ill-fated Article 48 and enacted in February, 1933, to which Hindenburg, blinded by Hitler's conservative, Christian-national promises, agreed, laid the foundations for the power through which the National Socialists were able almost at will to control and oppress the country.

This, however, could not be accomplished without doing some injury to legal process. Thus, a decree passed on February 6, 1933, giving Göring practically full control over Prussia was in clear violation of the findings of the State Court in the Prussian conflict of 1932. Also, the rigorous limitation on freedom of the press and assembly, and

[11] Count Lutz Schwerin-Krosigk, *Es geschah in Deutschland* (Tübingen and Stuttgart, 1951), p. 147.

[12] Ewald von Kleist-Schmenzin, "Die letzte Möglichkeit," *Politische Studien,* **X** (1959), p. 92.

above all the utilization of the Reichstag fire in the permanent abrogation of all basic civil rights, on which the Third Reich based its life-
long emergency powers, went far beyond existing constitutional
practices. But a façade of legality was preserved insofar as none of the
offices responsible or accountable for the preservation of the legal state
—from the President and the Army down to the ministries, the state
governments, the parties, the trade unions, and the courts—resisted or
effectively opposed these power grabs. Their failure helped to erect the
façade of a national revolution in the early weeks. Despite substantial
evidence to the contrary, Hitler's national partners continued to cling
to this fiction until by the end of June they were irrevocably outmaneuvered. They clung to this legend with almost fearful readiness in
the hope that they thereby could ward off the threatening alternative
of Nazi autocratic rule. That their behavior made this possible at all,
and without any risk for Hitler, was recognized too late by accomplices
like Hugenberg, and by men like Papen never at all.

Thus, the mistaken notion of the legal revolution was able to blossom
effectively only with the help of another mistaken notion—that of the
national revolution. For when the new Reichstag elections of March 5,
despite the propaganda and the terror, failed to bring Hitler his expected majority, he once more fell back on the national alliance. In
a gigantic display at Potsdam on March 21, he repeated the national-
conservative pledges of the early days which so deeply impressed
the middle class, civil service, and Army, and deflected their attention from the terrorist methods of the Nazi leadership. *"Wo
gehobelt wird, fliegen Späne"* (approximately, "You can't make an
omelet without breaking eggs") was a frequently heard saying meant
to reassure the people about the "unavoidable excesses" of this
national "turning point" (thus Papen). That is why, on March 21,
1933, the anniversary of the convocation of Bismarck's Reichstag
(1871), Goebbels, the new Propaganda Minister, staged a gigantic,
virtuoso show at the tomb of Frederick the Great in Potsdam. In the
presence of Hindenburg and the Crown Prince, before a chair set aside
for the Emperor, the Potsdam "touching comedy" (*Rührkomödie*) [13] successfully distracted monarchists and nationalists from the true nature
of the spreading National Socialist dictatorship. The black, red, and gold
national colors were replaced by the black, white, and red flag of the
national revolution, a violation of the Constitution which the German
National partners of Hitler could hardly object to, in view of their
demand that these colors of Bismarck's Reich replace the flag of the
Republic. Here, too, the apparent subjugation of National Socialist
ambitions to the common goal was preserved, since the swastika
banner was after all only one of the two flags of the national revolution.

But only two days after the Potsdam show, the veil was lifted, and
the reality of the National Socialist power-seizure stood nakedly re-

[13] Thus Friedrich Meinecke, *The German Catastrophe: Reflections and
Recollections* (Cambridge, Mass., 1950), p. 12.

vealed. The bourgeois parties, from the Liberals to the Center, had been so intimidated by the pressure of accomplished facts and so impressed by the appeal to nationalism that they felt they could not withhold their agreement to the Enabling Act. To be sure, this decision of March 23, 1933, in which the Reichstag, against the opposition of the persecuted Left, handed all legislative powers over to the Government, was an outgrowth of the permanent state of emergency proclaimed in the fatal Reichstag fire decree of February 28. It should also be pointed out that Hitler proceeded to violate the limiting provisions of the Enabling Act on which the bourgeois parties thought they could rely; alone the fact that the act was passed by a Reichsrat (the upper chamber of parliament) which, after the dismemberment of the state governments by coups, unquestionably was not properly constituted must be considered irregular. And the Center and Liberals probably were motivated also by the hope that in this way the regime could be brought back from government by radical decrees to the area of legislative rule. But precisely this fatal deception effected by the legal revolution enabled National Socialism to consolidate and expand its rule much more rapidly and more totally than Italian Fascism.

The enormous importance of the Enabling Act was rooted in this deception even more than in the concrete powers granted by it. It is true that the sanctions and acts of terror up to and including the brutal suppression and annihilation of the resistance movement were largely based on the radical decrees of the early days before the passage of the Enabling Act. But now the willing collaborators in the civil service and the courts, on which National Socialism, lacking its own specialists, was so dependent, were able to find reassuring legal provisions; after all, given such apparently unexceptional legal foundations, there was no basis for any real objections to a government, however turbulent and violent, and however regrettable some of its "excesses" (which were, however, "exceptions"). Wasn't it a good thing—so state the files of many a high official of that time—that the irresistible revolution was carried out in so legal a fashion? It was therefore only logical to do everything in one's power to assure this legal revolution every technical and administrative success.

This attitude obviously was responsible for the preparatory work by nonparty civil servants of the Ministry of the Interior in the drafting of the Enabling Act, and it was a factor in all important subsequent judicial and administrative efforts, as for example in the formulation of the basic Civil Service Act of April 7, 1933, by which all Jewish employees as well as all politically unreliable persons were removed from their posts. It also opened the floodgates of petty, sordid careerist ambition, personal enmity, and profitable denunciation. These motivations facilitated the National Socialist power drive in all areas of social and cultural life, particularly in the schools and universities, and sealed the guilty involvement of people in all walks of life, tying them to the regime through fear and preferential treatment and breaking their will—an essential presupposition of every totalitarian system.

The rapidity with which the political Left was overwhelmed, to the astonishment even of the new rulers, also was connected with deception and self-delusion. The reasons were manifold. Because of their refusal to take hold of the reins of government in 1930 and their capitulation before Papen's coup in Prussia, the Social Democrats found themselves excluded from the political arena even before 1933. And the Communists had not passed up any opportunity to stir up civil strife and weaken the democratic defenses. Contrary to the claims of present-day East German historians, it is an indisputable fact that the KPD's main attack was directed against "social fascist" Social Democracy. The Communist leadership, despite the antifascist propaganda campaigns, cooperated in the overthrow of the Social Democratic Government of Prussia, and on many occasions made common cause with the National Socialists against the Republic: in parliamentary votes of no confidence, in the Prussian plebiscite of 1931, during the Berlin transport workers' strike of November, 1932. This incongruous yet typical cooperation was based on the calculation that with the overthrow of the Republic, Germany would become ripe for a Communist revolution. Moscow, which sanctioned this policy, obviously did not count on the survival of the National Socialist dictatorship, but saw it merely as the executor of a preparatory function. This explains why Stalin immediately initiated efforts to establish friendly relations with Hitler, and even to continue the cooperation between the Reichswehr and the Red Army. In return, he was willing to accept without protest the persecution of Communists; one of the first international acts of recognition of the Third Reich (in April, 1933) was the renewal of a German-Russian trade agreement that had expired in 1931.

Moscow's strategy was based on a monumental misjudgment of the nature of the National Socialist takeover. By denying it the character of a true revolution and maintaining that it was simply a manifestation of the final crisis of monopoly capitalism, it served to paralyze and fragment the forces of resistance and steer them onto a false course. This held true particularly for the SPD, which in March, 1933, still had a large following and a strong organization. Hitler feared a general strike, but the SPD and the unions showed a touching faith in legality; their primary task, they thought, was to keep their organizations from being outlawed; to keep them intact for the moment when the new regime would collapse (a matter of months!). Contrary to all expectations, the SPD confined itself to legal opposition, and thus it, too, fell victim to the legality strategy. This miscalculation was intensified by yet another move of the Socialist leadership. Immediately after January 30, 1933, they announced that the fight against the reactionary capitalists, that is, against the Hugenberg camp, was the paramount issue. Apparently, Hitler's accomplices were held to be more powerful and dangerous. Thus, in its own way, the Left became the victim of the Marxist thesis of Nazism as mere counterrevolution and of the deceptive slogan of a national revolution. Real resistance began to form only after it was too late.

THE STEPS TO DICTATORSHIP

The confusion of specific events and motives that paved the way for the NSDAP and made possible the rapid transformation of Hitler's Presidential Cabinet into a one-party, one-man dictatorship is not easily unraveled even today. Some explanations tend to underestimate the complexity and multiplicity of causes as well as the role of accident and improvisation, and to see the establishment of the Hitler regime as the result of superior planning. On the other hand, explanations—which many look on as an apology—that fail to take seriously the stated goals of Hitler and his colleagues and that interpret National Socialist policy as mere reactions to chance and the challenge of the times (as is done by A. J. P. Taylor in his controversy with Trevor-Roper) are also misleading.[14] Such interpretations contradict the terrible realization that National Socialist ideology and doctrine of government achieved in the Third Reich—on both the domestic and foreign fronts. This had been the basic and fatal error of the non–National Socialists in Germany, and it was repeated after 1933 by the appeasement of the outside world. In this sense, the history of National Socialism from beginning to end is the history of its underestimation.

The dramatic events of the weeks leading up to January 30, 1933, were the result of individual decisions. Of course, the decisions reached were the product of and determined by the existing political situation, by a body of problems encompassing the entire history and prehistory of the Weimar Republic. Yet at this juncture, events still were not governed by any imperative necessity but rather were dependent more than ever before on the actions of a small group of men. In line with constitutional reality as well as the general trend toward an authoritarian state, the power of decision rested with Hindenburg. As matters stood, a decision could be made only by persons belonging to the inner circle around a President who for years had been preoccupied with authoritarian solutions. Schleicher was one of the important members of the clique around Hindenburg that also included ex-Chancellor von Papen, Hindenburg's son and adjutant, Oskar, and the President's State Secretary, Meissner. After becoming Chancellor and emerging from the shadows of planning and intrigue into the glare of publicity, Schleicher attempted to broaden the base of the Government. But the democratic parties distrusted Schleicher's abrupt change from authoritarianism to cooperation; the Socialist trade unions, which

[14] Hugh Trevor-Roper, "Hitler's Kriegsziele," in *Vierteljahrshefte für Zeitgeschichte*, No. 8 (1960), pp. 121 ff. Cf. the misinterpretation of A. J. P. Taylor, *The Origins of the Second World War* (London, 1961; New York, 1962), pp. 67 ff., 131 ff. The "revisionist" reinterpretation of the Reichstag fire, which overemphasizes the improvisational nature of the seizure of power, tends toward the same error. Fritz Tobias, *The Reichstag Fire* (New York, 1964), is particularly questionable, and Hans Mommsen, "Der Reichstagsbrand und seine politischen Folgen," in *VfZG*, No. 14 (1964), pp. 352 ff., as well.

initially had reacted favorably to Schleicher's advances, had to deal with the skepticism of the Social Democratic leadership. On the opposite side, Schleicher succeeded in winning over Gregor Strasser, still the most important man in the National Socialist party structure, to the idea of cooperation, but his hopes for splitting the NSDAP were dashed.

The start of the Schleicher Government had been quite auspicious. The new Reichstag (December 4, 1932), including the shrunken National Socialist delegation, refrained from a vote of no confidence; a return to Brüning's tolerative legislature seemed a possibility. But Schleicher's efforts to overcome Papen's heritage of isolation met with little success in the face of Strasser's indecisiveness and the paralysis of the democratic parties. On December 8, 1932, Strasser resigned from all his National Socialist positions; it was not a revolt against Hitler but an act of sheer frustration. In Hitler's monomaniacal view, however, it was a stab in the back for which he ultimately took bloody revenge —on Schleicher as well as on Strasser.

It soon became apparent that Schleicher's enemies had not been idle; through the initiative of a handful of key persons, new alternatives opened up which brought down Schleicher and with him the last hopes for preventing a Nazi takeover. To be sure, Hindenburg had resisted the appointment of Hitler to the Chancellorship almost to the very last. But apparently he was disappointed and disturbed about the seeming lack of success of Schleicher's efforts, and this is where Papen came in. The motives of the ex-Chancellor, whom Hindenburg now called his *homo regius,* were of a personal as well as a practical nature. Annoyance with and envy of his former friend and patron Schleicher combined with the ambition once more to play a role and with his unaltered vision of the authoritarian state, which, after Schleicher's refusal of support, he hoped to realize through an alliance with the NSDAP. This was the background of the historically decisive weeks of Papen's secret negotiations with Hindenburg and Hitler, beginning with the meeting with Hitler on January 4, 1933, in the home of the Cologne banker Kurt von Schröder. These negotiations were initiated by Papen with the support of heavy industry; later they received the support of Ribbentrop and Oskar von Hindenburg, and finally they were helped by Hugenberg, by agrarian interests, and by the Stahlhelm.

The resurgence of the Harzburg Front was primarily a consequence of Papen's efforts; all available proof overwhelmingly contradicts the self-seeking apologia of the Papen memoirs on this point as well. The fact is that the NSDAP, paralyzed by the dilemma created by the power vacuum and by its election losses, and weakened by internal conflicts and financial problems, suddenly and to its own surprise was boosted to the highest level of political activity, removed from the threat posed by Schleicher's opposing plans, and given a power role— and this at the very moment when the economic crisis was beginning to abate. Having come to power, the party on the decline now was bound to profit from the new world-wide economic recovery, while in the past it had profited from the worsening of the general situation. This may be seen as a fateful chain of circumstances, but it was a direct result of Papen's manipulations and of the plans for an authoritarian reorganization of the Government that he hoped to realize with Nazi help but under his aegis.

Contrary to the fears of the new alliance, Schleicher's defenses had become weak, partly because of the understandable hesitancy of democratic parties weakened internally and grown unaccustomed to the exercise of parliamentary and governmental power. They responded to the approaches of the agile General with deepest mistrust. They recalled his liking for intrigue and thought him incapable of a true return to regular government, a genuine disavowal of authoritarian experiments, and a determined defense against the National Socialist power claims. A second reason for Schleicher's weakness was the knowledge that despite the ready support given the Chancellor by General von Hammerstein (the chief of the Army command), the Reichswehr would never be called out against Papen's plans, and thereby against Hindenburg. That, however, did not prevent the circulation as late as January 29 of rumors of an imminent Reichswehr putsch, rumors finally used by the men around Hindenburg to accelerate the final negotiations with Hitler and the reorganization of the Government. A third reason was the lack of accurate information available to Schleicher, despite the many known details, about the scope and true direction of opposing plans. Up to the very last, he held the type of alliance that actually came into being impossible, relied on Hindenburg's dislike of Hitler, and devoted his attention to the threat of a new Papen Cabinet. But above all, he never expected to be replaced as Minister of Defense by General von Blomberg, a man susceptible to National Socialist ideas, and robbed of all control over and influence on the future Government.

These were the immediate stages by which Hitler came to power. In these final months of the Republic, personal moves took on historical importance. They determined the outcome of the conflict over the ban of the SA, the overthrow of Brüning, Hindenburg's turning his back on the democratic version of Presidential rule, Papen's coup in Prussia and his frivolous dictatorial experiments, and finally Hitler's unexpected summons to the Chancellorship at a time when the economic crisis had passed its nadir and the NSDAP was beginning to sustain tangible losses. Any attempt to reduce the dramatic interplay of events and developments between June, 1932, and January, 1933, to one common denominator would be an irrelevant oversimplification. There can be no doubt that the intensification of the organizational problems of the Republic in the seemingly insurmountable power vacuum of 1932—involving as it did the mutual blocking of the democratic parties, totalitarian attempts at overthrow, and authoritarian rule—made possible the rise of National Socialism. But against this historico-political background, the ultimately decisive importance of the autocratic intrigues of a minute minority around the one remain-

ing power pillar, Hindenburg—a man devoid of all understanding—
remains an indisputable fact. That this could happen at all and meet
with so little active resistance seems to confirm that the parliamentary
Republic, after being overwhelmed by authoritarian experiments, was
no longer able to function. Yet this very fact was the fatal reverse side
of Presidential rule.

Mishaps and errors, consequence and accident, became an almost
inextricable mass of causes of the National Socialist seizure of power.
It was not a "necessary" development; even at the very end, there still
remained a freedom of choice, but one which the political and intellectual elite relinquished, partly in tired resignation, partly frivolously,
and partly maliciously. The early trend toward authoritarian solutions
outside the framework of a still strange democracy undoubtedly stimulated the growth of a variety of factors that helped bring about the
events of January 30, 1933, and their aftereffects. Nonetheless, up to
the very last moment there existed alternatives which are historically
equally well-founded. The final blow was dealt by the irresponsible
activities of the Papen-Hugenberg-Hindenburg camp. This tiny minority, through its ambitious, overweening alliance with the totalitarian
mass movement, helped the National Socialists into those positions of
power which Hitler could never have captured on his own. Instead of
the hoped-for restoration of authoritarian rule, there came a totalitarian dictatorship that overwhelmed not only the Weimar Republic,
but also the proponents of a so-called third solution between democracy
and dictatorship.

The subsequent road to a totalitarian one-party state was covered in
three stages. The first was marked by a massive intensification of
executive power by means of Presidential rule, followed by the liquidation of the constitutional pluralistic state by the one-party regime,
and finally by the institutionalization of the total leader dictatorship.
Immediately upon his appointment on February 1, Hitler persuaded
Hindenburg to dissolve parliament once again. A recalcitrant parliament was suspended for seven decisive weeks and the stage was set for
rule via emergency decree. On this pseudo-legal basis, freedom of the
press and opinion were sharply curtailed (February 4), Prussia was
brought in line (February 6), basic rights were repealed (February
28), and the states that still resisted National Socialism after the elections of March 5 were subjugated. In each instance, political pressure
and terror were used in combination with the dicta of Presidential
emergency decrees. This method served not only to legalize the dictatorship of the Government, but at the same time opened up more room
for the advancing forces of the party and its manifold organizations,
headed by the rapidly growing civil-war army of the SA.

Administrative leveling and National Socialist penetration of society
were the methods by which this first stage in the power seizure was
carried out. The typical and highly successful method consisted of a
mixture of pseudo-legal official decrees, threats of revolution, and terrorist pressure. This approach also marked the Reichstag elections of

March 5, 1933, which were held against the background of the state of emergency declared on February 28, and were marked by intimidation and an overpowering propaganda campaign. In view of this, the election results are rather astonishing. Even at this stage, the NSDAP still failed to garner a majority of the votes (43.9 per cent). Its Government was able to claim a narrow majority only because of the fatal alliance with the DNVP (8 per cent). The middle parties (Center and Liberals) maintained their 1932 strength (18 per cent), and the Left managed to get more than 30 per cent of the votes, despite persecution, suppression, and mass arrests of its candidates. The National Socialists gained primarily from the recruitment of former nonvoters and new voters and the large voter turnout (89 per cent), not at all a sign of political maturity but the result of the hectic propaganda efforts of the NSDAP. In numerous Catholic and working-class strongholds, the National Socialists suffered clear-cut defeats; in many places, they polled less than 20 per cent, and in some less than 10 per cent, of the votes. Agrarian Protestant regions, small towns, and the lower middle class continued to furnish the majority of NSDAP votes.[15]

The ensuing *Gleichschaltung* * of the states also reflected the interplay of the "upper" and "lower" echelons. The "electoral victory" was said to justify the political "coordination." But this was in accord neither with the results of the election nor with the federalist constitutional structure. Rather, it reflected the embarrassment of the rulers toward the states in which the party had not gained a majority: Bavaria, Württemberg, Baden, Hesse, Saxony, and the city states. The Government proceeded according to the recipe of the pseudo-legal coordination of Prussia, and by resorting to pseudo-revolutionary methods: mobilization of the SA, ultimatums to state governments, terror, and blackmail.

It soon became apparent that whatever resistance existed was weak, scattered, and without any real hope of success. Only in Bavaria, the largest German state after Prussia, were serious countermoves attempted. These were supported by old conservative-monarchist restoration tendencies which, in union with Bavaria's strong federalist traditions, resulted in an effort to prevent the imminent National Socialist regime by establishing a constitutional monarchy under the popular Crown Prince, Ruprecht. The reasons for this move were twofold: first, to utilize the defeat of the Weimar Republic to restore the monarchy, and thereby also emphasize Bavaria's independence of Prussia and the centralizing tendencies of the Central Government; and second, this move seemed the only possible basis for resisting the threatened subjugation of all states under National Socialist centralization. The programmatic statements on federal reform in the party

---

[15] Voting pattern analysis in K. D. Bracher, W. Sauer, and G. Schulz, *Die nationalsozialistische Machtergreifung* (2 vols.; Cologne and Opladen, 1962), pp. 93 ff.

* The term used by the Nazis for the leveling of state and society.— TRANSLATOR'S NOTE.

program and in Hitler's *Mein Kampf* were ambiguous; they did not go beyond vague promises for a "strong central power." This was another issue on which differences with a diversified membership were best avoided. But after the "coordination" of Prussia on February 6 by the deposition of its government, Bavaria began to feel threatened. In view of the existing power relationships, Munich shied away from an open conflict; it confined itself to legal depositions, and despite all negative experience hoped for a constitutional ruling by the State Court. But, in the swiftly moving course of events, the court never ruled. By the middle of February, a number of smaller states— Thuringia, Mecklenburg-Schwerin, Oldenburg, Brunswick, Anhalt, Lippe, and Mecklenburg-Strelitz—in which the National Socialists were in the government were to all effects and purposes taken over politically. But even so, the National Socialist Reichsrat delegation was still a minority. Now, however, the Damocles Sword of coordination through Reich commissars, which Papen had wielded in 1932, and Hitler and Göring were now wielding so successfully in Prussia, hung threateningly over all other German states.

In order to prevent what had been tried out in Prussia, the Bavarian Government under Minister President Heinrich Held and the BVP leadership under Fritz Schäffer changed their strategy in the middle of February to launch a campaign against the imposition of Reich Commissars. No Reich Commissar, so the slogan went, would be allowed to cross the River Main. South German federalism seemed to have become the final bastion of resistance to National Socialism. Here, too, the main hope was Hindenburg. In 1932, the President had repeatedly promised not to permit the dispatching of Commissars to Bavaria. And on February 4, 1933, he had sent a reassuring reply to a renewed inquiry by Held. Neither the President nor the Central Government, he stated, planned to send a Reich Commissar to Bavaria. A similar assurance was given by Papen in a conversation with Schäffer the following day. Papen, however, hinted that the National Socialists were toying with the idea of sending Reich Commissars to states with Social Democratic Ministers of the Interior (Police), as for example Hesse and Saxony. And on February 12, Frick dispatched a Ministerial Councillor to Hesse. The Bavarian Minister President reacted to this first storm signal with energetic protests. On February 17, Schäffer returned from a conversation with the President with the renewed promise that no Reich Commissar would ever be sent to Bavaria. Consequently, Schäffer told a Bavarian election rally that any Commissar sent to Bavaria in violation of Hindenburg's assurances would be promptly arrested.

On February 24, however, Frick, himself of Bavarian descent, told a Hamburg gathering that the Government would proceed ruthlessly against all states which refused to submit willingly. The governments would have to accept the new conditions and be made to realize that the Central Government was determined to establish its authority everywhere, he said. Papen made another attempt to calm the waves of discord by paying lip-service to federalism. And Hitler stated at a mass meeting in Munich that he himself was after all a Bavarian and therefore would not treat Bavaria badly. But he also added: "I did not give in while in opposition, and now, as the representative of state power, I will have the strength to protect the unity of the Reich." The "unity of the Reich" remained the tactical formula for National Socialist subjugation.[16]

In this situation, the decree of February 28 was passed. Its second paragraph contained this handy provision, long before the adoption of the Enabling Act: "If a state fails to take the necessary steps for the restoration of public safety and order, then the Central Government is empowered to take over the relevant powers of the highest state authority." This, together with the rigorous stipulations about the suspension of basic rights, made possible the arbitrary interference in local government and consequently in the federal structure of Germany. Although the decree dealt only with temporary interventions, they were in fact of a permanent nature, as was the decree itself, which was never rescinded. The subjugation of the states was completed in short order; events followed one another in swift succession. The interpretation of the decree was left solely to the judgment of Minister of the Interior Frick. If he thought that a state he disapproved of because it had not yet been brought in line was not dealing harshly enough with opponents of the current course, he could order and justify executive action against that state even without Hindenburg's approval. When the Minister President of Bavaria on that same February 28 once more told Hindenburg of his misgivings, he again received the by then incredible assurance that the President had no intention of sending Reich Commissars.

But protests based on legality and rule of law had become futile. Clinging to the fiction of the inviolability of the state showed a fatal misunderstanding of the power situation. Such legal resistance by tested methods was hopelessly unequal to the technique of the pseudo-legal seizure of power. In essence, the counterplans devised in Bavaria sought to have the Bavarian Government ask the Crown Prince to serve as General State Commissar with broad governmental powers during the declared state emergency, as a step toward the proclamation of the monarchy. It was a hasty, problematical plan. Nonetheless, Fritz Schäffer supported it strongly and Crown Prince Ruprecht agreed to it. But Held hesitated to make a decision which, strictly speaking, was undoubtedly unconstitutional, even though it might protect the spirit of the Constitution far more ably than the pseudo-legality of the National Socialist takeover. His legal adviser was close to the German Nationals and knew how to paint the dangers of violating the Constitution in bold colors. And when advisers to the Crown Prince reported from Berlin that Hitler's position was far stronger and far

[16] See particularly Karl Schwend, *Bayern zwischen Monarchie und Diktatur* (Munich, 1954), pp. 506 ff.; Erwein von Aretin, *Krone und Ketten* (Munich, 1955), pp. 155 ff.

more decisive than Hindenburg's and Papen's, all hopes for German National and Presidential support from Berlin collapsed.

Here, too, the illusions and weakness of Hitler's partners vis-à-vis National Socialist policies had detrimental consequences. The Bavarian envoy discussed the possibilities of a restoration of the monarchy as a barrier against National Socialist autocratic rule with Neurath, Krosigk, and Gürtner, but these non-National Socialist ministers counseled waiting; as a result, the Bavarian Government could not make up its mind about the plan, particularly since the Reich Defense Ministry was threatening to replace the Bavarian Army commandant, General von Leeb, thereby putting the support of the Bavarian Reichswehr in doubt. On March 1, Held was summoned to Berlin and, in an official meeting with Hitler, given strong warning; the Chancellor even invoked the threat of calling out the Reichswehr against Bavaria's plans. Held retreated, so as to deprive Hitler of a pretext for intervention. Once again, the dilemma of the policy of legal opposition became evident: It could not prevent the final blow, which was not long in coming.

The National Socialist leadership, vastly overstating its election victory of March 5, on the very next day prepared for the final blow against the states not yet under National Socialist rule. The NSDAP still could not hope to come to power in Bavaria by parliamentary means. On March 8, with the forcible subjugation of the other states in full swing, Hindenburg reassured the Bavarian delegate once again, and stated almost indignantly that he would finally like to have his promise believed that no Reich Commissar would enter Bavaria. Even Hitler gave similar assurances; however, he added that even in Bavaria the pressure from below might become so great that the Reich would have to intervene. This outlined that interplay of a stage-managed revolution from above and a manipulated revolution from below which was to play such a vital role in the takeover and in the coordination of the states. Since the "unified political direction of Reich and the states" which Hitler and the National Socialist leadership were now demanding ever more categorically could not be achieved by parliamentary means, they now resorted to revolutionary putschist methods, to "pressure from below," while at the same time providing for the pseudo-legal protection of these methods from above with the help of the decree of February 28.

In this manner, the dual methods were brought into play. On the night of March 9, Adolf Wagner, the Gauleiter of Munich and the most important stage director of the putsch, returned to Munich from strategy meetings in Berlin. While Hindenburg was still making reassuring promises and Hitler pretended ignorance, the Munich SA stood poised to force the resignation of the Bavarian Government. On the morning of March 9, in response to renewed Bavarian protests, Berlin still pretended ignorance, though the Nazi coups were being carried out in all other states. While Held was still feverishly consulting with his Police Minister and the Police President of Munich, the SA was readying itself for the first blow. Chief of Staff Röhm and Gauleiter Wagner appeared in Held's offices in full regalia and presented him with an ultimatum to install General Ritter von Epp, that early National Socialist and Free Corps leader who, as General State Commissar, had been instrumental in crushing the Munich *Räterepublik* in 1919. Röhm spoke of the "revolutionary" mood of the SA, but refrained from invoking orders from Berlin. This was in accord with Hitler's tactic of seemingly staying in the background, letting events in Munich take their course—though in fact they were obviously stage-managed. The self-deposition of the Bavarian Government in line with the National Socialist legality strategy would undoubtedly have been the easiest way out.

Held tried to postpone a decision. But meanwhile, armed SA and SS detachments were marching everywhere; the swastika flag was hoisted on the spire of Munich's City Hall, and the situation began to assume a revolutionary character. In the afternoon, Held discussed with Reichswehr officers the possibility of resistance. But in reply to an inquiry, the order came from the Defense Ministry in Berlin that "the Reichswehr must stand at parade rest, since the affair in Bavaria was considered a purely internal matter, and the Reichswehr had to stay out of it completely." [17] This also made the employment of the state militia questionable, though the Bavarian Ministerial Council still rejected the demand for the immediate resignation of the Government and the appointment of Epp. Once again Röhm, Epp, Wagner, and Himmler had to leave with empty hands. But now Berlin intervened. The document appointing Epp had been in readiness at the Reich Ministry of the Interior all along, and the decree of February 28 was invoked. The Bavarian envoy learned of Epp's appointment at 7:00 P.M. through the press department of the Central Government, although the Bavarian Government had not yet been officially informed. Held immediately wired his protests to the President, stating that Frick had exceeded his jurisdiction, for conditions in Bavaria by no means justified intervention, and that Hindenburg's guarantees had thereby been violated. The only answer was a telegram from Frick to Held containing the official notification and making Bavaria the last German state to be politically coordinated. A similar telegram with the appropriate instructions was sent to Epp. When Held sent a telegram to Hindenburg expressing his bitter disappointment, he received a reply via Meissner the next day (March 10) making obvious the utter impotence of the President: Epp's intervention was "made by the Reich Government on its own competence," and Hindenburg would ask Held to refrain from calling on him and to address his complaints to Hitler directly. This message gave clear evidence of the withdrawal of Hindenburg and Meissner's growing reliance on Hitler.

That Epp's appointment meant the seizure of power, not simply a temporary police emergency measure, is shown by the extent to which

[17] Schwend, *op. cit.*, pp. 538 ff.

he interfered with and encroached upon the personnel and legislative
policies of the Bavarian Government. The Government and legislature
continued to lead a brief shadow existence, but the final decision had
been made, not through a popular revolution, as was claimed, but
through interference from above. All major power tools were in the
hands of the National Socialists, who promptly began to build their
own new executive, with Heinrich Himmler as chief of the SS taking
over the police powers. This was the beginning of his national police
career. The SA began its excesses immediately on the night of March
10; Fritz Schäffer and other political leaders were brought to the
Brown House; recalcitrant newspapers were forcibly brought to heel
and unyielding editors and publishers arrested. The resignation of Held
became a mere formality. On March 16, Epp vested all powers of government in the National Socialist "Ministerial Commissars"; fantastic
accusations (treason, separatism) were leveled against the former
government.

The coup-like events in Bavaria bore the typical earmarks of the
National Socialist policy of *Gleichschaltung*. Developments in Württemberg, Baden, Saxony, Hesse, Hamburg, Bremen, and Lübeck followed a similar pattern. Threats of violence (from below) and
telegraphic intervention by Frick intermeshed, until governments
were replaced, generally by Reich Commissars. Württemberg after
January 30 had an interim government headed by the Center Party
leader Eugen Bolz. When the Hitler coalition in Württemberg, despite
tremendous propaganda efforts, remained in the minority (46.9 per
cent)—the Center and Liberal parties even registered gains—the
NSDAP prepared for the forcible takeover of that state. On the
night of March 6, it called for the overthrow of the Bolz Government
before a mass gathering on the market square of Stuttgart, and the
next day National Socialist troops hoisted the swastika flag at the legislature, the ministries, and all other public buildings. And on the
evening of March 8, Frick, contrary to all his promises, appointed the
National Socialist ex-Lieutenant Dietrich von Jagow as Reich Police
Commissioner, on the stereotyped grounds that the "maintenance of
public safety and order in Württemberg was no longer assured under
the existing police administration." This simply meant that "public
safety and order" were identical with a National Socialist seizure of
power. This, too, leaves no doubt about the true meaning and reasons
of National Socialist decrees and the myth of the legal assumption of
power. The sense of the Constitution was violated (as it had been in
Prussia and was to be in Bavaria) when Bolz was forced under protest to accept the appointment of Jagow.[18]

That the National Socialists in Württemberg also were not concerned
with the restoration of constitutional rule but with capturing power

[18] Wilhelm Keil, *Erlebnisse eines Sozialdemokraten* (Stuttgart, 1948), II,
487 ff.; Max Miller, *Eugen Bolz* (Stuttgart, 1951), pp. 433 ff.; Waldemar
Besson, *Württemberg und die deutsche Staatskrise 1928–1933* (Stuttgart,
1959), pp. 344 ff.

was evident when Jagow blocked the election of a State President (scheduled for March 11), to which the government and the state legislature had agreed as a constitutional resolution of the conflict. Instead, the disempowered ministers were kept in office until Gauleiter Wilhelm Murr was elected State President under the pressure of the real rulers. Only now was the de facto seizure of power legalized. The true nature of the much-touted legality, however, was revealed in Murr's speech at the giant victory demonstration of March 15: "The government will brutally beat down all who oppose it. We do not say an eye for an eye, a tooth for a tooth. No, he who knocks out one of our eyes will get his head chopped off, and he who knocks out one of our teeth will get his jaw bashed in." [19]

In the other states, the political coordination was carried through in similar fashion—by planned terror of regional National Socialist organizations and the simultaneous appointment of Reich Commissars, helped by Berlin's invocation of the Reichstag fire decree. The earliest move was made in Hamburg, where on the evening of March 5, the SA and SS occupied the City Hall, while simultaneously the Ministry of the Interior decreed that the Senate had to carry out the wishes of the National Socialists. The only choice left to the city's long-term democratic mayor was to resign in protest; and on March 7, a new Senate consisting of six National Socialists, two German Nationals, and two Stahlhelm members took over under the National Socialist leadership of Karl Krogmann. A day later, the Social Democratic senators of Bremen were forced to resign after a similar decree of the Interior Ministry, while Frick appointed a Reich Commissar and the SA occupied the City Hall. In Lübeck, the Social Democratic mayor and senators resigned after Frick intervened by telegram and handed over police powers to the National Socialist Gauinspektor Walther Schröder.

In Baden, coalition talks between the Center Party and the NSDAP began on March 7, and it seemed as if there the government was to be reorganized legitimately. But on March 9, police powers in Baden were also handed over to a National Socialist Commissar (Robert Wagner), and two days later a National Socialist government was installed.

In Saxony, the same "solution" was arrived at on March 10, under the stage management of a Police Commissar (Manfred von Killinger), though for the time being the SA was called off, after a series of excesses on the streets and in the legislature.

In Hesse, Frick intervened on March 8 and installed a National Socialist Police Commissar. By the middle of March, with the suspension of the state legislature through the passage of a regional Enabling Act and the election of a National Socialist State President alongside the new Hessian State Commissar (the youthful author of the notorious Boxheim Documents, Werner Best), the political coordination of the German states had become a fact. The securing and consolidation of these regional takeovers, however, was a long-drawn-out process. That

[19] Miller, *op. cit.*, p. 440.

no clear-cut solution was ever found for the problem of the structure of the Reich showed the lack of concern of the National Socialist rulers with the crux of the matter. In this context, too, everything was seen from the vantage point of power, and all reforms and plans only served as a pretext for the total encompassing and penetration of public life in the sense of National Socialist dictatorial rule.[20]

The terrorist, profoundly unconstitutional intensification of the power thrust—the *first stage* of the seizure of power—reached its acme in the Enabling Act of March 23, 1933, abolishing the Reichstag and firmly establishing the dictatorship of the "national" government. This was yet another instance of the symbiosis of "legality" and terror, but now the objective was to discard the instrument hitherto utilized with such virtuosity, the Presidential decree. To the extent to which Hitler could do without the help of Hindenburg and his go-between von Papen, the sham alliance with the German Nationals became superfluous. By voting for the Enabling Act, the misguided Center Party as well as the Hugenberg-Papen group relinquished the base of its existence.

In its forward march to total power, the NSDAP concentrated on two major points: (1) the liquidation of the remnants of the democratic constitutional state insofar as their functions could not be accommodated in the new power structure, and (2) the creation of a total leader state, in which economy, society, and culture through coordination and supervision were to be transformed from free, pluralistic entities into pillars of the untrammeled rule of *one* party and a governmental apparatus subordinate to it. Neither goal was ever fully realized, either then or in later years. But the decisive shifts took place between the passage of the National Socialist Civil Service Act in April, 1933, and the emphatic declarations about "unity of party and state" in December, 1933.

The liquidation of the democratic constitutional state (the *second stage*) called for the "purge" of the civil service and judiciary, and, together with the smashing of the trade unions and democratic professional organizations (April-May, 1933) and the dissolution of all other political parties, resulted in the legal establishment of the one-party state (July 14, 1933).

Finally, the creation of the total state (the *third stage*) involved the alliance with the rapidly expanding Army and the taking over of the police and its incorporation into the SS. Simultaneous with this mobilization of power came that "engagement" of the population, which was given expression by the infiltration and "alignment" of organizations and the creation of all-inclusive monopoly organizations in the economic sector (German Labor Front) as well as in the cultural sector (Reich Cultural Chamber). Here, too, *Gleichschaltung*, this euphemistic and telling name for the implementation of the total claim of a dictatorial party in state and society, was the technical term used. The plebiscite of the one-party state on November 12, 1933, was the first of a series of "yes" plebiscites which in totalitarian dictatorships are

---

[20] Bracher, Sauer, and Schulz, *op. cit.*, pp. 427 ff.

among the preferred means of pseudo-legal, pseudo-democratic self-approbation.

The above review is in effect a list of the most important dates of the first year of the Third Reich. Rule by decree, which reached its highest point on February 28, and the conquest of the states were followed by the permanent suspension of the division of powers by virtue of the Enabling Act, which ended the Presidential dictatorship and marked the beginning of the one-man dictatorship. Contrary to the illusions and apologies of professors of public law then and now, the one-man dictatorship had as little legal validity as the rule by decree. The arrest of numerous left-wing Reichstag deputies was illegal, the manipulation of votes through deception and threat was illegal, the SA march into parliament was illegal, the political coordination of the Reichsrat (the instrument of ratification) as the representative of the states was illegal, the subsequent violation of all restrictive provisions of the Enabling Act and the grotesque self-prolongation of the powers Hitler granted himself in 1937, 1941, and finally in 1943 was illegal. Hitler never intended to keep his promise of having a national assembly draft a new constitution. Though the Weimar Constitution was never abrogated, the Third Reich from beginning to end was in effect ruled by emergency decree ignoring all constitutional restrictions.

What this "legalization" of dictatorship meant was shown by its first major law, which was based solely on the reality of power. March 31 and April 7 saw the promulgation of laws "for the coordination of the states with the Reich." As post facto justification of coups and as the basis for the future rule of the Gauleiter as Reich governor, they sealed the fate of any parliamentary-constitutional rule in the member states as well. At the same time, the reorganization of the personnel and administrative apparatus proceeded apace. In view of the shortage of qualified personnel, only some key positions were initially filled by National Socialists; for the rest, the cooperation of the majority of civil servants was won through firings and threats. Moreover, the new rulers were able to rely as much on opportunism, on concern for the safeguarding of "well-earned rights," as on the susceptibility of the civil service for nonparliamentary, hierarchical rule by a monocratic administrative state that had marked its ambivalence toward the Weimar Republic. Whatever one may think about the thesis that the determined resistance of the civil servants and "bureaucratic sabotage" might have impeded the success of such revolutionary change,[21] one fact remains: Hitler was able to rely on the smooth functioning of a machinery of government still largely non–National Socialist despite numerous "March casualties" * by combining the appeal to the national and antidemocratic, authoritarian traditions of the civil service with the promise that party and state would continue to coexist as the two

[21] Thus Herbert von Borch, *Obrigkeit und Widerstand* (Tübingen, 1934); Arnold Brecht, *op. cit.,* p. 77.

* *"Märzgefallene,"* opportunists who joined the party during the early part of 1933.

pillars of the Third Reich, that the revolution would be "carried out" administratively, so to speak.

In fact, skillful handling of the fiction of the legal and national revolution would in itself not have sufficed to smooth the transition from constitutional state to totalitarian dictatorship. This required yet another aspect of the technique of power seizure and rule, and Hitler now made use of it: the dualism of state and party, which continued to exist in the one-party state as well. Contrary to a widespread stereotype, total rule does not necessarily mean a closed, monolithic, single-track governmental structure. It is also not true that it operates more efficiently and effectively or that it is superior to the complicated pluralism of democracy. As a matter of fact, Hitler refrained from a complete fusion of party and state. Rival agencies continued to exist or even were newly set up at all levels of public life. Thus, for example, instead of the promised governmental reform, the states were turned into a vast system of satrapies in which frequently as many as three different governing bodies claimed primacy: Reich Governor, Gauleiter, and Minister President. Instead of simplifying the administration, the expansion of the principle of one-man rule only served to complicate jurisdictional relations. Friction, waste, duplication were the result, and it soon became apparent that this was not a childhood disease of the new system but intrinsic to it.

In fact, we are dealing with a largely conscious technique of rule which fulfilled an important function, particularly during the takeover phase, but later on as well. This approach facilitated the recruitment of technicians who were assured the continuation of the existing order. As in the case of the legal revolution, their satisfaction over their own importance in the new system blinded them to the fact that this duality granted them only relative freedom, which could be rescinded at any time, and that the Leader, in command of the tools of coercion and terror, had the decisive voice on all vital questions; thus, alongside the surviving system of law and justice, that deceptive façade, the system of protective custody, Gestapo, and concentration camps developed beyond the reach of any court. This hints at the second function inherent in this dualism, this frequently multifarious nature of the governmental structure even in the takeover phase. The Leader was the sole figure standing above the confusion of jurisdictions and command chains; on him rested the hopes of almost all concerned, National Socialists and non–National Socialists alike, and this tied them to the regime. He was the supreme arbiter whose omnipotent position was forever reaffirmed, through all the rivalries of party officials, all conflicts between state and party, Army and SA, economy and administration; by playing up one against the other and apparently supporting each, he was able to preserve and strengthen his position of power. As in the early years of struggle, Hitler used this principle of making all dependent on him with matchless virtuosity. It is a matter of dispute to what extent this was conscious intention or the expression of the erratic mood of the Leader and his movement, which was chaotic rather than orderly. At any rate, this planned chaos fatally influenced the grotesque, erroneous estimations of the National Socialist revolution on the part of Hitler's contemporaries.

The realities of power politics firmly established themselves in the governmental apparatus with the first civil-service decrees. After the prelude of the purge in Prussia and the Reich, the notorious Law for the Restoration of the Professional Civil Service was passed on April 7, 1933, a measure designed for the retroactive and providential legalization of numerous arbitrary acts. Its euphemistic name is typical of many National Socialist laws whose "positive" designations rarely gave an inkling of the terrible practices they instituted. The new civil service law, which was followed by numerous amendments and implementation decrees, made possible the dismissal of employees even in violation of existing laws if they did not possess the requisite "suitability," were not of "Aryan descent" (initially with the exception of war veterans), or "on the basis of their former political activities did not offer the assurance that they supported the national state without reservations." Also, "for reasons of administrative efficiency," measures such as these could be passed "outside regular legal channels." These arbitrary regulations showed that the true purpose of the law was not the restoration of the civil service but rather its intimidation and political leveling. Political purges, persecution of Jews, threats, and revenge coalesced. The nonlegal state of emergency dominated the reconstruction of the machinery of government, regardless of existing restrictions. The dual existence of party and state by no means signified that a counterweight to National Socialist rule had been preserved, but rather that the effectiveness and pseudo-legality of the totalitarian dictatorship was thereby given a measure of support which party rule alone could never have achieved.

The civil service legislation also served as the vehicle for the first incorporation of the officially mandated anti-Semitism into a tenet of law. Anyone with even one grandparent of Jewish origin was held to be "non-Aryan." National Socialist policy was as unscrupulous in its use of these regulations of dubious legal and scientific validity as in its general acceptance of the pseudo-scientific race theory, with its confused mixture of religious, socio-economic, political, and biological "proofs."

The incursions were, of course, particularly serious in the realm of the judiciary. There the purge along political and racial lines encompassed lawyers as well, who, even more than the courts, had been among the pillars of the Weimar Republic. On that same April 7, 1933, a Law on the Admission to the Practice of Law restricted the freedom of the legal profession: "Aryan articles" and the arbitrary imposition of prohibitions were the devices by which the rights of a citizen defending himself against encroachment by the state could be violated even more profoundly than was already the case under the state of emergency and political terror. On the heels of this law came the coordination of lawyers (as "Legal Protectors") in the Nazi-controlled Front of German Law and the Academy for German Law. Their chief, Hans Frank, the National Socialist legal luminary of the early days, now Bavarian Minister of Justice, and later the brutal Governor General of occupied Poland, was appointed to the position of Reich Commissar for the Coordination of Justice in the States and for the Renewal of Jurisprudence. The purpose of the reorganization was to put law at the service of National Socialism, based on the broadly interpreted general formula of the "healthy folk emotions" (*gesundes Volksempfinden*) and on the catchphrase, "Right is what's good for the people."

Efforts to preserve justice undoubtedly were made in the twelve-year rule of the Third Reich. Hitler singled out lawyers as a group guilty of undue objectivity, and in fact the dualism of party and state was most evident in the field of law. But at the same time, this dualism created the basis for the sort of legal justification and implementation of the dictatorial terrorism that found its strongest expression in the creation of special courts and people's courts and in the thousands of jail and death sentences meted out against "traitors and saboteurs."

The police agencies of the party and above all of the SS stood outside all legal control; they were in a position to translate the political orders into the terror justice of the concentration camps without recourse to legal process. This, too, began within the first days of the power seizure, with SA camps for political opponents. Even if a court showed compassion, defenseless political victims were at the mercy of this second track of official justice. Release from prison frequently was followed by transfer to a concentration camp. In the course of time the dual system of a formal state of law and a "decree state" with officially sanctioned arbitrary power [22] was overwhelmed by the totalitarian police-state system, until in the final phase the last remnants of legal, objective procedure disappeared and the citizen became the defenseless pawn of the summary justice of the SS terror.

CONTROLLED SOCIETY AND ONE-PARTY STATE

Beginning in April, 1933, Hitler was able to place the entire machinery of government under the almost totally unchecked jurisdiction of his autocratic policies. The existence of other political parties and a number of social, economic, and cultural organizations still barred complete Nazi control over state and society. The step from bureaucratic-authoritarian dictatorship to total rule required the smashing or absorption of all voluntary organizations as well. This was true particularly of the trade unions, where the National Socialists had not been able to gain a foothold prior to 1933, and against which—despite all socialist slogans—they had not been able to put up a significant organization of their own. The NSDAP had made its breakthrough as a petty-bourgeois and agrarian protest movement with the backing of nationalist and conservative circles and anti-union busi-

[22] See Ernst Fraenkel, *The Dual State* (New York, 1941), a basic work on the subject.

ness leaders. The attempt to win the workers with a National Socialist Shop Cell Organization (NSBO) had misfired, despite its aggressive bearing since its founding in 1929. Only among the (unorganized) unemployed was the SA able to make any inroads by promising pay, adventure, and future employment. A party relying so strongly on the middle class and the national Right and vying for the support of employers and the military could not develop a genuine trade-union policy.

The defeat of Otto and Gregor Strasser had also made it obvious that Hitler was not interested in socialism or the workers but only in the political manipulation of these powerful forces. Exponents of the NSDAP's left wing, relegated to the role of socialist embellishments, exercised no real influence after January 30, 1933. Strasser's successor, Robert Ley, who like the later Economic Minister Walter Funk had begun his career as a contact man with employers and banking circles, consistently worked toward the smashing of the unions. At first, Hitler seemed undecided on this point. The possible risk in such a course was the provocation of protest strikes that could endanger both the political and economic existence of the regime. But in the meantime, the unions had also been caught up in the powerful pull of the successful power grab. Weakened by the continuing unemployment and the division into socialist (4.5 million members), Christian (1 million), and liberal (500,000) organizations, they too were caught up in the wave of fear and opportunism. The number of defectors grew from week to week. This alone made a general strike most unlikely; no protest strike had been called even on July 20, 1932, the date of Papen's *coup d'état.*

Helplessness, false hopes, and resignation spread among the unions, and they began to offer the new rulers pledges of loyalty and cooperation in return for their continued existence. The unions, like the political parties, counted on a short life for the Hitler regime. They, Brüning, the Social Democrats, and the Communists all were convinced that it would founder on its inner contradictions, even though the expectations of each were very different. The preservation of their organization, not demonstrations, was the issue. That was the reaction of Theodor Leipart, a trade-union leader, to the events of January 30. The politics of legality set the tone and led to false hopes and defenselessness, while the terror of the pseudo-revolutionaries increased. The first to collapse were the white-collar organizations, already eroded by the pull of the victorious party. After a sweeping administrative coordination in early April, a series of laws and decrees deprived shop stewards and with them the unions and workers of their functions altogether. A great propaganda coup crowned the pseudolegal coordination, and this was followed promptly by the smashing of the unions. At Goebbels' initiative, Hitler declared May Day the Day of National Labor, a paid national holiday. This fulfillment of an ancient demand of the working-class organizations took the wind out of the sails of the unions. There was nothing left for them to do but welcome the act and ask their members to observe the holiday.

The shows staged on May 1, 1933, at which Hitler and his cohorts in the guise of the true champions of the workers proclaimed the realization of a "national socialism" paralyzed the unions. The very next day, May 2, the SA and SS, in line with well-laid plans, occupied union offices throughout the country. This act of force, unlike all preceding seizures, took place without any legal sanction. However, open resistance was out of the question. As the chief of the Action Committee for the Protection of German Labor—another typical euphemism for a violation of the law—Robert Ley proclaimed the formation of a German Labor Front (Deutsche Arbeitsfront, or DAF) of "eight million working people." In fact, the DAF was a compulsory organization subservient to the party, in which the concept "worker" was, in line with the people's community ideology, stripped of its class-sociological meaning. Employees and employers were locked into one joint, gigantic satellite organization, which ultimately embraced more than 25 million members, almost half the population. The organizational structure within a plant also was adapted to the leader-subject relationship of the pseudo-military hierarchy of the leader principle party. A Law for the Regulation of National Labor (January 20, 1934) and the official designation of the DAF as an "auxiliary of the NSDAP" and "member organization" of the party (March 29, 1935) made the DAF the sole organization of all "soldiers of labor," "depending solely on the will of the leadership of the NSDAP." [23]

Authoritarian regimentation and total mobilization was the purpose of this new regulation; it accorded with a theory in which all social organizations were assigned the function of transmitting the will of the party and its leaders to the masses. The elimination of the tradition-rich and, until recently, presumably powerful sociopolitical organizations of the working class was an important step toward readying the economic and social sector for rearmament. The events of May 1 and 2 were intended to show up the brittleness of the old system and, by contrast, the determination and irresistibility of the national and social dynamic of the victorious movement.

The overpowering of the member states, the suppression of the Left, the capitulation of the Reichstag majority, the progressive disintegration of the "old" parties, the willing cooperation of the "cleansed" machinery of state, the benevolent coexistence of the Army—this was the balance sheet of the first four months of Hitler's Chancellorship. Most professional and economic organizations had fallen victim to the pull of coordination even before the trade unions. It was a process carried out almost uniformly through the interlocking of two different developments. The demands of the National Socialist special organizations and auxiliaries which had been built up in cadrelike fashion within the party coincided with the desperate efforts of existing organizations to preserve their continued function through accommoda-

[23] Thus Robert Ley, *Deutschland ist schöner geworden* (Berlin, 1936), p. 275. Also, Hans-Gerd Schumann, *Nationalsozialismus und Gewerkschaftsbewegung* (Hanover, 1958), pp. 168 ff.

tion and reorganization, through personnel changes and adoption of the leader principle. The result depended on a variety of circumstances; the degree of coordination differed. In one case, the smashing of an organization may have been prevented through adjustment and the influence of individual persons, in another the new men were able to complete the capture or smashing.

Major personnel changes, far more sweeping than in the administration, changed the top structure of German society. The broader effects of this process deserve the name social revolution, though at first the economic elite seemed to be spared. They were granted the relative freedom of useful and willing henchmen. But Hitler was as little in the service of monopoly capitalism, if this oversimplification ever held any truth at all, as he was controlled by the military, who may have had similar expectations. To see National Socialism according to a monocausal formula as a veiled capitalist dictatorship is to misjudge its revolutionary impact on state and society; to call it militaristic defines only one aspect of its system of domination, only one part of a politically and socially far broader ideology of power.

In view of the fact that since 1929 the NSDAP had scored its greatest successes in agricultural regions, the subjugation of the agrarian organizations was accomplished in record time. The primary instrument of coordination was the "agrarian policy apparatus" of the NSDAP under the race and peasant ideologist Walter Darré. The peasantry as the agricultural "life motor" of National Socialist rule and as the "biological blood renewal source of the body politic" was finally to be used for the settlement of the "Eastern regions" to be taken from the Slavs, as Darré had proposed to Hitler back in 1930. In his very first official proclamations, Hitler himself stated that the peasantry "in fact was the future of the nation itself." The onslaught on the portions of the agrarian organizations still under the control of German Nationals in April, 1933, resulted in their coordination, the defeat of Hugenberg, and the ascent of Darré. It culminated in a series of incisive laws and regulations, beginning with the Entailed Farm Laws of May 15 and September 29, 1933 "for the preservation of the insoluble bonds of blood and soil." The same period saw the institution of a settlement policy "based on race," the central direction of agriculture, the control of market and price policies, and finally, the political organization of the peasantry under Nazi local, regional, and state peasant leaders in a pseudo-corporative roof organization, the Reich Nutrition Estate. The youthful and vain Darré, who himself delivered the dedication address at the unveiling of a plaque in the town in which he wrote his book *Lebensquell* (*Life Source*), was promoted to Reich Peasant Leader in January, 1934. Finally, *völkisch* agrarian romanticism, the counterpart to the National Socialist workers' ideology proclaimed on May 1, 1933, was given expression by designating the harvest festival as the party's own *Ehrentag* (Memorial Day) of the German peasantry. Hitler announced this article of the National Socialist faith on October 1, 1933, on the occasion of a mass demonstration of 500,000 farmers at the Bückeberg near Hameln; one year later, 700,000 persons were mobilized for the Bückeberg Memorial Day and in 1935, one million.[24]

The coordination of the organizations of handicraft, commerce, and industry in the spring and summer of 1933 was accompanied by similar ideological exaltation, but also by greater differences. In early 1932, Hitler had delivered a major speech before an assembly of business leaders in Düsseldorf, who were much impressed and some of whom became his backers.[25] For years, their money had flowed into the party treasury. At the end of 1932, influential industrialists and bankers had asked Hindenburg to form a strong "national" government that included the National Socialists, and at the crucial moment Hitler was the beneficiary of the liaison services of the banker von Schröder and of the support of the Reich Agrarian League. In the course of February, 1933, Hitler with the help of the influential former President of the Reichsbank, Hjalmar Schacht, who had come out for the national opposition in 1930, managed to win the support of still more industrialists and financiers. In a memorable meeting on February 25, they agreed to underwrite the National Socialist election campaign, after Hitler had told them of the advantages of a pro-business, authoritarian, anti-Marxist government. Ironically, Göring, then President of the Reichstag, told them that "industry would find the asked-for sacrifice easier if it knew that the elections of March 5 were bound to be the last in ten years, and presumably in a hundred." [26]

Although prior to the seizure of power the role of business was still an individual matter and feelings about National Socialism still were divided, the powerful industrial and employer organizations rapidly changed over to a position of full support. In part their personnel were infiltrated by National Socialists, and in part they were reorganized and coordinated. Despite the propaganda about the "corporate reorganization of German economic life," the result contradicted the romantic-conservative corporate idea; the regime only used and manipulated it to win support. In early May, 1933, the leader principle was introduced into the Reich League of German Industry, and in mid-June, in line with the corporate idea, it was combined with the League of German Employer Organizations into the Reich Group of German Industry. Influential executives became the victims of political and racist purges. But the extension of the principle of one-man rule to economic life and the "trustees of labor," appointed with the acquiescence of employers, both favored the anti-unionism of industry. Krupp remained at the helm, and Hitler's long-time patron Fritz Thyssen oc-

[24] Karlheinz Schmeer, *Die Regie des öffentlichen Lebens im Dritten Reich* (Munich, 1956), pp. 87 ff.

[25] George W. F. Hallgarten, *Hitler, Reichswehr und Industrie* (Frankfurt/Main, 1955), p. 94; Klaus Drobisch, "Flick und die Nazis," *Zeitschrift für Geschichtswissenschaft*, XIV (1966), 379 f.

[26] *Nürnberger Dokumente*, XXV, 47 f. For the role of business, see particularly Arthur Schweitzer, *Big Business in the Third Reich* (Bloomington, 1964).

cupied a particularly strong position; the mutually profitable association of industry and National Socialists was underscored by the creation of the Adolf Hitler Foundation of German Business by Krupp and Schacht (June 1, 1933), and by the convocation of a General Economic Council (July 13, 1933). Its growing power as well as a mutual interest in the imminent rearmament program assured industry of a measure of influence; more so than in other sectors, official coordination in this case meant cooperation, profits, and a still stronger voice for the captains of industry in the New State. Yet at the same time, this sealed their inclusion in the political-military expansionism, their acquiescence in the totalitarian system, and ultimately their complicity in the extreme consequences of slave-labor and concentration-camp policies. Therefore, National Socialism cannot be seen merely as the by-product of monopoly-capitalist interests.

While the expectations of large segments of big business seemed at first to be fulfilled, the high hopes of the middle class, whose fear of crisis made such a vital contribution to the victory of National Socialism, were rapidly dashed. On May 3, 1933, the National Socialist Fighting League of the Industrial Middle Class, under former Hitler Youth leader Theodor von Renteln, pushed through the establishment of an all-embracing chamber, the Reich Estates of Trade and Handicraft, which in June pre-empted the functions of the German Chamber of Industry and Commerce. Hope for the realization of expectations, let alone the smashing of department stores and consumer cooperatives, turned out to be a delusion; the organizations of the Fighting League were dissolved or incorporated into the DAF in August of that year. The unwelcome concrete demands of the passionately courted middle class were tabled once that group had played its assigned role in the seizure of power; its organizations were broken up and the middle-class movement put under party and state control.

Within weeks, the party system collapsed, against the background of a sociopolitical coordination that combined seduction and terror, opportunism and threats. July 14, 1933, was the date on which the one-party state was officially proclaimed.[27] The dissolution of the Reichstag, the abrogation of all basic rights, the wave of persecutions of February and March, 1933, and the subsequent self-suspension of the Reichstag and legalization of the dictatorship had destroyed the foundations of the multiparty democracy. The extraparliamentary *Gleichschaltung* in April and May put an end also to the existence of all other parties.

The first attacks naturally were directed against the Communist Party: press prohibitions, arrests of functionaries and deputies, and confiscation of party property preceded the official ban of the party which, probably for tactical reasons, was imposed only after the March 5 elections. Unlike Hugenberg, who had favored the immediate liquidation of the KPD, the National Socialists relied on the division of

[27] See the basic studies in Erich Matthias and Rudolf Morsey (eds.), *Das Ende der Parteien 1933* (Düsseldorf, 1960).

the Left, which in fact did prevent any effective resistance from forming in those first decisive weeks. Even the KPD was not immune to the National Socialist pulling power, and its illegal work was patterned on the Russian example, on the fight against the Czarist police state rather than attuned to the pseudo-plebiscitary technique of the Nazi takeover. The KPD was faced with turncoats and informers as well as with the anti-Communism of broad circles of the population. Moreover, Moscow held back its support for reasons of foreign policy; it was interested not in conflict with the new regime but rather in the preservation of German-Soviet relations, and indeed, the Berlin Treaty of 1926 was reaffirmed in May, 1933. And so the Soviet Union, by treating the fate of the KPD as a German domestic problem and concentrating its concerns on its missions and the unhindered conduct of their affairs, became the first foreign power to grant diplomatic recognition to the Hitler regime; this grotesque fact was outdone only by the *Realpolitik* of the Hitler-Stalin pact of 1939.[28]

The SPD's demonstrative adherence to the path of legality was able to prolong its existence for only some months. Its ultimate declaration of opposition, contained in Otto Wels' exemplary and brave speech in the Reichstag during the debate on the Enabling Act, was due perhaps more to the memory of the opposition to the Socialist Law (1878) than to insight into the true character of the new regime. Standing pat, saving the organization by steering a middle course, faith in the historically inevitable collapse of Fascism—those were the slogans, and not calls to open resistance against a supposedly short-lived mass movement. Paralyzed by legalistic stand-by tactics, weakened by persecution, flight, and organizational disintegration, this largest of the democratic parties increasingly lost touch with its membership. The death of the unions and differences with the exiled SPD leadership as well as within socialist resistance groups were followed by a last-ditch effort of tactical accommodation: a vote in the Reichstag on May 17, 1933, for Hitler's foreign policy statement on his peaceful intentions. It was the final delusion of the pursuit of legal methods by which a Social Democratic leadership too deeply committed to its own traditions thought it might preserve its substance even in the face of Göring's confiscation on May 10 of all its assets—buildings, newspapers, and party treasury. At this last meeting of a multiparty Reichstag, Hitler was able to demonstrate to the world the "legality" of his rule. Its numbers cut in half, the SPD Reichstag delegation capitulated to pressure as well as out of concern for its jailed comrades in voting for the resolution jointly offered by the NSDAP, DNVP, the Center Party, and the BVP on May 17. Yet despite this vote, the decimated SPD was held responsible for the increasing activity of exiled SPD leaders. On June 22, after a period of growing terror, the last blows fell: the outlawing of the SPD as a

[28] Karlheinz Niclauss, *Die Sowjetunion und Hitlers Machtergreifung* (Bonn, 1966), pp. 182 ff.

"party hostile to the nation and state," its explusion from the Reichstag, more arrests, and ruthless persecution of all oppositional activities.

The death of the remaining parties followed within days. Almost unnoticed, the formerly imposing structure of German liberalism crumbled. It had never fully overcome nineteenth-century divisions and the errors of the National Liberals. Save for a brief resurgence in 1919, it was reduced to splinter groups, particularly after the National Socialist breakthrough of 1929. Ever since the founding of the Harzburg Front, the DVP increasingly became a party of fellow travelers. The DDP's transformation into the State Party (July, 1930) was futile; it, too, bowed to the will of three of its five deputies and ultimately (against the advice of Theodor Heuss) voted for the Enabling Act. Its small, loose organization was no match for the new political reality; many of its middle-class supporters had already chosen the road to the Right years before. Its organizations and professional groups in business and administration were coordinated willy-nilly. On June 27, the State Party was ousted from the Prussian parliament; one day later, it announced its dissolution. At least the party, in its final statement, avoided paying obeisance to the Hitler regime. Not so the DVP, some of whose locals had already recommended going over to the NSDAP in April. After vain attempts to keep in step with the times, a decision to dissolve sealed the fate of Stresemann's party on July 4; its chairman, Eduard Dingeldey, in a rather eager letter, assured Hitler of his cooperation. The Christian-Social People's Service had taken a similar step on July 1. After Bismarck cult and war enthusiasm, the civic conscience of the old ruling elite, which had greatly facilitated and in many ways made possible Hitler's rule, died an inglorious death.

The capitulation of political Protestantism, whose monarchist, nationalist majority had never managed to arrive at a positive position toward the Weimar Republic, was followed by the death of the Center Party and the BVP, those pillars of the Republic and bastions of political Catholicism in the Reich and Bavaria. Flexible and adjustable toward Right and Left alike, the nucleus of all coalitions up to 1932, the Center Party in 1933 did not succeed in joining the Government. After the March elections, it lost its traditional key role in the formation of majority governments. It, too, was affected by the challenges of that era; acclimatization and the strong trend toward the Right urged accommodation. Its acceptance of the Enabling Act reflected internal pressures; external threats accelerated its disintegration. The recommendations over what its future course should be ranged from determined opposition to far-reaching collaboration. The continued existence of the party was deemed essential to the protection of the cultural life of the Catholic population even though the party was excluded from political life.

At this juncture, Hitler, with the help of Papen and former Center chief Ludwig Kaas, managed to outmaneuver the newly constituted Center leadership under Brüning. While the Catholic Church relented on its former verdict on National Socialism and a growing number of prominent Catholics sought to build bridges to the new regime, Hitler began negotiations on a concordat with Rome. This move appealed to the hearts of German Catholics and pulled the rug out from under the Center Party. Broad concessions, which Hitler of course did not honor, brought the National Socialists the support of this group as well—until it was too late and the political coordination had been completed. We know today that Hitler in union with Papen was determined from the very outset, probably since the Cabinet meeting of March 7, to storm the Center bastion through promises to the Curia, without any qualms about granting concessions on the problems of schools and organizations going far beyond any made by Weimar. Whether the safeguarding of some assets outweighed the sacrifice of the political organizations of Catholicism in the coming struggle of the Church is an open question. The widespread optimism, including that of Cardinal Faulhaber of Munich, turned out to be an illusion, hardly justifying the Vatican's joining the Soviet Union in certifying the Third Reich's acceptability as a partner in negotiations. At any event, the decision of the Center as the last of the parties to dissolve is closely related to this illusion. The announcement came on July 5, 1933, three days before the signing of the concordat in Rome, which traded the false promise of the retention of parochial schools for the ban on political activities of priests and Catholic organizations.

The formerly so self-assured German National allies of the national revolution long ere that had fallen victim to the NSDAP power grab. They failed to exploit the presumed superiority of their position in Government and Army, economy and society, and bureaucracy and Presidency, nor did they succeed in salvaging their parliamentary indispensability beyond the imposition of the Enabling Act. The pull of coordination worked for the benefit of the stronger, and Papen soon relinquished his confidently proclaimed role of overseer by giving up his position of mediator between Hitler and Hindenburg and by formally handing over full control of Prussia to Göring on April 7, 1933. Besides, Papen, although as Reich Commissar the highest Prussian authority, had done little to hinder Göring's de facto dictatorship. By April, the utter failure of his policy had become apparent.

This fact was not changed by differences over a number of posts still in the hands of German Nationals. The Stahlhelm, the most powerful ally, was completely paralyzed through the political coordination of its first chairman, Franz Seldte, who was rewarded with the Ministry of Labor, a post he held to the very end. The Stahlhelm's capitulation to the SA was not accomplished without conflict; its second chairman, Theodor Düsterberg, who, the National Socialists charged, had a Jewish grandfather, sought to preserve and expand the Stahlhelm by recruiting members of other parties and groups, including the Reichsbanner. But after some clashes and regional bans (for example, in Brunswick), Seldte won; on April 26, he put the Stahlhelm under the jurisdiction of the Supreme Leader of the SA, that is, Hitler. In early

July, the subjugation became formalized. The fact that some Stahlhelm leaders opposed Röhm's leadership claim and a few even found their way into active opposition was of little consequence.

The DNVP ended in similar fashion. There, too, at the last hour a faction sought to stem National Socialist coordination. The blind illusions of Hugenberg's policies became obvious only too late; Ernst Oberfohren, the head of the German National Reichstag delegation who had voiced misgivings and was replaced on April 11 by a Hugenberg man, Otto Schmidt-Hannover, was found dead on May 6. Whether it was murder or suicide is an open question. In the meantime, Hugenberg and the party executive committee were beginning to see their helplessness in the face of widespread excesses. In mid-April, Hugenberg still found words of praise for the alliance of January 30, but the honeyed words of this overweening yet impotent self-styled "economic dictator" could not obscure the campaigns of the SA against German National organizations. Complaints were futile. The arrogant delusions that the drummer Hitler could be used had led, via Munich (1923) and Harzburg (1931) and the January 30 sham victory of the national opposition, to catastrophe. The German National antidemocrats, insofar as they had not already become the handmaidens and fellow travelers of their more powerful junior partner, became its victims as well. Among the last convulsions of an outmaneuvered conservatism was the formation of a monarchist Fighting Ring (League of the Upright) on June 2, 1933. But monarchist appeals, initially still tolerated by Hitler, no longer offered any real alternative, however great their contribution to the collapse of the democratic Republic. Here the difference between National Socialism and Italian Fascism, which accepted the monarchy, is quite evident. Two or at most three weeks after its founding, the Fighting Ring was suppressed, in some instances after violent conflict. Here, as in the case of the Stahlhelm, the influx from other non-Nazi groups—though a much greater number joined the NSDAP and SA—served as the pretext for the smashing of all "counterrevolutionary" resistance movements, as proclaimed by Goebbels on June 21, 1933.

Having retreated into isolation, Hugenberg finally also capitulated on June 27. He made one last attempt to appeal to Hindenburg, but Hindenburg's son Oskar prevented Hugenberg's emissary, ex-DNVP chairman Oskar Hergt, from seeing his father. Hugenberg's provocative behavior at the International Trade Conference at London, where he tried to outdo the National Socialists with colonial and expansionist demands, furnished a welcome pretext to force that hollow economic dictator to resign his four (!) Reich and Prussian ministries. He had failed to exploit his powerful position either in the Cabinet or as administrative chief, and his conservative ministerial colleagues who had managed to keep their posts through a timely accommodation now left him in the lurch. On that same June 27, the German National Party decided to dissolve.

The policy of taming Hitler had been carried to the point of absurdity; the national revolution turned out to be a National Socialist power grab. The dismissal of Hugenberg violated the Enabling Act, that pseudo-legal constitutional surrogate for dictatorship which expressly ruled out any change in the existing government. But this was of little consequence after the abolition of parliaments and parties, the co-ordination of the civil service and judiciary, and the destruction of constitutional government. And in the ensuing months, Hitler also ig-nored the other restrictions of the Enabling Act—the Reichsrat, the Presidency, and the time limitation. Yet none of this prevented the per-petuation of this pseudo-legalistic myth in the Third Reich nor its later acceptance by public law and courts of the Bonn Republic. Even the Federal Constitutional Court has accepted the validity of the Enabling Act on the basis of a questionable theory of continuity.[29]

Contrary to Hugenberg's expectations, Hindenburg and the Reichs-wehr, its highest guarantors, accepted the breakup of the "national concentration" without demur. The remaining non–National Socialist ministers were allowed to stay in office, but only as specialists without specific political affiliations. The initially few National Socialists in the Cabinet were joined by Goebbels, who since March 11, 1933, held the post of Propaganda Minister, as well as by Kurt Schmitt and Darré, who took over Hugenberg's posts. In addition, Hitler also ordered Rudolf Hess to sit in on all Cabinet meetings. In this way, the number of Na-tional Socialists in the Government grew from three to eight; the con-servatives became a minority, a mere façade, rather than a counter-weight to a Chancellor heading the only existing party. The dream about the restoration of the monarchy had also come to an end. By order of the Propaganda Ministry, all observances of the seventy-fifth birthday of William II (January 27, 1934) were forbidden.

Hugenberg, embittered, withdrew to his estate in Westphalia, and, with reference to the death of Oberfohren, announced that no report of his having committed suicide was to be given any credence. This, however, did not prevent him from lending a helping hand to the Na-tional Socialist Reichstag delegation. Yet he did not play the role of handmaiden with the same opportunistic perseverance as Franz von Papen, whose way led from Center Party deputy to minidictator to creator of the Hitler Cabinet, from self-assured wirepuller of Hitler to willing helper. Not even the blows received in 1933 and 1934 could deter this Catholic Conservative from becoming Hitler's special envoy in paving the way for the takeover of Austria, or from serving the re-gime till the very end.

The creation of the one-party state, which put the final seal on the National Socialist seizure of power, was clothed in the sort of pseudo-legal sanctions with which the regime liked to adorn its authoritarian moves. The elimination of the political Left had been an irregular act, even though it was done by a decree of July 7 "for the protection of the state," which ousted the SPD and the State Party from all state legis-

[29] E.g., in the sentence of the concordat trial of 1957. On the theory of continuity, see Chapter IX.

latures and municipalities. The catalogue of laws proclaimed by the Cabinet on the all-important day of July 14, 1933, is an extensive one. Celebrated in France as the anniversary of the storming of the Bastille, as the symbol of rebellion against absolutism, this day formally sealed the establishment of the National Socialist dictatorship in Germany. Among the laws promulgated was one "on the confiscation of the property of enemies of the people and the state" legalizing arbitrary confiscation; laws on the constitution of the Evangelical Church and the concordat spelled out the new policies toward the churches; a "law on the remolding of the German peasantry" sanctioned the policy of resettlement; laws "for the prevention of defective progeny" and "on the revocation of naturalization and on the revocation of German citizenship" legalized cultural, population, and racial policies based on the blood and soil ideology. The keystone of the political *Gleichschaltung*, however, was the Law Against the New Formation of Parties. In terse language, it decreed the National Socialist one-party state and severely penalized all other political activity.

This, incidentally, was another violation of the provision of the Enabling Act protecting the "institution of the Reichstag as such." Now the one party appointed deputies from above. The Reichstag could no longer be formally considered a parliamentary representation; thus, the party law of July 14, ignoring Constitution and Enabling Act alike, was another link in the chain of thinly veiled violations of law and Constitution. The truly illegal nature of the emphatically stressed legality of the revolution is revealed by what followed. With the Enabling Act being stripped of yet another restriction, the state of emergency in fact became a permanent condition, for now it was no longer possible to give the impression of the existence of a legal opposition and parliamentary controls. The Reichstag ceased to be even the one remaining sham institution whose existence was guaranteed by the Enabling Act; according to a joke then current, it became the most expensive glee club in the country. Its only function was to celebrate feasts of acclamation, listen to the Führer's speeches, and extend the Enabling Act (1937 and 1939) if this was not done by Hitler himself (as was the case in 1943). National Socialist constitutional lawyers like Ernst Rudolf Huber consequently announced that the Reichstag "is neither an instrument of legislative powers nor a control organ of the Government. . . . It would be impossible for the Reichstag to propose and pass a law that did not originate with the Führer or at least had not been approved by him beforehand." In short, the Reichstag "is an institution that expresses the political agreement of nation and Government." Just as the plebiscites, it was to "document the unity of Führer and nation." [30] As in all modern dictatorships, the sole function of elections was to confirm one-party voting lists or approve authoritarian decisions already reached.

Although Hitler in *Mein Kampf* had posited the leader principle

[30] Ernst Rudolf Huber, *Verfassungsrecht des Grossdeutschen Reiches* (Hamburg, 1939), pp. 207 ff.

against the principle of popular elections, the Government continued to resort to the method of plebiscitary confirmation as an expression of popular support. A special law on plebiscites, also passed on July 14, substituted the effective confirmatory plebiscite, so beloved by dictatorships, for parliamentary decisions. Between 1933 and 1938, five such plebiscites were staged, with predictable results. In view of their utility of purpose, namely, the mobilization of the population and the confirmation of the self-proclaimed unity, Göring's assurance to his financial backers that the elections of March 5, 1933, were bound to be the last for ten years (and presumably for one hundred) was forgotten. Opportunities for soliciting contributions for elections continued to abound, even though the choice was limited to one party.

The effects of the pseudo-legal one-party decree of July 14, which Papen and his conservative colleagues also voted for without demur, were inestimable. The law violated the Enabling Act, in itself pseudolegal, on which Hitler's legislative dictatorship based itself. For this reason, Hitler's twelve-year reign must also in a formal juridical sense be considered unlawful. Regardless of the Enabling Act, Hitler now was able to command a two-thirds majority in his one-party parliament any time he wished to legalize the violation of restrictions still found in the Constitution and Enabling Act. Open, legal opposition against the rule of National Socialism had become impossible. And the possibilities of legalizing arbitrary acts insofar as this was considered necessary for the mollification and deception of the civil service and judiciary, the population and Army, the business community and the outside world, were unlimited. This perfected legalization machinery also made superfluous the drafting of a new constitution, which Hitler had mentioned in the past. It was far easier to operate with one's own laws, decrees, and regulations, in the course of which the Weimar Constitution was repeatedly violated and broken but never formally repealed. Even though this was nothing more than the "formal-juridical garb of legality" (Arnold Brecht) of an already accomplished act of government, it was highly effective in deceiving and mollifying a legalistically oriented civil service and judiciary. Even today, apologetic analyses and trials of National Socialists are surrounded by the fiction of legality with which the Third Reich was able to bind "loyal" jurists and specialists, civil servants and soldiers, to its despotic rule, beginning with the introduction of the mandatory Hitler salute to the legalization of the terror and murder decrees which were carried out, or at least respected, by those servants of state.

The many political consequences of the pseudo laws of July 14 included yet another important violation of the federal constitutional structure of Germany. One may minimize the creation of the one-party parliament as a mere reorganization of the Reichstag,[31] but it is nonetheless a fact that six months later both the Constitution and the

---

[31] E.g., Hans Schneider, "Das Ermächtigungsgesetz. . . . ," *VfZG,* I (1953), 197 ff.

Enabling Act were clearly violated. On January 30, 1934, the occasion of the first anniversary of the "national uprising," the upper house, the Reichsrat, was abolished by unanimous vote of the Reichstag under the pretext of governmental reform (which despite all promises never was carried out). This step not only violated specific guarantees, but more importantly, finally abrogated the sovereign rights of the states. At the same time, the Government was given the power to introduce new constitutional laws at will. It invoked that power to abolish the office of Reich President six months later. With this, the last remaining restriction of the Enabling Act was removed.

Hitler's one-man dictatorship thus based its legal existence largely on the party law of July 14. As a final consequence, the dual head of state was abolished one year later (August, 1934), when Hitler succeeded in uniting the offices of President and Chancellor in his person. In Fascist Italy, the monarchy continued to exist alongside the one-party regime of the Duce—and this fact made possible the dismissal of Mussolini in 1943—but in Berlin, the totalitarian principle of a unified, omnipotent leadership became a reality. That is yet another reason why the Nazi regime, despite frequent organizational and administrative chaos—the consequence of regimentation and arbitrary rule—was able to hold out until its total defeat.

V

The Formation
of the Third Reich

The consolidation of the totalitarian regime, following the establishment of the one-party state in the summer of 1933, brought with it problems bearing on the relationship of party and state, the institutionalization of domestic *Gleichschaltung*, the economy, rearmament, and foreign policy. On July 6, 1933, before the proclamation of the one-party decree, Hitler told his Reich governors that the task that lay ahead of them was the "winding-up of the revolution": "We now must eliminate the last remnants of the democracy. . . . The achievement of outward power must be followed by the inner education of the people." The next phase involved the consolidation and expansion of autocratic rule, the transition of the revolution "into the secure bed of evolution." Therefore, only replaceable specialists were to be gotten rid of. To "secure position after position," the National Socialists would have to "set their sights far ahead and make long-range plans." Instead of overthrowing existing ideologies and doctrines, what was needed was practical thinking and "clever and careful" action.[1]

The slogan "the winding-up of the revolution" was adopted for tactical reasons. It was meaningless as far as the radical long-range goals, the ideological content, and the revolutionary character of National Socialist rule were concerned. The barely veiled revolutionary acts of the first power-seizure phase were replaced by the principle of the "permanent revolution" as the policy tool of totalitarian rule. This is the meaning of the call for evolution and consolidation with which the power seizure was modified and restrained on all levels, with the result that new illusions supplanted the old. Many both inside Germany and abroad continued to see Hitler as a moderate statesman (in contrast to the "radicals," especially in the SA leadership) whom reality

[1] *Völkische Beobachter*, July 6, 1933.

would steer onto a sensible course. This error led to the fatal misjudgment of the "second revolution"—the bloodbath of June 30, 1934, and its consequences. The illusions found expression in sayings such as "the Leader knows nothing about this," which were meant to deflect any criticism of the regime; then as before, the brutal reality was explained as the regrettable but understandable excesses of lower-ranking chieftains, inevitable in the initial period of so dynamic a policy.

STATE AND PARTY

Vital to its successful seizure of power was the fact that the National Socialist leadership, through threat and seduction, was able to take over the machinery of state intact. The reluctance with which large portions of the civil service had accepted the democratic Republic was matched by their readiness to cooperate with a new regime that promised to substitute order, stability, efficiency, and "national values" for the disturbing innovations of a crisis-ridden, "unnational" parliamentary democracy. The national-authoritarian new order of 1933 derived its precepts, justification, and popularity from the tradition of the authoritarian state, and apparently followed this tradition, even though it might not bring the hoped-for restoration of the monarchy. Many a bystander (including Brüning) who expected the regime to collapse in short order because of its technical incompetence was hoodwinked. The new rulers could rely completely on the efficient functioning of the government machinery on which they were so dependent if: (1) They limited the administrative "purge" to a democratic minority, many of whom, being appointees, were looked on as irksome outsiders by the closed caste of civil servants (a fact which was cleverly exploited by the very name of the Law for the Restoration of a Professional Civil Service of April 7, 1933); (2) the relationship to the one and only party was regulated in such a way as not to impair the civil service's traditional claim to embody the "state above parties."

In the first months, the National Socialist leadership did everything in its power to ward off conflicts, above all those arising out of the violent activities of the SA, through a seemingly workable delimitation and consolidation of the relationship of party and state. Rigid control of the party from above and support of the civil servant's faith in status and order—these were the foundations of the solution offered by the new order of 1933–34 under the slogan "unity of party and state," once the "troublesome" parliaments and political pluralism had been wiped out. The solution was based on Hitler's ideological dictum: "The party now has become the state. All power rests with the Reich Government." [2] And even before the promulgation of the one-party law, Minister of the Interior Frick, in a letter to the Reich Governors and state governments (July 11, 1933), declared that the one-party state had been erected "for all eternity" and that through it "all power" was vested in the Hitler Government, "in which all vital positions are filled

[2] *Ibid.,* July 8, 1933.

by reliable National Socialists." The task now was "to provide intellectual and economic underpinnings for the total power incorporated in [the Hitler Government]."[3] This meant expansion instead of continued revolution, taut party discipline instead of arbitrary and overbearing acts on the part of commissars, the men who, as executors of the revolution, had played so vital a role in the political coordination of the country.

Everything was now directed toward protecting the power won against unchecked inroads by the party. Now and later, Wilhelm Frick, who as a not overly loyal civil servant had joined Hitler in 1923, championed not only the tactical line of the moment—the winning-over of the bureaucratic specialists and the regimentation of the revolution —but quite obviously also the self-interest of his office and of a ministerial bureaucracy concerned with self-preservation and cooperation. His objective was a strong civil-service state, and in fact the staff of the ministries multiplied within a few years. That is the explanation for Frick's sharply worded announcement that "any type of collateral government is incompatible with the authority of the total state." Soon thereafter (July 17), Goebbels also proclaimed the "winding-up of the National Socialist revolution" and warned against "camouflaged Bolshevik elements who talk about a second revolution." Hitler has "stopped our revolution at exactly the right moment. Now that we have possession of the state with all its powers, we no longer have to capture by force positions which are legally ours."[4] That most certainly was not an apt summation of the facts. It did not hold true for the legality which was being claimed, nor did the leadership in the future refrain from intimidation and force. But it did show up the fictitious character of the "unity of party and state," a slogan which was meant to resolve the tension between the sovereignty claims of the NSDAP and an indispensable state apparatus, between National Socialist ideology and traditional governmental practices.

In a speech at the fifth party congress in Nuremberg, the "Congress of Victory," Hitler sought to solve the problem by a sort of division of labor. The turgid phrases of the ceremonial opening address of September 1, 1933,[5] contained the statement that with the abolition of the parliamentary multiparty democracy and the right to public criticism, the NSDAP had become the "sole representative of state power" insofar as it now was charged with the intensive "political education of the German people." Its task was to establish authority, discipline, and the general validity of the leader principle. This, according to Hitler's grotesque definition, consisted of the exercise of "responsible authority downward and authoritarian responsibility upward." Whatever the specific intent of this may have been, it did mean the inversion of the democratic principle. The party was assigned the function of "finding and uniting the most capable persons in Germany through a

[3] *Ibid.*, July 12, 1933.
[4] *Der Angriff*, July 18, 1933.
[5] *Der Kongress des Sieges* (Dresden, 1934), p. 8.

selection conditioned by day-to-day struggle," to carry out the elitist training for the leadership hierarchy, to serve as the "political selection organization" for the authoritarian regime. That was to be the task of the NSDAP after the seizure of power. The state, on the other hand, was charged with the "continuation of the historic and developed administration of the governmental agencies within the framework and by virtue of the laws."

This sort of jurisdictional division into political training on the one hand and administration on the other opened up wide possibilities for a future dualism of party and state, and consequently for the discretionary powers of the Führer. Hitler continued to invoke vague formulas: "That which can be solved by governmental action will be solved by governmental action, and that which the state by its very nature is not able to solve will be solved by the movement." [6] A meaningless definition. The National Socialist idea of the state remained as vague as the promised and never realized new National Socialist constitution. The Third Reich remained in a state of permanent improvisation. True, the concept "movement," whatever that may have meant at any given moment, was placed above a state relegated to "administration." But the vast expansion of the administrative apparatus in the totalitarian *Obrigkeitsstaat,* which encompassed both the executive and legislative, left the dualism unresolved. The official commentary on the 1933 party congress was able to disguise this tension euphemistically but could not do away with it: "In this polarity between political movement and governmental bureaucracy, the life of the nation will in future find its expression." [7]

Such vague formulas could not define the relationship between party and state. But the National Socialist leadership was of course incapable of defining it, and probably not even interested in any ultimate clarification. Here as in other cases, it was easier and at the same time more effective to let the issue hang fire, to decide on competencies from case to case to demonstrate the superiority of a Führer ruling over both movement and state. The tension also was not really resolved by the apparently definitive Law on the Securing of the Unity of Party and State promulgated on December 1, 1933. To be sure, the law clearly stated that "after the victory of the National Socialist revolution," the NSDAP was to be "the representative of the German state idea and indissolubly linked to the state." The heads of the political and military party organizations—Rudolf Hess as Hitler's deputy and Ernst Röhm as chief of staff of the SA—were taken into the government to symbolize the close connection of party and state. The party also now dominated numerically in the Cabinet. But at the same time the autonomy of the NSDAP, now an institution of public law subordinate solely to Hitler, was confirmed and the party given its own legal jurisdictional sphere (including the imposition of prison sen-

[6] *Der Parteitag der Freiheit vom 10. bis 16. September 1935* (Munich, 1935), pp. 283 f.

[7] *Der Kongress des Sieges,* p. 7.

tences) ; in exercising this jurisdiction, it could call upon public officials. Party judges thenceforth were "responsible only to their National Socialist conscience . . . and subordinate only to the Füh-rer." The lapidary formula of unity of party and state as stated in the law did not clearly define the jurisdictional spheres, either. The pur-pose of the law was to confirm the coordination which offered continued opportunities to the dualism of a dynamic-revolutionary political move-ment and a regimented authoritarian state order. Amid this tension, the numerous existing personal and institutional conflicts were ex-acerbated and further complicated by the rise of the SS, with its own bureaucracy and quasi-governmental powers.

Numerous German constitutional lawyers, in a feat of rapid read-justment, tried to fit the reality of the one-party authoritarian state into a systematic theory encompassing all components of the regime. The first one to do so was the flexible, opportunistic Carl Schmitt, the leading professor of international and public law at Berlin University. Once a conservative Catholic, pupil of Erich Kaufmann, and admirer of Hugo Preuss, the author of the Weimar Constitution, Schmitt turned his back on his Jewish mentors to champion the Hindenburg-Papen version of authoritarianism. Now his essay *Staat, Bewegung, Volk (State, Movement, Nation;* 1933) celebrated the trinity of the new system, the "tripartition of political unity." Ultimately the Na-tional Socialist idea of the civil service was to bring the quadriparti-tion of Leader, movement, nation, state.[8] Other young law professors steered a direct course toward the "total state," as for example Ernst Forsthoff, in his *Der totale Staat (The Total State;* 1933). Yet none of the theoretical constructions for the sanctioning of National Social-ist rule solved the question of which functions were to be retained by the victorious monopoly party if it was to preserve its separate existence and continue to develop and escape complete absorption by the totali-tarian state.

The NSDAP of the "fighting years" had patterned its structure on that of the state, in line with Hitler's dictum "that all future institu-tions of this state must grow out of the movement itself."[9] Accord-ingly, separate departments on foreign policy, economics, finance, labor, agriculture, and military affairs were set up and staffed. But the rapid and smooth takeover of the governmental apparatus, which played so vital a role in the successful seizure of power, was not accom-panied by a merger of the state and party bureaucracies. In their drive for state office, only a few party heads succeeded in taking the hurdles, as for example Darré in his contest with Hugenberg. Generally speak-ing, the conflict between party and Government continued, and a num-ber of *"apparats"* became involved in costly rivalries. This sort of

[8] *Der Beamte im Geschehen der Zeit, Worte von Hermann Neess* (Berlin, 1936). (300,000 copies of this were distributed by the National Socialist Organization of Civil Servants.) Cf. also Hans Mommsen, *Beamtentum im Dritten Reich* (Stuttgart, 1966), pp. 21 ff.

[9] Adolf Hitler, *Mein Kampf* (Munich, 1925–28), p. 673.

"institutional Darwinism" [10] was strikingly exemplified by the coexistence of the Foreign Office under Neurath with the "unofficial" foreign policy pursued by the offices of Ribbentrop and Rosenberg and Goebbels' Propaganda Ministry. This situation prevailed until Ribbentrop's appointment to the Foreign Ministry in 1938. Of even weightier consequence was the coexistence of Army, the SA party troops, and later the SS.

All these instances involved both organizational and personnel problems; the fight of job- and influence-hungry party officials who saw the state as their booty continued even after the officially mandated unity of party and state. In the realm of military policy, the decision in favor of the state was reached within six months—in the summer of 1934—when Hitler sacrificed the ambitions of the SA leadership to the Army, although this decision also did not prove to be final. At the same time, the rise of the SS as the political-military elite organization of the party meant a new rival for the Army. And after consolidating his power, Hitler did not cease to assign central functions to the NSDAP. The tasks of the dictatorial monopoly party which he re-emphasized at the party congress of 1935 included above all the formation of a new elite and the "creation of a stable, self-perpetuating eternal nucleus of National Socialist teachings," the control and indoctrination ("education") of the masses, the linking and transmitting of the Leader's will to society and state to achieve coordination, and the consolidation and expansion of the new power and elite structure through the ever-present activities of the one party and its all-encompassing organizations.

The party of 1933–34, assigned this position and these tasks, was in the process of a profound transformation. The victory over all opponents and rivals, the rapid growth of membership and party auxiliaries, the personnel changes and the official functions acquired by the NSDAP on the road toward officialdom—all these confronted the "movement" for the second time since its breakthrough to a mass organization (1929–30) with the problem of how to carry out its dual function of elite and mass party. Between 1928 and 1932, the membership had grown from 108,000 to almost 1.5 million. Between January 30, 1933, and the end of 1934, it again increased by almost 200 per cent. The "old fighters," now one-third of the membership, were confronted with two-thirds new party recruits.[11]

The enormous change also was reflected in the social composition and background of the membership. The proportion of working-class members, though it still fell far below their share in the population (46 per cent), increased from 28 per cent in 1930 to 32 per cent in

[10] David Schoenbaum, *Hitler's Social Revolution* (New York, 1966), p. 206.
[11] Wolfgang Schäfer, *NSDAP, Entwicklung und Struktur der Staatspartei des Dritten Reiches* (Hanover, 1956), pp. 17 ff. Schoenbaum, *op. cit.*, pp. 71 ff., gives somewhat different figures on the basis of material in the Document Center Berlin (the main archive of the NSDAP), but the picture of the composition is the same.

1934, while the percentage of white-collar workers fell off (from 25.6 to 20.6 per cent), although it remained far above their share in the population (12.4 per cent). The number of independent businessmen remained disproportionately high (20 per cent, as compared to their population proportion of 9 per cent). The membership increase of civil servants and teachers was particularly steep (from 8.3 per cent to 13 per cent, compared with their 5 per cent representation in the population); they of course were most exposed to direct pressure. Farm membership, on the other hand, declined from 14 per cent to 10.7 per cent (population share, 10 per cent). It should be borne in mind that professional and class differences played a part in the proportion between followers and membership. The relatively small number of farmers in the party says nothing about the tremendous rallying of voters from this sector after the elections of 1929–30.

The middle-class structure of the NSDAP became even more apparent in the leadership. White-collar workers predominated, particularly among the Kreisleiter (district chiefs) (37 per cent), followed by civil servants and independent businessmen, while the farmers were found mainly in the many lower-ranking positions. The NSDAP continued to build its image as the "party of youth." More than 37 per cent of its members were under thirty; more than 65 per cent had not yet reached forty; barely 15 per cent were over fifty. The average age of the National Socialist elite also was below that of their forty-five-year-old Leader. The growth of the Hitler Youth was enormous, not least through the absorption of the pre-Hitler youth movement; in 1933–34, the membership increased from 108,000 to nearly 3.6 million.

Regional differences persisted both in the numerical strength of the party and in the relationship between old and new party members. Almost analogous to the elections after 1930, the NSDAP registered its relatively largest gains in the party regions of Schleswig-Holstein, southern Hanover, Main-Franconia, and Hesse (as well as in Danzig), and its smallest in Westphalia, Silesia, Pomerania, Baden, Berlin, Munich, and southern Bavaria. After 1923–24, the weight of the movement had shifted northward from its birthplace and the "capital of the movement" (Bavaria and Munich). Only Central and Upper Franconia, the land of Julius Streicher and the national party congresses, remained a stronghold of the NSDAP after the seizure of power.

The question of which party region showed the greatest membership increase after January 30, 1933, is of still greater interest. Here the lead was held by Main-Franconia, where by the end of 1934 the membership had multiplied more than sevenfold (740 per cent), followed by Cologne-Aachen (458 per cent) and Coblenz-Trier (448 per cent). In a process of rapid adjustment, these predominantly Catholic areas compensated for their initially low membership, while, conversely, the high membership of Schleswig-Holstein increased by a scant 80 per cent, though it continued to lead. The agricultural and middle-class regions retained their large lead over the industrial cities; even now, inroads into the working class were not as easily made as the program and propaganda of the party pretended.

The enormous increase in membership and restructuring of the NSDAP into the sole, official party not only altered the proportion between old and new party members but also made possible the eradication of sources of party strife and rebellion that had survived the bloody purge of June 30, 1934. Almost 20 per cent of the political leaders who had belonged to the NSDAP before 1933 had left by the end of 1934. Significantly, the turnover was greatest in Berlin (more than 50 per cent), followed by Main-Franconia (35 per cent), Hamburg and Düsseldorf (27 per cent each), and other large cities, in which the transition from "old fighters" to newly discovered "leaders" was most apparent. The "old fighters" were either replaced (more than one-fourth) or retired. The reasons for these changes were organizational and political, connected either with the old Left course of the Strasser camp, with socialism, or with the problem of the SA and revolution. At any rate, with the influx of new members, the NSDAP had turned into a mass organization which the state leadership was able to steer easily through the course changes of the early period. By the end of 1934, almost 80 per cent of the political leaders were people who had joined the party after 1933; only the Gauleiter corps was still made up of self-assertive, self-confident old fighters. Thenceforth the party became the instrument of totalitarian rule; not political conflict but personal and organizational rivalries marked the further expansion of the NSDAP—the victorious and all-embracing state party and the instrument of change of the Führer state all in one. Only the SS was able to develop an independent position as the avant-garde of the National Socialist empire, and it too never rebelled against Hitler.

The fact that even in the future the party never achieved clear-cut primacy testifies to the ambiguous character of the National Socialist system. The formula of the party issuing orders to the state was true of the Communist one-party state which had smashed the old governmental machinery and the traditional elite structure, although even there the future might see a return to dual structures. But in the Third Reich, where traditional and revolutionary elements continued to exist partly fused and partly as rivals, the primacy of the party was established only in specific instances; at times it almost seemed as if the opposite were the case, and often enough it was not even the party and state but rival party bigwigs who found themselves on opposite sides. The party did not issue orders to the state but rather gained quasi-governmental privileges and pushed through the total claims of the system in the social sphere as well by carrying out the extragovernmental functions of "education," coordination and control, and recruitment of youth.[12] The "state" itself also was divided into differ-

[12] Thus also Robert Pelloux, *Le parti national-socialiste et ses rapports avec l'état* (Paris, 1936), pp. 35 ff.

ent power groups. The claims of the Presidential and Führer dictatorship, of the corporate organizations, and of the growing police state
were in competition, while the Reich Cabinet lost its leading function
and after 1937 no longer even met.

The Führer constituted the only definite link between and above the
jurisdictional thicket of party agencies and state machinery. The
omnipotence of his position rested not least on the ill-defined relationship of party and state; he alone was able to solve the costly jurisdictional conflicts which were part of the system. Regardless of whether
this was an unavoidable dilemma of totalitarian dictatorship or a consciously wielded tool of dictatorial rule, the widespread idea about the
better organized and more effective "order" of totalitarian one-man
rule is a myth all too easily believed in crisis-ridden democracies. It is
the lie that animates all authoritarian movements, then and now; its
matrix is an ideology of order which vilifies the pluralistic character of
modern society, subjugating it to a misanthropic as well as unreal
ideal of efficiency modeled on technical perfection and military order.

ARMY AND SECOND REVOLUTION:
THE SEIZURE OF POWER COMPLETED

By the fall of 1933, National Socialist *Gleichschaltung* was officially
completed on all levels of public life. With the claim to the total incorporation of all citizens, accomplished with the help of the dismal, unresisting capitulation of the German elite, National Socialist doctrine
also captured the culture and values of German society. To what extent
total rule posturing as a revolutionary "upheaval" was actually realized rather than merely externally institutionalized in the social and
economic as well as in the intellectual and moral spheres is debatable.
There undoubtedly were unconquered areas, and not only with regard
to the churches. But by the end of 1933, it appeared that after the
complete collapse of the Weimar establishment, the regime was faced
with only two possible sources of disquiet: the self-assurance of the
Army, which based itself on the legendary authority of Hindenburg,
and the latent, persistent tensions among the activists in the NSDAP
and above all in the SA, to whom the proclamation about the "end of
the revolution" was addressed. The clash of these two power centers in
the brutal events of the summer of 1934 ended the final phase of the
seizure of power.

Between 1918 and 1945, the German Army went through four major
phases. The first, beginning with the revolutionary situation at the
end of World War I and ending with the fall of General von Seeckt in
1926, was marked by an almost forced though wavering cooperation
with the Weimar Government; in the ensuing course of events, the
gap between military and civilian power, which manifested itself in
the crises of 1920 (Kapp Putsch) and 1923, widened. Hindenburg's
presidency and the political role of General von Schleicher marked the

second phase—from 1926 to the National Socialist takeover—which saw the direct participation of the Army command in policy-making and, after 1930, its vital contribution to extraparliamentary crisis governments. The National Socialist regime, on the other hand, in the course of its rearmament policy sought to push the expanded Army back into a more limited, purely military realm and to exclude it from political decision-making. In this third phase, from 1933 to 1938, the Army wavered between the desire to protect itself against National Socialist encroachment and its readiness to make common cause with a regime so assertively military-minded (in contrast to Weimar). The final phase, following the ouster of Generals Blomberg and Fritsch in 1938, was marked by Hitler's increased interference in the Army command structure, which more and more became the tool of National Socialist war and extermination policies and simultaneously was threatened by the rival party army, the SS. The vacillation between acquiescence and resistance showed up the impotence of this proud, tradition-rich power; in the conditions of the totalitarian state, its claim to independence turned out to be an illusion.

In fact, the trend toward interference became apparent quite early, even though the Army seemed to be the only power factor outside the reach of *Gleichschaltung*, and even, so it was thought, seemed to offer the best opportunity for "inner emigration." As a matter of fact, the National Socialist takeover would probably not have been possible had it not been for the deep gulf and alienation between the Army and the Republic that began with Seeckt's command. The attitude of the military in many ways resembled that of the civil service. In line with his strategy, Hitler initially seemed to respect the Army's desire for separation and independence. This was made easier by his knowledge that in Werner von Blomberg and Walter von Reichenau he had two uncritical supporters in key positions, and that for the rest he could rely on the drawing power of his championship of revision and rearmament, which was as welcome to the military as the suspension of parliamentary democracy was to the civil service. In harmony with Seeckt's above-party ideology, Blomberg on February 1, 1933, in his first proclamation expressed his pleasure that the Army now finally would be able to rid itself of political intrigue and, standing "above parties," devote itself to its unique tasks.[13] There began that devotion to the special tasks of military reorganization and rearmament by which the officer corps thought it could avoid political coordination. This was in line with the "soldier only" attitude maintained by General Werner von Fritsch, the successor to General Kurt von Hammerstein during party intrigues in 1938, up to his ignoble end and alleged suicide during the Polish campaign in 1939. "We cannot change politics [only] do our duty," Fritsch told a high-level Army conference after the June, 1934, bloodbath.[14] Given this aloofness, the Army was as little able

---

[13] *Völkischer Beobachter*, February 2, 1933.
[14] Hermann Foertsch, *Schuld und Verhängnis* (Stuttgart, 1951), p. 58.

to cope with the dictatorship as earlier it had been unable to cope with its tasks in the democratic Republic.

Apologists maintain to this day that Hitler's real plans were unknown at that time, that his call for a revision of Versailles had been a legitimate demand, and that at any rate the Army had preserved greater independence than other institutions. In fact, however, at least at the top military level, there could have been little doubt about Hitler's designs for expansion and conquest. Even if one did not put much credence in what he had to say in *Mein Kampf*, copies of which were now being disseminated by the millions, Hitler had made himself unmistakably clear at his very first meeting with the military leadership. Any possible misgivings about the bellicose expansion plans the Chancellor revealed on February 3, 1933, before the Army and Navy command, only four days after his appointment, were dispelled by his simultaneous promises for the expansion and independence of the armed forces and the national defense in the New State. Seeckt's narrow, one-sided autonomy ideal was too deeply rooted to permit the development of any serious resistance to the new course and the dual National Socialist takeover strategy. Almost the only exception was Hammerstein's resignation at the end of 1933, but it had no further consequences. And moreover, there was a widespread feeling that with Hindenburg heading both state and Army, a political veto could if needed be exercised. But above all, the mutuality of interests with a regime dedicated to military (and pseudo-military) values continued to grow. Thus, contrary to the legend of an Army "above politics," cooperation with the new regime, emphatically called for by Blomberg, met with far less resistance than had cooperation with the Republic.

This collaborative course with all its delusions and illusions of a presumably equal partnership of Army and National Socialism reached its zenith when Hitler used the differences with the SA leadership seemingly to satisfy the interests of the Army, but in truth to make his monopoly position formally untouchable. The bloody purge of June 30, 1934, and the tacit complicity of the Army, together with Hindenburg's death, presented Hitler with the unique opportunity of realizing the idea of the total leader state much more fully than was the case in Italy.

What motivated the momentous collaboration of the Army command at this decisive turning point was the belief that the power struggle among the National Socialist leaders would do away with the military rivalry of the SA together with Röhm's power pretensions and assure the Army of the monopoly Hitler had promised. The old tensions between SA and party leadership, exacerbated by the rivalry between SA and Army, came to a head once more in the spring of 1934. It was consciously played up by various quarters, and particularly by Göring and Himmler. The myth of an imminent Röhm putsch against Hitler played a vital part in this. But the fact of the matter is that ultimately it was not the SA but the ascendant SS, with the benevolent tolerance of the Army, that promoted a conflict. Although Röhm himself repeatedly affirmed his loyalty to Hitler and finally, to calm things down, ordered a general vacation for the SA, the party and SS leadership managed through deceptive maneuvers to heighten the impression that a second revolution of the SA was in the offing. To this day, it still is unclear how the alarm to the Munich SA and the rumors of an alleged imminent overthrow of the Government came to be circulated.

At any rate, these rumors were used to persuade Hitler, who possibly may still have wavered, to break off a scheduled trip—probably undertaken for camouflage purposes—to Bad Godesberg at 1:00 A.M. on June 30, 1934, and have him appear unexpectedly in Munich three hours later to "settle accounts" with the SA leaders, to have Röhm and other SA leaders called out from their beds in Bad Wiessee and have six of them executed summarily that very same day in Munich. Röhm was executed the next day by Theodor Eicke and Michael Lippert, the commandants of the Dachau concentration camp. In addition to the charge of treason, the homosexuality of the victims was offered as justification for their deaths, even though their preferences had been known for years (and moreover homosexuals were among the executioners). More victims were added, also outside of the SA. Among them were such old adversaries of Hitler's as Kahr in Munich, Papen's associates Herbert von Bose and Edgar Jung (who were under Göring's direction in Berlin), Erich Klausener of the Catholic Action (Katholische Aktion), and, most important, General von Schleicher and his wife, General von Bredow, and Gregor Strasser.

With Röhm and Strasser, Hitler rid himself of his oldest military and political collaborators; with Schleicher, of his predecessor as Chancellor. Papen, the confident overseer of the Hitler Cabinet, who two weeks earlier had criticized the totalitarian trend in a speech in Marburg inspired by his adviser Edgar Jung, was put under house arrest. Later, after the murder of his friends, he gladly exchanged the post of Vice Chancellor for the office of special personal envoy of Hitler and went to Vienna to prepare Austria's annexation. This was typical both of the character of a man who so flaunted his Christianity and of the disastrous role played since 1932 by this irresponsible pacemaker of dictatorship.

The smoothness with which the murders of June 30 were carried out is eloquent proof that no Röhm putsch was imminent. There was no resistance encountered anywhere, not even among the armed elite formations of the SA; many victims unsuspectingly surrendered of their own accord, having faith in their "Führer" and in the eventual clarification of an obvious mistake. The only shots fired were those of the executioners; often enough the SS commandos were thereby also settling private feuds. The number of victims, officially set at 77, is estimated to have been between 150 and 200.

The main significance of the purge does not lie in the disputed number of its victims but in its methods and in its consequences. The population may have accepted it by saying that the revolution consumes its children, but the fact was that any possible opposition within the party as well as in the national-conservative camp was being nipped in the bud. Moreover, the arbitrary power of the Führer was formally turned into a principle. Within a month, Hitler's total dictatorship was further institutionalized when the Army took the oath of loyalty to Hitler personally and tolerated his usurpation of the Presidential office. These decisive acts rested on the mutuality of interests between Hitler and the Army, which permitted itself to be made an accomplice of Hitler's deeds.

One aspect was the legalization of the terror, which more clearly than anything else revealed the true nature of the takeover and what the future held in store. Hitler quite openly now claimed the "right" to rid himself of his opponents without either legal investigation or trial. If earlier terror acts, especially by the SA, had been accepted in the belief that they were inevitable albeit temporary by-products of a revolution, murder, carried out by the Government, now became part and parcel of official policy. Considering the lack of resistance, the Government could not possibly claim to be acting in "self-defense." But this was precisely how it justified itself in the formal "legalization" of the crimes after the event. This was done with the law of July 3, 1934, which contained only this one terse paragraph: "The measures taken on June 30 and July 1 and 2 to strike down the treasonous attacks are justifiable acts of self-defense by the state." The law was as grotesque as it was typical: a simple assertion in place of judicial investigation (although in the case of Schleicher's murder an investigation was begun but immediately cut off). By appointing itself judge in its own case, and turning violation of law into law through a pseudo-legal sham law, the Government also forced the courts to sanction the regime, or at least prevented them from instigating any moves against the murderers. The loudly proclaimed "lawful state of National Socialism" [15] was quite clearly a state of injustice, arbitrary rule, and government by crime.

Thus the internal consequences of this revolution from above go far beyond its power-political aspects. The Government's official condonation of crimes and the elevation of murder to a legal official act were tantamount to the formal erosion of the legal system and its subjugation to the will of a ruler who appointed himself "Supreme Judge of the German people" (speech by Hitler before the Reichstag, July 13, 1934). The legalization of crime in the name of the state was further underscored by the praise and rewards bestowed on Hitler's accomplices in murder. This was the beginning of the rise of Himmler and his SS, which by decree of July 20, 1934, replaced the SA as an inde-

[15] Thus Hans Frank, "Der deutsche Rechtsstaat Adolf Hitlers," in *Deutsches Recht IV* (1934), p. 120. In the eyes of Carl Schmitt, the "National Socialist state without doubt was an exemplary constitutional state, perhaps even more so than most countries in the world." For documentation, see Gottfried Dietze, "Rechtsstaat und Staatsrecht," in *Die moderne Demokratie und ihr Recht*, II (Tübingen, 1966), 37 f.

pendent organization and was even given the right to organize armed combat troops. Security Service (Sicherheitsdienst, or SD) and SS chieftains who had taken part in the crimes of the week of June 30, among them Sepp Dietrich, Christian Weber, and Emil Maurice, were promoted. Other henchmen were decorated by Himmler on July 4. Murder officially sanctioned and lauded became the norm for the smooth future annihilation of political enemies, Jews, and "inferiors." Later Himmler himself—at an SS leader conference at Poznan on October 4, 1943—specifically made the connection between June 30, 1934, and the policy of annihilation and confirmed the continuity of crime as a maxim of the regime. This would seem to contradict a still widespread tendency to divide National Socialist rule into "constructive" and "degenerate" (wartime) periods.

Even after June 30, it was still possible to find intellectual helpers willing to lend their influential names to the brutal rule. Carl Schmitt headed this list. In the *Deutsche Juristenzeitung* (*German Law Journal*) of August 1, 1934 (pp. 945–50) he proclaimed the quintessence of his years of undermining the legal state and the arbitrariness of the total state in a cynical article entitled "The Führer Protects the Law." Schmitt praised mass murder as the "justice of the Führer" meting out "direct justice," as "genuine administration of justice" and the "highest law" of the new order. Thus, more or less clever theories of authoritarianism and dictatorship merged with the crude sanctioning of the National Socialist claim to the total manipulation of society, state, and law. "The idea of law became simply a word for force." [16] It also spelled the opportunistic capitulation before the legalization comedy which Hitler performed on the stage of the Reichstag on July 13, when Göring in his role of President of the Reichstag ended Hitler's two-hour report to the nation with the dictum: "All of us always approve what the Führer does." [17] The mechanism of legalization ended with the order for the burning "of all files connected with the acts of the last few days." [18] The abortive Reichstag fire show trial in the autumn of 1933 apparently did not evoke any desire for a repeat performance. When, after the collapse of the regime, attempts were made to track down specific cases, it was found that almost all proofs had been destroyed.

The final stages of the seizure of power were incompatible with even the most generous view of the "legal revolution." Its terrorism was revealed also by the broader aspects in which the bloody events took place. The institutional consolidation of the Führer dictatorship brought down the barriers which the partners of January 30, 1933, had thought would protect them against National Socialist autocratic rule.

[16] Karl Dietrich Erdmann, *Die Zeit der Weltkriege* (3d ed.; Stuttgart, 1963), p. 198.

[17] *Verhandlungen des Reichstags*, CDLVIII (July 13, 1934), 32.

[18] Otto Meissner, *Staatssekretär unter Ebert-Hindenburg-Hitler* (Hamburg, 1960), p. 370.

Papen was pushed off the stage which he had so confidently mounted with Hitler. The last wraps fell off the national revolution; the conservative frame around National Socialism, the aristocratic-authoritarian nationalism surrounding its plebeian-totalitarian manifestation was destroyed. Hindenburg, the symbol of this illusion, was eighty-six years old, remote from political reality, and surrounded by advisers beholden to Hitler. Since the Day of Potsdam, he had been nothing more than a respectable front for the dictatorship, his last service in this capacity being the proclamation for a national plebiscite in November, 1933. His death brought a timely solution to a number of problems. On his deathbed in Neudeck, where he had been brought at the beginning of June, 1934, Hindenburg lent himself to one final service to the regime which he had so carelessly installed in power: On July 2, Hindenburg, probably at the instigation of his son and Meissner, sent Hitler and Göring a wire of congratulation on their handling of the events of June 30.

The highest sanctioning of the murders introduced a macabre drama, in which the highest offices of the state were merged in the person of the "Führer and Reich Chancellor" who was above all controls. Even before Hindenburg's death on the morning of August 2, 1934, the Cabinet passed a law ("signed" by the absent Papen) merging the offices of President and Chancellor, thereby once and for all smashing the hopes for a restoration of the monarchy voiced in Hindenburg's disputed last will and testament. This "legal" act also resembled a *coup d'état*, for it violated the restrictions of the Enabling Act on which the Government continued to base itself. The legality claim thus was shown up once again, however strongly later laws and decrees sought to buttress the new construction. A plebiscite was to bring the "express sanction of the German people," even though the reorganization had been designated as "constitutionally valid" prior to any such vote. This platonic act of approbation was explained by Hitler in the voice of the confirmed democrat: He was "convinced through and through that all state power must emanate from the people and [be] confirmed by them in free, secret elections." In explaining his new title, he followed the pseudo-democratic camouflage of his usurpation with the pathetic contention that Hindenburg had given "the title of Reich President unique significance" [19] and thus it should thenceforth not be used. Hence the usurpation of merging the offices of President and Chancellor: a constitutional somersault which numerous German legal theorists obediently parroted.

The oath of loyalty to the dictator sworn by every German soldier on August 2, 1934, the Army's confirmation of its alliance with Hitler, was equally significant. Perhaps not all officers acquiesced in this new course as spinelessly as Blomberg and Reichenau. But together with the satisfaction over rearmament and the dismantling of the SA, Hitler's repeated assurances that the party and the Army were to be the

[19] *Reichsgesetzblatt I*, 1934, pp. 747–51.

two sole pillars of the National Socialist state proved effective. And so the illusions on which the now broken alliance of the "national revolution" had been based lived on. The precipitate loyalty oath of the Army also was the result of couplike manipulation. It was administered with dispatch, without benefit of special legislation, merely by command of Blomberg, an order which unquestionably exceeded his authority. Only eighteen days later, after the plebiscite of August 19, was a law passed sanctioning the coup. The oath was irregular also because existing laws provided for the swearing-in only of new recruits; a new oath by the entire Army would have required a change in the Constitution. But even more serious than these formal violations were the wording and circumstances of the oath. The new text was tailored to Hitler personally, ignoring any allegiance to Constitution, legal institutions, and superiors. And the "sacred oath" sworn "before God" was linked up with the duty for "unconditional obedience."

This religiously sanctioned formula tied the Army absolutely to Hitler, though in his letter thanking Blomberg dated August 21, Hitler renewed his pledge to preserve the mutual-interest alliance and the relationship of mutual loyalty ushered in by the oath. Hitler for his part took on the obligation "to defend the existence and the inviolability of the Wehrmacht" and "to secure the Army as the sole weapons bearer of the nation." [20] But even after it became obvious that Hitler was ignoring these guarantees—as he also ignored those of the concordat with the Catholic Church—the oath continued to tie the Army to Hitler, a one-sided arrangement with dire consequences that continued to the very last day of the Third Reich. All charges of "breach of oath" raised against the military resistance movement ignore Hitler's own repeated breaches of his promises, by which he forfeited his claim to loyalty and obedience long before the revolt of July 20, 1944, sought to dissolve this misused relationship.

But ever since June 30, 1934, the National Socialist leadership, and above all Hitler, knew "what he could ask of the officer corps so long as he took care to avoid a public scandal." [21] The Army, by accepting the assassination of two generals without protest, by becoming the accomplice of the SS, and finally by rendering the oath on the day of Hindenburg's death, tied itself firmly to the National Socialist regime, "to which it felt committed in some dark manner." [22] Without the assistance of the Army, at first through its toleration and later through its active cooperation, the country's rapid and final restructuring into the total leader state could not have come about. While making the military coresponsible for his murders and coups, Hitler at the same time undermined the monopoly he had promised the Army by

[20] *Völkischer Beobachter*, August 21, 1934, p. 1.
[21] Wolfgang Sauer, in K. D. Bracher, W. Sauer, and G. Schulz, *Die nationalsozialistische Machtergreifung* (2d ed.; Cologne and Opladen, 1962), p. 965.
[22] Hermann Mau, "Die zweite Revolution," in *Vierteljahrshefte für Zeitgeschichte*, I (1953), p. 136.

building up the SS. Barely four years later, the fall of Blomberg and Fritsch, the resignation of Beck, and the continuing rise of the SS were to show which side had profited from the "second revolution." To be sure, in the interval, continued rearmament, universal military service, the remilitarization of the Rhineland, and finally the annexation of Austria stilled most doubts and further cemented the Army-Hitler alliance. The road to war made this alliance irrevocable up to the very end; after 1938, only a small minority of the officer corps planned and dared to offer the resistance which, in fatal misjudgment of the new regime and their own position, they had failed to offer in 1934.

The role of the Army in consolidating National Socialist autocracy cannot be overestimated. By comparison, the plebiscite of August 19, 1934, was nothing more than the final farce of the pseudo-legal revolution. The voter was given no genuine choice, either then or in the plebiscites of 1936 and 1938. The vote of August 19 was an act of confirmation without any alternative and without constitutional or political significance. Nonetheless the acclamation was not an unqualified success. Even a new wave of propaganda and psychological coercion, of intimidation and terror, of interference in the electoral process and fraud could not bring the votes up to the 99 per cent to which the plebiscitary acclamations of dictatorial regimes generally aspire. Taking into account the conditions of the elections, a disproportionately high number of no votes were cast, particularly in Hamburg and Berlin, where only 72.6 and 74.2 per cent, respectively, of the qualified voters cast affirmative ballots.[23] Let us keep in mind that in totalitarian "elections" nonvoters and invalid ballots generally should be considered as oppositional voices. As in November, 1933, the big cities with a traditional left-wing voting pattern showed the greatest resistance. But whereas in that November Catholics capitulated, following the support given by the Church fathers to their concordat partner Hitler, the number of no votes in some Catholic regions increased in 1934—clear evidence of a beginning disillusionment in that quarter.

Most importantly, in some areas assent to the total leader state remained significantly below the vote of the preceding "elections." November, 1933, had brought 87.8 per cent yes votes, while in August, 1934, these totaled only 84.6 per cent; the over-all vote also fell below that of 1933. The falling-off in the yes vote in Schleswig-Holstein, where the NSDAP had scored its greatest triumphs before 1933, and as early as 1932 had won an absolute majority, is particularly striking (84.1 and 80.3 per cent in 1933 and 1934, respectively). The smallest "assent" was won in some boroughs of Berlin (Wilmersdorf, 68.8 per cent; Charlottenburg, 69.6 per cent), in Wesermünde (69.4 per cent), and Aachen (65.7 per cent, as compared to 80.6 per cent in 1933), and in Ahaus in Westphalia (69.9 per cent, as compared to 88.3 per cent in 1933). "Unfavorable" election returns were also reported

[23] Election analyses in Bracher, Sauer, and Schulz, *op. cit.*, pp. 95 ff., 350 ff.

from Herford, Bielefeld, Bremerhaven, Lübeck, Iserlohn, Leipzig, Breslau, and rural districts of Münster and Olpe. This was the last time that traditional electoral patterns were discernible in the resistance of Socialist and Catholic voters, before the totalitarian perfecting of the plebiscitary method resulted in the meaningless monotony of 99-percent election results.

The true feelings about the regime, particularly among the workers, were made evident in the shop-steward elections of April, 1935; the results were not made public, but on the basis of available evidence it seems that frequently no more than 30–40 per cent of a plant voted for the single Nazi slate.[24] At issue here were not the great national acclamations of 1933, 1934, 1936, and 1938 connected with a specific political purpose, but the concrete reality of the system. Yet there can be no doubt that the majority of the population was no longer able or willing to resist the noise of the acclamatory propaganda. Stronger than any reservations was the pull of power and apparent success, the impression of order and unity, the recollection of the predemocratic authoritarian state, and the belief in the unlimited promises of the regime. And where manipulation failed to bring the desired results, as in the case of the shop-steward elections, facts were shelved and assertions substituted, as, for example, Robert Ley's, that "far more than 80 per cent of German industrial workers" had voted for National Socialism. Hence, a still-doubting citizen might ask himself, what purpose could be served by a risky opposition at the ballot box?

Thus, even under the still imperfect results of 1933 and 1934, the plebiscite was nothing more than one of many methods for the mobilization and manipulation of the population. It served the same ends as parades, demonstrations, mass rallies to listen to radio broadcasts, and collection campaigns—to create the atmosphere of "voluntary" compulsion, of manipulated consensus, of the unpolitical politicization to distract from the reality of the coercive system.

The Army, seemingly an independent power in the system, also saw this mobilization as contributing to its strengthening and rearmament. The fact that democracy and free elections were abolished together with the unlamented Weimar Republic after all spoke in favor of the new regime, even though one might have preferred a traditionally authoritarian, conservative monarchy. Thus it should come as no surprise that the notes on a conference in the Defense Ministry in the spring of 1934, at which possible moves against the SA were hinted at, mention that the following point met with great approbation: "New elections will be so phrased that everyone will have to say 'yes.' The only thing that will not be changed is the position of the Army." [25] The history of the Germany Army since 1918 is a history of self-delusion. What led them into the unequal alliance with Hitler, into war and catastrophe, was not the "nemesis of power," as John Wheeler-Bennett

[24] Theodor Eschenburg, "Dokumentation," in *VfZG*, No. 3 (1955), pp. 314 ff.
[25] Conference notes of Major Henrici, in *Zeugenschrifttum des Instituts für Zeitgeschichte* (Munich).

asserts in his book by that title (1954), but political ineptitude and unpolitical arrogance.

As early as August 20, 1934, Hitler was able to proclaim the victorious conclusion of his fifteen-year fight for power: "Beginning with the highest office of the Reich, through the entire administration down to the leadership of the smallest village, the German Reich today is in the hands of the National Socialist Party." And in fact what mattered was not so much a taking over of all positions, for this was not invariably the case: there was an astonishing degree of continuity, beginning with non–National Socialists in the Government to the civil service and judiciary to economic and cultural life, and above all in the "independent" Army. But state and society were nonetheless completely in the hands of the National Socialists, subject to their control and manipulation, serving a regime focused entirely on the one Leader; for the rest, it brought anything but order and security, but rather arbitrariness and frequently internal chaos. Hitler himself tailored his proclamation of August 20 to this dual aspect of the consolidation of power: "The fight for governmental power has ceased as of this day. But the fight for our precious people continues." [26] This melodramatic sentence meant nothing more than that only after the last remnants of pre- and non–National Socialist power had been eliminated could the total gathering-in of the nation, the instrumentalization in the service of Hitlerian goals, be fully realized.

This was also the framework within which the NSDAP was assigned its position and function as the ideological and ruling force above and within the conquered state. In the summer of 1933, it had become the only existing party and was entrusted with the task of educating a new elite. Rudolf Hess opened the Reich party congress of 1934 by stating that "the law of totality" was to be the guiding principle of all future National Socialist policy. Hitler ceremoniously recalled the epoch of the "final consolidation of National Socialist power in Germany." Since the summer of 1933, he said, they had, fighting a battle, "broken through and taken one enemy position after the other." Now, as already a year earlier, he declared "the National Socialist revolution . . . as a revolutionary power process is closed." Beginning now is the evolution, and since the leadership "in Germany today has the power to do everything," its actions in the future "cannot be inhibited by anything, except through impulses of a tactical, personal, and hence temporary nature." [27]

But herein lay problems. What did the declaration that the "final" conquest of Germany would be followed by "the realization of the National Socialist program directed from above" mean if that program was anything but clear and consistent, while Hitler's aims were directed toward the outside, toward race and *Lebensraum* policies, toward expansion and hegemony? When Hitler prophesied that "in the

[26] Gerd Rühle, *Das Dritte Reich* (Berlin, 1935), p. 278.
[27] *Der Kongress zu Nürnberg vom 5.–6. September 1934* (Munich, 1934), pp. 18, 22–24.

next thousand years there will be no revolution in Germany," this bombastic dictum was in keeping with the slogan of the Thousand-Year Reich or Göring's promise that in the next hundred years there probably would not be any election. History did not heed these prophecies. But the wrapping-up of the seizure of power opened up an area in which the consolidation of totalitarian rule could progress and the policy of expansion and domination in Europe, the essence of National Socialism, begin. National Socialist power and rule did not rest on a consistent political philosophy or on a detailed master plan. The thinking and conduct of this "movement" was eclectic and opportunistic, its ideas of power politics vulgarly Machiavellian. And yet it would be a mistake to see the spread and imposition of totalitarian rule as mere improvisation and response to favorable opportunities. Alone the pace of the power seizure, so much more rapid and more completely successful than that in Fascist Italy, bespeaks the purposeful logic of the Nazi power ideology. It was given its inner content by the immovable consistency with which Hitler had clung to his Weltanschauung since his Vienna years: above all, anti-Semitism and anti-Slavism. They formed the basis of the two primary aims toward which the consolidation and application of the power he had won were directed: annihilation of the Jews and eastward expansion.

WELTANSCHAUUNG AND IDEOLOGICAL *Gleichschaltung*

How was it possible that these ideas and aims were not only ignored or minimized, but even widely taken up and elaborated, that the intellectual *Gleichschaltung* also largely was self-imposed—completed almost more rapidly and more obligingly than in the social and political sphere? A reference to Hitler and an irresistible "demonization of power" does not explain the German phenomenon nor answer the question about the causes and the responsibility. Two reasons emerge. Hitler and National Socialism were in a long-standing tradition of German political thought. The mixture of Prussian-authoritarian and Austrian-*völkisch* political and expansionist ideologies found their radical outlet in Hitlerism. But the war-aim debates of 1914–18 already contained the essential elements, and behind them there was the development of the German sense of special destiny in the nineteenth century. Hitler and National Socialism—they were not unfortunate accidents, not incomprehensible derailments in the path of German history; they were, as Konrad Heiden said, a "German condition."

Furthermore, the development of National Socialism is the history of the underestimation of politics and the overestimation of order. It was widely believed in "educated circles" that National Socialism essentially was a movement of the forces of order and strong government against chaos and Communism. All that was needed was to support these decent forces, free them of the dross of everyday politics, and lift them up to the heights of culture and philosophy once the necessarily dirty fight for power was over. This summed up the ideas of

Realpolitik that developed after the failure of 1848 and whose moral justification was based on success. It led to the characteristic unpolitical illusion that the "idealistic" component of National Socialism could be furthered and used for a national, political purpose by refining and developing the crude statements of the functionaries, including the well-intentioned but clumsy notions of the "man of the people" Adolf Hitler: in other words, by showing the National Socialists what lay behind their blind drive, thus bringing about a "better" National Socialism. Some were impressed by the forcefulness of this anti-Communist, anti-union "movement"; others, from the camp of the "conservative revolution," were taken by the national-revolutionary, antiliberal component. It was a continuance of the illusion of the "national uprising" by other means, even after it had foundered on the level of political coalition.

The National Socialist camp considered such assistance from conservative and bourgeois circles presumptuous and at times even dangerous. The membership increase of 1933, partially the result of the idea that by going along the worst might be prevented and National Socialism remolded into something more acceptable, had brought similar problems. After 1934 there began the curt rejection and ultimately the ostracism of this sort of parlor National Socialism; some of these early proponents found their way into the resistance, the product of such a mixture of motives and tendencies. However, this does not alter the fact that intellectual fellow travelers at first rendered most valuable assistance. Goebbels, the "intellectual" among the Nazi leaders, was the one to see and exploit this most skillfully. The effective spread of propaganda and the rapid regimentation of cultural life would not have been possible without the invaluable help eagerly tendered by writers and artists, professors and churchmen.

Opportunism and coercion alone do not explain the process which subjugated German intellectual life to the Reich Cultural Chamber within a period of months. The events of the "golden twenties," if looked at dispassionately, may be seen to contain some seeds of this abject capitulation. Also, the blood-letting of the German intelligentsia in 1933 resulted in the collapse from which science and culture did not recover even after 1945. The expulsion of large portions of the critical intelligentsia, however, was only one side of the irreversible loss which made possible the autocratic rule of National Socialism. The other side of the coin was the process of self-destruction, by which the majority remaining behind in part accepted and in part even sanctioned the adaptation of cultural life and values to the nationalist and social-Darwinist power ideology of National Socialism.

A famous example of the very first period was the radio address of the poet Gottfried Benn, physician and exponent of literary Expressionism in the Weimar era; he broadcast to his persecuted, exiled friends a sardonic "Reply to the Literary Emigration," published under the title *Der neue Staat und die Intellektuellen* (*The New State and the Intellectuals*). In it he indulged in the then fashionable glorification of discipline and order. The book was announced in these typical words: "Gottfried Benn declares his allegiance to the new state and explains his step into the other camp—which for him was not 'another' but that with which he had always been in accord. For in truth his roots sprang out of the same soil in which the renewed Germany has its deepest roots. His confession of faith will be a confirmation for those members of the German intelligentsia who have already gone his way, and for those who are still standing aside it will be an exhortation to reflect and re-examine obsolete ideas." That the "new" was something "with which they had always been in accord" was now being proclaimed by many. The continuity of the National Socialist seizure of power, so emphatically denied after 1945, could hardly have found clearer expression. The fact that Benn later submerged himself in the Army, in "inner exile," in no way diminishes the effect and example of a process which was being repeated in many forms.

This is not the place for a detailed examination of this process of "accommodation" to power and its pseudo-intellectual, pseudo-scientific manifestation.[28] What matters here are primarily those aspects touching immediately upon the goals and power technique of National Socialism. Let us consider first the development and impact of ideology, as well as its aims, and second the organization and effect of cultural policy and propaganda within the system of the Third Reich. The two are intimately related. Not only were ideas manipulated in the usual sense and attuned to politics, but conversely, the ideologization of politics and finally the proliferation of insane notions, particularly in the area of race policy, played a decisive role. On the whole, one of the reasons for the disastrous underestimation of National Socialism in Germany, and later for the appeasement policy of the West and in 1939–41 of the Soviet Union, is the failure to take seriously the part played by ideology in National Socialist policy and to overestimate the opportunistic and manipulatory components in the sense of Machiavellian power politics. Hitler, a true revolutionary in this respect, was not the only one obsessed by the absolute truth of his basic ideas, even though they may not deserve the grandiose label "Weltanschauung"; his closest followers, the mafiosi of the fighting years as well as the dignitaries in party and state recruited shortly before and after the takeover, were completely committed to him and to the leader principle and simultaneously to the primacy of the ideology behind and above the policies of the total state. Unquestionably, there were occasional doubts and secret deviations. But the complete absence of ideological conflicts up to the time of catastrophe points up an important difference between this and other dictatorships. There was an abundance of conflicts and rivalries about competencies, but the singular position of the Führer and the primacy of his ideology remained untouched.

[28] For the decisive period 1933–34, see Bracher, Sauer, and Schulz, *op. cit.*, pp. 261 ff.

The primacy of ideology emerged most clearly in the policy on the Jews. Here all reservations about expediency and opportuneness, not to speak of minimal moral standards, had to be shelved from the very outset. Other aspects of National Socialist ideology occasionally would be embellished and carefully packaged. But after the conquest of the state, Hitler's *Mein Kampf*, Rosenberg's *Mythus*, and the racist-imperialist extremist literature of the "fighting years" remained for all to see and were offered up in millions of copies as official reading matter. When he tried to mollify the churches, Hitler was wont to say that the *Mythus* was a private work he himself had never read—which anyone who had ever tried to read that concoction could readily understand. The "unalterable" party program of 1920 also was variously interpreted for tactical reasons. This was true particularly of the agricultural policy statement on the expropriation and redistribution of land. Hitler had already scotched this provision in 1928 by his acquisition of property and by giving the provision an essentially anti-Semitic twist so as to win support in rural areas. But in the revised edition of his commentary to the party program, Rosenberg in 1937 was able to state: "On matters of principle almost nothing had to be changed; only on a few questions did the new Reich have to take different roads than we had visualized." This referred to the unfulfilled domestic promises; the "social-revolutionary" part of the program had become a mere accessory after the alliance with industry and the farmers and after the elimination of the Strasser wing.

But the basic racist and expansionist ideas and formulations called unalterably valid in Hitler's *Mein Kampf* were never officially rescinded or changed by the statesman of "peace" speeches in any of his domestic or foreign balancing acts. Among intimates there could be no doubt as to their validity, among the Army command either in 1933 and 1937, among an industry committed to rearmament, and certainly not on the part of the swaggering theorists of *Lebensraum* and war ethos at desks and lecterns. One simply did not want to admit the possible consequences. The theory of the totalitarian state demanded a militant ideological mobilization on behalf of an internally closed ruling system of maximal efficiency. Beyond that, however, the function of this theory lay in the conscious preparation for the goals of domination spelled out in the ideology. These goals, going beyond a revision of Versailles and a "Greater Germany," envisaged a *völkisch*-racist empire with an unlimited claim to *Lebensraum* resting solely on the needs of the "core nation" and the hegemony of the superior over the inferior race.

The syncretism of German intellectual life and the national revolution of Hitler was dismaying not only in view of the primitive conglomerate of ideas feeding the National Socialist ideology, but even more so because of the blind submission to an intolerant claim to exclusivity. This claim also was one already stated in *Mein Kampf:* "For the Weltanschauung is intolerant . . . and peremptorily demands its own, exclusive, and complete recognition as well as the complete adaptation of public life to its ideas" (p. 506). Many of the illusions that nonetheless persisted were discarded after the summer of 1933 with the control and regimentation of the written word, of art and science. But this did not stop the process of voluntary coordination encompassing lawyers and economists, historians and philologists, philosophers and scientists, publicists and poets, musicians and artists. For the interplay of Byzantinism, manipulation, and coercion would not have been effective had it not been for profound, historically conditioned relations based not so much on racial doctrines as on a pseudo-religious, exaggerated nationalism and on the idea of the German mission.

Das Reich als deutscher Auftrag (The Reich as German Mission; 1934), by the conservative sociologist Georg Weippert, was characteristic of the enthusiastic interpretation accorded to National Socialism in the camp of national-imperial romanticism. Weippert's Reich embodied the "principle of world order," was compelled to lay claim to the "totality of power," and could tolerate "only one ruler"; as "the expression of the German will and sense of mission" it was "all-embracing": "The Reich is not simply the form of order of the German people; rather the Reich is Germany's mission in this world." Given help such as this, which also came forth in introductions and postscripts to serious books and was proclaimed from renowned chairs of learning, almost anything could be justified. Once more the much-heralded "ideas of 1914" were being bruited about, but this time in connection with a political movement in possession of total power and unwilling to tolerate a discussion of aims. If political education was desirable, as Hitler held in *Mein Kampf,* this was only if it postulated an absolute state beyond criticism and a boundless national egotism. Such an "outline of German civics" bore the significant title *Deutschland, nur Deutschland, nichts als Deutschland (Germany, Only Germany, Nothing but Germany,* by W. Wallowitz; 1933).

An analysis of the voluntary coordination of 1933–34 would have to trace many connections which both temporally and essentially go beyond the secondary structure of National Socialist ideology. Such questions of continuity deserve more than mere cursory attention; they are significant for an explanation of the attraction of National Socialist ideology and its effectiveness among the "educated," even though their ready acceptance rested on a misjudgment. The simple schema into which flowed the conservative-authoritarian, antidemocratic, nationalist, irrationalist chain of ideas can be summed up as follows: Man can live only as a member of a nation, and therefore the nation transcends group interests. It is strong only as a cohesive unit, and therefore true "socialism" welds the classes together rather than dividing them; it upholds national idealism instead of Marxism and liberalism; duty, loyalty, and disciplined followers instead of human rights; and, instead of a selfish pluralism, the monolithic leader state, which alone is able to overcome the weaknesses of centuries of German division and ensure optimal power.

National Socialism intensified and sharpened these ideas harking back to Romanticism and the wars of liberation in two ways: by super-imposing a *völkisch*-racist concept of domination on the state and by making battle an absolute, basic principle of all political and social life. Biological social philosophies about the "struggle for survival" as pro-claimed by the Social Darwinists, the idea of politics as a friend-enemy relationship as postulated by Carl Schmitt, military concepts of authority and order—these were now linked to the National Socialist principle that the war in fact was still in progress, that the "frontline spirit" must govern the "rebirth of culture" as well. Hitler's central experience, the war, remained the determining factor, not only in the sense of a radical revisionism but even more so in the infusion of society and culture with a martial terminology and values: from the Labor Front and "work battle" to the marching columns as the expression of the German life-style. As Alfred Rosenberg stated in a speech before the senior officers in the War Ministry in 1935: "The German nation is on the way finally to finding its life-style. . . . It is the style of a marching column, regardless of where and for what purpose this marching column is employed." [29] Military and pseudo-military organization became an organizational and governing principle of the leader dictatorship in all sectors of political and social life.

But the real point of departure of National Socialist ideology was the realization of the racial doctrine. While National Socialist imperial-ism in the early years had to take second place behind the securing and internal consolidation of its rule, and domestic policy was given prim-acy, the terrorism of the regime was made clear quite early with bar-baric purposefulness in the persecution of political outcasts, and its ideological character in its Jewish policies. The eclectic racial anti-Semitic constructions of the pseudo-scientific and pseudo-philosophic concoctions of Ferdinand Clauss, Hans F. K. Günther, and Alfred Rosenberg were now translated into practice. Here, too, intellectual and social ideas of long standing culminated in the thesis of the "natural" hegemony of the Germanic-Nordic race, of which the German people were the nucleus. The corollary of the thesis was the "Jewish world plague," depicted most brutally in Hermann Esser's book by that name (1927) and in Julius Streicher's *Stürmer*—the works of Hitler's two old comrades.

The historico-social components of anti-Semitism were discussed in Chapter I. The Jew, stereotyped as a "parasitic creature," [30] was the personification of evil in National Socialist ideology. Here was the absolute enemy which a totalitarian system needs for the mobilization of political and social forces and as a distraction from its problems. The National Socialist program called for the disenfranchisement of all Jews; anti-Semitic activities were part of its early history. Once in

---

[29] Alfred Rosenberg, *Gestaltung der Idee* (Munich, 1936), p. 303.
[30] Walter Frank, "Die Erforschung der Judenfrage," in *Schriften des Reichsinstituts für Geschichte des neuen Deutschland*, V (Hamburg, 1941), 11.

power, the Nazis began the systematic organization of the persecution of Jews. No tactical considerations were allowed to interfere substantially with instituting the boycott of Jews, expelling them from public life, making them subject to special laws, and finally annihilating them.

As long as the regime was in need of external peace, it shrank from the most radical measures. In the summer of 1933, the flight of Jews from Germany had brought unwelcome reactions from abroad, and the people of Germany also still were something of a hindrance. Unlike nationalism, anti-Semitism existed only as a strong, latent feeling, not as a broad mass movement. Hence the first major boycott that spread across cities and villages on March 28, 1933, was prematurely broken off after only a few days. But meanwhile, anti-Semitic laws began to be introduced early that month (with the full support of the German Nationals) legalizing the "purge" of the civil service and judiciary, of universities and medicine, and setting in motion the machinery for depriving political and racial undesirables of their citizenship. The frantic efforts for accommodation by German-Jewish organizations brought only minor concessions for war veterans and for the organization of self-help and limited "self-government." The censure of National Socialist Jewish policy by the League of Nations on May 30, 1933, did not prevent the carrying-out of the first phase of Jewish exclusion from public life in the summer of 1933; only in the economic sector did considerations of expediency delay major inroads. By April, 1934, the restrictions affected hundreds of university teachers, about 4,000 lawyers, 3,000 physicians, 2,000 civil servants, and about the same number of actors and musicians of Jewish descent. In 1933–34, about 60,000 fled to the not exactly open arms of neighboring countries; by 1938, about one-fourth of Germany's 550,000 Jews had managed to escape oppression and future extermination.

The formal legalization of biological-racist anti-Semitism finally was accomplished by the Nuremberg Laws passed by the Reichstag by acclamation on the occasion of the National Socialist party congress on September 15, 1935. The laws had been hastily drafted only some hours earlier on bills of fare in a Nuremberg beer hall. The chief of the Reich medical chamber, Gerhard Wagner, was one of the prime movers for more severe laws. A Reich Citizen Law and a Law for the Protection of German Blood and German Honor disenfranchised all those citizens "not of German blood." In line with the long-standing agitation of the *Stürmer*, German-Jewish marriages and extramarital relationships were to be considered "race defilement" punishable by imprisonment, and after 1939 by death. This arbitrary act, annotated and given respectability by such non–National Socialist legal experts as Hans Globke was, from the National Socialist viewpoint, a consistent ideological policy; not only did it furnish persecution and discrimination with a legal foundation, it also provided a legalistic starting point for the later annihilation of the disenfranchised.

The brutal myth underlying Nazi racial doctrine was subsequently expanded to include the enslavement of the subjugated peoples, especially those of Eastern Europe. The counterpart to this was the idea of the "transnationalizing" (*"Umvolkung"*) of racially valuable elements, of the selection of blond, blue-eyed potential Germans from kindred peoples. In Germany, a racist population policy and "eugenics" were instituted, with measures ranging from barbaric sterilization to racially desirable breeding. Here, however, the regime did run up against some obstacles and even opposition, particularly from the churches. Whereas the Jewish policy was on the whole accepted, because the latent anti-Semitism found even in the churches condoned the principle if not all the measures, the "eugenic" plans of the animal breeder Himmler for a Nordic polygamy and the "Life Source" (*Lebensborn"*) brothels of the SS were never fully realized. However, tens of thousands were exterminated in a campaign euphemistically dubbed as "euthanasia"; it was based on older ideas and during the war justified with the argument that unproductive consumers had to be eliminated.

The implementation of racial policies as an essential part of National Socialist ideology had a dual aspect. On the one hand, the stereotype of *the* Jew did away with all individual, humane, social, and political differentiation in favor of a systematic, pseudo-religious persecution and extirpation of evil. To be sure, there were exceptions along the lines of Lueger's dictum "I will decide who is a Jew" (an idea Göring also toyed with, though in only a few scattered cases, as for example with respect to his State Secretary, Erhard Milch, technically of "mixed blood"). On the other hand, race policy was an instrument of total rule. The race concept "disseminated" by the National Socialists was devoid of all linguistic, logical, and scientific content; it was a fiction, a myth for the mobilization of subjective and psychotic mass emotions and associations. The employment or nonemployment of racist measures in the takeover phase and the proliferation of these measures in the wartime and liquidation policies were marked by a calculated arbitrariness. The fact that the race concept was not spelled out made the race myth an ideal instrument of rule over a people designated as a "race" engaged in combat with the absolute enemy, and for the supermoral justification of the subjugation and annihilation of undesirable groups, minorities, or even entire peoples: Jews, Poles, Russians—the "subhumans."

The regimentation of the educational system, universities, writers, artists, and also the churches was carried out against the background of race policies and intellectual capitulation. The total claim of the regime was pushed forward in all areas of cultural life with the help of the rapidly expanding system of monopolized propaganda. The alternatives offered were re-education or expulsion from public life. This process was systematized and manipulated through a far-flung system of institutionalized controls. It was expanded to include entertainment and leisure as well, through party auxiliaries and the German Labor Front; in particular, *"Kraft durch Freude"* ("Strength through Joy"), modeled after the Fascist *"dopo lavoro,"* was to ensure control over the private lives of workers and employees through communal leisure and vacation activities.

The first step was the regimentation of broadcasting, which was semiofficial to begin with; by the spring of 1933, it was largely coordinated in personnel as well as programming. National Socialism recognized and exploited the importance of this medium as had no previous regime. In the press, things developed somewhat differently. The regime continued to tolerate non-Nazi papers because it thought to turn their prestige to advantage at home and abroad. Not until August, 1943, was the last great paper of this kind, the *Frankfurter Zeitung,* abolished. But the expression of independent opinion, let alone criticism, called for the art of writing and reading between the lines. What set these papers apart from the party press was their individual style rather than additional information. Goebbels, through his system of internal press conferences and stream of "directives," succeeded in imposing a uniformity of news and interpretation soon after the creation of the Propaganda Ministry (March, 1933). He was a skilled enough journalist to appreciate the necessity of tolerating some variation to avoid the danger of boring the reader to death and consequently diminishing the propaganda value of the press. But the political scope permitted was extremely limited, and economic manipulation helped to make the press materially dependent and the political pressure almost irresistible.

The expansion of the National Socialist press combine, built by Hitler's former sergeant, Max Amann (the publisher of the *Völkische Beobachter* and now the powerful President of the Reich Press Chamber), on the foundation of the old National Socialist publishing house of Eher, played a major role in this sector. There were parallel and frequently conflicting pressures brought by regional party publishing houses and autocratic regional chieftains, particularly in the early days, to force intimidated publishers to give up their papers—not always successfully, since interests often overlapped and personal rivalries tended to blur political fronts. There exists an excellent special study on Amann's not infrequent role as the antagonist of separatist party ambitions, and his emergence as the powerful victor from these disputes.[31] And at any rate, the questions of ownership had little bearing on the political content and direction of the press; the primacy of the party was established regardless, and it would be sheer folly to see the internal conflicts of the Nazi establishment or the trifling individual tones of its papers as signs of opposition, as is the case in the rather apologetic pamphlet *Presse in Fesseln (The Fettered Press;* 1947).

[31] Oron Hale, *The Captive Press in the Third Reich* (Princeton, 1964), pp. 337 ff.

Goebbels formulated the concept of "total propaganda" in his speech at the Nuremberg party congress on September 7, 1934: "Among the arts with which one rules a people, it ranks in first place. . . . There exists no sector of public life which can escape its influence." [32] By that time, what Goebbels eighteen months earlier (May 8, 1933) had spoken of at a meeting of theater directors had become the norm and been institutionalized—namely, that after the capture of the state, the National Socialist idea "would link up all of cultural life with conscious political-ideological propaganda," would tear it out of the "Jewish-liberalistic" Weimar culture and steer it toward the presentation of the sound and strong, the typical and generally binding. The degree of tolerance which was conceded in accordance with tactical requirements [33] said nothing about the extent of control and direction—for example, in the case of the publication of an inexpensive edition of foreign Hitler caricatures, which grotesquely bore the inscription "authorized by the Führer," [34] and also in Goebbels' instructions to the press and to all other cultural media to be "monoform in will, polyform in the expression of the will," or his statement: "We don't want everyone to blow the same horn at all, but only want them to blow according to *one* plan . . . that not everyone has the right to blow what he pleases." [35] The tools used were: coordination of the news services, daily press conferences at the Propaganda Ministry, "dissemination" of binding "directives" and "terminology." In this way the uniform treatment of current issues had become a fact by the summer of 1933.

A high point in institutionalization was reached with the official installation of a "Reich Cultural Chamber" on September 22, 1933. The opening of this all-embracing control and censorship agency to which all "intellectual workers" had to belong may not have been the "event without precedent in the history of all peoples and ages" that self-serving announcements proclaimed, but it gave the Propaganda Minister the power to "organize" the whole of cultural life, which now existed in name and pretense only. Within the framework of the Cultural Chamber, Reich Chambers for Literature, Press, Broadcasting, Theater, Music, and Fine Arts were set up, and the already existing Film Chamber incorporated. Laws and decrees saw to it with bureaucratic thoroughness that anyone subject to the "intellectual influencing" of the Propaganda Ministry, anyone who in the broadest sense worked in "creation, reproduction, intellectual or technical processing, dissemination, preservation, circulation, or who assists in the distribution of the technical means of dissemination" had to join; this included even the "manufacture and distribution of technical means of dissemination." [36] The threat of nonadmission to or expulsion from

[32] *Der Kongress zu Nürnberg vom 5.–6. September 1934*, p. 134.

[33] Walter Hagemann, *Publizistik im Dritten Reich* (Hamburg, 1948), pp. 55 ff.

[34] *Hitler in der Karikatur der Welt. Tat gegen Tinte* (Berlin, 1938).

[35] In Hagemann, *op. cit.*, p. 35, and Rühle, *op. cit.*, p. 82.

the Chamber, tantamount to being barred from one's profession—and hence to economic death or possibly a concentration camp, underscored the degree of total absorption and control. Censorship and publication bans, the traditional tools of dictatorship, were made practically super-fluous by this up-to-date method of penetration and control.

This supervisory mechanism was supplemented by a stringent law which, by holding editors in chief responsible for everything published by them, subjected them to the arbitrary rule of the Propaganda Minister. Goebbels rounded out his triple position of power as Minister, President of the Cultural Chamber, and party propaganda chief by setting up a Reich Journalism School (1935) compulsory for young journalists. On November 15, 1933, speaking at the festive opening of the Cultural Chamber, he said: "The revolution we have made is a total revolution. . . . It is completely irrelevant what means it uses." [37] The appointed spokesmen of the new culture hailed the "parade of faith," the "steel romanticism" Goebbels conjured up. In addition to Benn and Heidegger, Richard Strauss also manifested his cooperation by accepting the Presidency of the Reich Music Cham-ber. The Literature Chamber was presided over by the Germanic peas-ant poet Hans Friedrich Blunck, who as late as 1952 let it be known that "he did not get overly indignant over rumors [!] of book burnings; such things are part of all revolutions." [38] Behind him there was a phalanx of "poets" willing to swear their allegiance to Hitler, among them many who in 1932 had petitioned for a Heine monument in Düs-seldorf but who did not shrink from replacing ousted cosignatories in the academies, from defaming persecuted Jews, or from transforming, crudely or sensitively, the theses of the rulers into "culture." These included Rudolph G. Binding, Max Halbe, Hanns Johst, Heinrich Lersch, Walter von Molo, Josef Ponten, Wilhelm von Scholz. The now defamed included Heinrich and Thomas Mann, Käthe Kollwitz, Max Lieber-mann, Stefan Zweig, Jakob Wassermann, and Alfred Kerr.

The "purge" of the academies was rivaled by the eagerness with which many publishers, headed by J. F. Lehmann (Munich), Han-seatische Verlagsanstalt (Hamburg), Diederichs (Jena), Korn (Bres-lau), Stalling (Oldenburg), Junker und Dünnhaupt (Berlin), and Langen-Müller (Munich), began to specialize in "national" and *völkisch* literature. Great opportunities opened up for writers who sought to remedy the regrettable lack of a genuinely National Socialist literature: Erwin Guido Kolbenheyer, Rudolf G. Binding, Emil Strauss, Hans Grimm, Hanns Johst, Wilhelm Schäfer, Jacob Schaffner (a Swiss), Werner Beumelburg, Will Vesper, Richard Euringer. The academies still tolerated some of the "old-timers," most notably Ger-hart Hauptmann, as window-dressing. However, the new literati, who

[36] Karl-Friedrich Schrieber, *Das Recht der Reichskulturkammer* (5 vols.; Berlin, 1935–37).

[37] *Deutsche Kultur im Neuen Reich* (Berlin, 1934), p. 23.

[38] *Unwegsame Zeiten* (Mannheim, 1952), p. 186.

in addition to those named above included Hermann Claudius, Gustav Frenssen, Agnes Miegel, Josef Magnus Wehner, and Hans Carossa, moved up the ladder. Those ousted, on the other hand, included Alfred Döblin, Leonhard Frank, Georg Kaiser, the Mann brothers, Alfred Mombert, Rudolf Pannwitz, Fritz von Unruh, Jakob Wassermann, and Franz Werfel. In February, 1935, a writer who still sought to maintain himself between the fronts, noted: "Result: in ten years we will no longer have a literature." [39]

Yet even the expulsion and disenfranchisement of the undesirables and the supervision of all others did not ensure the complete success of the vaunted cultural revolution. There remained the existing literature, art, and music. Blacklists were compiled ceaselessly and literary histories were revised; a *völkisch* German philology, developed with the assistance of numerous literary historians from Adolf Bartels to Hermann Pongs, set the tone. The "cleansing" of libraries and bookstores presented some problems, but the destruction and self-destruction of German literature was achieved within a matter of months through the substitution of second- and third-rate scribblers for first-rate writers and by inhibiting contacts with the outside. This process of attrition was to engulf many initially friendly conservative-national writers whom Himmler's Reich Security Office proceeded to unmask as "opportunists" with erroneous notions about race and Führer, despite the fact that the "adjustment" of 1933–34 had been marked by absurd efforts in "national" and church circles to lend meaning to the slogans of National Socialism. Among those who so exerted themselves were Reinhold Wulle, Richard Benz, Max-Hildebert Boehm, Hans Naumann, the disciples of Othmar Spann, Erich Rothacker, Hans Freyer, Ernst Jünger, and Rudolf Herzog.

But the exclusion of "Left," democratic, and Jewish literature took precedence over everything else. The blacklists that were being compiled beginning in April, 1933, ranged from Bebel, Bernstein, Preuss, and Rathenau through Einstein, Freud, Brecht, Brod, Döblin, Kaiser, the Mann brothers, Zweig, Plivier, Ossietzky, Remarque, Schnitzler, and Tucholsky, to Barlach, Bergengruen, Broch, Hofmannsthal, Kästner, Kasack, Kesten, Kraus, Lasker-Schüler, Unruh, Werfel, Zuckmayer, and Hesse. The catalogue went back far enough to include literature from Heine and Marx to Kafka. The book burnings staged on May 10, 1933, in the public squares of cities and university towns symbolized the auto-da-fé of a century of German culture. Accompanied by torchlight parades of students and passionate orations of professors, but staged by the Propaganda Ministry, this barbaric act ushered in an epoch which Heinrich Heine had summed up by the prophetic words that there where one burns books, one ultimately also burns people.

Anti-Semitism, antimodernism, and political functionalization also marked Nazi music policy. The denunciation of atonal experimenta-

[39] Oskar Loerke, *Tagebücher 1903–1939*, ed. by Hermann Kasack (Heidelberg and Darmstadt, 1955), p. 310.

tion, but also of classical romantic works by Jewish composers (Mendelssohn, Gustav Mahler) was matched by overemphasis of folk music and battle songs adopted by the youth movement. In June, 1933, Bernhard Rust, the Prussian Minister of Culture, appointed a commission composed of Wilhelm Furtwängler, Max von Schillings, Wilhelm Backhaus, and Georg Kulenkampff to supervise concert programs and associations. This did not proceed without major public controversies and clashes between Furtwängler and Goebbels over men like Hindemith, Reinhardt, Otto Klemperer, and Bruno Walter. The regime's effort to replace the "degenerate music" by a pompous, vacuous *"völkisch"* music met with little success.

In the field of art, interference made itself felt particularly in the personnel policies of the museums, exhibition halls, and art associations. Here, too, the starting point was an attack on modern schools—an approach with great popular appeal—on "decadent art," reviled and barred as un-German and Jewish. Exhibits designed to ridicule, with price tags dating back to the inflation, appealed to the lowest instincts of the general population. "Architectural Bolshevism," which included the great Bauhaus movement, was countered by the plans for a National Socialist "political architecture" in the style of the pompous pseudo classicism championed personally by the artist and architect *manqué* Hitler. With the self-confidence of a Nero, he inaugurated the gigantic public buildings of the Third Reich as the heralds of a "native (*arteigen*) art" and as monuments to "millennia" of National Socialist rule. Hitler's bombastic-primitive "culture address" at the party congress of 1933—proclaiming the thesis of the "racial basis" of all art —revealed more clearly than any theory both the enormous banality and the brutality of this ideologization and instrumentalization of culture. He was backed by such *völkisch* champions of art as Paul Schultze Naumburg, Alfred Rosenberg, H. F. K. Günther, and Walter Darré. The reactionary resentments of the semi-educated and the uneasiness of the traditionalists supported them; not infrequently the long-standing radical opposition to modern art of Rosenberg's Combat League for German Culture was carried out in unholy alliance with conservative critics. (The Austrian ideologue Othmar Spann had been the main speaker at the founding meeting of this group at the University of Munich in 1929.) The national revolution culminated in the arbitrary suppression, and finally, with the Law on the Withdrawal of Products of Decadent Art of May 31, 1938, in the destruction of the art of an entire epoch. The almost endless list of works despoiled, ranging from Beckmann, Chagall, Klee, and Kokoschka to Kollwitz, Barlach, Kandinsky, Gropius, Mies van der Rohe, and Oskar Schlemmer, included almost every artist of international renown.

THE NEW EDUCATION AND THE WORLD OF KNOWLEDGE

While National Socialism could substitute little more than ideology and second-rate imitation for the literature and art it expelled or destroyed, its main efforts from the very outset were directed toward the most important instruments of totalitarian policy: propaganda and education. The goal of "gathering in" the youth occupied first place in the National Socialist canon. The NSDAP had a youthful leadership corps, had built up strong youth and student organizations, and its propaganda played on the generation problem; "Make room, you old ones," was an effective battle cry against the Weimar establishment. The personnel changes after the seizure of power were in fact largely a change of generations; thirty-year-olds were given leading positions in state and society. The appeal of the revolutionary changeover lay not a little in the chances it opened up to a youth striving toward change, adventure, and more rapid advancement. The pseudo-military pageantry and close ties to the youth movement also were not without effect.

The ongoing debate about the need for school and university reform was perverted into demands for authoritarian-*völkisch* education by Nazi educators like the former liberal teacher Ernst Krieck and the Nietzschean Alfred Bäumler. This sector also had its precursors and presuppositions that facilitated a rapid coordination. George Mosse [40] has followed the process back to the nineteenth century; national-*völkisch* ideas of education permeated the German educational system long before the arrival of National Socialism. Krieck combined fantasies of a "Platonic disciplinary and educational state" which no longer possessed autonomous education or freedom of instruction with the demand for a *völkisch*-national political permeation of all teaching. Bäumler's idea of a "political school" was aimed at a purposeful one-sided political orientation and adjustment to the Führer principle; the "German community school" as a "*völkisch* ideological school" was the paradoxical formula.[41] The spring of 1933 saw the beginning of a stream of opportunistic pamphlets dealing with the *völkisch*-national reorganization of the schools. Coordination of teachers, uniformity of syllabi, ideological indoctrination of students were the fixed points, and their eager defenders even saw the teacher—this too in line with an older tradition—as the "leader and educator of the nation."

National Socialist policy sought to functionalize education in the service of totalitarian rule in two ways: first, through the stress on subjects bearing on racial, national, and political ideas (history, German philology, biology, geography, and sports) and their alignment with communal "race lore" and military values; and second, through the creation of elite schools, at which the future leaders were to be trained in a special National Socialist education program. Rust, Frick, Goebbels, Rosenberg, and Hitler himself sought through proclamations, laws, and decrees to accelerate the reorganization of the schools. This went hand in hand with the smashing of the old youth organizations and the promotion of the Hitler Youth to the only organization,

[40] *The Crisis of German Ideology* (New York, 1964), pp. 13 ff.
[41] Ernst Krieck, *Nationalpolitische Erziehung* (Leipzig, 1933); Alfred Bäumler, *Männerbund und Wissenschaft* (Berlin, 1934); *Politik und Erziehung* (Berlin, 1937).

under a Reich Youth Leader, the German philology student Baldur von Schirach. In April, 1933, Schirach usurped the leadership of the Reich Central Committee of German Youth Organizations; in December, 1933, the Protestant youth movement was incorporated into the Hitler Youth, and with the law of December 1, 1936, the last non–National Socialist youth organizations were dissolved and membership in the official youth organization made compulsory for all youth between the ages of ten and eighteen.

To be sure, there were limits to the reorganization. Interests and jurisdictions remained confusingly chaotic; conflicts between party, Hitler Youth, and state were numerous. The incompetence of the alcoholic former high-school teacher Rust, the Minister of Education, made itself strongly felt. Opinions also diverged on what subjects and educational principles did in fact make up the National Socialist ideology. The numerous pamphlets and textbooks seeking to revise the teaching of history proved of little help. The battle for the new history, in which scholars who took part covered themselves with little glory, often led to absurd results. Greek culture was Nordified, Sparta glorified, Caesar and Augustus made into modern "leaders." Charlemagne was the "Slaughterer of Saxons," the Hohenstaufens un-German admirers of Italy. Widukind, the Guelf emperor Henry the Lion, and "Frederick the Only One" (thus Rosenberg) were glorified, and the Jews were seen as the force behind every disaster. This was supposed to be "world history on a racial basis" (titles of books by the historian Wilhelm Erbt and the philosopher Wilhelm Wundt), going hand in hand with countless absurd attempts by historians and German philologists to relate all history to the highest point of National Socialism, to legitimize the Third Reich as the fulfillment of the medieval longing for the Thousand Year Reich (thus the noted Bonn professor Hans Naumann), or even in unintended humor to celebrate Hitler as the greatest *Volkskünstler* (folk artist) (Wilhelm Erbt). History was to be looked at "with the eyes of blood," under the perspective of the "leader idea of our time, which links up with the oldest models of the German past" (Frick). Its primary function was to serve the "political, intellectual, and spiritual mobilization of the nation." [42]

Recent studies have revealed the failure to produce any major scholarly work supporting the vague National Socialist picture of history, and the reasons therefor.[43] The effort remained bogged down in protestations of faith, in one-sided political pedagogy; any attempt at pseudo-scientific systematization was necessarily condemned to failure. Even the creation of a Reich Institute for the History of the New Germany (1935) under the ambitious anti-Semitic historian Walter Frank, despite support from highest quarters and the help of such

[42] See Bracher, Sauer, and Schulz, *op. cit.*, pp. 311 ff.

[43] For a comprehensive treatment, see Helmuth Heiber, *Walter Frank und sein Reichsinstitut für Geschichte des Neuen Deutschland* (Stuttgart, 1966); cf. also Karl Ferdinand Werner, *Das NS-Geschichtsbild und die deutsche Geschichtswissenschaft* (Stuttgart, 1967).

cooperative professors as K. A. von Müller of Munich (Frank's university teacher), produced nothing more than a few conferences and symposiums on the "Jewish question." Finally, the proposal of one of the authors of the official outline of history (Walter Gehl) to adopt a new calendar beginning with the first year of the regime was also turned down; apparently the examples of the French Revolution and of Fascist Italy did not invite imitation. What remained was the scheme of the view of the more remote past as the prehistory of National Socialism, the most recent past as an "interim Reich," and the new state as the fulfillment and redemption of German history and the most vital world historical point of reference.

The teaching of German and history was to be degraded to pure ideology; only the short span of National Socialist rule helped avert this and make possible a retreat to more harmless themes. Here, too, it was a case less of active resistance than of power conflicts among Nazi bigwigs. Thus, for example, Goebbels countered the extremist historical philosophies of his rival Alfred Rosenberg with a directive for propaganda officials stating that although the 1918–33 period was to be labeled "criminal," one could not apply "National Socialist yardsticks to all of German history and its heroes," and present "Goethe as a Freemason and poisoner of Schiller, and Mozart as a victim of poisoning . . . and all of them together as Freemasons." [44] Here the propagandist demurred against a "sellout of German history," which was "not in the interests of National Socialist public enlightenment." But transcending the tensions between state and party, between school and Hitler Youth, which made the extent and the actual success of totalitarian re-education so hard to gauge, there still remained the final pedagogical goal proclaimed by Schirach before a meeting of the Hitler Youth leadership in, of all places, the National Theater of Weimar: "The youth leader and educator of the future will be a priest of the National Socialist creed and an officer in the National Socialist service." [45]

In principle this goal was achieved in 1933. Just as teachers and parents capitulated to the pressures of the regime, so on the whole did the indoctrination of youth succeed. The young, who were receptive to heroic legends and black-and-white oversimplifications, were handed over to the stupendous shows of the regime. From earliest childhood, they were exposed to flag raisings, parades, nationwide broadcasts in the schools, hikes, and camps. The teacher, fearful of his civil-service status and subject to denunciation by pupils and parents alike, was rapidly coordinated.

The reorganization and manipulation of the existing educational system was, however, only one part of the process. From the very beginning, a separate elite school system was developed parallel to the

[44] Hagemann, *op. cit.*, p. 99.
[45] Baldur von Schirach, *Revolution der Erziehung* (Munich, 1938), p. 125. Cf. Rolf Eilers, *Die Nationalsozialistische Schulpolitik* (Cologne and Opladen, 1963).

National Socialist penetration of the old system, a process which set the Nazi revolution apart from the revolutionary transformation in Russia. Almost everywhere the regime operated on two planes simultaneously: penetrating and compromising the old institutions yet at the same time building up new, separate rival machineries above them. This characterized the relationship between the state, party, and SS bureaucracies, the coexistence of Army and SS, and the dual judiciary, in which the police state of the Gestapo and the concentration camps was erected behind the regular courts. As to a separate educational system, National Socialism was however only partially successful. Here, too, the briefness of its rule and the endless conflicts among the parties concerned played a part. But what was done clearly indicated the direction of the ideas on education and elite training.

The future National Socialist leadership corps was to be educated and trained in four different institutions, according to the age of the students as well as the type of training. The first such schools, Order Castles (*Ordensburgen*), were founded in 1933, at the same time as the National Political Education Institutes (*Nationalpolitische Erziehungsanstalten* [Napola]). Beginning in 1937, there also were Adolf Hitler Schools (AHS), and in 1941 Rosenberg's so-called Supreme School (*Hohe Schule*) was opened in Frankfurt/Main, the only one set up before the war.

The Napolas, boarding schools for boys between the ages of ten and eighteen, in some respects continued the tradition of the Prussian cadet training schools; as a matter of fact, three of the latter were taken over in 1933 as Napolas. They typified the National Socialist reorganization of established institutions. The program concentrated on the development of a military spirit, the fusion of Prussian and National Socialist values, the development of courage, dedication, and simplicity. Its administrators under the direction of a high-ranking SS officer were members of the SA and SS; however, unlike the other National Socialist special schools, the institutes were under the administrative control of the Reich Ministry of Education. The result was numerous jurisdictional conflicts which in the eyes of the party diminished the value of the Napolas. In the course of time, their number grew to more than thirty; there were Napolas in Austria, the Sudeten region, and Alsace-Lorraine, and finally also Napolas for girls. Theirs was a pseudo-military rather than a strict Nazi orientation; their purpose was the training of future SA, SS, police, and Labor Service leaders; there was great awareness of the coming war and the future need for officers. This awareness also was made obvious in the emphasis on competition, military indoctrination, and training with horses, motorcycles, cars, and glider planes, and it explains the expansion of these schools even after the outbreak of the war. They were meant to combine the old and new militarism, conservative-nationalist and National Socialist military training.

Not so the Adolf Hitler Schools. The twelve- to eighteen-year-olds in these "leadership schools," or "training schools of the party," were, according to Hitler's personal orders, above all meant to become Nazi functionaries; the party training institutes therefore were deeply involved in this program. But AHS graduates were given preference in nonparty posts as well. At the same time, the AHS were assigned the task of bringing National Socialist education into areas "in which the school authorities, for reasons of foreign or church policy (concordat) are unable to carry out and stress National Socialist propaganda with the proper degree of intensity." [46] The party here took over what the state was unable to do; in effect, Rust was quite obviously being outmaneuvered by Schirach and Ley. But that was only part of the constant conflict between state authorities and Hitler Youth or Reich Youth leadership, which gained jurisdiction over the AHS. The party interposed itself via its Central Educational Office, through which close contacts with the Order Castles were established.

The funding of free boarding schools of the AHS also took place via the party, although an "Adolf Hitler Fund" provided for the "voluntary" financial participation of the parents. The pupils were under the sole jurisdiction of the party; they could be discharged at will, whereas the parents could not take their sons out of the school without permission of the party. The party regions, through local and Hitler Youth leadership, annually selected twelve-year-olds showing special "leadership ability," of "healthy stock" and "racially pure"; intelligence and learning played only a minor part, and social background none at all. After thorough physical and political checks in questionnaires and by physicians and Hitler Youth leaders in regional camps, only a small portion of all applicants were selected by a special committee under the chairmanship of the regional political administrative chief. Admission ceremonies were held on April 20, Hitler's birthday.

Although social background allegedly played no part in the selection of students, nearly four-fifths of the AHS students came from the middle class; because all governmental posts eventually were to be filled by a Nazi elite, intelligence and learning gradually began to take on added importance. This tendency also began to assert itself in the choice of textbooks and of teachers, who in part were party functionaries with high Hitler Youth rank, paid by the NSDAP. As preparatory schools for the Order Castles, the AHS were to symbolize the National Socialist revolution in culture and education through new teaching methods and programs, and even in their buildings. (The plans, never executed, show barracks and castlelike projects in the preferred Germanic-Nordic style of Nazi architecture.) Their program stressed military-gymnastic drill, ideological-political training, particularly in such "core subjects" as biology, folklore, the study of foreign countries, and preparation as "administrative officials of the National

---

[46] Dietrich Orlow, "Die Adolf-Hitler-Schulen," in *VfZG*, No. 13 (1965), p. 273. On the Napola, see Horst Ueberhorst, *Elite für die Diktatur* (Düsseldorf, 1968). See also Harald Scholtz, "Die NS-Ordensburgen," in *VfZG*, No. 15 (1967), pp. 269 ff.

Socialist new order" (Orlow). The new approach included guided discussions with predetermined end results, "instinctive" evaluation of the students instead of report cards, as well as practical work in the conquered eastern and western regions which these young "leaders" were one day to administer as fanatically trained technicians of authority.

Though these goals were never realized, they clearly reflect the design for the National Socialist empire of the future. This is true particularly of the Order Castles. Their expansion was part of a glorification of a misrepresented German colonization and dominance in the Middle Ages. Selected graduates of the Napolas and AHS were to be trained in a series of these Order Castles. The most important prerequisite, however, was satisfactory completion of Labor Service and Army training as well as work in leading party positions. Only those meeting these requirements were admitted as candidates to the ruling elite, to the new "aristocracy of the nation."

The program of the Order Castles, which was to institutionalize this progression, had to be modified during the war. Originally it provided for a three-year course, beginning with race-biological and ideological indoctrination, followed by transfer to an Order Castle specializing in sports and physical training, including mountain climbing, shooting, parachuting, and mountain combat. The last period was to be spent at the rebuilt Marienburg in Western Prussia, in symbolic deference to the German Knights' Order, representing the German drive to the East in the Middle Ages; here political education with special emphasis on the "Eastern question" was to be emphasized, a programmatic finish to the preparation of the elite of the future Nazi empire. This plan for the future, pursued with much secrecy by its founder, Robert Ley, more and more came under the jurisdiction of Himmler and the SS. In a secret speech at the Sonthofen Order Castle on November 23, 1937 (eighteen days after the Führer's meeting on the coming war), Hitler gave a detailed outline of the historic-racist nature of the future Germanic Empire of the German Nation (*Germanisches Reich Deutscher Nation*), in which the graduates of the Order Castles were to take over leadership.

While a number of Order Castles were founded and run along the grandiose lines of Neogermanicism, particularly in the border regions, Alfred Rosenberg's pet project, the Supreme School, never came to play its projected role of National Socialist university. The functions spelled out at its festive opening in 1941 were practically a continuation of the controversial activities of the Institute for Research on the Jewish Question, which had been wrested from Walter Frank's hands. As the first branch of an enterprise presumably intended to reorient all of German scholarship, the Supreme School accomplished little. Further plans provided for institutes of Aryan intellectual history, race lore, and the study of Freemasonry. Rosenberg's special pride was the Library on the Jewish Question, whose shelves were filled with books and whole libraries looted from occupied countries. But the main emphasis of National Socialist educational policy was not on these unfinished projects, which operated in the shadow of jurisdictional conflicts and finally of war, but on efforts to bring the German universities themselves into line.

The situation of the universities after 1933 was shaped by the fact that the new rulers were helped by internal weakness, wishful thinking, and the willingness to be seduced—a frightening susceptibility to the manipulations and threats of National Socialism. Coordination measures, innumerable instances of voluntary *Gleichschaltung,* but also cases of refusal to knuckle under combine to give a somewhat diffuse picture. A major factor that facilitated the inroads of National Socialism was the "aberrant development of German political thought" since the second half of the nineteenth century,[47] as well as the deification of the concept of the state. Although the radical nationalist-*völkisch* tendencies which flowed directly into National Socialism were not strongly represented in the universities, there was admiration for successful power politics and for those great men outside the rules of ordinary morality, attitudes which ever since Bismarck's *Realpolitik* were considered quite proper and compatible with a humanistic education. The libertarian impulse of the university and student movement had, after the protest of the Göttingen Seven and the failure of the Frankfurt "parliament of professors" of 1848–49, given way increasingly to a doctrine of power politics and a national-imperialist ideology of catching up with others. This trend reached its first peak in 1914–18, with the manifestoes against Western democracy and the prowar activities of hundreds of professors. The defeat of 1918 was simply not accepted. Most of the critical examinations dealt with the question of war guilt and the democratic Republic, not with the stab-in-the-back legend and the true causes of the disaster. The slogans the student corps repeated in academic addresses and at national festivals, often consciously aimed against the Republic, reflected the profound self-delusions of large segments of German academic life. Its civic consciousness was oriented toward predemocratic values; its dedication after the interlude of Weimar was to the re-creation of the "Reich" as a major power, with or without an emperor.

The great sympathy shown for the German Nationals by a predominantly conservative-national body of professors, and for the National Socialists by an activist student body, symbolized the deeply troubled relationship between power and intellect, politics and values. The events had cast their shadow before them since 1929: in the student elections dominated by National Socialists, in anti-Semitic activities, in the defamation and boycott of Republican or pacifist lecturers. Once in power, the Nazis could claim that the hour for the synthesis of power and intellect, for the "political university," had come, as hasty acclimatization to the new climate was being propounded by philosophers like Hans Freyer and Martin Heidegger.

To be sure, the enormous number of those expelled and censured

---

[47] Rudolf Smend, *Staatsrechtliche Abhandlungen* (Berlin, 1955), pp. 364 ff.

showed that great resistance still had to be overcome to make the university amenable to the regimentation of scholarship and instruction. Yet the readiness to cooperate or to knuckle under and desert the persecuted minority of colleagues predominated. The idea of a state exempt from ethical yardsticks and of statesmanship justified by success was widespread. The great events of the spring of 1933 made personal reservations seem petty; the return of a strong authority and its far-flung goals made up for any disagreeable "side effects." This mentality, and not the relatively small number of active National Socialists, lay at the root of the helplessness of the universities. Admiration for imposing displays of power were coupled with the unpolitical idea of politics as a "dirty business," and this made for both resigned acceptance and the justification of cooperation. One's conscience could be appeased by saying, in a misinterpretation of Max Weber, that here the conviction ethic (of personal reservations) had to take second place to the responsibility ethic (for the national renewal). Ideologization of personal failure, blindness, misguided ideas, or opportunism predominated and were fed by that idealistic, romantic, or Machiavellian concept of the state which dominated in schools and universities, in textbooks and even scholarly works.

The natural sciences and medicine, those disciplines of detached sobriety, did not remain unaffected. Among the absurd fruits of nationalist and racist thought was the creation of a "German mathematics," of "German" or "Aryan" physics, to which renowned scientists like Philipp Lenard and Johannes Stark lent themselves both before and after the takeover—even if only in order to gain a powerful platform for their feuds with Einstein and other Jewish scientists. The consequence of National Socialist coordination and unpolitical acquiescence was a substantive loss which, long before the bloodletting of the war and postwar years, enormously weakened German science.

In addition to personal factors, social, professional, and institutional problems accelerated this process of coordination. The confrontation with National Socialism called in question a number of axioms on which the self-awareness of the German universities rested. The belief dating back to Wilhelm von Humboldt that scholarship and scientific knowledge also brought with them moral ennoblement was refuted, as was the idea that an unpolitical attitude as a prerequisite of scientific objectivity was the best safeguard against political manipulation and ideological susceptibility, and that scholarship so understood could survive as a repository of truth, independent of social and political change. In fact, professional specialization and seeming depoliticization contributed in no small measure to the defenselessness of the German universities and their inability to respond to the *Gleichschaltung* of entire branches of learning and the erosion of self-government. And this organizational misdirection also was responsible for the failure of a society with a deep respect for the university to recognize the importance of the political responsibility of the scholar, and consequently to permit that office to be handed over to the control and criticism of pseudo-scientific, pseudo-intellectual ideologies. Hence, professors in Munich in 1933 had to listen to their new Minister of Culture, the failed elementary school teacher Hans Schemm, tell them: "From now on, it will not be your job to determine whether something is true, but whether it is in the spirit of the National Socialist revolution." [48]

In the twilight zone of coercion and capitulation, rectors, deans, and university senates were replaced in the spring of 1933, objectionable professors boycotted and forced out, and scientific and personnel policies "revolutionized" in the spirit of national renewal. Official overseers of this "university reform" like the Hamburg historian Adolf Rein called for a university of "*völkisch* learning." In early March, 1933, hundreds of university teachers rushed to assure Hitler of their loyalty. Then came the professional organization of professors, the University League (*Hochschulverband*). Heidegger's assumption of the rectorship of Freiburg in May, 1933, created the biggest stir. The famous philosopher, author of *Sein und Zeit* (*Being and Time*), forgot his teacher Edmund Husserl, defamed as "non-Aryan," and sanctioned the regime in vigorous words of self-abdication: "Not theses and ideas are the laws of your being! The Führer himself, and he alone, is Germany's reality and law today and in the future." [49] The rise of Carl Schmitt, who also dropped his "non-Aryan" teachers, has already been mentioned. Additional "affirmations" by hundreds of professional signatories followed.

This did not prevent Nazi activists from criticizing the slow pace and incompleteness of "university reform." The objective was tersely defined as "the creation of a new genus of student, the creation of a new genus of university teacher, and the development of a new concept of scholarship." [50] Toward this end, the number of students was reduced along national and anti-Semitic guidelines; the admission of foreigners and women was restricted; the faculties were "purged," and the allegedly German original sin of unconditioned scholarship fought as an "obsolete unscientific idea." Research and learning were assigned their functions in the new regime: the future university, as the "supreme school of the state," would have to offer political education in the new spirit (Freyer), it could not recognize "any autonomy and freedom of the teacher, but only dedication," and "liberalistic scholarship as an end in itself" would have to give way to the "obligatory goal of *völkisch* Weltanschauung and unity" (Krieck).[51] The application of authoritarian and military principles of order to the universities

[48] Erdmann, *op. cit.*, p. 217.

[49] Martin Heidegger, *Die Selbstbehauptung der deutschen Universität* (Breslau, 1934), pp. 22 ff.

[50] Rühle, *op. cit.*, I, 151. On the subject of research policies, see Heiber, *op. cit.*, and Kurt Zierold, *Forschungsförderung in drei Epochen* (Wiesbaden, 1968), pp. 150 ff.

[51] Hans Freyer, *Das politische Semester. Ein Vorschlag zur Hochschulreform* (Jena, 1933), p. 40; Krieck, *op. cit.*, pp. 173 f.

accelerated the process. Elected academic bodies were abolished; the leader principle was extended to include the appointment of rectors and deans by outside bodies—with the Chancellor as "chief of staff." The historian Ernst Anrich (thirty years later again active as a leading NDP ideologue), in an essay with the telling title *Universitäten als geistige Grenzfestigungen (Universities as Intellectual Frontier Fortresses;* 1936), wrote: "The universities must become bodies of troops," and the professors must develop "trooplike cooperation."

The quantitative and qualitative consequences of this voluntary dismantling are immeasurable. Here, and not in 1945, began the decline of German scholarship. German intellectual life went into exile. Entire branches of knowledge were devastated; others were perverted. In 1933–34 alone, more than 1,600 scholars, including more than 1,100 professors and lecturers (approximately 15 per cent of the entire teaching body), became the victims of mass firings. Added to this there were countless demotions, threats, and indirect persecutions. Entire faculties and research units were seriously hit when outstanding scholars, including numerous Nobel Prize winners (alone in 1933, Otto Meyerhof, James Franck, Albert Einstein, Fritz Haber, Heinrich Hertz), were driven into emigration, which for intellectuals was a particularly harsh, uncertain fate. The numerical losses differed considerably from place to place. In the lead were Berlin and Frankfurt/ Main, with more than 32 per cent, Heidelberg with more than 24 per cent, Breslau with 22 per cent, and Göttingen, Freiburg, Hamburg, and Cologne with an 18–19 per cent loss of teachers. The universities were harder hit than the technical institutes (16.6 and 10.7 per cent, respectively); the highest numerical losses were sustained by the medical schools, the largest percentage losses by the law schools (21.2 per cent), which witnessed the greatest anti-Semitic persecutions and the simultaneous moving in of young National Socialist lecturers.

The forced transfers also broke up entire scholarly bodies; academic work stood under the constant shadow of informers among students and faculty, of fear and mistrust. The former security and continuity were constantly threatened by interference and demands from the outside, by manipulation of the curriculum, cancellation of the right to hold examinations, and denunciation. Outside political activity was demanded; adjustment and subjugation against one's better judgment collided with thoughts of persecuted colleagues and teachers. A new "spirit" moved into the faculties. The revisions along racist lines of the qualifying regulations for teaching (December, 1934) made the appointment to an instructorship dependent on nonscholarly qualifications: attendance at "communal camps" and "instructors' academies," political evaluation by the rector, Ministry of Culture, National Socialist University Teachers League, and the party now were prerequisites for an academic career. Ernst Sturm, the Rector of the Technical Institute of Berlin, made the following comment in the *Journal for National Socialist Education* (1934) : "The ministers of education in the new Germany will not admit any crude materialists or anemic paper pushers as university teachers. . . . Every vigorous instructor [*Dozent*] belongs in the SA . . . so that the alienated German scholar may soon become a thing of the past." The rise of the new university teachers as "leaders of youth" more surely than the mass firings completed the *Gleichschaltung* and political-ideological functionalization of the universities.

Here as well, the policy of coercion from above was helped by a "movement" from below. Intoxicated by the promises and activities of the regime, the majority of university students had supported and often intensified the "change" of the spring of 1933 with violent demonstrations: through boycotts, the wearing of uniforms, public attacks and political declarations in lecture halls. The *völkisch–*Pan-German, antidemocratic roof organization of German students had been in the tow of the National Socialist German Student League ever since the latter had captured control in 1931 at the student congress in Graz (Austria). They also gained many members from the student corporations; here too the traditionalist, socially exclusive university structure played a role. Under the system of privileged education which continued undisturbed under the Weimar Republic, the students were largely nationalistic, conservative, and moreover anti-Semitic, a promising recruiting ground for an antidemocratic movement. Just as many fraternities (*Burschenschaften*) in 1923 had hailed the Hitler Putsch, the last German student congress in 1932, which interestingly enough met in a military barracks in Königsberg, called for the abolition of academic self-government in favor of the leader principle.

The activities of 1933, initially directed against professors, ended up as voluntary coordination. While students called upon the rector of Berlin University to extirpate the "un-German spirit" (Jewish professors, for example, were to be permitted to publish in Hebrew only), firings were accelerated under threats, books of objectionable professors were removed from university libraries and bookstores and publicly burned, and guidance and regimentation from above was begun. Sharply worded decrees of April and May, 1933, extended the "order" of the totalitarian state to students as well. After their brief, violent flare-up came silencing by the dictatorship. The reorganization according to the leader principle, completed in 1935, also subjected the students to strict organization from above, under the control of the Ministry of Culture and the party. The "new genus of students" was to be created through semimilitary service. As early as August, 1933, Rust ordered the conscription of upper sophomores into the student Labor Service. Here, and not in the universities and high schools, so he told them, was to be found "the true great practical school . . . for here instruction and words end and deeds begin. . . . He who fails in the labor camp has forfeited the right to want to lead Germany as an educated man." [52] From that time on, admission to the universities was

[52] "Kundgebung der Deutschen Studentenschaft (Opernplatz Berlin), 16. Juni 1933," in *Dokumente der Deutschen Politik*, I (Berlin, 1939), 281 f.

made contingent on four months' compulsory service in the Labor Service and two in SA camps.

Analogous to the duality of party and state, the National Socialist German Student League remained as a National Socialist nucleus. But the one-sided measures and melodramatic declarations no longer had to compete with student elections and initiatives from below. Both the National Socialist Student League and the German Student Association were committed to guided activity and affirmation of the regime, to a nebulous synthesis of "university community" and "people's community." The end of academic freedom had come, for the students even more so than for teachers. The still-existing student organizations hurriedly proclaimed their loyalty to the National Socialist revolution (including the Catholic student organization and the Catholic fraternities, in January, 1934). Stirrings of resistance of conservative groups disappeared in the nether depths of illegality. On October 28, 1935, the association of German fraternities voted to disband; the National Socialist Student League fell heir to its remnants. Some traditional groups continued to eke out an existence, in part even inside the National Socialist student movement. On the whole, however, the "organization" and political functionalization of the students, helped along by rigid selection (through membership in the Hitler Youth) and promotion policies, was highly successful.

This did not mean, though, that a National Socialist scholarship now emerged triumphant. The fawning acclamations of an army of fellow travelers could not disguise the emptiness of the formulas and paucity of the results now dominating the field. More and more specialties were created, particularly in the "military sciences" (*Wehrwissenschaften*) and of course in the race disciplines and lore of foreign countries. Individual branches were transformed into "war science" (*Kriegswissenschaft*). There came into being a military chemistry and military geography, military geology and military mathematics, military physics and military technology, military history and military economics, military psychology and military medicine; the crowning touch was a "military philosophy." Beginning with the reorganization of the universities and economy in 1933–34, the total state oriented itself toward the coming war.[53] Especially after 1939, traditional university activities were increasingly reduced, and the "war propaganda engagement" assigned a growing role: philosophers, historians, Anglicists, philologists, and legal scholars collected appropriate quotations and "examples" for the use of press and party propagandists. Free academic exchange also was undermined by travel restrictions. Then, not in 1945, began the era of the questionnaire. Every traveling scholar had to report to the appropriate foreign Nazi organization, and

[53] Albrecht Erich Günther, "Die Aufgabe der Wehrwissenschaft an der Hochschule," in *Zeitschrift für die gesamte Staatswissenschaft*, No. 95 (1935), p. 568.

in line with a decree of April 20, 1937, even had to supply the Rust Ministry with two copies of his proposed lectures abroad.

The role accorded scholarship and universities in the "new order of Europe" was made clear in 1939, when the universities of occupied Czechoslovakia and Poland were closed and the majority of their professors sent to concentration camps. In 1941, with the help of the *Gau* leadership, a "Reich University" of Posen was founded, with chairs for race policy, Jewish history, the study of border and ethnic Germans, National Socialist intellectual history, and Germanic folk music; access to the Polish university library was barred to Poles. Similar arbitrary measures (e.g., the Reich University Strassburg, 1942) were intended also to decimate the universities of northern and western Europe, with the clearly stated purpose of depriving non-German countries of their intellectual centers, of reducing their powers of resistance and of making them amenable to their future roles as satellites (in the West) or slaves (in the East). These visions of the future, however, ran up against concrete obstacles and also against internal resistance. In particular, the efforts to give the race doctrine broad "scientific" underpinnings, to rewrite technical literature in a generally binding fashion, and to create new disciplines ultimately foundered on the inner contradictions which even a totalitarian regime could not overcome. It reacted with mistrust and the sort of abuse Julius Streicher hurled at the Berlin University in 1938: "If the brains of all university professors were put at one end of the scale and the brains of the Führer at the other, which end, do you think, would tip?" And in fact, he did have a point there. One only has to recall the statements of distinguished scholars, as for example a university address by the Göttingen historian Ulrich Kahrstedt in 1934: "We renounce international science, we renounce the international republic of scholars, we renounce research for the sake of research. *Sieg Heil!*" [54] This was a cruel refutation of the confident belief in the liberating value and effect of learning, which in the Enlightenment began its victorious march through the Western world. Hitler was given confirmation of his deep disdain for learning, intellectuals, and legal scholars.

THE NATIONAL SOCIALIST ELITE

If the composition of the political elite is to be considered a vital characteristic of any ruling system, then this is true to an even higher degree of National Socialism, with its elitist ideology, its idea of a "new aristocracy" (Darré) and an aristocratic leader order. The structure of the party and the National Socialist system rested on the validity of the leader principle, on its claim to being the realization of the new political and social order; this system was based on a

---

[54] Documentation in the journal *Politicon* (Göttingen), No. 9 (1965); on the subject of the Streicher speech, see Helmut Seier, "Der Rektor als Führer," in *VfZG*, No. 12 (1964), p. 108. On the resistance, see Chapter VII below.

pseudo-Germanic idea of leader and followers in a pseudo-military order-obedience relationship. The question of how real this organizational principle was and what its consequences were brings one to the composition and recruitment of the National Socialist elite. This in turn leads to the problem of the extent and method of the elimination, absorption, or modification of the existing elite structure.

In contrast to the Bolshevik Revolution, the National Socialist seizure of power rested its "legal revolution" on alliances and compromises with non-Nazi office and influence holders. This strategy became apparent not only in the Cabinet of January 30, 1933, but also in the absorption of the governmental bureaucracy. The multiplication of leaders in all areas of political and social life encompassed many members of the existing economic, cultural, and educational elite. To be sure, many confirmed democrats were fired and driven out together with the Communists; the restaffing showed traces of a revolutionary change. But at the same time, the strength of the antidemocratic forces in the Weimar establishment, the antidemocratic potential of pre-Nazi German society, became visible and operative.

Analysis of the *Führerlexikon* published in 1934,[55] which lists the new National Socialist elite as well as portions of the old, including bishops, gives statistical data about the structure. The first point of interest is the "male movement," the elimination of women from the new leadership. It also makes obvious the extent to which the ruling National Socialist elite differed socially from the "former German elite," how "marginal" it was, even though the encyclopedia deleted the SA leaders murdered in 1934. Here, too, one is confronted with a dual state, in which the top party elite exercised effective control over the cooperating, adjustable traditional elite. The biographies of those in leading administrative positions show the strongest deviations from the norm: from poor beginnings they rose highest. This holds true to a far lesser degree of the propaganda, police, and military elite. Moreover, the role of the border region and ethnic Germans, who invested National Socialist ethnic ideology with its special intensity, must be stressed, inasmuch as the pre-eminence of the *völkisch* idea over the idea of the state constitutes one of the major differences with Italian Fascism. A disproportionately high number of the National Socialist elite came from "marginal" regions oriented toward Pan-Germanic politics: from the eastern border states or Bavaria, but also from western border states and from foreign countries.

Two basic characteristics emerge: first, the age composition of the party membership (seven years below the national average), especially that of the leaders, whose average age in 1934 was eight years lower than that of the non-National Socialist elite and even five years lower than Germany's male population. A comparison with the elites of other Western countries also reveals to what extent the National Socialist leadership was characterized by extreme youth and lightning careers.

[55] Daniel Lerner, *The Nazi Elite* (Stanford, 1951).

The average age of the Cabinet members was forty, while in the United States it was fifty-six, and in England fifty-three.

Other data show that the National Socialist leaders, contrary to the official postulates, married late and long after joining the party, and still later—if ever—took regular jobs and had families, that they changed jobs frequently, and that they led "unstable" existences up to 1933. This observation is underscored by the fact that even though a relatively large number attended universities—although far fewer than the proportion in the traditional elite—many of them never completed their studies. The places of birth, age composition, family status, and job problems underscore the special character of the National Socialist elite—its dynamic restlessness, its urge for mobility and change.

The question remains, however, to what extent it is really true that the National Socialist movement was led and buttressed by marginal men,[56] i.e., that it was a nontypical group movement rather than an all-encompassing collective movement. If the vast differences between the old and new elite justify speaking of an administrative "revolution," the problem remains to what extent the victory of the NSDAP and the privileged position of its leaders simultaneously meant a revolutionary social change. This was undoubtedly true in the political area. Both the leadership and membership of the NSDAP were composed predominantly of the war and postwar generation; with the exception of the Communists, no other political organization was so decisively structured. The National Socialist elite, by virtue of personal background and values, was clearly oriented toward war, the postwar conflicts, the Free Corps, and opposition to the Republic. Working-class representation in both the membership and the leadership of the NSDAP was below average. Contrary to its original designation, the party was a movement of the middle class and petty bourgeoisie, and its leadership was recruited largely from among the "plebeians," [57] i.e., from the lowest middle class and farmers, not from among the industrial workers. The craftsmen and small businessmen, employees and peasants, found themselves in economic and social difficulties because of industrialization, the growing influence of the workers, the expansion of big business, and the growth of corporations and cartels. The discrepancy between the desire for status and the actual situation made for a crisis, for the sort of "social panic" (Theodor Geiger) which was directed primarily against socialism and the unions as the alleged causes of the crisis. The inflation of 1922–23 and the economic crisis of 1929–33 served to refine this reaction and make it receptive to the appeals of the National Socialist dictatorship. The appeals of the Nazis were aimed primarily at a stabilizing middle-class policy via domestic national "socialism" and the expansion of the state potential via foreign expansion.

The rootless middle class, of which the frustrated military and pro-

[56] *Ibid.*, p. 184.
[57] Franz Neumann, in *ibid.*, p. v.

fessionally dissatisfied intellectuals also were a part, furnished the mass following as well as the leadership of the NSDAP. They rebelled against the democratic-industrial society; the main dynamics of this trend were professional insecurity and the discrepancy between actual economic status and the desire for greater social prestige. All National Socialism had to do was to perpetuate the tradition of the nationalist, anti-Semitic middle-class movement which since the 1870's had developed in various combinations of conservative, Christian-social, and agrarian groupings; and finally, after 1929, the Nazis profited from the mass of unemployed who had listened to the demand for "work and bread"; this was true particularly of the many young unemployed males, who formed a major part of the new voters in the 1930–33 period and who could not be integrated at all into the social setting of professional and regular work and sought to find their roots in the adventurist-terrorist activities of the SA.

If one subdivides the National Socialist elite into mainstays of propaganda, organization (administrators), and violence (coercers), one gains a more differentiated picture of the relationship of social background to party leadership. The professionally frustrated, "alienated intellectuals" tended to come from the upper middle class; they were younger (even when joining the party), fewer of them had a military background, they were better educated, and they had been more consistently unemployed than any of the other groups. Yet as propagandists of the regime, they did not achieve much higher rank than pre-Nazi society would have offered them.

The National Socialist administrative elite, on the other hand—from party functionary and Gauleiter to the top bureaucrat of National Socialist cast—represented the types of the rapidly rising "revolutionary" plebeian from the urban and rural lower middle class. Coming from a lower level socially and educationally, they achieved higher and more powerful positions. These organizers of the "struggle for power" also had control over the monopolization and exercise of power in the Third Reich; their lightning careers, regardless of social or professional qualifications, represented the true revolutionary component of the reorganization of the German elite structure. These organizers saw themselves as being different from the rest of the National Socialist elite—as a group of proud "idealists" who early on had joined a still small, insignificant party, and who had given the party their full, loyal assistance. These old fighters may well be called the "actual," innermost corps of the National Socialist elite; in a sense, they were the Stalinists of National Socialism, the ruthless guardians and unswerving executors of a power to which they owed everything. Almost one-third of them had been active in the party since 1923, and more than two-thirds since 1930, whereas less than one-third of the remaining elite had belonged to the NSDAP before its ascent to power.

Members of this inner leadership corps, on the other hand, were generally somewhat older when they joined the party. Unlike the propagandists, they were not aspiring intellectuals but disappointed petty bourgeois who had already been engaged for some time in the futile pursuit of a career. There were additional signs to bear out this image. A disproportionately high number of these old-timers hailed from Bavaria (20.5 per cent), from border regions, and foreign countries, but only a very few came from the Ruhr area; Prussia, Baden-Württemberg, and Hesse-Nassau also were poorly represented. A large portion came from rural areas and small towns, which they had left for the cities; but they had not established themselves until comparatively late in life. A provincial, petty bourgeois background, limited education, military service, and job problems were common to almost all of them. Those with higher education and specialized training included a high proportion of military (29 per cent), teachers (15 per cent), architects, and business-school graduates, while the Nazi propagandists had the highest share of college graduates (59 per cent), and of these, 58 per cent were lawyers. Military training, which after 1918 was of little utility, left its mark on the style of the party, which contained an above-average number of functionaries with a Free Corps background. The National Socialist takeover and the organization of the Third Reich essentially was the social revolution of the professionally handicapped or unsuccessful petty bourgeois with military training or tendencies, who harbored great resentments against the establishments of both the Left and Right. Hitler was their perfect embodiment.

The military ranked behind the police among the pillars of violence (coercers) with a Nazi background. The year 1934 already saw the revolutionary shake-up: the displacement of the SA, which turned the police into an ideal instrument for the policy of repression and annihilation within the framework of the reign of the SS and the occupation. The Army officer corps, on the other hand, was part of the traditional image of the German elite, whose continued existence was a symbol of the legal revolution. This changed only with the rise of the young "party" generals during the war and with the Army's subordination under Himmler after the 20th of July, 1944.

This brief survey gives a picture of the dual structure that characterized the elite of the Third Reich. The Nazi leadership corps was the personification of a revolutionary shake-up of the political power elite which cannot be sloughed off with the simple Marxist label of "counterrevolution." At issue here was not merely the eradication of the November revolution and its consequences. The counterrevolutionary aspect of the National Socialist, and even more so of the Fascist, system lay in the partial toleration of the "unpolitical" and the conservative-nationalist segment of the traditional elite. They were fated to become the instrument and also the disguise and legitimization of a revolution that sought to achieve its goals—totalitarian rule and imperial expansion—not by outright putsch but by pseudo-legal methods. In the course of *Gleichschaltung*, the elites of both the old and the new states became intertwined. And the relationship of the two was made even more complicated by the presence of in-between groups like the propagandists and the military.

Thus, no clear division can be made between party and state, revolution and tradition, either with respect to the power-political and organizational or the social changes. Major elements of the traditional authoritarian state were retained and even considerably strengthened. The economic and social structure remained largely unchanged, though of course oriented toward mobilization and war. The jurisdictional chaos and rivalries faithfully reflected this dual structure. But the revolution of the nationalist elite remained the determining factor both in the aims and the distribution of power. The more far-reaching political, economic, and social consequences asserted themselves increasingly during the war and in the rise of the "SS state" as well as in the innermost reality of the National Socialist system. The end in 1945 did not come about as the internal collapse of a regime that had managed to survive all attempts at resistance and overthrow. Only the military defeat inflicted on it prevented the complete success of this new type of revolution.

The political and social structure of the National Socialist elite was a significant factor in that revolution and in the ties binding it to a system that could make and break it. Because the individual characteristics of the top leadership played a vital part in this dictatorship, we must briefly examine the careers and impact of Hitler's closest comrades. They can be divided into two groups: the men who had established themselves in leading positions before 1933, and the functionaries who rose to the top before and during the war era. Among the men closest to the Führer, all joined long before the big wave of newcomers in March, 1933 (*Märzgefallene*). This is true even of such "late bloomers" as Martin Bormann, who owed his final position as Hitler's "shadow" to Hess's defection, or of such opportunists as Ribbentrop, the least clearly delineated of all of them. Only in the military and the SS hierarchy, or in areas conquered later (Austria), could latecomers rise to the top positions.

Hitler himself and his early cohorts have already been discussed in Chapter II. Of these, the Strasser brothers and Röhm were among the great losers of the old elite. As far as the rest are concerned, Hitler held on to them even if—as in the case of Julius Streicher, for example, —they proved a considerable embarrassment for the party and the regime. The Strasser brothers may be considered the only top functionaries who consistently represented the Left component of the "movement." They became victims of the turn toward the Right in 1930 and 1932. Still more radical was the murder of Röhm, Hitler's earliest promoter; his elimination resolved the old conflict between political and paramilitary leadership.

Of the oldest comrades, Göring, Hess, Rosenberg, Himmler, Frick, and the newspaper czar Amann moved up into the highest echelon of the Third Reich, while a large proportion of second-rank leaders, particularly the Gauleiters, joined the party only after its reorganization in 1925. These included Goebbels, who however managed to move up to the top even before Himmler, and in the end outdistanced all the others. In this most intimate circle, which was involved in endless rivalries about the person of Hitler and the powers delegated by him, the influence of the younger men or those who had come to this group later—Ley, Schirach, Heydrich, Hans Frank, Darré, Ribbentrop—fluctuated. In addition to the powerful regional chieftains and ministers, the second level also included famous fellow travelers and opportunistic specialists who at times wielded considerable power—i.e., Blomberg, Papen, Schacht, Speer, and later also Keitel, Jodl, and, surprisingly, Dönitz. But behind these men, there was the increasingly influential work of the top functionaries of the expanded SS bureaucracy, the concentration-camp and occupation rulers who in effect ruled over the lives and deaths of millions: Kaltenbrunner, Seyss-Inquart, Müller, Höss, Eichmann.

Hermann Göring (1893–1946) was considered the hand-picked successor to the Führer. At the beginning of the war, Hitler had so stated officially. This designation did not, however, solve the cardinal problem of every dictatorship once and for all, as later events were to show. Two facets of Göring's personality emerged most strikingly during his tenure: his cunning, ruthlessly brutal quest for power behind the façade of the decorated, cordial, popular World War I officer who played a key role in the years of the takeover and *Gleichschaltung;* and his greedy, naïve ostentation, his pompous enjoyment of power, the manner of a "scented Nero," [58] which was to cost him his influence and, at the end, his position in the Third Reich. He has been called the perfect example of the "born" National Socialist who sees struggle as the basic principle and, in contrast to those who "turned into National Socialists" (for example, Rosenberg and Goebbels), considers questions of ideology and their realization as merely instrumental or subordinate.[59] In view of his upper-class background, Göring was the countertype of the frustrated petty-bourgeois who furnished most of the early National Socialist leadership, and for that reason he was of particular help in building bridges to the conservative, traditional elite.

His father, a Prussian officer and first governor of Southwest Africa, was General Consul in Haiti at the time of the birth of his son. Uniforms, parades, heroic tales, and the hope for a career as an officer were part of Göring's early life in Berlin and at the family estate in Bavaria. To the very last, he liked to speak of his allegedly aristocratic descent and to indulge his feudal tastes as an officer and gentleman-hunter. As in the case of Hitler, there was a discrepancy between aspiration and reality. An aggressive courage also asserted itself early in his life in his relations with his friends as well as in youthful attacks on Jewish merchants in Fürth; after frequent, turbulent changes of schools, he attended cadet training academies (Karlsruhe and Berlin) and entered on the longed-for military career. The war was his great chance; a daring fighter pilot (since 1916), he won the Order pour le Mérite, succeeded the flying ace Richthofen as commander of a fighter-

[58] H. R. Trevor-Roper, *The Last Days of Hitler* (New York, 1947), p. 15.
[59] Joachim C. Fest, *The Face of the Third Reich* (London and New York, 1970), pp. 71 f.

plane squadron, and found his purpose: battle, fame, and power. The end of the war brought profound disruptions, but Göring remedied this by becoming a circuit flyer. He married a wealthy Swedish baroness (Karin von Fock-Kantzow), briefly attended the University of Munich, together with other ex-officers tried his hand at politics, and in 1922 came across Hitler. Göring was interested primarily in the fight against Versailles, in militant aggression, and in the revolutionary quest for power. From the viewpoint of Hitler and his party, the recruitment of this husband of a wealthy woman with good military contacts was a prestigious gain; he was the ideal man for building up the SA as a paramilitary organization. Göring's ideological needs were satisfied by the nationalistic and anti-Communist slogans. After some hesitation, the "aristocrat" Göring decided to cast his lot with the obviously talented demagogue Hitler; he expected the revolution to bring him new authority and power.

The abortive Hitler putsch, in which Göring was wounded, drove him to Austria and then to Italy and Sweden. The political adventure seemed finished; he became addicted to narcotics. He did not establish contact with Hitler again until 1927, when Hitler's star was once more in the ascendancy. Now he made himself useful as a spokesman for the legality strategy. His money, bearing, and bonhomie made him an ideal liaison man with the Right; while he, as Reichstag deputy (since 1928) and President of the Reichstag (1932), finally saw himself on the road to status and power. The recipient of numerous titles and offices, Göring was the most active power seeker and purger. He ruled over the Reichstag and Prussia, over police and Gestapo (and hence also over the first concentration camps), over air policy and rearmament. Power for the sake of power, not growth or goals, was what interested this seemingly jovial man of action. He repeatedly demonstrated his ruthless fixation on force and power in word and deed. "I have no conscience," he said. "The name of my conscience is Adolf Hitler." "I thank my Maker that I do not know the meaning of objectivity. . . . I'd rather shoot too short or too wide of the mark, but at least I shoot." "My measures will not be sicklied by any legal misgivings. . . . My job is not to practice justice; my job is to destroy and to exterminate, nothing more." [60]

In the ensuing years, Göring continued to collect offices and titles: Supreme Commander of the new Air Force (1935), General Plenipotentiary of the Four-Year Plan (1936), and, finally, designated successor and first and only "Reich Marshal." Only when reaching out for control of the Army, prepared in 1938 by his intrigues against Blomberg and Fritsch, was he thwarted by Hitler. But while Göring, potentate by the grace of Hitler and pseudo-Renaissance prince, began to spend more and more time in his luxurious hunting lodge, Karinhall, amid looted treasures, he in effect lost power to his rivals, until the defeats suffered by the Air Force hit him in his most vulnerable spot, his military competence. From 1943 on, Hitler looked at him as a failure whom he

[60] *Reden und Aufsätze* (Munich, 1941), pp. 51 ff.; J. Hohlfeldt, *Dokumente der deutschen Politik und Geschichte*, IV, 25.

tolerated only for appearances' sakes. Even though Göring's last-ditch attempt to claim his heritage as the "second man" of the regime led to his deposition shortly before the end of the war, at Nuremberg he tried through his aggressive stance also vis-à-vis his fellow prisoners and his ostentatious suicide to preserve for all time the aura of the great patriot and wielder of power.

Rudolf Hess (b. 1896) was the other old fighter whom Hitler in 1939 named as his successor alongside to Göring. His career was that of follower without a will of his own and with well-nigh religious faith in the Führer; he represented the pseudo-religious component of the National Socialist leader principle, as Rosenberg did on the level of National Socialist ideology. The rise of this introverted student to the nominal position of third man of the regime can be explained only thus. Hitler came into his life like a vision; without special abilities, shy and inhibited, he clung to a burning faith until an equally fantastic decision led him to his parachute jump in Scotland and back to insignificance. But the burned-out believer remained faithful even in his closing words at Nuremberg: "It was given me to work many years of my life under the greatest son whom my people have brought forth in their thousand-year history." [61]

Hess, in contrast to the active totalitarian person who is capable of anything, has been called the passive totalitarian man to whom anything can be done, who effaces himself in complete "renunciation of criticism, judgment, and self-assertion, ideologized in such concepts as faithfulness, duty, and obedience," and whose guiding principle is: "One must want the leader." [62] His broken relationship with authority may have been the result of a too rigid upbringing, with an authoritarian father who forced him to study merchandising in preparation for his wholesale business in Alexandria. Having escaped this fate by volunteering for war service, Hess became involved in new dependencies; the end of the war prevented him from becoming an active pilot. Not until 1941 was he to gain world fame as an aviator. A student with fantastic ideas, this ethnic German followed his mentor, General Haushofer, into geopolitics. Ever since the first encounter in 1920, he literally, as even his wife has said, belonged to Hitler. His role seems relevant in only two respects: as the faithful secretary of *Mein Kampf*, he enriched the *Lebensraum* concept with geopolitical ideas, and as a guilelessly believing paladin of Hitler without self-seeking motives, he contributed much to the Führer cult.

Hess remained in the shadow of Hitler even when, after the fall of Gregor Strasser in 1932, he emerged from Hitler's private office to become his official deputy, and finally a Cabinet member. He was the blindly trusting servant, the instrument of the idol, the honest adjutant heralding the arrival of the Führer. In view of his pseudo-

[61] *Nürnberger Dokumente*, XXII, 425.
[62] Krebs, *op. cit.*, p. 170; Hannah Arendt, *The Origins of Totalitarianism* (New York, 1966), p. 383; Fest, *op. cit.*, pp. 187 ff.

religious relationship with Hitler, it is not surprising that he became increasingly preoccupied with occult pseudo sciences. The startling flight to Scotland on May 10, 1941, where he presented the old plan of a division of the world between Germany and Britain, was undertaken rather as a "sacrifice" or for the miraculous salvation of Hitler; it was anything but an act of resistance. That its third man suddenly had to be declared "insane" meant a great propaganda defeat for the Third Reich. For Hess it spelled the collapse of his dream; he has not been able to accept it to this day, either in Nuremberg, where he escaped execution, or in his letters from Spandau Prison, where this last of the Führer old guard leads an eerie existence.

Alfred Rosenberg (1893–1946), the administrative clerk of the National Socialist Weltanschauung, also was unable to compete with the second wave of old fighters (Goebbels, Himmler, Bormann) in the distribution of power in the Third Reich. It remained his fate to be overestimated ideologically and overlooked politically. His role in the fighting years as frustrated foreign-policy expert and as cultural-ideological coordinator has been discussed (Chapter II). Just as Hess unconditionally gave himself to the Führer, so Rosenberg gave himself to the pseudo system of his Weltanschauung. He undoubtedly was more than a mere "prop from the party's recruiting phase when ideology determined action." [63] Not only did he guard and stoke the terror against freedom of opinion in the Third Reich, but also in the battle against the churches; and he played an active and leading role in the art and cultural policies of the regime. But as far as concrete power politics was concerned, he more and more came to be looked on as an eccentric "philosopher" whom the practical men among the leadership did not take seriously. At the end it was considered good form by all, from Hitler on down, to say that one had not even read the *Mythus*.

The devaluation of Rosenberg seems to have been brought on by the dogmatism and introversion of this would-be philosopher and religion founder. However, one should not conclude from this that the relationship of National Socialism to its own ideology was determined by pure expediency. Hitler's tactical opportunism may have been in accord with the eclectic-syncretistic character of National Socialist ideology, but its racist-expansionist postulates, based on Rosenberg's widely distributed pseudo bible, became terrible reality. Whether he was actually read or taken seriously as a philosopher, Rosenberg has no reason to be disappointed. His printed revelations about Jews and Communists, Freemasons and Rome, and the *Protocols of Zion,* which he unearthed anew in 1923 and oddly enough republished as late as 1940, were as important a contribution to the insane Jewish policy, to the education of the annihilators and concentration-camp executioners (Rudolf Höss, the first commandant of Auschwitz, has specifically said so) as the orders of the rulers.

Rosenberg's disappointment hence was more the misunderstanding

[63] Fest's underestimation (*op. cit.,* p. 163).

of an impractical theorist; the regime did everything in its power to realize his bizarre ideology. He never was as close to Hitler as he would have liked, and an opportunist like Goebbels was able to dismiss his *Mythus* as an "ideological hiccough"; and these factors militated against his desire for position and power, for which he was ill-equipped. But he, with greater perseverance than any other National Socialist, conceived and prepared the theory for the annihilatory program of the Third Reich, that "noblest idea" which he still spoke of with enthusiasm at Nuremberg after 1945. He did not succeed in becoming either a leading power-political figure or founder of a religion; but he contributed more than any of the old and new fighters to the pseudo-scientific and pseudo-religious justifications of these power politics. The circle closed: in 1918, the failed student of architecture had come to Munich from the Baltics as "a man dedicated completely to art, philosophy, and history, who never thought of becoming involved in politics,"[64] and he went down in the history of political adventurers whom he there encountered not as a politician but as an ideologue.

Joseph Goebbels (1897–1945) came to the "movement" later. His career even in the fighting years, and certainly his position in the Third Reich, rested on the fundamental importance which Hitler from the very outset assigned to propaganda. Goebbels' was a propagandistic talent without peer. It was primarily thanks to him that the idea of the Führer found such a great response and that the masses could be mobilized so successfully. He made it possible for Hitler to assume his godlike position, and he also made possible a system of government resting on threats and coercion rather than merely on assent. Führer cult and modern propaganda methods combined to furnish the basis for mass recruitment from 1929 on, and the great consensus of 1933. Goebbels' strength lay not in personal convictions but in the manipulation of the convictions of others. He himself adjusted to changed situations often enough, even after his great conversion to Hitler in 1925–26. In the diary entries of that period he called himself "apostate" (January 20, 1926), and his flexibility is reflected in his belief in the total "directibility" of the people. Everything can be organized: jubilation and confidence, persecution and war moods, readiness for a volte-face (1939), and stoicism in total war.

Goebbels, the rationalist amid a group of ideological sectarians or crude irrationalists, compensated for his physical appearance, his Catholic upbringing, and the burden of a university background and intellectualism with his undoubted contribution to the construction and exploitation of the National Socialist propaganda machine. His career as Gauleiter of Berlin had rested on his propagandistic gifts, and as the "truth minister" of the National Socialist regime he came close to the model of Orwell's *1984*. But his craving for acceptance and renown was also compensation for the physical and intellectual differences which set him apart from the other "old fighters." He had been neither soldier nor Free Corps fighter; he found his métier, the surro-

[64] Alfred Rosenberg, *Letzte Aufzeichnungen* (Göttingen, 1955), p. 65.

gate satisfaction of his ambition, in the mobilization of the masses. For a time he tried to give the impression of having been wounded in the war and sought to assert his masculinity in erotic adventures, and that too fit into the picture. His sudden changes from self-assurance to self-pity were reminiscent of the youthful Hitler; but Goebbels even more so than Hitler kept a cynical distance from reality, concentrating on mass manipulation and seduction through propaganda—a basically meaningless and aimless method, as demonstrated by his changing attitude on Bolshevism or the remark: "I have never made independent politics." [65]

If Goebbels clung to Hitler to the very last, flooded the press and radio to the very end with effusive declarations of faith in the Leader, he showed greater insight than Göring and Rosenberg, Ribbentrop and Himmler, Ley and Streicher into the real consequences of defeat. As early as November 14, 1943, he wrote in his paper *Das Reich*: "As far as we are concerned, we have burned the bridges behind us. We no longer can turn back, but we also no longer want to. We are forced to extremes and therefore also ready for extremes. . . . We will go down in history either as the greatest statesmen or as the greatest criminals." Goebbels wrote a disgusting finish to a life dedicated to the manipulation of the "human beast"; worried about his posthumous reputation, he murdered his six children and wife before following Hitler in death.

Heinrich Himmler (1900–45) was the member of Hitler's inner circle representing the machinery of coercion and annihilation. During the takeover he was still in a secondary position; only with the ascendancy of the SS state over Göring's empire and the Army, in the course of the intensification of coercion and terror, did he gradually become the most powerful man after Hitler. Given his respectable background and bourgeois appearance, it seems hard to believe that he should have become one of the greatest criminals of all times. He saw himself as "a merciless sword of justice," yet at the same time he represented a type that predominated in the leadership and SS vanguard of National Socialism: the romantically overwrought petty bourgeois with the hint of the pedantic bureaucrat "who, under the specific conditions of a totalitarian system of government, attained exceptional power and hence found himself in a position to put his idiocies into bloody practice." [66] Colorlessly average and dependent, but devoid of feeling and overeager in the "carrying out" of all plans, that is how most who knew him characterized him. But at the same time, Carl Jacob Burckhardt found Himmler more sinister than Hitler, because "of his degree of concentrated subordination, of hidebound conscientiousness, something inhumanly methodical with an element of the automatic." [67]

---

[65] Joseph Goebbels, *Kampf um Berlin* (Munich, 1932), p. 39.

[66] Fest, *op. cit.*, pp. 111–12.

[67] Carl Jacob Burckhardt, *Mein Danziger Mission* (Munich, 1960), pp. 124 f.

Himmler was born in Munich and brought up in Landshut. His grandfather was a county police officer, his father a strict, devoutly Catholic schoolteacher and occasional tutor of Bavarian royalty. Educated in an authoritarian atmosphere, he became a star pupil in the Royal Wilhelmsgymnasium of Munich; a pedantically kept diary from his school days exists. He was physically not equipped to follow the career of his choice, agriculture. But he found fulfillment in the quasi-agricultural and biological ideologisms of his SS state; calling himself a peasant "by descent, blood, and nature," he transferred the ambitions of the chicken breeder of the 1920's to the breeding and destruction of human beings. He came into the NSDAP as ensign via radical right-wing soldiers' organizations. In the Hitler Putsch he carried the flag, standing next to Röhm, whose murder in 1934 was to clear the way for his ascent. Along with his faddist interest in homeopathy and herb medicine, his political-bureaucratic abilities came to the fore when Hitler in the beginning of 1929 entrusted him with the leadership of the SS, which he rapidly expanded from 300 members to 50,000 in 1933. But it was the methodical expansion of the police empire from his first seat in Bavaria that brought him, the true victor of June 30, 1934, into the top echelons of the National Socialist regime as the Reichsführer SS. His sphere of power grew step by step: 1935, chief of the political police; 1936, chief of the entire police; 1943, Minister of the Interior; 1944, commander of all reserve troops; 1945, Army group commander. In fact, the SS state, the incarnation of the Third Reich, could not have come into being without the help of Himmler's closest assistant, the ex-officer Reinhard Heydrich (1904–42). After the assassination of that ice-cold organizer of the SS empire and the extermination of the Jews (June, 1942), Himmler continued to expand the powerful machinery of a systematic total state within the state. There was hardly a sphere he did not penetrate with his own organizations.

Typical of Himmler's personality was the coexistence of sectarian lunacies (special mineral-water enterprises, the cultivation of herbs and roots, a Henry I cult, an institute for ancestor research) and the sober-pedantic terror and annihilation machinery, of love for animals and plants and planned extermination of human beings, of codes of honor and idealization of mass murder. In his speeches before the SS leaders entrusted with that task, Himmler celebrated mass extermination as a "glorious page in our history," as a "victory over one's self in the sense of a higher morality: to have remained decent through all this has made us tough." Mass murder becomes justice, theft of a cigarette a crime deserving of the death penalty: "On the whole, however, we can say that we have fulfilled this most difficult task out of love to our people. And we have suffered no harm to our spirit, to our soul, to our character through it." [68] One may argue whether this perverted morality was the ultimate result of National Socialist "idealism"

---

[68] Speech delivered in Poznan, October 4, 1943; *Nürnberger Dokumente*, **XXIX**, 122 f.; 145.

or the madness of a schoolmasterly quack. But that such ideas, which elsewhere remain bottled up in the outer reaches of society, were able under Hitler to poison thousands and come to power, and that their exponent at the end believed that he could save his skin by negotiating with the Jewish World Congress before trying to escape in disguise— this proves the political enormity as well as the ideological blindness of Nazi totalitarianism, and also the inner weakness of a society which capitulated to him.

Martin Bormann (1900–?) entered the inner circles of this "elite" only after the disappearance of Hess, also as Hitler's shadow, but enjoying incomparably greater power in the circle of the aging Führer now fixated on the war. Bormann was and remained the functionary in the background whose actual influence was known only to the most intimate Führer circle, the man who was in charge of Hitler's dwindling contacts with the outside world, the indistinct, indispensable bureaucrat whom Hitler shortly before his death called his "most faithful party comrade." Trevor-Roper has compared the institutionally indefinable role of Bormann, who may be said to personify the post-Hitler phase of the regime, with Stalin's power position shortly after Lenin's death.[69] This colorless, heavy-set Saxonian petty-bourgeois, the son of a post-office employee and master sergeant, began his career as estate manager in Mecklenburg and treasurer of the Free Corps Rossbach. As the instigator of the kangaroo-court murder of an elementary-school teacher, in which Rudolf Höss also played a part, Bormann made his acquaintance with prison—and Hitler. As party administrator and experienced secretary, his rise was inconspicuous yet purposeful. In July, 1933, as Reich and staff chief, the second man after Hess in the party headquarters, he built his position through manipulation of administrative programs and the allocation of jurisdictional spheres at the expense of old party leaders. The less Hess was able to handle the constantly growing tasks of the party command, the more indispensable did the hard-working nonsmoker and teetotaler, the unscrupulous racist and enemy of the church, become to Hitler.

If Bormann was hated by the rivals in the Nazi elite and considered Hitler's evil spirit by men like Rosenberg and Frank, then this was due not to his unscrupulous brutality, which all of them possessed in fair measure, but to his growing control of all access to the Führer, and his greater technical organizational skill and power of command. He had no desire to represent but "only" to head a bureau—though of course the highest, in view of his appointment as secretary to Hitler (1942)—one staffed by his own people dependent on him. He was the archetype of the functionary who is powerful because of the office he holds, and the archetype of the bureaucrat, who had his enthusiastic National Socialist wife, the mother of his ten children, keep a file of his mistress' letters.[70]

[69] Trevor-Roper, *op. cit.*, pp. 208 ff.

[70] Josef Wulf, *Martin Bormann—Hitlers Schatten* (Gütersloh, 1962), pp. 20 ff.; H. R. Trevor-Roper (ed.), *The Bormann Letters* (London, 1954).

The future toward which the Third Reich was being led was mapped out in the power positions of these desk criminals whom it created. Instead of following what he wrote in a letter to his wife of April 2, 1945—"as the Nibelungen of old going down in King Etzel's [Attila's] chamber"—Bormann disappeared after Hitler's suicide as silently and stealthily as he had risen twelve years earlier.

VI

Foreign Policy Between Revision and Expansion

TACTICS AND AIMS IN THE PERIOD OF TRANSITION

The foreign policy of the Third Reich derived directly from the ideological principles and long-range goals of National Socialism. But its implementation demanded first of all the consolidation of the take-over, as well as the assent of the population and the cooperation of the Foreign Office under its conservative chief, Konstantin von Neurath. With this in mind, the Nazi leadership resorted to a dual approach. It appeased, showed an apparent willingness to negotiate, and sought to win international recognition, while simultaneously initiating the strategy of threats, surprise moves, and *faits accomplis*. The interplay of these two approaches helped National Socialist foreign policy to master the critical early years. And after 1935, the Nazis, having consolidated their power domestically and in possession of greater military and arms potential, prepared a forcible shift to foreign affairs through treaties and military methods.

This approach was responsible for the widespread belief that up to 1938, Hitler had pursued a moderate, understandable course of peaceful revision, the same sort of delusion that had paved the way for his pseudo-legal seizure of power. Hitler's reiteration of his peaceful intentions fed the illusion that once saddled with the responsibility of government, he would act sensibly and not revert to the dilettantish, intemperate plans and demands of the early years. And in fact the appeasement practiced by the Western powers up to the very moment of war rested on the same disastrous belief in the possibility of a peaceful containment of the National Socialist dynamic as had the mistaken notions of Weimar domestic policy. Hitler, on the other hand, flexibly yet undeviatingly pursued a course which step by step won him freedom of maneuver, the total revision of Versailles, and ultimately hegemonic expansion.

287

The pattern was established quite early. The first steps included the smashing of the collective League of Nations system through unilateral acts, the isolation of France through alliances with Fascist Italy and "Germanic" Britian, and the creation of a Greater Germany, beginning with the annexation of Austria. Hitler never lost sight of the program first spelled out in *Mein Kampf:* the completion of the national state and revision of Versailles, however not merely the revival of Bismarck's Reich but the realization of a *"völkisch* state" representing "a sound, viable relationship between the size and the growth of the nation, on the one hand, and the size and quality of the land on the other." According to Hitler's racist-geopolitical ideology, a superior people like the Germanic nation needed adequate *"Lebensraum"* for reasons of both food production and military policy. "Thus we National Socialists are deliberately drawing a line under the foreign policy of our prewar years. We will resume where we left off six centuries ago. We are putting a stop to the old Germanic movement toward the south and west of Europe and turning our attention to the land in the east. We are putting an end to the colonial and trade policies of the prewar era and are going over to the soil policies [settling] of the future. But if we today speak of new land, we think above all of Russia and its subject border states." [1]

The racist and geopolitical national imperialism of *Mein Kampf* spelled out more clearly and in greater detail the unchanging though occasionally camouflaged *Lebensraum* policy than did the party program itself, which inclined to a Greater German revisionism. The essence of the *Lebensraum* idea was the fusion of the national and imperial principles and the natural claim of the German race to territorial expansion and rule. This objective also dominated Hitler's second book of 1928, which for tactical reasons had not been published, and he stated it in unmistakable words in his 1933 conversations with a group of intimates (recorded by Hermann Rauschning). In these, he apparently even went so far as to see nationalism only as a façade and an instrument for mobilizing a backward public opinion; backing it up was the more profound, forward-looking principle of race struggle as the world-shaping principle that would determine the political order of the future.[2]

There are those who say that although the ideology of *Mein Kampf* was quite obviously being perpetuated in Hitler's race and religious policies as well as in his propaganda, there were substantial differences between *Mein Kampf* and the foreign policy actually carried out.[3] That may be true of specific tactics, and of course Hitler ultimately did not succeed in forging the alliance with Great Britain, and consequently found himself fighting the feared two-front war. This, however,

---

[1] Adolf Hitler, *Mein Kampf* (Munich, 1925–28), pp. 728, 742.

[2] Hermann Rauschning, *Hitler Speaks: A Series of Political Conversations with Adolf Hitler on his Real Aims* (London, 1939), pp. 111 ff. The authenticity of this source has been questioned, however.

[3] Werner Maser, *Hitlers "Mein Kampf"* (Munich, 1966), pp. 159 ff.; 177 ff.

in no way alters the rigidity of the aims. The alliance with Italy and the isolation of France were pursued against all obstacles, and until the tactical shift of 1939 foreign policy was consistently in line with the alliance goals spelled out in *Mein Kampf*. And finally in the war, we learn from *Hitlers Tischgespräche (Hitler's Table Talks)* of 1941–42, the basic intentions again were clearly and irrevocably spelled out; Hitler clung to them with almost manic obsessiveness, up to the eerie end in the bunker of his Chancellery.

He never left any doubt that his totalitarian domestic policy was meant to serve the ends of the new foreign policy. In his famous speech in January, 1932, before the Düsseldorf Industrieclub, as well as in addresses, both before and after 1933, to generals, party functionaries, business leaders, and publicists, Hitler made clear that the function of National Socialist policy was to create the organizational, military, and psychological conditions for foreign moves. Inasmuch as this objective had a direct bearing on the consolidation of his rule, the interlocking of foreign and domestic policy was a significant attribute of National Socialist totalitarianism. The phenomenon of the "permanent revolution" (as described by the political scientist Sigmund Neumann) played a vital role. Total rule demands keeping the public under the constant pressure of major events and successes, distracting them from domestic coercion by holding out hope for external expansion, compensating for the loss of freedom by the constant acceleration of the sense of revolution and mission.

The beginnings of National Socialist foreign policy were marked by the difficult transition from the moderate Weimar revisionism to big-power politics. At a meeting with military commanders on February 3, 1933, Hitler pointed out the dangers inherent in this transition to a policy of "conquest of new *Lebensraum* in the East and its ruthless Germanization." If France has statesmen, he said, then "it will not give us time but attack us (presumably with eastern satellites)." [4] The camouflage tactics of 1933–34 succeeded in bridging this dangerous period of preparation and in warding off any possible setbacks by giving the impression that the goal continued to be the revisions sought by Weimar. The Foreign Office was treated most gingerly; Papen's and Schleicher's Foreign Minister, Konstantin von Neurath, stayed on at Hindenburg's request. The diplomatic corps remained largely unchanged; its primary task was to lay foreign misgivings to rest. And it soon turned out that Neurath, above all, immediately and unreservedly supported Hitler's policies, not only within the Cabinet but also in his dealings with the outside world, and even initiated a more intensive pursuit of revision.

This intensification found expression in the first major move of National Socialist foreign policy, the new push on rearmament and the break with the League of Nations in the fall of 1933. But even thus, the alleged continuity of foreign policy, the counterpart to the

[4] *Notizen des Generals Liebmann aus den Befehlshaberbesprechungen 1933/35*, Institut für Zeitgeschichte (Munich).

tactic of legal revolution, served to offset criticism of the new regime at home and abroad. As later in the Polish and Austrian questions, the Third Reich succeeded in breaking through potential opposition despite an initially critical deterioration of the situation and the threat of isolation. This was the result partly of the continuation of some aspects of Weimar foreign policy and partly of the retreats by the forces of appeasement which cleared the way for steadily mounting Nazi demands. The reparations issue had to all effects and purposes been solved at the Lausanne Conference of 1932, and the disarmament and parity talks by the Schleicher Government had progressed satisfactorily. These negotiations continued under Hitler. He answered objections of National Socialist activists with the assurance that "first he had to make all of Germany National Socialist, and that would take four years. Only then could he turn his attention to foreign policy." [5] The assurances of his peaceful intentions contained in his Reichstag addresses of March 23 and May 17, 1933, were rewarded by Mussolini's drive for a four-power treaty between Britain, France, Italy, and Germany. Though never ratified, this pact meant the tacit recognition of the National Socialist regime and its acceptance into the conclave of major powers; moreover, it also meant the discarding of the League of Nations principle in favor of old-fashioned power politics.

The progressive revision of the Versailles system now was in full swing. When the Third Reich began to break away from the League of Nations, its international position had been strengthened by the concordat with the Vatican. The stiffening French position on the secret rearmament of Germany and the critical treatment by the League of Nations of Nazi *émigré* and Jewish policies furnished the overt reasons. In fact, however, the example of Japan's withdrawal from the League in May, 1933, encouraged Hitler to take the step from the tedious multinational negotiations to the freedom of bilateralism and the room offered by it for the realization of his own goals. The secession from the League of Nations on October 14, 1933, which had been preceded by almost fifteen years of hostile revision propaganda, met with widespread approval in Germany. It was characteristic of the new style— close interweaving of domestic and foreign policy—that this first display of power in foreign affairs was used to stage the first great unity plebiscite of the regime (November 12, 1933). Acclamation of Hitler's policies was performed with much fanfare and the outspoken support of non-Nazi groups as well, up to the Catholic episcopate.

The secession from the League of Nations was similarly fraught with grave consequences. It meant the end of the apparently unbroken continuation of the Stresemann course and the beginning of Hitler's own foreign policy, though still shielded by the unequivocal support accorded this first coup by Neurath and the Foreign Office. The idea of disarmament was dead; the determination to rearm, the mainstay of National Socialist policy from the very beginning, now

[5] Rudolf Nadolny, *Mein Beitrag* (Wiesbaden, 1955), pp. 130 f.

emerged in the open. At the same time it became obvious that London and Paris were incapable of acting in unison, and Italy's vacillation completely ruled out any possibility of forming a counterfront. In Great Britain, influential forces took Hitler's claim to being a "bulwark against Communism" seriously, or at least believed that the dynamics of an allegedly inevitable German armament could, in line with the National Socialist program, be diverted toward the East—just as Japan's war policy was tying down Russia in the Far East. Although these ideas were never concretized, they probably influenced the course of appeasement and the passing over of Russian interests at the Munich Conference. Subsequently Moscow, inflating them disproportionately, was able to cite them as justification for the Hitler-Stalin Pact of 1939.

At any rate, resistance to the tactics of threat and surprise moves, which were being substituted for the policy of peaceful revision, was far less than expected. By conceding to Hitler in short order what had been denied Weimar far too long, the policy of appeasement contributed to the consolidation and strengthening of the regime, both domestically and abroad. It was the tragedy of this policy that it hoped to preserve peace by containing National Socialism through the revision of positions that had become untenable; instead, however, it erased existing doubts in Germany about Hitler's self-confident assertions and the "soundness" of his hazardous decisions and only encouraged National Socialist policy to renewed aggression. After the break with the League of Nations, which ended the era of constant contact with the outside world, the influence of experienced diplomacy more and more gave way to the erratic, high-handed, instinctive policies of Hitler. In view of his successes, he apparently always was right, unlike the timid traditionalists in the Foreign Office.

In the restructuring of Germany's *Ostpolitik* (Eastern policy)—the second major point of National Socialist foreign policy—the change from traditional diplomacy to the strategy of surprise began early. In concluding the treaties of Rapallo (1922) and Berlin (1926) and normalizing German-Soviet relations, the Weimar Republic had sought to counterbalance the Versailles front of the Western powers through close economic contacts and military cooperation. Political-ideological reservations took second place; as a matter of fact, conservative and military circles had been among those most interested in the cooperation of the two states isolated by and defeated in war. Added to this was the German fear of Poland and of French-Polish encirclement, the wish to eliminate the Polish Corridor, and, on the part of Russia, the claim to the Polish eastern regions lost in 1920. Some members of the military and proponents of geopolitics, using historical and strategic arguments, also proposed a joint German-Russian dismemberment of Poland and another Polish partition. Not only Alfred Rosenberg but also Seeckt favored such a course; however, it was not adopted until 1939, and then only temporarily. Like Brüning and Schleicher, Hitler seemed concerned only with the threat of Polish intervention and a

Polish-French two-front war against a (still) unarmed Germany. Although the degree of cooperation between Reichswehr and Red Army diminished in the course of the summer of 1933, both sides at first proceeded with great circumspection. Hitler specifically excepted relations with the Soviet Union from his anti-Communist propaganda. Stalin in turn attached great importance to the preservation of Russo-German economic relations, probably one of the reasons he refrained from giving effective assistance to the persecuted German Communists and from criticizing the Nazi regime. The extension in May, 1933, of the Berlin treaty (which had expired in 1931) went off more smoothly and rapidly than in the Weimar era.[6]

The fact that Moscow became the first to conclude a treaty with the Third Reich and the first to grant it international recognition demonstrated as clearly as the Hitler-Stalin Pact the futility of the bulwark thesis and the virtuosity with which totalitarian states can subordinate even the most violent ideological antagonisms to political self-interest, even if only temporarily. Here, too, the tactical continuation of Weimar policy did not last long. Almost simultaneous with the withdrawal from the League of Nations, Hitler, through a radical shift in German-Polish relations, discarded the revision policy of the past. In March, 1933, fear of intervention had still determined the pro-Russian position of the German Foreign Office; only a few weeks later, however, the authoritarian government of Poland began to revise its League of Nations and French policies, which at any rate seemed endangered by the negotiations over a four-power treaty, in favor of closer ties with Nazi Germany. Apparently Pilsudski was banking on the anti-Bolshevik and antidemocratic principles of the Hitler regime. Despite differences in their methods of government, both men were right-wing dictators. At the same time, Warsaw also seemed to figure that the top leadership of the Third Reich, predominantly South German and Austrian, would not pursue the traditional Prussian German-Russian policies at the expense of Poland.

These factors were responsible for the change of course by which Hitler, bringing into play his personal brand of instant diplomacy and outplaying the traditionalists in the Foreign Office, enlisted the interest of Poland. It was another demonstration of the flexibility of totalitarian rule. Regardless of the displeasure in diplomatic as well as in military and Prussian-revisionist circles over the radical shift from an anti-Polish course to German-Polish cooperation, it worked. In Danzig, National Socialists, who in the meantime had come to power in the Free City, had to acquiesce, and the propaganda machinery of both sides prepared the ground for the nonaggression pact of January 26, 1934; in Germany, the event was hailed as a blow against the Eastern policy of the Allies. The agreement, initially drawn up for a ten-year

[6] Karlheinz Niclauss, *Die Sowjetunion und Hitlers Machtergreifung* (Bonn, 1966), pp. 85 ff.

period, obligated the signatories to renounce the use of force and to negotiate directly on all mutual problems. Hitler honored this obligation as faithfully as all his other agreements; his basic idea remained unchanged by these tactical moves. On the contrary, this second act in the series of abrupt reorientations of German foreign policy following the secession from the League of Nations introduced the strategy of bilateral agreements which within a few years was to destroy all efforts for collective security and isolate the enemies of the Third Reich.[7]

The obverse side of this development was the acceleration in the revamping of Soviet policy, beginning with the ratification of a French-Soviet nonaggression and friendship treaty in May, 1933. Now the bottled-up German-Soviet propaganda war flared up. The advice of established German experts like Ambassadors to Moscow Nadolny and von der Schulenburg was passed over. The threat of isolation once more hung over Germany when Soviet Foreign Minister Maxim Litvinov sought to reorient Moscow toward the West and also forge an alliance against National Socialism, despite Moscow's and Berlin's memory of Rapallo. On the heels of the French-Russian *rapprochement*, underscored by a visit of Minister President Herriot to Moscow in September, 1933, came the overdue recognition of the Soviet Union by the United States; also, the West finally relented and, at the end of 1934, admitted Russia into the League of Nations in place of Germany.

Still a third National Socialist initiative brought the "new" Germany to the brink of isolation, namely its deteriorating relations with Austria and with Italy. Germany's Austrian policy of 1933–34 exemplified the increasing weight of ideological viewpoints and the interlocking of domestic and foreign-policy considerations. Hitler now was ready to shed his initial restraint and embark on the autocratic manipulation of foreign policy. This former Austrian national thought nothing more logical than to follow up the seizure of power in Germany with a National Socialist revolution in Austria and *Anschluss* to a Greater Germany. Ever since the ban on German-Austrian union in the Paris treaties, *Anschluss* was not only the goal of revisionists but a demand voiced in almost all political camps. The "Pan-German" idea was not invented by the National Socialists; after the end of the old Reich, in the movement of 1848, and again after the collapse of the Habsburg Empire in 1918, it was common property, from the nonmonarchist Right to the Social Democratic Left. To be sure, the National Socialist idea of the Reich of all Germans was not the same as the federalist concept of liberal democrats and socialists. Hitler wanted to bring Austria into the German Reich via forced incorporation into the coordinated unitary state, not via constitutional and lawful revision.

[7] Hans Roos, *Polen und Europa* (Tübingen, 1957), pp. 108 ff.

The spring of 1933 saw the beginning of massive assistance to the Austrian National Socialists, who despite their primogeniture had never achieved the strength of the German party. This political interference in Austrian domestic affairs was supplemented by economic pressure. Berlin's answer to the countermeasures of Vienna was to close its borders and impose a boycott with inevitably profound economic repercussions. But the immediate consequence was to intensify the isolation of Germany with regard to France and above all Italy. Hitler's policy of threats and blackmail drove the authoritarian government of Engelbert Dollfuss into the arms of Mussolini. Setting up an "Austrofascist" dictatorship modeled on and supported by Italy, Dollfuss set about to eliminate Nazis, democrats, Communists, and finally also Social Democrats and trade unions. Treaties with Italy and Hungary as well as solemn assurances given by Great Britain, France, and Italy on February 17, 1934, promised to preserve Austria's independence and inviolability.

This was the situation when the National Socialists began their forward push. On July 25, 1934, shortly after the bloody consolidation of the Hitler regime, Dollfuss was assassinated by Austrian Nazis while his wife and children were visiting Mussolini. But like Hitler's 1923 venture, this putsch failed. Germany denied any role in it, but without any doubt the enterprise was closely connected with Hitler's Austrian policy; the German and Austrian parties were working hand in glove. That Hitler was able to disengage himself from the abortive coup and proceed to long-range plans for "legal" *Anschluss* was due in no small measure to Papen's eager mediation. Notwithstanding the murder of his closest associates and his ouster from the Vice Chancellorship, this useful henchman of the Third Reich became the special envoy of the Führer, and, as a conservative Catholic, was instrumental in assuaging Vienna, thus successfully mapping out a less risky road for the absorption of Austria. And so in October, 1935, Papen was in a position to tell Hitler: "For the rest, we can leave further developments to the near future. I am convinced that the changing balance of power on the European chessboard will permit us to take up actively the question of our influence on the southeastern area in the not too remote future."[8]

Yet for the moment, not only the *Anschluss* but also Hitler's old plan of a united front of the two dictatorships through a close alliance with Italy seemed to have been put off indefinitely. The good relations with Rome predating 1933, the result of the French-Italian rivalry in the Mediterranean, were beclouded. Mussolini responded coolly to Hitler's friendly admiration (underscored by visits of Göring and Papen to Rome) at the first official meeting of the two dictators in Venice in June, 1934. Instead of the hoped-for alliance, Hitler was faced with yet another coalition: Italy-Austria-Hungary. Not only had his Aus-

---

[8] *Nürnberger Dokumente,* Doc. D-692 (October 18, 1935).

trian policy failed for the time being, but the Third Reich also seemed to be isolated in southern and southeastern Europe. A low point was reached on the day of the Austrian Nazi coup when Italian troops massed at the Brenner Pass and the Carinthian border. And in January, 1935, when France and Italy also concluded a treaty, the ring around the Third Reich seemed closed and its future most uncertain.

At this point, National Socialist propaganda was able to chalk up a fresh success: the reincorporation of the Saar on January 13, 1935. Although the basis for this had in fact been laid by the foreign policy of Weimar, the widespread jubilation over the outcome of the plebiscite was yet additional proof of the power of propaganda in the plebiscitary legitimization of National Socialist policy. Yet this solution of the Saar problem could neither bring the originally hoped-for improvement of German-French relations nor contribute to a loosening of the almost universal isolation of the Third Reich.

The normalization of German-Polish relations was the only real success National Socialist foreign policy could claim in the two years of transition from the policy of negotiation to the strategy of surprise. But coming after Russia's reorientation, even this move contributed to the deterioration of the general situation. The revision and minority policies of Weimar—however questionable they may have been with regard to Poland—were replaced by Machiavellian expediency. Foreign policy was changed without a second thought, and the German minorities manipulated and brought in line according to the dictates of expediency (for example, in the case of Danzig). Here the political coordination and exploitation of German ethnic groups throughout the Baltic area, in Poland, Czechoslovakia, and the Balkans—and regardless of differences in history, interests, and structure—proved its effectiveness.

That the National Socialist policy on Poland was nothing more than a transitional measure was borne out by the propaganda and actions of the regime. The Berlin-Warsaw agreement did not furnish a basis for the smashing of the great-power alliances, and though at times it was combined with an old plan for expansion in the Ukraine, it still conflicted with Hitler's basic idea of a connected *Lebensraum* in which there would be no place for an independent Poland. And five years later, German Polish policy had indeed served its purpose; its temporary protective function gave way to the true purpose of National Socialist policy. Perhaps this was a success in the National Socialist sense, but measured against the existing possibilities of German foreign policy, as well as the doctrines and goals of the National Socialist policy of alliances and revisionism, the Third Reich of 1934–35 seemed to have arrived at a dead end. Despite the domestic coordination and consolidation of totalitarian rule, internal repercussions were still within the realm of possibility. But all such calculations soon proved idle. Within a few months, in the spring of 1935, Europe underwent a realignment of forces, beginning with Britain's policy of appeasement and Mussolini's colonial-imperialist venture. This enabled Nazi foreign policy to break through its isolation and opened up the way to the German-Italian preparations for war.

BREAKTHROUGH INTO INTERNATIONAL POLITICS

The first great act of appeasement, namely the Anglo-German naval agreement of June, 1935, set in motion the momentous chain of events that prevented a possible anti-Hitler coalition and freed the Third Reich from the threat of isolation. Earlier, in the course of the disarmament talks, London had already shown a willingness to make changes and concessions. London took a more lenient view than Paris of a possible revision of the Versailles system, despite Germany's break with the League of Nations. French policy could ill afford to ignore this leniency, particularly in view of Britain's simultaneous efforts to withdraw from the problems of continental Europe and protect its own flank. London apparently was willing to accept the consolidation of the National Socialist regime, its progressive rearmament, and the open violation of the military provisions of the Versailles Treaty.

On March 16, 1935, Hitler risked another sudden move. He announced the institution of universal military service and the creation of an Air Force. This was the first overt blow against the principles of Versailles. While France and Italy tried to coordinate firm countermoves and hoped to win Soviet support, London's response to Hitler's move was separate negotiations and a naval agreement apparently favorable to Great Britain. The situation was now completely changed. In violation of the decisions of the League of Nations and without informing France and Italy, both naval powers, London agreed to the *fait accompli* instead of applying sanctions against treaty violations; it rewarded Hitler's unilateral act by accepting him as a partner in negotiations, believing that he could be held in check by concessions, even though these shook the foundations of the Versailles system.

Moreover, this first epochal act of appeasement, which spelled the beginning of the failure of European policy toward Hitler, also pulled the rug out from under those German diplomats who had been skeptical of Hitler's unilateral moves. It accelerated the rise of the subservient Ribbentrop, who had sat in on the London negotiations as envoy and now chalked them up as a personal success. And above all, Hitler felt himself confirmed in his belief that the time for bolder action had come, and that his success would not only help his revisionist plans but also serve to rally the German people. The revisionism of Weimar had become a thing of the past. Now unilateral moves and coups, threats and blackmail, had become the rule. The interrelation of the foreign and domestic policy of the total dictatorship became increasingly obvious.

It is only fair to point out that the naval agreement, whose symbolic significance was incomparably greater than its actual contents, was intended not only to satisfy Great Britain's quest for security but also to commit the Third Reich to an agreement. London fell victim to the same illusions in the second event that agitated the European political scene and directly played into Hitler's hands—the Ethiopian war. Mussolini's adventure shook the League of Nations and in the end forged a firm bond between Fascist Italy and the Third Reich. Here and in the Spanish Civil War, the basic constellation for the future war was taking shape. In addition to the continuation of a futile appeasement policy, only one other factor was needed to make the war Hitler wanted "inevitable": a temporary shielding off against Russia.

Even before the German-British agreement, Mussolini already had in mind the price he planned to demand for cooperating with the French in their policy to contain Germany: a free hand in Ethiopia. While plans for strengthening the security belt through Franco-Soviet and Czech-Soviet mutual assistance pacts progressed (May, 1935), the Duce believed the time had come to embark on a long-overdue imperial expansion. This broadening of *mare nostrum* imperialism to an anachronistic colonial imperialism was Mussolini's version of the land-based *Lebensraum* imperialism of Hitler. (Yet five years later, in the first flush of success, Hitler, in carving up the British overseas empire, summarily decided that Central Africa was to become his, and North and East Africa were to go to Italy.) [9]

But with the Italian expansion, an alliance of mutual interests of the two latecomers against the established colonial powers began to take shape; the two dictators came together in their demand for territorial redistribution, for the political rectification of the nineteenth century. That Mussolini's appetite should be fixed on Ethiopia, which in 1923 was admitted to the League of Nations with Italian support, went back to the abortive attempt of 1893 to expand the Italian colonies of Eritrea and Somaliland. The "crisis" was provoked by staged border incidents. Mediation efforts by the French Government, which saw its alliance structure endangered, were of no avail. On the other hand, Hitler, extremely interested in heating up the conflict, secretly supported Ethiopia with arms.[*] Paris and London were left with only one alternative to prevent international repercussions, particularly with regard to Germany: either to make a last-ditch effort to strengthen the League of Nations through determined action against the Fascist venture, or to tolerate it in the hope of tying Italy to a policy of European alliances that could deal with Hitler even without the League of Nations. Neither was done. That there were differences among the Western powers on Ethiopia as well as on the German problem soon became obvious. While Britain pushed for support of the League, France sought to prevent a conflict which inevitably would present Hitler with fresh opportunities.

[9] Talks with Molotov in November, 1940; minutes in Alfred Seidl, *Die Beziehungen zwischen Deutschland und der Sowjetunion 1939–1941* (Tübingen, 1949), pp. 254 ff.

[*] As documented in a doctoral dissertation (Bonn) on the Ethiopian war, by Manfred Funke (to be published in 1970).—K. D. B.

These differences gave Mussolini scope and time to prepare his war. Investigation committees, arbitration efforts, and British naval displays in the Mediterranean proved ineffective. Between October, 1935, and May, 1936, Italian troops, with incomparably superior forces and also with poison gas, overcame the fierce resistance of Ethiopia. In effect, this victory meant the end of the League of Nations. Labeling Italy the aggressor and imposing economic sanctions not only proved ineffective but even accelerated the European consequences of the crisis: the loss of prestige of the two great democracies and of the League of Nations.

Mussolini was able to claim a victory over "fifty nations" and have his King proclaimed Emperor of Ethiopia, thus confirming the imperial idea of Fascism. There now existed a model for the future course of action of the dictators; and as early as 1936, the lifting of sanctions and acceptance of *faits accomplis* testified to the effectiveness of this policy.

The international political significance of this debacle lay in the fact that it helped the Third Reich to work its way out of isolation and embark on its strategy of alliances and war preparation. Though there had been great sympathy in Germany for the brave fight put up by Ethiopia, the war of sanctions was an economic windfall; at the same time, Italy's shift and the paralysis of the League of Nations presented Hitler with the opportunity for a new surprise move which further strengthened his position at home and demonstrated anew the helplessness of the Western powers. On March 8, 1936, one year after instituting universal military service and creating an air force, Hitler used his tried and proved *Blitz* coup tactics to march into the demilitarized Rhineland. This was not only another blow against Versailles, but a clear violation of the Locarno Pact.

Again, the ability of a totalitarian regime to act quickly proved effective. The success of unilateral action was a persuasive answer to any existing misgivings of diplomats and military. At the same time, new opportunities were opened up for the now perfected plebiscitary self-approbation of the regime; the Reichstag "elections" of March 29, 1936, were the first in which the totalitarian ideal figure of 99 per cent was reached—or rather totaled up. The internal consolidation of totalitarian rule—which, according to Hitler's ideas of the relationship between domestic and foreign policy, was the basis of his external strength—had become an established fact.

To be sure, none of these moves was devoid of propagandistic justifications. The reason given for the violation of the Locarno Treaty, which Hitler had specifically recognized only a short time before, was the ratification of the Franco-Soviet pact. Moreover, Hitler told the customary acclamatory special Reichstag session that he was ready to conclude nonaggression pacts, along the lines of the German-Polish agreement, with France and Belgium as well as with his Eastern neighbors. Up to 1939, this was the tried method, after having broken agreements, of sugarcoating "immutable" decisions with new promises and guarantees of peace. France above all had to react if the principle of lawful acts, not to mention the structure of the Versailles system, was to be saved. Again there were protests and public statements, and again no effort was made to trade concessions for reliable security guarantees. Great Britain was even less interested in taking action. Foreign Secretary Eden, though denouncing the German move, merely counseled moderation and the avoidance of further conflicts. A conference of the Locarno powers in London also protested the treaty violation but limited itself to an appeal to the International Court at The Hague and an agreement on guarantees.

In a situation that held considerable dangers for its rearmament policy, the Third Reich had successfully taken another step on the road of revision through action and simultaneously on the road to the "reorganization" of Europe. The last good chance to put a stop to this Hitlerian strategy had been missed. There may be disagreement over the possibilities then open to the Western powers, but there can be no dispute that at the time Italy was still preoccupied with its own pursuits, that the other Locarno powers were still united in their opposition to Hitler, and that Germany—as the German military knew full well—was not yet ready for a conflict. True, Hitler's sure instinct for the opportune moment was not the only factor in this preliminary test of strength. France was suffering from the aftereffects of years of economic crisis and was pressed by semifascist movements in the transition to a Popular Front government; the country was shaken by mass strikes, its military preparations were stagnating, the differences over the "alternatives" of Communism and Fascism, reminiscent of the end of the Weimar Republic, confused public opinion on Germany, and the country concentrated its efforts on domestic problems.

Meanwhile, the alleged superiority of the dictatorships over the democracies, with their waning prestige and internal conflicts, became increasingly evident, as was borne out by the next test that arose: the Spanish Civil War. In the course of this conflict, the almost involuntary cooperation of the two great dictatorships that had begun after the Ethiopian war was accelerated. Italy, eager to win recognition of its conquest, had taken part in the conference of Locarno powers, but now the temptation of testing its success in further actions was too great. Consequently, Mussolini, despite his misgivings over the power aspirations of the Third Reich, began to move closer to Hitler and his anti–status quo policies. In the meantime, the main obstacle to Italo-German cooperation—German-Austrian tensions—had also been removed with Papen's help. Although the joint statements issued by Berlin and Vienna on July 11, 1936, merely postponed the *Anschluss* problem, they nonetheless cleared the way for a German-Italian *rapprochement*. The start of the Spanish Civil War, set off after years of internal conflict by the Spanish-Moroccan Army revolt under the leadership of General Franco on July 17, 1936, accelerated this trend. The outcome of the bloody Spanish war that raged for almost three years expanded the dimensions and impact of the antidemocratic forces of Europe.

Spain became the first great battlefield of the new political and ideological antagonists on which the system of Versailles and the power alliance supporting it were smothered.

Mussolini had lent support to the profascist enemies of the Spanish Republic even before the outbreak of the civil war. In addition to the political and ideological factors motivating him, there was his hope that a change in government would improve Italy's position in the Mediterranean and vis-à-vis France. The French Popular Front Government, on the other hand, despite its sympathy for the Spanish Republic, pursued a course of nonintervention, supported by London and, for appearances' sake, also by Rome. This stand-by position in fact equated the Spanish rebels with the legal government. It soon also became apparent that the committee meeting in London to supervise the observance of nonintervention had as little authority and effect as the League of Nations' sanctions during the Ethiopian war the year before. Italy had no scruples about supplying the rebels with arms and even sending troops under the transparent guise of "volunteers." German help also began immediately, most strikingly in the form of the equally "voluntary" Condor Legion, which distinguished itself in the bombing of Republican cities. On the other side, the Soviet Union tried to give the conflict a Communist coloration, and though it did not do quite as well, it did succeed in one vital respect: Franco now appeared as the savior of Spain from Communism, alongside those two other pioneers of anti-Bolshevism, Mussolini and Hitler. This strengthened Franco's position substantially, while Western assistance for the Republican side remained weak and ineffective.

The Third Reich profited from the conflict in two ways: As a dress rehearsal for the coming war, the Spanish war offered new possibilities for both political and military development; and more important, the close cooperation with Italy on which Hitler's plans rested took concrete shape. The high point was reached with the formation of the "Berlin-Rome Axis." Mussolini had coined this term on November 1, 1936; it was also meant as an announcement of the claim to hegemonic rule by Italy and Germany, the two new European power centers. This "axis," around which the other countries would rotate, was to be the nucleus and crystallization point of the new Europe between the "decadent" democracies of the West and the Bolshevik danger. The major alliance of World War II was beginning to take shape.

Three major events of 1936 may thus be said to have been the signal points of the road into catastrophe: the violation of the Locarno treaty, Ethiopia, and Spain. Each of these gave evidence of the helpless acceptance of fascist aggressiveness. The European peace order had collapsed, even though the façade continued to stand for another three years. In view of Hitler's overt goals, a new general war appeared probable if not inevitable. The rapid pace of German rearmament could leave no doubt that the Third Reich would soon become a power to be reckoned with. Everything now depended on gauging the National Socialist course correctly. We know today from the wealth of documentary evidence that

Hitler remained unalterably committed to an expansionist, aggressive *Lebensraum* philosophy. Such documentation was then not readily available, but millions of copies of *Mein Kampf* were circulating in Germany and accessible to the rest of the world, as were the proposals of Rosenberg and other top functionaries. The axioms of a national-imperialist, racist, totalitarian Weltanschauung which the Third Reich had made into a universally valid principle were clearly spelled out. On many levels of domestic life, where the stumbling blocks of the transitional period had on the whole been removed, this ideology had become a terrible reality, most strikingly in the persecution of the Jews; step by step, the complete elimination and finally the extermination of that "race" was becoming a fact.

It is true, foreign policy by comparison was still lagging; the consolidation of internal power and the total organization and mobilization of the human and material "potential" took precedence. Only after this was achieved could foreign policy be tackled. But that this vital aspect of Nazi ideology would also be pursued consistently and ruthlessly should have been obvious to anyone familiar with the course of domestic affairs. The only question was whether National Socialism would be given opportunities similar to those it was afforded by the dissolution of the Weimar Republic and the capitulation of German society. There are astonishing parallels between the pre-1933 domestic policy of restraining Hitler and foreign appeasement after 1933, both in the illusions fostered and in their ultimate failure. And Hitler's skillful employment of the legality tactic encouraged the former as greatly as his tactic of peaceful revision did the latter. But at the same time the reverse side was always apparent, in the terror acts of the party and SA before and after 1933 as much as in the coups and treaty violations of Nazi foreign policy.

A crucial factor was the manner in which Hitler's policies were attuned to Britain's increasing readiness to lend a friendly ear to Germany's demands for revision. This considerably limited the scope of France, which in many respects was as rent by internal problems as Weimar had been. In addition, there was the persuasiveness of the "bulwark" propaganda with which the National Socialists impressed leading circles throughout Europe. However unconvincing their claim to be the defenders of "European culture" or even of capitalist society, there were those who considered them the lesser evil. As a result, the Soviet Union, despite its obvious receptivity, was excluded from the efforts to contain Hitler Germany. The immobility of France, the only country with good contacts with Moscow, confined the Soviet Union to a policy of suspicious waiting. No wonder therefore that this suspicion turned into profound mistrust after the Munich conference and ultimately influenced Stalin's decision to arrive at an arrangement with Hitler—which turned out to be a major factor in unleashing the war.

The fact that the author of *Mein Kampf* and masterful wielder of totalitarian terror was not taken seriously soon enough, either in

Germany or outside, whether West or East, vitally contributed to the success of National Socialist policy. By seeking to differentiate between ideology and politics, fantasy and reality, ultimate goals and existing possibilities, and betting on the "good" or at least useful aspects of National Socialism—anti-Communism in the one case, anti-Western interests in the other—both West and East failed to see the interrelation of domestic and foreign policy, of dictatorship and expansion. In retrospect, the road to catastrophe, for Europe as well as for Germany, thus seems inevitable. This was true of the situation which had developed in 1936: an ineffective stand-by attitude on the part of Paris and London, the debacle of the League of Nations, successful unilateral action on the part of Italy, and the role of Spain as a battleground on which the victory of Fascist and Nazi intervention was taking shape. The ring of the French security treaties had been broken; the bilateral, isolating revision and agreements tactics of the Third Reich eroded and destroyed the multilateral peace and order principles of democratic Europe. The pull of success began to assert itself. Not only had the Versailles system, in need of major changes though it was, become a fiction, but international power relations became unsettled and unstable, with each country seeking to safeguard itself and harboring doubts about the feasibility of a joint solution and the principle of collective security, which had so obviously failed in the face of power politics and the *fait accompli*. The two great dictatorships were the founders and masters of a new style. After the successes scored by them in 1935–36, they began to acquire an aura of near invulnerability both at home and abroad. Two years later, they were imposing their will on Europe.

Throughout this period, the Third Reich, purposefully pursuing the postulates and visions of National Socialism, managed to catch up with Italy's lead and to gain the upper hand in the alliance. Hitler, showing far greater consistency than Mussolini, based his future policy on the realization—the wellspring of his highly touted "intuition"—that the West would not risk a war and bring its power to bear against judiciously applied blackmail, but, on the contrary, would retreat inch by inch. This was the experience of the past years, and it had also made the smaller states insecure and susceptible to the dual strategy of pressure and seduction. But in following this course, Hitler was not just being a Machiavellian tactician. He also held a conviction, almost like an article of faith, that the Western democracies were politically and racially decadent and ripe for decline.

Here too the confluence of politics and ideology was apparently borne out by events. The policy of appeasement of 1937–38 seemed to support Hitler. But later on—first in the unexpected decision of the West not to let Poland down—events also were to show to what extent ideological dogma can blind one to reality. This put an end to the strategy of the easy step-by-step achievement of individual expansionist goals, and finally the much-feared two-front war by which Hitler fell back on his original *Lebensraum* idea destroyed the Third Reich itself. And so in the end Hitler, by holding fast to his old, mad notions, foundered.

PREPARING THE EXPANSION

Three major stages mark the change on the international political scene by which the Third Reich, after five years of preparation, was given the opportunity to start on the road to expansion: the creation of the Berlin-Rome Axis, with increasingly adverse effects on the smaller states; the broadening of the European dictatorial alliance to include expansionist Japan in the Anti-Comintern Pact; and, in the opposing camp, the continued retreat into appeasement and the isolation of the Soviet Union.

In conjunction with this trend, German foreign policy was restructured, a process which institutionally found expression in the replacement of Neurath by the Nazi careerist Ribbentrop, the counterpart to Mussolini's thirty-two-year-old son-in-law, Count Ciano. (Like the parvenu Ribbentrop, Ciano was not an "old fighter" but had moved up from the directorship of the Fascist Propaganda Ministry to the head of the Italian Foreign Ministry, proudly noting that although it had taken Fascism fifteen years to capture the Foreign Ministry, it had now become the most Fascist of all ministries.) [10] Had it not been for this change, the foundation for the era of expansion could not have been laid so rapidly.

The creation and broadening of the Axis played a decisive part in all of this. The Ethiopian war almost automatically had brought about a union of interest of the two expansionist dictators which until then, despite all political and ideological affinity, had not been forged. But now the reciprocal advantages of such an alliance made themselves felt: Italy's venture interfered with Western reaction to the violation of the Locarno treaty, just as the year before, Hitler's violation of the Versailles military provisions had interfered with the imposition of sanctions against Italy. The institutionalization of the German-Italian alliance hence did not come as a surprise. What was surprising was that the *rapprochement* of the two related systems should have taken so long. Ethiopia, the Austrian agreement, and Spain ensured the priority of mutual interests over continuing conflicts of interest. And the fact that Hitler unreservedly recognized Italy's rights in the Southern Tyrol played a part as well. This was the only point on which the *völkisch* principle was modified in favor of the alliance principle; the problem was to be solved, in good totalitarian fashion, through resettlement.

Germany had promptly recognized the conquest of Ethiopia and the proclamation of the Italian empire; on October 24, 1936, Hitler re-

---

[10] [Count] Ciano, *Diario* (Bologna, 1948), pp. 40, 55.

ceived the new star, Ciano, to sign an agreement supporting Franco's claims and defining the boundaries between the Central European and Mediterranean spheres of interest of the two dictatorships. But above all, the popular "fight against Bolshevism," which in view of Russia's intervention in Spain had received a shot in the arm, now took center stage in the joint propaganda campaign: It provided effective leverage in influencing public opinion in many countries, not least of them Britain.

In view of the indecisive and unsuccessful policies of the West, the Axis, as the new power center, did not fail to make an impression on other European countries. As early as January, 1937, Hitler rewarded Belgian defection from the impotent French alliance system with his stated willingness to recognize the inviolability of Belgium and Holland. A formal guarantee of October, 1937, confirmed this ongoing process of eroding the counterfront. Similar considerations continued to govern the position of Poland, the attitude of prorevisionist countries like Hungary and Bulgaria, and ultimately even the *rapprochement* between a Yugoslavia threatened by Fascist expansionism and Italy. The Little Entente (Czechoslovakia, Rumania, Yugoslavia) also disintegrated. Only the French alliance with Czechoslovakia and the Soviet Union was still in force. The rapid shift in the balance of power and the fatal crisis of the Versailles system revived the manifold problems of the Paris treaties; the artificially secured status quo between the smaller powers also was shaken. At the same time, Western colonialism faced a crisis in the Middle East, North Africa, Indochina, and India. The West saw itself attacked on two fronts, while the strength and prestige of the forward-moving "young states," encouraged by the example of the successful policies of Mussolini and Hitler, increased from day to day.

In the fall of 1937, this development reached a high point. Mussolini demonstrated the power and confidence of the German-Italian alliance in a pompous state visit to Berlin in September, 1937, full of noisy totalitarian combative slogans. Two months later, Italy joined the German-Japanese Anti-Comintern pact and thereby fixed the ultimate fronts of World War II. At the same time, Hitler, at a secret military and political leadership conference, announced his "immutable decision" to begin the earliest possible expansion via force with the "lightning" destruction of Czechoslovakia and Austria, ending with the "acquisition of more *Lebensraum*." [11] These three events sum up the essence of the future policy not only of National Socialism but also of the war alliances of 1939 and 1941. To be sure, there still were major departures of a tactical and strategic nature, in which the Soviet Union in particular, but also the special interests of Italy and Japan, played a role. But events were to prove that with the change in the balance of power, a decision had already been reached in 1937 by one side,

[11] *Nürnberger Dokumente*, Doc. PS–386 (**XXV**, 403 ff.), Talks in the Reich Chancellery, November 5, 1937.

namely by the aggressors. Its consequences depended on the attitude of the other side, the defenders of the status quo.

Franco-Russian relations were formalized by agreements, but whether this meant a firm strengthening of the West seemed increasingly doubtful. While the inactivity of the Western powers added to Moscow's mistrust, opinions in London and Paris about Russia as an alliance partner were divided. With the Five-Year Plans, the expansion of heavy industry, and the collectivization of agriculture in full swing, Stalin pushed on with domestic political coordination, the great purges, and the show trials; the rigorous consolidation of the Stalinist dictatorship limited the Soviet Union in its foreign policy to the issuance of declarations and to the role of critical observer of events. While the rule of terror strengthened anti-Soviet voices throughout Europe, in Moscow there was growing fear of an anti-Communist front of Fascists and capitalists, of an accord between British appeasement and German *Drang nach Osten* (Drive toward the East), of a European understanding at the expense of Russia. Under these circumstances, would not the one who managed to steer clear of the threatening conflict with Fascism be at an advantage? Such speculations in the East and the West adversely affected a joint front against the Axis and later, after the disenchantment over Munich, contributed to the Soviet Union's independent position on Germany and Japan. And the Munich conference in turn was an expression of Western reservations about Russia.

Thus within two years the conditions for National Socialist power politics and their outward direction had improved substantially. During 1937, London continued its efforts for further compromises with Berlin on the basis of tacit acceptance of German treaty violations. Hitler, as a screen for past and more recent ventures, entered into friendly but noncommittal negotiations over a Western pact. Indisputably, Neville Chamberlain was profoundly mistaken in his belief that Hitler could be restrained and the threat of the Axis averted by accepting the "defensible" portions of Hitler's demands. On the contrary, appeasement only built up Nazi self-confidence and Hitler's determination to conquer. On the other hand, however, there also seemed to be good reason for the gullibility of the appeasers. Up to that time, the Axis powers had refrained from extending their unquestionably massive intervention in Spain to other aggressive acts; today of course we know that Hitler's war plans directly hinged on his Spanish venture. But at the time, Hitler missed no opportunity to impress the naively gullible new British Ambassador, Sir Nevile Henderson, with demonstrations of his friendly and peaceful intentions. Official British visits to Berlin increased; and in November, 1937, at the very moment when the Axis and the anti-Comintern pact were being consolidated and the war for *Lebensraum* was being definitely planned, Hitler received the future Foreign Secretary, Lord Halifax.

On January 30, 1937, the fourth anniversary of the takeover, the Führer went before the Reichstag with the solemn assurance that the politics of surprise was a thing of the past. Such "definitive" statements had been part of his tactical arsenal since the success of the 1933 revolution, and he continued according to the tried and true recipe of sweeping demands, secret plans, emphatic peace guarantees, and successful surprise coups, followed by glib assurances "to the world" that this was the last act to ensure Germany's vital rights, that thenceforth no further demands in that area would be made, and that on the contrary the obstacles on the road to friendship had now been removed. This was in line with Hitler's idea of *Realpolitik*, and inasmuch as it brought success, it expressed the ideas popular with all too many Germans since the time of Bismarck. Far from objecting to the moral reprehensibility and political danger of such behavior, which dictatorially ruled out all critical public participation, the people learned to accept sudden treaty violations with the sly satisfaction of accomplices and the unpolitical philosophy of the armchair politician: "That's politics; now we're better at it than the other guy; soon there'll be another coup; the Führer is always right." That of course did not mean that the prospect of war was popular. The crises of 1938 and 1939 showed that what rallied large segments of the German people behind Hitler was not readiness for war but admiration for successful blackmail. One may call this a misjudgment on their part, and Hitler repeatedly voiced his disappointment over it, the last time in the battered bunker of the Chancellery, when he damned the Germans as unworthy of him. But not only Hitler was guilty of such "misjudgment." The mixture of authoritarian and vulgar political thinking in Germany was among the essential preconditions for the domestic consolidation of National Socialism and its show of strength in foreign affairs.

Meanwhile Britain—with France, against its better judgment, in tow—was still inclined on the eve of German expansion to look at any outward sign of Hitlerean yielding as a confirmation of its own stand-by attitude, not as a screening maneuver of German rearmament. The man who went furthest in this was the future Foreign Secretary, Lord Halifax, who on November 19, 1937, at the Obersalzberg, and in the name of the other British Cabinet members, assured Hitler of his conviction "that the Führer not only had accomplished great things in Germany itself, but that through the extirpation of Communism in his own country had also erected a barrier in Western Europe, and that therefore Germany rightly had to be considered as a Western bulwark against Communism." Halifax also conceded further revisions of Versailles on the question of Danzig, Austria, and Czechoslovakia, provided "that these changes were carried out via a peaceful evolution." [12] London honored this hope for peaceful change by showing its good will two more times, once during the *Anschluss* of Austria and again at the dismemberment of Czechoslovakia. And if anything, the

[12] Karl Dietrich Erdmann, *Die Zeit der Weltkriege* (3d ed.; Stuttgart, 1963), p. 233.

warlike acts of Japan in the Far East, including the occupation of Shanghai and Peking at the end of 1937, contributed to the intensification of appeasement efforts; England's Far Eastern outposts were increasingly threatened. The West did not know or did not want to know that at that very moment the now presumably more realistic "statesman" Hitler, who in fact however understood all past experiences only in the sense of his *Weltanschauung*, was presenting his plans for aggressive expansion to the heads of state and Army.

The decision to unleash a war of aggression within the near future, regardless of when Hitler himself may have concretized it, was apparently discussed at the Berlin Reich Chancellery for the first time on November 5, 1937. By a lucky accident, the substance of this meeting has been preserved in the notes of Hitler's Army adjutant, Colonel Friedrich Hossbach.[13] Among those present at the secret meeting were Blomberg, Fritsch, and Raeder, as well as Göring and Neurath. The group was limited to the military command and the Foreign Minister, though Göring was wearing several hats—those of Supreme Commander of the Air Force, Cabinet Minister, business potentate, and party luminary. Still not included was Ribbentrop, who was in Rome celebrating Italy's joining the Anti-Comintern pact. In high spirits because of the favorable international situation, Hitler for more than four hours developed his ideas before the gathering. He stressed that he was basing himself directly on the experiences of his four and a half years of rule; this alone shows up the unsubstantiality of all theses of Hitler's "growth." The economic and demographic arguments on which the Führer based his military ideas were an almost verbatim reiteration of the expansionist-imperialist *Lebensraum* ideology of *Mein Kampf*. After national revisionism, which had proved useful in the period of camouflage and preparation and in the tactics of surprise moves, the strategic realization of the *Lebensraum* idea now moved into the area of direct planning, that second stage of Nazi policy which Hitler had told the military as early as February 3, 1933, was the true purpose of *Gleichschaltung* and rearmament.

The "basic principles about the possibilities and prerequisites of our foreign policy" should be both plan of action and also "testamentary legacy in case of my death," Hitler added with pathos. The substance was the mixture of Social Darwinist, geopolitical, and racist arguments advertised in *Mein Kampf*: preservation and multiplication of the "nation" as the first goal of National Socialist policy, which presupposed the expansion of the sphere of rule and influence around the "race nucleus"; from this followed the indisputable claim to expansion, since Germany's future, the solution of social problems, and the defense against race infiltration "were solely conditioned on the solution of the space problem." Hitler saw "the sole, perhaps illusory solution . . . in the acquisition of more *Lebensraum*, a search which since

[13] See Walter Bussmann, "Zur Entstehung und Überlieferung der Hossbach-Niederschrift," in *Vierteljahrshefte für Zeitgeschichte*, No. 16 (1968), pp. 373 ff.

time immemorial had been the reason for the creation of states and of migrations." But this room could be won only through economic and political expansion in Europe, not through a "liberalistic" colonial policy. At issue was the founding of a great world empire as a geographic entity around a strong "racial nucleus" braving all resistance.

Before going into detail on how the war might be set off, Hitler stated clearly and unmistakably that "for the solution of the German question . . . there is only the road of force," and this forcible solution would have to be sought as soon as possible for both military and political reasons. In line with his "immutable decision," he planned to bring about the "solution of the problem of space" no later than 1943–45, and in case of a favorable combination of circumstances—continuing conflict in the Mediterranean area or internal crisis in France—possibly as early as 1938; it was to begin with the "lightning" defeat of Czechoslovakia and Austria. Here in unmistakable language Hitler outlined the strategy and imperialistic nature of National Socialist policy. To be sure, actual events did not follow these calculations exactly. This was true particularly of the unleashing of the war itself. But the relentless consistency of Hitler's thinking on which everything rested is clearly evident. At the same time, he had stated clearly that the goal was not only the *völkisch*-national revision of the status of the Sudeten region but the absorption of all Czechoslovakia. This, too, throws an eerie light on Britain's endeavors and the Munich Conference. The majority of those present on that November 5 apparently listened to his outpourings "silent and uneasy." [14] This was true above all of Blomberg and Fritsch, who must have weighed the possible military consequences of a hitherto so welcome rearmament policy with some misgivings. And even so acquiescent and cooperative a conservative as Neurath, a more than willing coauthor of nationalist revisionism, was no longer considered sufficiently effective for the daring expansionist policies of the future. All three were in fact replaced in the great reorganization of military and foreign policy that preceded the first expansion, early in February, 1938. This reorganization in effect put the two departments most vital to the policy of expansion under the direct jurisdiction of the Führer. The ambitious Hitler sycophant Ribbentrop, at the head of the Foreign office, was nothing but a liaison man, and Hitler himself made the Army subordinate to him after Blomberg and Fritsch had been brought down by the underhanded intrigues of Göring and Himmler, but not without fault of their own. Now the first reservations among the higher officers began to appear, though for the time being Hitler had created the firm positions for his two first great ventures beyond Germany's borders.

The incorporation of Austria had not only remained the first and most popular objective of National Socialist expansionism, but since

[14] Alan Bullock, *Hitler—A Study in Tyranny* (London, 1951; New York, 1952), p. 336.

Mussolini's turning away from the West and concentration on a Mediterranean *mare nostrum* imperialism, it had also become the most promising starting point. The Greater German–nationalist demands for self-determination lent effective support to the National Socialist strategy. Versailles was a thing of the past; an effective defense by the West for this relic of a broken system was hardly likely. Still in April, 1936, Kurt von Schuschnigg, Dollfuss' successor, in vain sought to win British guarantees. His unsuccessful semidictatorial methods, including bans and persecution of Austrian Nazis, could not prevent the *Anschluss* propaganda, much less win popular support for an independent policy. The German-Austrian "agreement" of July 11, 1936, contained a secret provision, with Austria's concession to include members of the "national opposition," among them such "decent" National Socialists as Edmund von Glaise-Horstenau and later Arthur Seiss-Inquart, in the "Patriotic Front" and Government. This weakened the resistance against the downward trend as greatly as the dismissal on May 13, 1936, of the anti-Nazi exponent of the pro-Italian Right, Vice Chancellor Prince Starhemberg. Mussolini's shift had become obvious; a success "in that policy of capturing Austria by peaceful methods to which Hitler resorted after the failure of the putsch, in July, 1934," [15] was only a matter of time.

The pseudo-legal seizure of power in Germany served as a model for the planned peaceful conquest. The Austrian Government now tolerated the illegal NSDAP. And at the same time, the German Army was working on plans for the invasion of Austria. Finally, Papen succeeded in bringing a reluctant Schuschnigg, who had been strongly advised not to go, to a meeting with Hitler at Berchtesgaden on February 12, 1938. In a dramatic scene at which German generals formed an effective backdrop, Hitler, loosening the full arsenal of his threats, induced Schuschnigg to grant the National Socialists freedom of action and to appoint Seyss-Inquart to the post of Austrian Minister of Security and Interior. Efforts to resist and to stem the course of events by holding a plebiscite on the question of Austrian independence on March 13 came too late. The plan was dropped after pressure from Berlin. Now Göring took matters in hand. Ribbentrop reported to him from London that Britain would not act; a similar assurance also came from Mussolini. On March 11 followed the ultimatum from Berlin; Schuschnigg resigned in favor of Seyss-Inquart, who, after unmistakably clear telephone instructions from Göring in Berlin, opened the borders to the German troops on March 12, 1938, while the Austrian National Socialists took control of the regional governments. Moreover, before resigning, Schuschnigg had instructed the Austrian Army to withdraw without resistance in case of a German invasion.

So the coup worked, even if the first major deployment of the new German Army revealed a number of technical deficiencies. Amid enor-

[15] *Ibid.*, p. 318.

mous jubilation of a partly National Socialist, partly misled population, Hitler moved first into "his" Linz and then on to Vienna, where church bells rang out and swastika banners were hoisted on church spires. And on March 13, he proclaimed the "reunification of the *Ostmark* [East March]" with the Reich. In tried and true fashion, there followed a Greater German plebiscite on April 10, 1938, which yielded the routine 99 per cent "yes" votes. This was the fifth and last "election" under Hitler's rule. It confirmed the rapid success of both forced and voluntary *Gleichschaltung;* the Austrian bishops under Cardinal Innitzer issued a proclamation celebrating the "extraordinary accomplishments of National Socialism in the sphere of *völkisch* and economic reconstruction as well as social policy." [16] The voice of the small Protestant church sounded no different, and even leading Austrian socialists like Karl Renner let themselves be duped. The terror of Himmler's arrest and execution squads, which began their work even before the appearance of the Army, was drowned out in jubilation. Whatever feeble resistance existed was throttled even more rapidly and brutally than in 1933 in Germany; political persecution was organized, while a pack of party commissars that at times totaled 25,000, combined the expropriation of Jewish business with private looting. A new wave of refugees swept over non-German Europe. Sigmund Freud was among those who escaped; he lived out the last year of his life in England. The cosmopolitan culture of Austria disappeared in the Pan-German provincialization of the *Ostmark,* just as the very name of Austria disappeared in the designation of the new provinces of "Upper Danube" and "Lower Danube"; the capital city of Vienna became the seat of a German governor. And soon the popular enthusiasm gave way to the disillusionment of war.

This was the return of Hitler to the land of his birth and "education"; his life's work, so his propaganda proclaimed, was now fulfilled. Again the international reaction bore out the optimistic calculations of the man who only a year earlier had promised to refrain from any more surprise moves. In Britain, a tendency to be understanding prevailed, despite the disapproval of Hitler's methods; France, torn by internal crisis, was preoccupied with its own problems; Mussolini received an effusive message of thanks from Hitler; and even Chiang Kai-shek sent congratulations. The shaping of the "Greater German Reich" was a major, undisputed success of National Socialist policy. But this was not, as many then wanted to believe, the end of revisionism but the beginning of expansion.

THE ROAD TO WAR

Hitler, as we know, was quite certain of his next step: to move against Czechoslovakia. This was even less of a secret in view of the intensification of Sudeten German Nazi activity after Austria's an-

[16] Hohlfeld, IV, No. 176.

nexation. Hitler again succeeded in skillfully combining the inner weaknesses of the country involved—in this instance, Czechoslovakia—with the slogan *"völkisch* self-determination." The multinational state of 1919 had not solved the political, social, and psychological problems inherent in the incorporation of the German minority. The political structure was governed by nationality parties; the ruling Czech majority was confronted by national minorities. Perhaps greater autonomy or a solution à la Switzerland might have improved matters, but from the very outset the Germans in particular wanted to get out of the state. This tendency gained strength after Hitler's ascension to power; the Nazi program promised a policy designed to bring about the inclusion of the Sudeten Germans in the future Reich. Consequently, as in Austria, the two German nationalist parties (one of them the German National Socialist Workers Party, which as the German Workers Party had organized the first National Socialist groups in Bohemia before World War I) were banned in 1933. They were replaced by a catch-all group, the Sudeten German Home Front under the leadership of Konrad Henlein. Henlein had begun to pursue an openly National Socialist course as early as 1936. His revisionist movement, now calling itself the Sudeten German Party, was supported by the majority of the German-speaking population. Valid Czech fears were even more justified because the separation from Czechoslovakia of the fortified German-inhabited border regions would have left the country defenseless.

Adhering to his customary practice, Hitler followed his Austrian venture with prompt messages of reassurance to Prague. But in line also with his announced plans of November 5, 1937, he simultaneously had military orders drawn up in which he said that October 1, 1938, was the date for the realization of his "immutable decision to smash Czechoslovakia in the foreseeable future." [17] The Sudeten German question, the *völkisch*-national justification, was merely a pretext for the annexation. For the first time, he burst through the frame of revisionist policy and let the imperial expansionist claims of National Socialist policy show through. Only two weeks after his entry into Vienna, Hitler drew the Sudeten German National Socialists into his game. As in the case of Austria, a combination of factors—domestic and foreign-policy blackmail, inflated maximum demands by the Sudeten Germans, and military threats—was again brought into play. At the end of March, 1938, Hitler had already instructed Henlein to raise demands in Prague "unacceptable to the Czech Government." The purpose was clear: "We must always ask so much that we cannot be satisfied." In Germany itself, Hitler ordered the formation of a Free Corps "for the protection of the Sudeten Germans and the continuation of disorders and clashes" (!), while Ribbentrop simultaneously instructed Henlein "to avoid joining in the government by the magnitude and the step-by-step announcement of the demands to be

[17] *Nürnberger Dokumente,* Doc. PS–388 **(XXV, 433 ff.).**

made." [18] This was already done in April, 1938, in the "Karlsbad Program" of the Sudeten German Party. The planned stepping-up of tensions ultimately was to bring German intervention. On May 20, Prague mobilized, and Berlin followed. This time, however, the tactics ran up against an obstacle. The German Chief of Staff, Ludwig Beck, warned against the course being taken and finally resigned. Disturbed by the rapid German upsurge and the reaction to the Austrian move in southeastern Europe, Italy temporarily backed British mediation efforts, although London continued along its course of conciliation at almost any price. The dispatch of a mediator (Lord Runciman) meant increased pressure on Prague to accept the Sudeten German "demands." France was uncertain about the extent of its commitment under the treaty with Prague.

War seemed inevitable when Hitler, on September 12, at the last Nuremberg party congress to be held, in an impassioned speech promised the Sudeten Germans military assistance. Henlein now openly operated with the slogan "Home to the Reich." But Chamberlain's patience and his hopes of becoming if not Hitler's tamer then at least the preserver of peace were still not exhausted. He offered to go to Hitler. That, he thought, would prove the seriousness of his intentions, but in the German view it also proved his respect for Hitler's power politics. The British Prime Minister, without regard to prestige, visited the Führer at the Obersalzberg on September 15 and promised to support his efforts to incorporate the Sudeten area; Paris supported this move, and after vain protests Prague gave in to this dual pressure. The British and the French Ambassadors in Berlin (Henderson and François-Poncet), both conservative anti-Communists, played a questionable role in this escalation of appeasement. But now Chamberlain faced new demands by Hitler: At the Godesberg Conference (September 20–24), the British Prime Minister was asked to assent to the immediate entry of German troops into Czechoslovakia. In a furious, incendiary address in the Berlin Sportpalast, Hitler on September 26 underscored the threats of war with a forty-eight-hour ultimatum; now France and England also began to mobilize. That is how matters stood when Mussolini, aware of Italy's inadequate preparedness, at the last minute persuaded Hitler to accept Chamberlain's proposal for a four-power conference. The British head of government once more was prepared to make the trip to Hitler, this time to the "capital of the movement"; French Premier Daladier joined him.

The Munich conference of September 29, 1938, took place under most questionable circumstances. The participants acquiesced to military blackmail and accepted Hitler's final conditions without substantial change. German troops began to move into Czechoslovakia on October 1. Above all, this hastily convened meeting reached a decision in the absence of the party most directly involved, Czechoslovakia.

[18] *Akten zur Deutschen Auswärtigen Politik*, Series D, II, 158.

Moreover, the Soviet Union, with whom Prague had a mutual-assistance pact, was not consulted, a factor that contributed to Moscow's shift of policy and its justification for the pact with Hitler that triggered the war.

Back in March, 1938, after the Austrian move, the Soviet Union had offered "without delay, in the League of Nations or outside the League of Nations, to discuss practical measures with other powers, as circumstances dictated. Tomorrow it may already be too late, but today there is still time, if all states, particularly the great powers, will take a firm, unambiguous position on the problem of the collective preservation of peace." [19] But London, where Halifax had replaced Eden, who had resigned in protest, did not respond. The direct participation of the Soviet Union, which could reach Czechoslovakia only via Poland, seemed too risky. Poland would certainly refuse to agree; it was anti-Soviet, clung to its pact with Berlin, and moreover expected territorial gains from the dismemberment of Czechoslovakia. And above all, Chamberlain suspected that Moscow wished to involve the West in a war with Germany, just as the Soviet Union for its part feared a German incursion in the East. The creation of an East-West front, an alliance which might possibly have put a brake on Hitler even without the force of arms, since he had reason to fear a two-front war, foundered on these fears. Russia's exclusion from Munich also cannot be justified by pleading a concern for Polish interests. When the Western powers finally went to Moscow in early summer of 1939, it was too late; the Soviets were already veering toward Germany.

There is even less justification for the exclusion of Prague. For Prague, the Munich conference was a brutal dictate, without validity from the very beginning, not only after Hitler's treaty violation of March, 1939. And in fact the fate of Czechoslovakia was decided there. The guarantees of England and France for the preservation of a rump Czechoslovakia in no way changed this. Moreover, the consultative and peace agreements signed in Munich with Britain and later with France (December 6, 1938) were a mere formality. True, Chamberlain returned to London as the man who had saved the peace. And Hitler did not altogether achieve his goal; he complained to Schacht about Chamberlain, saying "that character has ruined my entry into Prague." [20] Not only the reservations of the military but also the cool reception accorded by the people of Berlin to a huge demonstration of arms may have contributed to Hitler's acquiescence. But that does not alter the fact that Munich overstepped the limits of a meaningful policy of appeasement. For the embryonic political and military opposition in Germany, which since Beck's demonstrative resignation had counted on the failure of Hitler's aggressive course, the Western capitulation to Nazi blackmail meant a great setback. The credibility of the Western powers had been badly damaged in the eyes of the world. Triumph-

[19] Erdmann, *op. cit.*, p. 238.
[20] Schacht's testimony, in *Nürnberger Dokumente*, XII, 580.

antly or (in the case of a few) resignedly, the Germans once more were led to believe that there were no limits to Hitler's purpose, instinct, and intuition.

Munich was no more than a breathing space. Only three weeks later, on October 21, Hitler issued the order for the miiltary "finishing off of all of Czechoslovakia," [21] in violation of his assurance to London that all that mattered was the self-determination and reunification of all Germans, and in violation of his declaration that this was "the last territorial demand which I have to make in Europe." "We don't want any Czechs anyway," he said in his speech of September 26. Once again, political and military preparations overlapped. While appeasement continued to lead a phantom existence in London and Paris (supported by Ribbentrop's visit to Paris on December 6, 1938), Slovak nationalism was being mobilized against Prague and the disintegration of the rump state helped along from inside and outside. The postponement of the Nazi war of aggression did afford the West a year in which to prepare itself, but this time interval was of even greater benefit to the Germans. The building of the Siegfried Line (*Westwall*), the expansion of the bases around Bohemia and Moravia, and the elimination of a possible East-West alliance brought Germany decisive advantages.

The true purpose of the National Socialist Sudeten policy became obvious very soon. Step by step, Prague had to bow to German wishes. Under pressure of Berlin and the neighboring countries avid for booty, Slovakia and the Carpathian Ukraine began to withdraw from the rump Czechoslovakia at the end of the year. Again, manipulated "provocations" helped the disintegration of the state along. As late as March 11, 1939, Hitler prodded the Slovak nationalist leader Josep Tiso to secede from Prague by threatening that in case he refused, Slovakia would be given to Hungary. And on the night of March 15, 1939, he informed Czech Minister President Hacha, who had been summoned to Berlin, that "for the safeguarding of calm, order, and peace in this part of Central Europe," German troops were on their way to Prague; in case of resistance, Göring threatened to have his Air Force bomb Prague. Amid the embittered silence of the population, the country was occupied, and on March 16, Hitler proclaimed the creation of the "Protectorate Bohemia and Moravia" from Prague's Hradschin Castle. Poland also accepted its share of the booty. This, then, was the consequence of the untenable solution of Munich. Hitler was confident that "in two weeks not a soul will bother to talk about it." [22] The international situation seemed to favor this. Franco's victory had been recognized by Paris and London in February, 1939. He promptly joined the Anti-Comintern pact and strengthened the front of the dictators. France's situation was becoming increasingly complicated.

But now for the first time, Hitler miscalculated. His new coup, an

---

[21] *Ibid.*, Doc. C–136, **XXXIV**, 388 ff.
[22] Erich Kordt, *Wahn und Wirklichkeit* (Stuttgart, 1948), p. 144.

obvious act of brute force devoid of all "just causes," had changed the situation completely. To begin with, the much-invoked principle of self-determination and of national-ethnic revision of the Versailles provisions had been clearly violated; the imperialist, expansionist objectives of National Socialist policy now stood revealed. And second, appeasement on the basis of negotiations over German revision demands had finally been carried ad absurdum. There could no longer be any doubt that neither concessions nor treaties—to Hitler nothing more than scraps of paper—could restrain or "satisfy" him. Not even Chamberlain could fail to recognize that Britain's illusions had been just that. Only Hitler seemed unaware of this turning point. He continued his tactics of isolating one objective after the other and readying it for the takeover from both inside and outside. His next goal was close by.

Poland was the last country where the pretext of national-political revision was still applicable. For five years, Berlin had held in check the Nazi Government in Danzig and the propaganda against the Polish Corridor. But immediately after the smashing of Czechoslovakia, which within a week was followed by the reincorporation of Memel, as per ultimatum to helpless Latvia on March 22, Warsaw was asked to join the Anti-Comintern pact and negotiate about Danzig; Hitler now also announced that the Danzig question had to be solved. It cannot be ruled out that he planned to move against the West first in order to keep his rear free for expansion in the East. His retrospective statements before the Army commanders on August 22, 1939, support this conjecture, as do Ribbentrop's hints in Warsaw at the end of January, 1939, about a Polish-German expansion into the Ukraine. Hitler also offered Poland a twenty-five-year extension of their agreement.[23]

But Hitler simply did not believe that the situation had undergone a basic change, not even when Chamberlain, on March 31, 1939, in a far-reaching guarantee to Poland in which Paris joined, addressed an unmistakable warning to him. The declaration that Britain would meet any new attack with force was followed with assurances to Rumania, Greece, and (in view of Italy) Turkey.

Hitler thought that all this was pure bluff. On April 28, he announced the abrogation of the German-Polish agreement as well as the Anglo-German naval agreement; in addition to Danzig, he now demanded an extraterritorial passageway through the Corridor. At the same time, following the pattern of his 1938 moves, he ordered the plans for the attack on Poland on September 1, 1939. He had told his top military leaders on May 23 that Danzig was merely a pretext for further expansion: "Danzig is not the object at issue. What is involved for us is the consolidation of *Lebensraum* in the East and the safeguarding of our food supply." [24]

[23] *Akten zur Deutschen Auswärtigen Politik*, V, 87 ff.
[24] *Nürnberger Dokumente*, Doc. L–079, XXXVII, 546 ff.

Hitler had good reason for his optimism. Even though the Western powers began to strengthen their military defenses and entered into political and military negotiations with Moscow while Roosevelt appealed to Hitler and Mussolini (April 14), the illusions of appeasement were not quite dead. Also, there could be little doubt about the superiority of modern German arms; only a postponement of the conflict could bring about a more favorable balance of forces. Mussolini, by making fresh demands on France and Britain with regard to Nice, Tunis, Djibouti, and the Suez Canal, committed himself more strongly than ever to the expansionist interests of the Axis. With the annexation of Albania in April, 1939, he grabbed his profits from the changed situation in Europe. Considering the state of its preparedness, Italy would have been well advised to delay a war. But the Duce, by signing a German-Italian armament pact ("steel pact") in Berlin on May 22 relating to problems of *Lebensraum* and "vital national interests" and pledging mutual assistance in case of war, had irrevocably committed himself to Hitler's intention to unleash the war that had been prevented in Munich that summer.

This state of affairs was further helped along by the changing Soviet stance. Signs of such a trend began to appear after Munich. In a speech on March 10, 1939, Stalin turned on the Western powers, yet he failed to react to Hitler's invasion of Prague. At the prodding of opposition voices in the Conservative Party led by Winston Churchill, Chamberlain finally bestirred himself to try to enlist Moscow in an alliance against Hitler. The real problem was Poland's fear of falling into the Soviet sphere of influence; Warsaw was satisfied with Britain's guarantees. The Baltic states also had misgivings about such a development. This was the situation when British-French-Soviet military negotiations got under way in Moscow on August 1, 1939. But all the issues became obsolete when Germany and Russia signed a pact on August 23. Two factors motivated the Soviets. The fear of an agreement by the others at the expense of Moscow, of a deflection of the German dynamic to the East, had not diminished after Munich. Moreover, in Russia's eyes, the loss of its western provinces and the Baltic states after World War I was only temporary. Russia, too, as Rapallo had shown, considered itself a revisionist power; the shift of 1933–34 had not really altered this. A return to a joint Soviet-German policy remained a possibility.

For totalitarian countries, regardless of their ideological differences, such changes of heart do not constitute insurmountable problems. In concluding the pact, Germany was motivated by military-strategic considerations and the desire to avoid a two-front war, as well as following the Bismarckian tradition of German-Russian cooperation. While Russia's neighbors persisted in their refusal to grant Russian troops right of way or to accept Russian help, thereby risking a possible Communist coup or a German attack, Stalin on May 3, 1939, replaced his long-time Foreign Minister Litvinov, thus serving notice that in his opinion "collective security" with the West was a failure. With the agility and heedlessness at the command of dictatorships, he turned to the other camp (and the better offer). The secret negotiations with the "Fascist beasts" brought quick results. Nazi propaganda shifted from attacks on Bolshevism to attacks on the Western "plutocracies"; the imminence of Hitler's self-imposed deadline for attack (September 1) accounts for the hasty conclusion of the pact. Just as the Western negotiators were hoping to conclude a military agreement with Moscow, Ribbentrop set out on his journey, and on the very night he arrived in Moscow (August 23), in the presence of Stalin and Molotov, he signed that German-Soviet nonaggression pact which startled the world and set off World War II.

The published text of the pact barred both powers from supporting any country at war with either of the signatories. The West was thereby isolated. But the gist and real political meat of the pact was a secret protocol defining the "boundaries of the mutual spheres of interest in Eastern Europe" and "in the case of a territorial-political reorganization," giving Finland, the Baltic states, the eastern part of Poland, and Bessarabia to the Soviet Union. The fact that the question of a Polish rump state was left open and that the protocol was "to be treated with the greatest secrecy by both sides" [25] was stressed makes obvious the immediate war aim of this booty pact. Hitler was offering Stalin more than the West, which had considered the interests of the other countries involved. The pact, however, gave Hitler a free hand to move against Poland and for the "territorial-political reorganization of territories belonging to the Polish state" up to the Narew, Vistula, and San rivers. German expansion now could begin its course, and at the same time the road to the West had been opened up for the Soviet Union. Not the highly touted "defense against Communism" but expansionism emerged as the motive force and content of the Hitler regime. For the next two years, the bulwark thesis was simply turned around. Ribbentrop told Stalin outright that the Anti-Comintern pact "essentially was not directed against the Soviet Union but against the Western democracies." [26]

The circumstances and consequences of the pact indeed bear out the contention that Hitler became "the greatest pacemaker of Bolshevism in Europe" (Hofer), nay in the world. The union of interests of the two mortal enemies, celebrated with toasts by Stalin to Hitler and accompanied by the about-face of propaganda and the belief that dictatorships "do not have to pay heed to vacillating public opinion" [27] was, at least on the part of Germany, totalitarian diplomacy of the purest water. Future war booty was distributed, complete turns could be made in a matter of hours, agreements could be torn up and new

---

[25] *Das nationalsozialistische Deutschland und die Sowjetunion 1939–1941* (Berlin, 1948), p. 86.

[26] Seidl, *op. cit.*, pp. 84 ff.

[27] Ribbentrop to Schulenburg (August 3, 1939), in *Nazi-Soviet Relations: 1939–1941* (Washington, D.C., 1948), p. 38. Cf. Walther Hofer, *Die Entfesselung des Zweiten Weltkrieges* (Frankfurt/Main, 1964), pp. 117 ff.

ones made. To be sure, there were reservations and dismay, not only in the German Foreign Office but also among National Socialists and Communists. The chief Nazi ideologue, Alfred Rosenberg, confided bitter thoughts to his diary,[28] and not every non-Russian Communist was able to make the somersault. But the Machiavellianism of this pact rested on the sure foundation of inner political coordination. The Soviet motives certainly were understandable, and Western appeasement as well as Polish intransigence undoubtedly bear a great share of the blame. Yet Moscow's unequivocal support of Hitler's aggression is no more justifiable than the West's sacrifice of Czechoslovakia the year before. The Russian occupation of eastern Poland and the invasion of Finland made it quite clear that an "aggression" pact had been concluded. To Hitler, it brought temporary protection; to Stalin, territorial gains and the prospect of the "inevitable" internecine war of capitalism and its "fascist afterbirth"; to Poland, a death sentence: the fourth partition.

The originator and prime beneficiary of the pact was Hitler. The details of his intentions remain an open question. (Was he planning an attack on the West, did he again believe in an accommodation with London and Paris, did he conclude the pact with his later attack on the Soviet Union in mind?) Much depended on the tactical situation. But apparently, even after the invasion of France, he continued to believe in the possibility of an accord with Great Britain and a return to the basic ideas of *Mein Kampf*. He believed this because London, by talks and mediation efforts at various levels and by offering considerable concessions almost to the very last minute, tried to prevent a war. In the eyes of Hitler and Ribbentrop, these were merely more signs of English weakness. They simply could not see that the British people were no longer prepared to accept appeasement.

Even though it became apparent barely two years later that the German-Russian coup conflicted with long-range National Socialist goals and could not last, it nonetheless fulfilled its immediate purpose: Within a week, it laid the basis for the destruction of Poland. Hitler reassured his generals thus: "I will furnish the propaganda cause for the start of the war." [29] Again the reason given was the self-determination of German minorities, Danzig's right to affiliate with the Reich, the "blood-drenched borders" in the East. Again the crisis was exacerbated by blown-up incidents, "provocations," and ultimative demands to Warsaw; finally, an "attack" on the German broadcasting station at Gleiwitz, staged by Himmler with concentration-camp inmates clad in Polish uniforms, furnished the needed incendiary headlines. Mussolini, informed of Hitler's Russian negotiations only late in the game, vainly tried to arrange a conference à la Munich. He com-

[28] H. G. Seraphim (ed.), *Das politische Tagebuch Alfred Rosenbergs* (Göttingen, 1956), p. 9.

[29] Speech on August 22, 1939, at the Obersalzberg, in *Nürnberger Dokumente*, Doc. PS–1014, XXVI, 523. Hitler continued: "The victor will not be asked later whether he had spoken the truth or not."

plained to Hitler that it was his impression that the war had been "scheduled for after 1942, and at that time I would have been ready on land, at sea, and in the air, in accordance with the agreed-on plans." [30] War had become inevitable solely because Hitler wanted war, and therefore he rejected a second Munich by invoking his "life's task." It no longer was a matter of revision. Hitler told his generals on August 22: "My only fear is that some dirty dog [*Schweinehund*] at the last moment will come up with a mediation plan." [31]

There is no question of war guilt for 1939. Germany bears full responsibility. Neither the many reasons of the early postwar years, Soviet coresponsibility, nor the West's failure in its dealings with Hitler can alter this. Chamberlain, in a letter to Hitler dated August 22, also left no doubt about Britain's determination to honor its Polish commitment. A proposal for a division of political spheres between Germany and Britain, still circulated by Hitler on August 25 in the spirit of *Mein Kampf*, completely misread British policy. Against the doubts of the generals and political experts, Hitler and his "England expert," Ribbentrop, apparently believed to the very last that the planned *Blitzkrieg* could be localized. It was the first major miscalculation of his allegedly infallible "instinct" which two years later was to plunge him irrevocably into catastrophe. After brief hesitation, Hitler fixed September 1, 1939, as the date of his attack. Last-minute mediation efforts that included Göring failed because of Warsaw's refusal to negotiate under pressure. German troops were on the march on September 3 when first the British and then the French ultimatum arrived. Twenty-five years after the beginning of World War I, Hitler's idea that the war had neither ended nor been decided in 1918 won out. This was the idea with which the ex-corporal had begun his political career in 1919, and on it rested the rise and policies of National Socialism. The second world war was not an unfortunate accident, it was a National Socialist war.

THE STRUCTURE OF NATIONAL SOCIALIST FOREIGN POLICY

Any study of the foreign policy of the Third Reich must concentrate on the plans and ideas of Hitler. Two questions, however, remain: the role of the German Foreign Office, and its relation to the institutions and undertakings promoting the foreign ambitions of the party at various levels. Once again we are faced with the central problem of the relation between state and party, between specialists and politicians. The same confusing mixture of claims and conflicts, tradition and revolution, ideology and *Realpolitik* that prevailed on the domestic scene marked the development of National Socialist foreign policy. To be sure, Hitler was in absolute, unchallenged control. In the last analysis, all internal conflicts and rivalries merely strengthened his posi-

[30] *Nürnberger Dokumente*, **XXXI**, 155.
[31] *Ibid.*, **XXVI**, 338. ff.

tion. Moreover, he took recourse in established principles and accepted advice and guidance only insofar as they served the realization of these principles. But within the framework of this basic structure, the tactical successes and later miscalculations can be understood only in connection with the political *Gleichschaltung,* in the close relationship of domestic and foreign policy.

A variety of explanations can be offered for the readiness of almost every German diplomat to serve the Third Reich. Their motives differed little from those of the rest of the bureaucracy. In addition to the ordinary concern for jobs and advancement, there were the arguments that a stable continuity of experts offered the best chance that Hitler, with the "responsibilities" of office, would convert from demagogue to statesman. Hindenburg, the conservative partners, and not least Neurath, as both the "old" and the "new" Foreign Minister, seemed to ensure this continuity. After all, had it not been preserved in 1918 by adjusting to the Republic, and had not the experts of the old establishment in Fascist Italy managed to prevent risky adventures by staying at their jobs? The conservative State Secretary Bernhard von Bülow, a diplomat of the old school, shared the opinion that Hitler, being an amateur in foreign affairs, was dependent on the Foreign Office. The tone of the first memorandums to the diplomatic missions consequently was one of reassurance and continuity. And the beginnings of Nazi foreign policy, which in 1933 was still overshadowed by domestic political consolidation, seemed to bear this out. The personnel changes made were minor; the ambitions of party functionaries were held in check. Thus, for example, the chief of the Geneva mission, Rudolf Nadolny, ordered two Nazi activists (one of them the SS leader Heydrich) who were acting independently back to Berlin. The only major oppositional gesture was the resignation of the Ambassador to Washington, Friedrich von Prittwitz und Gaffron.

But more to the point, the first stunning moves of the Third Reich were completely in accord with the wishes of the Foreign Office and were even supported by it. Only a few in the Foreign Office were critical of the break with the League of Nations; Neurath even advised Hitler to take this step. The solidarity of the Leader and his advisers was also demonstrated earlier, in the conclusion of the concordat. The only issue to cast a shadow over their rapport was the Austrian policy, in which the party for the first time displayed its own initiative alongside and also against the Foreign Office, and at the same time strained relations with Mussolini. But here, as in the attitude toward the German-Polish pact, with its dangerous effects on Soviet policy, there was hardly any opposition, despite misgivings. Only Nadolny, by then Ambassador to Moscow, resigned after a dispute with Hitler. Even if one were to assume that Nadolny's disagreement with this aspect of the new course was shared by others, perhaps by von Bülow as well, there can be no question of Neurath's complete support of Hitler. His political weakness and probably his desire to keep his position come what may became more and more apparent. These factors may also account for his relationship with Nadolny, who was thought of as a possible rival for Neurath's post. Hitler must have become increasingly convinced that the Foreign Office did not pose any greater problem than the domestic political apparatus.

In the course of 1934, the rivalry of party agencies began to make itself felt in the Foreign Office. Goebbels, Ribbentrop, Gauleiter Ernst Wilhelm Bohle, and Rosenberg displayed the greatest ambitions in this area. The Propaganda Ministry laid claim to a monopoly over public information. Goebbels largely succeeded in absorbing both the press and cultural functions of the Foreign Office. More serious than this loss of important jurisdictions, however, was the competition being developed by Ribbentrop. His "qualifications" in the realm of foreign affairs rested on the familiarity with foreign countries and languages of a traveler for the champagne merchant Henkell, into whose family he had married. Ribbentrop owed his title of nobility to the paid-for adoption by a relative. At the end of his life he wanted to be known simply as an "international businessman." [32] But he impressed Hitler, a man unfamiliar with foreign countries and languages, with his seeming sophistication and flattery; Ribbentrop considered himself the foreign-policy expert of the party, which he had joined during its 1932 upsurge. Vain and subservient, sticking close to Hitler, he set his hopes on a discord between Hitler and the Foreign Office. His first special missions as delegate to disarmament conferences in London and Rome in 1934 were without results, but in the meantime he had set up his own "Ribbentrop office" in rivalry with the Foreign Office—a "para-diplomatic" outfit [33] with agents in numerous countries, paid for with special funds and also with monies from the "Adolf Hitler Foundation," which together with a motley group of businessmen, party comrades, and adventurers drafted Ribbentrop's foreign policy for Hitler. It was a meeting ground for men who tried to operate outside official foreign policy or who, despite party honors, had not been able to gain a foothold in the Foreign Office. Here foreign-policy intrigues incompatible with the dignity of career diplomats could be spun. Hitler rewarded his adept colleague with the right to see all Foreign Office reports not addressed specifically to the Minister or State Secretary. The result was feverish activity on the part of Ribbentrop, who, using his direct contacts with Hitler, superseded and interfered with the Foreign Office by acting on his own. He concentrated primarily on one of Hitler's favorite themes—German-British relations—and counteracted the doubts of the Foreign Office by reaffirming the ideas and hopes of Hitler. During his visits to London, he made contact not only with skeptical observers like George Bernard Shaw but also with ad-

[32] G. M. Gilbert, *The Psychology of Dictatorship* (New York, 1950), p. 167.
[33] Carl Schorske, in Gordon Craig and Felix Gilbert (eds.), *The Diplomats* (Princeton, 1953), p. 479. See also Hans-Adolf Jacobsen's basic work, *Nationalsozialistische Aussenpolitik 1933–1938* (Frankfurt/Main, 1968), pp. 252 ff.

mirers of the "new Germany" like Lord Lothian. In this period of foreign isolation, Hitler welcomed Ribbentrop's assertion that almost everyone in England favored cooperation with the Third Reich. Hitler persuaded himself that Ribbentrop knew more about foreign countries and foreign affairs than all the experts in the Foreign Office and foreign embassies.

It was typical of the state of affairs at the Foreign Office that Neurath himself did little to counteract the bypassing and interference with official foreign policy by Ribbentrop's office. In the past he had even prevailed upon Hindenburg to entrust Ribbentrop with special missions, and he continued to follow the easy way of sidestepping all possible friction. Bülow for his part obviously had continued to underestimate the amateur diplomat by the grace of Hitler until it was too late. Contributing to Hitler's faith in Ribbentrop was the prestige he had gained in Hitler's eyes during the negotiations for the Anglo-German naval agreement. Contrary to the skeptical expectations of the diplomats in the Foreign Office in Berlin as well as in the Embassy at London, Ribbentrop, thanks to the hardly comprehensible decision by London, came home with an agreement which, like the concordat engineered by Papen, was a major step in the international recognition of the Third Reich and in the break-up of a potential anti-Hitler front.

Then as well as later, Hitler felt confirmed in his belief that diplomats were overcareful or even unrealistic. And so the unscrupulous toady Ribbentrop, the dynamic special envoy who in Hitler's opinion promptly delivered the goods, became the pioneer of the new-style foreign policy. In its pursuit, he imitated his master by making any promise whatever to lure country after country away from security agreements. For example, he promised Belgium to forgo all claims to Eupen-Malmedy if it would remain neutral in any future conflict. The Foreign Office had to deal with the consequences of such ventures without having had prior notice; from 1935 on, it increasingly lost contact with Hitler's opinions and intentions. It was told of the introduction of universal military service only belatedly; in the next German move, the remilitarization of the Rhineland, Ribbentrop's office also had the upper hand, and although the London Embassy warned of British countermeasures, Ribbentrop was proved right. In June, 1936, after Bülow's death, Ribbentrop moved up to the Ambassadorship in London, where a year before he had won his greatest success. Even now he retained his position as special envoy and remained under the direct jurisdiction of the Führer, just like Papen in Vienna. Great Britain and Austria were taken out of Foreign Office jurisdiction and turned into sectors of personal contact with Hitler. Neurath phlegmatically concurred in the undermining of the Foreign Office, and with the beginning of the expansionist era Ribbentrop reached his longed-for goal.

Another rival of the diplomatic service was the Foreign Countries Organization (Auslandsorganisation, or AO) of the NSDAP under Gauleiter Bohle, the son of a German professor in Cape Town, born in England in 1903. The AO, formed in 1931 as the special "region" of party members in foreign countries, developed foreign-affairs ambitions after 1933; it was concerned with the manipulation and coordination of ethnic German groups, and at the same time with spying on Germany's diplomatic missions. The AO, an increasingly influential and disturbing rival of the Foreign Office, by order of Hitler on January 30, 1937, was given an independent place in the Foreign Office, with jurisdiction over all Germans in foreign countries. The carefully protected independence of the Foreign Office from the party was thereby eroded, for Bohle was only formally under Neurath; as head of a Nazi organization, he was in fact under Hess; at the same time he was also given Cabinet status. As far as the diplomats were concerned, the AO was a sort of fifth column charged with the political alignment of the foreign missions, using stalwart ethnic German Nazis to pursue its own foreign policy, while Bohle, sitting in the Foreign Office, kept an eye on its staff.

The activities of the AO played a vital role in Austria and particularly later in Spain. Franco had the help of the AO even before the beginning of the civil war, and the subsequent German involvement was in large measure the work of the AO.[34] A letter from Franco transmitted to Hitler by AO officials immediately after the putsch brought Franco military assistance; the Foreign Office was superseded in this matter as well. Again we see the customary picture: skepticism and restraint in the Foreign Office and in part also in the Army; independent action of party activists supported by ethnic German contact men; opaque maneuvers followed by quick decisions of Hitler, whose success gives the lie to the warnings by Foreign Office and Army. Differences of opinion within the machinery of state favored this condition: Göring was interested in testing the Air Force in combat in Spain and in trading German arms for Spanish raw materials; Ribbentrop's office involved itself in its own fashion; the Propaganda Ministry continued to make its incendiary revelations; Admiral Canaris, the chief of intelligence, was an old friend of Franco's; and like the AO intermediaries between Franco and Hitler, the German envoy to Franco, an old party member and ex-general, also played his own political game. In short, one cannot possibly speak of Foreign Office control and decisions. This situation is yet another example of the internal chaos of the allegedly monolithic Hitler regime. Yet at the same time the lack of coordination obviously did nothing to change the feeling at home and abroad that Germany was following a strong, astutely planned Spanish policy. It was this persistent delusion about the nature of a totalitarian dictatorship that made possible Hitler's apparently unstoppable successes through "instinct."

The AO has been linked particularly to the creation of fifth columns in countries settled by ethnic Germans. Here too it can be said that no

[34] Manfred Merkes, *Die deutsche Politik gegenüber dem spanischen Bürgerkrieg 1936–1939* (2d ed.; Bonn, 1970), pp. 19 ff. On the AO, see Jacobsen, *op. cit.*, pp. 90 ff.

purposeful organization of powerful National Socialist subversive movements was ever carried out, but the myth itself was enough to spread fear and confusion.[35] But more importantly, alone the political coordination of the ethnic groups was a political factor that exerted considerable pressure on the political development of Eastern and Southeastern Europe. The bearing of this factor on both the Czech and Polish questions is self-evident. Of course, the historico-political presuppositions in the Baltic states, Rumania, and Yugoslavia were different. Unlike the Sudeten Germans and Polish Germans, the ethnic Germans in these countries could not simply be considered as part of the population of a future Greater Germany and made the targets of the appropriate *Anschluss* propaganda. But after some differences, the ethnic German organizations everywhere were rapidly coordinated. In countries where the League of Nations provisions for the protection of minorities had not always been an unmixed blessing, Nazi criticism of international agreements was particularly well received. Other political groupings were outmaneuvered by appeals to the cultural and *"völkisch"* community; the idea of the "ethnic community," of the primacy of *völkisch* over state ties, was likewise postulated and the Third Reich greeted as the protector of all Germans, even if a direct *Anschluss* was not possible. The expectations in many ways resembled the illusions that had made the triumph of National Socialism possible, except for the still greater distance from the reality of this movement and its rule.

The organizational *Gleichschaltung* was helped by the existing nonpartisan cultural organizations, many of which had been financed by German interests. In this, a vital role was played by the powerful League of Germans Abroad (Verein für das Deutschtum im Ausland, or VDA), which since Bismarck's time had enthusiastically supported schools, theaters, papers, and political activities of ethnic Germans throughout the world. The VDA, before 1933 a "national," nonpartisan organization presided over by the democratic ex-Minister Otto Gessler, was now put under the jurisdiction of a national chief (Reichsführer) and increasingly became a transmission belt of Nazi ethnic and coordination policies in the service of the new foreign policy. The first head was the Carinthian ethnic propagandist Hans Steinacher. Once the temporary solution had served its purpose, the organization was put under the SS and as part of an ethnic German office became a tool of radical Nazi ethnic policies. Nazification and German party politics were able to gain the upper hand largely because of German funding. Loyalty toward the host country dwindled proportionately. The ethnic Germans became more or less willing instruments of National Socialist foreign policy. In so doing, they dissolved their bonds to their homelands, and finally during the war had to accept the dubious blessing of resettlement in conquered territories

---

[35] Louis de Jong, *Die deutsche Fünfte Kolonne im Zweiten Weltkrieg* (Stuttgart, 1959).

(for example, the Balts to the Warthe region) and after the defeat, the fate of expulsion.

The border and ethnic German ideology played a central role in the genesis of National Socialism and later also in its foreign policy. Again and again, it was stressed that leading personalities of the Third Reich by birth belonged in the category of border and ethnic Germans, i.e., Hindenburg (Poznan), Hitler (Braunau), Rosenberg (Riga), Hess (Egypt), Darré (Argentina). At a VDA congress in 1933, Steinacher with pathos but not without some justification pointed out

> how much the ethnic German unity and defense movement of those years [after World War I] was also the root of the national revolution of Adolf Hitler. . . . The movement comes out of the depth of the ethnic community. Because it does, it is not a purely national movement, is therefore not limited to the boundaries of the state. It embraces the full extent of our people. . . . And there across the borders: from the Baltic to the mouth of the Danube, from Upper Silesia to the Egerland, from Burgenland to the Tyrol [this however against Hitler's plans!] and to Eupen-Malmedy, everywhere we see how the young generation is carried away by this movement. We can also see it across the ocean, in North America, in Brazil, and in South Africa, where with unparalleled ardor the simple people in particular have gained in self-awareness and go their way with growing faith and growing strength. The entire German ethnic community has been set in motion. Those who belong to it are being newly formed. A new epoch of German life has begun.[36]

This was then still a fanciful, idealized camouflage of a suprastate ethnic nationalism and its National Socialist orientation. But in the years to come, it became the manipulated instrument of expansionism and racist *Lebensraum* policies. In the brutally real fantasies of "transnationalization" (*Umvolkung*) pursued by Himmler and the SS, the aberration of the ethnic idea was carried ad absurdum. The ethnic and national German cultural ideology became the incubation chamber of vital impulses and pseudo justifications for the superiority doctrine and ruling claim of National Socialism.

The exalted ideas and frustrated ambitions of the Baltic German ideologue Rosenberg also contributed to the confusion of motives and jurisdictions under the Leader, in which National Socialist foreign policy developed partly in tandem with and partly alongside the Foreign Office. In the early years, Rosenberg had been Hitler's foreign-policy adviser; later he was chairman of the foreign-affairs committee of the Nazi parliamentary delegation. But instead of becoming the head of the Foreign Office as he expected, he was given only the foreign-affairs department of the NSDAP (Aussenpolitisches Amt, or APA). All his busy work in jurisdictional conflicts with the Foreign Office

---

[36] In Walter Gehl, *Der nationalsozialistische Staat* (Breslau, 1933), p. 218. On the *Gleichschaltung* of the League of Germans in Foreign Countries, see Jacobsen, *op. cit.*, pp. 162 ff.

as well as with Goebbels and Ribbentrop cannot hide the fact that his department was nothing more than a reception center for foreign visitors, particularly for non-German fascist groups. Göring practically made it official that "in questions of foreign policy it was never consulted." [37] Rosenberg's effort to take over the future generation in the Foreign Office with the help of a party school for diplomats also met with little success. He sought consolation for his frustrations in the realm of foreign policy in mobilizing the forces for the attack on "decadent art" and in exerting the Nazis' "sovereign right to the evaluation of all intellectual institutions." [38] The most bitter blow dealt him was his being passed over again in 1938 in favor of the careerist Ribbentrop, which brought the despised consequence of the Hitler-Stalin Pact. His influence remained negligible. It was he who in 1940 brought Quisling to the attention of Hitler, ordered the looting of conquered libraries, and drew up plans for the Supreme School of National Socialism. Even his appointment to the position of Reich Minister for the occupied Eastern territories was nothing more than a consolation prize; his jurisdictions were impinged on from all sides (Göring, Himmler, Sauckel); the office was sneeringly referred to by Goebbels as the "Ministry of Chaos."

Ribbentrop, on the other hand, developed different skills. After his successful entry into the diplomatic elite in 1936, he sought to seal his standing with Hitler by scoring another success over the Foreign Office. He became a commuter between London and Berlin (*Punch* called him the "wandering Aryan").[39] And he kept his office, which by now had a staff of 300, busy with the search for new coup possibilities. London was not a big enough stage for him, particularly not after he committed the faux pas of greeting the King with the Hitler salute. He therefore fell back on Hitler's sometime idea of Japanese-German cooperation. The most obvious goal was a joint policy of the two dynamic expansionist powers against the Soviet Union; anti-Communism formed the propaganda basis. Again the Foreign Office remained on the outside. It was Ribbentrop who signed the Anti-Comintern Pact with Japan in November, 1936. However, the German Ambassador in Tokyo, Herbert von Dirksen, apparently was involved in some double-dealings between the Foreign Office and Ribbentrop's office —a typical example of the susceptibility of the conservative career diplomat to power and success; in reward for his services, Dirksen was appointed to succeed Ribbentrop in London in 1938.

The Foreign Office could take solace in the insubstantiality of the Anti-Comintern Pact, though it did disturb the traditional German-Chinese relations and also affected the interests of the military, which had been cooperating with Chiang Kai-shek for years. But a

[37] *Nürnberger Dokumente*, XVIII, 83. On the Foreign Affairs Committee of the NSDAP, see Jacobsen, *op. cit.*, pp. 45. ff.

[38] Thus Alfred Rosenberg, *Weltanschauung und Glaubenslehre* (Halle Saale, 1939), p. 14.

[39] Paul Seabury, *The Wilhelmstrasse* (Berkeley, 1954), p. 91.

year later Ribbentrop also succeeded, behind the backs of the experts, in getting Italy to join and thus endow the Anti-Comintern pact with unsuspected political significance as the basis of the war coalition. Again the Foreign Office and the military had been outflanked and their China policy finally sacrificed.

The continuing power loss of the Foreign Office to Hitler's joint actions with Ribbentrop could no longer be overlooked. Within a few years, the office which had so self-confidently expected to steer Hitler toward the traditional conduct of foreign policy had been put in the role of a "technical apparatus," as State Secretary Ernst von Weizsäcker confessed.[40] And even on this minor level, it remained excluded from many matters, under supervision at home as well as abroad, insecure in the face of sudden moves from outside and of infiltration from within. The eager cooperation of the early days, the conservative-national orientation of the anti-Versailles course, and the bureaucratic, authoritarian mentality of an unequivocally "closed society" contributed in no small measure to the defenselessness and lack of resistance of the Foreign Office. The fatal role of Neurath cannot be ignored. True, there were instances of opposition, and these increased in the course of time. But neither the intervention of the party and the advent of Nazi diplomacy à la Ribbentrop nor the momentous switches of National Socialist blackmail and expansionism were ever checked. It was not merely a question of the defeat and failure of traditional diplomacy by a dictatorship wielding the tools of modern propaganda and manipulation with virtuosity. Many diplomats also displayed that frightening susceptibility to the idea of power and success, to nationalist slogans and narrow-minded subservience which made possible National Socialist autocracy and war.

A first low point had already been reached on the eve of overt expansionism when the despised and underestimated outsider Ribbentrop took over the Foreign Office, thereby removing any lingering doubts over the degree of actual *Gleichschaltung*. Like Papen, Neurath after being ousted let himself be used as a conservative window dressing in other high posts; the "superior" experts of the Foreign Office acted as instruments of the uncontrolled, instinctual policies of Hitler and of a satellite whom the party veterans dubbed "Ribbensnob" and of whom Goebbels said derisively, although not without envy: "He bought his name, he married his money, and he swindled his way into office."[41] Even at the Nuremberg trial, rivals like Göring still gave indications of the general disdain of the party elite for this Byzantine figure. Hitler, however, was known to have called him a genius and a "second Bismarck." [42]

---

[40] Ernst von Weizsäcker, *Erinnerungen* (Munich, 1950), p. 129; on Weizsäcker, see *The Diplomats, op cit.*, pp. 435 f.
[41] Joachim C. Fest, *The Face of the Third Reich* (London and New York, 1970), p. 179.
[42] Carl Jacob Burckhardt, *Meine Danziger Mission 1937–39* (Munich, 1960), p. 297; Otto Dietrich, *12 Jahre mit Hitler* (Munich, 1955), p. 259.

Even after Ribbentrop's appointment, the Foreign Office still found consolation and justification. Ambassador Dirksen, now in London, welcomed the end of the rivalry with Ribbentrop's office; Weizsäcker as the new State Secretary of the old school put his faith in Ribbentrop's accessibility to reason and the fact that foreign policy would again be concentrated in the Foreign Office.[43] But this also put an end to the possibility of exploiting jurisdictional conflicts. Ribbentrop immediately threw himself into an endless battle to recapture the spheres that were lost under Neurath. He succeeded in the ensuing years in isolating Bohle and the AO and in strengthening his position vis-à-vis the Propaganda Ministry. Though the Foreign Office owed him the preservation of its external existence in the welter of war politics, this sham success meant little in view of the disintegration of actual jurisdictions and the poor contents of a "foreign policy" the Foreign Office was called upon to carry out in the Ribbentrop era. New uniforms, the installation of old party comrades with high SA and SS rank, and the opening of an SS school for diplomats marked the new era. Ribbentrop informed Weizsäcker's successor, Gustav-Adolf von Steengracht, that the task of the State Secretary was to maintain routine contacts with foreign diplomats, to preserve discipline within the Foreign Office, and to protect its jurisdictions ruthlessly, but to leave policy to Hitler and to him, the Minister, and simply carry out orders.

Blind obedience rather than advice was expected of diplomats; even Ribbentrop himself only carried out Hitler's wishes and tried to protect the Leader against the influence of doubters and thus make himself indispensable. Only those reports and proposals that fit into this scheme were henceforth accepted. This also accounts for the growing blindness to reality that marked Hitler's war policies. After the summer of 1938, all efforts of Weizsäcker and his diplomats to halt or modify the course of events foundered on this. The leader principle ruled, according to which the Leader (and after him the Foreign Minister) was always right, and only after that was the Foreign Office listened to. Ribbentrop expected of the Foreign Office that it make the inspired infallibility of Hitler's foreign policy the sole basis of its existence. In the spring of 1939, he reputedly went so far as to threaten with execution any staff member who doubted that Poland would collapse within twenty-four hours and that England would not intervene.[44]

Ribbentrop's certainty was a momentous miscalculation growing out of disappointment over the failure of his crude England policies. Thus he contributed substantially to the decision to go to war, apparently convinced that Germany "had not exploited the war fear of the Western powers to its every depth" when it agreed to the Munich

---

[43] Herbert von Dirksen, *Moskau, Tokio, London* (Stuttgart, 1949), p. 199; Weizsäcker, *op. cit.*, pp. 152 ff.

[44] Erich Kordt, *Nicht aus den Akten* (Stuttgart, 1950), p. 372.

conference.[45] And so with his "personal foreign policy" he thwarted the last-ditch mediation efforts (for example, of the Swedish industrialist Birger Dahlerus), suppressed the reports of the London and Washington embassies, and interrupted contacts with Warsaw. Yet the monumental miscalculation of August, 1939, neither disturbed Ribbentrop's relations with Hitler nor put a stop to the partly voluntary, partly resigned acceptance by the German career diplomats of the violent and catastrophic course of National Socialist war policies.

Late in life, Weizsäcker arrived at this insight: "The fault lay with the system, in which such a figure could become the Minister of Foreign Affairs of a nation of seventy million and remain in office for seven years." [46] But it should be added that the system itself was not a puzzling phenomenon. It could not have survived without the German traditions and attitudes which made it possible, without the susceptibility and cooperation of the experts who supported it and kept it functioning, and without the failure of diplomacy and the illusions of the European powers who accepted it. Finally, it was obedience to "the state," this abstract entity of Prussian-German tradition, which put all misgivings to rest. To be sure, the methods of Hitler and his minions were not always approved of, but their aim —Greater German expansion and hegemony in Europe—was. The tactics and chances of success may have been points of contention, as in the crises of 1938 and 1939, but even such overt acts of terror and arbitrary rule as the November pogroms of 1938, which aroused international storms of indignation, did not change this hierarchy of ideas: first "the state," then the individual. The rather diminutive term "crystal night" helped one cope with the frightening happening. The bureaucratic ethic of service continued to predominate over political morality. Only a handful of men, among them the envoys in Rome and Moscow, Von Hassell and Count Schulenburg, managed to shed this traditional attitude and belatedly put resistance above the idea of the total state. The others survived.

[45] Weizsäcker, *op. cit.*, p. 191.
[46] *Ibid.*, p. 354.

VII

Domestic Mobilization and Resistance

ECONOMY AND SOCIETY IN TRANSITION

At no time did National Socialism develop a consistent economic or social theory. The catchwords of the party program (Articles 13–17) were a disjointed conglomeration of middle-class and semisocialist slogans; Hitler himself referred only to the *Volksgemeinschaft* (people's community) and the end of the class struggle, to war on both Marxism and liberalism; Gottfried Feder, his early mentor, and Feder's "war on finance capital" receded into the background after 1933, together with the "socialist" Strasser wing; and Alfred Rosenberg, the party's chief ideologue, thought it below the dignity of a philosopher to occupy himself with economic and social theories. By the summer of 1933, it had become obvious that not only were the anticapitalist appeals being sacrificed, but also the promises of a corporate order alleged to protect the middle class against socialism as well as against heavy industry and big business. The men who engineered the takeover were not swayed by the dismay of old Nazi ideologues or new Nazis dreaming of a corporate state modeled on Fascist Italy or on a preindustrial society.

Just as the "legal" revolution succeeded in overthrowing a political order with the instruments of that very order, the economic and social realm also was the scene of a unique, paradoxical revolution. It has been called a "dual revolution," [1] that is to say, in the final analysis ideological concepts determined the aim—the fight against bourgeois and industrial society—but at the same time, this fight was conducted with the tools of industry and technology and with the help of the

[1] David Schoenbaum, *Hitler's Social Revolution* (New York, 1966), pp. xxii f.

330

bourgeoisie. This ambivalence had already surfaced in the romantic pessimism of the precursors of National Socialism. As a political organization, and certainly as totalitarian rule, National Socialism made singularly effective use of modern industrial and technological methods. This was a presupposition both for the propagandistic and organizational *Gleichschaltung* and for the plans of expansion. The other basic precept, racism, that product of a pseudo-scientific naturalism resting on irrational foundations, culminated in the technical application of "eugenics" and mass murder. In its methods National Socialism was as up-to-date as any regime: Hitler's reverence of technology, the highly touted Autobahn, the Four-Year Plans and new industrial plants, and the rise of the technician Speer furnish ample proof. Only the bases of the objectives were reactionary and anachronistic: expansion leading to autarchy; race policies to solve the problems of a mixed, mobile population; the substitution of the utopia of a people's community for the social stratification of an expanding industrial society.

But these were theoretical problems. The practical problem lay in the contradiction between economic and social theses of revolution and the revisionist and later expansionist revolutionizing of a foreign policy dependent on the mobilization of a political apparatus. As a consequence, the economic and social structures were subject to profound political and administrative encroachment, but they were neither destroyed nor basically reorganized.[2] They were a mixture of private and state capitalism, which under conditions of rearmament and a war economy were increasingly directed from above and outside, but which never became anticapitalistic or antimonopolistic, let alone socialist. For contrary to the promises of the propaganda machine, the middle class and the workers never reaped the promised profits from this development. On the contrary. During 1933 and 1934, the destruction of the trade unions and the reserve army of 5–6 million unemployed were used to make working and wage conditions even more stringent. The programs for increased employment in connection with rearmament benefited big business rather than the small businessman, while the interests of the workers were diverted ideologically to the political successes of the regime and to the organization of leisure—a strategy involving strict controls and threats that protests or strikes would be seen as evidence of Marxist activities. One of the first laws of the Hitler regime (April 4, 1933) sanctioned the on-the-spot dismissal of Communist workers and all SPD and union shop stewards; this threat effectively hovered over all undesirable workers, who possessed neither representatives nor the right to strike nor funds.

But at the same time, efforts were made to win labor support and cooperation by sham reforms. At any rate, in 1933, almost one-third of the NSDAP membership—750,000—were workers. The NSDAP was not just another capitalist party, as some oversimplified analysis

[2] T. W. Mason, "Labor in the Third Reich 1933–1939," in *Past and Present*, No. 33 (1966), p. 112.

maintains. The founding and activity of the German Labor Front
(DAF) must be seen in this light. It had been formed to counteract
the special interests of National Socialist employees' organizations
(like the NSBO). For this reason, the DAF was put under the jurisdiction of the Chief of Party Organization, Robert Ley, and in November,
1933, the employers' organization was incorporated into it. All industrial enterprises were designated communities of a leader and his followers; trusteeship councils were set up to advise works managers and
intensify the new harmony; trustees of labor and honor courts were to
supervise these utopian class and unionless work communities and were
empowered to remove not only workers but also entrepreneurs from
their own plants. To be sure, the employer once more was master in his
own house, more so than in the days of the unions. But because of its
size and monopoly position, the DAF soon began to develop its own
power claims. Tensions developed between the DAF and the interests
and authority of the employers, as well as with the planners and directors of the arms programs, the economic and labor ministries, and the
offices of the Four-Year Plan. Here, too, guided jurisdictional chaos—
David Schoenbaum has called it the institutional Darwinism of National
Socialism—ruled. It turned out that the destruction of the unions
and the voluntary dissolution of the employers' organizations could not
in themselves make the class and wage conflicts of an industrial
society disappear. That which the DAF offered as a substitute for freedom—appeals to national pride and the work ethos of the "soldiers of
labor" (thus Ley), the beautification of work sites as well as cultural
and sports installations under the aegis of the DAF, a "Beauty of
Labor" division, vacation trips and various cultural activities after
1934 through the "Strength through Joy" (*"Kraft durch Freude"*)
program, and, finally, the promise of the Volkswagen (people's car)
—could not alter the fact that employer and employee continued to
stand in opposite corners, that with full employment after 1936, workers wanted higher wages, that work performance in the boom of the
arms and construction industries tended to decline, and that all
branches of industry and trade suffered under the pressure of price
competition and labor shortage. The highly touted "battle of labor" of
1933–35 was won largely by virtue of rearmament and universal military service; however, the regime profited psychologically from this
sham success. The fact that this upswing meant "guns instead of
butter" (in the words of Göring) was lost in the short-range self-
interests of the social partners. But along with full employment and
unprofitable weapons, Autobahn, and military construction, there
arose classic problems of wage and price policies, balance of payments,
raw materials, and the budget. Wages leveled off, conflicts between
employers and employees increased, and economic measures alone
could not hold the "socialism" of the people's community together.

Beginning in 1936, Göring's Four-Year Plan office drew up far-
reaching plans for wage and production controls, regulations barring
the hiring of workers employed in other jobs, and the stabilization of

working conditions. But the Government was hesitant about restricting the workers' job mobility. Plans to draft workers for war enterprises (Hermann Göring Works, Siegfried Line) were not implemented until June, 1938, and were expanded only after the beginning of the war. Before that time, it would have taken coercion to break worker resistance and this, given the labor shortage, would have had disastrous effects on the economy and rearmament. True, the Gestapo (Geheime Staatspolizei, the secret police) could ship intractable workers to concentration camps, but it could not replace them. The war seemingly solved the problem; in fact, however, it only covered it over. On September 4, 1939, comprehensive wage and price controls were instituted and the existing labor legislation largely modified. But the future saw protests and substantial modifications, proof that the Government was as dependent on a contented labor force as on the cooperation of big business. Of course, in addition to political and social controls, the Government also commanded harsher weapons to control labor and production: the labor and military draft, as well as a classic method of colonial rule—the employment of disenfranchised foreign and slave labor.

The basic principle of National Socialist economic policy was to use the traditional capitalist structure with its competent economic bureaucracy to coordinate and move toward its prime objective: acceleration of rearmament and safeguarding of the food supply. (This policy was modified, however, with the founding in 1937 of far-flung Government enterprises designed to expand and direct the arms potential like the Hermann Göring Works [steel industry] and the Volkswagen Works.) But even during the war, despite a trend toward vast monopolistic organizations, the private capitalist enterprises continued to exist, except that more determined official efforts were made to impose controls. The same spirit that bred profitable mutual-interest alliances with big business and the incidental enrichment of numerous Nazi chieftains also brought the dissolution of medium-sized and small enterprises. Their existence was made dependent on their contribution to the war effort; moreover, they were not able to keep up with the mammoth orders and the rationalization of modern giant plants and trusts. They were also at a disadvantage in the network of connections and influence-peddling; contacts with rival economic bigwigs were a vital part of the game. The Nazi leadership had respect for the top managers who faithfully paid their Adolf Hitler Fund contributions and gained entree into the circle of industrialists around Himmler. Capital concentration continued to increase. The confiscation of Jewish and captured economic holdings, which for reasons of the war economy went mostly to large firms like Krupp, Mannesmann, IG Farben, and Siemens, contributed considerably to this growing concentration.

The involved system of controls and interference and the creation of superagencies (Reich Economic Chamber) and planning councils could not, however, prevent either waste, jurisdictional conflict, corruption, or faulty planning. Detailed studies [3] have shown the gap that existed between objectives and reality in the economic preparations for the war despite the daring financial manipulations of Hjalmar Schacht. The development of synthetics could not alleviate the raw-material shortage, which played a vital part in the decision of industrial circles— whether or not they favored the autarchic ideology of National Socialism—to support and exploit Hitler's thesis of the necessity of expansion. More and more, the view that war was a near certainty for economic reasons as well gained ground. Long before the Hossbach meeting, in which Hitler cited Germany's food and raw-material situation as the compelling reasons for expansion, he had made this point in a secret memorandum on the Four-Year Plan (August, 1936). It was a vicious circle in which the German economy, blindly fixing its sight on greater production and efficiency, followed the regime: rearmament exacerbated the raw-material situation, which made aggression necessary, and which in turn resulted in the need for more arms. Thus from the very beginning, a permanent war economy in the guise of capitalism formed the backdrop of National Socialist economic policy.

In contrast, the solutions promised before 1933 played no role in either economic or social policy: nationalization of trusts, profit-sharing in big business, improvement of the old-age pension system, creation of a viable middle class, and the communalization of large retail enterprises and leasing them to small businessmen, expropriation of large landholdings and their distribution for common use, abolition of land mortgages and loan speculation. None of these partly radical, partly romantic-reactionary reform plans was ever seriously tackled, unless one considers the persecution of Jews, the "Aryanization" of their assets, and the resettlement of German farmers and businesses in occupied territories as fulfillment of these promises. In the course of mobilization for war other roads were taken to realize the social and political ideas of National Socialism. Power politics was the sole determinant in the course being followed: economic recovery as a prerequisite for the consolidation of power; this in turn called for huge sums and material as well as economic expansion, which could be gained most expeditiously through war—which, of course, in the end devoured everything.

Only the objectives, not their realization, were total. It would be misleading to speak of the economic policies of the Third Reich as a smoothly functioning system of planning and controls. But, conversely, to conclude from the obvious discrepancy between objectives and reality that the war mobilization was merely a gigantic hoax designed to

---

[3] *Die deutsche Industrie im Kriege 1939–1945* (Berlin, 1954). On this problem, see particularly Gerhard Meinck, *Hitler und die deutsche Aufrüstung 1933–1937* (Wiesbaden, 1957); Burton H. Klein, *Germany's Economic Preparations for War* (Cambridge, Mass., 1959); Alan S. Milward, *The German Economy at War* (London and New York, 1964); also, Dieter Petzina, *Autarkiepolitik im Dritten Reich* (Stuttgart, 1968), pp. 48 ff., 190 ff.

deceive the rest of the world would be as misleading as to say that the Nazi foreign policy was simply a conventional method of blackmailing the appeasers. The very fact that a capitalist economy could be led into war in so noneconomic a fashion and mobilized fully only during the war itself (after 1941–42) proves the absolute primacy of the political goals. Here, too, Hitler was anything but an instrument of the capitalists. Their cooperation followed the same pattern found in the governmental and cultural policies: the cooperating experts and economists were instruments and objects, not originators, of this policy. Economic efficiency and primacy of politics, not capitalist, middle-class, or socialist doctrines, determined the course. As never under Socialist governments, the economy was controlled by the Government and subject to the subsidies, retrenchments, plans, and controls of the Nazi regime. The voice of special interests disappeared; assent and cooperation offered the only chance for success—a clearly lopsided alliance of economy and dictatorship, and Hitler, contrary to the predictions of both Right and Left, did not become either capitalism's captive or its servant.

Next to the middle class, agriculture had had the greatest expectations of the new government. And in fact, National Socialism held fast to the romantic-racist peasant ideology even after 1933, despite the enormous contradiction between an agrarian ideal of state and society and accelerated industrialization. Hitler's, and particularly Himmler's, visions of the future (one of Himmler's offices was the chairmanship of the League of German Agriculturists [Reichsbund Deutscher Diplomlandwirte]), saw the issue of *Lebensraum* essentially as a battle for the establishment of Germanic farm settlements in the East and de-urbanization in line with the "blood and soil" ideology. One of the many paradoxical consequences of Nazi rule is the fact that its policies and ultimate defeat brought the exact opposite: less space and more industrialization, yet greater economic progress than ever before. A cynic willing to ignore the victims might speak of the cunning of reason, by which a rule of horror with anachronistic goals accelerated the modernization of Germany.[4]

Ideological and political-economic motives intertwined. Rural life as the *völkisch*-racist "source" was held up as a model against urban civilization; expansion via settlement simultaneously was to serve as strategic protection against the "East." It was a rather revolutionary though romantic conception, extending from the pre-Nazi ideologists to the aims of the SS state and its repopulating policies. Germanic race policies, a European political economy, a "new aristocracy of blood and soil" (Darré)—these central ideas of a future German empire were part of the Nazi agrarian ideology. And yet, National Socialism was by no means a rural movement, even though it had profited from the large influx of rural voters in the years

---

[4] Cf. Ralf Dahrendorf, *Society and Democracy in Germany* (Garden City, N.Y., 1967), pp. 402 ff.

1930–33. Farmers were not too strongly represented in the party, and they were greatly underrepresented in the SS, so committed to future resettlement. In this area, just as in the program for the middle class, the difference between ideology and practical politics soon became apparent. But unlike the short-lived middle-class ideology, the party's agrarian ideology remained a political objective which, in close alliance with the politics of war and expansion, was destined to lend support to the Nazi reorganization of Europe.

Like the rest of the economy and industry, agriculture after the *Gleichschaltung* of its organizations was made subservient to the political objectives through market and price controls. The more far-reaching plans for reform, on the other hand, remained incipient. Neither the entailed farm laws, introduced with great fanfare, nor the fragmentary measures for lifting indebtedness, for redistribution, and for resettlement brought alleviation, let alone the reagrarianization of Germany. Contrary to the anti-urban propaganda, which at any rate conflicted with industrial mobilization, the population of the big cities and industrial centers continued to grow, particularly in those cities with strategic chemical industries; between 1933 and 1938, the populations of Magdeburg, Halle, Halberstadt, Dessau, Bitterfeld, and Bernburg more than doubled. And the population of the future "world capital city" Berlin, in megalomaniacal contradiction to the de-urbanization ideology, was even expected to reach 10 million.

In fact, many fewer new farms came into being in the Third Reich than in the Weimar Republic; the opening up of land for military and industrial purposes (not to mention highways) clearly had priority. In line with the autarchic goals, imports of agricultural products were reduced, and thanks to substantial subsidies, the farmers could count on firmer prices and better incomes. But in contrast to the wages and profits of industry, farm income did not keep step with the growth of national income after 1935. After a brief recovery spurt, the indebtedness of the small and medium-sized farms in particular continued to increase; technological improvements and mechanization made as little headway as their precondition—a far-reaching consolidation of landholdings—and the shortage of farm labor increasingly made itself felt. In profound contradiction to the romantic agrarian ideology, agriculture lagged far behind the general standard of living, bringing with it a movement to the cities, the sale of farms, and declining agricultural production. The much-bemoaned "flight from the land" set new records between 1933 and 1938; the exodus has been estimated at almost 1 million.[5] A magnanimous decree "for the support of the rural population" (July, 1938), granting greater agricultural subsidies and credits, also did not bring an increase in farm production; the decline of farming, a consequence of National Socialist economic and rearmament policies, continued. Not the highly touted settlement movement but the ideologically undesirable landholdings of the Junk-

[5] Josef Müller, *Deutsches Bauerntum zwischen gestern und morgen* (Würzburg, 1940), p. 8.

ers shaped agricultural life east of the Elbe, though there, too, the continuing pressure of political planning and decisions made itself felt. Instead of reversing the trend of the industrial era, the Nazi power and war policies accelerated it, and the failure of the expansion finally sealed it. In the agricultural sector, the Nazi regime was unable to solve the built-in problems which it had inherited from the German economic crises of 1918 and 1929. To be sure, the dynamization and mobilization of German society, its political regimentation and psychological orientation toward war, substantially furthered Nazi economic policies. The help proffered by "unpolitical" experts and interested parties in business and bureaucracy dazzled by feelings of superiority and short-range prospects of success proved invaluable.

The social aspects of the political revolution of 1933 initially were determined by a negative aim shared by Nazi leaders as well as followers: the rejection of the status quo and the chance to overhaul everything. The conservative-national partners believed that these changes were directed only against the democratic-republican establishment of Weimar. But the National Socialist thrust went much further. It was revolutionary not only in the utopia of the "people's community" but also in the reality of a changed elite structure and a pseudo-egalitarian leveling of all strata under the leader principle. The emergence of youth, social awareness, productive society—those were the battle cries of the "newcomers" against the old, outmoded "system." The Third Reich saw itself as a unique system, and its new order clamorously called on two groups—peasants and workers—above all others. This invocation was given immediate expression in the institutionalization of appropriate holidays and mass demonstrations at harvest festivals (the slogan: "Blood and Soil") and on the "Day of National Labor" (the slogan: "Workers of Brawn and Brain"). Here both the romantic, anti-urban and the pseudo-proletarian, technological elements of Nazi ideology asserted themselves; the two met in the military ideal, which through such slogans as "soldiers of labor" and "battle of labor" was integrated into civilian life and made part of the combative and leader principle. A verbal "social revolution" took place, and under its sign both the old anticapitalism and the diverse new body of supporters could be manipulated. "Bourgeois," "capitalist," "intellectual" continued to be terms of derision, synonyms for reactionary; the reviled past became the "bourgeois epoch."

But the profound changes in the relationship of state and economy and of labor and capital took place on another plane. The aim of the much-invoked socialism was not genuine socialization or expropriation but a change in the social consciousness, unconditional cooperation with the political regime, and the leadership's irrevocable right to encroach and control. The right to property, like all other civil rights, became a function of dedication to the new state,[6] and in this sense

[6] Ernst Rudolf Huber, "Die Rechtsstellung der Volksgenossen," in *Zeitschrift für die gesamte Staatswissenschaft*, No. 96 (1936), pp. 446 f.

"national socialism" and "good" capitalism were held to be not only compatible but practically identical. In contrast, Western capitalism was derided as plutocracy in the manner of the old anticapitalist slogans, just as "German socialism" was contrasted to Marxism and Soviet socialism. The basic concept underlying all *Gleichschaltung* and mobilization plans was that of the equality of all "national comrades" regardless of class, limited only by the politically determined function of the leader principle. In this respect, the Nazi system, particularly during the war, did in fact help to remove social barriers and in a way played a modernizing role. The persistent myth about the "good" aspects of National Socialism is based on this no less than on the technical achievements. At the time, this point proved a persuasive propaganda issue.

The National Socialist system like no other demonstrated the superior ability of an ideology, however vague, to shape minds, whatever the social reality. Now every German had to be socialistic in the sense of "social." The *Winterhilfe* (Winter Help) and countless other fundraising drives, national labor competitions and model plants, "Strength through Joy" and nationwide one-pot meals, a people's car for everyone, and finally the classless society of the Hitler Youth and party organizations, of the DAF and Labor Service—all these active manifestations of the "people's community" were undeniably effective, even though they were purposeful tools of control, coordination, and war mobilization and relied on more or less gentle coercion. Designations like "worker" or "entrepreneur" were no longer supposed to indicate class differences, only functions. Not status but principles allegedly mattered; the model was Adolf Hitler, the man of the people, who lived simply and turned down honorary doctorates.

The position of women in this "new" social system also remained paradoxical. As a decidedly male movement, National Socialism sought to contain the emancipation of woman and reduce her role to biological and familial functions. In line with the anti-urban, antimodernist ideology of National Socialism, this generally was understood to mean motherhood, housework, and at best "feminine" professions. Politics, at any rate, was not a suitable field for women. The task of the Nazi women's organization was to lead women back into the traditional realms of the specifically feminine, to their "natural" duties and rights. Thus, the first step in the effort to create jobs in 1933 was to ease out women from the labor market and the universities. The introduction of the so-called household year, marriage credits, and child bonuses was part of the anti-emancipation campaign. But with the growing labor shortage after 1935, the anachronism of these efforts became patently obvious, above all in regard to unmarried women. They were reabsorbed into the labor process and continued their impotent role in the labor market as during the Weimar Republic. In addition, labor service for women was expanded. At first (from 1936) voluntary, and later (from January, 1939) compulsory, women under twenty-five, except those in essential jobs, served one-year labor terms, allegedly to alleviate the labor shortage on the land and in the factories, but in reality in order to involve them fully in the mobilized economy. The number of working women in 1938 rose to 5.2 million, from 4.24 million in 1933 and 4.52 million in 1936.[7] An increasing number of women were employed in industry. Among women there also was a growing trend to leave farms and migrate to the cities. With the beginning of the war, the number of women in the universities also increased.

In one respect, however, Nazi ideology remained consistent: Women's opportunities for advancement were much smaller, and they were paid incomparably less than men for performing the same work. They were also poorly represented in the civil service, although the war brought some loosening there. But the original intention—the ousting of women from the modern labor process—was defeated by the consequences of progressive industrialization and social and economic mobilization. Woman's economic emancipation continued and even gained momentum in the course of the war. True, the political rights of women in the Third Reich were limited to plebiscitary assent, but that essentially was true of everyone. The undesired social by-products of modernization implicit in the Nazi war policies affected women as well as men. Thus, in its fashion, the totalitarian state contributed substantially to the social mobility and equality which wrought changes in the social structure.

The paradox which enabled Nazi legal and social theorists to hail the equality of all "national comrades" and simultaneously champion a sharply defined, military-aristocratic command structure was made possible above all by two major organizational tenets: the leader principle in place of electoral and majority decisions, and the battle or war community as the prototype of the new social order. Labor and military service as the training ground of a classless nation not only were to be the visible supports of militarization but also models of the inner uniformity and mobilization of the "people's community." The single act of rearmament hit two targets, and the war community was already being offered and prepared as an answer to the social problem. These factors contributed substantially to changing German society both organizationally and psychologically, even though in fact the basic structures of income distribution, capitalism, and bureaucratic autocracy remained. To the many thousands who before 1933 either had become unemployed or had never been employed at all, the loss of trade-union organizations and social freedom was, in the final analysis, less important than the fact that with Hitler came full employment, mobility, and opportunities for advancement—regardless of the methods or consequences. This argument proved effective then, as it still does today; it served to sustain a regime which the great majority of workers had opposed in 1933.

From 1935 on, all employed persons had to register in labor offices, were increasingly regimented, and, as "soldiers of labor," were subju-

[7] Gustav Stolper, *Deutsche Wirtschaft 1870–1940* (Stuttgart, 1950), p. 150.

gated to the needs of rearmament, yet the pseudo-military order ideology of the regime profited psychologically from this. Neither labor nor social policy improved measurably—Autobahns and rearmament gobbled up too much—but both were effectively manipulated and used. Political spectacles and Strength through Joy "care" provided for leisure-time activities; thus, in 1938, Ley was able to announce triumphantly that the private citizen had ceased to exist; only sleep was still a private affair, and no longer could anyone do or not do whatever he wanted.[8] It was a renunciation of freedom in favor of the semblance of social order, security, and unity. At what cost and with what results was another matter.

LEADER PRINCIPLE AND STATE

The Third Reich claimed to be a social, classless community of all Germans and at the same time a superior command structure girded for battle. The function of the leader principle lay in the blending of these two order concepts. It combined the political-charismatic combat idea of the "movement" with the bureaucratic-military order idea of the authoritarian state.

The leader principle followed a deeply ingrained German tradition, which, having survived the overthrow of the monarchic authoritarian state, lived on in the Presidential system of the Weimar Republic, in the "surrogate monarchy" of Hindenburg, in the militarized structures of the youth and combat organizations, in widespread antidemocratic thinking, and in the hierarchic ideas of bureaucracy and Army. The crises of 1923 and 1930 in particular had given new impetus to the demand for a strong man, recalling older ideas about the savior and healer in times of crises. The modern form of the leader concept was a synthesis of authoritarian, military ideas of order and pseudo-democratic–plebiscitary legitimation which, manipulated by mass propaganda, concentrated on the person of the charismatic leader.

German legal science rushed to present the Third Reich with an airtight theory of the leader state, beginning with works like Ernst Rudolf Huber's *Verfassungsrecht des (Gross-) Deutschen Reiches (Constitutional Law of the German Reich;* 1937 and 1939). The list of works in which the theory of the legal state was perverted into unrestrained justification of the leader dictatorship as the "true" legal state is a long one: Heinrich Lange, *Vom Gesetzessstaat zum Rechtsstaat (From State of Law to Legal State;* 1934); Otto Koellreuther, *Der deutsche Führerstaat (The German Leader State;* 1934); Herbert Krüger, *Führer und Führung (Leader and Leadership;* 1934); Reinhard Höhn, *Der Führerbegriff im Staatsrecht (The Führer Idea in Political Law;* 1935). These were supplemented by countless enthusiastic pronouncements on the theme of leadership and administration. The link between the state-military and political-charismatic leader

8 Robert Ley, *Soldaten der Arbeit* (Munich, 1938), p. 71.

ideas was documented, for example, in an essay by Wilhelm Sauer, a specialist in international law, entitled *"Recht und Volksmoral im Führerstaat"* ("Justice and People's Morality in the Leader State") in the *Archiv für Rechts- und Sozialphilosophie* (1935) or Ernst Forsthoff's *Totaler Staat* (1933): "The hierarchical order of the National Socialist state is characterized by the link of the National Socialist leadership order with the bureaucratic administrative apparatus." And: "The new and decisive aspect of the leader constitution is that it overcomes the difference between the governed and those who govern in the unity formed by the Führer and his following" (pp. 35–37).

From the vantage point of legal science, the substantiation of the total leader state occurred in two stages. By designating himself "Leader and Chancellor" (1934), Hitler not only laid claim to the constitutional powers of the two highest offices but at the same time also made reference to the pre- and extragovernmental, even supragovernmental, powers personified by the "Leader" as the carrier of the historic mission of National Socialism. Compared to mere governmental power, the powers of the Leader were "all-encompassing and total . . . exclusive and unlimited." [9] The "sacred oath" by which the Army promised its "unconditional obedience" when it acquiesced in the bloody elimination of the rival SA was sworn to Hitler the "Leader," not to the head of state or to the constitution. In the later years of the Third Reich, Hitler's official designation logically was reduced to the laconic and omnipotent "Führer." Hitler thereby had erased not only the Republican President but also the Bismarckian Chancellor. The leader constitution, whose precise provisions were left open, demonstrated the revolutionary break with constitutional history. At the same time, it was an expression of dictatorial omnipotence far greater than even that of the Fascist Duce (who had a king next to him). Hitler's was not a circumscribed, institutionally defined office; both in theory and practice, Hitler was the sole representative of the people on all levels of political and social life. He claimed to embody the total unity of that people, leaving no room for opposition or criticism. All expressions of the national will were to be his. No representation of different groups, interests, and ideas was allowed to exist alongside him; that would have been unthinkable, given the totalitarian fiction that the "correct" ideas of National Socialism and their perfect representative, the Leader, simultaneously represented and canceled out all special interests. In place of conflicts and compromise, there was to be only the absolute enemy on whom the sights of the unified nation were fixed.

It was a grandiose as well as violent fiction, one ignoring the essence of man and of human relationships: "The Führer speaks and acts not only for the people and in their behalf, but as the people. In him, the German people shape their fate." [10] Being the sole representative and

---

[9] Ernst Rudolf Huber, *Verfassungsrecht des Grossdeutschen Reiches* (Hamburg, 1939), pp. 213, 320.
[10] Gottfried Neesse, *Führergewalt* (Tübingen, 1940), p. 54.

the personification of the people, this leader could act above all intermediate offices and his will alone counted; he could follow official norms, but he did not have to, because "the will of the leadership, regardless of the form in which it is expressed . . . makes for right and changes hitherto valid laws." [11] The Leader alone embodied the *volonté générale* by virtue of the self-granted authority from above and the consequent guided acclamation from below. He led the people out of the confusion of everyday life to the conscious awareness of his mission; he was in possession of salvation; he acted in agreement with the objective laws of national life.[12] The plebiscites that were staged had no binding effect, no power of decision over the actions of the Leader; they were nothing but an a posteriori demonstration of the presumed unity. The constitution of the Third Reich exhausted itself in the mystical agreement of Leader and nation. This theory of the National Socialist leader state, in many respects resembling the glorification of Stalin, reached heights of dithyrambic, pseudo-religious Leader deification which reality could live up to only inadequately. The task to be done was to educate a still imperfect people to acceptance, assent, and unconditional obedience. This required, in addition to the old, unconditionally loyal leadership corps, a new elite able to superimpose the validity of the leader principle on all sectors of German life.

The National Socialist leader principle determined the radical consequences of totalitarian rule not only internally but also toward the outside. It was based on the belief that the (German) people were essentially incapable of self-government. In place of self-government, there was by virtue of his own, sole "correct" will only one free will—that of the Leader. He could delegate power to aides, but they were and remained his unconditional subjects. He was always in complete control of the orders which they enforced: Germany was turned into a garrison state. At the same time, the absolute subjugation to the leader principle made possible the push beyond the borders. The forces pent up in the quasi-military Führer and coercive state found a surrogate for their urge to move, a reason for their subjugation, a chance of becoming themselves leaders and wielders of power in the promulgation of race policies, in imperial expansion, and in the exploitation of "inferior" peoples. The oppressed became oppressors, the subjugated became the master race which, though unable and not allowed to govern itself, could govern others. The solution to the problem of freedom and control posed by the leader theory of National Socialism thus lay in the diversion to the outside of the natural need for political growth and freedom. Racial and political persecution and war became the psychological safety valves and tools of self-affirmation, expansion, and social imperialism, the substitutes for internal reform and self-fulfillment. It is at this point that the National Socialist leader constitution and its war policies are most closely linked; the correlation became more and more

[11] Werner Best, *Die deutsche Polizei* (2d ed.; Darmstadt, 1941).
[12] Huber, *Verfassungsrecht des Grossdeutschen Reiches*, pp. 194 f.

pronounced with the intensification of totalitarian rule during the war.

There is no doubt that, in contrast to the Communist dictatorship, Nazi totalitarianism lived and died with the Leader and the leader principle. And in political practice, the unlimited power of the regime also rested on the absolute authority of the Leader. That was true of all three sectors in which the power and authority of the Third Reich were rooted: the monopoly party, which was to furnish "leadership"; the Army, which was to provide "defense"; the state, which was to be in charge of "administration." [13] The Führer controlled all three. Just as he had sole and unlimited control over the party, he also quite early gained control over the state (1934) and the Army (1938). The picture was the same in areas where the power of the Führer was not defined institutionally but politically and ideologically, where Hitler was bombastically celebrated as the "representative of the people, guardian of the Weltanschauung, protector of the Reich, first lawmaker of the Reich, and supreme judge of the nation," as the "first guardian of the people." [14]

Let us examine the effects of the leader principle first on the machinery of government and then on the monopoly party. In the party, the leader principle had formed the real foundation of Hitler's strength long before 1933. The fact that there were relatively few "purges" and no serious rebellions also marks the difference between the Nazi and the Soviet dictatorship, which, though it knew personality cult and one-man rule, institutionalized the party principle in place of the leader principle. Even when, at the end of the war, Göring and Himmler sought to save their skins, they did not attempt to rebel against Hitler; the structure of the leader dictatorship remained firm.

The position of the Leader vis-à-vis the Army was basically decided in 1934, when Hitler replaced Hindenburg as commander in chief. The Army, it is true, was able to ward off party encroachment much more effectively than the governmental bureaucracy, yet the reorganization of February 4, 1938, also gave the Führer formal jurisdiction over the War Ministry, and with the dismissal of Field Marshal von Brauchitsch during the Russian crisis (December 21, 1941), Hitler finally assumed direct command of the Army and its top echelons.

In the governmental bureaucracy, the application of the leader principle was somewhat more complicated. Here it found itself competing with the principle of administrative hierarchy. At the same time, however, members of the civil service were subjugated to the Führer by a personal loyalty oath and by close surveillance. The first step in this direction was the passage of the Civil Service Law (April, 1933), and the peak was reached in the Reichstag speech of April 26, 1942, in which Hitler, to enthusiastic applause, proclaimed his "legal" right to demand the resignation or dismissal of anyone who in his opinion failed to do his duty—without regard of person or his "well-earned

[13] Hans Frank, *Recht und Verwaltung* (Munich, 1939), p. 16.
[14] Neesse, *op. cit.*, p. 55.

rights." The National Socialist defenders of civil-service rights fighting for re-employment and benefits after 1945 forgot all too quickly that it was Hitler who pulled the rug out from under their claim to the right for tenured employment.

The leader principle was also employed as needed in foreign policy: in the promulgation of Hitler's surprise coups as in the unleashing of the war. The Führer alone could at will decide on the appointment of diplomats, on negotiations and alliances, on the breaking-off of diplomatic relations, on interventions and sanctions, on war and peace. In all matters, so declared a scholar in constitutional law, the "personal decision of the Führer" was what counted.[15] Accomplished facts were, if this served propaganda purposes, retroactively approved by the Reichstag: that happened after the attacks on Poland and on the many neutral states—Denmark, Norway, Holland, Belgium, Luxembourg, Yugoslavia, and Greece—overrun in 1940–41. Similarly, the fateful attack on the Soviet ally was a "personal decision of the Führer" retroactively sanctioned by the Reichstag.

Above all, legislation in the broadest sense was under the complete control of Hitler. Neither the ministries nor the Cabinet, neither the states nor the administrative courts, could act against his dictum. The ludicrous extension of the Enabling Act that preserved a faint aura of legality in the realm of legislation had in effect become quite superfluous. For, outside these remnants of the legal state, there stood the naked "right" of the Führer to issue orders and commands at will. Even his speeches were considered as binding sources of legislation and had the force of law when deemed expedient.

The Führer was also the "supreme judge" of the nation, as he had told an approving Reichstag and was applauded by legal scholars after the bloodbath of June 30, 1934. Judges and civil servants rendered loyalty oaths to him, and ultimately he assumed the power to dismiss any judge who passed sentences he thought too lenient or who failed to administer the law in accordance with National Socialist beliefs and interests. This power, enthusiastically confirmed by the Reichstag on April 26, 1942, destroyed an independent judiciary and revealed the façade of the dual state for what it was: a transitory, tactical concession. Instances of illegal transfers to concentration camps, even after acquittal by courts, multiplied; political interference in court proceedings became more and more frequent. The trials of the People's Courts and their predetermined outcomes were merely a final consequence of the subservience of law to the omnipotence of the leader principle. If, for example, the case of the graphic artist Erich Knauf was a matter of the personal vindictiveness of Goebbels, who felt insulted by a critical remark of Knauf's and persuaded Judge Freisler to pass a death sentence, it also was evidence of the total power wielded even by second-level leaders.[15a]

The pertinent organizational definitions of the powers of the leader

[15a] Cf. Leber, Brandt, Bracher, *Conscience in Revolt* (London, 1957), pp. 52 ff.

were in inverse relationship to their boundless applicability. During the seizure of power, they had become the basis of the system of rule, and for that very reason were insolubly connected with the person of Hitler. This was bound to create problems relating to the very real question of succession. The National Socialist system undoubtedly wanted to be more than the temporary rule of Hitler. It laid claim to the finality of the "Thousand-Year Reich" and wanted to have its "eternal" existence taken seriously. But all preparations for a succession invariably posed the question of whether efforts simply to change the person were not doomed to failure in view of the amorphous nature of the leader principle and its peculiar commixture with Hitler's career. The naming of Göring as Hitler's first successor and Hess as his second, in a speech delivered by Hitler after the unleashing of the war, was little more than a dramatic gesture. A "senate" which was to clarify the further succession was never formed. Hess dropped out of the race, and at the end of the war Göring's feeble attempt to take power also failed. Hitler himself nipped in the bud any possibility of Diadochian battles between such "strong men" as Goebbels and Himmler by his surprising decision of April, 1945, to reinstitute the leadership structure of 1933 and hand over the office of Reich President to a military man.

The Third Reich thereby was declared to be merely a transitional stage, and for the last time the extent to which the party, the political power structure, Himmler's SS state, as well as the leader principle and the total leader state were dependent on and linked to Hitler was clearly demonstrated. Without Hitler, this leader state lacked institutional continuity and binding force. Consequently, the efforts to install Admiral Dönitz as "Reich President" by appointment of the Führer and to accept him as the pillar of the continuity of the state were in vain. Even if the state bureaucracy believed in the continuity of its offices, Hitler's death indisputably put an end to the top office of the leader state. This rupture defined the unbridgeable gap between the total leader state and a democratic state of law and also delimits the theories of continuity so eagerly advanced by adaptable German legalists of the post-Hitler era.

If one turns from the rarified heights of Hitler's unlimited powers to the manifestations of the leader principle in the organizations of political and social life, the initial impression of a perfect monolithic order crumbles. In theory, the leader principle was supposed to govern the extension of total power to the lower levels. But the confusing multitude of leaders had to lead to bitter jurisdictional and power struggles. Once the enemy—parliamentary and democratic institutions—had been removed, the conflicts between political leader principle and governmental hierarchy broke out anew. The radical inroads were also felt in the 51,000 municipal administrations. A new municipal regulation of January 30, 1935, abolished self-administration in favor of the leader principle; mayors as the solely responsible and governing "leaders" of their community now were appointed from above. But at

their side stood the local party leader as deputy of the National Socialist leadership: The dualism of state and party was present on this level
as well.

The confusion and conflict of leadership and administrative hierarchy
was further complicated by the wide proliferation of leadership positions. The machinery of both party and state had to be expanded if the
all-encompassing supervisory functions of the totalitarian system were
to be carried out. The alleged inefficiency and corruption of the Weimar democracy were as nothing compared to the costly expansion of
the one-party state and the antagonistic coexistence of overlapping
top-level bodies. So long as the Führer did not interfere—and he gave
free rein to the policy of divide and conquer—nothing could stop this.
On the contrary. Over the years, Hitler, in the consolidation of his
leader dictatorship, created a vast special bureaucracy which in turn
had to collide with the "normal" agencies. Three offices were at his personal disposal: the Reich Chancellery, which in effect replaced the
Cabinet and whose chief, Hans Lammers, held ministerial rank; the
Presidential Chancellery, which under the eternally flexible Meissner
also was part of the structure of the leader state; and, finally, the
Führer Chancellery under Martin Bormann, who was in charge of
party affairs, and who, as a result of the shifting relationship of party
and state, exerted increasing influence on all aspects of Hitler's rule.

Parallel to these offices, numerous ad hoc special deputies set up their
own leadership staffs. Thus in 1936, Göring, as head of the Four-Year
Plan, was put above the ministers and specialists of the arms and war
production agencies, now reduced to executive functions. Aside from
the ministries and the Cabinet, supreme Reich offices had been created
which encroached on the jurisdictions of other bodies, fought for controlling powers, and issued orders over the heads of other agencies—as,
for example, the Inspector of Roads (Fritz Todt) and the Reich Youth
Leader, who imposed his educational reform campaigns on the cultural agencies. These supreme offices were directly under the Führer,
as were the Central Agencies of the Reich Administration. One such office
was the Reich Commissar for the Consolidation of the German Nation,
who on October 7, 1939, was charged by Hitler with initiating policies
for resettlement in the East, over the heads of numerous other agencies.
In the hands of Himmler, this turned into an instrument of Germanization, looting, and extermination. On the other hand, a Reich Commissar for Public Housing, appointed in 1940, was to open up visions
of a beautiful postwar world filled with lovely houses. On the same
plane was the appointment in 1937 of a General Building Inspector for
Berlin to plan the grandiose remodeling of the future "world capital
city." Hitler himself contributed megalomaniacal, imitative designs of

---

[16] Joachim C. Fest, *The Face of the Third Reich* (London and New York,
1970), p. 202; cf. also Gregor Janssen, *Das Ministerium Speer: Die deutsche
Rüstung im Krieg* (Berlin, 1968), and Albert Speer, *Inside the Third Reich:
Memoirs* (New York, 1970), pp. 132 ff.

"insane monumentality" [16] to this project, such as a 1,000-foot high people's assembly chamber with a seating capacity of 100,000.

Among the tasks of this office, at which Albert Speer, then a young architect, began his rapid rise as Hitler's protégé, was the construction of gigantic stadia in Nuremberg, the city of the Reich party congresses, and the artistic redevelopment of Linz, the city of the Führer's youth. With a dictator's certainty of his role in history, Hitler, in one of his bombastic "art addresses" at the party congress of 1937, called the former project the "imperishable confirmation" of the power of the Third Reich: "Therefore these edifices are designed not for the year 1940, and also not for the year 2000, but shall tower like the spires of our past into the millenniums of the future." [17] Only a few fragments still remained in 1945 as testimony to this nonstyle of pseudo-antique form, ponderous excess, and solemn emptiness. Speaking at the ceremonial laying of the foundation stone of the Nuremberg Assembly Hall, Hitler made clear the reasons for this project: "But if this movement should ever fall silent, then this witness here will still speak after millenniums. Amid a holy grove of ancient oaks, people will gaze at this first giant among the buildings of the Third Reich in awesome wonder." Hitler reputedly even had a sketch prepared showing what the building would look like as a weathered ruin,[18] and said that the "concrete mass and stone colossi which I am erecting here" were greater than the pyramids: "I am building for all eternity." And in a mood of Götterdämmerung, he added: "We are the last Germany. If we should ever go down, then there will no longer be a Germany." [19] Hitler's building mania already showed that identification of his fate with that of Germany which was to dominate the final stages of the Third Reich.

The leader principle also made itself felt, particularly during the war, in the roles of a multitude of additional top agencies that superseded the traditional machinery of government. The German Central Bank, for example, lost its independence when the arms program had to be financed, and in 1939 it, too, was put directly under Hitler. The special position of the "representatives of Reich sovereignty" in the occupied countries rested solely on the Führer. For example, the official in Prague's Hradschin Palace who governed Bohemia and Moravia held the euphemistic title "Reich Protector." The first Protector was Neurath, who had been ousted from the Foreign Office and like Papen let himself be used; he was succeeded by Heydrich (1941–42) and then by Police General Daluege. There was also the Governor General of rump Poland, Hans Frank, who, holding court in the castle of Cracow, administered the barbaric Jewish and Polish policies, though in endless conflict with the SS offices. The governments of other occupied countries were also directly under the Führer, even though, unlike

[17] *Kongressbericht* (Munich, 1936), p. 78.
[18] Walter Görlitz and Herbert A. Quint, *Adolf Hitler* (Stuttgart, 1952), p. 476.
[19] Frank, *Im Angesicht des Galgens* (Munich, 1953), p. 312.

Czechoslovakia and Poland, those countries were never fully under German legal and administrative jurisdiction, at least not formally.

Within the framework of the leader state, the monopoly party officially embodied the connection between Leader and people. The division of party and state remained, except in the person of the Führer, who combined the two. The party auxiliaries continued to be built up and institutionalized; they extended into all areas of social life. In addition, the party's special departments continued, frequently in uneasy coexistence with the governmental departments, even though they never built up a comparable hierarchical structure, and a party cabinet comparable to the Soviet Politburo was out of the question in view of the leader principle. Structured according to the leader principle, the party formed a tight net of office holders, of political "chiefs": block chiefs, cell chiefs, local chiefs, district chiefs, regional chiefs (Gauleiter). Up to 1938, there were thirty-eight regions; in the course of the war, the "Greater German" regions of Austria, Czechoslovakia, Poland, and Alsace-Lorraine were added, making a total of forty-five. The Gauleiter, the old guard of the party, were to gain special importance during the war, when they were given administrative and policy-making powers and finally were made Defense Commissars for their regions.

The determined independence of the monopoly party found expression not only in the development of a separate party judiciary but even more so in the prohibition of any criticism of the party, in the legal protection of its symbols, and in the secrecy surrounding its activities. And although the NSDAP was the state party, its finances were not under state control. In line with the leader principle, the millions of marks in membership dues, the collections and contributions, and the party's vast assets were outside public supervision or control. In this respect, too, the dictatorial "order" offered an opportunity for corruption far greater than anything possible under the "bossism" of the democracy.

The interlocking of party and government leadership was complex yet incomplete. Beginning with Hitler, there was a system of interlocking party and state positions, as for example in the dual functions of Goebbels, Hess, Himmler, Rust (also Gauleiter of Brunswick), Ley, Schirach, Bohle (AO and Foreign Office), and a number of Gauleiter who simultaneously held high party and governmental positions. This led to fresh conflicts with rival party officials in high government posts who were part of the old governmental and administrative hierarchy. But whereas the "unity of party and state" was never fully realized in the ministries, the interrelation was strong in the cities and municipalities. This is where a great many party veterans installed themselves in administrative posts. In 1935, they held almost 50 per cent of all municipal administrative positions and almost 30 per cent of all district offices. Thirty-one per cent of all party district leaders and 19 per cent of all local leaders were in national or communal executive positions, while the cell and block leaders were left out in the cold (only 2.5 per cent held official posts). And almost 60 per cent of those district leaders in official positions were mayors of cities; the local leaders were mayors of smaller towns.[20] Meanwhile, the size of the leader corps grew irresistibly. In 1935, there were 33 regional leaders, 827 district leaders, approximately 21,000 local leaders, and about 260,000 cell and block leaders. By 1937, the total number of political leaders had grown to more than 700,000; in addition, there were the vast number of auxiliaries and subsidiary organizations through which the party encompassed the social and professional life of the country. During the war, the total number of leader positions was around 2 million. Germany had become a nation of leaders. Although all had to obey, many could at least also give orders somewhere, could share in the leader principle: a gigantic *Obrigkeitsstaat* under a charismatic flag.

And indeed, the vast supportive apparatus of the political leader principle continued to edge closer to the machinery of state both on the personnel and organizational level. The new crop of civil servants almost in its entirety was at least nominally committed to the party; education, examinations, training programs, and advancement were increasingly made dependent on party or Hitler Youth membership, on party recommendation and years of membership. This meant that civil servants and judges more and more found themselves subject to the authority of party leaders of backgrounds very different from theirs. State and party hierarchy were rivals; there were extreme cases in which, by virtue of the leader principle, a subordinate would issue orders to his superior. Party comrades moved into the personnel offices of the administration, and conversely, expulsion from the party generally also meant dismissal from one's job. The Civil Service Law of January 26, 1937, gave the Leader the right to dismiss tenured employees whose loyalty was doubted by the party. An employee moreover also had to report anything whether on the job or outside that in his opinion might possibly be injurious to the party and National Socialism. He was, in effect, being turned into a potential Gestapo agent. However, though party affiliation of high-ranking employees was thought desirable, Hitler himself did not deem it an absolute prerequisite for advancement.[21] But given the combination of pressure and opportunism, the initial forbearance shown the bureaucracy gave way to the penetration of the administration by the party, at least nominally; continuing adaptation and expansion served to accelerate this process. As early as 1937, 86 per cent of all civil servants in Prussia, and 63 per cent in the rest of the country, belonged to the NSDAP, but of these, only 48 per cent in Prussia and 11 per cent in the rest of the country were old members. The percentage of civil servants in the NSDAP rose from 6.7 per cent before 1933 to 29 per cent by 1935.[22]

---

[20] Wolfgang Schäfer, *NSDAP, Entwicklung und Struktur der Staatspartei des Dritten Reiches* (Hanover, 1956), pp. 26 ff. Cf. also Peter Hüttenberger, *Die Gauleiter* (Stuttgart, 1969), pp. 75 ff.

[21] Schoenbaum, *op. cit.*, p. 225.

[22] Hans Gerth, "The Nazi Party," *American Journal of Sociology*, XLV (1940), 534 ff.; Karl Dietrich Bracher, Wolfgang Sauer, and Gerhard Schulz, *Die nationalsozialistische Machtergreifung* (2d ed.; Cologne-Opladen, 1962), pp. 509 ff.

Thus in the bureaucratic sector too, Nazification followed rather than preceded the seizure of power. The most rapid strides were made in Göring's Prussia and in the municipal and provincial administrations. But the top civil service, particularly in the Interior, Education, Agriculture, Justice, and, of course, in the new Propaganda and Air Ministries, was under great pressure. In addition, there were the many quasi–civil-service positions created by the party for the functionaries of its auxiliaries. For all these reasons, the tautening of the administrative structure, a reform clamorously advocated before 1933 as a vital necessity justifying dictatorship, was of course out of the question. Like state reform, it remained mired in political proclamations and maneuvers. And like the party, the state under the leader dictatorship did not become less costly; on the contrary, it became immeasurably more expensive, even before the regime gambled everything away during the war. The cost of government, with the able assistance of rearmament and party patronage, rose astronomically. Between 1934 and 1939, the budget of the ministries increased by 170 per cent overall, according to the degree of their involvement in rearmament and police-state surveillance and their closeness to the party. In view of their many new functions, the Justice and the Interior Ministries were way out front, followed by those involved in some aspect of remilitarization; the Foreign Office, whose powers had been so sharply curtailed, limped far behind. Yet the salary cuts made in Brüning's time were not restored; the increases were the result entirely of vast personnel expansion. The party, on the other hand, paid its employees an additional month's salary at Christmas time. As early as 1935, the Munich party headquarters alone employed 1,600 persons, housed in 44 buildings, and the national party 25,000, according to the proud proclamation of the national treasurer, Franz Schwarz.[23] In the meantime, beyond the unresolved dualism of party and state, a separate apparatus, one which was destined to become the true embodiment of the radical consequences of Nazi rule, was being formed: the SS state.

TOTALITARIAN TERROR: THE RISE OF THE SS STATE

The omnipotent power of the Führer, abrogating all state and legal norms and sanctioning all deeds, was the basic law of the Third Reich. The creation of the system of terror and extermination and the functioning of the police and SS apparatchiks operating that system rested on this overturning of all legal and moral norms by a totalitarian leader principle which did not tolerate adherence to laws, penal code, or constitution but reserved to itself complete freedom of action and decision-making: Political power was merely the executive of the Leader's will.

It would be misleading and simply echo the self-delusion of the state bureaucracy to dismiss the "regular" legislation of the regime as a lesser evil and perhaps to see the Nuremberg Laws and the pseudo-legal

[23] *Völkischer Beobachter*, February, 27, 1935.

commentary by jurists like Stuckart and Globke as freaks in the "non-official terrorism," [24] for in fact not only do the reasons for these laws defy belief, but they helped to supply the legitimation which even a totalitarian regime, for tactical reasons, cannot do without. A factor lending support to the many illusions of the population and the civil service, and one that played so disastrous a role in lulling their misgivings was, to a considerable degree, the meshing of the two sectors, the camouflage and screening of the terror and violence by formal state-juridical measures. This was the nature and function of the "dual state," in which norms of justice and law continued outwardly to exist but were subject to rescision and assigned the function of serving as the façade for the unrestricted "measures" of the total powers of the Leader.

The Reichstag fire decree of February 28, 1933, which furnished the pseudo-legal basis for the state of emergency, was not the "temporary" provision intended by the much-abused Article 48 of the Weimar Constitution; rather, it was in force throughout the life of the Third Reich and was the first opening for the extralegal policy of coercion and terror. It made possible the circumvention of the courts and the state bureaucracy and the building up of a separate bureaucracy of terror. This is the area in which the revolution actually took place, not in the changes of the traditional machinery of state; only in the build-up and encroachment of the police and SS state did the leader dictatorship prove to be a truly revolutionary system of rule. This new power alongside and outside the state has been called the "Führer executive": "To this machine were allotted all those political tasks in which Hitler was really interested; in particular the preservation of his own power, demographic policy, the policy for the occupation of conquered territory, persecution of all actual and supposed opponents of the regime." [25] The Gestapo became the institutional basis of this innermost reality of the Third Reich; the further institutional expansion was borne by the SS, which as the elite formation developed the multifarious structure of a separate state. Its beginnings go back to the "fighting years." Formed in 1925 as Hitler's personal guard, the SS was not in the tradition of combat groups like the SA, even if after 1926 it was under SA command. It saw itself as the heart of the NSDAP, as a sort of party police, and after 1931, Heydrich, in close association with Himmler, did in fact build up the Security Service (Sicherheitsdienst, or SD) as a secret police control organ of the NSDAP. In the seizure of power itself, SS Special Commandos acted as quasi police special guards and "security groups," from which came the later "Ordinance Troop" (Verfügungstruppe) and the Waffen SS (Armed SS). But the SS became a Führer executive in the true sense after it amalgamated

[24] Thus Hans Buchheim in his otherwise basic essay "The SS—Instrument of Domination," in *Anatomy of the SS State* (New York, 1968), p. 132. On the genesis of these "laws," see Bracher, Sauer, and Schulz, *op. cit.*, pp. 286 ff.

[25] Buchheim, *op. cit.*, pp. 139–140.

with the political police. Within that framework, it was possible to circumvent, and through surveillance put pressure on, the "normal" pillars of justice and administration through secret and special authorizations.

As early as March, 1933, Göring had put the old political police of Prussia under the chief of the police group of the Ministry of the Interior, Rudolf Diels, and given it broader powers; at the end of April, he formed the Gestapo in Berlin and set up Gestapo bases and "directorates" throughout the country. More and more, the Gestapo was made independent of the Prussian administration, while remaining under the jurisdiction solely of Göring. The other opening was in Bavaria. There Himmler, as Police President of Munich, together with his SD chief, Heydrich, managed to gain a foothold on March 9, 1933, the day of Bavaria's *Gleichschaltung;* a week later, Himmler was given control over the entire political police of Bavaria. Within months, he had gained control over the political police in all German states; only in Prussia was he still formally subordinate to Göring. The personal union of the now centralized Gestapo and Himmler's SS, formally independent since 1934, formed the power base of the SS state. Though the jurisdictional conflicts with the state administration continued for years, particularly in Prussia, the Gestapo was officially authorized "to root out and fight all pernicious efforts throughout the country," and its activities were not subject to court review.[26] The leading Gestapo lawyer, Werner Best, made the lapidary observation that the "division between the Secret State Police acting according to special principles and requirements and the administration working according to general and uniform legal regulations is hereby completed." [27]

This development was topped off by investing the Reichsführer SS with the newly created office of Chief of the German Police through a Führer decree of June 17, 1936. It meant the centralization of the entire police, which hitherto had been under the jurisdiction of the individual states, and at the same time the transfer of the police from administrative to SS control. The misuse of Article 48 (state of emergency and *Gleichschaltung* of the Länder), the snuffing out of the sovereignty of the German states (law of January 30, 1934), and the "centralization" (*Verreichlichung* was the technical term used)—all against the will of the Interior Ministry—resulted in the independence of the domestic terror machinery, which found institutionalized expression in Himmler's official titles: Reichsführer SS and Chef der deutschen Polizei (Chief of the German Police); in the jargon of the Third Reich, these were known respectively as RFSS and ChdDtPol. Himmler's subordination to Minister of the Interior Frick was a purely formal one, for in practice he was given Cabinet rank and himself claimed some of the powers of the Interior Ministry, and this long before his powerful position and the pre-eminence of the SS was formalized with

[26] Law of February 10, 1936, Paragraphs 1 and 7.
[27] *Deutsches Recht,* April 15, 1936, pp. 127 ff.

his taking over the Ministry and the entire administration (1943). Moreover, Himmler declined to become part of the civil-service structure. His conflicts with Frick showed quite early that not only was he independent, but by virtue of his close contact as Supreme SS Chief with Hitler himself, he was the stronger man in the Interior Ministry.

The personal union of SS and police control more and more turned into an actual union of leader powers and official position, consolidated by SS and police personnel. In June, 1936, Himmler ordered the division of the police into two main departments: the Order Police (Ordnungspolizei) under Daluege (as general of police), and the Security Police (Sicherheitspolizei) under Heydrich, who as SS Group Leader also continued as chief of the Security Service of the SS in charge of intelligence and ideological control. The fact that the criminal police as well became part of the Gestapo was also of major consequence. The divisions, beginning in 1938, of the political police within the framework of this "Main Office Security Police" give an inkling of the extent of surveillance and the scope of the groups whose persecution and extirpation was the purpose of the apparatus: II-A—Communism and other Marxist groups; II-B—churches, sects, émigrés, Jews, camps; II-C—reaction, opposition, Austrian affairs; II-D—protective custody, concentration camps; II-E—economic, agrarian, and sociopolitical affairs, and organizations; II-G—supervision of broadcasting; II-H—party affairs, groupings, and auxiliary organizations; II-J—foreign political police; II-Ber.—situation reports; II-P—press; II-S—fight against homosexuality and abortion (as a political task!); III—intelligence. Beyond this, a separate "political administration" alongside and above the state administration was built up. In the background there was a triple goal: SS departments for all political areas and the complete integration of the police into the SS and SS army, resulting in a ruling system with its own bureaucracy and coercive apparatus, with the police as the most important wedge. The subsequent division of the SS into three main pillars—General SS, Waffen SS, and police—was in line with this objective.

The process was formalized decisively when, shortly after the beginning of the war (September 27, 1939), Security Police and SD were coordinated in the Reich Security Office (Reichssicherheitshauptamt, or RSHA), thereby institutionalizing the personal union under Heydrich. In addition to the Political Police (under Heinrich Müller) and the Criminal Police (under Arthur Nebe), the RSHA among others also took over the SD offices for "enemy research" under Professor Franz Six (later "Ideological Research and Evaluation"), for "German Living Areas" (Otto Ohlendorf), and Foreign Intelligence (Heinz Jost). In the course of wartime expansion, the RSHA as the central agency of the SS state not only grew enormously but was repeatedly reorganized. First a "Greater German Areas of Influence" department was set up, and later departments for occupation and extermination policies, which were divided into "subjects" areas like Left and Right opposition, anti-sabotage work, anti-espionage, Jews and churches, special tasks, and protective custody. It was both vital and typical that this superagency could, as needed, appear in the guise of governmental, police, or SS agency; this made possible both tactical camouflage as well as the mobility required by the terror and extermination measures and policies of the metastate. Here as well as in the area of government, traditional structures and names lived on in the service of a purely formal legalization, which could be rescinded or changed at will and which, moreover, reality had long since made obsolete.

The giant apparatus was tested outside Germany for the first time in the occupation of Austria and Czechoslovakia. Here the SD and Gestapo Einsatzstab and Einsatzgruppe (special staffs and commandos) for the "safeguarding of political life," which were to play so crucial a role in the occupation and annihilation policies of the future, made their debut. Their appearance in the wake of the Army, a blueprint for the terror of the Einsatz commandos during the war, was quite openly described in the *Völkische Beobachter* of October 10, 1938: "At the same time, the men of the Secret Police within the Security Police, in close cooperation with the advancing Army units, immediately set about to purge the liberated territories of Marxist traitors and other enemies of the state." The procedure was also followed in the preparation of the Polish campaign. Each Army was supplemented with an Einsatz commando wearing the battle dress of the SS disposal troops, to "fight all anti-Reich and anti-German elements in the rear of the fighting troops." Thus by the time the war was started, the new power had been fully established. The second stage in the realization of an untrammeled will to rule now began, domestically as well as in other lands.

The development of the nucleus of a political administration from the police was a presupposition for the rise of the SS state. As early as 1937, Himmler quite officially—in a *Festschrift* for the sixty-year-old Frick, who presumably was a major victim of this move—had given the political police the task of *creating*, not merely of safeguarding, the new political order. And simultaneously he stressed that this independent activity, beyond any law and unfettered by formal restraints, would be carried out "only on orders of the leadership." This meant that in the political area, control lay not in the state bureaucracy but in the hands of the SS police, as the instrument of the will of the Führer and unhampered by law. Police power became political power, its protective role was transformed into a "positive" claim to make policy beyond the "legitimate" state power. Behind the pseudo-legal disguise, police power represented the permanent revolution; it no longer had to act in accordance with laws and decrees but instead based its actions on the "over-all mission allotted to the German police in general and the Gestapo in particular in connection with the reconstruction of the National Socialist State." [28] In the tactical application of this principle, one could, of course, whenever it was deemed opportune, fall back on legitimacy. "In principle," however, this was su-

[28] Decree of the RSHA of April 15, 1940, in Buchheim, *op. cit.*, p. 190.

perfluous: "Only in those cases in which it appears desirable that state police orders be given the protection of the penal code should the decree of February 28, 1933, be invoked." So even the Reichstag fire decree, pseudo-legal at best, was no longer essential.

Long before the primacy claim of the SS police state could be fully instituted and implemented in war and occupation, it was being substantiated in a stream of declarations and measures. On October 1, 1936, Himmler, addressing the German Law Academy, had this to say about the building up of police powers: "We National Socialists then . . . went to work not without right, which we carried within us, but, however, without laws." Führer orders as well as court decisions confirmed the right claimed by the Gestapo, or the RFSS and ChdDtPol, respectively, to act unfettered by legal restraints. The political "total assignment" justified any measure and any move to interfere with or supersede the state administration. Once the indefinite, elastic, and pervertible principle of "prevention" was substituted for the protective role of the police, all possible limits to the total claim to the right of surveillance, persecution, and extermination of potential enemies were removed; this was true even more of the so-called "positive" measures of National Socialist policies which rested on this terror. Even so passionate a National Socialist as Hans Frank had to recognize the complete arbitrariness of the police state in 1942, in which "any citizen can be consigned to a concentration camp for any length of time without any possibility of redress," the result of a "judiciary . . . almost completely dominated by the police machine." [29]

The revolutionary and totalitarian ruling claim of the Nazi regime was a constant presence in the apparatus and methods of the SS police state. As significant as the continuity of pseudo-legal structures and the chaotic rivalries of the Third Reich may be in an evaluation of the system, it was undeniably revolutionary and totalitarian insofar as that "second state" reversed all former concepts of order and value and at the same time laid claim to the total control of man and the reshaping of his functions in the service of the new order. (To what extent this definition also applies to other pseudo-legal revolutions of the twentieth century and to other terrorist one-party regimes should be made the subject of more probing studies of the fascist and Bolshevik systems.) The National Socialist regime was totalitarian not only in its ideological claim of the omnipotent leader dictatorship, but also in the reality of its terror system. And this was the decisive characteristic: that a police power having become SS rule and enjoying unlimited discretionary powers could take "preventive" action also against persons who at most were suspected of possible opposition or infractions. We are dealing here not "only" with the external coercive measures of a dictatorship, but with the creation of ideological and racial policing powers that encroach on every aspect of human life. The establishment of concentration camps, instruments of both re-education and terror, and their development

[29] Memorandum of August 28, 1942, in *ibid.*, p. 199.

into pillars of mass arrests and mass extermination were simply consequences of this totalitarian authority. It went considerably beyond
that of the Stalinist system of the 1930's.

In the opinion of the SS leadership, this total power necessitated
control also over presumably unpolitical problems of organization and
order. Heydrich believed that the SS police state guaranteed "the total and permanent check upon the situation of each individual," for he
was "responsible not only for executive security measures but also for
security in relation to the ideological and other aspects of life," [30] and
in line with Nazi ideology of rule and race, this terrible terminology
encompassed all aspects of life. This was not simply a belated interpretation on the part of a power-hungry SS leadership. The official party
publication *Das Recht der NSDAP* (*The Law of the NSDAP*) [31] proclaimed the totalitarian doctrine that "not only the 'warding off of
danger' in the liberalistic sense [was] the task of the police, but also
the control of the entire scope of duties of the individual vis-à-vis the
people's community." The appointment of the Reichsführer SS to the
post of chief of police in itself documented the "close relationship" that
had come into being "between the police as the protector of the people's
community and the NSDAP as the representative of the popular will."
And Himmler himself had said in the *Völkische Beobachter* of June 18,
1936, on the day of his appointment as head of the police, that the "battle for generations" would be led in the outside world by the Army
and domestically by "the police, fused with the Order of the SS." And
so at the 1938 Greater German Party Congress, the police marched in
the ranks of the SS.

The union of police and SS personnel into one State Protective Corps
(Staatsschutzkorps) was promoted step by step. This naturally created
certain problems for the SS and its claim to be an elite order: SS fitness, Aryan proof, marriage permits (if necessary retroactive) remained qualifying conditions. Yet the drive to put the police into SS
uniforms and its penetration by SS members was intensified during the
war; above all, its leadership lay in the hands of the SS. The personal
union was particularly apparent in the function of the so-called Higher
SS and Police Chiefs (HSSPF). It was probably no accident that this
was happening at the same time as Hitler was refining his war plans.
The SS police power, as the totalitarian counterpart to the Army, was,
in preparation for the mobilization in every *Wehrkreis* (defense sector, which was identical with the SS command sector), put under an
HSSPF whose relationship to the administrative offices and the war
organization was essentially undefined, despite his subordination to
Reich governors and provincial presidents.

After the beginning of the war, it became evident that here existed
yet another opening for the independent expansion of the SS state,
though it also opened up endless conflicts of interest with the military

[30] *Ibid.*, p. 202.
[31] Munich, 1936, p. 479.

and civilian administration, particularly in the occupied territories. Yet the direct connection with Himmler assured a measure of independence and arbitrariness, as exemplified particularly by the self-willed acts of the HSSPF of Poland (Friedrich Wilhelm Krüger) in opposition to Governor General Frank. This was true also for the HSSPF's relationship to the Army in East and West and was responsible for the creation of special SS and police courts paralleling the Army's judicial system. The terror machine was directed by one hand, and formal subordination meant little in the face of the real independence of the SS and its HSSPFs, which were equally feared by administration and Army; the HSSPF sections controlled the Order Police, Political Police (Security Police), SD, General and Waffen SS, and, finally, by order of Himmler of May 21, 1941, were to control the "political administration" (which Himmler equated with police powers)—the basis and ultimate purpose of the metastate SS state. What was being tested in the occupied territories was the preparation for the final promulgation of the total postwar command order. Only the SS power, the quintessence of National Socialism, was "political"; in the still traditional state structure of the Third Reich, which for tactical reasons had been preserved, it alone was the new and therefore completely reliable power validating the revolutionary and totalitarian claim of National Socialism and in a position to realize it unconditionally and with finality.

The role played in this connection by the development of the Waffen SS into an ultimately powerful rival of the Army will be discussed in the section on the war system. While this process gave increasing visibility to the total power claim of the SS, the concentration camps and Jewish persecution had, even before the war, formed the nub of the activities on which rested the expansion of the SS state. Here, too, the transition from the improvised terror of the early years to the gigantic concentration-camp system of the extermination era typified the interrelation of opportunistic power politics and purposeful totalitarian organization that marked the implementation of the "new order" generally. The significance of the concentration-camp system in Nazi rule has been excellently summed up in a basic study by Martin Broszat:

The fact that the concentration camps were retained after 1933/4 without objective necessity signified an intentional prolongation of the state of emergency, and it was not accidental that after the outbreak of the war they assumed gigantic dimensions. For even in internal affairs war was the element most characteristic of the National Socialist leadership: it was the great state of emergency which enabled it to carry through totalitarian control. The protective custody camps for enemies of the State became centres of forced labour, biological and medical experiments and the physical extermination of Jewish and other unwanted life.[32]

[32] Broszat, "The Concentration Camps 1933–45," in *Anatomy of the SS State,* p. 440.

The first departure from established legal norms came in March, 1933, with the institutionalization of "protective custody" as "political custody"—a preventive measure in the fight against potential enemies of the Nazi revolution. Here, too, the Reichstag fire decree, by suspending basic rights, formed the pseudo-legal basis. Before that time, protective custody had been a police measure limited in time as well as locally and legally, to be invoked in exceptional circumstances. Now it became an accepted preventive measure without any legal limitation. It was intended initially to help smash the Communist Party and "Marxism," an action which, according to Hitler's dictum in the Cabinet meeting of February 28, 1933, "was not to be dependent on legalistic considerations." But at the same time, it furnished the springboard from which the police could launch the unrestrained terror of the new regime throughout the country. The mass arrests of Communists and Socialists that began on February 28, 1933 (in Prussia alone, 25,000–30,000 persons were arrested during March and April), brought the first provisional concentration camps to relieve the overcrowded prisons. On March 20, 1933, Himmler opened a camp under SS control in the barracks of an old powder factory in Dachau, near Munich. The SA and SS "supplemented" the preventive police custody by their own brutal arrests. The settlings of old personal grievances, vicious destructiveness, and looting became commonplace; maltreatment and killings in overcrowded prisons and improvised concentration camps were everyday affairs. In addition to Dachau, camps were set up also in Oranienburg (near Berlin), Papenburg (Ems region), Esterwegen (Ems region), Dürrgoy (near Breslau), Kemna (near Wuppertal), Sonnenburg (Warthe, near Frankfurt/Oder), Sachsenhausen (near Berlin), Quednau (near Königsberg), Hammerstein (Pomerania), Lichtenburg (near Merseburg), Werden (Essen), Brauweiler (near Cologne), Börgermoor (Ems region), and the notorious SS Columbia House special prison (Berlin).

With the progress of *Gleichschaltung*, the wave of arrests was extended to other parties and groups, to trade unions and, above all, to Jews. A growing number of concentration camps were organized and financed as state institutions, as a "provisional" transitional solution pending the creation of permanent camps in which inmates were to be put to work at productive tasks. True, after the first wave, the number of arrests temporarily declined: according to official reports, there were about 27,000 political prisoners on July 31, 1933 (of which 15,000 were in Prussia). But the consolidation of the regime and the decline of the SA, accompanied by the tactical slogan of the "end of the revolution," merely signified the transition from planless terror to planned persecution. According to a memorandum of the Prussian Ministry of the Interior of October 14, 1933, persons in protective custody were no longer to be arbitrarily "kept" but transferred to state concentration camps or, if need be, to prisons. According to yet another memorandum (January 9, 1934), protective custody was not to be invoked against lawyers defending undesirable clients, and neither was it to be a substitute for legal proceedings, as apparently was the practice—anticipating the methods of the future.

After Himmler's assumption of police powers in 1934–35, the institutionalization of the persecution and concentration-camp system was completely integrated into the SS. Protesting ministries and governors (for example, Epp in Bavaria) were pushed aside in a series of jurisdictional conflicts. On June 30, 1934, the SS also replaced the SA guards in the concentration camps, and all future attempts of the judiciary or administrative apparatus to abolish the system of protective custody and concentration camps or bring them under control were doomed to failure. Through personal contacts with Hitler, Himmler was able to throttle repeated efforts to intervene, particularly on the part of the Ministers of Justice (Gürtner) and Interior (Frick). Alone between October, 1935, and May, 1936, the Gestapo arrested a total of 7,266 persons for "KPD and SPD" activity, and the vaguest reasons sufficed: behavior "hostile or harmful to the state," "political activities" or "seditious behavior," "spreading atrocity stories" or "insulting leading personalities," "defamation of the swastika" or "vilification of Gauleiter Streicher."[33] The threat of internment hovered over all who dared criticize the regime. For the time being, the Reichstag fire decree, which was expanded to include the indirect "Communist threat" allegedly posed by religious groups, was accepted by the courts also. And at the same time, the political-totalitarian, quasi-military basis of the concentration-camp system, according to which established legal norms no longer were expected to apply in the means used, gained ground; the props of this method of "protecting the state" saw themselves rather as members of a "combat league" charged to "root out" all dissent, to "ferret out enemies of the state, to keep watch over them and at the right moment render them harmless," and for that purpose, "independent of all past ties, to use every appropriate means"—the authorization for this "deriving solely from the new concept of the state, without requiring any special legitimation."[34] This theory, developed by Werner Best, the Gestapo's top legal expert, also furnished the broad framework for the institution of the far-flung concentration-camp system, the nucleus of the future SS state. The consolidation of the Nazi regime after the turbulent seizure-of-power phase set the pace for the organization and monopolization of a "regular," bureaucratically regulated concentration-camp system administered by the SS.

The model, Dachau, had been operated by the General SS since its inception. Crude "special regulations" sanctioned cruel and brutal "punitive" measures; summary proceedings were instituted and an SS camp court, under the chairmanship of the camp commandant, meted out punishment, including death sentences. In contrast to the arbitrariness of the SA camps, the SS here began the institutionalization of the terror which became the hallmark of its independent policies

---

[33] *Ibid.*, p. 425.
[34] Best, "Die geheime Staatspolizei," *Zeitschrift für Deutsches Recht,* 1936, pp. 125 ff.

outside the rule of law and government. Himmler was forced to drop the first Dachau commandant, Hilmar Wäckerle, in June, 1933, but his 41-year-old successor, Theodor Eicke, became the real pioneer of the new terror. A native of Alsace-Lorraine, active paymaster in World War I, discharged from the police because of antirepublican activities, later employed in the industrial counterespionage department of IG Farben in Ludwigshafen, Eicke began his rise in the SS in 1928. Sentenced to two years for his role in bomb plots, he fled to Italy. In February, 1933, Eicke was again at his post, although he had been held in temporary protective custody after a fight with his Gauleiter (Josef Bürckel) and was under psychiatric observation by Dr. Werner Heyde, the very man who later headed the euthanasia program. Himmler brought him to Dachau directly from the clinic at Würzburg. Within a year, Eicke, who had distinguished himself in the murder of Röhm and his comrades, rose to the position of Inspector of Concentration Camps and SS Guard Units and to SS Group Leader (July, 1934), and also remained in his post of camp commandant until 1935.

The structure of Dachau served as the model for the reorganization and consolidation of the concentration camps. The system of brutal punishments was expanded in Eicke's detailed instructions of October, 1933, to include lashings in the presence of guards and inmates; the death penalty was proposed among other things for incitement and spreading atrocity stories; every penalty increased the length of detention; and it was a basic rule that punishments were to be administered with the greatest harshness and inflexibility yet impersonally and in a disciplined fashion. Death's head insignia and ready weapons for use against the enemy—such were the precepts of the Alsatian former paymaster and executioner who embodied the combination of bureaucratic systematization and uninhibited violence typical of the SS state. The future Auschwitz commandant Rudolf Höss was among those who received their early training at Dachau.

Even at this early date (1934–35), the legal apparatus, despite some efforts at intervention, proved to be increasingly impotent against the concentration-camp system's claim to the right to pass and carry out sentences on its own. In most instances the explanation that a camp inmate had been shot while resisting a guard or trying to escape sufficed to ward off any possible investigation. And the guards shot without warning. The National Socialist idealization of combat found fulfillment in peacetime by conducting a permanent war against the internal "enemy." The claim to independence, which was also asserted by putting the political police outside the traditional machinery of state, won out over all attempts to impose controls. The close connection of the concentration-camp system and the political police was made evident by the "political departments" under Gestapo or police officers that were attached to every camp. These officers conducted interrogations, were in charge of the "registration" file of the inmates, of contacts with the judiciary, and of the issuance of death certificates and discharges. By the end of 1934, the SS guard units (also called

"Death's Head Units" because of their collar insignia) stationed in the camps were taken out of the General SS and established as a special branch of the armed SS under Eicke. In 1938, Eicke's camp administration moved from Berlin to Oranienburg, near the Sachsenhausen camp, and there it remained to the end of the war, in constant close touch with Himmler. Eicke thus was generally in a favorable position in any conflict with the General SS and with the Gestapo, which had jurisdiction over the sentencing and discharge of prisoners. Eicke himself, by then General of the Waffen SS (Death's Head Division), was killed in action in Russia in February, 1943.

One of the consequences of the consolidation of Nazi rule was that by the winter of 1936–37, the number of camp inmates had declined to fewer than 10,000. Of the seven camps operating in 1935, some were dissolved (Hamburg-Fuhlsbüttel, Oranienburg, Esterwegen, Columbia House, Sachsenburg) and the inmates transferred to new camps— Sachsenhausen and (after August, 1937) to Buchenwald (near Weimar) —as well as to Dachau. In addition to Lichtenburg, which was made into a woman's camp (after 1939 in Ravensbrück [Mecklenburg]), there thus were three camps in 1937–38, each of which served as headquarters of a Death's Head unit of 1,000–1,500 young men (mostly sixteen- to twenty-year-olds), while the camps themselves were staffed by 120 SS men. The persecution now was extended also to so-called antisocial parasitical (*volksschädigende*) elements, who under existing laws would have gone unpunished. "Asocials" (conveniently interpreted as the need arose), "work-shy elements" (a category encompassing the rejection of offers of work "without good reason"), homosexuals, and Jehovah's Witnesses were "preventively" detained in concentration camps, together with "habitual criminals," émigrés, Jews, and political prisoners who had served prison sentences or had been acquitted by regular courts(!). Chevrons of different colors worn by the prisoners indicated their respective "category." [35]

The admixture of political, criminal, punitive, and preventive considerations characteristic of the new phase of concentration-camp policy that began in 1937 brought an increase in the camp population. The relevant orders which Himmler issued in 1937, again on the basis of the Reichstag fire decree, once and for all burst through the provision limiting its application to political enemies and gave the political police and the camp system unlimited powers above and beyond the Ministry of Justice. How feeble the resistance to this was may be gleaned from the lame request of the Ministry of Justice in 1937 to the Gestapo to refrain from detaining Jehovah's Witnesses in protective custody (after they had served a jail sentence) under circumstances that might be considered detrimental to the standing of the courts.[36]

The expansion of the camp system rested above all on the claim that the concentration camps also served as "state reformatories and labor

[35] Details in Broszat, *op. cit.*, pp. 450 ff.
[36] *Ibid.*, p. 452.

camps" (as formulated in the April 4, 1938, directives for the prevention of crime of the Criminal Police Office). The reasons given for the "sudden" (*schlagartig*) moves against "asocials," "work-shy persons," and Jews with criminal records were economic and military. Mobilization and war were casting their shadow ahead; forced labor for SS projects and the construction of SS-owned industries lent fresh importance to the concentration camps. At first, it was a question primarily of building materials for the monumental structures of the Third Reich —slave labor for Hitler's pyramids. Able-bodied prisoners were in demand, and new camps were set up near quarries and SS building-material plants. Brick ovens were built near Sachsenhausen and Buchenwald and new concentration camps opened up near the granite quarries of Flossenbürg (Upper Palatinate) and Mauthausen (near Linz, Austria) and, in 1940, in Gross-Rosen (Lower Silesia) and Natzweiler (Alsace). And the foreign invasions of 1938 brought thousands of new prisoners. The Security Police raids and the wave of denunciations that swept over Austria and the Sudetenland were successful beyond all expectations. And, finally, the pogrom of November 9, 1938, brought about 35,000 Jews into the concentration camps. Even though most were released within weeks if they could document their intention to emigrate, the number of camp inmates at the beginning of the war was still around 25,000, and in the subsequent two years, despite a high death rate, the number grew to hundreds of thousands and later to millions. The numerous new Death's Head Units organized after 1937–38 formed the framework of this development, which strengthened the position of the SS with such irresistible force. "The war was used to embark on a new stage of the National Socialist revolution and the totalitarian transformation of society, which would complete the extermination of political opponents by so-called national political and biological cleansing operations." [37] The power of the SS and the concentration-camp system were the pillars of this process. Their growing influence, which began to assert itself early, built the foundations of the future commando and slave state.

DISENFRANCHISEMENT AND PERSECUTION

The social theory of the Third Reich, like its political theory of rule, was based on the friend-foe principle. Under the leader principle, the legal system also had to serve the closed people's community and the fight against minorities and outsiders. In the final analysis, the annihilation of the enemy was made a function of law. As early as March 23, 1933, Hitler told the Reichstag that the legal system must "first of all serve the preservation of this people's community." Demanding the "elasticity of judicial findings for the purpose of safeguarding society," he offered this yardstick: "Not the individual but the nation must be the focus of legal concern." And he granted equality

[37] *Ibid.*, p. 469.

before the law only to those who backed the national interest and did not stint in their support of the Government.

But even within this National Socialist people's community, there were gradations in the right to legal protection. The Führer had absolute control over it, since he had appointed himself supreme judge (July 13, 1934); the subleaders in turn enjoyed privileges downward, though being without rights upward; and in the end, the country still was divided into party members, civilians, and the disenfranchised. There was neither equality nor equal inequality before the law. The abolition of legal safeguards paralleled the authoritarian structure of state and society. As in the case of the relationship between domestic and foreign policy, the principle of distraction was operative here also. The still more discriminatory treatment meted out to politically and racially persecuted persons was to make the loss of basic and equal rights more palatable.

The manipulation and perversion of the legal system in the service of the National Socialist structure of leadership and subordination initiated mainly by Hans Frank and Roland Freisler, the new State Secretary in the Ministry of Justice, was embedded in numerous "reform" plans and formalized in the creation of a special court system. But practice lagged behind theory. Gaps remained, and the regime for the time being compromised and tolerated the continuation of legal traditions and the legal apparatus—and along with this, the perpetuation of the many illusions of the mass of fellow travelers and others who were eager to adapt themselves. (Hitler had made no secret of the fact that ultimately he wished to do away with the legal system and lawyers altogether insofar as they could not be completely politicized.) But in every basic respect, the principles of a society governed by law had been destroyed by the Third Reich in the very first weeks of its rule. The principle of "no penalty without law" had already been violated by the law of March 29, 1933, authorizing prosecution (of the Reichstag arsonists) on the basis of ex post facto penal regulations. And conservative lawyers helped to pave the way by writing expert opinions and cooperating. These early encroachments became general practice two years later when it was officially stated that anything that violated the "healthy national spirit" (*gesundes Volksempfinden*) was punishable even if no specific provisions existed that dealt with such violations. The arbitrariness of the leadership thereby was made a principle of law, and the leadership alone determined what this "national spirit" was supposed to be. The "people" could not and were not supposed to express their feelings, for that would have violated the tenet of the leader state.

Arbitrariness in the name of "national spirit"—that was an incredible innovation. Let all the later vocal critics of the Nuremberg trials who at the time kept silent ponder this. (In Nuremberg, actual crimes were being tried, whereas here we are dealing with the arbitrary persecution of dissenters on the basis of a thoroughly vague general provision.) Moreover, protective custody and trials by extralegal bodies even anticipated this perversion of justice. It has been pointed out how, in the early stages, the SS police powers eroded the remnants of the constitutional state, most noticeably where the Gestapo quite "legally" (in accordance with the decree of the Ministry of Justice of April 13, 1935) consigned "undesirable" persons who had served their jail sentences to concentration camps. And in so doing, they euphemistically transformed permanent "protective custody" into a positive act, justifying it as a measure to protect the individual against public anger as well as protecting the "people's community" against the individual. A Social Democrat, for example, might land in a concentration camp and die there "because his political record leads to the belief that he would, after serving a two-year sentence for plotting high treason, again take part in activities of a Marxist character. (Signed) Heydrich." [38] The best-known case is that of Pastor Niemöller, which ended with his acquittal in 1937—and subsequent consignment to a concentration camp.

A second great opening was the increasingly frequent exemption of governmental and police actions from court review. As these more and more came to rest on political authority and leadership, the individual's right to protection under the law also eroded. The permanent state of emergency was most evident in the core area of Nazi rule—the Gestapo actions free from legal restraints. "The old and the new concept of police authority" [39] most strikingly illuminated the transition from constitutional state to police state. Once an undertaking of the state was said to be "political" and a "leadership act," legal review was eliminated.[40] And what was "political" was determined solely by the interpretation of the respective National Socialist leaders. It was inevitable that the reviewing agencies, particularly the administrative courts, more and more became subjugated to the will of the Führer and the party and left with little freedom of movement against the monopoly of one-sided "political acts." The fact that after September, 1939, administrative actions were not subject to any review whatsoever sealed a development in which the authoritarian administrative state blended into the totalitarian leader state and cleared the way for the SS state. Thus in the beginning of 1943, the State Secretary in the Ministry of Justice, Carl Rothenberger, limited himself to the proposal that in order to preserve the "authority of the courts," no public announcement of executions was to be made in cases "in which a regular court has spoken and, in the absence of legal ways and means, the death penalty was not imposed, yet on the other hand the execution of the perpetrator was deemed necessary in agreement with the

[38] Annedore Leber, Willy Brandt, and Karl Dietrich Bracher, *Conscience in Revolt* (London, 1957), pp. 97 ff.
[39] Thus the memorandum of Werner Lehmann (Berlin, 1937).
[40] Siegfried Grundmann, "Die richterliche Nachprüfung von politischen Führungsakten," *Zeitschrift für die gesamte Staatswissenschaft*, No. 100 (1940), p. 537.

officials." [41] But this decision, Himmler informed him, also lay with Hitler, "who not only orders the execution but also its public announcement."

The functions of judges and courts, and of prosecutors and defense attorneys, had been mapped out early. The attempts to nail justice to its new role, the annihilation of "antisocial parasites," began with the appointment of Hans Frank to the Reich Commissariat for the "*Gleichschaltung* of Justice," and proceeded, via the transformation of penal law into "combative law," to the special jurisdiction and terror justice of the people's courts. Where this did not work, that is, where the National Socialist penal ideology could not develop a new system of law, the traditional agencies frequently were bypassed or ignored. That does not mean, however, that the existence of the meta-legal SS state excuses the failure of large sections of the judiciary to oppose the total claim of National Socialism. The capitulation of the judiciary before the persecution and terror, which all too many "preservers of justice" applauded in speech and in print, made German justice an accomplice of the system of injustice.

The persecution of the Jews offers the most striking demonstration of the legal and psychological consequences of the totalitarian social idea. Before and after the disenfranchisement of the Jews was formalized in the Nuremberg Laws, anti-Semitic terror "from below" and official sanctioning from above intermeshed. And though it became evident that the Government's Jewish policy was by no means so generally "popular" as the propaganda would have it, the pseudo-legal aura accorded with the inclination of an unpolitical citizenry to accept the measures as a "necessary evil" and to shut their eyes to the facts and true meaning of the Jewish persecution. This same attitude underlay the suppression of the knowledge of concentration camps and extermination policies. What may have aroused disapproval when it involved the treatment of individual Jews was accepted by a latent, widespread anti-Semitism when it was abstractly justified as warding off and shutting out Jewish influence, as an act of authority. The Jews not only were assigned the lowest legal status in the hierarchy of a leader state built on inequality, but since the promulgation of the Nuremberg Laws, police-administrative oppression and terrorization were superimposed on their "legal isolation." [42]

The legal and police disenfranchisement was accompanied by the declaration of open season on the Jews. Hamlets and towns vied with one

[41] Werner Johe, *Die gleichgeschaltete Justiz* (Frankfurt/Main, 1967). Cf. generally Hermann Weinkauff and Albrecht Wagner, *Die deutsche Justiz und der Nationalsozialismus* (Stuttgart, 1968); Ilse Staff (ed.), *Justiz im Dritten Reich* (Frankfurt/Main, 1964).

[42] Documentation in Hans Mommsen, "Der nationalsozialistische Polizeistaat und die Judenverfolgung von 1938," *Vierteljahrshefte für Zeitgeschichte*, X (1962), 68 ff.; Krausnick, "The Persecution of the Jews," in *Anatomy of the SS State*, pp. 23 ff.

another to become "free of Jews" (*judenrein*) and documented their zeal by posting signs such as "Jews Not Wanted Here," "Bathing Prohibited to Dogs and Jews," "Jews Enter at Their Own Risk." In this hostile atmosphere, the German Jews, cut off from the free pursuit of their professions and threatened in their dealings with "Aryans" by the biological, sexually charged Nuremberg Laws, found themselves in a situation which "gave a psychological boost to the later, more extreme forms of persecution by the Party leadership." [43] In 1935, Hitler acquainted a small circle of intimates with his real intentions, to which he held as firmly as to his expansionist aims: "Out with them from all professions and into the ghetto with them; fence them in somewhere where they can perish as they deserve while the German people look on, the way people stare at wild animals." As early as April 29, 1937, before an assembly of Nazi district leaders, he spoke about the further consequences. The final goal was fixed, but, for tactical reasons, could be realized only gradually: "I do not say, 'come on and fight because I want a fight.' Instead I say [shouting louder and louder], 'I mean to destroy you.' And then I use my intelligence to help to maneuver him into a tight corner so that he cannot strike back, and then I deliver the fatal blow."

This is an exemplary expression of the relationship between tactics and goals that guided the domestic and foreign policy of the Nazi leadership. In no other area did the real intent behind the pseudo-legal disguise emerge quite so clearly. Consequently, the co-responsibility of all Germans in the Jewish policies cannot be erased by any reference to "not knowing" and to having been deceived. The fact of the political, legal, and moral discrimination against the Jews was constantly present, and its final consequence—deportation and extermination—was merely a matter of time and opportunity. The fact that events like the 1936 Olympic Games in Berlin, which enhanced the international standing of the Third Reich, brought a temporary letup, does not alter this. By 1938, the Jews were almost completely shut out from German life through an almost endless series of regulations of professional and personal disenfranchisements. They were not admitted to public offices and hospitals, to pharmacies and restaurants, to schools and universities, nor were they eligible for any governmental or tax aid. The almost uninterrupted flow of amendments to the Nuremberg Laws between 1935 and 1938 constitutes a catalogue of complete and total discrimination. Moreover, beginning in mid-1938, Jews had to carry identification cards and passports and add the stereotyped first names "Israel" or "Sarah" to their given names. Open season was declared on them on the fifteenth anniversary of Hitler Putsch, when the pogroms of November 9–10, 1938, which became known by the bitterly ironic name "crystal night" (*Kristallnacht*)—a night of broken windows, looted stores, and burning synagogues—ushered in a still greater intensification of official anti-Jewish acts.

[43] Krausnick, *ibid.*, pp. 31 ff.; same source for subsequent passage.

These pogroms had a threefold purpose: to intensify the psychological combative mood; to exclude Jews from economic life, the last area of their curtailed activity; and to enrich a state treasury depleted by the costs of war preparation. The material motives had already become apparent in the "Aryanization" of numerous businesses, which often enough was nothing more than expropriation. "Aryans" who tried to help Jews save their businesses through sham transfers were threatened with imprisonment and fines. Beginning in April, 1938, Jewish assets had to be registered and put at the disposal of Göring, who headed the economic war preparation. The excuse for the massive assault of November 9 was the assassination in Paris on November 7, 1938, of the German diplomat Ernst vom Rath by a seventeen-year-old Jewish youth, Herschel Grünspan. An enormous propaganda campaign was set in motion: bombastic memorial services in schools and plants to the strains of the funeral march of Beethoven's *Eroica* symphony were followed by an inflammatory speech by Goebbels on November 9 in Munich. This set off the planned action in the pseudo-spontaneous manner which the supreme party court later summed up in these cynical words: "All party leaders present probably understood Goebbels to say that to the outside the party was not to appear as the originator of the demonstrations, but that in fact it should organize and carry them out." [44]

The "demonstrations" of party and SA troops in one night of barbarism destroyed almost all synagogues in Germany and more than 7,000 stores. The true purpose became apparent when subsequently the Jews were made to pay for the repair of the damages, were fined 1 billion marks, and also had their insurance compensations confiscated. The vandals as well as the murderers of nearly a hundred Jews, except those found guilty of "race defilement" (!) or of violating "discipline," went unpunished. In the words of the party court, they had "transformed the properly understood will of the leadership into deed"—and so, barely a year later, did the murder squads of the SS and police. The SS for its part devoted itself to the less noisy arrest of 30,000–50,000 "prosperous" Jews who were to be forced to emigrate (leaving everything they owned behind) after a stopover in concentration camps. The barbaric acts were anything but spontaneous and most likely were disapproved of by the majority of Germans, as the British chargé d'affaires reported at the time.[45] But neither the British nor the French government drew the consequences; four weeks later, Paris concluded a friendship treaty with Ribbentrop. Göring, however, did draw the consequences: He told a conference of all concerned ministries that Hitler had authorized him to "centralize the decisive steps" in the Jewish question.[46] Through Aryanization, ghettoization, and

---

[44] *Nürnberger Dokumente*, PS—3063 (**XXXII**, 20 ff.). Cf. Lionel Kochan, *Pogrom 10 November 1938* (London, 1957), pp. 50 ff.
[45] *Documents on British Foreign Policy*, Second Series, III, 277.
[46] *Nürnberger Dokumente*, **XXVIII**, 499 ff.

deportation, the terror against Jews became a part of the Four-Year Plan.

Numerous additional discriminatory decrees eliminating the last remnants of professional and property rights followed; theaters, concerts, museums, athletic fields, and public baths were barred to Jews; the ownership of gold, silver, jewels, radios, and telephones became illegal; Jews were ordered to move together into designated "Jewish houses," and forced labor was introduced. The November 24, 1938, issue of the SS paper *Schwarzes Korps* anticipated the consequences when it spoke of extermination "by fire and sword," "the actual and final end of Jewry in Germany, its complete annihilation." And Göring, in his booty conference of November 12, 1938, openly stated that in case of war (and Hitler had after all predicted war the year before at the Hossbach meeting), a major settling of accounts with the Jews would be the first order of business.[47] Barely two weeks later, on November 24, Hitler quite openly told a South African Cabinet member that "the problem would be solved within the near future. This was his unshakable intention." [48] Although he also stated that the Jews would have to disappear from Europe, he nonetheless refused to cooperate in drawing up viable resettlement plans and called anti-Semitism the most important idea of National Socialism.

It is doubtful that even at that time resettlement—that is to say expulsion—as an alternative to the extermination of Jews ever had a real chance, even though it had been practiced since 1938 under Adolf Eichmann, the pedantic organizer of the "Central Office for Jewish Emigration" in Vienna, as a combination of looting, blackmail, and deportation, and lived on in the Madagascar Plan until 1940–41. Discussions with the International Committee for Refugee Problems began toward the end of 1938, but the issue was not so much the people involved as problems of property and foreign currency. Meanwhile, Hitler's pronouncements about a radical "solution" of the Jewish problem became more frequent. Thus he told Czechoslovakia's Foreign Minister on January 21, 1939: "We will exterminate the Jews" and that November 9, 1918, would be "avenged." And on January 30, 1939, he quite openly told the Reichstag that the next war would bring "the extermination of the Jewish race in Europe." The Central Reich Agency for Jewish Emigration, which was set up in Berlin in February, 1939, in fact already was the nucleus for the radical solution. It was put under the chief of the Security Police Heydrich; in October, 1939, its first administrative chief, SS Standartenführer Heinrich Müller, was replaced by Eichmann (who in the meantime, in addition to the office in Vienna, had also set up a Central Office for Jewish Emigration in Prague).

This once and for all put Jewish policy in the hands of the SS police power. In close coordination with foreign-policy and war developments,

---

[47] *Ibid.*, 537 f.
[48] *Akten der deutschen Auswärtigen Politik*, Series D, IV, 291 ff.

the first step was the forceful expulsion of the Jews. Since other countries did not wish to admit propertyless Jews, and since Jews were refused permission to transfer funds, the idea of a Jewish reservation was temporarily under consideration. At the same time, a Foreign Office memorandum of January 25, 1939, brutally spelled out the policy of expulsion to all its foreign missions and opposed the support of a Jewish state in Palestine; the objective was the further splintering of "world Jewry" and, at the same time, the intensification of anti-Semitism in all countries to which impoverished Jews were now beginning to emigrate.[49] The war finally freed the Nazi regime of all tactical restraints and opened the way for the radical solution. As in Austria and Czechoslovakia, the Einsatz units of the SS and police moved in after the Army in Poland, not only to work out this solution but also to begin its ruthless execution. The Army still had some authority, but it proved weak in the face of orders by Himmler and Heydrich, who in disputes could always invoke the name of Hitler. Also, the growing formations of the armed SS and some Army units participated in the outrages committed against Poles and Jews; increasing in intensity from week to week, these culminated in mass executions after September, 1939.

Deportation of all Jews to the East and ghettoization was the next step, and Heydrich, referring to Hitler's will, issued the relevant special orders to the chiefs of the Einsatz units on September 21, 1939. That this was the road to the extermination of the Jews was generally agreed on. A number of SS commandos even then preferred a simpler solution than the complicated deportations: simply shooting victims who "attempted to escape." Heydrich also called the ghettoization the "anticipation" for the "strictly secret . . . final goal, which will take somewhat longer." [50] It had become a matter of millions of Jews (in addition to the decimation of the Poles). Expulsion turned into herding together, and the final goal became the final solution: mass murder.

It would be misleading to describe the persecution of the Jews as merely another method of mobilizing the population, as a function of the combative people's community of the Third Reich. Neither before nor after 1939 was it a matter solely of *Realpolitik* and Machiavellianism. But because this was thought to be the case, the ideological obsession of the Nazi leadership was not taken seriously; its consequences were dismissed as mere by-products, and the revolutionary-totalitarian component of the authoritarian order which most Germans favored after the "failure" of the Weimar Republic was underestimated. The support for the regime rested on the widespread longing for a strong state, a longing which was misused and subverted. It was the product also of propaganda and coercion, which were apparently justified by successful domestic and foreign policies, and

[49] Details in Krausnick, *op. cit.*, pp. 344 ff.
[50] *Nürnberger Dokumente*, PS—3363.

it found its final expression in the ideology of a war that was allegedly an act of national self-assertion in a "world of enemies." In the face of these arguments, the facts of disenfranchisement and persecution paled. The readiness for acclamatory agreement and pseudo-military obedience to a strong authoritarian state was far greater. Therein, and not only in coercion and terror, lies the explanation for the problems facing a German opposition to the Hitler regime.

PROBLEMS OF OPPOSITION AND THE LEFT

The pseudo-legal National Socialist seizure of power also casts a new light on the age-old question of resistance to tyrannical rule. Opposition to a state which had fallen into the hands of *one* party via apparently legal Presidential emergency laws, parliamentary Enabling Act, and the plebiscitary mobilization of the people had to count on other and greater difficulties than resistance against violent coups and overt usurpation. It was the purpose of the widely accepted Nazi thesis of the "legal revolution" to sow confusion and to weaken potential counterforces. This influenced the character and impaired the chances of opposition to a regime that in so short a time, with the help of pseudo-democratic methods, had gained so firm a grip on state and society. In addition, the intellectual and social presuppositions for shaping opinions and creating valid yardsticks concerning the National Socialist takeover were largely lacking. The Western tradition of the right to resist arbitrary power had suffered a setback in the development of the modern German state idea after 1848 and been covered over by the bureaucratic structure of the authoritarian state. This became particularly evident in the matter of the oath to Hitler.[51]

Against the background of the specific conditions of the German authoritarian state stand the misjudgments that paralyzed a possible resistance to the Nazi takeover. Even such perceptive foreign observers as Curzio Malaparte and Harold Laski believed in 1932 that Hitler, the failed putschist, though not sincere in his pledge to legality, still had no chance of realizing his total dictatorship. This illusion resurfaced in the days of appeasement. The basic problem faced by the other political leaders and parties in 1933 was to what extent they could influence or even control the new rulers through collaboration, at what point principled opposition became mandatory, and what form it should take. The illusions of the unions, the wait-and-see attitude of the SPD leaders, who repeated their mistake of July 20, 1932, the vain attempts at adjustment of the parties of the center, the retreat of the KPD—all these were reflections of that problem. But in acting thus they missed the moment when they still could have operated from

---

[51] Cf. Gerhard Schulz, "Über Entscheidungen und Formen des politischen Widerstandes in Deutschland," *Faktoren der politischen Entscheidung* (Berlin, 1963), pp. 73 ff.

their old positions of strength. Only after the parties were dissolved and political power crumbled did scattered centers of resistance begin to form, though even then they were inhibited by their conviction that Hitler's rule would collapse within months and that all they had to do was to survive a short period of oppression.

In the ensuing years, a number of opposition groups against National Socialism or against certain aspects of its rule emerged at different times, with different scope, and with different methods and aims. At first there were the old left-wing enemies of National Socialism on the one hand, and the disappointed conservatives on the other. Later the opposition was augmented by church groups, Government officials, and businessmen. And finally, in 1938, and again after 1942–43, the military moved into the center of resistance plans and acts.

An assessment of the opposition is both difficult and controversial because of the many yardsticks that can be applied. Should major emphasis be given to motives, to prospects of success, or to political objectives? These factors determine the assessment of the Left, bourgeois, church, conservative, and military opposition groups, their relationship to each other, and their tactics.

All past examinations have been burdened by the limitations political, social, and ideological considerations imposed on the history of the resistance after the events. The appraisals fall into four major categories. To begin with, there are the two extreme opinions which summarily dismiss either (1) the Communist resistance (as "treason")[52] or (2) the conservative-military opposition (as a mere falling-out with the regime).[53] Such anti- or pro-Communist circumscriptions of the idea of resistance are quite simply unhistorical. Both these oppositional tendencies posed equal threats to the Nazi leadership and its claim to total rule. Of course, it soon became obvious that after its final institutionalization the regime could hardly have maintained itself without the help of the Army. But there is no justification for (3) considering only the military resistance, which did not exist at all in the first half of the Third Reich, and even after 1938 must be treated in connection with other, political forces.

The idea (4) that the churches were a source of a popular movement against National Socialism and that the Catholic Church almost to a man opposed it [54] is as questionable as the contrary thesis of a Communist mass movement against Hitler. The church opposition, significant though frequently equivocal, was certainly also a political matter, but

[52] Thus, for example, Fabian von Schlabrendorff in the second edition (not yet in the first) of his book *Offiziere gegen Hitler* (Zurich, 1950).

[53] This is a position taken by almost all East German writings on the subject, with the slight exception of Kurt Finker, *Stauffenberg und der 20. Juli 1944* (Berlin, 1967), and the Russian book by Daniil Melnikov, *20. Juli 1944, Legende und Wirklichkeit* (Berlin, 1966).

[54] Thus Gerhard Ritter, *The German Resistance: Carl Goerdeler's Struggle Against Tyranny* (New York, 1958); also, Johannes Neuhäusler, *Kreuz und Hakenkreuz* (Munich, 1946) and most Catholic works.

only rarely did it go over from the defense of its own concerns and interests to political resistance. On the other hand, the justified criticism of the illusions of the conservatives ignores the fact that a popular uprising was not likely at any time during the Third Reich, but that a coup from above, like the one finally attempted on July 20, 1944, had to develop contacts with the state apparatus and parts of the establishment. This is not intended to deny or minimize either the moral aspects or the intellectual and social problems of such contacts. But a political study must deal first of all with actualities, with the conditions, problems, and limits of resistance insofar as they bear on the reality of the Nazi system of rule.

At no time did a unified resistance movement exist. The multiplicity of political and intellectual forces which sooner or later isolated themselves or even resisted National Socialist *Gleichschaltung* did establish contact at crucial junctures; but the differences remained great both in attitudes and plans, and after the collapse of the regime these differences reasserted themselves. At any rate, however, the opposition in prewar Germany was far greater than the Nazi proclamations of unity indicated. Tens of thousands of political enemies were and remained in prison; thousands were executed for active opposition. Even if one ignores the mass persecution outside the legal system, active opposition was far more prevalent than Nazi propaganda would admit; the secret surveillance reports of the Gestapo give an entirely different picture. But it was a giant step from widespread nonconformity, which under conditions of totalitarianism was unquestionably a political act, to nonobedience and active resistance.

The misgivings and the seeds of opposition at first were most clearly evident in the attitudes of the political parties. Their failure at the end of the Weimar Republic was typical of the weakness they displayed when confronted by the claims of the Nazi regime. True, at the end of March, 1933, they still held a great many positions of power: state governments and municipalities, trade unions and economic organizations had survived January 30 with their staffs intact, and even the March elections did not convert the National Socialist minority into a majority. But even then it became obvious that no controls, let alone an effective opposition, could be built on such formal positions of power so long as the legality fictions continued. Moreover, the non-National Socialist majority was deeply divided; it was anything but a prodemocratic or even an antidictatorial majority. That was true both of the parties and the electorate.

The political Right, either as part of the Hitler coalition or at least tending toward an authoritarian transformation of the Republic, possessed no political base on which to build a broad opposition. The restoration of the monarchy had never been a realistic alternative, particularly since the expectations vested in Hindenburg were illusory and since the Nazi regime offered the most consistent and promising program for the dictatorial solution popular in right-wing circles. To be sure, the Right in particular had mixed feelings about the rise of the NSDAP. It considered the National Socialists as rivals and resented the vulgarity with which they had outmaneuvered the conservative supporters of a restorational or authoritarian reorganization of Weimar Germany. But despite conflicts and splits, the overwhelming majority of the Right, under the rigid Hugenberg, cooperated with the National Socialists until it was too late.

Among the middle-of-the-road parties, the Liberals had declined to impotent splinter groups, while the Center Party, on the surface remarkably stable, was increasingly paralyzed by Catholicism's flirtation with the new regime. When the liberal bourgeoisie turned its back on the Republic before 1933, the National Socialists rather than the German Nationals reaped the benefits. In view of this development, the formal positions of power still held by the liberal State and People's parties (DDP and DVP) in the states and organizations had become meaningless. The "purges" of March and April, 1933, did the rest; only a few dared to remain aloof from National Socialism. The new regime was still thought to be the lesser evil compared to the "Marxist danger." This factor carried great weight with the Center Party as well as with the churches.

Splits and paralysis also characterized the attitude of the political Left. The SPD, the largest democratic party, had been in retreat ever since the Papen putsch of 1932. But criticism of the impotent legalism and resignation of the SPD leadership also gave birth to a spirit of resistance which in the end brought one of its younger Reichstag deputies, Julius Leber (born 1891), to the head of active resistance groups. Amid the ruins of the shattered party, opposition groups formed which sought to bridge the gulf between Socialists and Communists and to activate an antifascist Left front. Yet while the trade unions were debating whether, in view of the massive unemployment, they could invoke their most powerful weapon—the strike— the idea of a united front of the Left collapsed, a casualty of mutual distrust, the profound differences in aims, and not least, the catastrophic tactics of the Communist leadership, which hoped to benefit from the bankruptcy of democracy and hence did everything in its power to help it along. The KPD fought bitter street battles with the NSDAP, but in the battle against the Republic it all too often played into the hands of the radical Right and fought the Social Democrats as "social fascists." Small wonder that the Communist alternative to the Nazi dictatorship offered no basis for a united front with the Social Democrats in defense of the democratic constitutional state.

But it nonetheless is a fact that, predating all later opposition by the churches, military, and conservatives, the earliest resisters were those who felt the terror of the Nazi regime "first and most strongly, and at the same time were considered its most dangerous enemies, namely the organizations of the labor movement." [55] The extent of this resistance

[55] H. J. Reichhardt, "Möglichkeiten und Grenzen des Widerstandes der Arbeiterbewegung," in *Der deutsche Widerstand gegen Hitler* (Cologne, 1966), p. 169.

is, however, not easily determined. Generally, the persecution of the Left and émigré activities are treated as one; inadequate source material rules out a truly comprehensive analysis of this far-flung, anonymous opposition. In the conditions of totalitarian rule, the conspiratorial activity of Left resistance groups had to remain buried in the darkness of illegality and anonymity; their records consequently are sparser and much less informative than the documents and plans of the bourgeois and conservative opposition. Though countless trials testify to the extent and continuity of this "silent rebellion," [56] they frequently offer only the distorted picture the Nazi-controlled "legal system" wanted to present as the image of the Marxist enemy; and in many instances the persecution took place outside the legal structure, in the realm of the concentration-camp state.

Thus the extent and form of the Left opposition have remained a matter of controversy. The SPD was completely smashed on June 22, 1933. Although the attempt to organize an underground movement soon enough failed because of the SPD leadership's commitment to legality, its proponents emigrated (Erich Rinner and Curt Geyer) or were arrested (Kurt Schumacher), while, between the summer of 1933 and the fall of 1934, a committee in charge of illegal work tried to maintain contact with the scattered groups and also with the exiled party executive in Prague through couriers. Inexperienced and frequently dilettantish, but displaying great courage in the hostile atmosphere of their own country, they searched for ways of meeting the challenges of a totalitarian regime. Tactics and aims of the shattered groups differed. Some, recalling the era of the Socialist Law under Bismarck, believed that they might be able to save the remnants of their organization after a brief National Socialist interlude; others drew the lesson from the failure of their party's leadership and the stabilization of the Hitler regime that only a workers' movement newly forged in the crucible of illegality could cope with the threat of fascist dictatorships.

It was above all the younger Social Democrats who saw resistance against National Socialism as a rebellion against the failure of the older party leaders, as a renewal and modernization of socialism. Thus, out of the nucleus of the Socialist Youth and student organizations, there grew opposition groups such as the Red Patrol (Berlin) and the Socialist Front (Hanover), who wanted to be different also in name and whose aims reflected the lessons they believed they had learned from the failure of the old SPD. By the end of 1933, the Red Patrol, which developed a lively publicistic activity, had a membership of about 3,000 Socialists, divided into five-man cells. In place of the failed policies of the SPD and KPD, this group as early as June, 1933, called for a "complete reorientation on a revolutionary basis," led by a "highly disciplined illegal organization." [57] The so-called New Begin-

[56] See Günther Weisenborn, *Der lautlose Aufstand* (Hamburg, 1953).
[57] Reichhardt, *op. cit.*, p. 179.

ning group (so named after its program), which had been organized in 1932 by dissident SPD and KPD members, worked even more consistently for the reorganization of the divided working-class movement under the new conditions of illegal anti-Nazi activity. Here, though on a small scale, the attempt to build a bridge between the various socialist factions held some promise of success. Until 1938, New Beginning supported the popular front; after numerous factional conflicts and arrests, the trial and sentencing of some of its leaders (Fritz Erler, Hermann Brill, Otto Brass, Kurt Schmidt) by the People's Court also put an end to this attempt.

By the end of 1933, arrests had smashed many early Social Democratic resistance groups. But a number (for example, until 1937–38, the International Socialist Combat League [ISK]) and various liaison offices remained active; by now, of course, they were more careful and more experienced, and, as hopes for an early end of the regime crumbled, they developed longer-range objectives. Papers and leaflets brought in from Prague (such as *Neuer Vorwärts*) or printed in the country were evidence of the continued existence of the SPD even after 1934. Couriers and border secretariats maintained contact with the outside. But the continued consolidation of the Nazi regime also meant intensified surveillance and persecution. The expansion of the SS state after 1935–36 not only perfected the Gestapo's methods of surveillance and of smashing organized opposition but also its methods of thwarting illegal counterpropaganda. A network of informers hobbled opposition on a broader scale, particularly since, in this era of visible successes, the regime had the mass of people behind it. After 1936, all that remained was the self-sacrificing resistance of individuals and minute groups, mutual help, close contact with reliable friends, exchange of information, and the strengthening of one's own position with the aim of surviving the regime, which obviously could be toppled only from the outside. A Gestapo report of 1937 found that although the large illegal organizations had been checked, an effective whispering propaganda campaign against the regime was rapidly spreading, helped along by the fact "that many former party and trade-union officials are now working as sales representatives and travelers." [58] But after the tragic experience of these years, the active oppositionists who had survived persecution and arrest arrived at the conclusion that resistance was realistically possible only in cooperation with men having entrée to the state apparatus. Thus, in 1938, they established contact with the bourgeois and military opposition, and, undergoing turbulent ups and downs, worked for the overthrow of the Government and the establishment of a government ranging from Right to Left.

This wrote an end to the early efforts to mobilize a united front of Socialists and Communists against a Nazi dictatorship resting on bour-

[58] Weisenborn, *op. cit.*, pp. 153 f. On the ISK, see Werner Link, *Die Geschichte des Internationalen Jugend-Bundes und des Internationalen Kampf-Bundes* (Meisenheim, 1964), pp. 173 ff.

geois-conservative support and rooted in capitalism. Even in the emigration, such a united front operated only fitfully and was never really forged: mutual mistrust and the changing line of the Communists continued to thwart such efforts—most detrimentally, of course, after the Hitler-Stalin pact of 1939, which put the exiled Communists and those in countries threatened or occupied by the Nazis in an untenable position, for it seemed to give final proof that Communist resistance was not a genuine alternative to the fascist dictatorship. Of course, measured by this yardstick, the opposition of the at one time violently antidemocratic Right with its somewhat authoritarian concept of "order" is also questionable.

As against this, it cannot be denied that Communists everywhere, not least in Germany itself, carried a major share of the burden of the resistance. The Soviet course put many of them into a tragic situation. This was evident even in 1933, when the KPD, not really prepared, and, like the SPD, misjudging the new regime, had to watch the destruction of its organization. The road into illegality demanded great courage, even though the party had become more experienced in dealing with prohibitions and persecution. The bloody clashes of the early weeks and the fanfares of antifascist propaganda were not followed either by revolutionary uprisings or by the smooth transition to illegality. Left in the lurch by the temporizing tactics of the Soviet Union, the KPD became the victim of the brutal reach of the Nazi rulers, who on this point more than on any other knew themselves to be in accord with their conservative, bourgeois, and church constituents.

Not even the loudest exhortations were able to invest the slogan of the united front, to which the pre-1933 course of the KPD had given the lie, with overnight credibility. The Reichstag fire was followed by mass arrests, and the political police were helped in this by the records of numerous search actions conducted since 1931. Here, too, the efficiency of the new regime proved to be superior to the bureaucratized, centralized apparatus of the KPD, the older dictatorial party. Moreover, after the arrest of Ernst Thälmann, the KPD was torn by power struggles which even did not stop at denunciations. Extending into the emigration, they ended in the victory of the Moscow satellite Walter Ulbricht. Official statements mirrored both the delusive misjudgment of the situation, and at the same time, the questionable nature of the united-front slogans; for example, on April 1, 1933, the Executive Committee of the Comintern not only dismissed the Nazi regime as a "temporary phenomenon" but advanced the almost profascist argument that it had "destroyed the democratic illusions of the masses" and freed "the masses from the influence of Social Democracy." [59]

Despite such misjudgments of who the true enemy was, despite chaos among the leadership and the defection of many supporters,

---

[59] Siegfried Bahne, "Die KPD," in *Das Ende der Parteien 1933* (Düsseldorf, 1960), p. 731.

despite betrayal and brutal persecution, thousands of dedicated Communists accepted terror and torture—at a time when little thought was given to resistance either in Germany or abroad. Together with a smaller number of Social Democrats, and long before church and bourgeois opponents followed along this road, Communists populated the first concentration camps, many of them without suspecting that "they had been the victims of betrayal by their own comrades as well as the unrealistic policies and incredible irresponsibility of the party apparatus." [60] After the initial shock, ideological conviction and a rigidly disciplined party apparatus combined to form a Communist underground of considerable merit, even if often enough it played into the hands of a Nazi propaganda and terror that invoked the specter of Bolshevism as its most effective argument after anti-Semitism.

In the beginning, the Communist opposition, in line with its slogan of the imminent proletarian revolution, spent its energies on the distribution of illegal literature; a surprising number of printing plants (ten in Berlin alone) were turning out such material. Of course, the Communist calls for demonstrations and strikes met with little response; as a matter of fact, the losses the illegal organization suffered in 1933 as a result were great. Also, the attempt to build a Communist trade-union organization as a mass base after the smashing of the unions did not go beyond the old cadres of the Revolutionary Trade Union Organization (Revolutionäre Gerwerkschaftsorganisation, or RGO)—the pre-1933 Communist alternative to the Socialist and Christian trade unions—and by 1935, this effort had been effectively halted. By the summer of 1933, all top KPD functionaries had emigrated; the second echelon was brutally persecuted. More and more, the fight had to be directed from the outside, and this only added to the misjudgment of the actual conditions and possibilities. But bitterness and tensions between the illegal party in Germany and the émigré leaders did not prevent renewed attempts to activate the opposition, efforts which invariably ended in new arrests.

From 1935 on, the united-front slogans were relaunched with greater force; the adoption of the united front by the Comintern Congress in Moscow in summer, 1935, also affected the German party line. Up to that time, the policy had foundered on the Communist advocacy of a united front from below—that is, trying to pry the Social Democrats loose from their leaders and to win control over them. The new Moscow directives called for unity of action and a popular front. But this new course came three years too late. Efforts to make contact with the Prague SPD leadership in exile in November, 1935, brought no results. The gulf created by the past perversion of the united front had become too deep. The Social Democrats, not unreasonably, mistrusted the change of line, which they saw as nothing but a tactical maneuver without a change of objective, and after the heavy losses suffered by

[60] Reichhardt, *op. cit.*, p. 187; cf. Carola Stern, *Ulbricht: A Political Biography* (New York, 1965), pp. 49 ff.

the Left and the successful consolidation of totalitarianism in Germany, the prospects for the creation of a mass base seemed dim. The bloody Moscow trials that began in August, 1936, and finally the Hitler-Stalin pact, also were not designed to make an alliance with the Communists an attractive alternative to the Nazi dictatorship. Thus, apart from occasional contacts, the two parties went their separate ways.

By radically decentralizing their organization, the KPD now attempted to set up illegal cells in industry and even in Nazi mass organizations (for example, in the DAF). These self-contained units were to be the vehicle for the implementation of the "Trojan horse tactics" advocated by Georgi Dimitrov, the Secretary General of the Comintern—oppositional activity in the guise of cooperation and the infiltration of positions of power. This strategy, however, was bound to create confusion among the opposition; moreover, its actual value was dubious, particularly since it risked exposing its members to the Gestapo network of informers. And ultimately these efforts were defeated by a new wave of arrests in 1936–37, followed by years of trials before the People's Courts and other oppressive measures.

In the hard-pressed conditions of 1939–41, the surviving Communist groups followed a confusing dual course: opposition to the regime and support of the Soviet pact. Even after the break of 1941, efforts to set up an illegal party organization involving above all functionaries from Sweden and Holland had little chance of success. The war also brought intensified surveillance and persecution. It was the independently operating groups around Communists like Robert Uhrig, Anton Saefkow, and Franz Jakob which worked most effectively in Berlin and also made contact with resistance centers in other cities and among other groups, for example, with the circle around the former Free Corps leader Joseph (Beppo) Römer. Like Uhrig, Saefkow, after being released from prison and concentration camp in 1939, worked tirelessly to establish contacts with a wide range of opposition groups, organized illegal propaganda activities, and apparently sought to form a comprehensive democratic front against the regime. While the Communist Party organization itself was fragmented and isolated, certain contacts with the non-Communist resistance were effected. However, the contacts established by Social Democrats like Leber and Reichwein in June, 1944, and with Saefkow and Jakob, not only ended in the smashing of the Communist groups (which apparently had been infiltrated by informers), but also contributed to triggering the tragedy of July 20th.

Up to the very end, the hope that the united resistance of the Left could restore the unity of the working-class movement remained a significant factor. After 1945, the policies in countries under Soviet rule to forge antifascist blocs and unity parties sought to capitalize on the shared suffering and experiences in the fight against National Socialism. Now the "reunification" did take place, though of course under the pressure and coercion of an occupation regime that suppressed all opposition. The founding of the German Socialist Unity Party (Sozialistische Einheitspartei Deutschlands, or SED) in 1946 demonstrated what the slogan of the united front had been all about both before and after 1933: the Communist sovereignty claim as the sole alternative to fascism.

CHURCHES AND RESISTANCE

If the forces of the divided Left opposition (which encompassed approximately 10 per cent of its former membership) were too weak to set in motion a movement against National Socialism, this holds doubly true for all other political and social groups. Here the preconditions for illegal cells and organized resistance, which after all were part of the tradition of the parties of the Left, were completely lacking. But while resignation spread in the socialist camp, because the efforts to weld the illegal groups into a mass movement failed and the only thing left was individual opposition in union with a handful of fellow believers, the efforts of the bourgeoisie to use positions of influence in public and social life as a base of opposition and for the overthrow of the regime increased over the years. Such attempts manifested themselves primarily in three areas: in the partial resistance of the churches against *Gleichschaltung,* in the growing misgivings of liberal and conservative circles about the nature of Nazi rule, and finally, in the criticism by a disillusioned military of Hitler's risky war policies, voiced for the first time in the mid-1938 crisis.

The motives and forms of these oppositional stirrings cannot be reduced to one common denominator. They rested on both liberal and conservative traditions, on religious and humanistic ideas. But the real spur for breaking through the paralyzing and intoxicating spell that had been cast over all of German life was the troubled conscience awakened by the presence of tortured fellow men, by persecution and terror. Individual moral decisions led people of varied backgrounds away from mass prejudice to resistance. The first stirrings were probably on a personal level, a consequence of the immediate and pressing problem of helping the disenfranchised and persecuted. The next step was to make contact with others of like mind and to acquaint a brainwashed nation with the truth behind the propaganda clichés. Still more risky, and dared by only a handful, was the step to political conspiracy, to the organization and planning of active opposition, to cooperation with other individuals and resistance groups. In addition to the present danger, traditional German attitudes toward state authority imposed an inner inhibition. The decision to resist was reached in terrible loneliness in the midst of a mass society. It meant a constant burden of suspicion and secrecy, danger to family and friends, isolation from the vast majority of one's own people; unlike the later resistance movements outside Germany, it did not bring the comforting proud awareness of fulfilling a national duty. Most likely the churches, having escaped complete *Gleichschaltung,* were able to offer a measure of support. But that had not been true at the very beginning.

The development in the Protestant churches was particularly complicated and dramatic. Largely conservative and antirepublican in orientation, many churches welcomed the advent of the new regime. Initially, the National Socialists had emphasized the Christian-national character of their "revolution." Article 24 of the party program hailed "positive Christianity" as a factor in the fight against Marxist atheism; even before the takeover, a National Socialist Movement of German Christians had been organized, which now, with the help of party and state, sought to win control over the churches. Parallel with the *Gleichschaltung* in the spring of 1933, this organization worked for the political and "racial" purification of the church, its centralization and structuring according to the leader principle under one "Reich bishop," the abolition of all parliamentary bodies of the church—in short, the "coordination of state and church." [61] This program of the 1933 Easter conference of the German Christians (Deutsche Christen, or DC), which was attended also by Göring and Frick, was being promoted on all church levels.

The new course also won the support of many clergymen, bishops, and theologians not affiliated with the German Christians. In May, 1933, a fight broke out over the nominee for the new office of Reich Bishop. When the candidate of the German Christians, the Army Chaplain Ludwig Müller of Königsberg (who had brought Blomberg over to Hitler), was defeated by the church candidate Fritz von Bodelschwingh, the election was invalidated, a State Commissar for the Prussian Churches appointed, and the existing church leadership replaced by plenipotentiaries of the German Christians. Finally, Müller, through a Decree for the Alleviation of the Critical Situation of Church and State quite in keeping with the "legal" seizure of power, himself took control. The conflicts were apparently decided by the church elections held at the end of July, 1933, under massive pressure of Nazi propaganda and threats favoring the DC, who called themselves the "SA of Jesus Christ." The DC won by fraud and took over the church offices.

In this moment of apparent *Gleichschaltung,* accompanied by grotesque displays of a *völkisch* Nazi reform of Christian teaching, the divided opposition finally found their voice. The call for a Confessional Church "independent of the state and the pressure of all political power" was first heard during the church election campaign. On September 21, 1933, Martin Niemöller (born 1892), a Berlin pastor, ex-U-boat captain, and initially close to the National Socialists, appealed to his colleagues to fight the DC. He called on all clergymen to form an emergency league (*Notbund*) to fight the new anti-Jewish personnel practices of the church (the so-called Aryan paragraph) and to unite for theological reappraisal. Two weeks earlier, on September 7, he and the twenty-seven-year-old pastor and university lecturer Diet-

---

[61] *Kirchliches Jahrbuch für die evangelische Kirche in Deutschland: 1933–1944,* ed. Joachim Beckmann (Gütersloh, 1948), pp. 13 f. See also Günther van Norden, *Kirche in der Krise* (Düsseldorf, 1963), pp. 17 ff., 34 ff.

rich Bonhoeffer, who had already voiced criticism of the leader principle and Jewish policies in the spring of 1933, had issued a declaration against the Aryan paragraph of the church law of September 6. And at the National Synod at Wittenberg, which was dominated by the DC and which installed Reich Bishop Müller with great fanfare in the same church in which Martin Luther had preached, the new Emergency League of Clergymen, in the name of 2,000 oppositional pastors, declared its determination to protect the persecuted and to defend Evangelicanism against one-sided politicization and coercion.[62] The declaration of September 27, 1933, bravely distributed among participants of the synod and fastened to lamp posts, was the first major document of a broad church opposition. By the end of 1933, the Emergency League, whose direction was taken over by a Brethren's Council under the chairmanship of Niemöller, had won over almost a third of Germany's Protestant clergy. Even in the ensuing years, despite outside pressure and internal conflicts, 4,000–5,000 pastors belonged to this circle. In response to organizational and theological coordination, a counterfront known as the Confessional Church (Bekennende Kirche, or BK) was set up.

Two reservations should, however, be noted. Given the totalitarian ruling claims of the Nazi regime, the moves described above were political, but they did not constitute political resistance in the strict sense of the word, since they were not directed against the National Socialist "authority" but were concerned solely with the preservation of autonomy and the freedom to teach. And second, in the years to come, the fronts often became vague; many compromises and concessions were made which also limited the scope of active opposition in the churches and made it difficult to estimate its extent. The result was rather something like a truce: only few took the road to political resistance. Moreover, the Nazi rulers had nothing but disdain for theological disputes, for they led to doubts and criticism even among the German Christians and counteracted efforts at *Gleichschaltung.*

This was true particularly of the radical German Christian call for a "German reformation growing out of the spirit of National Socialism," for the abolition of the Jewish Old Testament and the purging of the New Testament of the "scapegoat and inferiority theology of the Rabbi Paul," for a "heroic Christ figure as the basis of an appropriate [*arteigen*] Christianity . . . purged of all Oriental distortion." These words were contained in a resolution passed by a mass rally of German Christians in Berlin on November 13, 1933. With the help of such proclamations, the DC maneuvered itself into a box, for this proved too much even for many of their supporters. A confusing mixture of factions marked later developments, and the weak Reich Bishop Müller soon lost control over them. The Government reacted with a "muzzle" decree that forbade all taking of sides from the pulpits

---

[62] See Eberhard Bethge, *Dietrich Bonhoeffer* (New York, 1970), pp. 248–50. Bracher, Sauer, and Schulz, *op. cit.*, pp. 363 ff. and notes.

(January 4, 1934). The Nazi party press also dropped its original support of a German-Christian "reformation," which so obviously had become bogged down. If religion was mentioned at all and was not merely the idolization of Hitler as the personification of providence, it was in the form of a Germanic-racist "God belief" rather than a National Socialist Christianity. Yet the eccentric plans of Alfred Rosenberg or of the Orientalist Wilhelm Hauer also never gained the standing of an official creed. Hitler ridiculed all these designs. He saw the role of religion far too pragmatically, as a tool of power politics, to let it become a needless source of opposition.

Hence the church opposition cannot be called a political resistance movement against the regime. It is true that within this limited framework, the *Gleichschaltung* of broad circles of the population was modified, and the criticism being leveled against certain aspects of Nazi rule was quite evident. And if the regime, for tactical reasons, kept out of "internal conflicts," this aloofness did not prevent close surveillance, mass punishments, and the persecution of objectionable clergy and church groups. But the inhibitions in the Protestant relation to the state, which a theologian involved in the resistance called an inability to render political resistance, remained: "The national-conservative prejudice; the absence of liberalism as a way of life and, applied to religion, the rejection of democracy under the label of 'Western Calvinism'; the acceptance of the Reich idea with the dream of a 'second,' Protestant-Lutheran Reich of the German Nation against the background of the synthesis of throne or nation and pulpit; the uneasiness about the Weimar Republic, or any republic at all; ideological anti-Marxism and the specter of Communism; the trauma of Versailles; and also, at least at first, the defense against a 'political Catholicism!' And in addition, a more than merely latent anti-Semitism. . . ."[63]

The church opposition did not completely shed these historical burdens, behind which, in the realm of theology, loomed in particular the Lutheran concept of authority. Only a minority in either of the two churches was able to overcome the involvement with a "pastoral nationalism" and the myth of Reich, Nation, and Fatherland. The church opposition against the Nazi state, which the churches initially had accepted, has been called an "involuntary resistance movement" which, forced into the defensive and repeatedly relapsing into conformity, simply tried to ward off "encroachments." [64]

In this limited framework, the decisions of the "resistance synods" held by the Confessional Church take on great significance. Their protests against *Gleichschaltung* and persecution reached a high point at the session in Barmen (May, 1934) and Berlin-Dahlem (October, 1934); at the same time, the Brethren's Council of Confessional Clergy-

[63] Ernst Wolf, "Zum Verhältnis der politischen und moralischen Motive in der deutschen Widerstandsbewegung" in *Der deutsche Widerstand gegen Hitler, op. cit.,* p. 273.
[64] *Ibid.,* p. 230.

men recommended that its members refuse to take the service oath ordered on August 9, 1934, which was analogous to the soldier's oath. These brave acts undoubtedly were a factor in the regime's retreat from a confrontation with the churches. The authority and reputation of the Third Reich seemed seriously threatened by the chaotic events and protests. Furthermore, ecumenical conferences such as the one held in Fanö, Denmark, in August, 1934, brought the Confessional Church a hearing outside Germany, despite the intensive efforts, official chicanery, and even denunciations by the Church Foreign Office. This office, headed by Theodor Heckel, a new bishop close to the regime, sought to prevent the appearance of the Confessional clergy (as, for example, Dietrich Bonhoeffer's) in Fanö.[65]

In this situation, Hitler refrained from launching an overt, new *Kulturkampf*. Some of the coercive measures of Bishop Müller, such as the dismissal of Bishop Wurm (Württemberg) and Bishop Meiser (Bavaria), were even rescinded. In November, 1934, the Confessional Church formed a church countergovernment (Temporary Head of the German Evangelical Church), and Müller's Nazi leadership beat a retreat. The creation of a Reich Church Ministry (July, 1935) under the former justice official Hans Kerrl, who after the Nazi takeover became Prussian Minister of Justice and later administered the Disposition of Space (*Raumordnung*), evidenced the new caution; the vain effort for *Gleichschaltung* from within gave way to rigorous political control from the outside. True, Reich Bishop Müller refused to resign, but, embittered and without influence, he withdrew with his title-without-office to Königsberg, where in the waning days of the Third Reich he committed suicide.

The DC split into numerous groups and came under attack by the *völkisch* God Believer ideologues around Rosenberg. Antichurch propaganda and the deification of Hitler, with slogans like "Adolf Hitler Yesterday, Today, and Throughout Eternity" (Gauleiter Kube), were commonplace. Rosenberg never ceased to point out that the party was not "the guardian angel" of any religious group, even if this group believed that it was "close to National Socialism." The SA, which had played so vital a role in the church campaigns of 1933, was finally barred from wearing uniforms at church feasts (1936); and the SS had always pursued an antichurch course. With the party's denunciations and its antichurch, anti-Christian turn, the difference between the German Christians and the Confessional Church diminished. Open discussion of questions of church policy gave way to strict surveillance and suppression of all politically relevant church events. The "church battle" (*Kirchenkampf*) more and more shifted to internal conflicts.

Even though the war revived the old illusions nurtured by pastoral nationalism, Hitler nonetheless was planning a radical "solution" of the church question, for as far as he was concerned the early indul-

[65] Dietrich Bonhoeffer, *Gesammelte Schriften*, ed. E. Bethge, I (Munich, 1959), 182–222.

gence shown the churches had been nothing but a political tactic. Martin Bormann, his most powerful accomplice, sent a confidential memorandum to all Gauleiter in 1941 spelling out the shift from the Christian-national tinge of the early days to the strategy of attrition and isolation of the churches: National Socialism and Christianity were incompatible, he said, and therefore "clerical particularism" should not be fought but preserved, intensified, and turned against the churches. For "just as the harmful influences of the astrologers, soothsayers, and assorted swindlers had to be eliminated and suppressed by the state, so the influence of the churches has to be completely eliminated." [66] What this was to mean for the future of a victorious Third Reich was apparent in the new Reich territories, for example, in the "model Gau" Wartheland, where the former Prussian Church Commissar August Jäger instituted a reign of anti-Christian terror in 1939.

Any analysis of the position of the churches must deal with the two aspects of the Protestant church battle. National Socialist infiltration and seduction, a policy of divide and conquer and persecution, created chaos within the churches and put relentless pressure on them. Although the plan of a coordinated, Nazified "National Church" was an obvious failure and the total claim of the Nazi dictatorship ran up against insuperable obstacles, it is also true that religious opposition all too often "was merely another way of 'evasion' and almost helped to delay political counteraction," [67] that it came too late, and that for far too long it heeded the taboos of respect for authority. This was stated quite plainly after the war in the Stuttgart Confession of Guilt of the Evangelical Churches (1945)—in contrast to the apologies with which other groups and institutions, including the Catholic Church, sought to cover up their coresponsibility.

As stated earlier, only a few individuals in the churches took unequivocal stands of opposition. This was evidenced most particularly in the ambiguous position on the Jewish question. Criticism of the Aryan paragraph did not prevent the survival of a traditional anti-Semitism; the Protestant and Catholic objections to euthanasia were not matched by any similar protests against the Jewish policy. Opposition was limited to scattered individual acts and assistance. The rejection of a traditional Christian state ideology, as defined theologically in the Barmen Declaration of May, 1934 (Article 5), did not find consistent political application: "We reject the false teaching by which the state is equated with the sole and total order of human life, and thus also made to fulfill the duty of the church, beyond its special assignment [to preserve law and peace]."

Only a few acted in accordance with Karl Barth's assertion that the preservation of a democratic constitutional state was the concern

[66] *Nürnberger Dokumente*, **XXXV**, 7 ff.; 12 f. On Hitler himself, *ibid.*, PS—1520, **XXVII** 286 f.; *Tischgespräche*, p. 348.

[67] Hans Rothfels, *Die deutsche Opposition gegen Hitler* (Frankfurt/Main, 1958), p. 47.

of Christianity. But in defensive form, this assertion was inherent in the continuing protest of numerous clergymen and church groups, and above all in a brave memorandum prepared by the Confessional Church in June, 1936. In it, the church broke through the past silence, assailing not only the Government's anticlerical course but also Nazi ideology, race anti-Semitism, and judicial arbitrariness, and openly criticized the "fact that in Germany, which calls itself a state of law, there still exist concentration camps and that the actions of the Gestapo are outside the scope of legal review." The memorandum also expressly turned against the Führer cult, which made Hitler's will "the norm not only of political decisions but also of the morality and the rights of our people."

The memorandum had not been intended for publication, and it cost some of its authors, among them the head of the Office of the Confessional Church, Friedrich Weissler, their freedom and even their lives. This document, together with a number of brave proclamations of the Brethren's Council (August, 1936) read from the pulpits, for the first time concretized also politically the protest against state authority. Only rarely, however, were clerical declarations of such general import attempted. In October, 1943, the Prussian Confessional Synod (Breslau) openly denied the Nazi state the right to pursue its annihilation policies: "Concepts such as 'rooting out,' 'liquidation,' and 'unworthy life' are not known to the Divine order. The extermination of people solely because they are related to a criminal or old or mentally disturbed or belong to an alien race is not a sword to be wielded by the state." That held true also for "the life of the people of Israel" and for taking refuge in the excuse of being merely the executors of official orders: "We cannot permit superiors to relieve us of our responsibility before God." [68]

The majority of those close to the church resistance failed to cope with three major problems. First, in the debate over the loyalty oath, only few severed the traditional ties to the state. Second, with the outbreak of the war, the churches largely fell back on their position of World War I and put patriotic duty and prayers for victory above possible reservations; during the Sudeten crisis of 1938, many of the Lutheran bishops had already begun to edge away from the Confessional Church. And third, the "fight against Bolshevism" proved an argument of overwhelming effectiveness even among critics; anti-Communism tied both Protestants and Catholics to the policies of National Socialism and neutralized much of the opposition against the regime. Only a few drew the logical consequence and like Karl Barth denounced the war, or like Dietrich Bonhoeffer confronted the Germans with the alternative "of either accepting the defeat of their nation so that Christian civilization can survive, or accepting victory and thus destroy our civilization." [69] Discussions about resistance before July 20, 1944, revealed how isolated views such as these were.

[68] Documentation in Wolf, *op. cit.*, pp. 234 ff.
[69] Bonhoeffer, *op. cit.*, I, 320.

The Protestant and Catholic churches, despite the differences in their structures, shared many impulses and prejudices. One of the differences was the incomparably greater organizational rigidity and dogmatism of Catholicism, and also its supranational character. Yet Catholicism's relationship to National Socialism was by no means unambiguous. The external cohesion of Catholicism did not prevent the Church from dropping much of its original opposition to National Socialism. On the contrary, it assisted in the acceptance of accomplished facts. Efforts were even made to win support for the regime. It is true that attempts to forge a bond between Catholicism and National Socialism never rivaled the intensity or scope of the German Christian movement. The confrontation with National Socialism did not, as in the case of Protestantism, create a major organizational crisis. But the process of voluntary *Gleichschaltung* did at times make considerable inroads on the Catholic Church. Just as in the case of Protestantism, the first plateau in this development was reached in the summer of 1933, and that position remained unchanged until the end of 1933.

Two problems above all marked Catholic reaction to National Socialism: the religious schism, which affected Germany more profoundly than any other nation, and the subsequent development of political Catholicism from the defensive movement of an embattled minority to the governing party of the Weimar Republic. With their polemic against "Rome," the National Socialists exploited popular anti-Catholic feelings, even though many of them were themselves Catholic and Hitler was an admirer of the authoritarian structure of the Roman Church. Its battle against a demonic non-German (*ultramontan*) power provided the regime with a still better platform than its fight with Protestantism.

This factor adds to the seriousness of the Catholic Church's attempt to protect its flanks in direct negotiations and its desertion of its political arm, the Center Party, shortly after the passage of the Enabling Act. On March 28, 1933, the Bishop's Conference at Fulda revised its previously negative attitude toward National Socialism. Despite all criticism of "certain religious-moral errors," the conference believed that in view of Hitler's Christian-national declarations "there was reason to be confident" that its previous "prohibitions and warnings may no longer be necessary." [70] At about this time, the head of the Center Party, the Reverend Kaas, turned up in Rome and, in conjunction with Papen, initiated negotiations for a concordat which promised to be advantageous to both parties. The idea of the coexistence of State and Church ignored the reservations of numerous clerical and political exponents of Catholicism. And the continuing encroachments on Catholic organizations also did not prevent the negotiations from continuing up to their successful conclusion on July 8, 1933, three days after the dissolution of the Center Party. The Vatican negotiations,

[70] Gerd Rühle, *Das Dritte Reich, I* (Berlin, 1934), 250.

conducted by its Secretary of State, Cardinal Pacelli (the future Pope Pius XII), recognized the Hitler regime and agreed to restrictions on political and social Catholic organizations in Germany; the National Socialists guaranteed freedom of religion, the protection of Church bodies, the right to the dissemination of pastoral letters, and the preservation of parochial schools.

It soon became obvious that Hitler was interested only in the tactical advantages won by the concordat. With respect to foreign policy, this meant the recognition and nonviolability of the takeover; domestically, it served to placate the Catholic opposition and to sanction the *Gleichschaltung*. Moreover, the agreement lent support to those groups which, prodded by Papen and other right-wing Catholics, urged active participation in the "national revolution" and close cooperation with National Socialism, as for example through the Cross and Eagle League, the Working Group of Catholic Germans, and the Catholic League for National Politics. The pamphlet series *Reich und Kirche* (*Reich and Church*), published in Münster, as well as *Germania*, a Center paper close to Papen, and other Catholic publications featured the opinions of reputable theologians and publicists lauding the "Catholic entrée to National Socialism." Initially, most Church dignitaries enthusiastically shared the illusions of the Vatican and the German clergy with regard to the agreement, which apparently made greater concessions to the Church than any of the Weimar governments had offered. The political organizations, to be sure, had been sacrificed, and this proved of crucial importance when it came to the implementation of the Nazi guarantees. When the Church began to press for the fulfillment of the promises made, Hitler altered his earlier tactics. In his Advent sermons of 1933, Cardinal Faulhaber took issue with the anti-Christian ideology and totality claim of National Socialism, and prior to that, an election appeal by the Bavarian Bishops on the plebiscite of November 12, 1933, had been suppressed.[71]

It has been argued that the concordat gave the Catholic Church better leverage in its fight for life and in its protests against the total claim of the Nazi regime. At the time, Cardinal Pacelli declared that the offer had to be accepted in order to save the Church in Germany.[72] But the political and moral price extracted was high. The recognition of the regime prevented a clear-cut confrontation and put a burden on the Catholic opposition similar to that borne by the Protestant resistance. Although the concordat was repeatedly violated by the Nazis from the very beginning, faith in the feasibility of close cooperation nonetheless persisted and was voiced by such high dignitaries as Archbishop Gröber (Freiburg), Bishop Berning (Osnabrück), and the

---

[71] Ernst-Wolfgang Böckenförde, "Der deutsche Katholizismus im Jahr 1933," *Hochland*, LIII (1960–61), 215 ff.; *ibid.*, LIV (1961–62), 217 ff.; cf. Bracher, *Nationalsozialistische Machtergreifung und Reichskonkordat* (Wiesbaden, 1956), pp. 44 ff.

[72] *Documents on British Foreign Policy*, Second Series, V, 524 f.

Papal Nuncio. The effects of this policy made themselves felt particularly in Catholic regions where the Center Party had been able to block the Nazi advance up to 1933. Thus the President of the Rhine province informed the Prussian Minister of the Interior on September 27, 1933, that as a result of the concordat "a substantial portion of the Catholic population, which up to now has shown an inner reserve toward the Reich Government, has now been unconditionally won over to allegiance to the new Reich," and he put particular stress on "the effectiveness of the abbot of Maria Laach"; but that is precisely why a "smaller number of Catholics" deplored the conclusion of the concordat—"because it robbed them of one of their most effective tools of agitation." [73]

And, in fact, the possibilities and limits of Catholic opposition lay between these two points of view. The conflict over the organizational and spiritual position of the Catholic Church intensified almost at the same time as the Protestant church fight. Criticism of scattered official acts began to be voiced at the highest level, and it was never to cease. But the basic decisions had been made, and just as in the case of Protestantism, opposition remained selective and restricted to Church-connected matters; only in special instances was there political resistance to the regime. The selective opposition undoubtedly was also a political matter, if only because of the extent and depth of the reservations which the pastoral letters in particular and the open conflicts with Rosenberg aroused or kept alive in Catholic congregations. Rosenberg's *Mythus* was put on the Catholic Index of forbidden books in February, 1934; the Catholic Action and Catholic Youth League became centers of opposition, and finally, the famous papal encyclical *With Burning Concern* (March, 1937) broadened the basis of criticism of National Socialist ideology and oppression. Although the Gestapo was able to prevent the encyclical from being distributed in printed form, it could not prevent its being read from the pulpits.

But the shortcomings and limits of such opposition were evident. To begin with, there was the contention that it was possible to be loyal to the state and also criticize the regime. Thus the Catholic Church supported the return of the Saar and contributed to the Nazi victory in the Saar plebiscite (January, 1935); and three years later, despite past experience, the Church similarly gave all-out support to the *Anschluss* of Austria through a momentous proclamation of Vienna's Cardinal Innitzer. A second factor was the Church's support of the war and the subsequent appalling displays of its willingness to cooperate. Closely allied with this was its support and sanctioning of anti-Communism. The bulwark theory laid to rest many misgivings about the ideology and methods of Nazi rule and encouraged the sort of ambiguous attitude that prevented Pope Pius XII from openly censuring National Socialism during the war. To argue that he failed to do so out of deference to the exposed position of the German Church and the con-

[73] Cf. Bracher, Sauer, and Schulz, *op. cit.*, pp. 344 ff. For a selection of documents from the Catholic vantage point, see Gerhart Binder, *Irrtum und Widerstand* (Munich, 1968).

flict of conscience of soldiers merely underscores the problem. And, finally, because anti-Semitism was part of the Catholic tradition, the Church failed to take a principled position on National Socialist Jewish policy, though individual criticism of the forms and methods of this policy was voiced. Only the work of the most recent Ecumenical Council (1965) marks a departure from this anti-Jewish position, while simultaneously proving its continued existence to this day.

For all these reasons, one cannot equate the Catholic Church with resistance. In contrast to the Evangelical Church, the Catholic Church issued no proclamation of guilt in 1945, nor did it engage in any critical discussion—a fact which has become an issue since the debate over the concordat that began in 1956 and over the Pope's role in the war (raised in particular by Rolf Hochhuth in his play *The Deputy* [1963]).

Aside from these reservations, the Catholic opposition played an impressive role. It fought a ceaseless battle against the *Gleichschaltung* of the youth organizations. The protests of the Bishop of Münster, Count Galen, against the "continuing murder" of euthanasia (1941) evoked so great a response that the leadership feared large areas of Westphalia would revolt if he were silenced—thus proving that overt protest was not impossible. Nazi campaigns against bishops and priests in disfavor frequently brought intensified resistance and the esteem of their congregations. Thousands of priests and laymen were sent to prisons and concentration camps; defamation campaigns against the cloistered clergy culminated in show trials for alleged moral and monetary crimes (1935). In the meantime, groups of the Catholic workers' movement found their way into the political resistance; Christian trade unionists like Otto Müller, Josef Joos, Nikolaus Gross, Bernhard Letterhaus, and Jakob Kaiser established close contacts with Socialist trade unionists around Wilhelm Leuschner and with the former German National Employees Association leader Max Habermann. The factors uniting the churches in their defensive battle and their contact with the political opposition involved them in the discussions of the Kreisau Circle and in the plans for the overthrow of the Hitler regime. In this respect the Catholic Church was, generally speaking, better able to protect its flanks than Protestantism, which contained a far more powerful group that made common cause with the country's rulers.

It can thus be said that misgivings and criticism of the regime possessed a greater potential force within the churches than in other sectors. The policy of ideological coordination here was limited, and Hitler himself believed that he would not be able to break through these limits until after he had won the war. Until such time, the regime relied on organizational restrictions and press prohibitions, the arrest of exposed leaders like Niemöller (after 1936), the shutting down of theological faculties, and pressure on all members of the clergy who used their pulpits to read oppositional proclamations of the Confessional Church or pastoral letters. Illegal activity and organization was the response to this, particularly in the divided Evangelical churches. The Confessional Church maintained its own divinity schools, in which theologians like Dietrich Bonhoeffer, officially barred from speaking and writing, were able to teach; in addition, there were projects such as Provost Grüber's Church Aid for Jewish Christians and a network of contacts with churches in foreign countries. What mattered was whether beyond the theological-ideological conflict and the protection of independent organizations those involved realized that the Christian churches, as Karl Barth had admonished, had to speak and act not only on their own behalf.

After many errors and delusions, a minority became persuaded of the validity of this position. In this area, too, the Nazi tactic of hastening capitulation to spiritual coordination through pseudo-Christian, pseudo-religious camouflage proved singularly effective. Ridding themselves of the churches' illusions about National Socialism, theologians like Dietrich Bonhoeffer and the Jesuit Alfred Delp moved into the forefront of the political resistance and played an active part in the plans for the overthrow of the Government and for a new political order. The churches never saw their way clear to sanctioning these efforts. Revolution and tyrannicide violated their basic legalistic, conservative position. But Christian motives, together with moral-humanistic, liberal, socialist ideas of democracy, played a large part in the conspiracy of July 20, 1944. The Nazi rulers to the very end were greatly concerned about the actual or potential resistance of the churches, which, according to the 1940 census, still counted 95 per cent of the population as nominal members. The elimination of this obstacle to total domination was a prime postwar objective of the regime.

Between Civilian and Military Opposition

The consolidation of the Nazi regime in 1933–34 severely curtailed the possibilities of resistance of socialist and church groups. In the absence of contacts with persons in positions of power as a step toward bringing influence to bear on official policy, there was little hope for a popular uprising or for a change. It soon became obvious that the possibilities of activating a popular opposition under conditions of totalitarian rule were slight indeed. The attitude of both the working class and the bourgeoisie made it clear that illegality and resistance did not exert mass appeal. At no time did an opposition movement develop able to unite the various groups and individuals into one joint planning and organizational body. In view of the diversity of resistance groups, the antitotalitarian impulses that emanated from the initially not democratically inclined civil service and the military circles take on added significance.

The first gesture from this circle came in Hindenburg's lifetime, with the bloody suppression of the attempt by the Munich lawyer and writer Edgar Jung to persuade Vice Chancellor von Papen to form a Christian-conservative opposition to Nazi autocratic rule. But Papen failed in this effort as well. Although he delivered the speech drafted for this purpose at Marburg University on June 17, 1934, he deserted his colleagues when the regime moved in—and he continued to serve it. Of greater import was the ceaseless activity of the Lord Mayor of Leipzig, Carl Goerdeler, a former German National. He worked in three directions: he sought to influence the Government through memorandums; he maintained contacts with various groups in the nascent bourgeois and conservative opposition; and he influenced the state bureaucracy. And, in fact, as a civil servant who worked for the regime out of a national, traditionally "unpolitical" sense of duty, while being indispensible as a specialist, he possessed greater insight than any of his contemporaries into violations of individual rights and arbitrariness, into the reality of Nazi rule. In the face of intensified coercion, persecution, and finally the threat of war, a growing number of men who initially had been sympathetic to the "national revolution" began to toy with the idea of civilian opposition. As they became more convinced that the overthrow of the Government from below was out of the question and that a *coup d'état* from above was the only feasible answer, these efforts began to center on the Army.

The Army was anything but ready for this. Contrary to the hopes of many conservatives, the Army had acquiesced unprotestingly in the seizure of power, the murder of Generals von Schleicher and von Bredow, and the oath to Hitler. Its illusions helped to consolidate Nazi rule. This was not only a consequence of Blomberg's policies. Seeckt's ideal of the "unpolitical soldier," which in fact was an antidemocratic concept, determined the Army's attitude; by promising military autonomy, Hitler had satisfied the old-type officers. In addition, there was the alleged mutuality of interests of the military and National Socialism: rearmament and eradication of the restrictions of Versailles were the goals, and for these, one was willing to accept the aberrant practices of National Socialist rule. But above all, the expansion of the Army also facilitated its Nazification. The introduction of universal military service (1935) necessarily altered the structure of the hitherto closed Army; the formation of the Air Force accelerated a development which opened up the middle and lower echelons of the Army in particular to the massive influence of National Socialism.

Apart from the Hitlerian orientation of Blomberg and his closest coworker, Walther von Reichenau, the top leadership, to be sure, remained initially untouched. The skepticism of the generals about the occupation of the Rhineland (1936) was typical of the aloof watch-and-see attitude of the top officers. But with each new success, Hitler's course, pursued in defiance of all warnings, undermined the position of the skeptics. Their attitude remained ambiguous and uncertain. But military class-consciousness and self-esteem, and the concomitant disdain for the "plebeian methods" and demagogic, hazardous policies of Hitler, did not prevent the top echelons from yielding to the seductive appeal of Nazi successes, and the rapidly growing "people's army" further strengthened the National Socialist impact. After the limited opportunities of the Weimar era, the officer corps found itself with unprecedented chances for promotion—though of course at the price of collaboration, for the formal independence of the Army did not stop Hitler from pushing through vital decisions as early as 1935 without paying much heed to the advice or objections of the military.

Even before formally taking over command of the Army, Hitler by his personal decisions had landed a blow against the Prusso-German military tradition from which it never recovered. How greatly the leadership and responsibility of the senior officer corps was thereby undermined became increasingly evident in the war itself, when Hitler interfered also in minor military command decisions and, over the heads of responsible officers and staffs, arbitrarily exercised his supreme powers. He staffed the top military leadership with complaisant generals who owed their rapid rise to him: the High Command (Oberkommando der Wehrmacht, or OKW), headed by the blindly subservient Generals Keitel and Jodl was the most blatant example. Ultimately the resistance of independent officers also failed because of these generals. The Army had ceased to be able to act independently after the failure of 1934. And military resistance also was fated to remain fragmented, limited to a minority which, though at times occupying vital positions and in possession of important contacts, never gained sufficient influence on the highest military levels. This determined the form and limited the possibilities of the military opposition.

As became evident, the German military tradition in the last analysis did not constitute a real foundation for political resistance. Opposition remained confined to the personal initiative of intellectually and morally independent officers. Its basis was not the tradition of the Army but the conscience of individuals whose eyes were opened by the reality of the new regime, who grew aware of the problem inherent in unquestioning military obedience, and, finally, who were ready to step out of the narrow framework of military thinking and make contact with the civilian resistance. Undoubtedly, existing conflicts about military policy also served as a springboard. One such early act was the resignation of General von Hammerstein at the end of 1933. The years to come saw much criticism directed against the War Ministry's subservience to Hitler. The Chief of Staff (Ludwig Beck) and the Commander in Chief (Werner von Fritsch) repeatedly accused Blomberg of yielding too readily to the party. But whereas Beck turned his back on Hitler with greater frequency between 1934 and 1938, Fritsch continued to play the part of the soldier who kept aloof from party matters, but ultimately he disappointed the expectations of the opposition and failed politically. His conduct in the crisis of 1938 again proved his helplessness when faced by political problems. After June 30, 1934, he also avoided all political entanglements and told his officers laconically: "We cannot change politics; we must do our duty silently." [74] The events of summer, 1934, remain a dark chapter casting a shadow on subsequent developments. All too many used the oath to Hitler as the

[74] Ulrich von Hassell, *Vom anderen Deutschland* (rev. ed.; Frankfurt/Main, 1964), p. 39.

justification or pretext for evading the issue of conscience and obedience and for refraining from resistance to the very last.

The first shift in the attitude of the military took place in 1936–37, when Hitler embarked on his expansionist course. The tensions between the military and political leaderships which put an end to the Blomberg era became pronounced, and at the same time they seemed to offer the first opening for overt criticism and opposition. In the center of this shift stood the Chief of Staff, General Ludwig Beck, born in 1880 as the son of a Rhenish industrialist. A conservative supporter of Hitler since 1930, Beck in 1934 underwent the change which one had looked for in Fritsch. He demanded explanations for the murder of Schleicher and Bredow; his misgivings over political developments were further strengthened by his contacts with Bernhard von Bülow, the Foreign Office's conservative State Secretary, In May, 1935, Beck threatened to resign if a report on the possible occupation of Czechoslovakia he had been asked to prepare was to serve as a blueprint for a coming war. Despite all Nazi successes, Beck stuck to his repudiation of military adventurism when, at about the time of Hitler's peace address of January 30, 1937, he was asked for his views on the possibilities of intervention in Austria. Significantly enough, Beck based his opinion on memorandums by Goerdeler, which furnished him with the economic arguments against a war. These early contacts with civilian opposition efforts became closer as time went on.

Beck, a careful, deliberate General Staff officer, possessed few of the gifts of the confirmed conspirator. Motivated by moral and military considerations, he was not made for coups, let alone revolutions. But he began to pay closer attention to the political developments and plans brewing outside his immediate area, and demanded of Blomberg that he act in consultation with those sharing military responsibility. Opposed to the evolving war course, which was becoming obvious to his trained eye, he drafted numerous memorandums calling for a morally responsible leadership. By the start of 1938, the critical point was reached: the so-called Blomberg-Fritsch crisis made it obvious that Hitler was determined to eliminate all formal obstacles on the road to military action (as mapped out in the Hossbach conference of November 5, 1937). The marriage of Blomberg and a filthy intrigue against Fritsch, behind which the fine hand of Göring and Himmler was discernible, brought the longed-for opportunity in February, 1938. The humiliation of the officer corps remained even after the refutation of the homosexuality charges against Fritsch. Fritsch, having been suspended, resigned; his successor, Brauchitsch, was further hobbled in his freedom of action because upon taking office he accepted a contribution to pay for his divorce. The officer corps acquiesced both in its loss of power and its humiliation. It settled for a vindication of Fritsch, but the *fait accompli* remained. The matter was covered over by the invasion of Austria, which so enhanced the prestige of the regime that the protest contemplated by Beck and Goerdeler seemed hopeless. The extent of the Army's loss of its vaunted "autonomy" was amply demonstrated by the manner in which the party, Göring, and Himmler organized the Austrian campaign, practically shutting out the General Staff (and the Foreign Office).

But this experience and Hitler's instructions to the military to prepare the smashing of Czechoslovakia (May, 1938) finally brought on the maturing of the first military resistance plan around Beck and Goerdeler. Carl Goerdeler, born 1884 in Schneidemühl of a conservative Prussian family, was among those big-city mayors who were conversant with the problems of modern life and experienced in working with liberals and socialists. This proved most useful in his tireless efforts to win cooperation across ideological and political barriers, regardless of his coworkers' justified reservations about his corporate-etatist ideas. He went on to establish contacts with persons in the administration, economic life, and the military. His was the classic example of the new type of opposition from *within* the establishment and the attempts to effect a change of government from within and above by taking off from existing positions of power. As the Deputy Mayor of Königsberg and (since 1930) Lord Mayor of Leipzig, this antirepublican nationalist had become a politically moderate administrator who first under Brüning and later also under Hitler (1934–35) held the important office of Reich Price Commissioner. However, he soon came into conflict first with the economic policy and later also with the political ideas of National Socialism. In 1934, in an effort to counteract the Government's course, he began to write a series of memorandums, including some to Hitler personally.

Behind Goerdeler's effort there stood up to the very last the illusory belief in the possibility of nonviolent change. But unlike others of his background, Goerdeler combined the mentality of the loyal civil servant with the rare courage of a man unafraid to speak his mind and to stand by his beliefs, a trait made evident by his conflicts with the Leipzig NSDAP and particularly with its rabid Gauleiter, Martin Mutschmann. Shortly after the beginning of Goerdeler's second, twelve-year term as Lord Mayor came the final turning point. At the end of 1936, when, against his will and in his absence, a statue of Mendelssohn was removed from its place in front of the Gewandhaus, the hall in which this greatest German-Jewish composer had conducted, Goerdeler with heavy heart but great spirit resigned his office. From that day on, helped by his wealthy connections, among them industrialists like Robert Bosch (Stuttgart), he began the ceaseless travels and writings which contributed so greatly to the marshaling of the bourgeois and conservative opposition. It was a one-man diplomacy, and between 1937 and 1939, his work repeatedly took him to Belgium and Holland, France and England, to the United States and Canada, to Switzerland, the Balkans, the Near East, and North Africa. Wherever he went, he tried to get talks under way and to establish contacts. He wrote comprehensive reports warning and admonishing like-minded friends and the military, but also Göring and Hitler.

The growing threat of war and the encroachments on the Army

and the Foreign Office convinced the bourgeois opponents of the regime of the urgency of concretizing their plans. In trying to assess the role of the military in the resistance, one must keep in mind that the consolidation and objectives of the Third Reich from the very outset rested on economic-military rearmament and aggressive expansion. The events of 1934 found the Army occupying a key position which at first remained unaffected by the rise of the SS. Even the dethronement of the Army leadership in 1938 did little to change the Army's confidence that it was vital to Hitler's plans and that it still occupied a strong, unique position. This fed the hope of Beck and Goerdeler that the Army offered a sound basis from which to influence the Hitler regime. In a series of memorandums and speeches, which in turn drew on Goerdeler's travel reports, Beck tried via Brauchitsch to change Hitler's mind. In this he was supported by General Georg Thomas, who, as the Chief of Economic Warfare and Rearmament in the OKW, entertained serious misgivings about the course being pursued. And furthermore, Beck began to prepare a show of resistance which burst through the framework of the Prusso-German tradition of the "unpolitical soldier." He justified the decision for political action with the exceptional nature of the situation: the threatening war and the awareness that only the Army was in a position to stop Hitler's aggressive politics, since the totalitarian regime had eliminated all other controls and counterforces.

It was Beck's intention to throw the weight of military judgment into the scale of political decision-making, and if need be, to force Hitler to heed this judgment. The weakness of this plan lay in Beck's connecting link: Brauchitsch. Although Brauchitsch on the whole agreed with Beck, he shied away from making good his promise to try to influence Hitler. Beck himself never managed to talk at length with Hitler. The entreaties, objections, and protests which he raised against Hitler's course were rejected by the Führer in this typical fashion: "What kind of generals are these which I as the head of state may have to propel into war? By rights, I should be the one seeking to ward off the generals' eagerness for war." And he succinctly defined the relationship which the military had arrived at with the regime through its alliance of mutual interest: "I do not ask my generals to understand my orders but only to carry them out." [75]

Beck's effort reached a climax on July 16, 1938. In a strongly worded memorandum of that date, he tried to persuade Brauchitsch to summon the top generals and, together with them, to bring influence to bear on Hitler. He suggested that they threaten to resign unless a halt was put to the war preparations. Beck made this suggestion more than once, and at the same time he put it into the broader framework of civilian opposition movements which, during these critical months, branched out in all directions. Behind the moral and military arguments there stood political viewpoints: the confrontation with

[75] Wolfgang Foerster, *Generaloberst Ludwig Beck* (Munich, 1953), p. 97.

the total state. To be sure, the basic note was not the deposition of Hitler and revolution but prevention of war and reinstitution of the rule of law. A military putsch was considered the last resort. This was the tenor of the address which Beck prepared at the beginning of August, 1938, for delivery by Brauchitsch to the assembled generals.

But even this minimal program rested on two presuppositions which no longer prevailed, namely, that Brauchitsch's cooperation was indispensible to any action from above, and that only the firmness of the West could stem Hitler's course. Since neither happened, the action was doomed to fail. Brauschitsch permitted Beck to present his arguments before an assembly of generals on August 4. Beck made a deep impression on the gathering; only Reichenau and Busch voiced reservations. But Brauchitsch himself shied away from the consequences. He neither delivered the prepared address nor did he set in motion a protest by the generals. And the fact that he subsequently showed Beck's memorandum to Hitler was sure to be damaging. The man who had sounded the warning was isolated and a "general strike of the generals" frustrated. Embittered and without support, Beck drew the consequence: to forestall being dismissed like Fritsch, he resigned on August 18, 1938.

Of course, the failure of the generals to act though they knew better was only one side of the coin. Another reason was the apparent success of Nazi blackmail and war threats during these months. Although Hitler retreated temporarily under the impact of the reservations of the military, still the events leading up to the Munich conference refuted the claims and plans of the opposition, which were based on the belief that Hitler was facing a crisis. From this vantage point as well, the Munich concessions were of crucial significance, because the German people were no more ready for war than were the generals. The situation was entirely unlike that of 1939, when the occupation of Czechoslovakia and the Soviet pact surrounded the Nazi war plans with an aura of irresistibility. Thus appeasement and the failure of the generals combined to reduce the civilian resistance which was gathering force in mid-1938 to ineffective opposition against a victorious government.

Skeptical appraisals of Beck's plans ignore the fact that they promised to be more than merely an isolated protest of generals which the regime could have counteracted by promoting Nazi careerists. This military opposition was in touch with a resistance which for the first time encompassed almost all political groups that were planning to topple the regime in the moment of the expected military and political crisis. The contacts of the conspirators extended from SPD and trade unionists to the higher civil service and the semicivilian secret service of the Army. These preparations, which reached a peak after Beck's resignation, also involved the new Chief of Staff, General Franz Halder. It was therefore quite obvious that a retreat of the West would diminish the chances of an effective resistance in the same degree in which it would enhance Hitler's popular image. Liaison men tried to make this point in England and France. Ewald von Kleist, for example, went to England in August, 1938, to speak to Winston Churchill. However, Churchill was unable to dissuade Chamberlain from his chosen course.[76]

In these weeks the nucleus of the active conspiracy was a circle that was forming around the Intelligence (Abwehr) section of the OKW, a department possessing profound insight into the true situation. Its motive force was the Chief of the Central Division of Intelligence, Colonel Hans Oster. Unlike his colleagues, this son of a Dresden clergyman (born 1888) had been critical of National Socialism even before 1933. After Schleicher's murder, Oster increasingly put the Intelligence network at the disposal of the opposition. He had formed a close relationship with Beck at the time of the Fritsch affair, when he furnished Beck with the documentation to fight the intrigue against Fritsch.

In the ensuing years, this determined enemy of the regime, with his far-flung connections and sources of information, a man of decision, flexibility, and cunning, became the soul of the military opposition. His position was practically unassailable so long as the Chief of Intelligence, Admiral Canaris, protected him. The feverish activity which Oster developed in the summer of 1938 substantially contributed to the bridge between the military and civilian opposition. Under the protection of the Abwehr, contacts were established and plans coordinated. Oster was the liaison to Halder, which Beck had arranged before his resignation. The contacts with the oppositionists in the Foreign Office were of major importance. These men—Adam von Trott zu Solz, Otto Kiep, Hans-Bernd von Haeften—also played a vital role in the future activities leading up to July 20, 1944.

Central to all the plans was the intention to arrest Hitler following his issuance of the order to unleash the war and the expected declaration of war by the West. It was assumed that these events would frighten the German people, win broader support for the planned putsch, and diminish the risk of civil war. If, so the thinking went, the criminal, catastrophic course of Hitler were made plain, then the resistance could hope to win the support also of the bourgeoisie and military circles committed to upholding the authority of the state, and a refusal to obey would not be thought of as sabotage and treason. The experience of November, 1918, served as a warning example. Two dangers obviously had to be avoided: a civil war whose outcome was uncertain in view of the power of the party, and a reverse stab-in-the-back legend, which might poison all future efforts by asserting that the Army and opposition had stabbed Hitler in the back at the height of success. How right these fears were was proved later by the defamation of the men of July 20, 1944, who, had they succeeded, would after all merely have put an end to a lost war.

The plans specifically called for the occupation of key positions by the military and the arrest of Hitler by the commander of the Berlin

[76] Cf. Bodo Scheurig, *Ewald von Kleist-Schmenzin* (Oldenburg, 1968), pp. 155 ff.

Defense District, General von Witzleben, to be followed by a trial of Hitler. Oster's closest collaborator, Hans von Dohnanyi, Dietrich Bonhoeffer's brother-in-law, had been compiling a file of Nazi crimes ever since 1934, and this was to be made public and distributed throughout the country. In order to make sure of the arrest, Oster and Dohnanyi had also established contact with the heads of the Berlin police. Police President Count Helldorf's initial enthusiasm for National Socialism and that of his top assistant, Count Fritz von der Schulenburg, had turned into skepticism. Contacts also were made with other disenchanted early supporters of the regime (like Hjalmar Schacht), but above all with prominent Socialists like Ernst Leuschner, Ernst von Harnack, and Julius Leber (who had just come back from prison). One of the alternatives being considered was to have Hitler declared insane and institutionalized. In this they counted on the cooperation of the director of the psychiatric clinic of the Berlin Charité hospital, Professor Karl Bonhoeffer, the father of Dietrich and Klaus (the latter a trustee of the Lufthansa who had also become involved with the conspirators). Other right-wing groups toyed with the less realistic plan of a restoration of the monarchy, and former Free Corps and Stahlhelm officers even thought of dispatching troops to Hitler's Chancellery and in the course of this military action shooting him.

But these were marginal plans. The ideas of the conspirators around Oster involved a brief period of military dictatorship, followed by the convocation of a national assembly to decide on the future political order. It was a risky, hurriedly improvised plan for a rapidly deteriorating situation. And it stood and fell with the threat of war brought on by the Nazi regime. Hitler's triumph at Munich knocked the bottom out of all these plans. In the next three years the regime went from one success to another, which weakened the ranks of the opposition and made any counteraction almost hopeless. Any attempt to stage a putsch now would have had the feared consequences of civil war and stab-in-the-back legend. On September 28, 1938, the convocation of the Munich conference on the heels of general mobilization wrote an end to the only plan which held out promise for preventing the war and for blocking the further expansion of the rule of terror. The at best problematical participation of a hesitant military, on which all the planners depended, was thereby made far more complicated. Consequently, renewed efforts were made to influence those in power, primarily Göring, on whose alleged moderation Goerdeler above all pinned his hopes.

The continuing war preparations nonetheless kept the idea of a military countermove alive. Now General von Hammerstein as well as Ulrich von Hassell, until recently German Ambassador to Rome, were brought into the plans, which were to deal with the changed situation. In addition, contacts were established with the Prussian Minister of Finance, Johannes Popitz, who was steering an independent course between collaboration and opposition, and Papen's former State Secretary, Erwin Planck, the son of the renowned physicist. Hammerstein, however, was highly skeptical of the Army, which he said had been beheaded and castrated, and the representatives of the Left were still more dubious after all the experiences with the vacillating military. And finally, events immediately before the war demonstrated the impotence of an opposition which despite the efforts of Oster and others could not influence the course of events. In addition to diplomatic efforts to prevent the war, two coup plans deserve mention. According to one, Witzleben, who had been transferred to Frankfurt, was to be brought back to Berlin to head the military putsch, and Halder, once the order for war was given, was to be persuaded to resign in protest—as Beck had done a year earlier in connection with the proposed strike of the generals. This plan failed also because of a change in the date for the order to attack. The second project rested on Hammerstein, who in the meantime had been reactivated as the leader of an Army unit near Cologne. He planned to invite Hitler to visit his headquarters and arrest him. But the visit did not come off, and Hammerstein, who was anyway under suspicion, was once more relieved of his office. The war presented the resistance with new presuppositions.

VIII

The Wartime Regime

World War II was the consequence not only of daring revisionist exploits. It was also the logical outgrowth of National Socialist ideology and rule—a factor that must be kept in mind when examining the causes and events leading to the war. Three points in particular deserve special mention: (1) as far as Hitler was concerned, World War I had never ended; (2) the acquisition of *Lebensraum* presupposed aggressive expansion; (3) totalitarian rule depended on a prepared mobilized community which diverted its internal conflicts to the outside. Improvisation and tactical moves undoubtedly also played a major role, particularly since, as 1938 had shown, most Germans were by no means enthusiastic about the prospect of war, despite the propaganda inroads on all areas of life, despite popular admiration for Hitler's successes, and despite the appeal of revisionist goals. However, the impotence of "public opinion," the effect of political coordination, and the extent of internal mobilization overshadowed all misgivings. Perhaps the Führer's highly touted "intuition" was right this time as well.

Within four weeks, the German armies, supported by the most modern European Air Force, overran the Polish defenses from three sides; by prearrangement, the Red Army moved in from the East on September 17, 1939. A further German-Soviet agreement (September 28, 1939) divided the territories and spheres of interest between the two powers. On September 19, Hitler proclaimed triumphantly at Danzig: "Poland will never rise again. This is guaranteed not only by Germany but in the final analysis also by Russia." Once again it appeared as if the Western powers had been outmaneuvered, and once again Hitler demanded the acceptance of accomplished facts as the price for "final" peace. And although this time London and Paris refused to play the game, the West stood by and watched as the Soviet Union forced its "protection" on the Baltic states and dictated its territorial and military conditions to Finland after a winter war, and the German occupation of Denmark and Norway (April 9, 1940) broadened the strategic basis of the Third Reich. A month later, the Western front was smashed in a major campaign through Belgium and Holland, in violation of all neutrality agreements. The German attack on Rotterdam (May 14) began the bombing of civilian populations which was to come down so terribly on Germany herself. The *Blitzkrieg* of the German tanks and planes seemed unstoppable; the only thing that marred their record was the incredible evacuation at Dunkirk, which rescued 200,000 British and 100,000 French troops from the Germans—an expression of a new British will to resist, exemplified by Churchill, who on May 10, 1940, had replaced Neville Chamberlain, the Prime Minister of the era of appeasement.

The fall of France brought Hitler to the height of power. At the same spot in the forest of Compiègne and in the same railroad carriage in which Germany had capitulated on November 11, 1918, the French were forced to accept the truce conditions of June 21, 1940. A scant ten months after unleashing the war, Hitler had reversed the defeat of 1918 and achieved hegemony in non-Russian Europe; moreover, Italy was assigned the role of a subordinate partner. The National Socialist–Fascist doctrines of a "new European order" could now unfold freely. Britain was isolated, the United States not yet prepared to intervene, and the Soviet Union still intent on preserving its union of interest with Berlin and on compensating for the losses of World War I by occupying eastern Poland, the Baltics, and Bessarabia.[1] But in July, 1940, Hitler was already toying with the idea of attacking Russia the following spring, while at the same time, in a speech before the Reichstag on July 19, 1940, in tried and true fashion calling the German-Russian relationship "firmly rooted." What contributed to his decision to move against Russia was the fact that Churchill's England, contrary to Hitler's expectations and "peace offers," was not prepared to arrive at an accommodation and that German plans to invade England were doomed because of the inferiority of the German Navy and the ineffectiveness of the London air raids. Following on the heels of the "miracle of Dunkirk," Britain's determination was the first turning point, comparable to the battle of the Marne of 1914. Hitler found himself in a situation similar to that of Napoleon. The move of 1938–40 turned into a drawn-out war. The attack on Russia was as much a forward push as it was a consequence of the *Lebensraum* idea.

Meanwhile, the Nazi regime tried to transform Europe into a hinterland of its aggressive policies through occupation, pressure, and sham treaties; Italy's advances in the Balkans and in North Africa enlarged the terrain of expansionism; the three-power treaty with Rome and

[1] For a basic discussion of this aspect, see Gerhard Weinberg, *Germany and the Soviet Union, 1939 to 1941* (Leiden, 1954). Together with the work of Walther Hofer, *War Premeditated, 1939* (London, 1955), the best treatment of the controversy on Hitler's road to war is Alan Bullock, *Hitler and the Origins of the Second World War* (Oxford, 1967).

Tokyo (September, 1940) aimed at a world-wide "new order." But England proved to be invincible in the Mediterranean as well. Although Franco proclaimed his sympathies for the Axis and later even agreed to furnish volunteers for the Eastern Front (the so-called Blue Division), he could not be induced to take an active part in the war; thus he turned out to be the only dictator to survive the war. Gibraltar and Malta remained powerful fortresses of British sea and air power; attempts to stir up Arab nationalism failed; the effective control of the French colonies proved to be impossible; and the Axis strategy in Africa could not, even at the height of military success (1942), push forward to the Suez Canal and the Near East. To be sure, German troops overran Yugoslavia and Greece (April-May, 1941), and Bulgaria and Croatia followed Hungary, Romania, and Slovakia in signing the three-power treaty. At the same time, however, the "new order" of southeastern Europe under Axis rule contributed to the exacerbation of German-Soviet tensions and to the subsequent delay in the attack on Russia, which turned out to be critical.

Already the talks held with Soviet Foreign Minister Molotov in Berlin in November, 1940, had in effect failed. In return for joining the three-power pact, Moscow demanded influence in the Balkans and free exit from the Black and Baltic seas, while protesting against the stationing of German troops in Romania and Finland. Ribbentrop and Hitler countered with a magnanimous offer to divide up the British Empire, even though British planes forced the talks to be conducted in the air-raid shelters of the Reich Chancellery and—as Molotov pointed out—testified to Britain's vitality. The idea of a German colonial empire in Central Africa was discussed, Italy was promised East and North Africa, and Russia, South Asia. But even then, Hitler was already determined to return to the essence of the National Socialist program temporarily shelved in 1939 and to seek a way out of the war and the realization of the *Lebensraum* claim by overpowering Russia.

Hitler's attack on Russia came on June 22, 1941. Though Moscow knew of the plans, Stalin may possibly have believed to the very last in a postponement. He had concluded a Soviet-Japanese nonaggression treaty on April 13, 1941, which relieved the pressure on Russia's eastern border and diminished the effectiveness of the three-power agreement. Moscow had fulfilled all its obligations toward Berlin to the letter, had recognized all of Hitler's conquests, and had not been sparing in its displays of amity—in Hitler's eyes, all of this was proof of Russia's weakness. The massive German troop movements in Poland and East Prussia could not have been a secret. Like Napoleon 129 years earlier, Hitler was able to advance rapidly. By late fall of 1941, German troops stood before Moscow; the "new *Lebensraum*" of the Ukraine was opening up. But now for the first time, the "greatest general of all times" was unable to refute the warnings of the experts by an immediate success. His expectations of bringing Russia to heel within three months turned out to be a pipe dream. His enormous territorial gains proved to have as little bearing on the course of the war as Napoleon's, and when the Russian winter set in earlier than anticipated and Hitler's armies suffered their first defeats, the Third Reich had arrived at its utmost limits. Yet another factor was added to Britain's stand and the defeat at the gates of Moscow: Japan's attack on Pearl Harbor on December 7, 1941, and Hitler's declaration of war on the United States on December 11, which turned the European war into a world war. And even though Japan's conquest of Southeast Asia initially bolstered Hitler's hopes, the mobilization of the underrated American war potential soon threw all his calculations overboard. December, 1941, was the turning point in the short life of the Third Reich. Hitler was beginning to pay the price for the ideological rigidity responsible for the misjudgment of Britain, America, and Russia. At first, this turn of events brought simply an acceleration of Germany's military efforts and above all a brutal intensification of totalitarian rule; particularly in the newly occupied territories, the most extreme consequences of Nazi ideology were being translated into reality.

In an eerie Reichstag speech on the day he launched the attack on Russia, Hitler referred to the Russian war as "the most difficult decision of my life." It was both a forward push and the consequence of ideological obsession. After years of success, the reverse side of the unrestrained leader dictatorship was becoming evident. In place of the strategically advantageous position of 1939, there was the war on many fronts which Hitler had so sharply criticized in *Mein Kampf*, and in place of isolated enemies, there was a powerful anti-Hitler coalition, which also helped the Communist underground movements to shake off their confusion and paralysis. Nor did the expansion of Germany's *Lebensraum* into the vast eastern territories bring the expected benefits. On the contrary, Nazi expansionism and ideology proved highly detrimental both to the conduct of the war and to the "new order." The material potential won in conquest was destroyed by the racist, dogmatic oppression and extermination policies of the Nazi governors and SS terror commandos, driving the peoples "liberated" from Communism, after brief periods of high hopes, into resistance and partisan warfare. The contradiction inherent in totalitarian ideas and totalitarian policies was evident here as it was in the irrational yet bureaucratic mass murder of the Jews. Hitler's drive for territorial expansion and the relentless expansion of the SS state simultaneously ushered in the final phase of National Socialist rule.

The further course of the war was marked by constant, disconcerting changes in command structure and the increasing concentration of the decision-making process in Hitler's hands. In this respect, also, the winter of 1941–42 was the turning point. Brauchitsch, together with other high officers, was fired as the scapegoat for the fiasco before Moscow; Hitler took over as Supreme Commander of the Army. Strategic planning now became his major preoccupation. He dismissed and appointed four chiefs of staff in succession (Halder, Zeitzler, Guderian, Krebs) and replaced the head of the Navy, Admiral Raeder, with the U-boat commander Karl Dönitz (January, 1943)—symbolizing the stress on U-boat warfare. In the course of the war, almost half of all generals in top positions were dismissed, transferred, or disciplined. Yet the conflicts between Hitler and the generals did not induce the military experts to hold their ground against the mistakes of the stubborn Führer, and the restrospective efforts of apologetic military memoirists to put all blame for the failures on Hitler do not come to grips with the real problem. The successes of the first two war years riveted Hitler on a strategy which had to fail under the completely different conditions of the Russian war. Here, too, the reverse side of the leader principle, which did away with consultation and permitted neither coordination of committee work nor judicious planning of the war effort, was evident. Everything was subordinate to the erratic "genius of the Führer," to his idolized intuitive and improvisational talents, while the generals resignedly accepted the role of handmaidens (like Keitel and Jodl in Hitler's headquarters) or of limited, unpolitical specialists. Their self-inflicted impotence, a consequence of the delusion which in 1934 had led them into the short-sighted union with the Nazi regime, was apparent not only in their helpless acceptance of Hitler's catastrophic strategy but also in their growing apathy in the face of the SS terror behind the frontlines.

An example of this is the handling of the so-called Commissar Order (*Kommissarbefehl*) of June 6, 1941, by which the Army was told even before the attack on Russia of the plan to liquidate all "Bolshevik leaders and commissars" immediately upon capture and without court martials.[2] Reservations and objections were voiced, as they were in the case of the treatment of the civilian population and the mass executions of Soviet prisoners of war, but they dealt largely with the effect on troop discipline, just as political reservations voiced by Rosenberg were based solely on the effects on the organization and efficiency of the administration in the East. Canaris and Tresckow, who raised principled objections, were the great exceptions. As a rule, jurisdictional conflicts resulted at best in partial modification of the rigid course; more frequently, the Army closed its eyes to the reality and the consequences of the war rule, limited itself to the efficient conduct of its trade, and avoided all strategic and political disputes. To be sure, doubts among the officers increased. Though only the younger "party generals" clung unconditionally to their faith in the leader, only a few others spoke out, let alone resisted. And the future resistance was the work of just a small minority; the vast majority stood by and waited to see whether resistance would succeed.

The fact that 1942 was a turning point became evident in all aspects of the war. The intensified deployment of U-boats, after their initial successes, could not keep pace with Allied ship construction and improved defenses; by 1943, the value of the U-boats lay more in their

[2] Hans-Adolf Jacobsen, "The *Kommissarbefehl* and Mass Executions of Soviet Russian Prisoners of War," in *Anatomy of the SS State* (New York, 1968), pp. 505–34.

propaganda potential than in their strategic successes. The losses in U-boat warfare (of 1,200 boats, more than half were sunk) were matched by air losses. The battle over Britain had shown up the limitations of the German Air Force. Though it fought over Russia and the Mediterranean, it proved unequal to the British, and later the American, bombing attacks from the west and south. Beginning in 1942, Germany's large cities and industrial centers were hit with increasing severity. Yet these raids failed to have the anticipated effect on war production and morale, for Goebbels managed to turn the "terror attacks" into a new source for rallying the nation. But the fact that the German Air Force was tied down to defensive tasks and sustained heavy losses did affect the conduct of the war. Behind Göring's braggadocio there stood miscalculations, misplannings, and shortages of raw materials and personnel. In November, 1941, the officer in charge of the production of aircraft, General Ernst Udet, committed suicide, and so, in August, 1943, did the Air Force Chief of Staff, General Hans Jeschonnek. New technical developments and rockets came too late; Hitler had neglected atomic research, considering it too long-range.

German arms production was not geared to a long war; it was expanded to full capacity only late, achieving its full potential in the autumn of 1944, despite bombings and defeats. Though German arms production was augmented by 6 million foreign workers, it still could not match the production capacity of its adversaries, not even after the confusion of commands was reduced by the proclamation of total war and production concentrated in Speer's armaments ministry. At the end of 1942, military defeats began to take on catastrophic dimensions. Stalingrad, where almost 200,000 men were lost, meant the final turning point in Russia, and after the capitulation in Africa and the capture of 250,000 men, the aggressors were confronted by a second advancing front, which inflicted heavy losses and forced Italy out of the alliance. At Casablanca, in January, 1943, Churchill and Roosevelt laid plans for the invasion of France in 1944; their demand for unconditional surrender ruled out a separate peace, though it also furnished Goebbels' propaganda machine with effective arguments. From now on, Hitler sustained blow after blow. Although the blow dealt by Mussolini's fall, which showed up the weaknesses of his dictatorship, had been softened by his abduction and the setting-up of a Fascist republic in northern Italy, Italian resistance movements began to spring up. June, 1944, brought the invasion and the attack on the Atlantic Wall and "Fortress Europe"; the German armies in the east were pushed back to Poland, and in the south to the Po Valley. Japan, too, began to suffer defeats. The outcome of the war could no longer be in doubt. At Teheran (December, 1943) and Yalta (February, 1945), plans for post-Hitler Europe were worked out.

In the meantime, however, one segment of the National Socialist program had become terrible reality. In the summer of 1942, Europe's "new order" reached its peak through occupation and satellite regimes. The ideas and forms of rule differed; there was an unholy confusion of improvisation and planning; rivalries dominated imperial rule in Europe as they did Germany's internal rule. Three major patterns emerged: barbarous enslavement and decimation governed in Poland and occupied Russia; a hegemonic policy of sham alliances was practiced in the satellites of southeast Europe; and western and northern Europe were ruled by military governments and collaborators.

On the eve of the war, Hitler had assured the British Ambassador once more that a German border revision in the West was completely out of the question. That same day (August 25, 1939), he sent his assurances to Premier Daladier via the French Ambassador (Robert Coulondre) that Germany did not lay claim to Alsace-Lorraine.[3] The truce conditions after the fall of France granted the authoritarian Vichy Government under Marshal Pétain a measure of independence, though of course within the framework of German-French cooperation set down by Germany. Consequently, Hitler had refused to accede to Italian and Spanish expansionist demands. The final shape of the "new order" was to come only after the war. Nazi ideologues like Otto Abetz, the German envoy in Paris, combined that vision with dreams about a European understanding that would put an end to centuries of enmity. Yet at the same time, Germany annexed Alsace-Lorraine, and soon the aims of World War I were being restated and expanded. Resorting to pseudo-historical arguments, Germany maintained that France north of the Somme and Burgundy was part of the ancient Germanic empire, and the grotesque Germanization of the names of the French cities (e.g., Nanzig for Nancy, Bisanz for Besançon) was meant to pave the way for their re-Germanization. The final disposition was left open, but the Allied invasion of French North Africa in November, 1942, was followed by the German occupation of all of France; all that remained was the Free French Army in London under the command of General de Gaulle.

By his declaration of war on the United States, Hitler provoked his own fall. For the second time, he sought to break through an impasse by forging ahead. The resistance of Britain, followed by the bogged-down Russian campaign, had made a shambles of all his calculations. Against all warnings of the Army, he postulated that the West did not have the tonnage to transport an expeditionary force to the Continent. But now Hitler was dealing with a foreign power beyond his military reach. And even though engaged in a war with Japan, the United States considered the Third Reich its Number One enemy. Hitler himself had turned the war into a radical ideological conflict. The rule of terror in Europe merely increased the determination of his enemies to fight until the unconditional capitulation of the Third Reich. The Western powers fought the war as a crusade for the liberation of Europe, and Nazi propaganda cooperated by the increasing raucousness

[3] *Akten zur deutschen Auswärtigen Politik, 1918–1945*, Series D, VII, No. 265 (Baden-Baden and Frankfurt/Main, 1956–); *Französisches Gelbbuch, Diplomatische Urkunden, 1938–39*, No. 242 (Basel, 1940). See also Eberhard Jäckel, *Frankreich in Hitlers Europa* (Stuttgart, 1966), pp. 25 ff.

of its ideological and racist claims that it was waging the "final battle" against Bolshevism and against the "plutocracies," both of them instruments of the world rule of "international Jewry"—in line with the fixed ideas of *Mein Kampf*.

As a consequence of this superwar—an ideologically determined, international civil war (Sigmund Neumann)—the resistance movements in the occupied countries grew stronger daily. Patriotism and treason lost their traditional meaning in this supernational conflict, in Germany even more so than in the satellite countries. Everywhere, opposition groups were locked in bitter, secret battles with collaborators; non-German SS troops were formed to demonstrate the new order in Europe, while partisans in Russia and Poland, in Yugoslavia and Norway, in France and finally also in Italy, formed inner defenses against Nazi rule.

In the decisive winter months of 1941–42, Hitler himself ordered that the conversations in his East Prussian headquarters be recorded, thus offering us a fantastic, unequivocal, banal outline of his plans for his postwar rule.[4] The only peace he could conceive of was one giving Germany practically unlimited influence. The first goal was a Germanic empire stretching from Norway to the Alps, from the Atlantic to the Black Sea, linked by a gigantic network of highways lined with Germanic defense settlements to secure the conquered territories. Berlin (or perhaps another, new city) was to be made into a gigantic "world capital" called Germania, overshadowing London and Paris, "comparable only to ancient Egypt, Babylon, or Rome." Leningrad, the symbol of Russian resistance, was to be razed; the Crimea, once ruled by Goths, was to be turned into a Nordic cultural and recreation area, and resettled by South Tyrolese: "All they have to do is sail down a German river, the Danube, and they'll be right there." Russia itself was to become in part a vast army camp and in part an area in which Nordic "Reich peasants," racially selected from all countries of Europe according to a master plan, were to be settled; however, the Swiss, whom Hitler despised, would be allowed only as innkeepers, if at all. The entire East was to become one gigantic colony, a Germanic India directly connected with the German heartland. The 180 million Russians, on the other hand, would have to die out. They were to be prohibited from procreating; their schools were to be closed to prevent the development of an educated class and of resistance; Russians were not to be permitted "to learn more than at most the meaning of traffic signs"—and, of course, to understand German orders. Hitler reduced the projected rule to this formula: Once a year, a group of Kirghiz was to be taken through the Reich capital to impress them with the power and grandeur of German monuments. In case of difficulties, the ghetto populations would be rounded up and liquidated by a handful of bombs "and the matter is settled."

Such visions of the future, offered at the height of war expansion,

---

[4] *Hitlers Tischgespräche* (rev. ed.; Stuttgart, 1963).

were not the fantasies of megalomania but horribly real facts and plans. The system of slave labor, the race and Jewish policies, and German rule, particularly in the eastern territories, testified to their reality. Himmler, the teacher's son and chicken farmer, directed their execution with pedantic care and intensity, even after it was patently obvious that the war was lost. In this context, too, the ideological aims constituted an absolute, which, regardless of its effect on the progress of the war, determined Nazi policy even after the loss of all strongholds. To be sure, in 1941–42 Hitler seemed to be in the process of creating the empire which he believed the Germans, because of their number and race, were destined for and urgently in need of. Yet up to the very end, Hitler continued to believe in the right of the stronger and in his predestined victory. Even in the final, eerily grotesque scene in the bunker of the bombed-out Reich Chancellery, the lost war moved him only to the observation that the German people were not worthy of him or of the tasks put to them.

Thus there was no ambiguity about the essence of Europe's new order and the objectives of National Socialism. On April 5, 1940, before the invasion of Denmark and Norway, Goebbels, more flexible than Hitler and Himmler, told invited representatives of the German press that the war would realize "the same revolution" in Europe "which on a smaller scale we have carried out in Germany." This speech, kept secret, clearly showed the extent to which domestic and foreign policy overlapped in the power ideas of National Socialism. The same tactics used in the era of the power seizure—"We had our plans, but we did not offer them for public appraisal"—were used again: "Certainly we have an idea" of the new Europe, but it will be spelled out only at the moment of its realization. "Today we say *Lebensraum!* Everyone can interpret it however he wants. . . . Until now we have succeeded in leaving the enemy unclear about the real objectives of Germany, just as our domestic opponents until 1932 did not know what we were aiming at, that the oath of legality was only a stratagem." [5] The rule of terror in the occupied territories made these aims obvious, but, just as in a Germany of *Gleichschaltung*, persecution, and disenfranchisement, illusions lived on and a crude worship of success helped to make palatable the "inevitable" brutality of the regime; now, too, the vulgar contention that one cannot make an omelet without breaking eggs, that nothing great can be accomplished without blood and tears, was heard in the land.

Tough and determined, even with catastrophe imminent, the Nazi leadership clung to its conviction that Russia must be destroyed, that the Slavs must be decimated, resettled in Siberia, and made into slave labor, and that the Jews must be exterminated. The new Europe was conceivable only as a "Greater Germanic Reich" built on racial foundations (into which Scandinavians and Dutch were to be incorporated through vast resettlement, not as a federative union of the peoples of

[5] Hans-Adolf Jacobsen, *Der Zweite Weltkrieg* (Frankfurt/Main, 1965), pp. 180 f.

Europe). What Hitler had said in his book of 1928 had become part of his war and ruling policies. The new Europe, he had written in criticism of the Pan-European idea, could come into being only through the hegemony of the best race and most powerful nation, just as ancient Rome had unified Italy; once that was done, Europe could hold up its head as a world power and face North America.[6] A racially "structured" Europe under German rule was to be the instrument of the National Socialist claim to world hegemony—this was the concept of domination to which all other tactical concepts and temporary solutions were subordinated, whether they were related to the statehood of western Europe, the breaking up of Russia into separate territories, or the temporary demarcation of the German-Italian power sphere.

Occupied Russia was the great laboratory for the experiments of translating the master plan into reality. There the new-style political administration, the exploitation, terror, and extermination machinery of the SS state, was employed consciously and with relentless logic. From the very outset, Russia was ruled not by military administrations and military commanders, as were western and northern Europe, but by a confusing multiplicity of party and SS offices. The Army opened up the territory for them and tolerated their activities, albeit with a troubled conscience. Therein, rather than in its acquiescence in the poor strategy of the Führer, lay the profound delusion and coresponsibility of the military leadership, which so high-ranking a spokesman as Field Marshal Kesselring still proclaimed proudly and uncomprehendingly long afterward (1953) in the title of his memoirs: *Soldat bis zum letzten Tag* (*Soldier to the Last Day*).

THE SYSTEM OF DOMINATION AND EXTERMINATION

The aggressive expansion of German rule accelerated the internal reorganization of the Third Reich and the consolidation of the totalitarian system. In this it differed considerably from the Stalinist dictatorship in Russia, where the war led to a loosening of the totalitarian system in favor of a wave of patriotism. True, the welter of jurisdictions and rivalries so characteristic of the Nazi leader dictatorship continued in the war, and new offices and command chains even were added to those already in existence. The Reich Government had not met since 1936. The effort to impose a supercabinet as the highest official agency above the confusion of commands was doomed by the nature of the Hitler dictatorship. On August 30, 1939, even before the war was started, a Reich Defense Council had been formed under the chairmanship of Göring, in which major spheres were represented: Hess (Party), Lammers (Führer), Keitel (OKW), Funk ("General Plenipotentiary" for economic affairs insofar as they were not under Göring as Chief of the war economy), and Frick (Plenipotentiary for the central administration, who simultaneously was overseer of the Justice, Cultural Affairs, and Church Ministries). Foreign and military affairs

[6] *Hitlers zweites Buch* (Stuttgart, 1961), pp. 129 f.

were Hitler's domain. But this Reich Defense Council was nothing more than another institution with little practical impact, which intensified the possibilities for conflict and further reduced the ministries to technical apparatuses.

The new chain of command was also extended to the regional level via the Reich Defense Commissars, who were in charge of the eighteen defense districts into which the country was divided. New conflicts with the regular administration, with the party and SS, and with business and the military were added to the existing overlapping jurisdictions. Generally, the Gauleiter took over these new defense command posts; in this way they (and through them the party) could assume control functions over the governmental apparatus and the military. This was only one of the consequences of the fact that under conditions of totalitarianism, emergency laws like the Reichstag fire decree and the dictatorial "Leader constitution" (of August, 1934) tend to blur the difference between war and peace. Whether in peace or war, the regime lived and functioned in a permanent state of emergency and mobilization.

Other special laws cropped up everywhere. Fritz Todt, Speer's predecessor, set up a Ministry for Arms and Munitions; there was also the Organisation Todt, formed to handle essential building tasks, which had the power to encroach on the jurisdiction of the military commanders in the occupied territories. The position of the new East Ministry under Rosenberg, composed entirely of rival jurisdictions, was never clarified. The Special Deputy for the Labor Draft (Fritz Sauckel) appointed in 1942, whose influence extended into a number of ministries and special staffs, was more powerful. But above all of them stood the Führer; his omnipotent position, beyond law and constitution, was confirmed by the Reichstag on April 26, 1942. However, in 1941 the conduct of the war became his sole preoccupation, clearing the way for Himmler and the further consolidation of the SS state.

The rule over occupied territories provided the framework for this consolidation. The attack on Poland introduced a policy of utter brutality, allegedly dictated by the requirements of war. The first step was the expansion of the Reich territory far beyond the revision of the Versailles borders. The new "Warthegau," extending to Poznan, as well as the Zjechanow and Suwalki districts, were torn off Poland and added to West and East Prussia; Upper Silesia was expanded to include the entire industrial region of southwest Poland as well as the former Czech region of Tesin. The expulsion of the Polish population, the settlement of ethnic Germans from the Baltic states and southeastern Europe, and the "Germanization" of "racially valuable" stock was to bring about the extension of the "ethnic borders." This went so far that in the fall of 1942, through precipitate forcible evacuation and mass arrests of Polish peasants in the Lublin area, the SS created the space for a German "mass settlement area." [7] In the West, Alsace-Lor-

[7] Martin Broszat, "The Concentration Camps 1933–45," in *Anatomy of the SS State.*

raine and Eupen-Malmedy were "reincorporated," and Lower Styria and a part of Carniola (both with only German minorities) were taken from Slovenia. But the protectorate of Bohemia and Moravia and the Polish Government General also were considered part of the Reich.

The status of the other eastern regions remained basically undecided. They were divided into two Reich Commissariats—Ostland, composed of the Baltics and Belorussia, and the Ukraine—under Gauleiter Erich Koch and Hinrich Lohse, respectively, and turned into military operational areas as well as proving grounds for the SS race and extermination policies. Their future as countries remained undecided. As early as July, 1940, Hitler, in planning the Russian campaign, had told the Army command that he wanted Russia broken up into a number of territories.[8] In March, 1941, he again spoke of dividing Russia into a series of states rather than setting up a "national Russia" in the place of Communist Russia. It soon became evident that the new order, to be carried out with "most brutal force," aimed at the total domination and exploitation of Russian territory to the Urals, as was stated unequivocally in the table talks of 1941–42. This pulled the rug out from under Rosenberg's visions. Russia was given over to the power struggle of the various agencies dealing with the East. The general confusion resulting from this was resolved on the backs of the people. Cooperation with "liberated" Russians on the basis of a mutual anti-Communism, which the group around Rosenberg visualized, was an illusion, even though individual efforts to deploy Russian auxiliary forces (such as the Vlassov Army and Cossacks) continued to the end of the war.

The treatment of and functions assigned to the Polish and Russian populations were spelled out in numerous public statements by leading Nazi functionaries. Governor General of Poland Hans Frank repeatedly said from 1939 on that the "epoch of the East," a "time of monumental new colonizing and resettlement," had begun for Germany. Poland was the "bridgehead in the advance into the limitless expanse of the eastern territory," and had to be made to realize the "difference between the living standards of the master race and of the subject people": "no Pole should attain higher rank than that of foreman (*Werkmeister*). In November, 1940, he summed up thus: "What we have here is nothing but a gigantic labor camp in which everything that signifies power and independence rests in the hands of the Germans." A year earlier, in October, 1939, immediately after the occupation, Frank had said: "Only those educational opportunities should be available to the Poles which show them the hopelessness of their national fate." [9] Toward the end, shortly before he had to evacuate his seat in the Cracow castle, Frank had visions of National Socialism's victorious peace: "When we have won the war, then as far as I am concerned they can make mincemeat

---

[8] Franz Halder, *Kriegstagebuch* (Stuttgart, 1963), II, 32 f., 49 f.

[9] Josef Wulf, *Das Dritte Reich und seine Vollstrecker* (Berlin, 1961), pp. 352 ff. Martin Broszat, *Nationalsozialistische Polenpolitik, 1939–1945* (Frankfurt/Main, 1965), is a basic work on the subject.

of the Poles and Ukrainians and everything else floating around here. Anything at all." [10]

More significant still are the statements of the highest executor, which at the same time are expressions of the close link between internal terror and foreign expansion. The pedant Himmler and fanatical, bureaucratic henchmen like Eichmann took Hitler's fantastic ideas of history and domination literally and sought to realize them "totally." Thus Himmler sponsored "consanguine fishing expeditions among the Germanic population of France" and other countries to rob them of their future leaders, which, true to ideology, he identified with the blond, blue-eyed "race." On the other side, he used his brutal apparatus to put the Czechs and Poles into the "steel pincers of German nationdom" and systematically to work toward their "nordification" or their enslavement and annihilation.[11] Planned with pedantic exactitude, ruthlessly "implemented," and when possible supported pseudo-scientifically by the card indexes of the Main Office for Race and Settlement (Rasse- und Siedlungshauptamt), these measures were as real and terrible for the victims as they were unrealistic in view of the actual happenings and conditions of a war which in 1942 had already been lost.

All this emerged in its final, naked consequence in a secret speech by Himmler at Poznan before the central and regional chiefs of the NSDAP on August 3, 1944, after the defeat of the July uprising. Following speeches by Goebbels and Speer dealing with the general mobilization for the total war, Himmler decried the foul blow the Army had allegedly dealt National Socialism and the SS; reversing the classic stab-in-the-back legend, he made the Army responsible also for the defeat of 1918 and bragged about the bloody liquidation of the July 20 resistance movement.[12] But even amid the collapsing Eastern Front, he clung to the romantic-brutal utopias of the future "Germanic Reich" and the "seedbed of Germanic blood in the East." According to Himmler, rearmament and expansion, the foundation and content of National Socialist policy, had repeatedly been hampered by the reservations and opposition of the generals. But now, after the remaking of the Army into a "National Socialist people's army" under Himmler, and effecting its complete reorganization under the SS, the empire in the East could be reconquered and consolidated. This is what the future would look like:

We don't even have to discuss the problem of whether we will regain the hundreds of thousands or millions of square kilometers which we have lost in the East. It is irrevocable that we will move our national boundaries forward by 500 kilometers, that we shall settle here. It is irrevocable that we shall found a Germanic Reich. It is irrevocable that the 30 million other Germanic peoples will be added to our 90 million, so that we shall increase our blood base to 120 million Germans. It

[10] Wulf, *op. cit.*, p. 371.

[11] Paul Kluke, "Nationalsozialistische Europapolitik," in *Vierteljahrshefte für Zeitgeschichte* (hereinafter *VfZG*), III (1955), 257 ff.

[12] *VfZG*, I (1953), 357 ff.

is irrevocable that we shall be the ruling power in the Balkans and the rest of Europe, and that we shall organize and regulate this entire people economically, politically, and militarily. It is irrevocable that we shall populate this territory, that we shall found the seedbed of German blood in the East, and it is irrevocable that we shall move our border defenses far into the East. For our grandchildren and great-grandchildren will have lost the next war, which is sure to come, be it in one generation or two, unless our Air Force in the East—we may just as well say this openly—stands at the Urals. . . . Moreover, I think it is wonderful that we are clear about this: that our political, economic, humane, and military tasks lie in the wonderful East. If the Cossacks were able to push their way through to the Yellow Sea for the Russian Czar and gradually conquer this whole territory, then our sons, in three devils' name, will manage, year after year, generation after generation, to fortify our farmlands and build bases along several hundred kilometers behind our military borders and gradually settle the land and push the others out. That is our task. The East out there will be our army encampment, and every winter so and so many divisions will hold their field exercises there in ice and snow and cold. Like their fathers in the year 1941, so the sons in years to come will hold maneuvers there, will put up their tents, will live in them, and every generation will practice its marksmanship there, will prove itself, so as to avert the danger inherent in victory of becoming prosperous and with it soft and comfortable in decades and centuries to come.

This speech, which went on to invoke the "selection process of nature," revealed the yardsticks and basic concepts of National Socialist policies of conquest and rule. Himmler stated them even more precisely and pedantically than Hitler, in keeping with the SS empire of the future based on the breach of all national principles and on the consolidation of a Greater German Reich.

The fate of the other occupied territories remained unresolved. Holland and Norway were put under Reich Commissars; the local administrations remained; collaborators like the Norwegian fascist leader Quisling were installed in "office." Belgium and unoccupied France were ruled by military commanders, and Denmark by a "Reich Plenipotentiary" (since 1942, the Gestapo lawyer Werner Best).

With the attack on Russia, the mobilization of Europe for the fight against Bolshevism was made the basis of the "new order," and Hitler was celebrated as "Europe's general." The formation of volunteer corps was to underscore the European breakthrough into the East, and in fact this "European policy" did meet with some response in conservative anti-Communist circles of Western Europe. In truth, however, what was really meant was a function of the *Lebensraum* policy; not "Europe" but the idea of the "Reich" was in the forefront of the propaganda.[13]

For the rest, the concrete policies followed in northern and western Europe gave the lie to the Nazi slogans. Thus through the expansion of

[13] Kluke, *op. cit.*, pp. 240 ff.

the "Westmark" (Germany west of the Rhine) under Gauleiter Bürckel, 70,000 French inhabitants of Lorraine were driven into occupied France,[14] and as early as 1941, repression and hostage executions were introduced to cope with the growing French resistance. As the opposition movements grew stronger in all occupied territories and the prospects of a German victory grew more doubtful, the terror increased. The greater the need of the German arms industry for foreign workers, the more slave laborers were shipped to Germany, but at the same time this brought with it growing resistance in the countries involved, via sabotage and even mass strikes. The deportation of the Jews exacerbated the tensions, and after the assassination of Heydrich and the "retaliatory" action against the Czech village of Lidice (June, 1942), in which the entire male population was murdered, National Socialist rule put its indelible stamp on the Czech protectorate as well. In the years to come, similar outrages were also committed in the West —as for example the murder and extermination campaign of Oradour, near Limoges, in July, 1944.

The most consistent terror, however, developed in Poland and Russia. The Polish campaign had already seen conflicts between Army and the Einsatz units of the SS police, for which Heydrich retrospectively held the "ignorance of the ideological position of the enemy" responsible; the instructions for police intervention had been "extraordinarily radical," so that the Army commands "could not be informed of this order." Consequently, "the actions of the police and SS on the surface seemed arbitrary and brutally independent." [15] In extenuation, Heydrich also added that "in the beginning, the Self-Defense [ethnic German militia under SS control], out of understandable bitterness against Polish atrocities, committed some inadmissible, uncontrollable revenge acts, which were then laid at the door of the police and SS." But even thus, future occupation policy of having SS police power operating behind the façade of Army and administration was clearly outlined. It is, however, highly significant that the secrecy of the terror and extermination measures was stressed and their viciousness used to justify the creation of a special command and administrative structure. The further extension and legitimation of the SS state was thereby guaranteed.

On the military level, this meant the expansion of the Waffen SS; on the administrative level, it meant the expansion of the SS police apparatus and the closely connected extermination system of the concentration camps. (The promise Hitler gave after June 30, 1934, that the Army would be the sole military force of the nation had already been broken that same year when he armed his Bodyguard regiment [under

---

[14] Kluke, "Nationalsozialistische Volkstumspolitik in Elsass-Lothringen 1940 bis 1943," in *Festgabe für Hans Herzfeld* (Berlin, 1953), pp. 629 ff. Cf. Eberhard Jäckel, *Frankreich in Hitlers Europa* (Stuttgart, 1966), pp. 79 ff.

[15] Marginal note on official document by Heydrich, dated July 2, 1940, in Helmut Krausnick, "Hitler und die Morde in Polen," *VfZG*, XI (1963), 206 ff.

Sepp Dietrich], the "political squads" [*Verfügungstruppen*], and the concentration-camp guards of the SS [Death's Head units].) The build-up of the Waffen SS proceeded somewhat more slowly than that of the SS police; Himmler had to show consideration for the Wehrmacht, on whose good will Hitler was dependent. The armed SS troops therefore were classified as special police units and, by secret order of Hitler (August 17, 1938), given special status directly under the Leader for "special internal political tasks that are the responsibility of the *Reichsführer-SS und Chef der deutschen Polizei* . . . [or] for mobile employment under the Army in the event of war."[16] But after this secret "legalization," the expansion of the Waffen SS proceeded rapidly once the war had begun. Hitler defined its function in 1940: As a "state police," the Waffen SS after "proving itself in the field" should repre-sent "authority" in a Greater German Reich which would also encom-pass recalcitrant "national bodies," while the Army "in future is solely and only to be used against the Reich's external enemies."[17] In the Polish campaign, SS political squads and Death's Head units had still fought within the framework of larger Army groups, but now, separate divisions with names like Viking, Reich, SS Death's Head Division (under Eicke) were formed; an additional nine Death's Head units stationed in Austria, Czechoslovakia, and Poland later were also turned into separate combat divisions, while noncombatant SS men were assigned to concentration-camp guard duty. Beginning in 1940, all these detachments, *including* concentration-camp staffs, became part of the Waffen SS, not only the fighting troops, as was claimed in self-de-fense by the SS veterans organization (Hiag) after the war. Between May, 1941, and May, 1942, the strength of the Waffen SS increased from around 73,000 to 147,000 men. As Himmler's position became more powerful, and with the radicalization introduced by the total war, the Waffen SS, formed as a political-ideological special troop in conscious opposition to the Army, was able to assert itself over the Army as forcefully as the SS administration was to assert itself over the state apparatus.

Himmler's powers had already been substantially broadened on October 7, 1939, through his elevation to Reich Commissar for the Strengthening of the German Nationhood (Reichskommissar für die Festigung des deutschen Volkstums, or RKF). A loosely worded Hitler decree charged him with bringing back and resettling ethnic Germans in the Reich, as well as with excluding "nationally alien populations constituting a threat to the Reich and the German people's commun-ity."[18] This put Himmler above the Army and the civilian administra-

---

[16] Hans Buchheim, "The SS—Instrument of Domination," in *Anatomy of the SS State*, p. 262.

[17] *Ibid.*, pp. 264–65.

[18] *Nürnberger Dokumente*, PS–686. Cf. Robert L. Koehl, *RKFDV, German Resettlement and Population Policy, 1939–1945* (Cambridge, Mass., 1957). On the Vomi, see Hans-Adolf Jacobsen, *Nationalsozialistische Aussenpolitik 1933–1938* (Frankfurt/Main, 1968), pp. 234 ff.

tion, responsible only to Hitler, and he used this power to consolidate his own apparatus. The resettlement office for South Tyrolese—opened in June, 1939, under SS Oberführer Ulrich Greifelt—offered an opening for this consolidation; Himmler also took over the apparatus set up by the Reich Security Office in 1938 for the confiscation of land owned by Jews and "state enemies" in occupied territories and which had grown into a separate land administration (Central Land Office). Himmler's Nationhood Commissariat became an SS central office, and together with other SS central offices (such as the SS Economic and Administrative Central Office) and their numerous subdivisions became a state within the state whose officers, particularly the top SS and police heads, could encroach on all sectors of the administration and at the same time had control over police and SS. This, too, affected the rule of terror in Poland and Russia.

But beyond that, included in the RKF was an SS organization administering expropriated settlement land and other "affiliated offices," some of which had been formed earlier by other party and SS divisions. The central agency since 1936 for ethnic German and national affairs was the Ethnic German Office (Volksdeutsche Mittelstelle, or Vomi) of the NSDAP, which, through the *Gleichschaltung* of older ethnic German organizations (VDA, Gustav Adolf League, League of Catholic Germans Abroad, etc.) sought to assure Nazi control of all ethnic groups. The Vomi was under the SS, at first because its head, Obergruppenführer Werner Lorenz, was an SS officer and later because it was raised to the level of SS central office. A huge apparatus controlling hundreds of resettlement camps came into being, bringing with it the usual overlapping with departments of the RKF and the Reich central office; the latter in particular was responsible for political and police aspects of resettlement, for the non-German population in the Reich and in occupied territories, and also for the race-biological selection of potential resettlers. Thus the SS Security Police played a decisive role in this selection as well as in the expulsion of the native population. By contrast, the Race and Settlement Central Office, founded in 1931, increasingly was restricted to bureaucratic, internal SS matters such as issuing marriage permits and certificates of racial purity. Himmler in his role of RKF was the center of everything; according to his own interpretation, he had "total" jurisdiction and "absolute powers," since "in the new Eastern regions there are no areas of life which do not fall under the special province of the consolidation of German nationhood." [19] Here the SS administration not only could gather up, dispose of, confiscate, and distribute over the heads of ministerial offices, but it also expanded its influence over the ministries of Agriculture, Interior, and Eastern Territories, until it reigned almost supreme over the "human material" in the occupied Eastern regions.

With its increasingly extensive system of "offices and central offices," the SS leadership ultimately sought to penetrate almost every sector of Nazi rule to realize the rigid ideological ideas of a racist-expansionist

[19] Ulrich Greifelt, in *Deutsche Verwaltung*, 1940, pp. 17 ff.

National Socialism via a military-bureaucratic, totalitarian police state. Parallel and separate organizations oversaw the various aspects of political, social, and economic life and increasingly championed such pet Himmler projects as Germanic prehistorical and war research (with institutions like *"Ahnenerbe"*) and maternity homes for SS wives and unmarried mothers (*"Lebensborn"*). The steady widening of its role gave rise to an independent SS bureaucracy: police, concentration camps, SS troops, Germanization, administration of vast assets and economic enterprises, còntrol of "human material" for war work, deportation and extermination of Jews and Slavs—these were the launching platforms and stations of the SS state with a gigantic economic and administrative central office, a military SS leadership central office, the Reich Security Office, the Commissariat for the Consolidation of German Nationhood, and numerous other "administrations." [20] Since the beginning of the war, the Hitler terror regime had at its disposal an institutional apparatus that overshadowed all governmental and military control.

The effects of this development asserted themselves most forcefully in the administration of concentration-camp and Jewish policies. In 1939, the structure and function of the concentration camps began to change. More and more foreign nationals joined the German inmates; the number of both camps and inmates began to increase particularly since 1941, and the detention and labor camps were augmented by extermination camps. The beginning of the war saw a new "protective-custody" drive buttressed by numerous new decrees and laws. On September 3, 1939, broad powers for the "internal protection of the State" were given the SS police, intensifying the special judicial powers it already enjoyed. These broad powers permitted the ruthless suppression of any attempt "to destroy the determination and fighting spirit of the German people" and the arrest of any person who "voices doubt about the victory of the German people or the just cause of the war"; "if need be such elements will be brutally liquidated upon instruction from above." [21] This applied particularly in cases having dangerous "propaganda effects." Among these, Himmler included not only sabotage and "Marxist work" but also the "demoralizing [*Zersetzung*] of members of the army or of a substantial group of persons, hoarding . . . etc." Such persons "will have to be liquidated absolutely ruthlessly [by execution] without regard to person." "Special treatment" was the euphemistic term applied by the bureaucracy to these executions, which began in September, 1939, in an intentional effort to sidestep legal procedures. They were carried out in the concentration camps by the Security Police without legal trial or conviction, and thus they also bypassed special court martials.

The concentration camps were thereby turned into sites of physical extermination outside the legal system; the SS police was both judge

[20] See particularly Enno Georg, *Die wirtschaftlichen Unternehmungen der SS* (Stuttgart, 1963).
[21] Circular issued by the Chief of the Security Police, in Broszat, *op. cit.*, p. 465.

and executioner. The Reichsführer SS and the Gestapo had final jurisdiction over executions; a steadily growing number of political undesirables, persons who refused to work, etc., began to be consigned to concentration camps and executed. The abdication of the legal system was sealed when Reich Minister of Justice Gürtner, on October 14, 1939, accepted the Führer's assertion that although he had given no general instructions to the Security Police, these executions were necessary in individual cases "because the courts (military and civil) were not equipped to deal with the special conditions created by the war." [22] For the time being, the legal façade was preserved, but the door had been opened to the lawless system of extermination; the measures for the "safeguarding of the state" could be extended at will to include mass extermination. Parallel with this, the ideological-racist collective murder to "cleanse the body politic," which in peacetime was still too risky, found a place in the new functions assigned to the concentration camps. Political and criminal persecution and extermination on "purely" ideological grounds proceeded apace. The state without justice marched toward its logical realization in the SS and concentration-camp state.

To begin with, an increasing number of former Communists and Social Democrats were again taken into "protective custody" in concentration camps. They were joined by "suspect" Polish citizens in Germany, more and more Jews, and also idlers, gypsies, and so-called psychopaths with criminal records "who because of mental disorders may be suspected of causing unrest among the population." [23] The Chief of the Security Police had tersely stated as early as October 24, 1939: "In general, prisoners will not be released from protective custody during the war." [24] Police action against churches also intensified, and arrests of clergy mounted. The National Socialist claim to total control, which presupposed not only unconditional obedience but ideologically based "extermination" regardless of guilt and responsibility was in full swing. War was not only the aim but also the precondition for the flowering of the regime: completion of *Gleichschaltung*, expansion of the machinery of terror, "positive" transformation of the body politic. In October, 1941, the number of monthly arrests by the Gestapo in Germany reached 15,000, ten times that of 1935–36.

But above all, the war meant expansion; masses of new concentration-camp inmates poured in from the occupied territories. Hitler's infamous "Under Cover of Night" (*"Nacht-und-Nebel"*) decree of September, 1941, which three months later also went out as an OKW decree signed by Keitel, ordered that anyone suspected of resistance be brought to Germany; after having served their sentences or being acquitted by special courts, such suspects were, on the basis of further decrees, to be handed over to the Gestapo.[25] By this method, about

[22] *Nürnberger Dokumente*, NG–190.

[23] Circular issued by the Criminal Police, dated September 12, 1939, in Broszat, *op. cit.*, p. 469.

[24] *Ibid.*, p. 494.

[25] *Nürnberger Dokumente*, PS–1733, NOKW–2579, NG–226.

7,000 prisoners, mostly from France, were sent to concentration camps either directly or via prisons. Another group of camp inmates were Soviet prisoners of war, for whom special sections were set up in the camps; there the vast majority died of starvation.

Numerous new camps were opened in 1940, the largest of these near Auschwitz, in the newly acquired part of Upper Silesia; it was set up in February by Eicke's disciple Rudolf Höss. The camp initially was housed in vacant barracks, but after March, 1941, it was turned into a mass camp for more than 100,000 inmates (the plans called for 200,000). Himmler, in his capacity as Reichsführer SS and RKF, could now translate his dreams into reality with complete impunity. Here on confiscated land, the SS set up its experimental stations and production sites, and also the Buna (synthetic rubber) works of IG Farben, which, like other large industrial firms, became an accomplice in the concentration-camp system. And here, East European "human material" could be literally consumed. Prisoners were also assigned to nearby industrial plants: a total of thirty-nine labor subcamps of Auschwitz were set up in the area. And here, too, the "final solution"—the extermination of the Jews—became a reality. For that purpose, a vast, unspeakably primitive barracks camp was opened in nearby Birkenau (Brzezinka), a concentration-camp settlement of more than 175 hectares, divided into sections by electrically charged barbed-wire fences and ditches. In 1943, about 100,000 men, women, and children were "living" there, while another 18,000 were crowded together in Auschwitz itself. Birkenau was the site of the gas chambers and crematories in which the spirit of National Socialism found fulfillment through the mass murder of millions.

New concentration camps were also set up in 1940 in Neuengamme, near Hamburg (up to then a subcamp of Sachsenhausen), an area of confinement for Scandinavians and West Europeans rounded up after their countries were overrun, as were the camps at Bergen-Belsen, Gross-Rosen (Lower Silesia), Stutthof (near Danzig), and Natzweiler (Alsace). Other concentration camps (in East and West Prussia, Styria, and Lorraine) served primarily as transit and resettlement camps or for "labor training" (for recalcitrant foreign workers). These camps were supplemented by unofficial ones set up at the behest of local SS and police chiefs; though not called concentration camps, they strongly resembled them. These local camps also fell under the jurisdiction of the Inspector of Concentration Camps, or rather the SS Central Office for Administrative and Economic Affairs, and their simultaneous function as sites for long-range SS work projects justified their existence as permanent institutions. They, too, exhibited the usual combination of terror and forced labor. Outside the (new) Reich territory, these types of concentration camps were "recognized" only from 1943 on—for example, the Lublin and Plaszow (near Cracow) labor camps, to which "work Jews" for SS enterprises temporarily spared the final solution were sent; also, the police-detention camp near 's Hertogenbosch (Holland) was converted into a concentration camp. In April, 1944, there were 20 officially designated concentration camps and 165 affiliated labor camps. But this fine, bureaucratic differentiation could not alter the fact that both the East and the West contained a vast number of detention camps which were part of the SS state and representative of it. The plans even called for their later expansion and use in "peace reconstruction tasks." But above all, they were used for whatever purpose seemed compelling, and in all of them death reigned—through the vicious "medical" experiments of ambitious SS doctors; through the "selection" of sick and unfit prisoners for "special treatment," an extension of euthanasia on another plane; through the mass executions of Soviet officials and prisoners of war; through the brutal practice of eleven-hour work days on construction sites frequently at great distance from the camp; and above all, through the systematic extermination of the Jews. In addition to Auschwitz (which was also a labor camp), Chelmno, Treblinka, Belzek, Majdanek, and Sobibor specialized in the extermination of Jews. In 1941, these camps were turned into factories of death; most prisoners were murdered immediately upon arrival, although in Auschwitz, SS leaders and doctors conducted selections, and those found fit for work were given at least temporary hope of survival.

This explains why, despite the constant flow into the concentration camps, the figure of (living) prisoners up to 1942 was given as "only" 100,000, and the highest number, in January, 1945, as 714,211 (511,537 men and 202,674 women).[26] But millions went through the camps, and the overwhelming majority met their death. The average mortality rate in labor camps was 60 per cent; in the extermination camps it was almost 100. With increasing frequency, collective death lists took the place of individual notifications of survivors; the official cause of death was "simplified" and standardized. The statement made by the Auschwitz detention-camp leader Aumeier in 1942 that prisoners unfit for work had to be liquidated "to lighten the load on the camp" is typical of the cynical yet bureaucratic mentality of the executioners. "Appropriate action," he went on to say, "is, however, complicated by the instructions of the RSHA, that, unlike Jews, Poles must die a natural death."[27] The "problem" was solved not only by shootings and starvation, but also by the "nonmedical work of the SS doctors" (thus Commandant Höss), by lethal injections called "hygienic" measures, and by other forms of camouflaged execution. And the chaotic evacuations, forced marches, and executions in the last months of the Nazi regime took the lives of yet hundreds of thousands more prisoners.

THE MURDER OF THE JEWS

SS ideology glorified the extermination of the Jews as a "historical task" which had to be "gotten over with" bravely.[28] The two basic

[26] Broszat, *op. cit.*, p. 504.

[27] *Ibid.*, p. 502.

[28] Himmler's notes on a conference with Hitler, June 19, 1943, in the Federal Archives, Coblenz.

precepts were: "Keep it secret and don't soften." In this vein, Himmler again and again reminded his executioners not to recoil from the most brutal logical consequence: the murder of women and children. Because what was at stake was "the unequivocal solution" of the Jewish question, he did not feel that he "should be justified in getting rid of the men—in having them put to death, in other words—only to allow their children to grow up to avenge themselves on our sons and grandsons. We have to make up our minds, hard though it may be, that this race must be wiped off the face of the earth." But since the mass of Germans was not (yet) ready for this, the SS "should carry this burden for our people . . . should take the responsibility upon ourselves . . . and carry the secret with us to the grave." [29]

Thus we are dealing not simply with coercion from above, not simply with a military execution squad's "condition of compulsion to carry out orders" (*Befehlsnotstand*), but rather with the ideology and mentality of the kangaroo court and Free Corps murderers raised to the plane of monstrosity, prepared to do anything for the sake of an "idea," putting obedience to the Führer above everything, finding its justification in the "higher law" of a permanent revolution, of a permanent state of emergency superseding all justice and all morality. SS members obeyed not only military but also "ideological" orders; their methods were not the product of a war conducted with military means within the framework of legal limitations; instead, the ideological, suprastate goals of a totalitarian system furnished the foundation for the use of force, and hence for the unrestrained and unscrupulous wielding of power. SS "morality" sought the heroic victory over the self as the victory over all moral and religious scruples. And so the SS, as the avantgarde of totalitarian rule, protected the "secret" of National Socialist policy and carried out commands for which neither the machinery of state nor the mass of the population was ready. That this was particularly "difficult," that it demanded many "sacrifices" and high "idealism," was the proud yet self-pitying special feeling on which Himmler, with Hitler's approval, wanted to build his SS state of the future. In a probing study, Hans Buchheim discusses the consequences of this SS ideology, which, by creating a world of "new" values, sought to cover over the perversion of human values that formed the basis of National Socialist racial and expansionist goals.

Himmler's secret speeches are superb illustrations of this perversion of both the moral and military order, a perversion which laid down the absolute order-obedience principle in the service of ideological-political objectives and legitimized the total militarism of the SS state. Himmler made clear that (and why) the SS had to act outside the state and military order and that therefore it was secretly and unconditionally committed only to the ideological commandment of the National Socialist Weltanschauung personified by the Führer. Consequently, the SS,

[29] Krausnick, "The Persecution of the Jews," in *Anatomy of the SS State*, p. 123, and Buchheim, "Command and Compliance," in *ibid.*, p. 359.

unlike the Army, had to be a voluntary organization; the admission of conscripts toward the end of the war was the exception. The rise and acts of the SS represented the "overlap into the official sphere of the right to issue orders on ideological matters." [30] Resting on secret Führer orders and camouflaged instructions, or even only on vaguely hinted wishes of the Nazi leadership, the policy of mass extermination, for which state and military warfare served as a façade, was organized and "implemented" by the "political administration" of the SS. On September 7, 1940, Himmler told the leaders of the SS: "In many cases it is considerably easier to lead a company into battle than to command a company responsible for some area where it has to hold down a hostile population, probably one with a long history, to carry out executions, to deport people, to remove shrieking, weeping women . . . to do this unseen duty, to maintain this silent activity[!] . . . to be always consistent, always uncompromising—that is in many cases far, far harder." [31]

He unfolded the SS ideology in a speech before SS leaders in Poznan on October 4, 1943:

> It is completely wrong for us to offer up our ingenuous soul and spirit, our good nature, our idealism, to other peoples. This holds true beginning with Herder, who probably wrote his "Voices of the Peoples" in an hour of crapulence and therefore brought us, his descendants, immeasurable suffering and misery. . . . The SS man is to be guided by one principle alone: honesty, decency, loyalty, and friendship toward those of our blood, and to no one else. What happens to the Russians or the Czechs is a matter of total indifference to me. If good blood of our type is to be found among the [other] nations, we will take it, if need be by taking their children and bringing them up ourselves. Whether other peoples live in plenty or starve to death interests me only insofar as we need them as slaves for our culture; for the rest it does not interest me. Whether 10,000 Russian women keel over from exhaustion in the construction of an antitank ditch interests me only insofar as the ditch for Germany gets finished. We will never be savage or heartless where we don't have to be; that is obvious. Germans after all are the only people in the world who treat animals decently, so we will also know how to treat these human animals [*Menschentiere*]; but it is a crime against our own blood to worry about them and instill ideals into them, only to create problems for our sons and grandsons. If someone comes to me and tells me: "I cannot dig these antitank ditches with children or with women, it is inhuman, they will die on the job"—I must say to him: "You are a murderer of your own blood, be, use if the antitank ditch is not dug, German soldiers will die, and they are sons of German mothers. They are our blood." [32]

This sort of perverted "beer-hall heroism" also permeated Himmler's comment on the liquidation of the Polish elite:

[30] Buchheim, *ibid.*, p. 319.
[31] *Ibid.*, pp. 265–66.
[32] *Nürnberger Dokumente*, PS–1919 (Vol. XXIX, 122 f.).

They had to go, there was no choice. . . . I can tell you, it is hideous and frightful for a German to have to watch such things [executions]. . . . It is, and if we would not find it hideous and frightful, then we should no longer be Germans. Hideous though it is, it has been necessary and in many cases will continue to be necessary. . . . Because if we now lose our nerve, our children and grandchildren will have to pay for our loss of nerve. [Therefore] let us not weaken. Let us never become soft, but grit our teeth and carry on.[33]

SS morality and secret orders culminated in the "going through" with the extermination of Jews. In the Poznan speech, Himmler lauded it as a "glorious page of our history."

I want to tell you about a very grave matter in all frankness. We can talk about it quite openly here, but we must never talk about it publicly. . . . I mean the evacuation of the Jews, the extermination of the Jewish people. It is one of the things one says lightly [!]— "The Jewish people are being liquidated," party comrades exclaim; "naturally, it's in our program, the isolation of the Jews, extermination, okay, we'll do it." And then they come, all the 80 million Germans, and every one of them has his decent Jew. Of course, the others may all be swines, but this particular one is an A-1 Jew. All those who talk like this have not seen it, have not gone through it. Most of you will know what it means to see 100 corpses piled up, or 500, or 1,000. To have gone through this and—except for instances of human weakness—to have remained decent, that has made us tough. This is an unwritten, never to be written, glorious page of our history.[34]

While a combination of oppression, forced labor, and liquidation marked the fate of non-Jewish prisoners, the "final solution of the Jewish question" meant the extermination of every single Jew. The mass deportation from the new German Eastern regions began in 1939, while the Foreign Office was still debating Eichmann's deceptive plan for the creation of a "huge ghetto" for 4 million Jews under an SS police governor in Madagascar, which allegedly also would serve as a "pledge for the future good behavior of their race brothers in America." [35] German and Austrian Jews began to be shipped to Poland, where they were turned into slave labor, made to wear the Jewish star, and confined to ghettos. These ghettos, set up in 1940–41 (Lodz, Warsaw, Cracow, Lublin, Radom, Lvov), marked a transitional phase; their closing ushered in the mass shipments to labor camps (about 500,000 of the 2.5 million Polish Jews had already died in the ghettos and labor camps) [36] and later to extermination camps.

[33] *Ibid.*, PS–1918 (Vol. XXIX, 109).
[34] *Ibid.*, PS–1919.
[35] Thus the plan drawn up in June, 1940, by Rademacher, chief of the Foreign Office's section on Jewish affairs, in *Nürnberger Dokumente*, NG–2586.
[36] Raoul Hilberg, *The Destruction of the European Jews* (Chicago, 1961), p. 173.

Hitler apparently decided on the actual form of the final solution while planning the Russian war; however, he did not put down this most secret objective of his career in writing. As early as March, 1941, the Army command was notified about the powers and "special assignments" held by Himmler "for the preparation of the political administration . . . by order of the Führer . . . independently and on his own responsibility." Though these special tasks were not spelled out, the chiefs of the Einsatz units received the order in May, 1941, for the execution of all male Jews, as well as of all Communist functionaries, "second-class Asiatics," and gypsies.[37] The reports of the Einsatz units proudly tell of their determination "to solve the Jewish question by any means and with all decisiveness, as ordered." Not only did the "purging by the Security Police, in line with the basic orders, aim at the broadest possible liquidation," but on Heydrich's orders "native anti-Semitic forces were encouraged to stage anti-Jewish pogroms."[38] In addition to the males, vast numbers of women and children now became the victims of the almost uninterrupted executions. By early 1942, Einsatz Group A alone had a record of 229,052 executions by poison gas. According to bureaucratically precise "progress reports" on the "state of liquidation," more than 1 million Jews were murdered in this fashion.[39]

In a conference with Göring, Rosenberg, Lammers, Keitel, and Bormann, held on July 16, 1941, Hitler gave as a reason for the mass executions the pacification of the "vast terrain": "This can best be done by shooting dead anyone who even looks askance." The partisan warfare also offered "opportunity to liquidate anything which stands against us."[40] But pacification and security were not the determining factors; on the contrary, such a policy only made them more of a problem. Ideology and racism were behind these rationalizations. The measures were directed not against individuals and individual acts but primarily against the stereotype of *the* Jew, and after him, *the* inferior peoples of the East. Helmuth Krausnick[41] cites an example which makes the terrible obsession clear: after inquiring in Berlin, Ohlendorf's Einsatz unit spared the Crimean Karaimes, a sect of practicing Jews but not of Jewish "race," while the Krimtschaks, another Crimean sect which did not or no longer adhered to the Jewish faith, were said to be "unquestionably of Jewish race" and were exterminated. And so the reply to a question about "race theory" decided over the life and death of an entire ethnic group.

According to Hitler's early testimony, the "idea" of the extermination, concretely expressed in the gassing of the Jews, goes back to World War I and to old resentments over his gas poisoning in 1918. In *Mein Kampf* (p. 772), were written these words for all to see: "If at

[37] For details, see Krausnick, "The Persecution of the Jews," pp. 62 ff.
[38] *Nürnberger Dokumente*, XXXVII, 672, 682, 687.
[39] Hilberg, *op. cit.*, p. 256.
[40] *Nürnberger Dokumente*, XXXVIII, 87 f., 92.
[41] Krausnick, "The Persecution of the Jews," p. 67.

the beginning of the war and during the war, twelve or fifteen thousand of these Hebrew defilers had been put under poison gas, as hundreds of thousands of our very best workers from all walks of life had to endure at the front, then the sacrifice of millions at the front would not have been in vain. On the contrary: twelve thousand scoundrels eliminated in time might perhaps have saved the lives of a million decent, valuable Germans."

That systematic extermination plans were being laid was made clear by an order of the RSHA (May 20, 1941) instructing the Security Police to block the emigration of Jews from France and Belgium "in view of the imminent final solution of the Jewish question." [42] The program received its final "legalization" through the involvement of official agencies, after hundreds of thousands had already been executed by SS commandos. It was Göring who, as chairman of the Ministerial Defense Council, on July 31, 1941, sent a written order to Heydrich "to prepare a master plan for the measures—organizational, concrete, and material—preparatory to the implementation of the sought-for final solution." [43] The SS bureaucracy, however, continued to employ Aesopian language, for example, referring to deportations to concentration camps as "having been emigrated"; [44] and evacuation and deportation, "special treatment" and "disposition," meant extermination. Yet letters by the Minister of Justice, Otto Thierack, contained clearer phrases like "annihilation through work," "settlement of the Eastern question," "liberation of the German body politic," and "extermination." [45]

Himmler explained the "first phase" with Hitler's wish "that the Altreich and the Protectorates should be cleared of Jews from west to east." [46] Those who had survived the first wave of murder in occupied Russia were assigned to forced labor in ghettos and camps until such time as the capacity of the extermination camps was able to cope with the demands of the final solution. This had priority before everything else: "Economic considerations are not to be taken into account in the settlement of the problem"; so the East Ministry informed Reich Commissar Lohse in December, 1941.[47] Executions by shooting, introduced in prison camps, met with only feeble protest on the part of the Army. But more and more, the regime began to resort to gas vans and gas chambers in its mass killings, a method requiring fewer men and promising greater secrecy. After June, 1942, a Special Commando even

---

[42] *Nürnberger Dokumente*, NG–3104.

[43] *Ibid.*, NG–2586, PS–170.

[44] Telegram by Himmler to the Inspector of Concentration Camps, dated January 26, 1942, in Broszat, "The Concentration Camps 1933–45," p. 483.

[45] Letter from Thierack to Himmler, dated September 18, 1942, in *Nürnberger Dokumente*, XXVI, pp. 200 ff.; letter from Thierack to Bormann, October 13, 1942, in *ibid.*, NG–558.

[46] Memorandum from Himmler to Gauleiter Arthur Greiser, dated September 18, 1941, in Krausnick, "The Persecution of the Jews," p. 69.

[47] *Nürnberger Dokumente*, XXXIII, 435 ff.

exhumed and incinerated the victims of mass shootings in an effort to remove all traces of the crimes.[48]

The large-scale deportation of disenfranchised Jews of Germany began in October, 1941, and their government-controlled organization, the Reich Association of Jews in Germany, was compelled to cooperate. This "collaboration," as well as the role of the "Jewish councils" in the occupied territories, has in recent years led to bitter controversy, stirred up largely by Hannah Arendt's book on Eichmann.[49] But regardless of individual incidents of perhaps unfortunate moral lapses, the fact remains that built into the plans for the final solution were the ways and means for its realization. Only an earlier end to the war and the overthrow of the regime could have saved the millions who were murdered still in 1944–45.

Hitler had proclaimed the goal of the "extermination of the Jewish race in Europe" from the very beginning (for example, in his Reichstag address on January 30, 1939). Göring's order to Heydrich of July 31, 1941, read: "Total solution of the Jewish question in the German sphere of influence in Europe." The extension of the final solution to the satellite countries was the subject of the Wannsee Conference held, on January 20, 1942, after repeated postponements, under the chairmanship of Heydrich at Wannsee (Berlin), ironically enough in the headquarters of the Interpol. The subject was the "parallel lines of action" of all departments directly involved in the final solution: RSHA (Müller, Eichmann), Race and Settlement Main Office (Hofmann), Security Police (Schoengarth, Lange), Party Headquarters (Klopfer), Reich Chancellery (Kritzinger), East Ministry (Meyer, Leibbrandt), Interior Ministry (Stuckart), Justice Ministry (Freisler), Four-Year Plan (Neumann), Government General (Bühler), and Foreign Office (Luther). Eichmann was Recording Secretary. The fourteen high party officials and civil servants present took note of Göring's "installation" of Heydrich as the "deputy for the preparation of the final solution of the European Jewish question"; "over-all direction," regardless of geographic boundaries, rested with Himmler.

Heydrich explained that emigration had been replaced by evacuation to the East and that the practical experience being gained in this evacuation would prove most profitable in the approaching final solution of the Jewish problem. In bureaucratic terminology, Heydrich then reported that "in pursuance of the final solution, special measures will apply to conscript Jews for labor service in the East," that they "in large labor groups, with the sexes separated . . . while constructing roads [will be] directed to these areas, whereby undoubtedly a large number will drop out through natural elimination. . . . The possible remainders, and they undoubtedly will be the toughest among them, will

---

[48] Krausnick, "The Persecution of the Jews," p. 74.

[49] Hannah Arendt, *Eichmann in Jerusalem: A Report on the Banality of Evil* (rev. ed.; New York, 1965); on this, see *Die Kontroverse, Hannah Arendt, Eichmann und die Juden* (Munich, 1964).

be treated accordingly, for they, being a natural selection, would if released become the germ cell of a new Jewish reconstruction (history teaches us that). In the course of the practical implementation of the final solution, Europe will be combed through from West to East."

These sentences—cold, primitive, bureaucratic—combine the vulgar philosophy of National Socialism with the murder vocabulary of the SS state: "natural elimination," "remainders," "natural selection," "practical implementation," "combing through," "treated accordingly." The extermination, according to the inflated estimate of the RSHA, was to encompass more than 11 million "practicing Jews," including those of Great Britain and Turkey. However, "Jews working in essential enterprises could not be evacuated so long as no replacements were available." State Secretary Bühler of the Government General pointed out, moreover, that the "majority" of Jews scheduled for the final solution were "unfit for work." At any rate, continued secrecy was considered imperative, and the discussion of the various "possible solutions," which Eichmann at his trial in Jerusalem (1961–62) quite frankly described as "possible methods of killing," was governed by the concern that "upsetting the population must be avoided." [50]

Heydrich's announcement at the conference about the creation of an "old-people's ghetto" for Jews over sixty-five in the former garrison of Theresienstadt (northern Bohemia) was part of this ambiguity. In line with the murder terminology of the SS bureaucracy, these Jews were not to be "evacuated" but "transferred." That meant that death was camouflaged with the harmless term "change of address" and with the order that Jews awarded the Iron Cross Class I and "notable" Jews were to be allowed to go to this privileged camp. H. G. Adler in a basic study has analyzed the structure and reality of this "privileged camp." Its purpose was clearly tactical: "to save face," as Eichmann explained at a meeting of the RSHA on March 6, 1942.[51] It was meant to deceive the Jews of other countries as well as to placate those German departments which had intervened in individual "evacuations." The deception went so far that, after appropriate preparations, the Red Cross was allowed to inspect the camp in 1942. In addition, Eichmann, via his instrument, the Reich Association of Jews in Germany, prepared a so-called home-purchase scheme—a maneuver to deceive and rob Jews who, on the pattern of old-age-home contracts, were promised living quarters, food, and medical care [!] in Theresienstadt if they signed over their assets to the Reich Association—i.e., the RSHA. Yet another approach to the financial independence of the SS state! In fact, however, Theresienstadt was nothing but a concentration camp, and for most simply a way station on the road to extermination camps. Of the 141,000 German, Czechoslovak, Austrian, and Dutch Jews brought to this "privileged camp," only 23,000 (16 per

---

[50] *Nürnberger Dokumente*, NG–2586 (XII, 210 ff.); Leon Poliakov and Josef Wulf, *Das Dritte Reich und die Juden* (Berlin, 1955), pp. 119 ff.
[51] H. G. Adler, *Die verheimlichte Wahrheit* (Tübingen, 1958), pp. 9 f.

cent) survived; 33,000 died in Theresienstadt, and 85,000 in Auschwitz, Lublin, Minsk, and Riga.

Beginning in 1942, the extension of the final solution to the satellite states was pursued energetically, with the cooperation of the Foreign Office. At first, efforts (some successful) were made to get the various governments to act on their own; later, the RSHA intervened more and more by assigning "Jewish advisers" to the German missions. Finally, Eichmann and his helpers organized the roundup and transport of hundreds of thousands of Jews from Slovakia and Hungary, Croatia and Romania. He was least successful in Italy, until Mussolini's rump republic sought to smooth the way there as well.

The theory and methods of mass murder revealed the racist ideology of National Socialism as being an end in itself. Practical considerations connected with the need for slave labor played only a minor role. And ultimately they too were overshadowed by the final goal—extermination, "implemented" first and most stringently in Poland. There the methods of extermination promising the most rapid and unobtrusive success were tested and "mechanized." In 1940, Governor General Frank regretfully informed an appreciative audience that he had made great strides, "but of course in one year I could eliminate neither all lice nor all Jews."[52] And in December, 1941, he announced that "one way or another," the Jews "had to be finished"; Berlin had told him that the Reich Commissariat in the East "also couldn't do anything with them, liquidate them yourselves"! And so Frank continued: "Gentlemen, I must ask you to arm yourselves against all feelings of pity. We must destroy the Jews wherever we meet them and wherever possible." Frank believed that executions on the vast scale required (2.5–3.5 million) were impossible, but he hinted at "steps which in one way or another can lead to success in extermination."[53]

The point of departure was the experience with "gas chambers" gathered in the murder of 70,000 mentally ill Germans organized by the office of the Leader (by Victor Brack) between 1938 and 1941. After this "euthanasia" was halted in response to protests, the method was employed in the liquidation of concentration-camp inmates unfit for work. The selection remained in the hands of unscrupulous doctors. One of them, Dr. Fritz Mennecke, described the methods used in Buchenwald in a letter to his wife dated November 25, 1941: "The next contingent consisted of about 1,200 Jews, who were not put through any preliminary test. All we had to do was to copy the reasons for their arrest (plenty of them, as a rule) from the reports and on to the forms. Simply theoretical paper work."[54] In rapid order, extermination sites at which this method of serial mass murder was perfected were set up in Poland. The office of the Führer made the staff of the euthanasia experiment available to the man in charge, SS General Odilo Globocnik. The personnel were sworn to strict secrecy by Himmler: "He

52 Wulf, *op. cit.*, pp. 352 ff.
53 *Nürnberger Dokumente*, **XXIX**, 502 f.
54 *Ibid.*, NO–907; Krausnick, *op. cit.*, p. 96.

was making a superhuman-inhuman demand on them. But it was the order of the Führer." [55] As early as December, 1941, an SS special commando in Chelmno, near Lodz, used camouflaged gas vans in which more than 150,000 Jews were poisoned; here, as elsewhere, the job was done by Jewish work commandos who were subsequently shot. The victims were driven into the gas vans or gas chambers, which they were told were baths, by deception or force. Frequently the machinery did not operate properly or the motor refused to start, and so they had to stand for hours crowded together waiting for their death. This method, as had already been pointed out in earlier reports, had two great "advantages": secrecy and the number of persons that could be gassed in a single operation.[56]

The remote Lublin district, where the SS was setting up large industrial enterprises of its own, was a center of these activities. There in Belzec, mass extermination in camouflaged gas chambers began in March, 1942. Within months, hundreds of thousands of Polish and Czech Jews were sent to this factory of death; the traces of the murders were carefully obliterated by Jewish work commandos and the corpses incinerated.[57] The extermination camp in Sobibor "functioned" in like manner; 250,000 East and West European Jews were liquidated there. The number of victims of Treblinka was still greater—between 700,000 and 800,000. And the shootings also continued. In November, 1943, under the code name "Operation Harvest Festival," tens of thousands of Jews who had worked in munitions plants were machine-gunned in predug ditches near Lublin. Increasingly, camps which primarily served the "extermination through labor," among them Majdanek (in Lublin), were equipped with extermination facilities. The largest extermination mill was Auschwitz-Birkenau, to which Jews from all over Europe were brought for immediate gassing or for forced labor and subsequent gassing. The reports monotonously followed this pattern: "Transport from Berlin, arrived on March 5, 1943, total strength 1,128 Jews; of these, 389 men and 96 women were selected for work (Buna); 151 men and 492 women and children received special treatment." By November 2, 1944, in addition to Poles, gypsies, and Soviet prisoners of war, around 2 million Jews (Höss put the figure at 3 million)—70–80 per cent of all those deported—were killed, following the "successful experiments" of Höss and his camp leader Fritzsch with the prussic-acid derivative Zyklon B, "which was used in the camp as an insecticide and of which there was always a stock on hand." [58] In addition, countless others were shot, injected with phenolic acid, and subjected to "medical" experiments.

[55] *Nürnberger Dokumente*, XLII, 546.

[56] Memorandum of the East Ministry, October 25, 1941, in *ibid.*, NO–365.

[57] Details in Gerald Reitlinger, *The Final Solution* (rev. ed.; Cranbury, N.J., 1961). Gerstein report on the mass gassings of August 18, 1942, in *VfZG*, I (1953), 189 ff. On the Gerstein report, see also Saul Friedländer, *Kurt Gerstein* (Gütersloh, 1969).

[58] *Commandant of Auschwitz: The Autobiography of Rudolf Höss* (London, 1959), p. 146.

The genocide of the Jews—according to Eichmann's figures more than 6 million (4 million in extermination camps) had been murdered by the summer of 1944 [59]—was not the result of either war or terror. Neither individual guilt nor internal conflicts, neither a deterrent function nor the necessity of war was the determining factor. The extermination grew out of the biologistic insanity of Nazi ideology, and for that reason it is completely unlike the terror of revolutions and wars of the past. Here we are faced by the completely impersonal, bureaucratic "extermination" of a people classified as a species of inferior subhumans, as "vermin," a problem which the farmer Himmler handled as though it were a biological disease.

The tempo of the mass murder of Jewish men, women, and children was constantly accelerated up to 1944. Attempts at resistance in Sobibor, in Treblinka (in the fall of 1943), and particularly in the heroic resistance of the Warsaw ghetto in April–May, 1943, were brutally put down. Himmler, who personally witnessed only one mass murder, in Auschwitz-Birkenau (July 17, 1942), in utter silence,[60] now moved heaven and earth to achieve his goal quickly. He wrote imploring letters to the State Secretary in the Transport Ministry (Theodor Ganzenmüller) to ensure the rail transport; he waged bitter jurisdictional battles to win the release of Jews from labor assignments and away from the protection of Army and armaments departments to bring them to his camps. Himmler stressed "that alone for reasons of camouflage one must work as quickly as possible," and the Chief of the Lublin SS and Police, Globocnik, added "so that we don't get stuck in the middle." [61] And with all this, Himmler and the SS leadership continued to use euphemistic language even among themselves, talking in terms like "Jewish resettlement," and Goebbels in his diary noted ironically on March 27, 1942, that "a pretty barbarous procedure—one would not wish to go into detail—was being used [in the East], and nothing much remains of the Jews themselves." Globocnik (though Goebbels does not mention him by name) was doing the job "with a good deal of circumspection, and his methods do not seem to be attracting much publicity. . . . One simply cannot be sentimental about these things. . . . Here too the Führer is the moving spirit of a radical solution both in word and deed." [62]

But the stage management rested in the hands of the SS police, which thereby was able to consolidate still more its position as the real pillar of a consistent National Socialist policy, to expand its administration and its enterprises, to manipulate slave labor at will, and to wield the actual power in the Eastern territories, particularly in the Government General. The Army command, especially Keitel, on the whole acquiesced in the extermination of the Jews, or at least closed its

[59] Estimates of the total losses range from 5 to 7 million. At any rate, the total number of Jews in Europe declined from 9.2 to 3.1 million.

[60] *Commandant of Auschwitz*, pp. 207–8.

[61] *Nürnberger Dokumente*, NO–205; Krausnick, *op. cit.*, p. 102.

[62] Krausnick, *op. cit.*, pp. 103–4.

eyes to what was happening. Consequently, it could not object to the removal of Jewish workers from munitions plants and the destruction of the Warsaw ghetto, whatever the economic effects. True, the Army commander in Poland, General von Gienanth, informed Keitel that in view of what was happening, Poles could no longer be spared for work in Germany and "the Jews released only after substitutes had been trained, that means gradually." But at the same time, the High Command ordered "in entire agreement with the Reichsführer SS that all Jews employed by the armed forces in military auxiliary services and in the war industries are to be immediately replaced by Aryan workers." [63] Only very few high-ranking officers lodged more than the sort of indirect protests entered by Gienanth (who incidentally was replaced a few days after having spoken up).

In many places the Army worked closely with the SS offices, which now had complete jurisdiction over the Jews and the labor camps, just as they were in complete control of the Polish and Russian population by virtue of their police and special powers. Once again, as had happened so frequently since 1933, however now on a very different scale, the Army became the accomplice of a policy which a majority of its officers, frequently against their better judgment, followed to the end, in blind obedience to the Leader. The victory of the SS over the Army, which after the summer of 1944 was obvious even to outsiders, had in fact been decided at the beginning of the war, when the Army accepted the SS murder system. Only a few brave individual officers like Stauffenberg sought to counteract the paralysis of the Army. The others served if not Himmler at least Hitler, who, even after the systematic murder of millions of Jews, in his "testament" of April 29, 1945, fanatically clung to his "basic idea," admonishing all who came after him, "leaders of the nation and followers," also in future "above all . . . to hold fast to the race laws and to the relentless resistance against the poisoner of all peoples—international Jewry." [64] The reality and irreality of National Socialism were given their most terrible expression in the extermination of the Jews.

RESISTANCE PLANS DURING THE WAR

The problems faced by an internal resistance in a totalitarian regime differ substantially from the conditions of legal opposition and also from the illegal fight against a dictatorial foreign occupation. This was brought home forcefully during the war and the steady intensification of National Socialist rule. The success of conspiracies and actions depends largely on the fissures and conflicts that exist even in an apparently monolithic dictatorship and its tendencies toward a pluralistic structure. Hitler's unique position and the leader principle

---

[63] *Ibid.*, p. 111.
[64] J. Hohlfeldt, *Dokumente der deutschen Politik und Geschichte*, V, No. 210.

delimited this tendency inherent in practically every ruling system. But even the Third Reich, which persecuted all opposition, rested on rival power centers—economic, military, and bureaucratic. And it was within this framework that the typical forms of resistance emerged. Opposition from the outside had become almost impossible since the consolidation of the regime in 1933–34. But with the growing visibility of the direction and aims of Nazi rule, new chances for an opposition from within opened up. Hitler's policy of divide and rule gave him absolute control, but at the same time it created the openings and beginnings for opposition, particularly as problems arose in the conduct of foreign affairs.

Any systematic study of the German resistance must take various factors into account.[65] It must differentiate between motives, means, and effectiveness of the opposition. Passive resistance is a broad, hard-to-define area. It extends from job resignations, emigration, desertion, and suicide to certain forms of collaboration, which were often summed up by the phrase that one stayed on in office "in order to prevent something worse." To be sure, this had its questionable side, for the collaboration of the civil service and military first made possible the consolidation of the regime. More overt forms of opposition included both spontaneous and organized sabotage and obstruction, disobedience, and strikes. Active resistance in the strict sense ranged from intellectual and propaganda opposition against the regime to violence. The various possibilities open to the opposition were already taking shape before the war. Goerdeler and Beck in particular wrote a series of memorandums in an effort to persuade the rulers to change their course. The illegally circulated leaflets reporting on events and the plans for a new government, later on particularly those of the Kreisau Circle,* went considerably further. Long before the war, resistance groups gathered and disseminated information in circulars, sermons, and draft statements about what was happening in the country, in the hope of influencing popular opinion and of winning over like-minded persons. The conspirators themselves met in secret; among their primary objectives was the dissemination of political and military information. Reliable information and personal contacts to counteract the official propaganda were the presuppositions for an active resistance beyond simple protest and individual opposition.

There now arose the political and moral problem of when and how opposition should and could resort to violence. The churches were not alone in their reservations, and with only few exceptions rejected the use of violence, including the assassination of Hitler. But many conservative oppositionists, from Goerdeler to the Kreisau Circle, also were undecided on this point and left the matter of assassination to the military, the majority of whom held fast to their loyalty oath. This not only proved a hindrance in the preparation of a *coup d'état* but

[65] See particularly Dieter Ehlers, *Technik und Moral einer Verschwörung* (Bonn, 1964), pp. 27 ff., 100 ff.

* For a discussion of the Kreisau Circle, see pp. 438–41 below.

also in the communication between various opposition groups, and ultimately seriously hobbled the putsch attempt. To the very last, too much reliance was placed upon the elements of deception and surprise. The putsch plans of September, 1938—between Beck's resignation and the Munich conference—served as the basic model: first, win assurance of military support for a bloodless action, if possible; then, win over the population through announcements and information about the criminal nature and catastrophic course of the Hitler regime.

The war both complicated and helped the work of the opposition. On the one hand, it became increasingly difficult to draw a dividing line between National Socialism and Germany. The appeal to patriotism was stronger than the reservations about the regime. In addition, there was the growing regimentation of wartime life, the excessive controls and the general intensification of all problems. On the other hand, the war also called for a greater measure of improvisation and pragmatism; it tended to loosen and open up the ruling structure in the civilian and military sector, potentially a boon to the organization and spread of resistance. But above all, the Army, which despite all its past errors nonetheless had kept aloof from the party, and certainly the SS, gained in strength. Moreover, many civilian enemies of the regime now found themselves in military posts. That was true particularly of the Abwehr, which had played the role of a central liaison between military and civilian opposition already in 1938. Protected by Admiral Canaris, General Oster had recruited men like Hans von Dohnanyi and later Dietrich Bonhoeffer into the Abwehr. Klaus Bonhoeffer, his brother-in-law, Justus Delbrück, a businessman and son of the renowned historian Hans Delbrück, and numerous ministerial officials also contacted this circle. The Army High Command of Zossen (near Berlin) also housed some supporters. General Stülpnagel, who was to play a leading part in the Paris putsch attempt of 1944, joined, as did the vacillating Quartermaster General, Eduard Wagner, and Oster's contact man, Colonel Hans Groscurth. Contacts were made even inside the Police, SS, and Gestapo. This, however, brought problems which substantially complicated relations within the resistance.

The first efforts of the resistance were directed toward stopping the regime from continuing the war. When the West refrained from acting and handed Hitler an easy victory in Poland, Hitler's successful daring once more refuted the warnings of the military, as in 1936 and 1938. Public opinion, initially critical of the war, changed, particularly in view of official propaganda claims that Hitler's sole desire was peace— but now of course a peace based on the conquest and domination of Europe. That is why all speculation about the chances of a negotiated peace in 1939–40 were unrealistic. But Hitler knew how to turn an uninformed public's longing for peace into support of his war course. He thereby also overrode the reservations about the Soviet pact, which had been sharply criticized by Goerdeler, Hassell, and Beck. The faint hope that anti-Communist sentiment in the West could be enlisted in support of the anti-Hitler resistance was shattered by the impact of the *fait accompli*. And inside Germany, the opposition found itself up against a wall of gullible prejudice and intensified national self-confidence. It is questionable whether even a successful opposition move would have brought the hoped-for result. The prospect of winning back the people now seemed utterly hopeless.

Nonetheless, efforts multiplied in the fall of 1939 to forestall the attack on France Hitler had ordered for October 9, 1939, which was to bring the "final military defeat of the West."[66] And in fact, the attack was postponed repeatedly in response to objections by the military, in which threats of resignation and plans for coups à la 1938 played a part. The above named conspirators were joined by Joseph Müller, a Munich lawyer with contacts at the Vatican which Oster hoped would prove helpful in consolidation of a post-Hitler government. Diplomats of the opposition made contacts abroad to win assurances that the West would refuse to conclude a peace with Hitler but would do so with a new German government. These efforts were made primarily to counter the objections and reservations of wavering generals. Thus the thirty-year-old legation councillor Adam von Trott zu Solz, a Rhodes scholar with good contacts in England and the United States, made use of a lecture tour to acquaint American officials with the plans of the German opposition, while Goerdeler sought to influence British, French, and American political leaders. Numerous contacts were established via Switzerland, in part through the mediation of former Chancellor Joseph Wirth and former Defense Minister Otto Gessler. These efforts won British and French guarantees for friendly relations with a non–National Socialist government, provided that it did not include any Nazi ministers and that it renounced all expansionist plans. Müller's efforts at the Vatican, undertaken with the support of Beck, Oster, Dohnanyi, and Dietrich Bonhoeffer, also met with a positive response.

The fact that despite these favorable developments the German Army command failed to act in the spring of 1940 was responsible for the understandable Western mistrust of all subsequent efforts. The military's hesitation to follow up the negotiations with action points up the problems facing the conspirators then and later. On the one hand, the generals demanded Western guarantees prior to any action, and on the other, they had grave misgivings about the "treasonous" contacts which made such guarantees possible. When Halder presented Brauchitsch with the results of these foreign soundings in early April (in a résumé by Dohnanyi), Brauchitsch again did not act. This profoundly unpolitical Army officer simply did not understand the National Socialist perversion of the concept of treason. Unlike Beck, he simply could not grasp that extraordinary situations called for extraordinary methods. The most that can be said in his defense is that he knew of the plans and did not report them. The talks were broken off for good by Hitler's fresh success—the occupation of Denmark and Norway in

[66] Jacobsen, *Dokumente zur Vorgeschichte des Westfeldzugs* (Göttingen, 1956), p. 6. On the subsequent passages, see Harold C. Deutsch, *The Conspiracy Against Hitler in the Twilight War* (Minneapolis, 1968).

April, 1940, undertaken over the objections of the military. This, as
far as the West was concerned, put the opposition in a bad light. Its
contact men were practically suspected of being Gestapo agents who,
by misleading the Western powers, made the German attack possible.

That was among the reasons that Oster, in the final hours before the war, sought to establish the reliability of the opposition.
With the help of a friend, the Dutch military attaché, he transmitted
the dates of the planned attacks on Scandinavia and France to Holland. This effort, which like all contacts abroad has been called "treason" by critics of the opposition after the war and even has been used
to fan the flames of a new stab-in-the-back legend, was the expression
of Oster's implacable opposition to the regime and his determination to
do everything in his power to end the war and overthrow the Government. He felt that such "treason" against a relentless dictatorship was
justified by the fact that Hitler was about to overrun five neutral
countries to which he had given specific guarantees of inviolability.
Oster's actions were politically and morally motivated; he was extremely well informed about the unscrupulous preparations for Nazi
aggression. If treason presupposes the intention to harm one's country, then right in this extraordinary step was on the side of those who
used all means at their disposal to fight against the breach of agreements and the defeat of justice. Treason and violations of oaths can
have no meaning in a land without justice, one that violates all its
commitments to its own people as well as to the outside world. At the
same time, Oster's act was a concrete and desperate attempt to salvage
the shaken faith in the German opposition. He failed because his warnings were not taken seriously and because the military efficiency of the
German operations brought an unexpectedly speedy victory in the West.

Hitler's new triumphs wrought a basic change in the situation. The
victory over France also meant a major defeat for the opposition. Now
began the hardest test for a resistance movement trying to keep alive
in the heady atmosphere of a victorious dictatorship. Its contacts with
the West and the hopes for an early end to the war and for the overthrow of the Government had been dashed. Isolated and without hope of
winning popular support, the opposition was reduced to moral and
legalistic positions; the rug had been pulled out from under overt action. This makes the continuity by which the opposition was organized
and expanded in the ensuing years all the more remarkable, and it
refutes later contentions that the German resistance was motivated
solely by fear of defeat, by a sort of last-minute panic. That may hold
true for some of its military exponents, but certainly not for those
who bore the burden of the suicidal battle against Hitler and his apparently invincible rule at a time when the Third Reich was scoring
its greatest successes.

New plans for overthrowing the Government could not be drawn up
within the existing framework; the chances of gaining the support
of a victorious, successful, much-decorated military were even slighter
than before 1940. And the swelling ranks of junior- and middle-rank-

ing officers, now of a younger generation devoted to Hitler, inevitably had a negative effect on the generals' readiness to act. Furthermore, as the power of the SS increased, so did the protective measures of the regime. After the beginning of the Russian campaign, Hitler lived almost exclusively in the hermetically sealed-off bunkers of the Führer headquarters in East Prussia and the Ukraine; plans for his removal involved a most complicated combination of circumstances. This was doubly serious because it had become unmistakably evident that under the conditions of war and Hitler's position of power, his assassination was the *sine qua non* for a change of government.

Two vital problems put their stamp on future developments. One was the fact that every German victory diminished the prospects of the internal opposition as much as it buttressed the foreign-policy position of its German National wing, from Goerdeler to the Foreign Office: "As long as Hitler's triumphant progress continued, revolution to most Germans would appear nothing but sabotage and treason. A change would come when the war was seen to be hopeless, and then it would be too late. The enemy demanded 'unconditional surrender' and to them the Opposition leaders were no more than nationalist opportunists whose only aim was to let Germany escape the punishment which her shameful deeds merited." [67]

The second problem was connected with the debate over the political and moral implications of the plan to assassinate Hitler. The consideration of the future of Germany, which took on even greater urgency as the atrocities piled up, brought to the fore the differences in the political and social ideas of the opposition. After the failure of all "regular" efforts to change the regime, after the profound convulsion of all traditional values, a basic re-evaluation of the situation seemed even more imperative than before the war. Was a joint program for the future possible? A look at the diverse political and social ideas of the resistance movement of 1940–43 reveals the limits of this aspect of the opposition.

The foreign-policy ideas of the "conservative-national notables who between 1938 and 1942 [determined] the nature of the potentially active part of the resistance movement" [68] seem particularly problematical. They differed from the Greater German, hegemonic pretension of the National Socialists only in scope and method, not in principle. Hitler was seen as a gambler who had sacrificed a justified revisionism and the true national interests of Germany to his quest for power. Goerdeler, Beck, Hassell, and Popitz for a long time accepted Germany's special position in the world, its leading role in Europe, and the preser-

[67] Gerhard Ritter, *The German Resistance: Carl Goerdeler's Struggle Against Tyranny* (New York, 1958), p. 210. See the recent detailed work by Peter Hoffmann, *Widerstand, Staatsstreich, Attentat* (Munich, 1969), pp. 130 ff.; 639 ff.

[68] Hermann Graml, "Die aussenpolitischen Vorstellungen des deutschen Widerstandes," in *Der deutsche Widerstand gegen Hitler* (Cologne, 1966), p. 19.

vation of the boundaries of Greater Germany as a self-evident fact. Even after his arrest in 1944, Goerdeler still believed that Germany had to keep its 1914 boundaries in the East, that it had a right to Austria and the Sudetenland, that it was entitled to the South Tyrol and to colonies. Of course, this position may have been dictated by tactical considerations; he possibly may have hoped to the very end to influence the rulers through his memorandums. And on the other hand, he had for years been a champion of peaceful cooperation in Europe and the revival of the League of Nations.

Generally speaking, an evaluation of the conservatives' position must take into account the special motives and circumstances of such plans, and here two aspects above all take on special significance. First, the tactical position of the opposition, which rested on cooperation with the military and conservative civil servants, did not permit a complete renunciation of conquered territories if it was to gain adequate support; this was true at any rate until 1942–43, the turning point in the war. And second, these plans reflected ideas which the German elite and large segments of the population had held in World War I and since in the "fight against Versailles"; they were in the tradition of the Bismarck Reich and of big-power thinking, which was perpetuated in the revisionism of the Weimar Republic and accepted by the appeasement of the West. It would be wrong to equate this "national" position with approval of National Socialist revisionism and to contend that the opposition objected only to the imperial expansionism of Hitler. The fact is that the decision to resist was triggered in 1938 by the forcible military expansion of the German borders. It was a decision against war as a means even for achieving desired, territorially limited revisions. Beck in particular believed a war in Europe to be anachronistic and militarily ill-advised. But on balance it would have to be said that most of the discussions and plans of this group were profoundly attuned to the dominant national mood.

On the other hand, it should be kept in mind that neither these ideas nor the social and political beliefs of Goerdeler were at all typical of or binding on the entire opposition. Many historians are inclined to judge the importance of any one group by the volume of written evidence—a most inadequate method of evaluating conspiratorial movements. Gerhard Ritter also did not succeed in avoiding this pitfall in his book on Goerdeler. These studies fail to make clear that the mountains of memorandums (Goerdeler), the records of conversations, letters, or coded diaries (Hassell), and even the draft plans for post-Hitler governments (Kreisau Circle) were by no means *the* program of even one segment of the German resistance movement, but simply expressions of individual opinion. Insofar as these plans were given to the other groups at all, they were either subjected to severe criticism or accepted as nonbinding proposals that were discussed merely for the sake of day-to-day cooperation. It should come as no surprise that the work of the political-minded activists of resistance is not nearly so well documented. What emerges from an analysis of the various programs is the extent to which all plans of the opposition, from Right to Left, were weighed down by inhibitions, illusions, and misjudgments, and that resistance and conspiracy against Hitler did not automatically mean a vote for democracy or the renunciation of nationalistic power politics.

This is made evident by the alternative programs for the new order of Europe drafted particularly by the Kreisau Circle. While the political ideas of the Goerdeler group have quite properly been subjected to sharp criticism—it has even been charged that they did not offer a real alternative to Hitler—the European ideas of the Kreisau Circle have been idealized and equated with the integration policies of the postwar era. But they too had a problematical connection with the European claims of National Socialism, and under the influence of the Goerdeler group their original rejection of nationalism at times gave way to ideas of a synthesis of Reich and Europe. In memoranda of July, 1940, and again after a temporary resurgence of illusions at the beginning of the Russian campaign, Goerdeler advanced the claim to a "German leadership" of Europe. Hassell spoke of the "German leadership of the West," and Popitz still more equivocally granted Germany "certain special rights" vis-à-vis other countries in the European "sphere of influence." To be sure, Hassell and his friends stressed that other nations were not to be subjugated to Germany, that their unique political and cultural character was to be preserved, and that their interests were to be protected.[69] But these ideas offered hardly any alternatives to Hitler acceptable to the outside world. As political programs for contact and discussion with the other European resistance movements, they were unrealistic. They bore a certain resemblance to the National Socialist ideology of the Reich and Europe. Though differing substantially in method and objectives from the ideas of Hitler, there was some coincidence in the argument that technical and economic development called for greater political units.

But at the same time, these programs offered the opening for the ideas developed by the younger and more broadminded oppositionists of the Kreisau Circle for the abolition of the national state. Their approach gained ground after 1941, when the spokesmen for the national-conservative opposition, alarmed by the turn the war had taken and by the terror which had completely discredited the name and the mission of the "Reich" in Europe, also began to stress the idea of a European union of independent and equal states.

The Kreisau Circle, an opposition group that first gathered in 1940, continued to meet in 1942 and 1943 at the estate of Count Helmuth James Moltke in Kreisau (Silesia). It differed from the group around Goerdeler in two respects: its participants, in the thirty-to-forty-year age group, were of another generation and even though coming from the nobility, the civil service, and the officer corps were less firmly wedded to national-conservative traditions; and both by background

[69] *Ibid.*, pp. 37 ff.

and conviction, they spanned a wide spectrum from Right to Left.[70] A Christian-Socialist reformist mood dominated the talks and discussions at Kreisau about Germany's future at home and abroad. The strong representation of old Prussian nobility was one of the striking features of this group. Count Moltke (b. 1907) was a great-grandnephew of a famous general; as consultant on problems of international law for the Army High Command, he tried, in close cooperation with the Abwehr, to bar the maltreatment of prisoners of war and civilian populations in other countries. Count Yorck von Wartenburg, another member and a relative of Moltke, was a descendant of the great general of the Napoleonic wars and of renowned philosophers and scholars. As a lawyer and later as an officer, Yorck was assigned to the Eastern Department of the Army's Economic Warfare Division, which after the summer of 1942 presented him with the opportunity to travel and make contacts, until finally he became actively involved in the putsch plans of his cousin Stauffenberg. Carl Dietrich von Trotha, one of the few members of the Kreisau Circle to survive, came from a progressive wing of the youth movement.

The Kreisau Circle established contact with members of the Socialist resistance, some of whom also came from the youth movement, among them Adolf Reichwein, who after World War I and work in the Socialist youth movement, was active in adult education groups and work camps. Later Professor of History and Civics in Halle, he was "transferred" in 1933 to a one-room village school. He had met Moltke during the Weimar era while both worked in voluntary labor camps. Reichwein introduced his Socialist friends Carlo Mierendorff and Theo Haubach to the Kreisau Circle and established contact with Julius Leber, who being a political activist, was critical of the theoretical plans of the Kreisau Circle. In the days of Weimar, Haubach had been an editor and later Press Chief of the Prussian Government; beginning in 1933, he spent two years at hard labor; after his release he went into business. His school friend Mierendorff, more emotional and brilliant than he, also a rebel within the SPD, had been a member of the Press Section of Hesse's Socialist Government. He spent the years from 1934 to 1938 in prison and forced-labor camps. After his release, he, too, was employed in private business; he became one of the driving forces in the coup plans. His death in an air raid in December, 1943, spared him the fate of his friends, but it also deprived the resistance of one of its most spirited members.

In addition to the Socialists, the Kreisau Circle also had Christian representatives. Its most active Catholic member was Father Alfred Delp, a young Jesuit who had converted to Catholicism in his high-school years. Passionately involved in the problems of the times, he did not permit the conservative, dogmatic position of his Church to hamper his quest for political and social reform. The Protestant side was

[70] For a comprehensive treatment, see Gerd van Roon, *Neuordnung im Widerstand* (Munich, 1967). Also, O. H. von der Gablentz, "Der Kreisauer Kreis," *Politische Vierteljahresschrift* (PVS), IX (1968), 592 ff.

strongly represented by the other members, and they were joined by the Berlin prison chaplain Harald Poelchau. Eugen Gerstenmaier, representing the Lutheran Bishop Wurm of Württemberg, made contact with the group after having played a somewhat ambiguous role in the Church's Foreign Office under the politically dubious Bishop Heckel. Furthermore, there were a number of professors, local government officials (like Theodor Steltzer), and diplomats, among them Hans Berndt von Haeften, a nephew of Brauchitsch but a very different sort of man, and his friend Adam von Trott zu Solz, who to the very last worked closely with Stauffenberg.

At the center of the discussions of this multifaceted group were the internal reforms, the basis of the new post-Hitler order. The approach to foreign policy mentioned earlier points up the unique qualities but also the limitations of the Kreisau Circle: the break with nationalism; the movement toward a European internationalism rejecting both the French hegemony of Versailles and the old and new ideas on German hegemony; German-French and German-Polish understanding in the place of disputed territorial demands. These ideas were largely the work of the Socialists (Haubach, Leber, and Reichwein); Leber had consistently maintained that the principles of economic cooperation and democratic domestic policy must also govern international relations.[71] But Moltke and his friends, also departing from the historico-political traditional ideas of their class, spoke of the Europeanization of political thought and of the need for revising the idea of the state as an end in itself. The problem of East German and East European nationality policies gave rise to the idea of a supranational, federalist solution. Moltke quite early had devoted himself to the problem of the minorities. This formed the basis on which cooperation with exponents of Socialist, internationalist concepts could be worked out. In some respects Moltke went even further by raising the seemingly utopian idea of the division of Germany and Europe into small, self-administered bodies. This type of radical federalism, which invoked the sovereignty of a European federation, meant a revolutionary break with nineteenth- and twentieth-century modes of thought, according to which the defense against "particularism" and support for the national unitary state was the highest law.

The practical proposals of the Kreisau Circle lagged far behind such radical models. But even more "realistic" supporters of a moderate national idea like Trott zu Solz made the preservation of the existing states dependent on a restricted sovereignty in favor of a European federation. While Moltke represented the most consistent moral and legalistic position and was highly critical of appeasement and its disregard of international principles of law in favor of national revisionism, Trott believed that concessions to the traditional national principle were indispensable. But in 1939 he, too, unlike Goerdeler, came out

[71] Julius Leber, *Ein Mann geht seinen Weg* (Berlin, 1952), p. 54 and *passim*.

for the 1933 borders and against territorial claims; central to his idea of Europe was German-British cooperation. Beyond that, Trott expressly stressed the role of the working class, in which "a strong tradition of international cooperation and rational politics" still lived on.[72] Apparently he had in mind in particular the example of the United States, and he visualized a unified Europe with a common economic policy and citizenship, a "joint highest court," and possibly also a European army. Leaving aside the question of whether or not some of the visionary details were realistic, the basic idea of a non-nationalist Europe in which neither a strong France nor a strong Germany would tip the scales offered a more constructive vision of the future and also a more persuasive alternative to Hitler than the regressive ideas of Goerdeler.

While Goerdeler's political ideas, and even some of the Kreisau Circle, retained elements of the idea of Reich and nation, against the wishes of the Socialists,[73] the conservative-national group from 1942 on also began to be influenced by other notions. The idea of a supranational and European order started to move into the foreground of Beck's and even of Goerdeler's thinking. With characteristic impulsiveness and optimism, Goerdeler, ignoring the contradiction of the two principles, tried to combine the preservation of the system of national states with the demand for a European union with supranational ministries of economics, defense, and foreign affairs.[74] The reactions of the skeptical diplomat Hassell to the Kreisau plans were similarly ambivalent (and not uncritical). Both Goerdeler and Hassell wavered between a greater emphasis on European unity and a traditionalist holding fast to "Germany's lifeblood," the Bismarckian state and its key position between West and East. Because they were innately conservative, their ideas were strongly influenced by their fear of the Soviet threat. Despite their awareness of Hitler's responsibility for this development, they nonetheless clung to the bulwark idea and the belief that Western understanding would still open up a possibility for saving the German state. For this reason, Goerdeler tried to get the military to act while the German armies were still able to hold the Polish eastern border. Goerdeler and Hassell misjudged the firmness of the compact of the Allies and their commitment to the demand for unconditional surrender put forth after the January, 1943, Casablanca meeting. These ideas of Goerdeler's and Hassell's were partially realized after the war, as the Cold War intensified—but then they brought the division of Germany.

Even though the proposals on the conduct of foreign affairs—the visionary as well as the "realistic"—of the resistance were overtaken by the rapidly deteriorating situation, they nonetheless offered some

[72] *Denkschrift* for Lord Halifax (late 1939), in H. Rothfels, "Trott und die Aussenpolitik des Widerstands," *VfZG*, XII (1964), 313.

[73] Theodor Steltzer, *Von deutscher Politik* (Frankfurt/Main, 1949), p. 156.

[74] Ritter, *op. cit.*, pp. 222–23.

remarkable ideas for the future. The domestic program, which in retrospect seems in part predemocratic-restorational and in part utopian and contrived, invites even greater skepticism. However, one must remember the circumstances and the tactical considerations involved, as for example the wooing of the generals, and one must also differentiate between the ideas of individual groups and the forces that would actually have had a voice in formulating the new German order after the overthrow of Hitler. The Left and the liberals were far less strongly represented in the known plans than indicated by their potential strength. Here, too, the assumption that the ideas of Goerdeler or Kreisau were representative of the entire resistance and of the reform plans of a post-Hitler government is erroneous. These reservations must be taken into consideration in dealing with reform ideas of the anti-Hitler opposition before contending that many appear to be an extension of the antidemocratic opposition to Weimar.[75]   As it turned out, this approach to constitutional reforms lost out after 1945.

The real problem facing the opposition was the coup, and with it the role of the Stauffenberg-Leber group, which at any rate did not trouble itself overly with theory but instead concentrated its energies on the three major, pressing problems: deposing the Hitler regime, ending the war, restoring justice and freedom. That was also the primary concern of Dietrich Bonhoeffer, who as early as 1942, in a radical departure from Goerdeler and others, had said that the guilt of Nazi Germany no longer permitted an "evasive foreign policy." The resistance must make it clear that it was simply performing an "act of penitence." [76] Bonhoeffer as well as Leber and Moltke believed that Germany's unconditional surrender was inevitable. Thus Moltke at the end of 1943, "for moral and political reasons," considered "the unequivocal military defeat and occupation of Germany absolutely necessary." [77]

The young students who in 1942–43 rebelled against the political failure of the German educators were motivated by a similar awareness. February 18, 1943, was the day on which they bravely launched their rebellion against the lies of the regime in Munich and elsewhere. The thousands of leaflets which had been prepared in the course of months, the appeals calling for the fight against Hitler and for freedom posted on walls and at the entrance of Munich University, were mainly the work of a resistance group known as the White Rose, formed in Munich in the spring of 1942 by Hans and Sophie Scholl, Christoph Probst, Willi Graf, Alexander Schmorell, and the professor of philosophy and musicology, Kurt Huber. The group established contacts with other universities (Hamburg, Berlin, and Vienna). Rejection and optimism

[75] Stressed by George R. Romoser, "The Politics of Uncertainty," *Social Research*, XXXI (1964), 73 ff.; and Hans Mommsen, in *Der deutsche Widerstand gegen Hitler*, pp. 74 ff.

[76] Dietrich Bonhoeffer, *Gesammelte Schriften*, ed. Eberhard Bethge (Munich, 1959), I, 395; see also Eberhard Bethge, *Dietrich Bonhoeffer* (New York, 1970), pp. 585 ff.

[77] Roon, *op. cit.*, pp. 457, 584.

motivated the students of the White Rose—rejection of the subjugation of the spirit by lies and brute force, and faith in the power of conscience and truth. Before she and her friends were executed, Sophie Scholl, a twenty-two-year-old philosophy student, told the People's Court: "What we have written and said is in the minds of all of you, but you lack the courage to say it aloud." [78] Her declaration sums up the situation of the German universities; they remained silent to the very end, despite growing criticism, despite the arrest and murder of students, despite the injustices and lies that engulfed them. "The Spirit Lives," proclaimed the posters affixed to the walls of Munich. But the University of Munich, its professors and students, did not dare to say one single word; they did not even petition for the pardon of their colleagues.

Resistance continued to be a lonely and disreputable affair, even in most places of learning. Shackled by German tradition, scholars were as little prepared as generals to risk conflict with conventional notions of patriotism and obedience. Fear of persecution and of the odium of treason frightened off men who should have known better because they were in daily contact with the realities of political and military life or with the world of intellectual and moral values. We know, of course, that there were limits to the possibilities of *Gleichschaltung*. What remained constant was the mistrust with which the rulers looked at all those whom they branded with their special term of invective: "intelligentsia." In August, 1934, the *Stürmer* admonished: "There is constant complaining and whispering in the halls of the universities. One thing is very noticeable: the reading of foreign newspapers. At least 60 per cent, probably even more, are in opposition." And in 1935, the Reich Governor of Hamburg, Karl Kaufmann, complained that no more than 10 per cent of all students were actively cooperating. One can cite numerous examples of independent thought and teaching; even eloquent silence holds significance if joining the chorus is what is being demanded. However, this refusal to be coordinated, manifested by retreating into passive resistance, generally took place in hopeless isolation, and withdrawal into scholarly realms seemed to imply the inability to form broader political judgments. The scattered cases of protest in the face of mistrust and surveillance were doubly courageous. But only a broadly based declaration for freedom could really have affected a regime so dependent on the cooperation of specialists.

In their first call to resistance, Hans and Sophie Scholl summed up the dilemma: a beginning had to be made; the vicious circle in which "every one waited until the other would begin," thus heaping guilt on everyone, had to be broken. The significance of this overt protest also lies in the warning example provided by the fate of the resistance in the Third Reich. Education and scholarship may capitulate to seductions and manipulations which pave the way for a regime like Hitler's —if the political passivity of the educated stratum is responsive to the

[78] Inge Scholl, *Die weisse Rose* (Frankfurt/Main, 1955), pp. 104 ff.; cf. Christian Petry, *Studenten aufs Schafott* (Munich, 1968).

tendencies which flourished in the partly unpolitical, partly antidemocratic atmosphere of the German schools and universities. What proved fatal were not only the crimes of a National Socialist minority and its petty-bourgeois fellow travelers but also the failure of a majority of the "educated." It is they, so Theodor Heuss stated, who failed to act decently, who heaped collective shame on themselves. This must be said to all those who now dismiss the disquieting symbol of the White Rose as naïve idealism and blindness to the harsh realities of political life. Behind the symbol of the White Rose stood an awareness of the reality of National Socialism that saw beyond the paralyzing influences of the time. The Munich leaflets voiced this awareness more freely and less ideologically than most plans of either the Right or Left opposition: "Even though we know that National Socialist power must be broken militarily, we want to achieve the renewal of the badly wounded spirit from within. This rebirth, however, must be preceded by the acceptance of the guilt which the German nation has heaped upon itself and by a ruthless battle against Hitler and his all too many accomplices." [79]

The brutally throttled demonstration of the White Rose was the "settling of accounts of German youth with the most despicable tyranny our nation has ever suffered"—so read the leaflet of February 18, 1943. It dealt with the dangerous deception of a generation which the Third Reich, through Hitler Youth, SA, and SS, "tried, in the formative years of our lives, to make uniform, revolutionize, and anesthetize" in order to make this youth into "godless, shameless, unscrupulous exploiters and murderers . . . to blind, stupid Führer followers." And it called on the students to strike against and sabotage the tyrants, who "in the name of freedom and honor of the German nation have inflicted and still inflict daily . . . this terrible bloodbath on all of Europe." The resistance of youth was given expression in a great number of other groups that in part came out of the old youth movement and in part arose in opposition to the Hitler Youth.

THE ROAD TO THE 20TH OF JULY

In the last year of war, the German resistance readied itself for a *coup d'état.* The fact that it had not done so earlier and the utopian nature of many of its plans gave rise to the contention that the overthrow of the regime was not given serious consideration until the war was irrevocably lost. It cannot be denied that a paralyzing conformism ruled the population to the very last, and that only a handful of officers, essential to such a move, dared to act. Many who joined the opposition, as for example Hans Scholl, arrived at the decision to resist after having witnessed German occupation policies, particularly in the East. This moral and political factor motivated also a portion of the military opposition. Further impetus was furnished by the conflicts in the lead-

[79] Scholl, *op cit.,* p. 145; pp. 151 ff. for subsequent citation.

ership which emerged into the open for the first time after the Russian winter offensive of 1941–42.

The prospects of the opposition at that time were dimmer than ever: Hitler stood at the height of his career; the resistance was cut off from contact with the outside world, and the Western powers did not put any credence in it, or at best thought it ineffective. Neither contacts with Switzerland nor independent ventures such as Dietrich Bonhoeffer's meeting with Bishop Bell of Chichester in May, 1942, repercussions of which reached all the way into the British Government, could alter this. Isolated both inside the country and abroad, the opponents of Hitler—unless they were possessed of Goerdeler's indestructable optimism—held little hope for success. All that was left to them was the moral certainty of being in the right.

And yet not only was the continuity of the opposition preserved, but its network spread—and that long before the regime had suffered any real setback, let alone defeat. The war, occupation, and Jewish policies of the National Socialists persuaded a number of militant younger officers, more determined than the tradition-bound generals, to join the resistance movement after 1941. The most notable example of this reorientation, which opened up a new chapter in the efforts to overthrow the regime, was Colonel Count Claus Schenk von Stauffenberg. Born the same year as Moltke (1907), a scion of the Swabian nobility, related to the families of Gneisenau and Yorck, Stauffenberg had at one time been close to the circle around Stefan George. After the outbreak of the war, this brilliant young General Staff officer gradually turned into an implacable foe of Hitler; in this, he had the support of his older brother Berthold, like Moltke an international lawyer, who was aware of the magnitude of the Nazi crimes. Going outside the sphere of the military and conservatives, Stauffenberg made contact with the activist Left, above all with Julius Leber. He soon found himself at odds with the ideas of the Goerdeler-Beck circle. It was his belief that all plans for a new order, a subject much debated by most opposition groups, must begin with the removal of Hitler and the overthrow of the Government. Unlike the theological, bureaucratic, and military legalists and authoritarian ideologists, he believed that tyrannicide and violations of oaths were justified, and, like Tresckow and Dietrich Bonhoeffer, he was not reluctant to bring down the charge of treason upon himself.[80]

Stauffenberg's far-flung activities and contacts bridged divergent opinions, plans, and objectives. He concentrated his efforts on building reliable strongholds inside the Army and on preparations for a coup. In this he had the help of friends in the civilian resistance and some oppositional generals, but above all of a group of younger officers personally committed to him and not hamstrung by the reservations of the older military and civil servants. They knew that in view of the un-

---

[80] Ernst Wolf, in *Der deutsche Widerstand gegen Hitler*, pp. 252 ff. On Stauffenberg, see the comprehensive treatment by Christian Müller, *Oberst i.G. Stauffenberg* (Düsseldorf, 1971).

conditional surrender demand of the West, a new stab-in-the-back legend and accusations of national and military opportunism were distinct possibilities, and indeed, these charges were promptly leveled against them both at home and abroad. That Stauffenberg and his friends knowingly accepted these risks speaks for their determination to topple the regime even without foreign guarantees.

Of course, the real problem was how, under these circumstances, the military leaders could be won over. Although the crisis of the winter of 1941–42 and the brutal murder of Soviet officials and Russian civilians had given rise to widespread indignation among the officer corps, the Bonhoeffer-Chichester meeting and a Goerdeler memorandum transmitted via Sweden in May, 1943, made clear that the British Government was no longer responsive to peace overtures. The world had united for unconditional war on Hitler Germany. All that was left to the opposition, insofar as it did not believe that the Nazi regime should and could not be relieved of the final responsibility, was the narrow base of an internal, morally justified coup. Thus the efforts launched after 1942 were acts of desperation aimed at putting a stop to a brutal regime, a criminal war, and the further erosion of the moral fiber of Germany.

Besides Stauffenberg, two younger generals furnished the main impetus for the planning and organization of the coup. Friedrich Olbricht, the chief of the Army Office (*Heeresamt*) at Berlin, made use of his far-flung connections in the Army to feed the growing indignation of the Army command over Hitler's terror orders and their execution by the SS. A friend of Goerdeler's, he became an energetic military champion of the coup plans.

The strongest exponent of these plans at the Russian front was General Henning von Tresckow. He gathered a group of like-minded officers of his staff, tried to win over his commander, General von Kluge, and was the driving force behind various assassination plans. None of the front-line generals, however, could be persuaded to desert Hitler. After the dismissal of General Hoepner and other critics of Hitler's Russian strategy, General Witzleben and Chief of Staff General Halder were also relieved of their commands, and thus the new, energetic efforts were reduced to plans of action inside Germany.

With that, the headquarters in Berlin and the Home Army moved into the center of the plans. After repeated consultation with Tresckow, Olbricht placed reliable officers in the Army commands in Germany; in Berlin, Vienna, Cologne, and Munich, surprise coups against the party and SS were to be staged on the day of Hitler's removal. These coups were to take the form of measures against "internal unrest." Operation Valkyrie, the code name for the planned action, was to make available all troops inside Germany to complete and consolidate the putsch. Because no outstanding front-line commander could be won over, and because two assassination attempts in March, 1943, had failed and the opportunity opened up by Stalingrad had been frittered away by the indecisiveness of General Paulus, the initiative remained with the

Berlin group. Stauffenberg's transfer to Berlin—he had been seriously wounded in Africa in April, 1943—strengthened this group enormously.

But in the meantime a vital link—the Abwehr—had been put out of action. Early in April, 1943, the Gestapo occupied Oster's department, arresting his most important collaborators, including Dohnanyi, Dietrich Bonhoeffer, and Josef Müller. Though Canaris succeeded in staving off their trial, and thus warding off the potential danger to the entire opposition, the Abwehr, under the suspicious surveillance of the rival SS and Gestapo, had become largely ineffective. Canaris, who still managed to hold the fort until February, 1944, found that his sphere of operations had been severely curtailed. And at the same time, Beck, incapacitated by a serious illness, underwent major surgery, which left him partially disabled.

Popitz meanwhile was pushing his efforts on another, admittedly problematic level. As a member of the Prussian Government, he sought to win over key officials to a plan for toppling the Government. Initially he had set his hopes on persuading Göring to stage a palace revolution. When that failed, he even tried to recruit the powerful central figure of the terror—Heinrich Himmler himself. Popitz apparently believed that the burning ambition and fears of the Reichsführer SS could be enlisted against Hitler and thus effect at least a weakening of Nazi rule. On August 26, 1943, Himmler's lawyer, Carl Langbehn, who was edging toward the opposition, arranged a meeting between Himmler and Popitz—a dangerous venture, which the adroit Popitz handled with great diplomatic skill. He came away confirmed in his suspicion that even Himmler was beginning to waver in his belief in final victory.

But the meeting brought no other result. A man so heavily burdened by guilt, and moreover so incapable of independent action, could not possibly be expected to rebel. Popitz's effort proved as problematical as it was illusory—and moreover, such an undertaking could only harm the nature and the objectives of the resistance. Any contact with Himmler would have hopelessly compromised the opposition at home and abroad and thrown it into confusion. Of course, once he had won Himmler over, Popitz planned to outmaneuver him and the SS— Popitz obviously was still blinded by the same dangerous illusions which in 1932–33 led the conservatives to believe that they could use Hitler and the NSDAP. Fabian von Schlabrendorff reports that the anti-Hitler officers in Kluge's headquarters told Canaris that they would refuse to shake hands with him if he made good his intention of having a confidential talk with Himmler: "One can't touch the hand of anyone who has shaken hands with that filthy dog without oneself becoming dirty." [81]

The Popitz-Langbehn venture evoked considerable misgivings and mistrust even among the men around Beck, Goerdeler, and Olbricht,

[81] Fabian von Schlabrendorff, *Offiziere gegen Hitler* (rev. ed.; Frankfurt, 1966), p. 75.

who were not categorically opposed to daring intrigues in the service of the ultimate objective. Although this group welcomed the possibility of a split within the SS and the top Nazi leadership, it did not want to have any direct contact, let alone cooperate, with it, and certainly not with Himmler, the personification of the terror. But the plan failed spectacularly anyway: Langbehn was arrested by the Gestapo soon thereafter, and the contacts with Himmler possibly may have laid the groundwork for the wave of arrests that summer. Popitz, like Schacht, remained isolated within the resistance movement. Not that there was doubt about his reliability—he gave his life for his beliefs—but there was mistrust of the daring conspiratorial methods of a man who, as a Prussian Minister, was a colleague of Göring.

In the meantime, the various opposition groups and leaders sought to reach agreement on the composition of a provisional government. Numerous lists, many of them the work of Goerdeler, were considered and discussed in 1943–44. It was generally agreed that Beck should become head of the new government. And despite many reservations and differences, Goerdeler was the favored candidate for the post of Chancellor. The Cabinet lists circulating among the opposition contained the names of a number of qualified experts representing the many groups and tendencies of the resistance. It was proposed that the new ministers and their state secretaries come from different political groups. The last Cabinet list presented, prepared by Jakob Kaiser in July, 1944, contained the following names: Head of State, Beck; Chancellor, Goerdeler; Vice Chancellor, Leuschner; Interior, Leber; Economy and Labor, Lejeune-Jung (a business executive); Culture, Bolz (or possibly Schuschnigg); Reconstruction, Letterhaus; Finance, Loeser (Popitz had been proposed earlier); Justice, Wirmer; Foreign Affairs, Hassell or Schulenburg; Agriculture, Hermes; President of the Reichstag, Loebe and an Austrian representative. Other lists mentioned Brüning as Foreign Minister and Leuschner as President, to succeed the provisional government. Stauffenberg in particular wanted to see Leuschner, or possibly Leber, as Chancellor after Goerdeler. Tresckow was mentioned for the post of Police Chief, Hoepner as Defense Minister, with Olbricht and Stauffenberg as the respective State Secretaries, and Mierendorff as Press and Propaganda Chief. After Mierendorff's death, Haubach's name was entered.[82]

By 1943, the military and political situation of Germany had greatly deteriorated. The defeats at Stalingrad and Tunis were followed by more defeats in Russia, and after Mussolini's overthrow, Italy capitulated. No one in his right mind still thought in terms of a final victory. It was conceivable that the expected invasion of the Continent by the Allies would seal Germany's defeat by the spring of 1944. Under these circumstances, the opposition again found the generals more receptive

---

[82] Details in Gerhard Ritter, *Carl Goerdeler und die deutsche Widerstandsbewegung* (rev. ed.; Stuttgart, 1964), pp. 575 ff. (Appendix, Document IX).

to its plans. According to Goerdeler's notes, Tresckow assured him in August, 1943, that all three Army Group Commanders in the East (Manstein, Kluge, and Küchler) favored early action. However, they thought only, or at most, in terms of protesting to Hitler. And nothing more should have been expected from Kluge, even though in September, 1943, he had come to Berlin to meet with Beck, Goerdeler, and Olbricht in Olbricht's apartment. At that time, aware of the desperate military situation, Kluge favored an early end to war and apparently was even persuaded by Beck of the necessity of Hitler's assassination. Goerdeler, who still resisted the idea of assassination, said that the plot of the 20th of July was born at this meeting; however, in view of the earlier plans and attempts at Hitler's life, this is not completely accurate.

But an accident also frustrated the plan developed here. Now that an outstanding front-line commander willing to support a coup had apparently been found, Kluge, in October, 1943, had a serious automobile accident and had to be counted out, at least for the time being, and with him others as well, above all Tresckow, whose new superior, Field Marshal Busch, was loyal to Hitler. Tresckow also failed in his efforts to join the Army High Command as General Heusinger's deputy and thus gain the opportunity for a direct attempt on Hitler's life. Daring plans of some younger officers failed either because of Hitler's well-guarded isolation or because of last-minute changes in his plans. A further problem was posed by the fact that the conspirators wanted to eliminate other leaders, for example Himmler and Göring, at the same time as Hitler, so as to avert a possible civil war and battles with Berlin-based SS and Air Force units. But at any rate, Stauffenberg had won his point: Hitler's elimination was the presupposition for a military coup and for winning over the front-line generals. With Stauffenberg, the resistance movement had gained its first determined activist in the military camp, one neither plagued by the conflicts, doubts, and hesitations of Beck nor bogged down in talks and memorandums. And Stauffenberg's relationship with Leber, who similarly criticized the hesitant opposition leadership from the vantage point of the civilian, grew steadily closer. And so when Leber was arrested, Stauffenberg at the last moment galvanized the opposition into action. Beginning in the fall of 1943, he, as Olbricht's aide, drew up and supervised a comprehensive plan of action. Because Kluge was incapacitated and because the commander of the Home Army, General Fritz Fromm, vacillated, the retired Field Marshal von Witzleben was recruited to head the military operation. It was he who signed the troop orders prepared by Stauffenberg, to be put into effect after the coup.

In the meantime, the Gestapo was bearing down on the opposition: The arrest of Count Moltke had broken up the Kreisau Circle, and the elimination of the powerful Canaris bastion in February, 1944, removed the last counterweight to Himmler's SS and police apparatus. At this juncture, the Stauffenberg group took a firm stand against the reservations and hesitations of the Goerdeler camp. A network of military and civilian officials stood ready to direct operations throughout the country once the coup in Berlin had ousted the Nazis from power. It is astonishing that secrecy was preserved despite the travels and contacts by which men were recruited into the conspiracy. Proclamations, leaflets, and broadcasts were prepared, decrees drafted for the critical hours right after the coup, plans drawn up to acquaint the public with the significance of and reasons for the coup and the truth about the Nazi regime, and preparations made for the defense against a possible Nazi counterblow.

Tensions among the conspirators increased; the differences between Leber and Goerdeler and signs of mistrust against the vacillating military became more overt. The conspirators lived with the constant fear that their plot would be uncovered, particularly after Leber and his friends intensified their efforts to expand the network of Socialist and trade-union resistance cells to give the military putsch a functioning, broader political base. Numerous contact men in plants and local districts were alerted and stood ready to make contact with local Army posts and volunteer their services to the new government. The Socialist unionists were joined by representatives of the old Christian trade unions; they, as well as representatives of the Liberal and German National organizations (Lemmer and Habermann, respectively) were determined to avoid the political and religious division of the trade-union movement of the past. Plans for a united German Trade Union organization, with Leuschner as chairman and Kaiser and Habermann as deputy chairmen, were well advanced.

The pro-Communist groups were also active. They certainly did not play the leading role that has been claimed for them since, but the Communist opposition cannot be dismissed as treasonous; those who continue to do so to this day either intend to defame the resistance as a whole or to draw a dividing line between Communist and other resistance groups. After the war, violent controversy raged around the espionage activities of the so-called Rote Kapelle (Red Orchestra)—a label the National Socialists pinned on a circle of left-wing intellectuals, some of whom were in radio contact with Moscow. The focus of this circle was an Air Force officer, Harro Schulze-Boysen, and Arvid Harnack of the Ministry of Economic Affairs and his American wife, Mildred. About 100 members of this diverse group were arrested in August, 1942, and half of them were executed. Their liquidation was the work of the notorious Judge Manfred Roeder, who later tried to brand them, and by implication the opposition as a whole, as Communist traitors.[83] But both Ritter and Schlabrendorff, by failing to include such radical left-wing opposition groups in their studies, have oversimplified the situation. These were realities which had to be considered in the overthrow of the government and the formation of a new one. Leber and Reichwein, though with some misgivings, decided to acquaint

[83] In his book *Die rote Kapelle* (1952); cf. Günther Weisenborn, *Der lautlose Aufstand* (Hamburg, 1953), pp. 203 ff. Gilles Perrault, *The Red Orchestra* (New York, 1969), contains much detail, though also questionable in its political appraisal.

themselves with the goals and plans of Communist resistance groups and with the role of the Free German National Committee operating out of the Soviet Union, and so they made contact with that camp as well. The Gestapo apparently got wind of the very first meeting, on June 22, 1944, between them and Anton Saefkow, Franz Jacob, and Ferdinand Thomas in the apartment of a Berlin physician, and just before the next meeting, scheduled for July 4, it struck. The arrest of Leber and Reichwein just as the Allied invasion was beginning, while the conspirators were still debating possible courses of action, struck like a bolt of lightning and with dramatic suddenness brought a maturing of plans.

The only alternative the conspirators had was either to act as soon as possible and end the war in the West or to resign and put the full responsibility for the catastrophe squarely in Hitler's lap. Even Stauffenberg seems to have wavered for a while and to have felt that it was too late. At that very moment, Tresckow sent him a message which more clearly than any ex post facto judgments shows the moral core of July 20, 1944, and refutes the charge of opportunism or cowardice leveled against them first by Nazi propaganda and later by German and foreign critics. Tresckow pleaded with Stauffenberg that the attempt on Hitler's life had to be made, at whatever cost: "Should it fail, we will still have to act in Berlin. Because it is no longer a question of the practical purpose, but of whether the resistance has dared to make the decisive move before the eyes of the world and of history. Next to that nothing else matters." Whereupon Stauffenberg sent this message to Leber's wife: "We know our duty." [84]

In this situation, spurred on by the progress of the Allied invasion, the conspirators turned to Field Marshal Rommel, whom Goerdeler had sought to win over earlier. With the help of Rommel's chief of staff, General Speidel, they now tried to gain the support not only of the divisions in France but also of the most popular Army officer. In view of the military situation, Rommel on July 15, 1944, finally agreed to present Hitler with an ultimatum that he end the war and, failing that, to support a move to have Hitler arrested and put on trial. The plan had the support of the Army commander in France, General Stülpnagel, headquartered in Paris, though not of General von Rundstedt, the Commander in Chief in the West. The plan called for a truce in the West, for the evacuation of the occupied territories, and for the deployment of troops to support the new government. When Kluge replaced Rundstedt in early July, 1944, the prospects for success seemed much improved, even though Kluge continued to insist that he would act only after Hitler was removed. A cousin of Stauffenberg, Colonel von Hofacker, attached to Stülpnagel's staff, was in charge of coordinating the activities of Berlin and Paris.

A stroke of luck helped their preparations. Stauffenberg was pro-

---

[84] Citations based on Schlabrendorff, *op. cit.*, p. 175; Leber, Brandt, Bracher, *Conscience in Revolt* (London, 1957), p. 260.

moted to Fromm's chief of staff. This put him into the position of issuing orders to Home Army units and temporarily even enabled him to act over the head of his vacillating boss. But above all, he could now attend Hitler's strategy meetings. And so the much-criticized but inevitable decision was made that Stauffenberg, though indispensable to the conspiracy, would himself make the attempt on Hitler's life. For this purpose, the Abwehr had supplied him with a British-made bomb. Ever since December, 1943, when a fairly sizable stock of explosives had blown up and endangered the conspirators, it had become almost impossible to get hold of and transport suitable explosives. The advantage of the bomb used by Stauffenberg was that he could carry it in his briefcase and set it off with the three fingers of his left hand (he had lost his right arm, two fingers of his left, and an eye). In defense of this plan, it must be pointed out that it offered the only possibility of prompt action. Stauffenberg had already taken the bomb with him on July 11 to a conference at Berchtesgaden, but had not set it off because Himmler was not present; both Kluge and Rommel demanded that Himmler and Göring be eliminated with Hitler. The same thing happened on July 15, when he attended a meeting in Hitler's East Prussian headquarters. Both times the troops for the occupation of Berlin were put on alert, and both times the very risky maneuver had to be called off and camouflaged as a "field exercise."

When Rommel was critically wounded in an accident on July 17, and when the Gestapo issued an arrest order for Goerdeler on July 18, action could no longer be postponed. Stauffenberg ordered Goerdeler to go into hiding so as not to endanger the plan at this crucial moment; thus began Goerdeler's flight through Germany. In the morning of July 20, 1944, Stauffenberg, accompanied by his adjutant and friend, Lieutenant Werner von Haeften, boarded a plane for Hitler's East Prussian headquarters. After their arrival in Rastenburg, they arranged for a plane to be readied for their return flight to Berlin. The meeting began in the hermetically sealed Führer headquarters at around 12:30 P.M.; Mussolini was expected to arrive there at 2:30. Stauffenberg was late for the meeting; he had stopped off at another building for a few minutes to release the timer of the bomb with a pair of pliers, a risky undertaking. The bomb was set to go off ten minutes after the release of the timer. It took him three minutes to pass through the last guard ring around the barracks in which the meeting was being held. It was under way when he came into the room. Himmler and Göring again were missing; about twenty-five persons in all attended. Stauffenberg was announced by Keitel, and Hitler greeted him; he tried to get as close to Hitler as possible and put down his briefcase near the map table, while General Heusinger, as representative of the Chief of Staff, continued reading his report. Stauffenberg left the barracks immediately (according to some reports, under the pretext of having to place an urgent phone call). He was being paged for some point of information—Hitler had just bent over the table to peer at a map—when the bomb exploded, some time between 12:40 and 12:50 P.M. Stauffenberg and Haeften watched the explosion seated in a car. Although the guard tried to prevent them from leaving, they managed to get out; by a ruse involving a mysterious telephone message, they also managed to outsmart the guards at the outer gates. At 1:15 P.M., before a message from the headquarters could head them off, the waiting plane took off with the two officers.[85]

But a number of security problems had not been solved. The return flight of Stauffenberg and Haeften took two-and-a-half hours—possibly a vital interval of inaction. The Chief of Intelligence at the Führer headquarters, General Erich Fellgiebel, a co-conspirator, was unable to silence the news media long enough; also, his prompt report to Berlin that Hitler had not been killed in the attack did not reach the conspirators. On his arrival at the Rangsdorf airport, near Berlin, Stauffenberg learned that the signal for the coup had not yet been given. He asked for immediate action and rushed to Berlin to the War Ministry at the Bendlerstrasse (the street has since been renamed Stauffenbergstrasse). In the forty minutes between Stauffenberg's call and his arrival at the Ministry, Olbricht issued the orders to the Army units. Simultaneously, he ordered the Commandant of Berlin, General Paul von Hase (who was acquainted with the plans and was an uncle of Dietrich Bonhoeffer), to take personal charge of the troops required in Berlin. While Beck, as the presumptive chief of state, was being called for at his apartment, Olbricht informed Fromm that Hitler had been killed and asked him immediately to spread the news of Operation Valkyrie to the general commands. Fromm hesitated. He wanted confirmation of Hitler's death, whereupon Olbricht unsuspectingly placed a call to the Führer headquarters. Keitel told him shortly after 4:00 P.M. that though an attempt on Hitler's life had been made, the Führer had suffered only minor injuries. Fromm, who knew nothing, was unable to answer Keitel's inquiry about Stauffenberg's whereabouts, while Olbricht, filled with grave misgivings, left the room.

Meanwhile, the signals for the coup were being passed down the line. Beck, wearing civilian dress, had arrived at the Ministry, and Stauffenberg also rushed in to report. Keitel's information, he said, was false; he himself had seen the explosion and was convinced that the attempt had succeeded. He urged immediate action, and via a telephone call to Hofacker, who had just returned to Paris, he gave the signal for Stülpnagel's operation. The Police President of Berlin, Count Helldorff, one of the initiates, arrived at the Ministry and was given appropriate instructions. However, the doubts were growing stronger. What persuaded them to continue the operation was Beck's unequivocal stand that they must not let denials from the opposing side sow confusion about whether or not Hitler was dead. It would take hours for headquarters to prove beyond any doubt that the man said to be alive was Hitler and not a double, and by then the Berlin opera-

[85] Details in Peter Hoffmann, *Widerstand, op. cit.*, pp. 466 ff., and (with important corrections) Christian Müller, *op. cit.*, pp. 476 ff.

tion had to be concluded. To win over Fromm before he himself could act, Olbricht together with Stauffenberg again went into Fromm's office. When Fromm was told that the signal for the operation had been given, he was furious. He demanded of Stauffenberg that he shoot himself on the spot. And when he said that he would order the arrest of all involved, he and Olbricht came to blows. Haeften together with some other younger officers rushed in with drawn pistols; Fromm was locked into an adjoining office and his telephone lines were cut.

In the meantime, Hoepner took over Fromm's functions, while Stauffenberg had the Ministry guarded by troops under the command of a friend of Haeften's. No one was allowed to enter or leave the building without Stauffenberg's permission. An SS officer from Kaltenbrunner's office who arrived at around 5:00 P.M. with an arrest order for Stauffenberg was himself arrested together with his men. Subsequently, Beck clashed with the commanding general of Berlin, Joachim von Kortzfleisch, who protested vehemently against the troop alert, and thereupon he too was taken into custody. By 5:30 P.M., the area housing the Government offices was, as planned, closed off by the guard regiment under Major Remer, who, however, was ignorant of the plan. The orders to troops outside the country and to the general commands within the Reich were transmitted with some delays. These orders, bearing the signature of von Witzleben as the new Supreme Commander of the Army, unequivocally stated opposition to the regime. They instructed the troops to seize all communications faci'ities and to arrest all Nazi officials down to the rank of Kreisleiter, as well as all Cabinet members, provincial presidents, police presidents, and Gestapo chiefs. Also, they called for the immediate occupation of all concentration camps, the arrest of camp officials and guards, as well as the taking over of the Waffen SS (by force if necessary), the seizure of Gestapo and SD offices, and cooperation with the "political delegates" of the future government.

But while these orders were still arriving at regional defense offices, Radio Germany at 6:00 P.M. brought the first report of the abortive assassination attempt. Beck still believed that this was a calculated misinformation, but now the fact that the plan to seize the broadcasting house had not been carried out made itself felt. An uninterrupted stream of urgent inquiries poured in from commanders in all parts of Germany who, having heard the radio reports, did not know what to make of the Berlin orders. Again Stauffenberg assured them that Hitler was dead and sent an urgent teletype message to all commanders. But only a small minority of those present at the War Ministry knew what was going on; the conspirators were in a minority here as well, and newly arriving officers had to be taken into custody and guarded. While the first of the alerted units began to arrive in Berlin, Witzleben himself came to the Ministry. In a talk with Beck and Stauffenberg, he criticized the obvious shortcomings of the operations, which he apparently believed to be a failure, for he left the Ministry immediately. Anxiety and uncertainty mounted. Teletype messages testifying to the conflicting sentiments of the alerted commanders continued to pour in; in the meantime, Keitel, at the headquarters, stated emphatically that no order emanating from the Ministry was to be obeyed.

But the most fatal flaw was that the operation in Berlin itself was proceeding only very sporadically; by 8:00 P.M., not even the priority goals, particularly the occupation of the broadcasting station and the Propaganda Ministry and the arrest of important SS officials, had been realized. And in fact, Major Remer, instead of isolating Goebbels and occupying the Government offices, had been persuaded by Goebbels to make a phone call to the Führer headquarters, and from there had been ordered by Hitler personally to squash the putsch. A bitter price was paid for the failure, despite repeated efforts in the preceding weeks, to replace the colorless Remer with a man from the opposition. In his postwar neo-Nazi activities, Remer has capitalized on the part he played in saving the Nazi regime. But the fact of the matter is that one of his officers (Hans Hagen), a Nazi functionary, after learning that the attempted assassination of Hitler had failed, pushed Remer into his "historic" position. The reports filed by Remer, who was promoted to general on the spot, and two of his officers immediately after the 20th of July for their own exoneration and to stress the services they had rendered also show how narrow was the margin between success and failure and how great the role of happenstance.

Remer's telephone call did in fact bring on the crisis. After that, Stauffenberg's and Hoepner's frantic efforts to enlist troop support in Berlin ran up against fearful officers of nearby units, even though some had already begun to move toward the city. The same situation obtained throughout Germany. The troops had already begun to withdraw when they received orders from Himmler, whose appointment to the post of Commander in Chief of the Home Army was broadcast at 9:00 P.M. At 10:30 P.M., Olbricht once more met with the oppositional officers and asked for their complete support. But by then a countergroup had been formed in the Ministry, spearheaded by Colonel Pridun, an Austrian, who reminded them of their oath to Hitler and asked those who supported him to help squash the putschists. Shortly after Olbricht ordered the still cooperative commandant of the Döberitz Infantry Academy to occupy the radio station, the counterforces went into action. At around 11:00 P.M., wielding pistols, guns, and hand grenades, they stormed Olbricht's office. In the scuffle that followed, Stauffenberg was wounded in the arm. The conspirators hastily tried to destroy their written records before Pridun's men overwhelmed them, and Remer's guard regiment now joined the loyalists. Fromm reappeared on the scene and summarily "sentenced" Olbricht, Stauffenberg, Haeften, and another conspirator, Colonel Mertz von Quirnheim, to death. The sentence was carried out shortly after midnight in the courtyard of the Ministry; under the glare of a car headlight, Remer's execution squad aimed its machine pistols at the four men.

Fromm ordered his old friend Hoepner removed to an Army prison and his one-time superior, Beck, shot by a sergeant of the guard regiment after Beck's unsuccessful suicide attempt. Then Fromm, standing in the yard next to the bodies of the four executed men, accepted the report that his orders had been carried out, saluted the Führer, and drove home. He soon found out, however, that he was mistaken if he believed he could save his own skin by silencing those who knew of his vacillation. His efforts to cover his tracks were too transparent; he was held responsible for not handing over the organizers of the conspiracy. He too was sentenced to death, even though by his indecisiveness and then by his hasty liquidation of his old friends he had successfully undermined the putsch and had sought to align himself with the winning side. At around 1:00 A.M., the War Ministry was occupied by SS troops led by Otto Skorzeny, the famous kidnaper of Mussolini. The other conspirators were arrested and brought to the Gestapo prison. The five executed men were buried that same night; later, Himmler's special commission disinterred and cremated the bodies and scattered the ashes to the four winds.

No study of this attempt can ignore the fact that although many Army commanders vacillated,[86] the conspirators in Paris, Vienna, Prague, Kassel, and Frankfurt continued to implement their plans even after the reported failure of the Berlin coup. The Paris operation was the most enduring. When the go-ahead was received from Berlin at 4:00 P.M., Stülpnagel assembled his generals and ordered them to isolate all SS and SD units immediately. His officers loyally carried out his orders, and the SS and SD quarters were occupied without a shot being fired. The surprised SS and Police Chief of France, General Oberg, was arrested, as was the chief of the SD and about 1,200 men. Within the space of one hour, the counterforces were immobilized. Only Kluge began to waver again when, after a series of telephone conversations with Berlin and the Führer headquarters, he became convinced that the attempt on Hitler's life had failed. He could not decide on giving the signal for the Army in France, even though matters in Paris were taking a more favorable turn than anywhere else. Stülpnagel, and above all Hofacker, fervently pleaded with Kluge to put an end to the hopeless war in the West that night, as long as the SS and SD were still out of action, by offering a truce to Eisenhower and Montgomery. They believed that in this way the abortive operation in Germany might still be salvaged. But their impassioned pleas went unheeded, even though bad news from the front continued to pour in. When the full extent of the catastrophe in Berlin became known, and the SS and Navy began their countermeasures, the cause in Paris also was lost. Stülpnagel was ordered back to Berlin; his fate was sealed. Kluge sent a wire of submission to Hitler. Soon thereafter, he committed suicide.

[86] Cf. Hoffmann, "Der 20. Juli im Wehrkreis II (Stettin). Ein Beispiel für den Ablauf des Staatsstreichversuches im Reich," in *Das Parlament*, B 28/65, July 14, 1965, Appendix, pp. 25 ff.; and Hoffmann, *Widerstand* . . . , pp. 520 ff.

Let us return to the Führer headquarters and see what had gone wrong. Stauffenberg had put his briefcase next to Hitler, but it had been pushed to the end of the table, where it exploded after a few minutes. The barracks was destroyed and four men in it were killed. Hitler suffered sprains, burns, and a shattered eardrum, but the table had shielded him. The wooden barracks was too flimsy a structure for the bomb used; in addition, the windows were all open, and the very large, massive oak table further helped to reduce the pressure. The fact that Haeften, who also carried a bomb with him, was not able to gain entrance to the barracks was another blow. (The experts who examined the explosives on July 21 concluded that if both bombs had gone off the outcome would have been very different.) The immediate reaction at the headquarters, before Stauffenberg's absence was noticed, was that a construction worker was responsible for the attack. At first it was thought that Stauffenberg had been hurt and hospitalized, but then the guards mentioned his hasty departure. Some believed that he had flown to the Russian positions, which were only 60 miles from the East Prussian frontier. Himmler, who appeared on the scene immediately, ordered Stauffenberg's arrest. While Mussolini, who had arrived at 4:00 P.M., was inspecting the site of the attack with Hitler, the first news began to come in from Berlin hinting at the extent of the operation.

Initially it was planned to hush up the attempt as the act of one individual. But when calls began to pour in from perplexed commanders and it became apparent that the War Ministry housed the center of a far-flung conspiracy, political countermeasures were instituted. Hitler's talks with Goebbels and Remer followed on the heels of Keitel's denials that Hitler had been killed; subsequently, Himmler was put in charge of the counteraction, and finally, at 1:00 A.M. the next morning, Hitler's furious speech was broadcast over all German stations. It began with these words:

> A tiny clique of ambitious, unscrupulous, criminal, and stupid officers forged a plot to remove me and together with me the entire staff of the German Army command. . . . The group which these usurpers represent is very small indeed. It has nothing to do with the German Army command and certainly not with German soldiers. It is a tiny coterie of criminal elements which is now being ruthlessly rooted out. . . . I see in this also a sign that providence wants me to continue my work, and therefore I shall continue it.

He was followed by Göring, speaking for the Air Force, and Dönitz, for the Navy, both in a similar vein. Göring called for the "extermination of these criminals"; Dönitz gave thanks to "providence," which "has protected our beloved Führer" from an "insane, small clique of generals, the handmaidens of our enemies"; the Navy, he said, unconditionally stood behind the Führer and "would ruthlessly destroy all who turn out to be traitors." Thus, on the morning of July 21, began the massive persecution of the German resistance movement which brought the terror trials of the People's Court, the butcher hooks and gallows of the prisons and concentration camps, the slaughter of thousands from all walks of life and all political camps, while the Third Reich itself was nearing its bloody end.

The terror was directed against all suspects, whether active participants or not. Although Hitler had spoken of a "tiny clique of ambitious, unscrupulous officers," the Gestapo sweep, conducted by the huge "Special Commission July 20," was evidence of the scope and diversity of the opposition. Around 5,000 persons were executed after civil trials (in addition to those court martialed). Some of the groups and persons had been under surveillance all along, but the events of July 20 and the extent and ramification of the opposition came as a surprise. Documents, appeals, lists of names, and diaries were found which the conspirators did not have time to destroy. In addition, men were made to talk in uninterrupted interrogations employing the most sophisticated methods of breaking man's spirit—through the arrest and collective punishment of their families, through beatings, torture, and drugs.

The case of Tresckow is an example of the methods used. Tresckow had committed suicide on July 21 at his post in the East. At first, he was still mentioned honorably in the Army report and his body was brought to Germany. But subsequently his body was taken from the family tomb in the presence of his relatives and used in Berlin interrogations, in an effort to break down the resistance of his friends who refused to confess. Stülpnagel's case was handled with like brutality after his unsuccessful suicide attempt en route from Verdun to Berlin. Blinded, he was operated on, only to be executed after weeks of suffering. With the help of the surveillance apparatus of the Special Commission, which expanded in proportion to the failing power of the Third Reich, the ferreting out of all under suspicion offered few problems. The climate of fear, general mistrust, and denunciations facilitated the hunt.

Goerdeler's fateful journey had begun on July 18, the day of his last meeting with Stauffenberg, Jakob Kaiser, and Leuschner. He crisscrossed the country, seeking shelter with relatives and friends. None seemed to offer enough safety. The warrant for his arrest had been published in every newspaper; a price of 1 million marks had been put on his head. One friend after another was arrested; his relatives, like those of Stauffenberg, Hofacker, Leber, and many others, were taken into custody. On the morning of August 12, Goerdeler was seen by an Air Force clerk in an inn in Marienwerder (West Prussia), to which he had come after having spent the night in the open. The woman who turned him in had once met the Goerdeler family in her village near Königsberg. A spent and exhausted Goerdeler was arrested by two Army paymasters summoned by the informer.[87] His apprehension sealed the

[87] For more detailed information on this and numerous crimes in the final phase, see *Justiz und NS-Verbrechen. Sammlung deutscher Strafurteile wegen nationalsozialistischer Tötungsverbrechen 1945–1966* (Amsterdam, 1968), I, 709 ff.

fate of numerous friends who had helped him during his odyssey.

The magnitude of the persecutions threatened to endanger the conduct of the war. Speer, the Minister of Armaments, tried to hold on to indispensable employees. But the Special Commission almost without exception continued to round up all suspects and hand them over to the People's Court. Initially, Hitler had wanted huge show trials with films, broadcasts, and press coverage, as a deterrent. But on the advice of Himmler, the trials were closed to the general public. He feared that in public trials, despite all security measures, defendants might criticize the regime or appeal to the popular desire for peace. The war hero Rommel had been forced to take poison and was given an ornate official funeral; Hitler even had a monument designed for him. The others were brought before an "Army honor court" presided over by Rundstedt and assisted by Keitel and Guderian. That tribunal ousted the officers brought before it from the Army, thus removing them from military court jurisdiction, so that they might be tried by the People's Court. As to the trials, Hitler demanded harsh and speedy action. The defendants were to be allowed to make only very brief statements and were to be sentenced to death by hanging. If possible, the sentences were to be carried out within two hours.

By no stretch of the imagination can this process be called the administration of justice. The purpose of these trials was the liquidation of all enemies. Hitler, confident that he could rely on his instruments, told a strategy session after July 20: "Freisler will handle this. He is our Vishinsky"—the Vishinsky of the Stalinist show trials, which served as the model. Trials and executions were filmed for Hitler to watch so that he could satisfy his pathological need for self-affirmation. He read all the daily reports of Freisler and the Special Commissions, intervened in the proceedings, and met not only with Freisler but also with the executioner, to satisfy his profound interest in the extermination of all real and imagined enemies. He would not let any pardons be granted; accompanied by the hum of the motion-picture cameras, the victims were to hang from hooks like cattle, so that none would ever be tempted to make them into martyrs. Yet significantly enough, although the first executions were publicized, the murder of thousands during the final months of the war was kept as secret as the terrible fate awaiting thousands more in prisons and camps.

In the final days of the war, many of these prisoners were taken out by SS commandos, killed, and thrown into mass graves. In particular, the regime tried to bring down with it all prisoners of prominence.[88] Consequently, on the night of April 9, 1945, Walter Huppenkothen, a special deputy of Kaltenbrunner at the Flossenbürg concentration camp, ordered the execution of Canaris, Oster, Dietrich Bonhoeffer, and other resistance leaders who had been dragged through countless prisons and camps; a similar fate befell the ailing Dohnanyi, a prisoner at Sachsenhausen. And on the night of April 23, 1945, practically on the eve of liberation, a group of select inmates in the Berlin-Moabit

[88] See Bethge, *Dietrich Bonhoeffer*, pp. 703 ff.

prison, including Albrecht Haushofer, Klaus Bonhoeffer, and his brother-in-law, Rüdiger Schleicher, were taken from their cells to a nearby park under the pretext of being released, and shot in the back of the neck by an SS squad. Not one of the principal conspirators of the 20th of July, and only a handful of their helpers, survived the slaughter that accompanied the departure of the National Socialist regime from the stage of world history.

Breakdown and Continuity of National Socialism

At the End of the Hitler Regime

The outcome of the 20th of July, 1944, wrote a bloody end to internal German resistance and opened up the way for a last intensification of Nazi rule. This spurt may account in part for the fact that Hitler and Himmler failed in their effort to make the 20th of July into a new stab-in-the-back legend and thus relieve National Socialism of its responsibility for the final catastrophe. But it also accounts for the fact that, in the climate of terror and fear, the overwhelming majority of Germans followed to the bitter end a regime whose leader issued his insane orders for holding out and for destruction from the isolation of his Berlin bunker. Once again, the German people were spared having to answer the question with which a successful coup would have confronted them, namely, how they felt about the horrors and crimes committed in their name. The settling of accounts between the German people and the Nazi criminals which Stauffenberg had hoped for did not come to pass: "The fact that this demand for a moral, autonomous, active decision for or against the Hitler regime was not put to the German nation on July 20, 1944, that they were irretrievably deprived of it, will remain the mark of Cain of the German people, the sting of a past that can never be mastered. That, at any rate, is how the conspirators of the 20th of July saw it." [1]

Had the putsch succeeded, millions of lives would have been saved and much devastation in Europe and Germany averted. In the final stages of the war, the deportation and murder of persecuted men and

[1] Dieter Ehlers, *Technik und Moral einer Verschwörung* (Frankfurt/Main, 1964), p. 173.

461

women, and Hitler's "total mobilization of all Germans," culminating
in the formation of a "people's army" of persons unfit for military service and in the ruthless conscription of adolescents, inflicted heavier
losses than in all the preceding war years combined.[2] When the Allies
advanced into western Germany in the fall of 1944, not even the
National Socialist leadership could still entertain any doubts about the
outcome of the war. But Hitler clung to his plan that, unlike 1918,
every city, every village, and finally "every square meter" would have
to be defended or left behind as "scorched earth." The destructive
dynamic of the terror system now came down on Germany in all its
force. More and more, the Army was held in distrust and subjugated
to the ideas and encroachment of the SS, and thus Himmler became
the most powerful figure in the Army as well. This development was
responsible also for the placement of "National Socialist guidance officers" in the Army—informers and propagandists modeled on the
commissars of the Red Army. Ideological-political reliability and
fanaticism became the highest ideals, transcending all considerations
of military expediency; costly, sacrificial defensive battles and hopeless
offensives led deeper and deeper into chaotic self-destruction; this, for
Hitler, was the only possible alternative to "final victory."

With Goebbels as their obsessive conductor, the Nazi propagandists
shouted their victory slogans and their unalterable faith in the Führer to the very end. And when Hitler, eighteen days before his death
in the bunker of the Chancellery, received news of Roosevelt's death,
he saw in this one last "sign of providence." Once more, in his order
of the day of April 17, 1945, he called for war on the "Jewish-Bolshevik
mortal enemy" and prophesied that "at the moment in which fate has
removed the greatest war criminal of all times from this earth, the
last onslaught of Asia will have been shattered." And so he pinned on
Roosevelt the label which he himself deserved as no other man did.

And, in fact, Nazi propaganda to the very last counted on a division
within the Allied camp and stirred up memories of the miracle of the
Seven Years' War (when Prussia almost single-handedly defeated a
great-power coalition), comparing Roosevelt's death with the death of
the Empress Elisabeth of Russia (1762), which changed the course of
history. To this day we can hear the echoes of the Nazi thesis that only
the myopia of the Western powers prevented a last-ditch stand against
Bolshevism. But in fact Hitler never for a moment intended to give up
the Western front in favor of a defense in the East. And there could
not have been the slightest chance that the Western powers, after all
their experiences since 1938 with Nazi policies of rule and conquest,
would take Hitler's completely discredited bulwark theory seriously. It
was Hitler himself who opened up the gates to the Soviet Union, first
in 1939 and then again in 1941; it was he who pushed the West into a

---

[2] Thus the Chief of the SS and Police in German-occupied Poland issued
an order on July 20, 1944, to liquidate prisoners and Jews "in the event
of unexpected developments" and to dispose of the corpses. See *Nürnberger
Dokumente*, **XXXVII**, 487 (L–053). Hitler's order for the mobilization of
a home guard, dated September 25, 1944, in *RGBl*, I (1944), 253 ff.

wartime alliance with Moscow, and it was his reign of terror which first brought down the misery on the countries of Europe, particularly in the East, as Eastern Europe fell under the Russian occupation which now was beginning to engulf Germany itself.

Hitler's claim of fighting the "war against Bolshevism," which was to loom so large in the postwar myths not only of old and new fascists, simply does not warrant belief. As late as December, 1944, Hitler ordered a last desperate offensive, which consumed the remainder of the reserves, in the West (Ardennes), not in the East. The much-touted "secret weapon," which a whispering propaganda prophesied would bring victory at the last hour, had, in the shape of the V-rockets, been employed against the West since June, 1944. The Government's science program was responsible for hindering rather than promoting atomic research. Soldiers and civilians in both West and East were subjected to the terror of kinship arrests, summary justice, and executions. Phrases like "on-the-spot liquidation," "putting down without further ado," "extermination" now began to appear in official orders and decrees, without the customary circumlocutions.

Hitler originally had planned to retreat to his Bavarian-Tyrolese "Alpine redoubt" for the final battle, but on April 22, 1945, he changed his mind and decided to remain in Berlin. After finally accepting how fantastic were his hopes for the relief of the encircled capital, and after macabre final scenes combining a Wagnerian Götterdämmerung mood with the petty-bourgeois marriage to his long-time secret mistress Eva Braun, he committed suicide with his wife on April 30, 1945. The myth of the Führer continued to work its anesthetizing spell over the population to the end. And Hitler's commitment to the continuation of a lost war shows the extent to which he himself was the victim of his claim to godlike omnipotence. In the course of the war, all life functions of the Third Reich had been tailored to the one and only Leader, so that his only contact with the outside world was through completely subservient accomplices. Hitler began to lose or disregard his undeniable instinct for political tactics; he would listen only to those reports that supported his rigid, ideologically determined wishful dreams. By identifying with the will of "providence," he finally eliminated altogether the corrective force of reality and ordered the execution of anyone who spoke a single dissenting word.

The reverse side of this was a belief that he alone could see and understand what was good for the German people and what their birthright was, and that his will was to be the sole guide in the conduct of politics and in the planning of strategy. This led to a conviction that the Third Reich was declining because Hitler could not be everywhere, because he could not personally lead every batallion. In fact, however, this consistent exacerbation of the situation revealed the inherent flaws of the dictatorial leader principle. The result was chaos, a paradoxical lack of leadership in the total leader state, the complete self-destruction of political life. But here, too, Hitler could offer only his one monomaniacal explanation: betrayal, failure of the generals, failure of the German people as a whole—with the one notable exception. And so, in a final manifestation of his hybrid claim to omniscience and unconditional obedience, he equated his own fall with the death of the German people.

But on this point, he could not enlist the support of even his closest comrades and accomplices. In the fall of 1944, for example, Speer still proudly claimed that the increased war production was due to the efficiency of his organization. But on March 15, 1945, he wrote a memorandum not only taking issue with the charge that the German people had failed but also opposing Hitler's orders to destroy everything; he repeated this still more strongly in a final radio address recorded in Hamburg on April 21 and broadcast to the nation on May 3. Very late, alas too late, this technocrat recognized the hopelessness of a policy which he had followed blindly. Not so Himmler. At the last hour, on April 23, he tried to save his own skin by offering to capitulate to the West, a proposal forwarded to Count Bernadotte of Sweden by General of the SS Schellenberg. Hitler thereupon expelled him from the party and stripped him of all official posts. Göring, who was at the Obersalzberg, suffered a similar fate when, that same day, he inquired of his Leader, who was in his bunker in Berlin, whether, in view of Berlin's isolation, he should not assume the leadership of the Reich, in accord with the succession decree of June 29, 1941. Bormann on his own changed Hitler's order for the ouster of Göring into a death sentence; Bormann himself became Party Minister. The promotion of this last remaining Hitler vassal except for Goebbels made him the most powerful man at a time "when the Third Reich held sway only over a few heaps of rubble and a bunker twenty-five feet below ground in the center of Berlin." [3] These hesitant stirrings of independence were completely meaningless; the Nazi elite, molded by the leader state and the Hitler cult, was not capable of a palace revolution.

Instead, before his death, Hitler himself altered the structure of the leader state by appointing Admiral Karl Dönitz to succeed him as Reich President, Commander in Chief of the Armed Forces, and Minister of War, and Goebbels to succeed him as Chancellor—one final manifestation of the arbitrary dictatorial rule which had dominated the Third Reich above all pretensions to legality. Dönitz's position was founded solely on Hitler's dictum. All continuity claims with which National Socialist exponents of the legality thesis have tried to invest Dönitz's position fail to recognize three facts: that Hitler's omnipotence ended with his death; that the Weimar Constitution formally still existed; and that, aside from all this, with the occupation of Germany, the Third Reich came to an end.

By the end of April, the German armies began to capitulate with or without Dönitz's consent; on May 7, the total capitulation was signed in Reims (the Western headquarters) and on May 8, in Berlin-Karlshorst (the Russian headquarters). Although Dönitz continued to keep a "government" in office in Schleswig-Holstein, headed by the former

[3] Joachim C. Fest, *The Face of the Third Reich* (London and New York, 1970), p. 135.

Minister of Finance Lutz von Schwerin-Krosigk, its members were ousted and arrested two weeks later by the occupiers, who exercised full governmental powers. The end of the Hitler regime also meant the end of the sovereign German state. That this loss of sovereignty would be only temporary was not readily apparent at the time. That is a later construction of the so-called continuity theory. The astonishingly rapid emergence of semisovereign governmental structures was the result of Cold War pressures, and in its wake came the insoluble problem of Germany's division.

The collapse of National Socialism was sealed legally by the Allied Control Council, which on June 4, 1945, formally dissolved the NSDAP and ordered the arrest and internment of its functionaries. The sum total of Nazi rule was as obvious as its end. Even its own measure of value—success—refuted the effectiveness of Nazi policy. But at what a price! More than 6.5 million Germans dead, twice that number of refugees, the truncation and division of the country, the end of its existence as a state—such was the German balance sheet of the Third Reich. The European balance sheet, leading off with the murder of about 6 million Jews, exceeded these figures by far. While France suffered the loss of about 800,000 dead and Britain 400,000, at least 20 million died in the Soviet Union, 4.5 million in Poland, and 1.7 million in Yugoslavia. Germany's guilt, particularly toward the peoples of Eastern Europe—and the retaliatory expulsion of Germans from these territories is not, despite the plaintive cries now heard, of comparable magnitude—will remain the eternal heritage of National Socialism.

The reality and consequence of Nazi rule also refute the popular belief that a totalitarian dictatorship which sweeps away all political and moral controls, and as a result is able to operate quickly and spectacularly, guarantees a larger measure of order and efficiency and greater security and stability than complex democratic systems. Behind the rigorous pseudo order of the Third Reich stood a confusion of job and personal rivalries, the arbitrary commands of the Leader, insecurity and widespread fear of surveillance and terror. The result was a temporary enhancement of power, followed by the withering of reality which culminated in the chaos of the final phase.

The excesses accompanying the decline of the Third Reich showed up the true character of a system which, contrary to the seductive theory of dictatorship, did not bring its citizens political order and effective government or greater security and opportunities, but rather rested solely on organized despotism and pseudo-legal, ill-concealed crimes. Hitler had only one, egomaniacal answer: the German people had failed their historic test and thereby forfeited their national existence. He was obsessed with one idea to the end: that he would never capitulate, that what happened in November, 1918, would never recur in German history. In his political testament of April 29, 1945, he repeated the fixed ideas which had governed the rise and rule of National Socialism, beginning with the ferocious hatred of "international Jewry and its helpers," who in Hitler's world were responsible for everything that was happening. While embarking on his flight from responsibility, he sought in eerie monomania to commit the future leadership of the nation and its followers to a strict adherence to the racial laws and relentless resistance to the universal "poisoner of all peoples—international Jewry." At the same time, in mock-heroic, banal self-glorification, he attempted to lay the foundation for the continuation of National Socialism. Hitler announced that the "honorable men" of the new government would "through their work and their comradely loyalty be just as close [to him] after death as I hope my spirit will live among them and always accompany them." In the pseudo-religious tone of the early years, he prophesied the rebirth of the movement: "Out of the sacrifice of our soldiers and out of my own identification with them unto death, the seed for the glorious rebirth of the National Socialist movement will one way or another be replanted in German history." And he expressed the hope "that our task of the building up of a National Socialist state will be the work of coming centuries." [4]

The attempt to enshrine the fall of National Socialism in myth, to make it the launching pad of a Hitler cult and a renaissance of the "movement," resorts to a series of legends. The official radio bulletin of May 1, 1945, planted the first of these legends by which the bulwark theory was carried over into the postwar period: Hitler, it was announced, "died this afternoon in the Reich Chancellery for Germany, fighting Bolshevism to his dying breath." This lie, together with the long-range elements of a Hitler myth, was underscored that same day by Dönitz in a broadcast address to the German people. "Our Leader, Adolf Hitler, has fallen. The German people bow down in deep sorrow and reverence. He recognized the terrible threat of Bolshevism early and dedicated his life to the battle. His heroic death in the capital of the Third Reich put an end to this fight and to his undeviating, purposeful life, a life dedicated to the service of Germany. His fight against the tidal wave of Bolshevism, however, served all of Europe and the entire civilized world."

The second myth was related to the first. In line with Nazi propaganda, Dönitz held that it was now up to the "Anglo-Americans" to "drive out the Bolsheviks from Europe," and insofar as they were continuing the war against Germany, they were helping the "advancing Bolshevik foe." The deleterious effects of this argumentation, which obscured the fact that National Socialism bore the primary responsibility for the advance of the Red Army, should not be underestimated. And the extravagant praise which, in the moment of Germany's capitulation, Dönitz, Schwerin-Krosigk, and the last Army communiqué showered on the steadfastness of soldiers and population added to this, while Dönitz dismissed the Nazi rule with these laconic words: "The unity of state and party no longer exists. The party has left the scene of its activities" (May 8, 1945). Thus the responsibility for and causes of

[4] *Nürnberger Dokumente,* PS–3569.

the disaster continued to be veiled, and even after Hitler's death the people were spared a close look at the real circumstances of the German catastrophe. The last head of government, Schwerin-Krosigk, even linked the paean to the "heroic battle" in which Germany was defeated by the "overwhelming power of the enemy" with a reminder of the values "which have always been the mainspring of the essence of Germany's existence: unity and right and freedom."

After the bloody smashing of the German resistance, which thwarted a settling of accounts with National Socialism from within, sloganeering about the future covered over the bankrupt policies and the war of the Third Reich, and the continuity from heroic battle to postwar work was established. Schwerin-Krosigk himself, the conservative Nazi fellow traveler and member of all Cabinets since the Papen Government (1932), equated unity with the "idea of the people's community" and the "front-line comradeship," which had to be "salvaged and preserved [from the] failure of the past" rather than letting it disintegrate again into "warring classes and groups." Not one of these proclamations [5] contained a single word of regret or of awareness of what Nazi Germany had been and had done to others; but there was vociferous lament about the "atmosphere of hate which today envelops Germany in the world." The Third Reich was surrounded by an aura of tragedy and put squarely in the midst of Western culture: "We will proudly combine the heroic battle of our nation with the desire to make a contribution as a link of Christian, Western culture in an honest effort that does justice to the best traditions of our people."

To be sure, 1945 left very little leeway for the lie about a stab in the back. The military defeat of the Third Reich was total. Exhaustion and worry about sheer survival were the common lot. One might think that disillusionment and depoliticization would have ruled out a perpetuation or resurgence of National Socialism, that what happened after World War I could not happen again. But the myths lived on. The measures for the liquidation of National Socialism could not fully prevent an inner continuity, based on self-justifying apologetics and the catchword about the "good in National Socialism." A number of factors—the tendency to minimize and suppress facts, the desire to forget—militated against a discussion of the past and favored the survival of the tatters of Nazi ideology. The dispute over the postwar order revived the latent differences between West and East on which the Third Reich had banked in vain. Perhaps, so some said, Hitler had been right after all. As time went on, the occupation powers granted West Germany sovereign statehood and opened up room for a resurgence of German self-confidence much more rapidly than had been anticipated. Those who had stressed the continuity of the Reich rather than a break with the National Socialist past felt their position confirmed. The feeling of the "zero hour," the "farewell to the past"

[5] J. Hohlfeldt, *Dokumente der deutschen Politik und Geschichte*, V.

which even history-oriented scholars of the stature of Alfred Weber, Karl Jaspers, and Friedrich Meinecke were calling for, the rejection of nationalism and militarism, supported by most public figures in the early postwar years including Konrad Adenauer and Franz-Joseph Strauss, almost precipitously gave way to a reversion to political and military power.

While these rapid changes were taking place, Nazi leaders and functionaries were being called to account only fitfully, and if, then only by outside, superior forces, as in the Nuremberg trials, which Germans tended to see as "victor's justice," or in the blanket de-Nazification procedure, which because of its lack of differentiation failed to make the desired impact on the millions of "involved persons"; moreover, as a rule there was no follow-up. Many of the responsible and active members of the regime went underground, or, with the help of underground organizations, reached the safe shores of South America, the Near East, and Spain. Only belatedly did Germany itself begin a more systematic punishment of Nazi crimes, but by then the time that had elapsed worked against an effective prosecution.

In the Soviet-occupied part of Germany, the liquidation of National Socialism was in fact carried out more purposefully. But the alternative SED * rule, to which the population bowed reluctantly and resignedly, suppressed some of the historical and psychological problems of which National Socialism was the expression. Although the collectivization of industry and agriculture deprived fascism of its economic basis, the actual rule of *Obrigkeitsstaat,* one-party regime, and totalitarian ideology also rested on an authoritarian structure of political behavior, on the antidemocratic traditions of a Germany that had never known a successful revolution. And at any rate, the question about the effectiveness of the Communist "mastery" of National Socialism within an all-German framework becomes more hypothetical as the prospects of Germany's reconstitution as a national state become increasingly remote. Only West Germany offers the possibility for an empirical study of the survival or resurgence of National Socialist ideas or organizations, for only in that part of Germany can popular political ideas and attitudes be tested in open elections, opinion polls, and writings.

Three major stages of development are discernible:

1. Between 1946 and 1951, right-wing extremist and neo-Nazi groups continued to gain in strength. Initially, they were hampered by the occupation powers and their licensing requirements, but after the founding of the Federal Republic they developed great activity in some sectors. The growing prosperity put a brake on their growth, and in 1952, the invocation of Article 21 of the Basic Law (West Germany's constitution) in outlawing the Socialist Reich Party (Sozialistische

---

* The Socialist Unity Party (SED) was and is the instrument of dictatorial rule installed in the Soviet-occupied part of Germany, now the German Democratic Republic.—TRANSLATOR'S NOTE.

Reichspartei, or SRP) apparently blocked the renaissance of Nazi movements.

2. The following years saw the absorption of the radical Right potential by the established parties. The continuity of National Socialism and its adaptation to the changed conditions were manifested in a constant stream of literature that brought the ideas and arguments of the radical Right to a substantial readership.

3. These journalistic activities furnished the starting point for a new gathering and organization of right-wing extremism that profited from the transition crisis at the end of the Adenauer era. Among the major forces at work were the unrest over the change in international policy from determined anti-Communism to *détente*, the resurgence of nationalism in the wake of French Gaullism, the crisis of German reunification and the idea of Europe, and finally, the fear of economic depression, which eventually was to lead to the "crisis government" of the Grand Coalition. This was the situation at the end of 1964, the year of the founding of a party which for the first time since the war was able to gather the divided forces of right-wing extremism and appeal to potential supporters and voters: the National Democratic Party of Germany (Nationaldemokratische Partei Deutschlands, or NPD).

RIGHT-WING EXTREMISM IN THE SECOND DEMOCRACY

The catastrophe of 1945 was the hour of truth for National Socialism. The majority of the German people accepted Germany's collapse, some disillusioned, others resignedly. Prohibitions, purges, and political and constitutional safeguards sought to prevent a repetition of Weimar. True, there was no revolution, and the debate with National Socialism took place primarily on the institutional level. Under the impact of defeat and de-Nazification, the great mass of Nazi followers, disappointed and embittered, withdrew from political life. But not surprisingly, a hard core of convinced National Socialists soon recovered from the shock. They tried, in changed form, to reactivate the political and ideological ideas with which they had grown up. The efforts for democratic re-education pursued by the occupation powers more or less intensively after the war necessarily came from outside and above. That was an artificial revolution. The Second Republic came into being under the protective umbrella of international politics. It was spared the birth pangs of the Weimar Republic; the new democracy contrasted more sharply with the negative balance of the Third Reich than the Weimar Republic had with the collapsing monarchy. But when this protective period came to an abrupt halt with the intensification of the Cold War, it immediately became apparent that changes in political mentality occur even more slowly than is generally assumed.

The German Rights Party (Deutsche Rechtspartei, or DRP), founded in 1946, furnished the first platform for keeping the ideas of National Socialism alive and for reactivating Nazi officials and supporters. It conformed to the times by taking on a decidedly conservative coloration and by paying lip-service to the democratic state of law; but its criticism of National Socialism was confined to an indictment of the "un-German" aspects of fascism. In fact, however, the party, according to the findings of the Federal Constitutional Court in 1952, tried "to organize the members of earlier right-wing parties."[6] Its leadership included a number of known Nazi propagandists; the conservative-German national façade of the DRP and of its successor parties was motivated by the same tactical considerations as the pre-1933 "national opposition." And in fact in later years this was openly proclaimed. The self-confidence of the new Right, which registered gains in municipal and provincial parliamentary elections in northern Germany (particularly in Wolfsburg) and sent five deputies to the Bundestag, the new West German parliament, was made overt in the founding of the SRP in October, 1949. Among its founders were a number of DRP members, former ranking Nazis, including its head, the ex-district leader and indoctrination officer Fritz Dorls, and the former political chairman (*Politischer Leiter*) Fritz Rössler, who in the meantime had assumed a new identity and a new name—Dr. Franz Richter. In addition to other "old fighters" like the Nazi student ideologue Gerhard Krüger, the new group sported the living exponent of the stab-in-the-back legend, the "hero" of the 20th of July, Otto-Ernst Remer. This new edition of the NSDAP profited from the abolition of political licensing as well as from the social and economic problems of ex-Nazi-party members in the immediate postwar years.

In addition, numerous small groups and organizations sprang up in which confirmed Nazis joined together with others critical of the "excesses" and "errors" but not the political doctrine of National Socialism. At the same time, the first efforts were made to undermine other political parties, particularly the Free Democratic Party (Freie Demokratische Partei, or FDP). The Right, in part conservative and in part in national guise, split into a profusion of small rival groups; this, despite many differences, was reminiscent of the early days of Weimar. The similarities became even stronger after 1950, when the turn to remilitarization saw the emergence of vociferous veterans' organizations which glorified military tradition and war exploits to counteract the "defamation" of the Wehrmacht. Numerous cross-connections, revisionist writings, and a greater self-assurance earmarked the growing tendency of nationalist and neo-Nazi activity. Among the many groups were some with names like German Community, First Legion, Free Corps Germany, German Brotherhood, and National Concentration, which were affiliated with youth organizations such as the Socialist Reich Youth, Young Nation, Young German Community, National Youth, German Youth, and Reich Youth Corps. The organizing fervor of right-wing sectarians and old Nazis had little impact on

[6] *Entscheidungen des Bundesverfassungsgerichts* (Tübingen, 1953), II, 28 f. The most comprehensive treatment is found in Kurt P. Tauber, *Beyond Eagle and Swastika* (2 vols.; Middletown, Conn., 1967).

the political-party situation, but both as a symptom and as a vehicle for the continuity of National Socialist ideology this temporary renaissance was of continuing significance. In addition to the DRP, the first Bundestag also contained a Hessian splinter group, the National Democrats; the two constituted the "National Right," until, after complicated conflicts, a National Reich Party split off; subsequently, in 1950–51, the Rights Party and National Democrats joined to form the German Reich Party (Deutsche Reichspartei, or DRP). Initially, the DRP was overshadowed by the SRP, which was celebrating short-lived triumphs, particularly in Lower Saxony. In May, 1951, the SRP won 11 per cent of the votes in the provincial diet elections of Lower Saxony, and it also made inroads in Bremen and Schleswig-Holstein. The SRP propaganda concentrated on a vague "popular socialism" in which the old National Socialists rediscovered well-worn slogans, and also on a nationalism whose championship of Reich and war was but a thinly disguised continuation of the *Lebensraum* ideology. The preservation of the stab-in-the-back legend also was reminiscent of the early days of the NSDAP. The Führer may have been missing, but in a series of noisy meetings complete with guards and combat leagues, the SRP succeeded temporarily in presenting Remer as the protector of the Third Reich against the "traitors" of the resistance. The party acted as the gathering point for available National Socialists, to whom it turned for support. Its 20,000 members (of which 12,000 were in Lower Saxony) were subject to a hierarchical command structure from top to bottom. The declared intention of the party leadership was the formation of "cadre organizations"; [7] the numerous auxiliaries were modeled on the NSDAP. Both the party's national leadership and the heads of the state units had the power to expel individuals and groups; the maneuverability thus gained, so they believed, would protect their legality tactics modeled on those of the Nazis. However, their profession of legality did not prevent them from openly proclaiming their faith in Hitler and the Third Reich, which the party leadership then tried to camouflage through formal declarations opposing dictatorship.[8] This move was related to provisions of the constitution of the Federal Republic. Drawing a lesson from the experiences of 1933, the Basic Law provided for the prohibition of parties with undemocratic organizations and goals (Article 21). Despite its efforts at camouflage, the neo-Nazi character of the SRP was so obvious that in October, 1952, the Federal Constitutional Court, after carefully exposing the flimsiness of the party's professed dedication to legality, found legal grounds for outlawing it.

The shades of Weimar seemed to be laid to rest, even though committed functionaries and followers went over to similar groups, particularly to the seemingly more moderate DRP. The leadership of the DRP typified the National Socialist functionaries who waited for a

[7] Letter by the party executive of December 25, 1950, in *Entscheidungen des Bundesverfassungsgericht, op. cit.,* p. 50.

[8] *Ibid.,* 64.

new chance by traveling the road via the postwar groups and the SRP.[9] But the DRP never was able to become more than a splinter group supported by barely 1 per cent of the electorate. Split into warring factions and short-lived new organizations, the radical Right seemed reduced to a minute group of incurable fanatics, the sort of lunatic fringe one finds on the margin of all multiparty systems. The effort, after a few sensational forays, to infiltrate larger parties, particularly the FDP, where Goebbels' State Secretary, Werner Naumann, turned up in 1953, also was not particularly successful. The German Party (Deutsche Partei, or DP) and the Union of Expellees (BHE) seemed to offer the best chance for gaining a foothold in the right wing of the Bonn party structure. But these two suffered the same fate as the other minor parties, and ultimately, as they vainly looked for survival in a fusion of conservative and national forces (All-German Party [Gesamtdeutsche Partei]), their fiasco contributed to the realization of an old plan, namely, the founding of an all-embracing national right-wing party—the NPD—with the unflinching DRP guard as its core (1964).

The decade in which political and economic stability reduced the chances of the radical parties to a minimum was bridged by the writings of the radical Right. Its journalistic output continued to grow in the 1950's. Its readership included the hard core of National Socialists as well as a substantial segment of passive yet potential supporters of radical Right ideologies. This output was not limited simply to papers with direct links to the DRP and championing their middle-class, pseudo-social, nationalist program, a more careful version of the SRP program. There were the early efforts, particularly by the FDP, to make use of the popular appeal of some Nazi slogans among the electorate in the parliamentary elections of 1953, which resulted in some dubious alliances. These tactics, so reminiscent of the illusions of the Weimar era, have recently been revived, particularly by Franz-Joseph Strauss and the CSU (the Bavarian sister organization of the CDU), in an effort to gear political party propaganda to that of the NPD, to keep abreast of the "national wave." This approach boosted the circulation of radical Right publications at a time of political low tide and helped to give them respectability. The results of the 1953 elections, however, proved that the expectations of cashing in on National Socialist longings were overconfident. And the comparatively small membership of the neo-Nazi groups also dampened the hopes of those who thought they could undermine the Federal Republic by infiltrating the bourgeois parties. The revisionism of conservative-national expellee politicians, who found their spokesman in Hans-Christoph Seebohm (DP), for many years the Federal Republic's Minister of Transportation, seemed to offer the most promising prospects.

But more important, the journalistic output after 1952–53 helped to

---

[9] Cf. Reinhard Kühnl, *Die NPD* (Berlin, 1967), pp. 19 ff.

keep alive National Socialist emotions and ideas. In this respect, German right-wing extremism differed from the lunatic fringe in other countries, for its literature could fall back on ideas and arguments unique to the past experience of the Third Reich. In the area of "International Fascism" (assuming the nationalist base of fascist movements, a questionable concept at best), the German case, because of its recent past, occupied a special position. In view of the optimistic hopes of the 1950's, warnings remained in order.[10] Despite the changed conditions, which were to prevent a repetition of 1933, there was a real possibility that the underground, neo-Nazi potential might blossom forth into political activity in the event of socio-economic crises or international problems.

The mainstays of the continuity of National Socialism included a number of newspapers, periodicals, books, and publishers. The *Reichsruf (Reich Clarion)* had been the official organ of the DRP since 1951; on January 1, 1965, it became the NPD paper *Deutsche Nachrichten (German News)*; in addition to news and articles, the *Reichsruf* published a series of pamphlets. The backers of these papers were largely identical with the DRP leadership, and under new auspices they later dominated the publishing activities of the NPD. Working closely with this group, Heinrich Härtle, Alfred Rosenberg's ex-secretary, published the *Deutsche Wochenzeitung (German Weekly)*. Härtle took up the anti-Bolshevik theme of the Third Reich; in 1955, a new edition of his 1944 book on the Soviets was published, though this time pseudonymously and without Rosenberg's preface. The publisher of the *Reichsruf* and the *Wochenzeitung* and a great many of their contributors were (and are) identical. The papers differed only in makeup and appearance: the *Reichsruf*, and later the *Nachrichten*, addressed itself to DRP members; the *Wochenzeitung* seeks the support of and plays on the resentments of unaffiliated nationalists. Both conduct intensive "documentary" campaigns against the "war-guilt lie" and ceaselessly publish apologetic accounts of the Nazi past glorifying the Nuremberg defendants or suggesting that Hess be awarded the Nobel Peace Prize.[11]

There were numerous small papers of other radical right-wing sects, as for example the *Freie Nation (Free Nation)* of the German Freedom Party (Deutsche Freiheitspartei), the *Deutsche Gemeinschaft (German Community)* of the party by that name, or the short-lived periodical *Widerhall (Echo)*, in which the pseudo-religious adoration of the Führer led to a comparison of the fates of Hitler and of Christ (including the betrayal by disciples). But two publications above all have for twenty years propounded the old and new theses of right-wing extremism to a regular, dedicated "readership." They are the monthly *Nation Europa* and the *Deutsche Soldatenzeitung (German Soldiers'*

[10] K. D. Bracher, "Rechtsradikalismus in der Bundesrepublik," *Colloquium*, X, Nos. 2–4 (1956); Otto Büsch and Peter Furth, *Rechtsradikalismus im Nachkriegsdeutschland* (Berlin, 1957); H. H. Knütter, *Ideologien des Rechtsradikalismus im Nachkriegsdeutschland* (Bonn, 1961).

[11] Thus the *Reichsruf*, No. 13 (1958).

Journal), later renamed *Deutsche Nationalzeitung und Soldatenzeitung*. *Nation Europa,* the mouthpiece of European fascism, founded with the substantial assistance of Scandinavian fascists (Carlberg, Engdahl, Essen), combines elements of nationalism and the Nazi concept of the European idea. It interprets the European idea as the fruit of National Socialist expansionism, but at the same time, skillfully camouflaged, rides the wave of contemporary European slogans. Literary and cultural guilds like the German Cultural Work of the European Spirit under the auspices of the SA poet Herbert Böhme, which in addition to a reader's service operates about fifty "training homes" in town and country, run mostly by old party members, use similar approaches.

The *Soldatenzeitung* concentrates on that aspect of the National Socialist heritage which lent itself to revival in the Federal Republic: German military tradition and the glorification of war. These issues merely provided effective starting points, a legitimate façade. Once the paper won the temporary support of the veterans' organizations and even of the Government in Bonn, it rapidly became the most widely read political paper in the nationalist camp, distributed in every town and hamlet in the country.

Nation Europa claimed to be—as did most publications of the radical Right, with their traditional emphasis on "culture"—the paper of an intellectual elite thwarted in the realization of its national and European goals by a "forcibly imposed 'democratorship'" (*Demokratur*).[12] This "monthly publication in the service of European renewal" (thus its subtitle) founded in 1950 seeks to set right the alleged falsification of the historical role of National Socialism (as, for example, by stressing the "European" role of the SS formations which were organized in other European countries and sent to the Eastern front) and to pit the true heritage of National Socialism against the degeneration of a world overwhelmed by "alien" democratization and Americanization— the dictatorship of an elite against democratic popular government. Working closely with the remnants of European Quisling governments, this camp pursues a determined campaign of exoneration and revival of the ideas and deeds of National Socialism on the international level, only thinly camouflaged by expressions of regret over some "excesses" or "errors" of the Third Reich, but voicing approval of Hitler's race policies and of his war.

The regular contributors to *Nation Europa* included such political and literary luminaries of the old regime as Hans Grimm, the author of *Volk ohne Raum* (*A People Without Space*), General Hermann Ramcke of parachute troop fame, the Nazi authors Bruno Brehm, Will Vesper, Gerhard Schumann, and Erwin Guido Kolbenheyer, Ribbentrop's widow, and the wife of Rudolf Hess. In addition, there were foreign fascist leaders like Oswald Mosley and Maurice Bardèche, the

---

[12] Thus Peter Kleist, publisher of the *Wochenzeitung*, former SS Obersturmführer and functionary in the Ribbentrop Office, in his widely distributed book *Auch Du warst dabei* (Heidelberg, 1952), pp. 396 ff.

editor of *Défense d'Occident, Nation Europa*'s French counterpart, which continued to express the hope for a German-led Europe to stave off the Communist threat. These groups ceaselessly discuss the "European" nature of the past war against Russia and the part played by the non-German SS formations, and step by step a new stab-in-the-back legend is being constructed; the resistance generally, and the German resistance in particular, is reviled as treasonous; pseudo-scientific articles and victorious references to the South African "solution" revive racial theories; the Arab stand against Israel is celebrated; statistics are manipulated to minimize the extermination of the Jews; and finally, a great deal of space is devoted to the "war-guilt question" of 1939. And on contemporary issues, both its contributors and the "letters from readers" also support extremist positions. For example, they do not simply demand the reconstitution of the 1937 borders but call for bringing Czechoslovakia and Poland to their knees; the writers like to point to the efficiency of the National Socialist new order agreed on at the Munich Conference (as for example in the July, 1957, issue).

The editors skillfully propound the most radical theses in long letters from "readers," thus protecting themselves against a possible ban—so far successfully. The December, 1959, issue, for example, contained a three-page "letter" in which a book denigrating the horrors of the concentration camps was effectively cited to shift the burden of guilt. Asserting that "there was good reason for the detention of many concentration-camp inmates and that their suffering and deprivation were no greater than that of the German combat troops," the letter went on to describe the misery of the Russian war, without, however, saying who was responsible for it or for the rule of terror in the East. It ended thus: "If the German soldiers and the German people, defending themselves against the international rabble and its henchmen who in 1914 and again in 1939 did in fact maneuver the nations into war, shouldered such suffering and deprivation for Europe, then criminals and people aiding the enemy simply couldn't be coddled and nursed in camps." In conclusion it sounded a note of Nazi morality: "Obviously Germans were more concerned with the fate of their comrades and their own people than with that of concentration-camp inmates who had stood on the side of the enemy. We therefore have no reason to feel the special collective shame recommended by Mr. Heuss" (the first President of West Germany).

This is but one of innumerable examples of the arguments and methods of right-wing journalism and Nazi propaganda and apologetics. At first, tactical considerations dictated caution in the treatment of Hitler. But in May, 1955, on the tenth anniversary of his death, *Nation Europa* devoted an entire issue to Hitler; under a solemn headline it attempted a complete rehabilitation of the Führer and at the same time a high-flown testimonial. The moving spirit behind this effort was the paper's publisher, Arthur Ehrhardt, a former Coburg elementary schoolteacher, Free Corps soldier, and SS officer, and a minority shareholder in the international consortium that owns the journal. For almost two decades, *Nation Europa* has been engaged in establishing the continuity and the revitalization of the National Socialist "world of ideas." Thus, when Nazi inscriptions were painted on walls and synagogues in Germany at the end of 1959, they were the old slogans and symbols.

In addition to elitist journals, a flood of pamphlets and best-selling reminiscences of fallen idols kept the Nazi legend alive, and a multitude of organizations passed it on to politically ignorant youthful followers. The most important role in this area was played by the *Soldatenzeitung* (later *Nationalzeitung*), since 1960 published and edited by Dr. Gerhard Frey. With him a generation which had not been active in the Third Reich moved into radical Right journalism. That may be why the paper, although Frey owns a substantial share of *Nation Europa,* remains somewhat aloof from the outspoken neo-Nazi camp, a fact which has extended its effectiveness to wider circles. In contrast to the other products of the radical Right, Frey's paper, with its explosive banner headlines in red, enjoys nationwide newsstand distribution. Whatever Frey's political ambitions—and his competition with the "old fighters" establishment in the DRP and NPD is probably also due to economic reasons—the influence of the *Nationalzeitung* on the potential radical Right vote cannot be overestimated. Its circulation is far greater than that of any of the other party papers. Aside from the pictorials, it is frequently the only non-local paper offered in the newsstands of small towns and villages. Analyses of the *Nationalzeitung* have shown that its news coverage and commentaries are not devoted solely to typical neo-Nazi or radical Right issues but also play on the more timely frustrations of contemporary everyday life. This indicates an adaptation to a changed situation, a modernization of the nationalist authoritarian emotional setting, whose effectiveness was demonstrated by the success of the NPD propaganda campaign against foreign workers, as substitutes for Jews. The *Nationalzeitung* quite appropriately has been called the "strongest non-party power factor of German right-wing extremism." [13] Behind the seemingly progressive façade, the basic ideas of National Socialism have been carried over into the postwar period, only now they appear in a veiled yet effectively updated union with contemporary issues: Barry Goldwater and the cause of South Tyrol are championed ("South Tyrol is Suffering for Germany"),[14] restitution and "world Jewry," are denounced ("Blackmailed for All Eternity? Capitulation Before World Jewry"),[15] a radical revisionism is indulged ("Breslau, Königsberg, Eger, Danzig, and Stettin Will Again

[13] Kühnl, *op. cit.,* p. 39.
[14] *Deutsche Nationalzeitung,* Nos. 51 and 52 (1963).
[15] *Ibid.,* No. 32 (1962).
[16] *Ibid.,* No. 7 (1965).

Be German"),[16] and a tireless battle is waged against the "war-guilt lie"—a struggle supported by not a few conservative national publicists. Since 1960, a Society of Free Publicists has devoted itself to the same general theme. It created a stir in 1964, when, together with DRP functionaries it sponsored a German tour by the American historian David Hoggan, whose book, *Der erzwungene Krieg (The Forced War)*, published only in Germany and full of distortions, shifts the blame for the war from Hitler to the British and the Poles. In this instance, as in the German anti-Roosevelt campaign, the assistance of like-minded Americans was apparently welcome.

Above all, the years 1952–64 saw the publication of many right-wing radical books which helped to preserve or revive the Nazi ideology until the successful founding of a unified party. Naïve or apologetic memoirs of politicians and military men, as well as "scholarly," or at any rate fact- and footnote-filled studies, continued to glorify the Third Reich and the war. The publication of Hoggan's book was sponsored by the *Deutsche Hochschullehrerzeitung (German University Teachers' Journal)*, an enterprise dedicated to the rehabilitation of ousted Nazi professors, under the direction of Herbert Grabert, a former Würzburg university lecturer in "German Weltanschauung." Publishers in Göttingen (Plesse Verlag, Göttinger Verlagsanstalt), Starnberg (Druffel-Verlag), Lippoldsberg (Klosterhaus-Verlag), and elsewhere brought out a number of similar works, which are made known to their audience by like-minded papers and periodicals. True, the scope is smaller, the influence less direct, and the language more cautious than in the Weimar Republic. But the tendency and tone is in many ways reminiscent of the conservative, nationalist, and *völkisch* literature which paved the way for and supported the rise of National Socialism. Then as now there was the myth of the stab in the back and of treason, the demonization of "seditious" intellectuals and democrats as handmaidens of Bolshevism, and the rejection of the "system" as "un-German" and imposed by the victors. Then as now, *Volk* and fatherland, nation and community, race and elite, authority and order, and the reconstitution of the Reich were postulated as the highest values of the German state.

It is hard to tell what influence radical Right journalism has had on the developing political mentality of the Germans. Of course, the political ideas and propagandistic indoctrination on which the Third Reich rested continued to reverberate even without direct influences. But the fact remains that behind the façade of democratic stability in the 1950's, National Socialist ideas were liquidated more slowly and less thoroughly than the simplified formula "Bonn is not Weimar" would admit, and this failure was due in part to the journalistic activities of the radical Right. Almost no restraints were imposed. After the prohibition of the SRP, the attention and emphasis of official surveillance concentrated largely on the Communist movement; its writings were much more rigorously controlled.

Resentments, ignorance, and indolence are the primary factors which in time of crisis exacerbate the threat to democracy. If economic prosperity, Adenauer's prestige, and the functioning of democratic institutions accelerated a positive reorientation of the population of the Federal Republic—unlike in the days of Weimar—then the following points take on added significance: Opinion polls showed that in 1953, 32 per cent of the people of West Germany thought that Hitler, aside from some mistakes, had been an outstanding statesman, possibly even the greatest statesman of this century. Five years later, when Adenauer's prestige was at its peak, 15 per cent still said that they would be willing to vote for a man like Hitler; and generally, Hitler was held to be one of the three greatest German statesmen. At the same time, a majority was of the opinion that it was better for Germany not to have any Jews in the country. In 1961, still more Germans disapproved than approved of the anti-Hitler resistance (32 and 29 per cent, respectively), while the number undecided or without an opinion was significantly large (39 per cent). In some instances, disputes arose between parents and school and municipal administrations over the naming of schools after resistance fighters; polls showed that the population did indeed overwhelmingly reject such names (49 versus 18 per cent); here, too, one-third of those polled were undecided.[17]

Since the young do not share the apologetic motives of their elders, the fact that the ideas of the young generation were not too different underscores the potential survival of National Socialist thinking and myths. In 1956, young men were asked whether in their opinion National Socialism had been a good or bad idea; 33 per cent said partly good and partly bad, while only 22 per cent responded negatively, and 16 per cent were unequivocally positive. Again it is interesting to note that almost one-third (29 per cent) offered no opinion at all. No less significant was the fact that throughout the years, only one-fourth of all persons polled expressed a determination to oppose a revival of a National Socialist party. On the other hand, the number of those who expressed a readiness to welcome or to support a new edition of National Socialism remained stable (12-13 per cent). Thus the radical Right potential by no means was limited to old National Socialists, and the expectation that the problem would solve itself as a new generation came of age was a doubtful one. The attitude toward the problem of neo-Nazism in the nineteen to twenty-eight age group was if anything less promising. Among them remarkably few came out in support of the resistance to National Socialism and a remarkably large number were indifferent. An informed observer should therefore not have been surprised that more than two decades after the end of the Hitler regime, during the first economic and governmental crisis of the Federal Republic—a crisis far less serious than any faced by Weimar—a radical Right party could within months poll 6 to 10

[17] *Jahrbuch der öffentlichen Meinung 1947–1955* (Allensbach, 1956), pp. 132 ff.

per cent of the votes in one state after the other. The solid 1 per cent electoral base was supplemented by a voting potential from which a protest movement, given the right political and organizational climate, could profit.

THE NPD—A NEW STARTING POINT?

The manifestations of right-wing extremism in Germany are quite comparable to those of the nationalistic, racist, and fascist movements in many other countries. However, none of these countries has had a regime comparable to National Socialism, with many of its founders, fellow travelers, and victims still living. The special situation of the second German democracy is made evident particularly in the activist aspects of right-wing extremism: propaganda and electoral politics. The extent to which the radical Right latches on to surviving patterns of Nazi thought and behavior is evidenced by the unbroken continuity of its publications from their inception to the propaganda arsenal of the NPD, which laud the "good" in National Socialism and minimize its consequences.

That the base created by the rise of the antidemocratic Right in the Weimar Republic has survived was shown after 1965 as well as before 1952, when radical Right voters were mobilized in those social groups and regions which had proved most susceptible to National Socialism. Any critical study of the relationship of the "new" right-wing radicalism to the "old" National Socialism must therefore consider particularly two aspects of the NPD: its structure and the sociology of its electoral gains.

Contrary to its claims, the NPD is not a new party. It was founded in November, 1964, after twelve years of effort (subsequent to the ban of the SRP) on the part of the DRP to form a coalition. The new though not highly original approach was the union of conservative–German national and radical-fascist elements, which the party broadened still more by making "democratic" part of its name. This of course was purely a tactical move, which sought to pre-empt any possible action or ban by the constitutional courts. At the same time, the new label meant the adaptation to democratic forms, which by comparison with Weimar had proved more stable and been more widely accepted, or at least tolerated. While the Reich Party had called itself socialist and German and had steered clear of the democratic parties, the NPD nominally adjusted to the Bonn party system. Tactical and psychological considerations went hand in hand; they offered the illusion that one could vote for the radical Right without being judged an undemocratic outsider or possibly even a neo-Nazi; the party claimed a place among the democratic parties and yet, as in the past, opposed the "system" and promised to break the "Bonn cartel of monopoly parties." All this is reminiscent of the time when the National Socialists, calling themselves a "workers' party," and the German Nationals, calling themselves a "people's party," had similarly adapted to the democratic spirit.

The NPD, which cynics have called the "NSDAP without the SA," owes its existence largely to the efforts of the old DRP guard. In the parliamentary elections of 1961, the DRP still was unable to expand beyond that hard core which had "kept faith" since 1953. It received a mere 0.8 per cent of the total vote. Subsequently, plans were laid for winning over the dissatisfied voters other than the old Nazis with the help of a pseudo-democratic movement, a potential whose strength could be gleaned from the circulation figures of radical Right publications. In June, 1964, the DRP party congress in Bonn decided to form a "union of all national-democratic forces." As events were to prove, the founding five months later took place at exactly the right moment: the problems of the Erhard Government signified a transition crisis, the DP and BHE had been dissolved, a German Gaullism was taking root, and conservative-nationalist stirrings, to which the CSU and the mass-circulation tabloids of the powerful Springer publishing house actively contributed, were being felt. The NPD stood ready in 1966, at a time when signs of economic stagnation and recession multiplied, when the stability of the Western system of alliances, on which the Federal Republic depended in such large measure, began to waver, when the demand for domestic stabilization of the state brought forth vague schemes for a conflict-free "controlled society" reminiscent of Carl Schmitt's models, and when the SPD opposition increasingly gave in to calls for political cooperation, thereby making room for a "new" opposition. The demands for emergency legislation and electoral reform also contributed to a growing feeling of uneasiness and radical criticism of the "system"; the retreat into the Grand Coalition in November, 1966, was justified by talk of a crisis of democracy; shades of Weimar appeared on the horizon.

The NPD developed in this setting of an overdramatized crisis of Bonn democracy. Half of its membership was recruited from the DRP, although that group continued its separate existence for another year; old National Socialists with too vulnerable a past remained in the background for the sake of the "democratic" façade. Its first chairman and conservative German National frontman was the Bremen industrialist Fritz Thielen, until 1958 a member of the CDU and later affiliated with the DP. In a political advertisement in the *Deutsche Wochenzeitung* (*German Weekly*), he called for the creation of an "effective party of the Right, which was lacking in West Germany's constantly shrinking party structure." The party was formed on November 14, 1964; the founding meeting of the "all-embracing party of national, libertarian, and social principles" took place two weeks later in Hanover, in the DRP stronghold of Lower Saxony, and was attended by approximately 700 invited guests. The DRP activists were joined by delegates of the All-German Party (Gesamtdeutsche Partei, or GdP), a DP–BHE creation, and by remnants of the DP. The broad back of Thielen shielded a number of deputy chairmen and executives, among them the

Lower Saxonian DRP functionary Adolf von Thadden, a skillful tactician and scion of a prominent family who since the end of the war had been tirelessly active in right-wing affairs and who moreover had the advantage, rare among that crowd, of not having been a Nazi functionary; the Baden-Württemberg GdP leader and old NSDAP functionary Wilhelm Gutmann, who had previously worked with the DRP; Heinrich Fassbender (until 1956 a member of the FDP), the leader of the minute German National People's Party of Hesse; the former rector of the University of Königsberg, Professor von Grünberg, an old NSDAP member and spokesman for ousted Nazi university teachers; the ideological "consultant on university problems" to the NPD Executive Committee, Professor Ernst Anrich, under the Nazis a historian in Bonn and Strasbourg as well as Educational Director of the National Socialist Student League, now chief of "political education" of the NPD; the notorious Nazi orator, high-ranking SA officer, and later deputy chief of the DRP, Otto Hess (who committed suicide in 1967 because of financial difficulties); the Strength through Joy official and SA officer Emil Meier-Dorn, now also deputy DRP chairman; and finally the party's propaganda and press chief, Waldemar Schütz, publisher of the official party papers *Reichsruf, Deutsche Wochenzeitung,* and *Deutsche Nachrichten,* owner of the publishing houses Schütz-Verlag and Göttinger Verlagsanstalt, director of the Plesse-Verlag and Nationalverlag, former Hitler Youth official and SS officer. More than two-thirds of the party's executive officers were active National Socialists, as were a majority of its regional officers.

With this army of experienced activists and by drawing on the membership of the DRP, the party was able to build up an organization throughout West Germany before the September, 1965, elections. The DRP furnished the cadres and technical apparatus; local offices sprang up all over, with Lower Saxony and Bavaria in the lead. Membership also increased rapidly; by the end of 1966, it had grown to 23,000, more than the SRP had at its peak; a year later it exceeded 30,000. The field of NPD activities and its appeal went far beyond this framework. Numerous small groups and special-interest associations of radical-Right persuasion (e.g., Böhme's Kulturwerk, the Waffen SS League, the Victims of Internment and De-Nazification) worked closely with the party; right-wing, in part illegal, youth organizations also helped to recruit members; "national-democratic" student groups came into being, and the *Deutsche Studentenanzeiger (German Student Reporter)* disseminated the propaganda message at the universities. And finally, the Army and even the police offered opportunities for the recruitment of young, "respectable" supporters.

The organizational structure of the NPD also was given a decidedly democratic façade. Its statutes sought to obscure the significant Nazi component in its leadership, propaganda, and following. Going far beyond the legality strategy of the NSDAP and the SRP, the NPD strongly objects to the "charge" of being a Nazi successor party. This must put a great burden on the tactical discipline and gifts of persuasion of its functionaries and followers. The authors of the statutes pledged "unequivocal" allegiance to the "libertarian principles of our political, spiritual, and economic life." They know they can count on the understanding and interpretative talents of the experienced party fighters. At the same time, however, great restraint is asked of the "old fighters." Under conditions very different from those of Weimar, the new legality policies find expression in the training of speakers and the preparation of arguments, in instructions to practice restraint in meetings, and in rigid disciplinary measures. Otto Hess summed up the requisite deception in this highly significant sentence: "Beware of the tone you once learned!" [18]

The democratic façade of the (since revised) statutes could not obscure the authoritarian nature of the party structure. "In case of danger," the chairman could "without delay" order the expulsion of a party member, "also without a hearing of those involved"; all he had to do was to obtain the retroactive assent of the executive committee within sixty days. In addition, the leadership was given the power to proclaim a state of "organizational emergency," thus enabling it to dissolve party auxiliaries, a tool skillfully wielded by the SRP. The fear of proscription was in no small measure responsible for such throwbacks to the leader principle, thus allowing the party to disavow any condonation of "undemocratic" behavior. In the fight that erupted between Thielen and Thadden, this led to grotesque situations, and not even the invocation of this provision was able to halt the ultimate victory of the DRP faction. The wealth of directives, draft speeches,[19] and the restriction of interviews to a handful of virtuoso party tacticians showed the authoritarian structure of opinion-making behind the democratic façade. The eagerness to preserve this front led to the promulgation of such interesting directives as the one requiring all hand votes to be taken with the left arm, to avoid any possible public "misunderstanding" and to guard against the reassertion of a powerful habit on the part of older members.

The victory of the Nazi and DRP guard around Thadden, Hess, Schütz, and Meier-Dorn over the Thielen group in the spring of 1967 revealed the true power relations. A few disillusioned conservative-national followers like the Bavarian NPD leader Franz Florian Winter were left with no alternative but to resign. Winter's book *Ich glaubte an die NPD (I Believed in the NPD;* 1968) offers deep insights into the practices of its leadership. For the time being, the new leadership under Thadden emerged stronger from its court battles with Thielen, whom it castigated as fomenting dissent harmful to the party. Its claim to being a democratic, non-Nazi party has to be balanced against the progressive radicalization of the party structure; the leadership crisis, contrary to predictions, resulted in a higher degree of discipline rather than in confusion. During 1967–68, the inroads into the pro-

[18] Cf. *Die Zeit*, March 17, 1967.
[19] Documentation and example in Kühnl, *op. cit.*, pp. 225 ff.

vincial parliaments continued unabated. In 1965, at its first appearance in national elections, the NPD was still limited almost completely to the hard core of radical Right voters, even though it polled considerably more votes than the old DRP. Like the NSDAP in 1928 with its 2.6 per cent of the total vote, it got only 2.1 per cent of the votes. Six months later (March, 1966), it more than doubled its votes in Hamburg. Though the party carefully refrained from participating in the July, 1966, North Rhine–Westphalian elections, successes began to mount—a situation in many respects reminiscent of the regional rise of the NSDAP in 1929.

Its ascent began in Bavaria, where the NPD registered substantial gains in the municipal elections of March, 1966. On November 20 of that year, 7.4 per cent of Bavaria's electorate cast its vote for the NPD; two weeks earlier, 7.8 per cent of the voters of Hesse had made the same decision. Of special interest were the spectacular inroads in Central Franconia. In 1967, the voters of Bremen (8.8 per cent), Lower Saxony (7 per cent), and Rhineland-Palatinate (6.9 per cent) confirmed the extent of the party's electoral gains. Only in Schleswig-Holstein, where the elections were held on the heels of the Thielen-Thadden conflict, did the results fall below expectations (5.8 per cent). The growing strength of the party was again confirmed in Baden-Württemberg in 1968 (9.8 per cent). This chain reaction has been ascribed to the impact the enormous publicity given the emergence of the NPD had on potential voters. Nothing succeeds like success. However, what is far more important is that the radical Right, for the first time since the war, proved on a national level that it could hurdle the obstacle of being a splinter party and that the ballots cast for it were not wasted. (According to the modified proportional system of the German electoral law, only a party polling more than 5 per cent of the votes [in Bavaria, 10 per cent of a district] or winning at least three seats is granted proportional representation in parliament.) And so the voters discarded their reservations and skepticism—a tendency strengthened by real and alleged crises of government and economy. At this point, the setting in which the radical Right vote was cast became clearly evident. The socio-economic structure of the electorate and traditional regional voting patterns confirmed unequivocally that a parallel with Nazi election results had been preserved over three decades.

The NPD's emphatic efforts to avoid any identification with National Socialism are refuted not only by its ideology and activists. More persuasive still is the degree to which the "national-democratic" election campaigns follow the sociological voting patterns of the emergent National Socialism between 1929 and 1933. The parallels in population and regional structures are particularly remarkable in view of the profound changes wrought by the influx of expellees and the progress of industrialization and urbanization since 1945. The NPD concentrated its propaganda on those groups and areas where the NSDAP had its strongest support: Central Franconia, Lower Saxony,

Schleswig-Holstein, and the Palatinate. At the same time, it succeeded, for the first time since the war, in mobilizing a substantial radical-Right following also outside these centers (Hesse, Baden-Württemberg), thus apparently improving its chances for success in the federal parliamentary elections of 1969. The potential, with 10–15 per cent (in the strongholds) and 4–6 per cent (in the weakest regions), has certainly not yet been fully exploited. The NPD itself has stated forcefully and optimistically: "Our objective: the 40 per cent nonvoters; our chances: excellent." [20] Sociological and demoscopic analyses of the NPD reservoir offer a wide leeway, but they confirm without exception that in proportional elections the party may get between 15 and 20 per cent of the vote, and that a gain of direct votes in potential strongholds cannot be ruled out. In 1967, the proportion in hundreds of communities exceeded 20 per cent, as for example in 198 communities in Rhineland-Palatinate and 342 in Lower Saxony. Still greater is the number of protest votes which, in the absence of other oppositional alternatives, might be cast for the NPD in socio-economically threatened regions, just as in 1932–33 many of the unemployed shuttled back and forth between the NSDAP and the KPD.

A glance at the social and political background of the NPD voters and the existing reservoir of a radical Right party with National Socialist overtones does not preclude such predictions. In its 1967 program, the NPD appealed to the "peasantry, middle class, skilled workers, and daring, independent entrepreneurs."[21] And, in fact, election results show similarities with the last stages of the Weimar Republic, with voters in middle-class regions manifesting a greater inclination for right-wing radicalism. Small businessmen, lower-and middle-level white-collar workers, civil servants, and self-employed persons are disproportionately well represented among the NPD supporters, members, and candidates. Although the NPD has not been as successful as was the NSDAP after 1929 in appealing to the peasantry, it nonetheless has been able to make contacts with the German Peasants' Association, whose powerful chairman, Edmund Rehwinkel, threatened to throw his support to the NPD when the Government contemplated a cut in farm subsidies. The agricultural crisis undoubtedly has opened up another potential, similar to that which the NSDAP was able to mobilize so successfully. An intensified propaganda campaign helped to make the NPD known in the rural regions as well, an effort rewarded by the electoral successes scored in April, 1968, in Baden-Württemberg.

The traditional weakness of right-wing radicalism in the large cities, and particularly among the industrial workers, no longer constitutes an adequate counterweight. The fact that the workers have the same aspirations as the middle class and behave in like manner has affected

---

[20] *Deutsche Nachrichten*, February 3, 1967, p. 9.
[21] *Politik in unserer Zeit*, p. 6.

this traditional situation. In the provincial parliamentary elections of 1967 the SPD held its own, while in the elections of 1968 it suffered substantial losses. Opinion polls during that period showed that the NPD was making substantial inroads among workers. Moreover, the NPD found itself operating under more favorable conditions than those of the NSDAP in the Weimar Republic, which was confronted with a strong Left alternative (SPD *plus* KPD) with a more developed class-consciousness. The briefness of the time since its founding and the decline of the NPD since the fall of 1969 make exact findings difficult, but there can be no doubt that the NPD resembled the NSDAP both in membership and electorate. As far as working-class participation is concerned, the NPD seemed to be in an even more favorable position.

The continuity was also apparent with regard to regional differences. In the Bavarian parliamentary elections of November, 1966, the NPD concentrated its efforts on the former Nazi stronghold of Central Franconia, and it did in fact manage to exceed the 10 per cent vote needed to enter the Munich parliament by 2.2 per cent. Individual returns hint at future growth: Nuremberg, 13 per cent; Schwalbach, 13.5 per cent; Ansbach-Land, 14.9 per cent; Hersbruck, 15.3 per cent; Neustadt-Aisch, 16.8 per cent. In Upper Franconia's Bayreuth, the mecca of the Richard Wagner cult, the continuity of the radical Right was also apparent (13.9 per cent). The former Nazi strongholds in Upper and Central Hesse, in the Palatinate and Lower Saxony, and in northern Württemberg-Hohenlohe present a similar picture. All of these are mixed middle-class and agrarian regions whose population, now as then, shows great susceptibility to the appeals of the radical Right. But substantial breakthroughs were also made in the large cities (Stuttgart, Mannheim, Nuremberg). Initially, the NPD, as the NSDAP earlier, was least successful in industrial and Catholic rural regions. Early demoscopic surveys concluded that Catholic and trade-union ties offered the greatest obstacle to the parties of the radical Right. But today these ties no longer have the same force as in the days of Weimar. True, the Protestants furnish the majority of NPD followers, and the party has made least progress in Catholic areas. But much depends on the attitude of the Church, and in some instances it has even supported the NPD. Thus in November, 1966, voters of the Würzburg diocese were urged to oust the anticlerical FDP from the provincial parliament and to vote for the NPD. Also, the number of Catholics who obey Church instructions is diminishing; in general, the SPD in Catholic rural regions has profited from this development, but it may benefit other parties as well.

Some further observations are essential to an evaluation of the NPD and its chances. Despite the missed opportunities to institute far-reaching reforms, the situation at the universities and colleges has changed; the institutions of higher education no longer present the same openings for right-wing radicalism. The number of students and professors open to modern social and political ideas and critical of nationalist slogans is greater than in the Weimar era. In the summer of 1967, only 2 per cent of students polled favored the NPD. The efforts for political education seem to have been remarkably successful here.

The same cannot be said of the Army, where the danger of a relapse from the reform of progressive generals like Count Baudissin into pre-democratic traditions looms large. The appeal of the NPD to the soldierly qualities of the Germans has met with favor. Thus the activities of Wolfgang Ross, a young Army captain, created quite a stir: Ross was the chief architect of the NPD election campaign in Central Franconia and was elected to the Bavarian parliament. Officers and noncoms (including, of course, some of the "old soldiers") have been very helpful to the new party both as propagandists and as candidates; professional soldiers made up a disproportionate share of the NPD's membership. The seductive powers of authoritarian ideology lend themselves particularly well to exploiting the tension between an open society and a military command structure, between liberal democracy and national-conservative tradition.

The appeal the NPD holds for expellees, who no longer have their own party to represent them, is not surprising. No one sounded the slogan "the right to the homeland" (*Recht auf Heimat*) or the demand for border revision more loudly than the NPD, which even went beyond the official position on the reinstitution of Germany's 1937 borders. Not surprisingly, the party made substantial electoral inroads in areas with strong expellee populations. In Kaufbeuren (Bavaria), for example, the expellee district of "New Gablonz" furnished the majority of NPD voters and helped the party win 14.8 per cent of the votes. The Bavarian parliamentary list of the NPD also contained many more expellee politicians, mostly Sudeten Germans, than other parties; they call for border reform beyond the 1937 boundaries and seek to win the support of the younger generation, despite all efforts to "integrate" the expellees. Parallel to the spirit of nationalism and revisionism, parallel to the pro-Arab, anti-Israel brand of anti-Semitism, is the anti-Slavism supported by anti-Bolshevism, once such an essential part of Hitler's thinking and of National Socialist ideology.

The voters of the NPD were drawn not only from the reservoir of splinter groups and nonvoters, but in growing measure from the three major parties. As before 1933, bourgeois liberalism, now represented by the FDP, has been the major victim. But the CDU, which has the farm vote, also stands in danger of losing voters to the NDP, as does the SPD. As a radical protest movement against socio-economic crises, the NPD nourished the hope of winning working- and middle-class voters not only in Rhineland-Palatinate and Baden-Württemberg but also in industrial regions like the Ruhr. The vague program, ideology, propaganda, and social structure of the NPD are, as had been the case with the NSDAP, attuned to the "panic of the middle class," to its fear of the threat from above (capitalism) and from below (socialism). The lesson of 1923 and 1930—that German voters threatened by crisis tend toward the Right rather than the Left—has not been refuted. In addition, social change has weakened the immunity of the Catholic and Socialist voters, the twin barriers to the rise of National Socialism, and the potential for susceptibility has been increased by the expellees and the professional soldiers (who under Weimar were supposed to be "unpolitical"). An interim balance sheet of the pseudo crisis of 1967 arrived at this conclusion: "The depoliticization of the broad mass of the population has reached such proportions in the Federal Republic that even a minor disturbance of the hitherto boundless confidence in the durability of the economic miracle is sufficient to cause panic reactions." [22]

The members and voters of the NPD continue to include a great number of former Nazis who fill most of its leading positions, particularly in the areas of ideology, propaganda, public speaking, and speechwriting. "Old fighters" and Nazi functionaries are amply represented. Contrary to the claims of the NPD (and unlike the NSDAP), the younger generation is not yet as well represented as the middle-aged voters, who were active in the Third Reich or at least had come of age under National Socialism. The forty-five to sixty-year-olds constitute the strongest group; those under thirty the weakest. The NPD appeals particularly to the middle-aged combat soldiers of World War II, just as it seeks to win over the younger members of today's Army with its militaristic slogans. Though this differs from the Weimar situation, it comes rather late. In this respect, the NPD does not find itself in as favorable a position as did the NSDAP. Although a male party like the NSDAP (the ratio of men to women is approximately 10 to 6), it is anything but a party of youth; the average age of its members is higher than that of the other parties.

These factors, though responsible for the strength and continuity of the Nazi element in the NPD, at the same time show its limits. This became apparent in the general elections of September, 1969, when the party, despite expectations, failed to garner the requisite 5 per cent of the votes and (with 4.3 per cent of the votes) remained excluded from the Bundestag. The party's decline corresponded closely to the general feeling of economic well-being and political progress; it continued in the state diet elections during 1970 and 1971 in Bremen (2.8 per cent), Hamburg (2.7 per cent), Lower Saxony (3.2 per cent), Northrhine-Westphalia (1.1 per cent), Rheinland-Pfalz (2.7 per cent), Saar (3.4 per cent), and Schleswig-Holstein (1.3 per cent). However, the limits of NPD expansion presuppose an intensification in the efforts for a critical and rational political education of young voters and a more determined documentation of credibility of the democratic claims made by the other political parties. Such efforts involve the unequivocal rejection of the nationalistic and authoritarian slogans of the NPD rather than a toying with the fatal illusion that the wind can be taken out of the NPD's sails by indulging a noisy neonationalism. Such a policy only adds grist to the mills of the radical Right, which after all has been far more successful in this area.

[22] Kühnl, *op. cit.*, p. 77.

The real danger lies in the possible contamination of the democratic parties, which in their efforts to compete with the NPD add to the popular political appeal of the slogans of the radical Right. The NPD is a throwback to anachronistic modes of thinking and behavior, a phenomenon of the past, not of the future. And it will remain just that if the primacy of democracy over all nationalist and etatist catchwords is preserved. The NPD is one of those marginal national movements which in the past have claimed to represent a "true," specifically German, democracy. National Socialism, through its pseudo-legal strategy of plebiscitary self-affirmation, also pretended to be such a "true democracy," as opposed to the Western "plutocracies." The NPD, by posing as the pillar of a new national consciousness after "twenty-two years of imposed self-befoulment and self-castigation," as the "organized spearhead" of the "national wave," [23] resorts to the same catchwords and resentments and seeks to mobilize the same groups against democracy and international cooperation as did the National Socialists. If the symptoms of the alliances with, and utilization of, this "national potential" should multiply, then the NPD, even though the situation is very different, can become a threat—even if it only complicates parliamentary decision-making and disturbs the very slow development from the authoritarian and National Socialist past to the establishment of a democratic tradition in Germany. Opinions may differ over the proscription of political parties. However, inasmuch as the constitution of the Federal Republic, drafted to safeguard democracy, has twice been invoked to ban political parties, the perpetuation of the poison of National Socialism by NPD and related organizations, albeit camouflaged, offers sufficient grounds for checking it in time. If this is not done, the logical conclusion is that such organizations are accepted as democratic and their "legality" tactics taken at face value, even according to the strict yardsticks of the Basic Law. History teaches.

GERMANY AND NATIONAL SOCIALISM

This survey, which began with the precursors of National Socialism and the antidemocratic movements of Germany and Austria and ends with the offshoots and new attempts of the present, spans more than a century. The repercussions of the Nazi movement and its rule in Germany and Europe were felt even in the shadow of the Cold War and the rapid changes of political and social structures. Scattered throughout the world, countless of its victims and many of its perpetrators are still alive. And the presuppositions which made possible the birth and rise of National Socialism have not disappeared altogether. Nationalism and racism, authoritarianism and imperialism, have remained problems to this day.

This holds true particularly for divided Germany. In West Germany,

[23] *Deutsche Nachrichten*, February 17, 1967.

the motive forces of National Socialism have been pushed back; in East Germany, they have been covered over by an authoritarian system. But the social crisis which at the turn of the century brought forth fascism and National Socialism out of radical nationalism has not been mastered. The process by which modes of behavior and thinking are changed is indeed slow and lags behind political events; the fear of crises makes visible the social and ideological potential inherent in radical Right movements even after they have been vanquished. The new efforts of the NPD resort to many of the old premises, however shopworn and disreputable: emotional paeans to heroism and soldier-dom, to the rural and simple life; the escape into a reputedly better past, and its counterpart, the promotion of an irrational feeling of dis-may over modern society and normal political life; cultural pessimism and demonization of everything alien, and authoritarian disdain for compromise and peaceful solutions. Even today these are the positions from which the "national opposition," clad in pseudo-democratic garb, launches its attack on modern democracy—that allegedly un-German, artificial, soulless essence of a dreaded modernization.

History has reduced to absurdity many of the historical presupposi-tions which made possible the rise of National Socialism, particularly in the area of international politics. National Socialism contributed considerably not only to an even more decisive refutation of Germany's great-power claim than happened in World War I, but also to the replacement of Europe as the center of the structure of international politics by two superpowers, with the European countries playing only a secondary role. The type of autarkic nationalist foreign policy preva-lent in the nineteenth century and the era of the world wars has become a fiction, and not even the potential of highly developed indus-trial states like France or Germany can alter that. International economic and social contacts have created a nexus of interests on both sides of the no longer hermetically sealed Iron Curtain in which the national-expansionist ambitions of the middle countries as well as absolute sovereignty have become anachronistic illusions.

Yet the internal presuppositions of National Socialism still exist, above all the unsolved problem of the national state. This latter issue will continue to convert every European political crisis into a potential crisis of democracy in Germany as long as the solution of the German problem remains focused on the creation of a national state. More-over, the truism that history does not repeat itself and that the inter-national situation has changed fails to deal with the problem of the survival of National Socialism. The internal factors that made pos-sible the origin of that movement are still with us—the social and ideological feelings of imminent crisis, antidemocratic and *völkisch*-nationalist emotions, authoritarianism and antimodernism, and finally, the technical possibilities of the total organization of state and society. It is undoubtedly true that without Hitler and his successful forging of the diverse components of an antidemocratic movement into the seemingly monolithic structure of the leader party and leader government, the phenomenon of the German dictatorship could not have come to pass. The various political, sociological, and intellectual analyses of National Socialism explain the *realization* of this totalitarian rule only in the context of the presuppositions of the leader dictatorship. This, however, arose and died with Hitler. Alan Bullock's classic biography of Hitler quite rightly refers to traditional tyrannies which rest in large part on the demagogically manipulated alliance between a leader and social groups threatened by crisis. In the Third Reich, this emotional alliance drew sustenance in no small measure from the invocation of popular resentments: of capitalism, foreigners, and Jews, of a class society and a feudal elitist structure, of educational privileges and "intellectualism." It considered itself revolutionary even though for the most part it served to cement the existing order.

The phenomenon of the German dictatorship is at present being discussed in two major contexts: within the framework of a renaissance of the fascist idea of the 1920's and 1930's, and in the debate about the totalitarian idea of the war and postwar eras. The explanations and interpretations coming out of this continuing controversy mirror not only the progress made in the study of National Socialism, but also the trends of a political debate on the problem of dictatorship in an age of universal democratization. The current theory of fascism takes up the arguments explaining the crisis and overthrow of the democracies that came into being in 1918, particularly under the impact of Mussolini's takeover. Under the changed conditions of the second postwar era, this theory serves as a generalizing evaluation both of the past "epoch of fascism" as well as of continuing and new radical Right tendencies, especially as the doubts about the validity of former theories of totalitarianism multiplied in the post-Stalin era.[24]

The strength of the theory of fascism is at the same time its weakness. It offers a comprehensive theoretical explanation of the conditions and structure of antidemocratic movements and systems, thus making possible a comparison and categorization of similar phenomena in various countries. And it cannot be denied that in the interwar period as well as in the early postwar years, comparable manifestations of right-wing extremism cropped up under very different political and socio-economic preconditions. All had in common an anti-Communist direction and a destructive utilization of bourgeois democracy.

But inherent in these parallels are the difficulties of trying to establish a generalized concept of fascism. These are threefold. As an idea

---

[24] In addition to the works of Ernst Nolte and Eugen Weber, see also Iring Fetscher, "Faschismus und Nationalsozialismus. Zur Kritik des sowjetmarxistischen Faschismusbegriffs," *PVS*, III (1962), 42 ff.; Wolfgang Sauer, "National Socialism: Totalitarianism or Fascism?," *American Historical Review*, LXXIII (1967), 404 ff. Cf. the interesting theory of fascism as development dictatorship, in A. James Gregor, *The Ideology of Fascism* (New York, 1969).

of political militancy, which Communist polemics in particular tries to extend to established democracies as well, fascism is hard to delimit. It deals with numerous transitional forms of authoritarian rule which bear little or no resemblance to the model of Italian, let alone German, "fascism": Unsolved problems are posed by the attempt to categorize Iberian, Balkan, and Latin American dictatorships, to differentiate between "classical" military dictatorships, oligarchies, or antidemocratic fledgling dictatorships, from the interwar period to the Greek, Arabic, and African military and one-party states of the present day. Another difficulty arises from the fact that the socio-economic explanations have to be very broad to permit the inclusion of the various types of right-wing dictatorships in one causal formula. And finally, in subsuming the process by which ideologies are formed and political positions are concretized in systems with very different national traditions and frames of reference under general sociopsychological concepts like "authoritarian" or "fascist syndrome," one loses sight of the specific characteristics of right-wing extremism.

The undifferentiated concept of fascism also ignores the fact that we are dealing with a radical nationalist movement which neither ideologically, politically, nor socially recognized any overlapping international connections. Its various shapes were the product of specific national conditions that are not readily comparable or exportable. The attempt to arrive at a generally valid definition of fascism (anti-Marxism, antiliberalism, extreme nationalism, oligarchical capitalism, dirigism or guided society) creates even more problems and when concretely applied to new-style dictatorships is even more questionable than the attempt of the theory of totalitarianism formally to determine features and methods of dictatorial rule. The theory of totalitarianism is more comprehensive and able to make comparative evaluations of the functional structures of ideologically and socio-economically diverse movements and governments; yet at the same time, it is less able to interpret the goals, content, and above all, presuppositions and genesis of modern dictatorships. The weaknesses and limits of general ideas are obvious: neither the theory of fascism nor the theory of totalitarianism, both of which lend themselves to political abuse, fully live up to their claim of furnishing a common denominator for *the* phenomenon of dictatorship in the twentieth century, just as no general theory of communism can deal with the changing realities of present-day dictatorships of the Left. Only if the limitations of these general theories are kept in mind do they offer yardsticks for comparative studies: the concept of fascism should be applied to uncover the interplay of right-wing dictatorship and bourgeois democracy in crisis-ridden parliamentary and capitalist systems, and the concept of totalitarianism, to illuminate structural principles in the rule and methods of both right- and left-wing dictatorships so opposed to the political process in pluralistic, multiparty democracies.

The wide-ranging debate has had the laudable effect of fostering a more critical approach toward the random application of the concept of totalitarianism to modern dictatorships.[25] A similar critical stance should also govern the theory of fascism. However, any analysis of the Nazi dictatorship must deal with the totalitarian components in its self-view and methods and weigh them against other systems. A more differentiated study of totalitarianism which refutes the cliché about its monolithic, conflict-free reign will discover substantial differences between totalitarian and traditional autocratic governments or dictatorships—in both the Third Reich and the Stalinist regime, the two "classic" manifestations of totalitarian dictatorship. Both show many of the same vital characteristics: an absolute, exclusive ideology with revolutionary pretensions; the legalization of unrestrained, directed terror along the lines of the friend-foe principle and the exaltation of force in the service of a chiliastically conceived future; monopolistic "control" of power and the simultaneous total direction of society to create the "new man" for this future order; the negation of all social conflict and the suppression of any opposition in the service of a technologically conceived and ideologically sanctioned operative principle; and finally, the abrupt, irrational equation of the rule of an uncontrolled leadership—be it dictator or clique—with the interests of "all," a postulated people's community or a postulated class claiming absolute worth as against individuals and groups. Here no facile distinction between totalitarian and authoritarian systems can be made: dictatorship, whether "fascist" or "communist," will have to be classified according to its totalitarian-revolutionary or authoritarian-traditional elements.[26]

These were the considerations that governed my approach to the German dictatorship. National Socialism came into being and into power under conditions which permitted an alliance between conservative-authoritarian and technicistic, nationalistic, and revolutionary-dictatorial forces. The story of right-wing movements in Germany from their inception to this day is made up of a tangle of different tendencies, groups, and motives which effectively rule out any precise delineation. National Socialism also encompassed the most heterogeneous elements; the prehistory and posthistory of the Hitler movement unfold against a backdrop of far-flung, not easily overseen

---

[25] Cf. the modifications in Carl J. Friedrich, "The Changing Theory and Practice of Totalitarianism," *Il Politico*, XXXIII (1968), 53 ff. Peter Christian Ludz, *Studien und Materialien zur Soziologie der DDR* (Cologne-Opladen, 1964), pp. 19 ff., and *Parteielite im Wandel* (Cologne-Opladen, 1968), pp. 11 ff. Otto Stammer, *Politische Soziologie und Demokratieforschung* (Berlin, 1965), pp. 259 ff.; Herbert J. Spiro, in *International Encyclopedia of the Social Sciences* (New York, 1968), XVI, 106 ff. Also, Martin Greiffenhagen and Klaus Hildebrandt, in *PVS*, IX (1968); B. Seidel and S. Jenkner (eds.), *Wege der Totalitarismus-Forschung* (Darmstadt, 1968).

[26] An attempt at delimitation has been made by Martin Drath, in Ernst Richert, *Macht ohne Mandat* (2d ed.; Cologne-Opladen, 1963), pp. xxvii ff.

authoritarian emotional forces pitted against liberal-democratic as well as left-wing socialist official and social policies. Conservatism, nationalism, and *völkisch* radicalism are the mainstays of the 150-year-old countermovement that brought forth the ideas of the German dictatorship. They developed in the reaction of the Romantics to the Enlightenment and the French Revolution, to a rapidly changing industrial society, and to the problems of the belated, never-completed German national state.

The ramifications of the phenomenon of the "German Right" were threefold: the specifically German anti-Western ideology, social tensions arising out of anachronistic feudal structures and rapid economic and social emancipation, and a political constitution hemmed in and distorted by the discrepancy between a traditional authoritarian order structure, national-imperial power ambitions, and democratizing multiparty trends. Isolated studies of German intellectual and state history, which have dominated German historiography for a long time, fail to see the complexity of the "German problem." Above all, they fail to point out why the course of the radical Right in Germany, its development and triumph, constitute a special case in international history, why it was unique in its realization, regardless of the importance of parallel developments in the conservatism and fascism of Italy, Spain, the Balkans, or even France.

This holds true not only for the historical considerations discussed in the first chapter of this book. It was borne out by the emergence and development of the Third Reich itself. As the consummation of a German dictatorship both internal and external, National Socialist rule neither followed the Marxist formula of the monopoly-capitalistic counterrevolution nor confirmed the conservative contention that Nazism stems from the radical-democratic consequences of the French Revolution. Finding a tenable explanation is a far more difficult matter. Such an interpretation must beware of the one-track simplifications of both Left and Right, which tend to substitute historical-philosophical schemas for scholarly analysis. But the opposite danger to which German explanations searching for a defense against the incomprehensible are prone must also be avoided—namely, a historical dissection of the fatal event into details, with specific reference to the temporary nature of National Socialism, the attempt to explain it as a product of its time or even apologetically to reduce it to the appearance of an evil genius. This approach dodges the obligation to find an explanation and to prevent a repetition of what has happened, an obligation which National Socialism has imposed on the German people before the entire world.

Thomas Mann has called politics a part of the human existence. The inhumanity of the national-totalitarian regimes also was rooted in the fact that they were essentially unpolitical. They rested on political oppression rather than growth, on an unpolitical commitment to the false idea of race rather than on civic responsibility. Fascism and National Socialism brought this development to its peak, with these consequences:

political coordination and oppression internally, aggression and extermination abroad. It is essential that we recognize that nothing basically new was evolving, that everything that was happening was inherent in the development of nationalism in the nineteenth century. As impermissible as is the attempt to draw a clear line leading, say, from Fichte to Hitler, nationalism toward the turn of the century without any doubt contained the two basic postulates of National Socialist ideology: the doctrine of race and the theory of *Lebensraum*. Their spread is closely connected with the social and economic crises of the great depression of 1873–96. But only in the upheavals of World War I and in the crises of the Weimar Republic could the theorems of extreme nationalism be transplanted from the desks and armchairs into the realm of political reality and become the foundation stones of a system of government. The intellectual as well as economic, the moral as well as sociopsychological causes of this concretization of a political mania will have to be probed far more deeply than they have been if we wish to be better prepared in case of a possible relapse. To limit the probe to the Weimar Republic or the war aims of World War I is a mistake. The entire formative development of the German national consciousness must be called into question if we wish to understand the road to catastrophe. This, and not the refutation of a Nazi ancestor's gallery, is the task confronting any renewal of the national idea in Germany; such a gallery, incidentally, is a German creation, developed, long before foreign critics took up the theme, by the National Socialists and their fellow travelers, when they claimed a direct line leading from Luther via Frederick II and Bismarck to the Third Reich.[27]

The call for a normal, healthy German national consciousness must be preceded by the question of how normal and "healthy" (if this biological concept is at all permissible) are the historical manifestations being invoked. In view of the German experience, the relationship of the national idea to democracy must become the yardstick. National Socialism, which led from nationalism to a ruthless *völkisch* war to racist extermination policies, reduced the absolutely posited national state to absurdity. In its total claim superseding all values, in its imperialist onslaught, in the hegemonic claim of the "core nation," and in the enslavement of non-German peoples, the idea of the national state always reigned supreme; the nationalization, enslavement, or extermination of subjugated peoples, through which the living space of the German nation was expanded, meant that the elastic principle of the national state was, as it were, superimposed on imperialist expansion.

Is it possible to return to a pre-existing situation? Karl Jaspers believes that the brief history of the German national state does not constitute a basis for the renewal of a German national consciousness.

----

[27] Cf. also Hajo Holborn, "Origins and Political Character of Nazi Ideology," *Political Science Quarterly*, LXXIX (1964), pp. 542 ff.

The doubts he voiced in his controversial essay *Freiheit und Wieder-vereinigung* (*Freedom and Reunification;* 1960) remain valid. There is a deep gulf between national consciousness and democracy in Germany. On the other hand, the nationalist counterblow by the peoples oppressed by the Third Reich, namely the expulsion of 12 million Germans in 1945, also raises doubts about the quality and suitability of the principle and idea of the national state. Too much has been destroyed by it. In the early years of the German second democracy, it seemed obvious that " 'national consciousness' was by no means to be considered as 'natural,' but simply as a special historical example of man's effort to gather within definite boundaries." [28] This awareness was part of the supranational political orientation of the immediate postwar era. But when the temptations of the ideas of sovereignty resurfaced, the political problems more and more became intertwined with ideas of a German national state—in the question of reunification, in the sublimating formula of the right to one's homeland, and finally in the slogans of the NPD which a big nationalist publicity campaign had been preparing for years. The real danger lies in the tendency shared by the major parties to adjust to a "national wave" and to concede the failed effort to establish a German national state fresh ammunition at the expense of democracy. In this respect, it is truly remarkable that the new Brandt Government (1969) has recognized the reality of two German states, though the "continuance of one nation" still poses major problems.

But it may be assumed that the era of the national state does not represent a final stage. The national state as a structural principle of Europe has long ago been called in question. The passion with which the peoples of Asia and Africa, in part in union with a temporarily nationally tinged communism, clothe their striving for independence in national-state forms, almost in the nature of an effort to catch up, will in the long run not disguise the fact that nationalism and the principle of national sovereignty are merely transitional phases. Nationalism offered long suppressed and newly awakened intellectual and political forces a chance to break through, to liquidate rigid forms of government, and established a firm, contemporary framework for the adjustment of political structures to a rapidly changing economy and society, particularly in the nineteenth century. But in the long run a democratic policy can prevail only if nationalism is subjected to democratic principles, to accommodation and compromise, and within a larger framework is limited to its constructive aspects. The German experience has shown that the idea of internal freedom can be throttled by the striving for national unity and a nationalist foreign policy. This should serve as a warning example for the "latecomer" nations and spare the United Nations the fate of the League of Nations, which was murdered by the selfishness of its members. The supranational conflict

[28] Christian Graf von Krockow, "Nationalbewusstsein und Gesellschafts-bewusstsein," *PVS*, I (1960), 143.

of ideologies which breaks through all historical and ethnic boundaries has eroded national sovereignties and the concomitant concept of loyalty. True, present-day national-communist tendencies show that national feelings have remained a significant political factor; the appeal to national feelings remains an effective instrument of rule even in this age of supranational, ideological conflicts, even when this rule may have broken through or abused the classical national idea. Hans Kohn has this to say about contemporary nationalism: "At one time it was a great life-promoting force, a spur to the growth of man; today it can turn into an obstacle to human progress." In the developing countries, nationalism perhaps might still be "an element of human progress." But "today, at least in the West, man's individual freedom must be organized on a supranational basis. Democracy and industrialism, the two forces which grew along with nationalism and spread out across the world, have both outgrown national ties." [29]

If other countries today face problems similar to Germany's or show even greater evidence of traditional nationalism, this cannot serve as justification, let alone as an example. Germany's position at the intersection of the East-West confrontation offers little prospect that ideologies of a national state will bring solutions. Instead, the second German republic relies on furthering a critical civic consciousness understood as consciousness of the value, rights, and duties of the citizen in a democracy, as the expression of a democratic awareness. Anything else brings with it the danger that political thinking, as was the case after 1848 and 1918, once again will turn from the concrete to the unrealistic. Thus the problem of "reunification" no longer is primarily a problem of the national state but of democracy and of supranational cooperation.

In political practice and in the efforts for political education, the question of the relationship between national consciousness and democracy can be answered in two ways. Consciousness means "clarity, self-criticism, sobriety, a sense of reality, rationality." Internally, it calls for participation in the development of a libertarian-democratic, social community, and toward the outside, for the recognition of the true situation and the possibilities in the modern world. A politically mature, "enlightened national conscience" does not see the "adolescent beginnings" of the German national state as a "model on which to orient ourselves." "If it can be defined at all, then only from the vantage point of the future." [30] Whereas the old national idea emphasized divisiveness, the present demands that nationalism everywhere be replaced by an international policy attuned to the rules of democracies, to discussion and compromise. This would meet the need for a universal domestic policy resulting from the increasingly closer interrelation of international life, which today is determined not so much by the

[29] Hans Kohn, "Das Wesen des Nationalismus," *Das Parlament*, February 14, 1962, Appendix.
[30] Thus Georg Picht, "Grundlagen eines neuen deutschen Nationalbewusstseins," *Merkur*, No. 21 (1967), pp. 4 ff.

rivalries of national states as "by the competition of social systems and systems of government." [31] So long as even democratic foreign policy is primarily attuned to ideas of national sovereignty, so long as nationalism and national egotism emphasize the differences between states, the unifying and moderating tendencies of democracy will not be able to blossom. It is true, a European or Atlantic communal consciousness cannot simply become a substitute for a nonexistent German national state. In view of the reverses suffered by the idea of European integration that would be a dubious matter. But supranationalism will be in step with international developments if war ceases to be an instrument of politics and if the mutual interdependence of states replaces ideas of nationalist sovereignty and autarky that cannot cope with the tasks of modern economy and society. Even Raymond Aron, while sympathetic to Gaullism, is of the opinion that those who see national units as the only lasting historical entities unwittingly put "the seal of eternity on the historical philosophy of the nineteenth century." And so conservative a historian as Hans Rothfels has called the past epoch an "exceptional period of nationalism." [32] Why for once should Germany not be among those with progressive national ideas instead of again following along the path of backward ideologies?

More immediate, of course, is the internal problem in the development of democracy of converting national consciousness into political consciousness, demonstrated by a concern for social and educational problems and a readiness to support a credible democracy and oppose authoritarian tendencies. Every German has heard the worried question by foreign observers about how he would act in case the rights and dignity of individuals were again at stake as in 1933, when personal choices and civil courage were needed. The personal and civic courage at issue presupposes a political education that offers understanding and knowledge, not only beliefs, and in any case goes far beyond a mere national education.

The basis of such efforts is a stronger, credible democracy. This means a higher degree of political participation and a sense of responsibility for the free interplay of the various social forces. Such an identification with democracy is still lacking. Pride in its institutions and its functioning must be awakened, pride that democracy is the opposite not only of dictatorship but also of authoritarianism. Here the inroads of government and administration along predemocratic lines governed solely by considerations of administrative efficiency create a problem. The warning signals are the diminishing power of parliament and preferences for a guided society instead of a pluralistic, open democracy. The result may be a still greater depoliticization and the concomi-

[31] Manfred Hättich, *Nationalbewusstsein und Staatsbewusstsein* (Mainz, (1966), p. 84.

[32] Raymond Aron, *Peace and War: A Theory of International Relations* (New York, 1966); Hans Rothfels, *Zeitgeschichtliche Betrachtungen* (Göttingen, 1959), pp. 55 ff.

tant danger of opening up room for pseudo-political authoritarian-nationalistic movements. Instead of revising the constitution to achieve greater efficiency at the expense of parliamentary democracy, instead of extending political command centers, as Carl Schmitt's disciples, who confuse politics with administration and authority, are demanding, the democratic-parliamentary process should be improved. "The national consciousness must become social consciousness," [33] particularly in divided Germany; it must be understood as a concrete effort for a more just social order, because "it is the lack, not of a strong sense of nationhood, but of a cohesive and confident society in Germany that weighs so heavily on her recent history." [34] After the aberrations of German nationalism, social and political consciousness could open up the way to democracy and put an end to the long history of the unpolitical citizen. Only then will we Germans have grasped the opportunity which the defeat of 1945 has given us. Only then will Thomas Mann's debatable declaration of 1918 no longer apply: "I declare my deep conviction that the German people will never be able to love political democracy for the simple reason that they cannot love politics, and that the much-decried *Obrigkeitsstaat* is and will remain the form of government suited to, deserved, and basically desired by the German people." [35]

And Mann's gloomy forecast of 1945 can be refuted only if the concept of freedom in Germany is not again directed toward the outside but understood and realized as a "moral domestic concept," and if Germans develop a concept of nationhood "which, incorporating the idea of humanity, in domestic affairs means freedom and in foreign affairs, Europe." [36]

The fear of the "restless Germans" lives on in the world. The problem of the German national state has not been solved; the susceptibility to crisis reactions, which the "economic miracle" only covered over, was evidenced by the rise of the NPD in 1966–68; there is still the trend toward a self-pitying, stubborn idea of self-worth which complains of an "unending fascination with the horrors of the Hitler dictatorship" (Gerhard Ritter) and instead of a "perpetual expiatory Germandom" asks for a "greater national consciousness" (Franz-Joseph Strauss).[37] What has also remained is a tendency toward a horrified rejection of political differences, the glorification of order and effectiveness, the denigration of pluralism and opposition in favor of a patriarchal chancellor democracy or a Grand Coalition "above" the parties. But even the principled opposition of the extraparliamentary New Left,

---

[33] Krockow, *op. cit.*, p. 152.

[34] Ralf Dahrendorf, *Society and Democracy in Germany* (Garden City, N.Y., 1967), pp. 274–75.

[35] Thomas Mann, "Betrachtungen eines Unpolitischen," in *Politische Schriften und Reden* (Frankfurt/Main, 1968), I, 23.

[36] Mann, "Deutschland und die Deutschen," in *ibid.* III, 170.

[37] Gerhard Ritter, in letters on the Spiegel affair, in *Frankfurter Allgemeine Zeitung*, November 10 and 16, 1962; Franz-Joseph Strauss, in *Der Stern*, No. 1, 1967.

which castigates such remnants of authoritarianism in the thinking and behavior of a "postfascist" society, has not shed the traditional traits of German political thinking if, beyond the liberal and parliamentary reality of libertarian democracy, it aspires to the allegedly more consistent but in fact dictatorial perfection of a "total" democracy.

The survival of prefascist and authoritarian conditions and modes of behavior is closely connected with the refusal to accept historical experience. However, the frantic efforts to "master the past" have at times also led to an unhistorical blindness toward reality. The radical Right continues in its pride in authoritarian tradition and minimizes the failure of the German dictatorship; a radical Left responds with the renewed belief that "true democracy" can be realized only through revolutionary violence and a transitional dictatorship.

The growing force of these two tendencies, which under adverse conditions might conjure up the dilemma of the first German republic, calls for strong countereffort. The most promising approach in counteracting such a development includes political education by way of unrestricted information and enlightenment, and via an authentic democratization instead of the popular appeal to state ideology and national consciousness. For too long have plaints over the undeserved fate of Germany, in which leading politicians have chimed in, deflected public attention from the causes and realities of the German problem. In Germany, general familiarity with the 150-year history of travail of German democracy is still in the beginning stage. Attempts to break through the limits of conservative-national interpretation become "self-defilement"—witness the reaction of leading German historians to critical studies like Fritz Fischer's well-known books on German aims and responsibilities in World War I—or they are charged with "unhistorical" contemporaneousness if they seek to discuss lines leading from the development of authoritarian and nationalist structures of absolutism and the Bismarckian state to the Third Reich.

The demand for political reform and democratization is closely allied with these problems. Because the Federal Republic has claimed that it rests on the continuity of the German national state and even the Reich, the second German democracy must stand and fall with the awareness of the consequences of 1871 and 1914, of 1933 and 1945. Not too much but too little democracy, not the danger from the Left but from the Right, have led to catastrophe.

The Adenauer era offered little more than a transitional solution. By combining democratic and authoritarian elements, Adenauer's chancellor democracy bridged the gap between the vacuum of defeat and a stable system of government; for the first time, Germans were shown that parliamentary democracy can bring security and economic progress. But the rapidly growing identification with the system of the chancellor democracy was made possible also because basic political problems (reunification, the eastern border, social reforms) were shelved, and because Adenauer's style perpetuated an unpolitical, bureaucratic-authoritarian tradition which many critics felt was reminiscent of the Wilhelminian era. Political participation and a voice in government were limited to elections; political education was relegated to formal courses in governmental institutions or diverted to the black-and-white categories of the Cold War. What was lacking was a testing by example, the experience of governmental crises, which when mastered prove the superiority of a mature democracy over authoritarian ideas of order; what was lacking was the preparation for a time of normalization in which political acceptance is no longer won via the simplified alignments of the Cold War, when democratic consensus can no longer base itself on an overriding anti-Communism.

The weaknesses of a system which put off important vital problems, preserved or restored authoritarian structures, and in large measure depoliticized public life were bound to emerge. When conditions changed in the 1960's and a postwar generation began to question old forms, the inevitable reaction set in: after Adenauer's departure, demands for internal reform and in the end attacks on the "system" began to mount. Shades of Weimar loomed.[38] A chancellor who had conducted politics in the highly personal style and along the authoritarian lines accepted since the days of Bismarck and Hindenburg was no longer there. The transition to normalcy showed up the problems which even so stable a multiparty system, in comparison with Weimar, experienced in its efforts to integrate the political and social mobility into the political process and to realize fundamental, long-overdue social and educational reforms. The Grand Coalition of 1966 was in no small measure an expression of this problem, and its by-product—NPD and extraparliamentary opposition—show the extent to which a past not mastered is still alive: in the fear of crisis and in an ideology of order, in slogans of unity and utopias of perfection.

The Weimar Republic collapsed fourteen years after the end of World War I. Almost twice as many years have passed since the end of World War II. The Federal Republic is already one-and-a-half times as old as the Weimar Republic. This would seem to speak not only for its stability, but also for the expectation that adjustment to a better-functioning system of parliamentary democracy will bring about a firmer entrenchment of democratic consciousness and the acceptance of the political system that was so sadly lacking from 1918 to 1933. But more probing polls and studies indicate that election results and external stability do not automatically assure strong democratic feeling. Susceptibility to economic and social crises has survived, and it has led to the justification of a questionable Grand Coalition and at the same time brought forth right- and left-wing antisystem movements. With the changed conditions in the international situation, the crisis in the reunification idea, and the emergence of a new generation, the un-

[38] Cf. Bracher, "Wird Bonn doch Weimar?," *Der Spiegel*, March 13, 1967, pp. 60 ff., and *Das deutsche Dilemma* (Munich, 1971). See also Alfred Grosser, *Deutschlandbilanz* (Munich, 1970).

finished, problematical aspects of the Bonn democracy are becoming evident.

Here the year 1969 meant an important turning point. Forty-four years after the death of Friedrich Ebert in 1925, a Social Democrat, Gustav Heinemann, became head of state. And after two decades of Christian Democrat leadership the country was able to pass the democratic test of a complete change of government. In 1930, the fall of Chancellor Hermann Müller (SPD) paved the way to the end of the first German Republic; now the election of a Social Democrat Chancellor, Willy Brandt, signalled the end of the postwar era. It was a test of the stability of the Bonn Republic as a parliamentary democracy—fully capable of a constitutional change between government and opposition and of opening the way to political alternatives. The democratic test of government change was significant also in view of the fact that the new Chancellor, an émigré with an antifascist and internationalist record, persecuted by the Third Reich and often defamed by nationalist propaganda during the fifties and sixties, had gained considerably in sympathy and respect during the previous years. The leadership of Heinemann-Brandt signifies a further step on the long road of mastering the heritage of the German past. This involves domestic and social reforms but also an Eastern policy prepared to recognize the consequences of 1945 with regard to the German and border questions. Only by discarding the provisional arrangement of the unfulfilled national state will the Second Republic be able to achieve the definitive arrangement of a libertarian-social democracy that has cast off the shadows of 1870, 1918, and 1933.

The German dictatorship has failed, but German democracy has not yet been secured. Securing it remains a task that demands full awareness that the road to a real and realistic democratization is a narrow one, still strewn with many obstacles. It runs between the continuing burden of the past and the increased demands of the future, between the threats of an authoritarian tradition and the exaggerated promises of ideological right- and left-wing radicalism which prevented the maturing of democracy in Germany and paved the way for the most terrible dictatorship mankind has known. The heritage of National Socialism lives on—negatively in the dangers of a relapse, positively in the opportunities of an educational process drawing on the experience of the past. In this special situation Germany—West and East— will have to live as long as national sovereignty and ideological cleavages remain the motive forces in contemporary political life. But the conditions and perspectives of the second democracy are infinitely better than before 1933: Bonn is not Weimar.

Bibliography

Since 1953, the Bibliography of Contemporary History under the editorship of Thilo Vogelsang, published as a supplement to the *Vierteljahrshefte für Zeitgeschichte (VfZG)*, has been the standard current source on the growing body of literature on National Socialism. For the preceding years, see F. Herre and H. Auerbach, *Bibliographie zur Zeitgeschichte und zum Zweiten Weltkrieg für die Jahre 1945–1950* (Munich, 1955).

The following selection of the most important works on the subject follows the subdivisions of this book.

I. THE PRECONDITIONS

PROBLEMS OF INTERPRETATION

ARENDT, HANNAH. *Origins of Totalitarianism.* New York: Harcourt, Brace, 1951.

Autoritarismus und Nationalismus—ein deutsches Problem? (Politische Psychologie 2). Frankfurt/M., 1963.

BRACHER, K. D. *Deutschland zwischen Demokratie und Diktatur.* Bern and Munich, 1964.

BOSSENBROOK, WILLIAM J. *The German Mind.* Detroit, Mich.: Wayne State University Press, 1961.

BROSZAT, MARTIN. *Der Nationalsozialismus.* Stuttgart, 1960. Published in English as *German National Socialism: 1919–1945.* Santa Barbara, Calif.: Clio Press, 1966.

BUTLER, ROHAN D'OLIER. *The Roots of National Socialism, 1783–1933.* London: Faber & Faber, 1941.

CRAIG, GORDON A. *The Politics of the Prussian Army: 1640–1945.* New ed. Oxford: Clarendon Press, 1964.

FETSCHER, IRING. "Faschismus und Nationalsozialismus," *Politische Vierteljahresschrift,* No. 3 (1962).

FRIEDRICH, CARL J. *Totalitarian Dictatorship and Autocracy.* Cambridge, Mass.: Harvard University Press, 1956.

GLUM, FRIEDRICH. *Der Nationalsozialismus.* Munich, 1962.

———. *Philosophen im Spiegel und Zerrspiegel.* Munich, 1954.

GREBING, HELGA. *Der Nationalsozialismus.* Munich, 1959.

HOFER, WALTHER, ed. *Der Nationalsozialismus.* Frankfurt/M., 1958.

JACOBSEN, H. A., and JOCHMANN, W., eds. *Ausgewählte Dokumente zur Geschichte des Nationalsozialismus.* Bielefeld, 1961.

LUKÁCZ, GEORG. *Die Zerstörung der Vernunft.* Berlin, 1954. Neuwied, 1962.

MEINECKE, FRIEDRICH. *Die deutsch Katastrophe.* Wiesbaden, 1946. Published in English as *The German Catastrophe: Reflections and Recollections.* Cambridge, Mass.: Harvard University Press, 1950.

NEUMANN, FRANZ L. *Behemoth. The Structure and Practice of National Socialism: 1933–1944.* 2d ed. New York and Toronto: Oxford University Press, 1944.

———. *The Democratic and the Authoritarian State: Essays in Political and Legal Theory.* Ed. HERBERT MARCUSE. Glencoe, Ill.: The Free Press, 1957.

NEUMANN, SIGMUND. *Permanent Revolution.* 2d ed. New York: Praeger, 1965.

RITTER, GERHARD. *Staatskunst und Kriegshandwerk.* 4 vols. Munich, 1954. Published in English as *Sword and Scepter: The Problem of Militarism in Germany.* 2 vols. Miami, Fla.: University of Miami Press, 1969.

SAUER, WOLFGANG. "National Socialism: Totalitarianism or Fascism?," in *American Historical Review,* LXXIII (1967).

SHAPIRO, LEONARD. "The Concept of Totalitarianism," in *Survey,* No. 73 (Autumn, 1969).

SHIRER, WILLIAM L. *The Rise and Fall of the Third Reich.* New York: Simon & Schuster; London: Heinemann/Secker & Warburg, 1960.

TALMON, J. L. *The Origins of Totalitarian Democracy.* New York: Praeger; London: Secker & Warburg, 1961.

TAYLOR, A. J. P. *The Course of German History: A Survey of the Development of Germany Since 1815.* London: Hamish Hamilton, 1945.

The Third Reich, A Study Published under the Auspices of the International Council for Philosophy and Humanistic Studies with the Assistance of UNESCO. New York: Praeger, 1955.

VERMEIL, EDMOND. *L'Allemagne contemporaine, sociale, politique et culturelle, 1890–1950.* 2 vols. Paris, 1952–53.

WHITESIDE, ANDREW G. "The Nature and Origins of National Socialism," in *Journal of Central European Affairs,* No. 17 (1957).

THE EUROPEAN BACKGROUND

ALATRI, PAOLO. *Le origini del fascismo.* 3d ed. Rome, 1962.

BAUER, O., MARCUSE, H., and ROSENBERG, A. *Faschismus und Kapitalismus.* Frankfurt/M., 1967.

CARSTEN, FRANCIS L. *The Rise of Fascism.* Berkeley: University of California Press, 1967.

CONRAD-MARTIUS, HEDWIG. *Utopien der Menschenzüchtung.* Munich, 1955.

Faschismus-Nationalsozialismus. Brunswick, 1964.

FAUL, ERWIN. *Der moderne Machiavellismus.* Cologne, 1961.

HUGHES, H. STUART. *Consciousness and Society: The Reorientation of European Social Thought, 1890–1930.* New York: Knopf, 1958.

LAQUEUR, WALTER, and MOSSE, GEORGE L., eds. *International Fascism, 1920–1945.* Magnolia, Mass.: Peter Smith, 1966.

NOLTE, ERNST. *Der Faschismus in seiner Epoche.* Munich, 1963. Published in English as *The Three Faces of Fascism: Action Française, Italian Fascism, and National Socialism.* New York: Holt, Rinehart & Winston, 1966.

———. *Die Krise des liberalen Systems und die faschistischen Bewegungen.* Munich, 1968.

———, ed. *Theorien über den Faschismus.* Cologne, 1967.

PLUMYÈNE, J., and LASIERRA, R. *Les Fascismes français 1923–1963.* Paris, 1963.

ROGGER, HANS, and WEBER, EUGEN J., eds. *The European Right: A Historical Profile.* Berkeley: University of California Press, 1965.

ROTH, JACK J. "Sorel und die totalitären Systeme," in *VfZG,* No. 6 (1958).

WEBER, EUGENE J. *Action Française: Royalism and Reaction in 20th Century France.* Stanford, Calif.: Stanford University Press, 1962.

———. *Varieties of Fascism: Doctrines of Revolution in the 20th Century.* Princeton, N.J.: Van Nostrand, 1964.

WOOLF, S. J., ed. *The Nature of Fascism.* New York: Random House, 1969.

ZMARZLIK, HANS-GÜNTHER. "Der Sozialdarwinismus in Deutschland als geschichtliches Problem," in *VfZG*, No. 11 (1963).

THE PROBLEM OF GERMAN STATEHOOD

BRACHER, K. D. "Staatsbegriff und Demokratie in Deutschland," in *Politische Vierteljahresschrift*, No. 9 (1968).

BUCHHEIM, KARL. *Leidensgeschichte des zivilen Geistes.* Munich, 1951.

DAHRENDORF, RALF. *Gesellschaft und Demokratie in Deutschland.* Munich, 1965. Published in English as *Society and Democracy in Germany.* Garden City, N. Y.: Doubleday, 1967.

FRAENKEL, ERNST. *Deutschland und die westlichen Demokratien.* Stuttgart, 1964.

HALLGARTEN, GEORGE W. F. *Imperialismus vor 1914.* 2d ed. Munich, 1963.

HAMEROW, THEODORE S. *Restoration, Revolution, Reaction. Economics and Politics in Germany 1815–1871.* Princeton, N.J.: Princeton University Press, 1958.

KEHR, ECKART. *Das Primat der Innenpolitik.* Ed. HANS-ULRICH WEHLER. Berlin, 1965.

KOHN, HANS. *The Mind of Germany: The Education of a Nation.* New York: Scribner's, 1960.

KRIEGER, LEONARD. *The German Idea of Freedom.* Boston: Beacon Press, 1957.

PLESSNER, HELMUTH. *Die verspätete Nation. Über die politische Verführbarkeit bürgerlichen Geistes.* Stuttgart, 1959.

PROSS, HARRY. *Die Zerstörung der deutschen Politik. Dokumente 1875–1933.* Frankfurt/M., 1959.

ROSENBERG, HANS. *Bureaucracy, Aristocracy and Autocracy. The Prussian Experience: 1660–1815.* Cambridge, Mass.: Harvard University Press, 1958.

SELL, FRIEDRICH C. *Die Tragödie des deutschen Liberalismus.* Stuttgart, 1953.

STADELMANN, RUDOLF. *Deutschland und Westeuropa.* Laupheim, 1948.

WEHLER, HANS-ULRICH, ed. *Moderne deutsche Sozialgeschichte.* Cologne-Berlin, 1966.

THE GERMAN AND VÖLKISCH SENSE OF SPECIAL DESTINY

CHAMBERLAIN, HOUSTON STEWART. *Die Grundlagen des neunzehnten Jahrhunderts.* Munich, 1899. Published in English as *The Foundations of the Nineteenth Century.* 2 vols. New York: Howard Fertig, 1968. (First English ed., 1911.)

GLASER, HERMANN. *Spiesser-Ideologie.* Freiburg/Br., 1964.

HANCKE, KURT. *Deutscher Aufstand gegen den Westen.* 2d ed. Berlin, 1941.

LOUGEE, ROBERT W. *Paul de Lagarde (1827–1891), A Study of Radical Conservatism in Germany.* Cambridge, Mass.: Harvard University Press, 1962.

MOSSE, GEORGE L. *The Crisis of German Ideology: Intellectual Origins of the Third Reich.* New York: Grosset & Dunlap, 1964.

STERN, FRITZ. *The Politics of Cultural Despair: A Study in the Rise of the Germanic Ideology.* New York: Doubleday, 1961.

THEISEN, HELMUT. *Die Entwicklung zum nihilistischen Nationalismus in Deutschland 1818 bis 1933.* Munich, 1955.

THE TRANSITION TO NATIONAL-IMPERIALIST IDEOLOGY

BAKKER, GEERT. *Duitse Geopolitiek 1919–1945.* Utrecht, 1967.
BÖHME, HELMUT. *Deutschlands Weg zur Grossmacht.* Cologne, 1966.
FISCHER, FRITZ. *Griff nach der Weltmacht.* Düsseldorf, 1961. Published in English as *Germany's Aims in the First World War.* New York: W. W. Norton, 1967.
———. *Krieg der Illusionen.* Düsseldorf, 1969.
HEUSS, THEODOR. *Friedrich Naumann.* 3d ed. Munich and Hamburg, 1968.
HEYDEN, GÜNTER. *Kritik der deutschen Geopolitik.* Berlin, 1958.
KRUCK, ALFRED. *Geschichte des Alldeutschen Verbandes 1890–1939.* Wiesbaden, 1954.
LÜBBE, HERMANN. *Politische Philosophie in Deutschland.* Basel and Stuttgart, 1963.
MANN, THOMAS. *Betrachtungen eines Unpolitischen.* Frankfurt/M., 1956.
MEYER, HENRY CORD. *Mitteleuropa in German Thought and Action 1815–1945.* The Hague, 1955.
PROSS, HARRY. *Die Zerstörung der deutschen Politik 1870–1933.* Frankfurt/M., 1959.
SAUER, WOLFGANG. "Das Problem des deutschen Nationalstaates," in *Moderne deutsche Sozialgeschichte.* Ed. HANS-ULRICH WEHLER. Cologne, 1966.
SULZBACH, WALTER. *Imperialismus und Nationalbewusstsein.* Frankfurt/M., 1959.

THE ROLE OF ANTI-SEMITISM

ADLER, H. G. *Die Juden in Deutschland. Von der Aufklärung bis zum Nationalsozialismus.* Munich, 1960.
ADORNO, TH. W., et al. *The Authoritarian Personality.* New York: Harper, 1950.
ANDICS, HELLMUTH. *Der Ewige Jude. Ursachen und Geschichte des Antisemitismus.* Vienna, 1965.
BEIN, ALEXANDER. "Die Judenfrage in der Literatur des modernen Antisemitismus als Vorbereitung zur 'Endlösung,'" in *Bulletin Leo Baeck Institute,* No. 6 (1963).
BETTELHEIM, BRUNO, and JANOWITZ, MORRIS. *Dynamics of Prejudice.* New York: Harper, 1950.
COHN, NORMAN. *Warrant for Genocide.* London: Eyre & Spottiswoode, 1966; New York: Harper, 1967.
ESSER, HERMANN. *Die jüdische Weltpest.* 6th ed. Munich, 1943.
FRANK, WALTER. *Hofprediger Adolf Stoecker und die christlich-soziale Bewegung.* Berlin, 1928.
FROMM, ERIC. *Escape from Freedom.* New York: Holt, Rinehart, 1941.
HUSS, H., and SCHRÖDER, A., eds. *Antisemitismus.* Frankfurt/M., 1965.
KAMPMANN, WANDA. *Deutsche und Juden.* Heidelberg, 1963.
LESCHNITZER, ADOLF. *The Magic Background of Modern Anti-Semitism: An Analysis of the German-Jewish Symbiosis.* New York: International Universities Press, 1956.
MASSING, PAUL W. *Rehearsal for Destruction: A Study of Political Anti-Semitism in Imperial Germany.* New York: Harper, 1949.
MÜLLER, JOSEF. *Die Entwicklung des Rassenantisemitismus in den letzten Jahrzehnten des neunzehnten Jahrhunderts.* Berlin, 1940.
PULZER, PETER G. *The Rise of Political Anti-Semitism in Germany and Austria: 1867–1918.* New York: John Wiley, 1964.
REICHMANN, EVA G. *Hostages of Civilization: The Social Sources of National Socialist Anti-Semitism.* London: Victor Gollancz, 1950; Boston: Beacon Press, 1951.

ROSENBERG, HANS. *Grosse Depression und Bismarckzeit*. Berlin, 1967.
RUDOLPH, E. V. VON. *Georg Ritter von Schönerer. Der Vater des politischen Antisemitismus*. Munich, 1942.
SILBERNER, EDMUND. *Sozialisten zur Judenfrage*. Berlin, 1962.
THIEME, KARL, ed. *Judenfeindschaft*. Frankfurt/M., 1963.

II. THE ORIGINS OF THE NATIONAL SOCIALIST MOVEMENT

AUSTRIAN PRECURSORS

BIBL, VICTOR. *Der Zerfall Österreichs*. Vienna, 1924.
CILLER, A. *Vorläufer des Nationalsozialismus*. Vienna, 1932.
FUCHS, ALBERT. *Geistige Strömungen in Österreich 1867–1918*. Vienna, 1949.
McGRATH, WILLIAM J. "Wagnerianism in Austria." Unpublished Ph.D. dissertation, University of California, Berkeley, 1965.
MOLISCH, PAUL. *Die deutschen Hochschulen in Österreich und die politisch-national Entwicklung nach 1918*. Munich, 1922.
——. *Geschichte der deutschnationalen Bewegung Österreichs*. Jena, 1926.
PICHL, EDUARD. *Georg von Schönerer und die Entwicklung des Alldeutschtums in der Ostmark*. 3 vols. Oldenburg, 1938.
REDLICH, JOSEF. *Das österreichische Staats- und Reichsproblem*. Leipzig, 1920–26.
SCHORSKE, CARL E. "Politics in a New Key: An Austrian Triptych," in *Journal of Modern History*, XXXIX (1967).
WANDRUSZKA, ADAM. "Österreichs politische Struktur," in *Geschichte der Republik Österreich*. Munich, 1954.
WHITESIDE, ANDREW G. *Austrian National Socialism Before 1918*. The Hague, 1962.

ADOLF HITLER

BULLOCK, ALAN. *Hitler: A Study in Tyranny*. Rev. ed. New York: Harper & Row, 1964.
DAIM, WILFRIED. *Der Mann, der Hitler die Ideen gab*. Munich, 1958.
FRANK, HANS. *Im Angesicht des Galgens. Deutung Hitlers und seiner Zeit auf Grund eigener Erlebnisse und Erkenntnisse*. Munich-Gräfelfing, 1953.
GISEVIUS, HANS BERND. *Adolf Hitler, Versuch einer Deutung*. Munich, 1963.
GÖRLITZ, WALTER, and QUINT, HERBERT A. *Adolf Hitler*. Stuttgart, 1952.
HANFSTAENGL, ERNST. *Hitler, The Missing Years*. London: Eyre & Spottiswoode, 1957.
HEER, FRIEDRICH. *Der Glaube des Adolf Hitler*. Munich, 1968.
HEIBER, HELMUT. *Adolf Hitler*. Berlin, 1960.
HEIDEN, KONRAD. *Adolf Hitler*. Zurich, 1936. Published in English as *Hitler: A Biography*. New York: Knopf, 1936.
——. *Der Fuehrer: Hitler's Rise to Power*. Boston: Houghton Mifflin; London: Victor Gollancz, 1944.
HITLER, ADOLF. *Mein Kampf*. Munich, 1925–28. Published in English under the same title. New ed. Boston: Houghton Mifflin, 1962.
JENKS, WILLIAM A. *Vienna and the Young Hitler*. New York: Columbia University Press, 1960.
JETZINGER, FRANZ. *Hitlers Jugend*. Zurich, 1956. Published in English as *Hitler's Youth*. London, 1958.
KOTZE, H. VON, and KRAUSNICK, H. *Es spricht der Führer*. Gütersloh, 1966.
KUBIZEK, AUGUST. *Adolf Hitler. Mein Jugendfreund*. Graz, 1953.
McRANDLE, JAMES H. *The Track of the Wolf. Essays on National Socialism and Its Leader, Adolf Hitler*. Evanston, Ill.: Northwestern University Press, 1965.

OLDEN, RUDOLF. *Hitler.* Amsterdam, 1936. Published in English as *Hitler, the Pawn.* London: Victor Gollancz, 1936.
RÖHRS, HANS-DIETRICH. *Hitlers Krankheit. Tatsachen und Legenden.* Neckargemünd, 1966.
SMITH, BRADLEY F. *Adolf Hitler: His Family, Childhood, and Youth.* Stanford, Calif.: Hoover Institution, 1967.
WIEDEMANN, FRITZ. *Der Mann, der Feldherr werden wollte.* Velbert, 1964.

PROBLEMS OF THE REVOLUTION AND THE REPUBLIC

BERGHAHN, VOLKER R. *Der Stahlhelm.* Düsseldorf, 1966.
BRACHER, K. D. *Die Auflösung der Weimarer Republik.* 4th ed. Villingen, 1964.
CARSTEN, FRANCIS L. *Reichswehr und Politik 1918–1933.* Cologne, 1964. Published in English as *Reichswehr and Politics: 1918–1933.* London and New York: Oxford University Press, 1966.
DEMETER, KARL. *Das deutsche Offizierkorps in Gesellschaft und Staat 1650–1945.* Frankfurt/M., 1962. Published in English as *The German Officer Corps in Society and State: 1650–1945.* New York: Praeger; London: Weidenfeld & Nicolson, 1965.
ESCHENBURG, THEODOR. *Die improvisierte Demokratie.* Munich, 1963.
EYCK, ERICH. *Geschichte der Weimarer Republik.* Erlenbach and Zurich, 1954–56. Published in English as *A History of the Weimar Republic.* 2 vols. Cambridge, Mass.: Harvard University Press, 1962–63.
FRIEDENSBURG, FERDINAND. *Die Weimarer Republik.* Hanover and Frankfurt/M., 1957.
GAY, PETER. *Weimar Culture: The Outsider as Insider.* New York: Harper & Row, 1968.
GORDON, HAROLD J. *The Reichswehr and the German Republic: 1919–1926.* Princeton, N.J.: Princeton University Press, 1957.
GROENER, WILHELM. *Lebenserinnerungen.* Ed. F. HILLER VON GÄRTRINGEN. Göttingen, 1957.
GROENER-GEYER, DOROTHEA. *General Groener, Soldat und Staatsmann.* Frankfurt/M., 1955.
HEIBER, HELMUT. *Die Republik von Weimar.* Munich, 1967.
JASPER, GOTTHARD. *Der Schutz der Republik.* Tübingen, 1963.
KAUFMANN, WALTER H. *Monarchism in the Weimar Republic.* New York: Twayne, 1953.
KNIGHT, MAXWELL E. *The German Executive: Eighteen Ninety to Nineteen Thirty-Three.* Stanford, Calif.: Stanford University Press, 1952.
KOLB, E., and RÜRUP, R. *Der Zentralrat der Deutschen Sozialistischen Republik.* Leiden, 1968.
KOLB, EBERHARD. *Die Arbeiterräte in der deutschen Innenpolitik 1918–1919.* Düsseldorf, 1962.
NEWMAN, KARL J. *Zerstörung und Selbstzerstörung der Demokratie. Europa 1918–1938.* Cologne, 1965.
OBERMANN, EMIL. *Soldaten, Bürger, Militaristen. Militär und Demokratie in Deutschland.* Stuttgart, 1958.
OERTZEN, FRIEDRICH WILHELM VON. *Die deutschen Freikorps 1918–1923.* 6th ed. Munich, 1930.
OERTZEN, PETER VON. *Betriebsräte in der Novemberrevolution.* Düsseldorf, 1963.
PAETEL, KARL O. *Jugend in der Entscheidung 1913, 1933, 1945.* Godesberg, 1963.
ROSENBERG, ARTHUR. *Entstehung und Geschichte der Weimarer Republik.* Frankfurt/M., 1955.
ROSSBACH, GERHARD. *Mein Weg durch die Zeit.* Weilburg/Lahn, 1950.

SCHMIDT-PAULI, EDGAR VON. *Geschichte der Freikorps 1918–1924.* Stuttgart, 1936.
SCHÜDDEKOPF, OTTO-ERNST. *Das Heer und die Republik.* Hanover, 1955.
SCHULZ, GERHARD. *Revolutionen und Friedensschlüsse.* Munich, 1967.
TROELTSCH, ERNST. *Spektator-Briefe. Aufsätze über die deutsche Revolution und die Weltpolitik 1918–1922.* Tübingen, 1924.
VAGTS, ALFRED. *A History of Militarism.* Rev. ed. New York: The Free Press, 1967.
WAITE, ROBERT G. L. *Vanguard of Nazism. The Free Corps Movement in Postwar Germany 1918–1923.* Cambridge, Mass.: Harvard University Press, 1952.

THE BEGINNINGS OF THE NSDAP

BRONDER, DIETRICH. *Bevor Hitler kam.* Hanover, 1964.
CASSELS, ALAN. "Mussolini and German Nationalism 1922–1925," in *Journal of Modern History,* XXXV (1963).
DEUERLEIN, ERNST. "Hitlers Eintritt in die Politik und die Reichswehr," in *VfZG,* No. 7 (1959).
DORST, TANKRED. *Die Münchener Räterepublik.* Frankfurt/M., 1966.
DREXLER, ANTON. *Mein politisches Erwachen.* Munich, 1919; rev. ed., 1937.
FEDER, GOTTFRIED. *Das Manifest zur Brechung der Zinsknechtschaft des Geldes.* Munich, 1919.
———. *Das Programm der NSDAP und seine weltanschaulichen Grundgedanken.* Munich, 1931.
FRANZ-WILLING, GEORG. *Die Hitlerbewegung.* Hamburg-Berlin, 1962.
FREKSA, FRIEDRICH, ed. *Kapitän Ehrhardt, Abenteuer und Schicksale.* Berlin, 1924.
HALLGARTEN, GEORGE W. F. *Hitler, Reichswehr und Industrie. Zur Geschichte der Jahre 1918–1933.* Frankfurt/M., 1955.
HEIDEN, KONRAD. *Geschichte des Nationalsozialismus.* Berlin, 1932. Published in English as *A History of National Socialism.* London: Methuen, 1934; New York: Knopf, 1935.
HOEPKE, KLAUS-PETER. *Die deutsche Rechte und der italienische Faschismus.* Düsseldorf, 1968.
JOCHMANN, WERNER. *Nationalsozialismus und Revolution. Ursprung und Geschichte der NSDAP in Hamburg 1922–1933.* Frankfurt/M., 1963.
MASER, WERNER. *Die Frühgeschichte der NSDAP.* Frankfurt/M., 1965.
MITCHELL, ALLAN. *Revolution in Bavaria 1918–1919: The Eisner Regime and the Soviet Republic.* Princeton, N.J.: Princeton University Press, 1965.
PHELPS, REGINALD. "Before Hitler Came. Thule Society and Germanen Orden," in *Journal of Modern History,* XXXV (1963).
———. "Hitler and the DAP," in *American Historical Review,* LXVIII (1963).
RÖHM, ERNST. *Die Geschichte eines Hochverräters.* Munich, 1928; 5th ed., 1934.
SCHUBERT, GÜNTER. *Anfänge nationalsozialistischer Aussenpolitik.* Cologne, 1963.

THE RISE OF HITLER

BOEPPLE, ERNST. *Adolf Hitlers Reden.* Munich, 1925.
DEUERLEIN, ERNST. *Der Aufstieg der NSDAP in Augenzeugenberichten.* Düsseldorf, 1968.
FABRY, PHILIPP W. *Mutmassungen über Hitler, Urteile von Zeitgenossen.* Düsseldorf, 1969.
FELICE, RENZO DE. *Mussolini.* 2 vols. Turin, 1965–66.

JOCHMANN, WERNER. *Im Kampf um die Macht, Hitlers Rede vor dem Hamburger Nationalklub von 1919.* Frankfurt/M., 1960.
PESE, W. W. "Hitler und Italien 1920–1926," in *VfZG*, No. 3 (1955).
PHELPS, REGINALD H. "Hitler als Parteiredner im Jahre 1920," in *VfZG*, No. 11 (1963).
SALVATORELLI, L., and MIRA, G. *Storia d'Italia nel periodo fascista.* Turin, 1964.
THYSSEN, FRITZ. *I Paid Hitler.* New York: Farrar; London: Hodder, 1941.

AGITATION AND ORGANIZATION

BENNECKE, HEINRICH. *Hitler und die SA.* Munich, 1962.
KILLINGER, MANFRED. *Die SA in Wort und Bild.* Leipzig, 1933.
NYOMARKAY, JOSEPH. *Charisma and Factionalism in the Nazi Party.* Minneapolis: University of Minnesota Press, 1967.
ORLOW, DIETRICH. *A History of the Nazi Party Nineteen Nineteen to Nineteen Thirty-Three.* Pittsburgh: University of Pittsburgh Press, 1969.
TYRELL, ALBRECHT. *Führer befiehlt. Selbstzeugnisse aus der Kampfzeit der NSDAP.* Düsseldorf, 1969.
VOLZ, HANS. *Die Geschichte der SA von den Anfängen bis zur Gegenwart.* Berlin, 1934.

THE CRISIS OF BAVARIA AND THE REICH

BUCHRUCKER, ERNST. *Im Schatten Seeckts, Die Geschichte der Schwarzen Reichswehr.* Berlin, 1928.
FRAENKEL, ERNST. *Zur Soziologie der Klassenjustiz.* Berlin, 1927.
GESSLER, OTTO. *Reichswehrpolitik in der Weimarer Zeit.* Stuttgart, 1958.
GUMBEL, EMIL J. *Acht Jahre politische Justiz.* Berlin, 1927.
——. *Verräter verfallen der Feme.* Berlin, 1929.
——. *Verschwörer. Beiträge zur Geschichte und Soziologie der deutschen nationalistischen Geheimbünde seit 1918.* Vienna, 1924.
——.*Vier Jahre politischer Mord.* Berlin-Fichtenau, 1922.
——. *Vom Fememord zur Reichskanzlei.* Heidelberg, 1962.
HANOVER, H. and E. *Politische Justiz 1918–1933.* Frankfurt/M., 1966.
HERTZMAN, LEWIS. *DNVP. Right Wing Opposition in the Weimar Republic: 1918–1924.* Lincoln: University of Nebraska Press, 1963.
HOEGNER, WILHELM. *Die verratene Republik.* Munich, 1958.
KILLINGER, MANFRED. *Ernstes und Heiteres aus dem Putschleben.* Munich, 1927.
MEIER-WELCKER, HANS. *Seeckt.* Frankfurt/M., 1967.
RABENAU, FRIEDRICH VON. *Seeckt. Aus seinem Leben 1918–1936.* Leipzig, 1940.
SALOMON, ERNST VON. *Der Fragebogen.* Hamburg, 1951. Published in English as *The Answers of Ernst von Salomon to the 131 Questions in the Allied Military Government "Fragebogen."* London: Putnam, 1954.
——. *Die Geächteten.* Gütersloh, 1930.
SCHWEND, KARL. *Bayern zwischen Monarchie und Diktatur.* Munich, 1954.
SENDTNER, KURT. *Rupprecht von Wittelsbach Kronprinz von Bayern.* Munich, 1954.
SINZHEIMER, HUGO, and FRAENKEL, ERNST. *Die Justiz in der Weimarer Republik.* Neuwied, 1968.
WHEELER-BENNETT, JOHN W. *The Nemesis of Power: The German Army in Politics, 1918–1945.* New York: St. Martin's Press; London: Macmillan, 1953.

THE HITLER PUTSCH

Der Hitlerprozess vor dem Volksgerichtshof in München. Munich, 1924.
DEUERLEIN, ERNST. *Der Hitler-Putsch.* Stuttgart, 1962.

HOFMANN, HANNS HUBERT. *Der Hitlerputsch.* Munich, 1961.
VOGELSANG, THILO. "Die Reichswehr in Bayern und der Münchener Putsch 1923," in *VfZG*, No. 5 (1957).

III. THE NEW PARTY IN THE "ERA OF STRUGGLE"

FORCES AND TRENDS: 1924-28

DORPALEN, ANDREAS. *Hindenburg and the Weimar Republic.* Princeton, N.J.: Princeton University Press, 1964.
FISCHER, WOLFRAM. *Deutsche Wirtschaftspolitik von 1918 bis 1945.* Cologne-Opladen, 1968.
HAGMANN, MEINRAD. *Der Weg ins Verhängnis, Reichstagswahlergebnisse 1919 bis 1933, besonders aus Bayern.* Munich, 1946.
MILATZ, ALFRED. *Wähler und Wahlen in der Weimarer Republik.* Bonn, 1965.
SCHULZ, GERHARD. *Zwischen Demokratie und Diktatur.* Berlin, 1963.
WHEELER-BENNETT, JOHN W. *Wooden Titan: Hindenburg in Twenty Years of German History, 1914–1934.* New York: Morrow, 1936. Published in England as *Hindenburg: The Wooden Titan.* London: Macmillan, 1936.

MEIN KAMPF AND NEW BEGINNINGS

DORPALEN, ANDREAS. *The World of General Haushofer: Geopolitics in Action.* New York & Toronto: Farrar & Rinehardt, 1942.
HAMMER, HERMANN. "Die deutschen Ausgaben von Hitlers 'Mein Kampf,'" in *VfZG*, No. 4 (1956).
JÄCKEL, EBERHARD. *Hitlers Weltanschauung.* Tübingen, 1969.
KALLENBACH, H. *Mit Adolf Hitler auf Festung Landsberg.* Munich, 1933.
LANGE, KARL. *Hitlers unbeachtete Maximen. "Mein Kampf" und die Öffentlichkeit.* Stuttgart, 1968.
LURKER, O. *Hitler hinter Festungsmauern.* Berlin, 1933.
MASER, WERNER. *Hitlers "Mein Kampf."* Munich, 1966.

THE STRUCTURE OF THE NEW PARTY

BROSZAT, MARTIN. "Die Anfänge der Berliner NSDAP 1926/27," in *VfZG*, No. 8 (1960).
BURDEN, HAMILTON T. *The Nuremberg Party Rallies: 1923–39.* New York: Praeger; London: Pall Mall, 1967.
HEIBER, HELMUT, ed. *Das Tagebuch von Joseph Goebbels 1925/26.* Stuttgart, 1960. Published in English as *The Early Goebbels Diaries: 1925–1926.* London:Weidenfeld & Nicolson, 1962; New York: Praeger, 1963.
KÜHNL, REINHARD. *Die nationalsozialistische Linke 1925 bis 1930.* Meisenheim, 1966.
———. "Zur Programmatik der nationalsozialistischen Linken: Das Strasser-Programm von 1925/26," in *VfZG*, No. 14 (1966).
NOAKES, JEREMY. "Conflict and Development in the NSDAP 1924–1927," in *Journal of Contemporary History*, I (1966).
ORLOW, DIETRICH. "The Conversion of Myth into Power: The NSDAP 1925–1926," in *American Historical Review*, LXXII (1967).

IDEOLOGY AND PROPAGANDA

BRAMSTEDT, ERNEST K. *Goebbels and National Socialist Propnganda, 1925–1945.* East Lansing: Michigan State University Press, 1965
FEDER, GOTTFRIED. *Der deutsche Staat auf nationaler und sozialer Grundlage.* 5th ed. Munich, 1932.

GOEBBELS, JOSEPH. *Der Nazi-Sozi. Fragen und Antworten für den National-sozialisten.* Elberfeld, 1927.
GÜNTHER, HANS F. K. *Rassenkunde des deutschen Volkes.* Munich, 1922.
KLEMPERER, KLEMENS VON. *Germany's New Conservatism: Its History and Dilemma in the Twentieth Century.* Princeton, N.J.: Princeton University Press, 1957.
KROCKOW, CHRISTIAN GRAF. *Die Entscheidung. Eine Untersuchung über Ernst Jünger, Carl Schmitt, Martin Heidegger.* Stuttgart, 1958.
LAQUEUR, WALTER Z. *Young Germany.* New York: Basic Books, 1962.
MOHLER, ARMIN. *Die konservative Revolution in Deutschland 1918–1933.* Stuttgart, 1950.
NEUROHR, JEAN. *Der Mythos vom Dritten Reich.* Stuttgart, 1957.
NIECKISCH, ERNST. *Gewagtes Leben.* Cologne and Berlin, 1958.
PROSS, HARRY. *Jugend—Eros—Politik. Die Geschichte der deutschen Jugend-verbände.* Bern, 1964.
REUPKE, HANS. *Der Nationalsozialismus und die Wirtschaft.* Berlin, 1931.
REVENTLOW, ERNST GRAF. *Deutscher Sozialismus. Civitas Dei Germanica.* Weimar, 1930.
ROSENBERG, ALFRED. *Der Mythus des 20. Jahrhunderts.* Munich, 1930.
————. *Wesen, Grundsätze und Ziele der NSDAP.* Munich, 1930.
————.*Das Wesensgefüge des Nationalsozialismus.* Munich, 1932.
SALLER, KARL. *Die Rassenlehre des Nationalsozialismus in Wissenschaft und Propaganda.* Darmstadt, 1961.
SCHÜDDEKOPF, OTTO-ERNST. *Linke Leute von rechts.* Stuttgart, 1960.
SCHULTZE-NAUMBURG, PAUL. *Kunst und Rasse.* Munich, 1927.
SCHWARZ, HERMANN. *Nationalsozialistische Weltanschauung.* Berlin, 1933.
SCHWIERSKOTT, JOACHIM. *Arthur Moeller van den Bruck und der revolu-tionäre Nationalismus in der Weimarer Republik.* Göttingen, 1962.
SONTHEIMER, KURT. *Antidemokratisches Denken in der Weimarer Republik.* Munich, 1962.
SPANN, OTHMAR. *Der wahre Staat.* Leipzig, 1921.
————. *Hauptpunkte der universalistischen Staatsauffassung.* Berlin, 1930.

TOWARD A MIDDLE-CLASS MASS PARTY

CRONER, FRITZ. *Soziologie der Angestellten.* Cologne and Berlin, 1962.
FRIED, FERDINAND. *Das Ende des Kapitalismus.* Jena, 1931.
GEIGER, THEODOR. *Die soziale Schichtung des deutschen Volkes.* Stuttgart, 1932.
KREBS, ALBERT. *Tendenzen und Gestalten der NSDAP. Erinnerungen an die Frühzeit der Partei.* Stuttgart, 1959.
LEBOVICS, HERMAN. *Social Conservatism and the Middle Classes in Germany: 1914–1933.* Princeton, N.J.: Princeton University Press, 1969.
SCHUMPETER, JOSEPH A. *Aufsätze zur Soziologie.* Tübingen, 1953.

THE BREAKTHROUGH OF 1929

BLEUEL, H. P., and KLINNERT, E. *Deutsche Studenten auf dem Weg ins Dritte Reich.* Gütersloh, 1967.
BRANDENBURG, H. C. *Die Geschichte der HJ.* Cologne, 1968.
DARRÉ, R. WALTHER. *Das Bauerntum als Lebensquell der nordischen Rasse.* Munich, 1929.
————. *Erkenntnisse und Werden. Aufsätze aus der Zeit vor der Machter-greifung.* Goslar, 1940.
————. *Neuadel aus Blut und Boden.* Munich, 1930.
GIES, HORST. "NSDAP und landwirtschaftliche Organisationen in der End-phase der Weimarer Republik," in *VfZG*, No. 15 (1967).
HEBERLE, RUDOLF. *Landbevölkerung und Nationalsozialismus.* Stuttgart, 1963.

————. "Zur Soziologie der nationalsozialistischen Revolution," in *VfZG*, No. 13 (1965).

LEPSIUS, RAINER. *Extremer Nationalismus. Strukturbedingungen vor der nationalsozialistischen Machtergreifung.* Stuttgart, 1966.

NILSON, STEN A. "Wahlsoziologische Probleme des Nationalsozialismus," in *Zeitschrift für die gesamte Staatswissenschaft*, No. 110 (1954).

STOLTENBERG, GERHARD. *Politische Strömungen im schleswig-holsteinschen Landvolk.* Düsseldorf, 1962.

IV. THE ROAD TO POWER

DEMOCRACY IN CRISIS

BESSON, WALDEMAR. *Württemberg und die deutsche Staatskrise, 1928–1933.* Stuttgart, 1959.

BORN, KARL-ERICH. *Die deutsche Bankenkrise 1931. Finanzen und Politik.* Munich, 1967.

BRACHER, K. D. *Die Auflösung der Weimarer Republik.* 4th ed. Villingen, 1964.

BRAUN, OTTO. *Von Weimar zu Hitler.* Hamburg, 1949.

BRECHT, ARNOLD. *Prelude to Silence: The End of the German Republic.* London and New York: Oxford University Press, 1944.

CONZE, WERNER, and RAUPACH, HANS, eds. *Die Staats- und Wirtschaftskrise des Deutschen Reiches 1929/33.* Stuttgart, 1967.

Der Weg in die Diktatur 1918–1933. Munich, 1963. Published in English as *The Road to Dictatorship: Germany 1918–1933.* Ed. LAWRENCE WILSON. London: Wolff, 1963.

DEUTSCH, JULIUS, ed. *Der Faschismus in Europa.* Berlin and Vienna, 1929.

FLECHTHEIM, OSSIP K. *Die KPD in der Weimarer Republik.* Offenbach, 1948.

FRANÇOIS-PONCET, ANDRÉ. *The Fateful Years. Memoirs of a French Ambassador in Berlin.* London, 1948; New York: Harcourt, 1949.

GROTKOPP, WILHELM. *Die grosse Krise.* Düsseldorf, 1954.

GRZESINSKI, ALBERT. *Inside Germany.* New York: Dutton, 1939.

HELLER, HERMANN. *Europa und der Faschismus.* Berlin and Leipzig, 1931.

HEUSS, THEODOR. *Erinnerungen 1905–1933.* Tübingen, 1963.

JASPER, GOTTHARD, ed. *Von Weimar zu Hitler 1930–1933.* Cologne and Berlin, 1968.

KALTEFLEITER, WERNER. *Wirtschaft und Politik in Deutschland.* Cologne and Opladen, 1966.

KEIL, WILHELM. *Erlebnisse eines Sozialdemokraten.* Stuttgart, 1948.

KESSLER, HARRY GRAF. *Tagebücher 1918–1937.* Frankfurt/M., 1961.

KIRCHHEIMER, OTTO. *Weimar—und was dann?* Berlin, 1930.

LANDAUER, CARL, and HONNEGGER, HANS, eds. *Internationaler Faschismus.* Karlsruhe, 1928.

LEIBHOLZ, GERHARD. *Strukturprobleme der modernen Demokratie.* Karlsruhe, 1958.

LÜKE, ROLF E. *Von der Stabilisierung zur Krise.* Zurich, 1958.

MATTHIAS, ERICH, and MORSEY, RUDOLF, eds. *Das Ende der Parteien 1933.* Düsseldorf, 1960.

MEISSNER, OTTO. *Staatssekretär unter Ebert–Hindenburg–Hitler.* Hamburg, 1950.

MORSEY, R., ed. *Protokolle der Reichstagsfraktion und des Fraktionsvorstands der Deutschen Zentrumspartei 1926–1933.* Mainz, 1969.

MOSSE, WERNER E., ed. *Entscheidungsjahr 1932.* Tübingen, 1965.

NEUMANN, SIGMUND. *Die Parteien der Weimarer Republik.* Rev. ed. Stuttgart, 1965.

PAPEN, FRANZ VON. *Der Wahrheit eine Gasse.* Munich, 1952.

————. *Vom Scheitern einer Demokratie.* Mainz, 1968.

PETZINA, DIETER. "Hauptprobleme der deutschen Wirtschaftspolitik 1932/ 33," in *VfZG*, No. 15 (1967).

PIRKER, THEO. *Komintern und Faschismus 1920–1940*. Stuttgart, 1965.

POETZSCH-HEFFTER, FRITZ. "Vom Staatsleben unter der Weimarer Verfassung," Part III, in *Jahrbuch des öffentlichen Rechts der Gegenwart*, No. 21 (1934).

PÜNDER, HERMANN. *Politik in der Reichskanzlei. Aufzeichnungen aus den Jahren 1929–1932*. Stuttgart, 1961.

ROSSITER, CLINTON L. *Constitutional Dictatorship: Crisis Government in the Modern Democracies*. Princeton, N.J.: Princeton University Press, 1948.

SCHMITT, CARL. *Positionen und Begriffe im Kampf mit Weimar–Genf–Versailles 1929–1932*. Hamburg, 1940.

———.*Verfassungsrechtliche Aufsätze aus den Jahren 1924–1954*. Berlin, 1958.

SCHULTES, KARL. *Die Jurisprudenz zur Diktatur des Reichspräsidenten nach Art. 48 Abs. II der Weimarer Verfassung*. Bonn, 1934.

SCHULZ, GERHARD. "Die grosse Krise in der Zeitgeschichte," in *Neue politische Literatur*, No. 4 (1959).

SEVERING, CARL. *Mein Lebensweg*. 2 vols. Cologne, 1950.

Stahlhelm-Handbuch. 4th ed. Berlin, 1931.

STAMPFER, FRIEDRICH. *Die 14 Jahre der ersten Deutschen Republik*. Hamburg, 1953.

VOGELSANG, THILO. *Kurt von Schleicher*. Göttingen, 1965.

———. *Reichswehr, Staat und NSDAP*. Stuttgart, 1962.

NATIONAL SOCIALIST TACTICS BEFORE THE SEIZURE OF POWER

ALLEN, WILLIAM S. *The Nazi Seizure of Power: The Experience of a Single German Town 1930–1935*. Chicago: Quadrangle Books, 1965.

CALIC, EDOUARD. *Ohne Maske. Hitler—Breiting Geheimgespräche 1931*. Frankfurt/M., 1968.

DIETRICH, OTTO. *Mit Hitler in die Macht*. Munich, 1934.

———. *Zwölf Jahre mit Hitler*. Munich, 1955.

DOMARUS, MAX, ed. *Hitler, Reden und Proklamationen*. Würzburg, 1962.

DÜSTERBERG, THEODOR. *Der Stahlhelm und Hitler*. Wolfenbüttel and Hanover, 1949.

GOEBBELS, JOSEPH. *Der Angriff. Aufsätze aus der Kampfzeit*. Munich, 1935.

———. *Revolution der Deutschen*. Oldenburg, 1933.

———. *Signale der neuen Zeit*. Munich, 1934.

———. *Vom Kaiserhof zur Reichskanzlei*. Berlin, 1933. Published in English as *My Part in Germany's Fight*. London: Hurst & Blackett, 1935.

GÖRING, HERMANN. *Aufbau einer Nation*. Berlin, 1934. Published in English as *Germany Reborn*. London: Matthews & Marrot, 1934.

HAMMERSTEIN, KUNRAT VON. "Schleicher, Hammerstein und die Machtübernahme 1933," in *Frankfurter Hefte*, No. 11 (1956).

HEUSS, THEODOR. *Hitlers Weg*. Stuttgart, 1932; rev. ed.,1968.

HOFER, WALTHER. *Die Diktatur Hitlers bis zum Beginn des Zweiten Weltkrieges*. Konstanz, 1959.

KLEIN, FRITZ. "Zur Vorbereitung der faschistischen Diktatur durch die deutsche Grossbourgeoisie (1929–1932)," in *Zeitschrift für Geschichtswissenschaft*, No. 1 (1953).

LOHMANN, HEINZ. *SA räumt auf! Aus der Kampfzeit der Bewegung*. Hamburg, 1933.

MALAPARTE, CURZIO. *Coup d'Etat, the Technique of Revolution*. New York: Dutton, 1932.

MEISSNER, HANS O., and WILDE, HARRY. *Die Machtergreifung*. Stuttgart, 1953.

ROLOFF, ERNST-AUGUST. *Bürgertum und Nationalsozialismus*. Hanover, 1961.

Bibliography

STRASSER, GREGOR. *Kampf um Deutschland.* Munich, 1932.
STRASSER, OTTO. *Hitler und ich.* Konstanz, 1948.

REFLECTION: THE "LEGAL REVOLUTION"

DILLER, ALBERT. *Die Legalität der nationalsozialistischen Revolution.* Erlangen, 1935.
MAU, HERMANN, and KRAUSNICK, HELMUT. *Deutsche Geschichte der jüngsten Vergangenheit 1933 bis 1945.* Tübingen and Stuttgart, 1956.
RAUSCHNING, HERMANN. *Gespräche mit Hitler.* Zurich and Vienna, 1940. Published in the United States as *Voice of Destruction.* New York: Putnam, 1940. Published in England as *Hitler Speaks: A Series of Political Conversations with Hitler on His Real Aims.* London: Butterworth, 1939.
————. *Die Revolution des Nihilismus,* 1938. Published in English as *The Revolution of Nihilism.* London: Heinemann, 1939; New York: Garden City Publishing Co., 1940.
RÜHLE, GERD. *Das Dritte Reich.* Berlin, 1933–38.
RYSZKA, FRANTISZEK. *The State of Emergency* (in Polish). Warsaw, 1964.
STEINBRINK, KONRAD. *Die Revolution Adolf Hitlers.* Berlin, 1934.
WALZ, GUSTAV ADOLF. *Das Ende der Zwischenverfassung. Betrachtungen zur Entstehung des nationalsozialistischen Staates.* Stuttgart, 1933.

THE STEPS TO DICTATORSHIP

BECKER, JOSEF. "Zentrum und Ermächtigungsgesetz," in *VfZG,* No. 9 (1961).
BELOFF, MAX, ed. *On the Track of Tyranny.* London: Vallentine, Mitchell, 1960.
BRACHER, K. D., SAUER, W., and SCHULZ, G. *Die nationalsozialistische Machtergreifung.* 2d ed. Cologne-Opladen, 1962.
BUCHHEIM, HANS. *Das Dritte Reich.* Munich, 1958.
DIELS, RUDOLF. *Luzifer ante portas.* Stuttgart, 1950.
HOCHE, W., ed. *Die Gesetzgebung des Kabinetts Hitler.* Berlin, 1933.
HEIDEN, KONRAD. *Geburt des Dritten Reiches.* 2d ed. Zurich, 1934.
HEUSS, THEODOR. *Die Machtergreifung und das Ermächtgungsgesetz.* Ed. E. PIKART. Tübingen, 1967.
JUNKER, DETLEF. *Die deutsche Zentrumspartei und Hitler.* Stuttgart, 1960.
MORSEY, RUDOLF. "Hitlers Verhandlungen mit der Zentrumsführung am 31. Januar 1933," in *VfZG,* No. 9 (1961).
POETZSCH-HEFFTER, FRITZ. "Vom deutschen Staatsleben vom 30. Januar bis 31. Dezember 1933," in *Jahrbuch des öffentlichen Rechts der Gegenwart,* No. 22 (1935).
RÖHM, ERNST. "SA und deutsche Revolution," in *NS-Monatshefte,* No. 31 (1933).
SCHNEIDER, HANS. *Das Ermächtigungsgesetz vom 24. März 1933.* 2d ed. Bonn, 1961.
TIMPKE, HENNING, ed. *Dokumente zur Gleichschaltung des Landes Hamburg 1933.* Frankfurt/M., 1964.
TOBIAS, FRITZ. *Der Reichstagsbrand, Legende und Wirklichkeit.* Rastatt, 1962. Published in English as *The Reichstag Fire.* New York: Putnam, 1964.
WHEATON, ELIOT B. *Prelude to Calamity: The Nazi Revolution 1933–1935, with a Background Survey of the Weimar Era.* London: Victor Gollancz, 1968.

CONTROLLED SOCIETY AND ONE-PARTY STATE

ARETIN, K. O. VON. "Prälat Kaas, Franz von Papen und das Reichskonkordat von 1933," in *VfZG,* No. 14 (1966).
BÖCKENFÖRDE, E. W. "Der deutsche Katholizismus im Jahre 1933," in *Hochland,* No. 53/54 (1961–62).

BRACHER, K. D. *Nationalsozialistische Machtergreifung und Reichskonkordat.* Wiesbaden, 1956.

DEUERLEIN, ERNST. *Der deutsche Katholizismus 1933.* Osnabrück, 1963.

DUDERSTÄDT, HENNING. *Vom Reichsbanner zum Hakenkreuz.* Stuttgart, 1933.

EDINGER, LEWIS J. *German Exile Politics: The Social Democratic Executive Committee in the Nazi Era.* Berkeley: University of California Press, 1956.

————. "German Social Democracy and Hitler's National Revolution of 1933," in *World Politics*, No. 5 (1953).

FRANZ, LEOPOLD. *Die Gewerkschaften in der Demokratie und in der Diktatur.* Karlsbad, 1935.

FURTWÄNGLER, JOSEF. *ÖTV. Die Geschichte einer Gewerkschaft.* Stuttgart, 1955.

HEINRICHSBAUER, AUGUST. *Schwerindustrie und Politik.* Essen-Kettwig, 1948.

KLÖNNE, ARNO. *Hitlerjugend. Die Jugend und ihre Organisation im Dritten Reich.* Hanover, 1955.

OPITZ, GÜNTER. *Der christlich-soziale Volksdienst.* Düsseldorf, 1969.

REPGEN, KONRAD. *Hitlers Machtergreifung und der deutsche Katholizismus.* Saarbrücken, 1967.

SCHUMANN, HANS-GERD. *Nationalsozialismus und Gewerkschaftsbewegung.* Hanover, 1958.

STARCKE, GERHARD. *NSBO und Deutsche Arbeitsfront.* Berlin, 1934.

V. THE FORMATION OF THE THIRD REICH

STATE AND PARTY

BORCH, HERBERT VON. *Obrigkeit und Widerstand. Zur politischen Soziologie des Beamtentums.* Tübingen, 1954.

BROSZAT, MARTIN. *Der Staat Hitlers. Grundlegung und Entwicklung seiner inneren Verfassung.* Munich, 1969.

DIEHL-THIELE, PETER. *Partei und Staat im Dritten Reich.* Munich, 1969.

EBENSTEIN, WILLIAM. *The Nazi State.* New York and Toronto: Farrar & Rinehardt, 1934.

FIJALKOWSKI, JÜRGEN. *Die Wendung zum Führerstaat.* Cologne and Opladen, 1958.

FORSTHOFF, ERNST. *Der totale Staat.* Hamburg, 1933.

FRAENKEL, ERNST. *The Dual State.* London and New York: Oxford University Press, 1941.

GEHL, WALTHER. *Die Jahre I–IV des nationalsozialistischen Staates.* Breslau, 1937.

GERTH, HANS. "The Nazi Party: Its Leadership and Composition," in *American Journal of Sociology*, XIV (1940).

HAUS, WOLFGANG. "Staatskommissare und Selbstverwaltung 1930–1933," in *Der Städtetag*, No. 9 (1956).

HOHEFELD, JOHANNES, ed. *Dokumente der deutschen Politik und Geschichte.* Vols. 4 and 5. Berlin, 1954.

HÜTTENBERGER, PETER. *Die Gauleiter.* Stuttgart, 1970.

LINGG, ANTON. *Die Verwaltung der NSDAP.* 4th ed. Munich, 1941.

LOHMANN, KARL. *Hitlers Staatsauffassung.* Berlin, 1933.

LÜKEMANN, ULF. *Der Reichsschatzmeister der NSDAP. Ein Beitrag zur inneren Parteistruktur.* Berlin, 1963.

MEDICUS, FRANZ A. *Das Reichsministerium des Innern. Geschichte und Aufbau.* Berlin, 1940.

MEHRINGER, HELMUT. *Die NSDAP als politische Ausleseorganisation.* Munich, 1938.

MOMMSEN, HANS. *Beamtentum in Dritten Reich.* Stuttgart, 1966.

MORSTEIN MARX, FRITZ. *Government in the Third Reich.* 2d rev. ed. New York: McGraw-Hill, 1937.

NEESSE, GOTTFRIED. *Partei und Staat.* Hamburg, 1936.
NICOLAI, HELMUT. *Der Staat im nationalsozialistischen Weltbild.* Leipzig, 1933.
————. *Grundlagen der kommenden Verfassung.* Berlin, 1933.
Organisationsbuch der NSDAP. 2d ed. Munich, 1937.
PELLOUX, ROBERT. *Le parti national-socialiste et ces rapports avec l'état.* Paris, 1936.
PETERSON, EDWARD N. *The Limits of Hitler's Power.* Princeton, N.J.: Princeton University Press, 1969.
PFUNDTER, HANS, ed. *Dr. Wilhelm Frick und sein Ministerium.* Munich, 1937.
SCHÄFER, WOLFGANG. *NSDAP, Entwicklung und Struktur der Staatspartei des Dritten Reiches.* Hanover, 1956.
SCHMITT, CARL. "Ein Jahr nationalsozialistischer Verfassungsstaat," in *Deutsches Recht,* No. 4 (1934).
————. *Staat, Bewegung, Volk.* Hamburg, 1933.

ARMY AND SECOND REVOLUTION: THE SEIZURE OF POWER COMPLETED

BENNECKE, HEINRICH. *Die Reichswehr und der "Röhmputsch."* Munich, 1964.
CASTELLAN, GEORGES. *Le réarmement clandestin du Reich 1930–1935.* Paris, 1954.
FABER DU FAUR, MORIZ VON. *Macht und Ohnmacht. Erinnerungen eines alten Offiziers.* Stuttgart, 1953.
HEUSINGER, ADOLF. *Befehl im Widerstreit.* Tübingen and Stuttgart, 1950.
MAU, HERMANN. "Die 'zweite Revolution'—der 30. Juni 1934," in *VfZG,* No. 1 (1953).
"Promemoria eines bayerischen Richters zu den Junimorden," in *VfZG,* No. 5 (1957).
RAEDER, ERICH. *Mein Leben.* Tübingen, 1956.
SCHWEPPENBERG, LEO GEYR VON. *Gebrochenes Schwert.* Berlin, 1952.

WELTANSCHAUUNG AND IDEOLOGICAL *Gleichschaltung*

BENN, GOTTFRIED. *Der neue Staat und die Intellektuellen.* Stuttgart-Berlin, 1933.
BERNING, CORNELIA. *Vom "Abstammungsnachweis" zum "Zuchtwart." Vokabular des Nationalsozialismus.* Berlin, 1964.
BLUNCK, HANS FRIEDRICH. *Unwegsame Zeiten.* Mannheim, 1952.
BOVERI, MARGRET. *Wir lügen alle. Eine Hauptstadtzeitung unter Hitler.* Olten, 1965.
BRENNER, HILDEGARD. *Die Kunstpolitik des Nationalsozialismus.* Hamburg, 1963.
Deutsche Kultur im Neuen Reich. Wesen, Aufgabe und Ziel der Reichskulturkammer. Berlin, 1934.
DREWS, R., and KANTOROWICZ, A., eds. *Verboten und verbrant. Deutsche Literatur, 12 Jahre unterdrückt.* Berlin and Munich, 1947.
ERBT, WILHELM. *Weltgeschichte auf rassischer Grundlage.* Leipzig, 1934.
FAUL, ERWIN. "Hitlers Über-Machiavellismus," in *VfZG,* No. 2 (1954).
GAMM, HANS-JOCHEN. *Der braune Kult.* Hamburg, 1962.
————. *Führung und Verführung. Pädagogik des Nationalsozialismus.* Munich, 1964.
GEISSLER, ROLF. *Dekadenz und Heroismus. Zeitroman und nationalsozialistische Literaturkritik.* Stuttgart, 1964.
GRENSEMANN, HEINRICH. *Leitfaden für den Geschäftsbetrieb der Reichskulturkammer.* Berlin, 1937.
HADAMOVSKY, EUGEN. *Propaganda und nationale Macht.* Oldenburg, 1933.
HAGEMANN, WALTER. *Publizistik im Dritten Reich.* Hamburg, 1948.
HALE, ORON J. *Captive Press in the Third Reich.* Princeton, N.J.: Princeton University Press, 1964.

HÄRTLE, HEINRICH. *Nietzsche und der Nationalsozialismus.* Munich, 1942.
KLEMPERER, VICTOR. *LTI (lingua tertii imperii).* Berlin, 1949. Rev. ed., *Die unbewältigte Sprache.* Darmstadt, 1966.
LANGENBUCHER, HELLMUTH. *Nationalsozialistische Dichtung.* Berlin, 1935.
LOERKE, OSKAR. *Tagebücher 1903–1939.* Ed. H. KASACK. Heidelberg and Darmstadt, 1955.
MOSSE, GEORGE L., ed. *Nazi Culture: Intellectual, Cultural and Social Life in the Third Reich.* New York: Grosset & Dunlap, 1966.
MÜLLER, GEORG-WILHELM. *Das Reichsministerium für Volksaufklärung und Propaganda.* Berlin, 1940.
MÜLLER-BLATTAU, JOSEF. *Germanisches Erbe in deutscher Tonkunst.* Berlin, 1938.
MUSCHG, WALTER. *Die Zerstörung der deutschen Literatur.* Bern, 1956.
NADLER, JOSEF. *Nation, Staat, Dichtung.* Munich, 1934.
PETERSEN, JULIUS. *Die Sehnsucht nach dem Dritten Reich in deutscher Sage und Dichtung.* Stuttgart, 1934.
POHLE, HEINZ. *Der Rundfunk als Instrument der Politik. Zur Geschichte des deutschen Rundfunks von 1923–1938.* Hamburg, 1955.
POLIAKOV, LÉON, and WULF, JOSEF. *Das Dritte Reich und seine Denker.* Berlin, 1959.
Presse in Fesseln, Eine Schilderung des NS-Pressetrusts. Berlin, 1948.
RAVE, PAUL ORTWIN. *Kunstdiktatur im Dritten Reich.* Hamburg, 1949.
ROH, FRANZ. *"Entertete" Kunst. Kunstbarbarei im Dritten Reich.* Hanover, 1962.
ROSENBERG, ALFRED. *Gestaltung der Idee.* Munich, 1936.
SCHLEMMER, OSKAR. *Briefe und Tagebücher.* Munich, 1958.
SCHMEER, KARLHEINZ. *Die Regie des öffentlichen Lebens im Dritten Reich.* Munich, 1956.
SCHONAUER, FRANZ. *Deutsche Literatur im Dritten Reich.* Olten, 1961.
SCHRIEBER, KARL FRIEDRICH. *Das Recht der Reichskulturkammer.* Berlin, 1935.
SCHULTZ, WOLFGANG. *Grundgedanken nationalsozialistischer Kulturpolitik.* Munich, 1939.
SCHULTZE-NAUMBURG, PAUL. *Kunst aus Blut und Boden.* Leipzig, 1934.
———. *Rassegebundene Kunst.* Berlin, 1934.
SCHWARZ, E., and WEGNER, M., eds. *Verbannung. Aufzeichnungen deutscher Schriftsteller im Exil.* Hamburg, 1964.
SERAPHIM, HANS-GÜNTHER. *Das politische Tagebuch Alfred Rosenbergs aus den Jahren 1934/35 und 1939/40.* Göttingen, 1956.
STERNBERGER, D., STORZ, G., and SÜSKIND, W. E. *Aus dem Wörterbuch des Unmenschen.* Rev. ed. Munich, 1962.
STROTHMANN, DIETRICH. *Nationalsozialistische Literaturpolitik.* 2d ed. Bonn, 1963.
WALDMANN, GUIDO. *Rasse und Musik.* Berlin, 1939.
WULF, JOSEF. *Die bildenden Künste im Dritten Reich.* Gütersloh, 1963.
———. *Literatur und Dichtung im Dritten Reich.* Gütersloh, 1963.
———. *Musik im Dritten Reich.* Gütersloh, 1964.
———. *Presse und Funk im Dritten Reich.* Gütersloh, 1964.
———. *Theater und Film im Dritten Reich.* Gütersloh, 1964.
ZEMAN, Z. A. B. *Nazi-Propaganda.* London and New York: Oxford University Press, 1964.

THE NEW EDUCATION AND THE WORLD OF KNOWLEDGE

BÄUMLER, ALFRED. *Männerbund und Wissenschaft.* Berlin, 1934.
———. *Politik und Erziehung.* Berlin, 1937.

BANSE, EWALD. *Wehrwissenschaft, Einführung in eine neue national Wissenschaft.* Leipzig, 1933.
BERNETT, HAJO. *Nationalsozialistische Leibeserziehung.* Schorndorf, 1966.
BÖHM, MAX HILDEBERT. *Volkstheorie als politische Wissenschaft.* Jena, 1934.
Deutsches Geistesleben und Nationalsozialismus. Tübingen, 1965.
Die deutsche Universität im Dritten Reich. Munich, 1966.
EILERS, ROLF. *Nationalsozialistische Schulpolitik.* Cologne-Opladen, 1963.
FEICKERT, ANDREAS. *Studenten greifen an. Nationalsozialistische Hochschulreform.* Hamburg, 1934.
FERBER, CHRISTIAN VON. *Die Entwicklung des Lehrkörpers der deutschen Universitäten und Hochschulen 1864–1954.* Göttingen, 1956.
FRANK, WALTER. "Deutsche Wissenschaft und Judenfrage," in *Forschungen zur Judenfrage.* Hamburg, 1941.
FREYER, HANS. *Das politische Semester. Ein Vorschlag zur Universitätsreform.* Jena, 1933.
GIESE, GERHARDT. *Staat und Erziehung.* Hamburg, 1933.
GLUNGER, WILHEM. *Theorie der Politik. Grundlehren einer Wissenschaft von Volk und Staat.* Munich and Leipzig, 1939.
GUMBEL, E. J., ed. *Freie Wissenschaft.* Strasbourg, 1938.
HARTSHORNE, EDWARD Y. *The German Universities and National Socialism.* Cambridge, Mass.: Harvard University Press, 1937.
HAUPT, JOACHIM. *Neuordnung im Schulwesen und Hochschulwesen.* Berlin, 1933.
HEIBER, HELMUT. *Walter Frank und sein Reichsinstitut für Geschichte des Neuen Deutschland.* Stuttgart, 1966.
HILLER, FRIEDRICH, ed. *Deutsche Erziehung im neuen Staat.* Langensalza and Berlin, 1934.
Humanistische Bildung im nationalsozialistichen Staate. Leipzig and Berlin, 1933.
KAHLE, PAUL E. *Bonn University in Pre-Nazi and Nazi Times.* London, 1945.
KLAGGES, DIETRICH. *Geschichtsunterricht als nationalpolitische Erziehung.* Frankfurt/M., 1936.
Nationalsozialismus und die deutsche Universität. Berlin, 1966.
NAUMANN, HANS. *Wandlung and Erfüllung.* Stuttgart, 1934.
OLENHUSEN, ALBRECHT GÖTZ VON. "Die 'nichtarischen' Studenten an den deutschen Hochschulen," in *VfZG*, No. 14 (1966).
ORLOW, DIETRICH, "Die Adolf Hitler-Schulen," in *VfZG*, No. 13 (1965).
ROSENBERG, ALFRED. *Weltanschauung und Wissenschaft.* Munich, 1936.
SCHALLER, HERMANN. *Die Schule im Staate Adolf Hitlers.* Breslau, 1935.
SCHIRACH, BALDUR VON. *Die Pioniere des Dritten Reiches.* Essen, 1933.
————. *Revolution der Erziehung.* Munich, 1938.
SCHOLTZ, HARALD. "Die 'NS-Ordensburgen,' " in *VfZG*, No. 15 (1967).
SEIER, HELMUT. "Der Rektor als Führer," in *VfZG*, No. 12 (1964).
UEBERHORST, HORST. *Elite für die Diktatur. Die Nationalpolitischen Erziehungsanstalten 1933–1945.* Düsseldorf, 1969.
WALLOWITZ, WERNER. *Deutschland, nur Deutschland, nichts als Deutschland, Grundriss einer deutschen Staatsbürgerkunde.* Leipzig, 1933.
WERNER, KARL F. *Das NS-Geschichtsbild und die deutsche Geschichtwissenschaft,* Stuttgart, 1967.
ZIEROLD, KURT. *Forschungsförderung in drei Epochen.* Wiesbaden, 1968.

THE NATIONAL SOCIALIST ELITE

ACKERMANN, JOSEF. *Himmler als Ideologe.* Göttingen, 1970.
ANGRESS, WERNER T., and SMITH, BRADLEY F. "Diaries of Heinrich Himmler's Early Years," in *Journal of Modern History*, XXXI (1959).

BAYLE, FRANÇOIS. *Psychologie et éthique du nationalsocialism. Étude antropologique des dirigeants SS.* Paris, 1953.

Das deutsche Führerlexikon 1933–34. Berlin, 1934.

FEST, JOACHIM C. *Das Gesicht des Dritten Reiches.* Munich, 1963. Published in English as *The Face of the Third Reich: Portraits of the Nazi Leadership.* New York: Pantheon; London: Weidenfeld & Nicolson, 1970.

GILBERT, GUSTAVE MARK. *Nuremberg Diary.* New York: Farrar, Straus, 1947.

GÖRING, HERMANN. *Reden und Aufsätze.* Munich, 1941.

HEIBER, HELMUT. *Joseph Goebbels.* Berlin, 1962.

———, ed. *Reichsführer. Briefe an und von Himmler.* Stuttgart, 1968.

KEMPNER, ROBERT M. W. *Das Dritte Reich in Kreuzverhör.* Munich-Esslingen, 1969.

LASWELL, HAROLD D. "The Psychology of Hitlerism," in *Political Quarterly,* IV (1933).

LERNER, DANIEL. *The Nazi Elite.* Stanford, Calif.: Stanford University Press, 1951.

MANVELL, ROGER, and FRAENKEL, HEINRICH. *Göring.* New York: Simon & Schuster, 1962. Published in England as *Herman Göring.* London: Heinemann, 1962.

ROSENBERG, ALFRED. *Letzte Aufzeichnungen.* Göttingen, 1955.

SPEER, ALBERT. *Erinnerungen.* Berlin, 1969. Published in English as *Inside the Third Reich: Memoirs.* New York: Macmillan; London: Weidenfeld & Nicolson, 1970.

VIERHAUS, RUDOLF. "Faschistisches Führertum," in *Historische Zeitschrift,* No. 198 (1965).

WULF, JOSEF. *Martin Bormann, Hitlers Schatten.* Gütersloh, 1962.

ZAPF, WOLFGANG. *Wandlungen der deutschen Elite.* Munich, 1965.

VI. FOREIGN POLICY BETWEEN REVISION AND EXPANSION

TACTICS AND AIMS IN THE PERIOD OF TRANSITION

BLOCH, CHARLES. *Hitler und die europäischen Mächte 1933/34.* Frankfurt/M., 1965.

BRACHER, K. D. "Das Anfangsstadium der Hitlerschen Aussenpolitik," in *VfZG,* No. 5 (1957).

DICKMANN, FRITZ. "Machtwille und Ideologie in Hitlers aussenpolitischen Zielsetzungen vor 1933," in *Festschrift Max Braubach.* Münster, 1964.

Die Erhebung der österreichischen Nationalsozialisten im Juli 1934. Frankfurt/M., 1965.

Documents on British Foreign Policy 1919–1939. London: H. M. Stationery Office, 1947–.

Documents on German Foreign Policy 1918–1945. Washington, D.C.: U.S Department of State, 1950–.

GILBERT, FELIX. "Mitteleuropa—The Final State," in *Journal of Central European Affairs,* VII (1947).

GOLDINGER, WALTER, and WANDRUSZKA, ADAM, in *Geschichte der Republik Österreich.* Edited by H. BENEDIKT. Munich, 1954.

HILDEBRAND, KLAUS. *Vom Reich zum Weltreich, Hitler, NSDAP und die koloniale Frage 1919–1945.* Munich, 1969.

LASPER, KAROL. *The Pilsudski-Hitler Pact* (in Polish). Warsaw, 1962.

NADOLNY, RUDOLF. *Mein Beitrag.* Wiesbaden, 1955.

NICLAUSS, KARLHEINZ. *Die Sowjetunion und Hitlers Machtergreifung.* Bonn, 1966.

PRITTWITZ UND GAFFRON, FRIEDRICH VON. *Zwischen Petersburg und Washington. Ein Diplomatenleben.* Munich, 1952.

RENNER, KARL. *Österreich von der erster zur zweiten Republik.* Vienna, 1953.

ROBERTSON, ESMOND M. *Hitler's Pre-War Policy and Military Plans.* New York: Citadel, 1957; London: Longmans, 1963.
ROOS, HANS. *Polen und Europa.* Tübingen, 1957.
ROSENBERG, ALFRED. *Der Zukunftsweg der deutschen Aussenpolitik.* Munich, 1927.
ROSS, DIETER. *Hitler und Dollfuss. Die deutsche Österreichpolitik 1933–34.* Hamburg, 1966.
SCHMIDT, PAUL. *Statist auf diplomatischer Bühne 1923–1945.* Bonn, 1950.
SCHMOKEL, WOLF W. *Dream of Empire: German Colonialism 1919–1945.* New Haven, Conn.: Yale University Press, 1964.
STORITZ, EKKEHART. *Die West-Ostbewegung in der deutschen Geschichte. Ein Versuch zur Geopolitik Deutschlands.* Breslau, 1935.
TREVOR-ROPER, HUGH R. "Hitlers Kriegziele," in *VfZG,* No. 8 (1960).
WEINBERG, G., ed. *Hitlers zweites Buch.* Stuttgart, 1961.
WISKEMANN, ELIZABETH. *Europe of the Dictators 1919–1945.* New York: Harper & Row; London: Collins, 1966.

BREAKTHROUGH INTO INTERNATIONAL POLITICS

BRACHER, K. D. *Zusammenbruch des Versailler Systems und zweiter Weltkrieg.* Vol. IX of *Propyläen-Weltgeschichte.* Berlin, 1960.
BRAUBACH, MAX. *Der Einmarsch deutscher Truppen in die entmilitarisierte Zone am Rhein im März 1936.* Cologne-Opladen, 1956.
CRAIG, GORDON, and GILBERT, FELIX, eds. *The Diplomats: Nineteen Nineteen to Nineteen Thirty-Nine.* Princeton, N.J.: Princeton University Press, 1953.
Das Dritte Reich und Europa. Munich, 1957.
Germany in the Third Reich, as Seen by Anglo-Saxon Writers. Frankfurt/M., 1936.
GRANZOW, BRIGITTE. *A Mirror of Nazism: British Opinion and the Emergence of Hitler 1929–1933.* New York: International Publishers; London: Victor Gollancz, 1964.
HIRSCH, HELMUT. *Die Saar von Genf.* Bonn, 1954.
HOARE, SAMUEL. *Neun bewegte Jahre. Englands Weg nach München.* Düsseldorf, 1955.
MALANOWSKI, WOLFGANG. "Das deutsch-englische Flottenabkommen vom 15. Juli 1935 als Ausgangspunkt für Hitlers doktrinäre Bündnispolitik," in *Wehrwissenschaftliche Rundschau,* No. 5 (1955).
SCHWEPPENBURG, LEO GEYR VON. *Erinnerungen eines Militärattachés. London 1933–1937.* Stuttgart, 1949.
SOMMER, THEO. *Deutschland und Japan zwischen den Mächten 1935–1940. Vom Antikominternpakt zum Dreimächtepakt.* Tübingen, 1964.
THOMAS, HUGH. *The Spanish Civil War.* New York: Harper & Row; London: Eyre & Spottiswoode, 1961.
WATT, D. C. "The Anglo-German Naval Agreement of 1935," in *Journal of Modern History,* XXVIII (1956).

PREPARING THE EXPANSION

BROOK-SHEPHERD, GORDON. *Anschluss: The Rape of Austria.* New York: Lippincott; London: Macmillan, 1963.
BRÜGEL, J. W. *Tschechen und Deutsche 1918–1938.* Munich, 1967.
CELOVSKY, BORIS. *Das Münchener Abkommen 1938.* Stuttgart, 1958.
DIRKSEN, HERBERT VON. *Moskau, Tokio, London.* Stuttgart, 1949. Published in English as *Moscow, Tokyo, London: Twenty Years of German Foreign Policy.* Norman: University of Oklahoma, 1952; London: Hutchinson, 1961.
EICHSTÄDT, ULRICH. *Von Dollfuss zu Hitler.* Wiesbaden, 1955.
EUBANK, KEITH. *Munich.* Norman: University of Oklahoma Press, 1963.

FEILING, KEITH. *The Life of Néville Chamberlain.* London: Macmillan, 1946.
FOERTSCH, HERMANN. *Schuld und Verhängnis. Die Fritschkrise im Frühjahr 1938 als Wendepunkt in der Geschichte der nationalsozialistischen Zeit.* Stuttgart, 1951.
GEHL, JÜRGEN. *Austria, Germany and the Anschluss 1931–1938.* New York and London: Oxford University Press, 1963.
GILBERT, MARTIN, and GOTT, RICHARD. *The Appeasers.* Boston: Houghton Mifflin; London: Weidenfeld & Nicolson, 1963.
HOSSBACH, FRIEDRICH. *Zwischen Wehrmacht und Hitler 1934–1938.* Wolfenbüttel and Hanover, 1949.
KEREKES, LÁJOS. *Anschluss 1938. Austria and International Diplomacy 1933–1938* (in Hungarian). Budapest, 1963.
KOERNER, RALF R. *So haben sie es damals gemacht. Die Propagandavorbereitung zum Österreich-Anschluss durch das Hitlerregime 1933–1938.* Vienna, 1958.
LOEWENHEIM, FRANCIS. *Peace or Appeasement? Hitler, Chamberlain and the Munich Crisis.* Boston: Houghton Mifflin, 1965.
NOGUERÈS, HENRI. *Munich ou la drôle de paix.* Paris, 1963.
RÖNNEFAHRT, HELMUTH. *Die Sudetenkrise in der internationalen Politik.* Wiesbaden, 1961.
WAGNER, D., and TOMKOWITZ, G. *Ein Volk, ein Reich, ein Führer. Der Anschluss Österreichs 1938.* Munich, 1968.
WENDT, BERNDT-JÜRGEN. *Appeasement 1938.* Frankfurt/M., 1966.
WHEELER-BENNETT, JOHN W. *Munich: Prologue to Tragedy.* Rev. ed. New York: Viking Press, 1963. Published in England as *Munich.* London: Macmillan, 1963.
WISKEMANN, ELIZABETH. *The Rome-Berlin Axis: A Study of the Relations Between Hitler and Mussolini.* Rev. ed. New York: Hillary House; London: Collins, 1966.

THE ROAD TO WAR

BRAUBACH, MAX. *Hitlers Weg zur Verständigung mit Russland im Jahre 1939.* Cologne-Opladen, 1960.
BULLOCK, ALAN. *Hitler and the Origins of the Second World War.* London and New York: Oxford University Press, 1967.
BURCKHARDT, CARL JACOB. *Meine Danziger Mission 1937–39.* Munich, 1960.
DENNE, LUDWIG. *Das Danzig-Problem in der deutschen Aussenpolitik 1934–1939.* Bonn, 1959.
HENDERSON, NEVILE. *Failure of a Mission.* New York: Putnam; London: Hodder, 1940.
HILGER, GUSTAV. *Wir und der Kreml. Deutsch-sowjetische Beziehungen 1918–1941.*
HOFER, WALTHER. *Die Entfesselung des Zweiten Weltkrieges.* Rev. ed. Frankfurt/M., 1964.
JASPER, GOTTHARD. "Über die Ursachen des zweiten Weltkrieges," in *VfZG,* No. 10 (1962).
METZMACHER, HELMUT. "Deutsch-englische Ausgleichsbemühungen im Sommer 1939," in *VfZG,* No. 14 (1966).
Nazi-Soviet Relations 1939–1941. Washington, D.C.: U.S. Government Printing Office, 1948.
PERROUX, FRANÇOIS. *Des mythes Hitlériens à l'Europe Allemande.* 2d ed. Paris, 1940.
SNELL, JOHN L., ed. *The Outbreak of the Second World War—Design or Blunder?* Boston: D. C. Heath; London: Harrap, 1962.
Soviet Documents on Foreign Policy. Vol. III (1933–1945). London and New York: Oxford University Press, 1959.
STRAUCH, RUDI. *Sir Nevile Henderson.* Bonn, 1959.

TAYLOR, A. J. P. *The Origins of the Second World War*. London: Hamish Hamilton, 1961; New York: Atheneum, 1962.

TREUE, WILHELM. "Rede Hitlers vor der deutschen Presse (10. Nov. 1938)," in *VfZG*, No. 6 (1958).

THE STRUCTURE OF NATIONAL SOCIALIST FOREIGN POLICY

BIBER, DUSAN. *Nacizan in nemici v jugoslaviji 1933–1941*. Lujbljana, 1966.

BROSZAT, MARTIN. "Faschismus und Kollaboration in Ostmitteleuropa," in *VfZG*, No. 14 (1966).

EHRICH, EMIL. *Die Auslands-Organisation der NSDAP*. Berlin, 1937.

Das grenzdeutsche Schrifttum. Ein bibliographisches Verzeichnis. Berlin, 1933.

JACOBSEN, HANS-ADOLF. *Nationalsozialistische Aussenpolitik 1933–1938*. Frankfurt/M., 1968.

JONG, LOUIS DE. *Die deutsche fünfte Kolonne im Weltkrieg*. Stuttgart, 1959.

LACHMANN, GÜNTHER. *Der Nationalsozialismus in der Schweiz 1931–1945*. Berlin, 1962.

LEUSCHNER, JOACHIM. *Volk und Raum. Zum Stil der nationalsozialistischen Aussenpolitik*. Göttingen, 1958.

RIBBENTROP, JOACHIM VON. *Zwischen London und Moskau. Erinnerungen und letzte Aufzeichnungen*. Leoni, 1953.

RIMSCHA, HANS VON. "Zur Gleichschaltung der deutschen Volksgruppen durch das Dritte Reich," in *HZ*, No. 182 (1956).

SEABURY, PAUL. *Wilhelmstrasse: A Study of German Diplomats Under the Nazi Regime*. Berkeley: University of California Press, 1954.

STRAUSZ-HUPÉ, ROBERT. *Geopolitics: The Struggle for Space and Power*. New York: Putnam, 1942.

WEIZSÄCKER, ERNST VON. *Erinnerungen*. Munich, 1950. Published in the United States as *Memoirs*. New York: Regnery, 1951. Published in England as *The Memoirs of Ernst von Weizsaecker*. London: Victor Gollancz, 1951.

VII. DOMESTIC MOBILIZATION AND RESISTANCE

ECONOMY AND SOCIETY IN TRANSITION

BETTELHEIM, CHARLES. *L'économie allemande sous le nazisme*. Paris, 1946.

BEYER, JUSTUS. *Die Ständeideologien der Systemzeit und ihre Uberwindung*. Darmstadt, 1941.

BÜLOW, FRIEDRICH. *Der deutsche Ständestaat*. Leipzig, 1934.

DUBAIL, RENÉ. *Une experience d'économie dirigée: L'Allemagne national-socialiste*. Paris, 1962.

ERBE, RENÉ. *Die nationalsozialistische Wirtschaftspolitik 1933–1939 im Lichte der modernen Theorie*. Zürich, 1958.

ESENWEIN-ROTHE, INGEBORG. *Die Wirtschaftsverbände von 1933 bis 1945*. Berlin, 1965.

FEDER, GOTTFRIED. *Kampf gegen die Hochfinanz*. 6th ed. Munich, 1935.

FRAUENDORFER, MAX. *Der ständische Gedanke im Nationalsozialismus*. Munich, 1932.

FRIED, FERDINAND. *Die soziale Revolution*. Leipzig, 1942.

FROBENIUS, ELSE. *Die Frau im Dritten Reich*. Berlin, 1933.

GERSCHENKRON, ALEXANDER. *Bread and Democracy in Germany*. Berkeley: University of California, 1943. London: Cambridge University Press, 1944.

GUILLEBAUD, C. W. *The Social Policy of Nazi Germany*. London: Cambridge University Press, 1942.

GURLAND, A. R. L., KIRCHHEIMER, O., and NEUMANN, F. *The Fate of Small Business in Nazi Germany*. Washington, D.C.: U.S. Government Printing Office, 1943.

GUTH, KARL. *Die Reichsgruppe Industrie.* Berlin, 1941.

HASE, GÜNTHER. *Der Werdegang des Arbeitsdienstes.* Berlin and Leipzig, 1940.

HOLTZ, ACHIM. *Nationalsozialistische Arbeitspolitik.* Würzburg, 1938.

KLEIN, BURTON H. *Germany's Economic Preparations for War.* Cambridge, Mass.: Harvard University Press, 1959.

KROLL, GERHARD. *Von der Weltwirtschaftskrise zur Staatskonjunktur.* Berlin, 1958.

LEDERER, EMIL. *State of the Masses: The Threat of the Classless Society.* New York: W. W. Norton, 1940.

MASON, T. W. "Labour in the Third Reich 1933–1939," in *Past and Present,* XXXIII (April, 1966).

MEINCK, GERHARD. *Hitler und die deutsche Aufrüstung 1933–1937.* Wiesbaden, 1957.

MEYSTRE, F., ed. *Sozialismus, wie ihn der Führer sieht.* Munich, 1935.

MILWARD, ALAN S. *The German Economy at War.* London and New York: Oxford University Press, 1965.

MÜLLER, KARL VALENTIN. *Aufstieg des Arbeiters durch Rasse und Meisterschaft.* Munich, 1935.

MÜLLER, WILLY. *Das soziale Leben im neuen Deutschland unter besonderer Berücksichtigung der Deutschen Arbeitsfront.* Berlin, 1938.

Organisation der Deutschen Arbeitsfront und der NS-Gemeinschaft Kraft durch Freude. Berlin and Leipzig, 1934.

PETZINA, DIETER. *Autarkiepolitik im Dritten Reich. Der nationalsozialistische Vierjahresplan.* Stuttgart, 1968.

SCHACHT, HJALMAR. *76 Jahre meines Lebens.* Bad Wörishofen, 1953. Published in English as *Confessions of "the Old Wizard."* Boston: Houghton Mifflin, 1956.

SCHOENBAUM, DAVID. *Hitler's Social Revolution: Class and Status in Nazi Germany 1933–1939.* New York: Doubleday, 1966. London: Weidenfeld & Nicolson, 1967.

SCHWEITZER, ARTHUR. *Big Business in the Third Reich.* Bloomington: Indiana University Press, 1964. London: Eyre & Spottiswoode, 1964.

———. "Die wirtschaftliche Wiederaufrüstung Deutschlands von *1934–1936,*" in *Zs.f.d. ges. Staatswiss.,* No. 114 (1958).

———. "Organisierter Kapitalismus und Parteidiktatur 1933–1936," in *Schmollers Jahrbuch,* No. 79 (1959).

SOMBART, WERNER. *Deutscher Sozialismus.* Berlin, 1934.

SÖRGEL, WERNER. *Metallindustrie und Nationalsozialismus.* Frankfurt/M., 1965.

STOLPER, GUSTAV. *Deutsche Wirtschaft 1870–1940.* Stuttgart, 1950.

STUCKEN, RUDOLF. *Deutsche Geld- und Kreditpolitik 1914–1953.* 2d ed. Tübingen, 1953.

TREUE, WILHELM. "Hitlers Denkschrift zum Vierjahresplan 1936," in *VfZG,* No. 3 (1955).

UHLIG, HEINRICH. *Die Warenhäuser im Dritten Reich.* Cologne-Opladen, 1956.

LEADER PRINCIPLE AND STATE

DAHM, GEORG, and SCHAFFSTEIN, FRIEDRICH. *Methode und System des neuen Strafrechts.* Berlin, 1937.

Der Beamte im Geschehen der Zeit. Berlin, 1936.

"Die Rechtsentwicklung der Jahre 1933 bis 1935/36," in *Handwörterbuch der Rechtswissenschaft,* VIII. Berlin-Leipzig, 1937.

FRANK, HANS, ed. *Deutsches Verwaltungsrecht.* Munich, 1937.

FRANK, HANS, HIMMLER, HEINRICH, BEST, WERNER, and HÖHN, REINHARD. *Grundfragen der deutschen Polizei.* Hamburg, 1937.

HOPPE, WILLY. *Die Führerpersönlichkeit in der deutschen Geschichte.* Berlin, 1934.

HUBER, ERNST RUDOLF. *Verfassungsrecht des Grossdeutschen Reiches.* Hamburg, 1939.
KOELLREUTHER, OTTO. *Der deutsche Führerstaat.* Tübingen, 1934.
———. *Volk und Staat in der Weltanschauung des Nationalsozialismus.* Berlin, 1935.
LEISS, LUDWIG. *Grossdeutsches Abstammungsrecht.* Berlin, Leipzig, and Vienna, 1943.
NICOLAI, HELMUT. *Die rassengesetzliche Rechtslehre.* Munich, 1934.
SCHAFFSTEIN, FRIEDRICH. *Politische Strafrechtswissenschaft.* Hamburg, 1934.
SCHORN, HUBERT. *Der Richter im Dritten Reich.* Frankfurt/M., 1959.
STAFF, ILSE. *Justiz im Dritten Reich.* Frankfurt/M., 1964.
SUREN, F. K., and LOSCHELDER, W. *Die Deutsche Gemeindeordnung vom 30. Januar 1935.* 2 vols. Berlin, 1940.
WEINKAUFF, HERMANN, and WAGNER, ALBRECHT. *Die deutsche Justiz und der Nationalsozialismus.* Stuttgart, 1968.

TOTALITARIAN TERROR: THE RISE OF THE SS STATE

BEST, WERNER. *Die deutsche Polizei.* 2d ed. Darmstadt, 1941.
BUCHEIM, HANS. "Die SS in der Verfassung des Dritten Reiches," in *VfZG,* No. 3 (1955).
———. *SS und Polizei im NS-Staat.* Duisdorf and Bonn, 1964.
———, et al. *Anatomie des SS-Staates.* Olten and Freiburg, 1965. Published in English as *Anatomy of the SS State.* New York: Walker; London: Collins, 1968.
DELARUE, JACQUES. *Geschichte der Gestapo.* Düsseldorf, 1964.
GEIGENMÜLLER, OTTO. *Die politische Schutzhaft im nationalsozialistischen Deutschland.* Würzburg, 1937.
GEORG, ENNO. *Die wirtschaftlichen Unternehmungen der SS.* Stuttgart, 1963.
GÜTT, A., LINDEN, H., and MASSFELLER, F. *Blutschutz- und Ehegesundheitsgesetz.* Munich, 1936.
GÜTT, A., RUDIN, E., and RUTTKE, F. *Gesetz zur Verhütung erbkranken Nachwuchses vom 14. Juli 1933.* Munich, 1934.
HAENSCH, WALTER. *Der organisatorische Weg zur einheitlichen Reichspolizei seit 1933.* Berlin, 1939.
HÖHNE, HEINZ. *Der Orden unter dem Totenkopf.* Gütersloh, 1967.
KERSTEN, FELIX. *Totenkopf und Treue.* Hamburg, 1952.
KOGON, EUGEN. *Der SS-Staat und das System der deutschen Konzentrationslager.* Munich, 1946. Published in English as *The Theory and Practice of Hell: The German Concentration Camps and the System Behind Them.* New York: Farrar, Straus; London: Secker & Warburg, 1950.
LANGHOFF, WOLFGANG. *Die Moorsoldaten. 13 Monate Konzentrationslager.* Zurich, 1935.
NEUSÜSS-HUNKEL, ERMENHILD. *Die SS.* Hanover, 1956.
PAETEL, KARL O. "Geschichte und Soziologie der SS," in *VfZG,* No. 2 (1954).
SEGER, GERHARD. *Oranienburg. Erster authentischer Bericht eines aus dem Konzentrationslager Geflüchteten.* Karlsbad, 1934.

DISENFRANCHISEMENT AND PERSECUTION

BALL-KADURI, KURT J. *Das Leben der Juden in Deutschland im Jahre 1933.* Frankfurt/M., 1963.
BLAU, BRUNO. *Das Ausnahmerecht für die Juden in den europäischen Ländern, 1933–1945.* New York, 1952.
GENSCHEL, HELMUT. *Die Verdrängung der Juden aus der Wirtschaft im Dritten Reich.* Göttingen, 1966.
GRAML, HERMANN. *Der 9. November 1938, "Reichskristallnacht."* Bonn, 1953.
HEIBER, HELMUT. "Der Fall Grünspan," in *VfZG,* No. 5 (1957).
KOCHAN, LIONEL. *Pogrom 10 November 1938.* London: Deutsch, 1957.

LAMM, HANS. *Die innere und äussere Entwicklung des Judentums im Dritten Reich.* Erlangen, 1951.

LÖSENER, BERNHARD. "Das Reichsministerium des Innern und die Judengesetzgebung," in *VfZG,* No. 9 (1961).

LÖSENER, BERNHARD, and KNOST, F. A. *Die Nürnberger Gesetze.* 3d ed. Berlin, 1939.

Persecution and Resistance Under the Nazis. 2d rev. ed. New York: Lounz; London: Wiener Library, 1960.

POLIAKOV, LÉON, and WULF, JOSEF. *Das Dritte Reich und die Juden.* Berlin, 1955.

ROSENSTOCK, WERNER. "Jewish Emigration from Germany," in *Publications of the Leo Baeck Institute,* Yearbook I. London, 1956.

SCHEFFLER, WOLFGANG. *Judenverfolgung im Dritten Reich.* Berlin, 1964.

SCHOENBERNER, GERHARD, ed. *Wir haben es gesehen. Augenzeugenberichte über Terror und Judenverfolgung im Dritten Reich.* Hamburg, 1962.

SIMON, ERNST. *Aufbau im Untergang. Jüdische Erwachsenenbildung im nationalsozialistischen Deutschland als geistiger Widerstand.* Tübingen, 1959.

STUCKART, WILHELM, and GLOBKE, HANS. *Reichsbürgergesetz, Blutschutzgesetz und Ehegesundheitsgesetz.* Munich-Berlin, 1936.

PROBLEMS OF OPPOSITION AND THE LEFT

ABSHAGEN, KARL HEINZ. *Canaris, Patriot und Weltbürger.* Stuttgart, 1954. Published in English as *Canaris.* London: Hutchinson, 1956.

Der deutsche Widerstand gegen Hitler. Four historico-critical studies by H. GRAML, H. MOMMSEN, H. J. REICHHARDT, and E. WOLF. Cologne, 1966.

DONOHOE, JAMES. *Hitler's Conservative Opponents in Bavaria 1930–1945: A Consideration of Catholic, Monarchist, and Separatist Anti-Nazi Activities.* Leiden: Brill, 1961.

EHLERS, DIETER. *Technik und Moral einer Verschwörung.* Frankfurt/M., 1964.

ESTERS, HELMUT, and PELGER, HANS. *Gewerkschafter im Widerstand.* Hanover, 1967.

GROSSMAN, KURT R. *Die unbesungenen Helden.* Berlin, 1957.

KLEPPER, JOCHEN. *Unter dem Schatten Deiner Flügel.* Edited by H. KLEPPER. Stuttgart, 1956.

KLÖNNE, ARNO. *Gegen den Strom. Bericht über den Jugendwiderstand im Dritten Reich.* Hanover, 1957.

KLOTZBACH, KURT. *Gegen den Nationalsozialismus. Widerstand und Verfolgung in Dortmund 1930–1945.* Hanover, 1969.

KOPP, OTTO, ed. *Widerstand und Erneuerung.* Stuttgart, 1966.

LEBER, ANNEDORE, BRANDT, WILLY, and BRACHER, K. D. *Das Gewissen entscheidet.* Berlin and Frankfurt/M., 1957.

———. *Das Gewissen steht auf.* Berlin and Frankfurt/M.,1954.Published in English as *Conscience in Revolt: Sixty-four Stories of Resistance in Germany 1933–45.* Westport, Conn.: Associated Booksellers; London: Vallentine, Mitchell, 1957.

LEBER, JULIUS. *Ein Mann geht seinen Weg.* Berlin, 1952.

LEIBHOLZ, GERHARD. *Politics and Law.* Leiden: Humanitas, 1965.

LINK, WERNER. *Die Geschichte des Internationalen Jugendbundes (IJB) und des Internationalen Sozialistischen Kampfbundes (ISK).* Meisenheim, 1964.

MATTHIAS, ERICH. *Sozialdemokratie und Nation.* Stuttgart, 1952.

———, and LINK, W. *Mit dem Gesicht nach Deutschland. Eine Dokumentation über die sozialdemokratische Emigration.* Düsseldorf, 1968.

MILLER, MAX. *Eugen Bolz, Staatsmann und Bekenner.* Stuttgart, 1951.

PECHEL, RUDOLF. *Deutscher Widerstand.* Erlenbach and Zurich, 1947.

PRITTIE, TERENCE. *Germans Against Hitler.* Boston: Little, Brown, 1964.

RITTER, GERHARD. *Carl Goerdeler und die deutsche Widerstandsbewegung.* Stuttgart, 1954. Published in English as *The German Resistance: Carl Goerdeler's Struggle Against Tyranny.* New York: Praeger; London: Allen & Unwin, 1958.

ROTHFELS, HANS. *Die deutsche Opposition gegen Hitler.* Rev. ed. Frankfurt/ M., 1958. Published in English as *German Opposition to Hitler.* Chicago: Regnery, 1962; London: Wolff, 1963.

SCHLÖSSER, MANFRED, ed. *An den Wind geschrieben. Lyrik der Freiheit 1933–1945.* Darmstadt, 1961.

VOLLMER, BERNHARD. *Volksopposition im Polizeistaat.* Stuttgart, 1957.

WEISENBORN, GÜNTHER. *Der lautlose Aufstand.* Hamburg, 1953.

WEISSBECKER, MANFRED. *Gegen Faschismus und Kriegsgefahr. Ein Beitrag zur Geschichte der KPD in Thüringer 1933–1935.* Erfurt, 1967.

WINZER, OTTO. *Zwölf Jahre Kampf gegen Faschismus und Krieg. Ein Beitrag zur Geschichte der KPD 1933 bis 1945.* 2d ed. Berlin, 1955.

Zur Geschichte der deutschen antifaschistischen Widerstandsbewegung 1933–1945. Berlin, 1957.

CHURCHES AND RESISTANCE

ACKERMANN, KONRAD. *Der Widerstand der Monatsschrift Hochland gegen den Nationalsozialismus.* Munich, 1965.

BARTH, KARL. *Theologische Existenz heute.* Munich, 1933.

BECKMANN, J., ed. *Kirchliches Jahrbuch für die evangelische Kirche in Deutschland 1933–1944.* Gütersloh, 1948.

BETHGE, EBERHARD. *Dietrich Bonhoeffer.* Munich, 1967. Published in English as *Dietrich Bonhoeffer: A Man for Others.* New York: Harper; London: Collins, 1970.

BIELFELDT, JOHANN. *Der Kirchenkampf in Schleswig-Holstein 1933–45.* Göttingen, 1964.

BINDER, GERHART. *Irrtum und Widerstand.* Munich, 1968.

BONHOEFFER, DIETRICH. *Gesammelte Schriften.* 4 vols. Ed. EBERHARD BETHGE. Munich, 1959.

BUCHHEIM, HANS. *Glaubenskrise im Dritten Reich.* Stuttgart, 1953.

Die zweite Bekenntnissynode der Deutschen Evangelischen Kirche zu Dahlem. Göttingen, 1958.

DIPPER, THEODOR. *Die evangelische Bekenntnisgemeinschaft in Württemberg.* Göttingen, 1966.

FAULHABER, MICHAEL. *Judentum, Christentum, Germanentum.* Munich, 1934.

GAUGER, JOACHIM. *Chronik der Kirchenwirren.* Elberfeld, 1934.

GÖTTE, KARL-HEINZ. *Die Propaganda der Glaubensbewegung "Deutsche Christen."* Munich, 1957.

GRÜBER, HEINRICH. *Erinnerungen aus sieben Jahrzehnten.* Cologne and Berlin, 1968.

GURIAN, WALDEMAR. *Der Kampf um die Kirche im Dritten Reich.* Lucerne, 1936.

GÜRTLER, PAUL, *Nationalsozialismus und evangelische Kirche im Warthegau.* Göttingen, 1958.

HARDER, G., and NIEMÖLLER, W. *Die Stunde der Versuchung. Gemeinden im Kirchenkampf 1933 bis 1945.* Munich, 1963.

HAUGG, WERNER. *Das Reichsministerium für die kirchlichen Angelegenheiten.* Berlin, 1940.

HERMELINK, HEINRICH. *Kirche im Kampf.* Stuttgart, 1950.

HIRSCH, EMANUEL. *Das kirchliche Wollen der Deutschen Christen.* Berlin, 1933.

KEMPNER, BENEDICTA M. *Priester vor Hitlers Tribunalen.* Munich, 1966.

KLÜGEL, EBERHARD. *Die lutherische Landeskirche Hannovers und ihr Bischof 1935–1945.* Berlin, 1964.

KUPISCH, KARL. *Zwischen Idealismus und Massendemokratie. Eine Geschichte der evangelischen Kirche in Deutschland von 1815–1945.* Berlin, 1955.

LEWY, GUENTER. *The Catholic Church and Nazi Germany.* New York: Mc-Graw-Hill; London: Weidenfeld & Nicolson, 1964.

LORTZ, JOSEPH. *Katholischer Zugang zum Nationalsozialismus, kirchengeschichtlich gesehen.* Münster, 1933.

LUCKEN, WILHELM. *Kampf, Behauptung und Gestalt der Evangelischen Landeskirche Nassau-Hessen.* Göttingen, 1963.

MÜLLER, ALFRED. *Die neugermanischen Religionsbildungen der Gegenwart.* Bonn, 1934.

MÜLLER, HANS. *Katholische Kirche und Nationalsozialismus.* Munich, 1963.

NIEMÖLLER, WILHELM. *Die Evangelische Kirche im Dritten Reich. Handbuch des Kirchenkampfs.* Bielefeld, 1956.

————, ed. *Texte zur Geschichte des Pfarrernotbundes.* Berlin, 1958.

PORTMANN, HEINRICH. *Kardinal von Galen.* Münster, 1950.

Prophetien wider das Dritte Reich. Munich, 1946.

REIMERS, KARL FRIEDRICH. *Lübeck im Kirchenkampf des Dritten Reiches.* Göttingen, 1965.

RITTER, EMIL. *Der Weg des politischen Katholizismus in Deutschland.* Breslau, 1934.

ROSENBERG, ALFRED. *Weltanschauung und Glaubenslehre.* Halle/S., 1939.

SCHMAUS, MICHAEL. *Begegnungen zwischen katholischem Christentum und nationalsozialisticher Weltanschauung.* Regensburg, 1933.

SCHMIDT, KURT DIETRICH. *Die Bekenntnisse und grundsätzlichen Äusserungen zur Kirchenfrage 1933–1935.* 3 vols. Göttingen, 1934–36.

SCHOLDER, KLAUS. "Die evangelische Kirche in der Sicht der nationalsozialistischen Führung bis zum Kriegsausbruch," in *VfZG*, No. 16 (1968).

STASIEWSKI, BERNHARD. "Die Kirchenpolitik der Nationalsozialisten im Warthegau 1939–1945," in *VfZG*, No. 7 (1959).

TÄSCHNER, FRANZ. *Der Totalitätsanspruch des Nationalsozialismus und der deutsche Katholizismus.* Münster, 1934.

VOLK, LUDWIG. *Der bayerische Episkopat und der Nationalsozialismus 1930–1934.* Mainz, 1965.

WURM, THEOPHIL. *Erinnerungen aus meinem Leben.* Stuttgart, 1953.

ZIPFEL, FRIEDRICH. *Kirchenkampf in Deutschland 1933–1945.* Berlin, 1965.

BETWEEN CIVILIAN AND MILITARY OPPOSITION

BECK, LUDWIG. *Studien.* Stuttgart, 1955.

BETHGE, EBERHARD. "Adam von Trott und der deutsche Widerstand," in *VfZG*, No. 11 (1963).

BRAUBACH, MAX. *Der Weg zum 20. Juli 1944.* Cologne-Opladen, 1953.

FOERSTER, WOLFGANG. *Generaloberst Ludwig Beck.* Munich, 1953.

GISEVIUS, HANS BERND. *Bis zum bitteren Ende.* Tübingen, 1947. Published in English as *To the Bitter End.* Boston: Houghton Mifflin, 1947.

KORDT, ERICH. *Nicht aus den Akten. Die Wilhelmstrasse in Frieden und Krieg.* Stuttgart, 1950.

KRAUSNICK, HELMUT. "Vorgeschichte und Beginn des militärischen Widerstandes gegen Hitler," in *Vollmacht des Gewissens*, I. 3d ed. Munich, 1960.

SCHEURIG, BODO. *Ewald von Kleist-Schmenzin.* Oldenburg, 1968.

VIII. THE WARTIME REGIME

WAR AND WAR AIMS

BOECKE, WILLY, ed. *Deutschlands Rüstung im zweiten Weltkrieg.* Frankfurt/M., 1969.

————. *Kriegspropaganda 1939–1941.* Stuttgart, 1966.

DEAKIN, FREDERICK WILLIAM. *The Brutal Friendship: Mussolini, Hitler, and the Fall of Italian Fascism.* London: Weidenfeld & Nicolson, 1961; New York: Harper & Row, 1963.

ERFURTH, WALDEMAR. *Die Geschichte des deutschen Generalstabs von 1918–1945.* Göttingen, 1957.

FRIEDLÄNDER, SAUL. *Hitler et les États-Unis, 1939–1941.* Geneva, 1963. Published in English as *Prelude to Downfall: Hitler and the United States, 1939–1941.* New York: Knopf, 1967.

GRUCHMANN, LOTHAR. *Der Zweite Weltkrieg.* Munich, 1967.

GUDERIAN, HEINZ. *Erinnerungen eines Soldaten.* Heidelberg, 1951.

HALDER, FRANZ. *Hitler als Feldherr.* Munich, 1949.

———. *Kriegstagebuch 1939–42.* 3 vols. Ed. H. A. JACOBSEN. Stuttgart, 1962–64.

HEIBER, HELMUT, ed., *Hitlers Lagebesprechungen.* Stuttgart, 1962.

HILLGRUBER, ANDREAS. *Hitlers Strategie, Politik und Kriegsführung 1940–1941.* Frankfurt/M., 1965.

———. *Staatsmänner und Diplomaten bei Hitler.* Frankfurt/M., 1967.

HUBATSCH, WALTER, ed. *Hitlers Weisungen für die Kriegführung.* Frankfurt/M., 1962.

JACOBSEN, HANS-ADOLF. *Der Zweite Weltkrieg.* Frankfurt/M., 1965.

KESSELRING, ALBERT. *Soldat bis zum letzten Tag.* Bonn, 1953.

KLUKE, PAUL. "Nationalsozialistische Europaideologie," in *VfZG*, No. 5 (1957).

MEINCK, GERHARD. "Der Reichsverteidigungsrat," in *Wehrwissenschaftliche Rundschau*, No. 6 (1956).

MICHAELIS, HERBERT. *Der Zweite Weltkrieg.* Konstanz, 1965.

RUGE, FRIEDRICH. *Der Seekrieg 1939–1945.* Stuttgart, 1954.

SCHRAMM, P. E., et al. *Kriegstagebuch des OKW.* 4 vols. Frankfurt/M., 1963–64.

SNELL, JOHN LESLIE. *Illusion and Necessity: The Diplomacy of Global War, 1939–1945.* Boston: Houghton Mifflin, 1963.

WEINBERG, GERHARD L. *Germany and the Soviet Union, 1939 to 1941.* New York: Lounz, 1954.

WRIGHT, GORDON. *The Ordeal of Total War: 1939–1945.* New York and London: Harper & Row, 1968.

THE SYSTEM OF DOMINATION AND EXTERMINATION

BÖBERACH, HEINZ. *Meldungen aus dem Reich. Auswahl aus den geheimen Lageberichten des Sicherheitsdienstes der SS 1939–1944.* Neuwied, 1965.

BÖHME, HERMANN. *Der deutsch-französische Waffenstillstand im Zweiten Weltkrieg.* Stuttgart, 1966.

BROSZAT, MARTIN. *Nationalsozialistische Polenpolitik 1939–1945.* Frankfurt/M., 1965.

———. *Zweihundert Jahre deutsche Polenpolitik.* Munich, 1963.

DALLIN, ALEXANDER. *German Rule in Russia, 1941–1945: A Study of Occupation Policies.* New York: St. Martin's Press; London: Macmillan, 1957.

DESSOUKI, M. K. *Hitler und der Nahe Osten.* Berlin, 1963.

DÖRING, HANS-JOACHIM. *Die Zigeuner im NS-Staat.* Hamburg, 1964.

DÖRNER, KLAUS. "Nationalsozialismus und Lebensvernichtung," in *VfZG*, No. 15 (1967).

EHRHARDT, HELMUT. *Euthanasie und Vernichtung "lebensunwerten" Lebens.* Stuttgart, 1965.

FRANK, HANS. *Im Angesicht des Galgens.* Munich, 1953.

GOEBBELS, JOSEPH. *Tagebücher aus den Jahren 1942–43.* Ed. LOUIS P. LOCHNER. Zurich, 1948. Published in English as *The Goebbels Diaries, 1942–43.* Garden City, N.Y.: Doubleday, 1948.

GRUCHMANN, LOTHAR. *Nationalsozialistische Grossraumordnung.* Stuttgart, 1962.

HORY, LADISLAUS, and BROSZAT. MARTIN. *Der kroatische Ustaschastaat 1941–1945.* Stuttgart, 1965.

JÄCKEL, EBERHARD. *Frankreich in Hitlers Europe.* Stuttgart, 1966.

KOEHL, ROBERT L. *RKFDV: German Resettlement and Population Policy 1939–1945.* Cambridge, Mass.: Harvard University Press, 1957.

KRÁL, VÁCLAV. *The Germans in Czechoslovakia 1933–1947* (in Czech). Prague, 1964.

KRANNHALS, HANNS VON. *Der Warschauer Aufstand 1944.* Frankfurt/M., 1962.

KRAUSNICK, HELMUT. "Hitler und die Morde in Polen," in *VfZG*, No. 11 1962.

KWIET, KONRAD. *Reichskommissariat Niederlande.* Stuttgart, 1968.

LOOK, HANS-DIETRICH. "Zur grossgermanischen Politik des Dritten Reiches," in *VfZG*, No. 8 (1960).

MITSCHERLICH, A., and MIELKE, F. *Medizin ohne Menschlichkeit.* Frankfurt/M., 1961.

PICKER, HENRY. *Hitlers Tischgespräche im Führerhauptquartier 1941–1942.* Bonn, 1951. Rev. ed. by P. E. SCHRAMM. Stuttgart, 1963.

SCHMIDT, GERHARD. *Selektion in der Heilanstalt 1939–1945.* Stuttgart, 1965.

STADLER, KARL. *Österreich 1938–1945 im Spiegel der NS-Akten.* Munich, 1966.

STEIN, G. H., and KROSBY, H. P. "Das finnische Freiwillingenbataillon der Waffen-SS," in *VfZG*, No. 14 (1966).

TILLMAN, HEINZ. *Deutschlands Araberpolitik im Zweiten Weltkrieg.* Berlin, 1965.

WACHENHEIM, HEDWIG. "Hitler's Transfers of Population in Eastern Europe," in *Foreign Affairs* (July, 1942).

WARMBRUNN, WERNER. *The Dutch Under German Occupation 1940–1945.* Stanford, Calif.: Stanford University Press, 1963.

WIEDER, JOACHIM. *Stalingrad und die Verantwortung des Soldaten.* Munich, 1962.

THE MURDER OF THE JEWS

ADLER, H. G. *Die verheimlichte Wahrheit.* Tübingen, 1958.
———. *Theresienstadt 1941–1945.* Tübingen, 1955.

AMÉRY, JEAN. *Jenseits von Schuld und Sühne.* Munich, 1966.

ARENDT, HANNAH. *Eichmann in Jerusalem: A Report on the Banality of Evil.* New York: Viking; London: Faber & Faber, 1963.

BALL-KADURI, KURT J. "Berlin Is 'Purged' of Jews," in *Yad Vashem Studies*, No. 5 (1963).

BISCHOFF, FRIEDRICH. *Das Lager Bergen-Belsen.* Hanover, 1966.

Blackbook of Localities Whose Jewish Population Was Exterminated by the Nazis. Jerusalem, 1965.

BLUMENTHAL, NACHMAN, and KERMISH, JOSEPH. *Resistance and Revolt in the Warsaw Ghetto.* Jerusalem, 1965.

FALCONI, CARLO. *The Silence of Pius Twelfth.* Boston: Little, Brown, 1970.

FRIEDLÄNDER, SAUL. *Kurt Gerstein oder die Zwiespältigkeit des Guten.* Gütersloh, 1969. Published in English as *Kurt Gerstein: The Ambiguity of Good.* New York: Knopf, 1969.

———. *Pius XII. und das Dritte Reich.* Hamburg, 1965. Published in English as *Pius Twelfth and the Third Reich.* New York: Knopf; London: Chatto & Windus, 1966.

HILBERG, RAOUL. *The Destruction of the European Jews.* Chicago: Quadrangle, 1961; London: W. H. Allen, 1961.

HOCHHUTH, ROLF. *Der Stellvertreter.* Hamburg, 1963. Published in the

United States as *The Deputy*. New York: Grove Press, 1963. Published in England as *The Representative*. London: Methuen, 1963.
HÖSS, RUDOLF. *Kommandant in Auschwitz*. Ed. M. BROSZAT. Published in English as *Commandant of Auschwitz*. London, 1959. New York: World, 1960.
KOLB, EBERHARD. *Bergen-Belsen. Die Geschichte des "Aufenthaltslagers" 1943–1945*. Hanover, 1962.
MARK, BERNARD. *Der Aufstand im Warschauer Ghetto*. Berlin, 1959.
MOLHO, MICHAEL, and NEHANNA, JOSEPH. *The Destruction of Greek Jewry 1941–1944*. Jerusalem, 1965.
NAUMANN, BERND. *Auschwitz*. Frankfurt/M., 1965. Published in English under the same title. New York: Praeger; London: Pall Mall, 1966.
POLIAKOV, LÉON. *Auschwitz*. Paris, 1964.
PRESSER, J. *Ondergang. De verfolging en verdelging van het Nederlandse Jodendom 1940 bis 1945*. The Hague, 1965.
REITLINGER, GERALD. *The Final Solution*. Rev. ed. New York: Barnes, 1961.
SCHNABEL, REIMUND. *Die Frommen in der Hölle. Geistliche in Dachau*. Frankfurt/M., 1965.
SAUER, PAUL. *Dokumente über die Verfolgung der jüdischen Bürger in Baden-Württemberg*. 2 vols. Stuttgart, 1966.
STEINER, JEAN-FRANÇOIS. *Treblinka*. New York: Simon & Schuster; London: Weidenfeld & Nicolson, 1967.
WUCHER, ALBERT. *Eichmanns gab es viele*. Munich and Zurich, 1961.

RESISTANCE PLANS DURING THE WAR

BAUER, FRITZ. "Oster und das Widerstandsrecht," in *Politische Studien*, No. 15/154 (1964).
BAUM, WALTER. "Marine, Nationalsozialismus und Widerstand," in *VfZG*, No. 11 (1963).
BONHOEFFER, DIETRICH. *Widerstand und Ergebung*. Munich, 1951.
DELP, ALFRED. *Im Angesicht des Todes*. Frankfurt/M., 1947.
———. *Kämpfer, Beter, Zeuge*. Berlin, 1954.
DELZELL, CHARLES F. *Mussolini's Enemies: The Italian Anti-Fascist Resistance*. Princeton, N.J.: Princeton University Press, 1961.
DEUTSCH, HAROLD C. *The Conspiracy Against Hitler in the Twilight War*. Minneapolis: University of Minnesota Press, 1968.
European Resistance Movements 1939–1945. 2 vols. Oxford: Pergamon, 1960–64.
GRAML, HERMANN. "Der Fall Oster," in *VfZG*, No. 14 (1966).
HASSELL, ULRICH VON. *Vom anderen Deutschland*. Rev. ed. Frankfurt/M., 1964.
KOSTHORST, ERICH. *Die deutsche Opposition gegen Hitler zwischen Polen- und Frankreichfeldzug*. Bonn, 1957.
KREBS, ALBERT. *Fritz-Dietlof Graf von der Schulenburg. Zwischen Staatsräson und Hochverrat*. Hamburg, 1964.
PETRY, CHRISTIAN. *Studenten aufs Schafott. Die Weisse Rose und ihr Scheitern*. Munich, 1968.
ROMOSER, GEORGE K. "The Politics of Uncertainty. The German Resistance Movement," in *Social Research*, XXXI (1964).
ROON, GER VAN. *Neuordnung im Widerstand. Der Kreisauer Kreis innerhalb der deutschen Widerstandsbewegung*. Munich, 1967.
SCHEURIG, BODO. *Freies Deutschland. Das Nationalkomitee und der Bund deutscher Offiziere in der Sowjetunion 1943–1945*. Munich, 1960.
SCHOLL, INGE. *Die weisse Rose*. Frankfurt/M., 1961.
Strafdivision 999. Erlebnisse und Berichte aus dem antifaschistichen Widerstandskampf. Berlin, 1966.
Vollmacht des Gewissens. 2 vols. Frankfurt, 1960–65.

THE ROAD TO THE 20TH OF JULY

BAUMONT, MAURICE. *La grande conjuration contre Hitler.* Paris, 1963.
FINKER, KURT. *Stauffenberg und der 20. Juli 1944.* Berlin, 1967.
FRAENKEL, H. and MANVELL, R. *Der 20. Juli.* Berlin, 1964.
HAMMERSTEIN, KUNRAT VON. *Flucht. Aufzeichnungen nach dem 20. Juli.* Olten, 1966.
HOFFMANN, PETER. "Zu dem Attentat im Führerhauptquartier 'Wolfsschanze' am 20. Juli 1944," in *VfZG,* No. 12 (1964).
———. *Widerstand, Staatsstreich, Attentat.* Munich, 1969.
JEDLICKA, LUDWIG. *Der 20. Juli in Österreich.* Vienna, 1965.
Justiz und NS-Verbrechen. Compiled by A. RÜTER-EHLERMANN and C. F. RÜTER. Vol. I. Amsterdam, 1968.
KRAMARZ, JOACHIM. *Claus Graf Stauffenberg.* Frankfurt/M., 1965.
"L'opposition Allemande à Hitler", in *Revue d'histoire de la deuxième guerre mondiale,* No. 36 (1959).
MAIER, HEDWIG. "Die SS und der 20. Juli 1944," in *VfZG,* No. 14 (1966).
MELNIKOW, DANIIL. *20. Juli 1944.* Berlin, 1964.
SCHEURIG, BODO. *Klaus Graf Schenk von Stauffenberg.* Berlin, 1964.
SCHLABRENDORFF, FABIAN VON. *Offiziere gegen Hitler.* Rev. ed. Frankfurt/M., 1966.
SCHRAMM, WILHELM VON. *Aufstand der Generale. Der 20. Juli in Paris.* Rev. ed. Munich, 1966.
TRAVAGLINI, THOMAS. *Der 20. Juli 1944. Technik und Wirkung seiner propagandistischen Behandlung nach den amtlichen SD-Berichten.* Karlsruhe, 1963.
ZELLER, EBERHARD. "Claus und Berthold Stauffenberg," in *VfZG,* No. 12 (1964).
———. *Geist der Freiheit. Der 20. Juli.* Rev. ed. Munich, 1963.
ZIMMERMAN, E., and JACOBSEN, H. A., eds. *20. Juli 1944.* Bonn, 1961.

IX. BREAKDOWN AND CONTINUITY OF NATIONAL SOCIALISM

AT THE END OF THE HITLER REGIME

BESYMENSKI, LEW A. *Der Tod des Adolf Hitler.* Hamburg, 1968.
BRACHER, K. D., ed. *Nach 25 Jahren. Eine Deutschland-Bilanz.* Munich, 1970.
DÖNITZ, KARL. *Zehn Jahre und zwanzig Tage.* Bonn, 1958.
DOLLINGER, HANS, ed. *Die letzten 100 Tage.* Munich, 1965.
HANSEN, REIMAR. *Das Ende des Dritten Reiches.* Stuttgart, 1966.
IRVING, DAVID. *The German Atomic Bomb.* New York: Simon & Schuster, 1968.
KÜHNL, REINHARD. *Deutschland zwischen Demokratie und Faschismus.* Munich, 1969.
KUBY, ERICH. *Die Russen in Berlin 1945.* Munich, 1964. Published in English as *The Russians and Berlin: 1945.* New York: Hill & Wang, 1968.
LÜDDE-NEURATH, WALTER. *Regierung Dönitz.* Rev. ed. Göttingen, 1964.
PETWAIDIC, WALTER. *Die autoritäre Anarchie. Streiflichter des deutschen Zusammenbruchs.* Hamburg, 1946.
STEINERT, MARLIS. *Die 23 Tage der Regierung Dönitz.* Düsseldorf, 1967.
TOLAND, JOHN. *The Last Hundred Days.* New York: Random House, 1966; London: Barker, 1966.
TREVOR-ROPER, H. R. *The Last Days of Hitler.* 3d ed. New York: St. Martin's; London: Macmillan, 1966.

RIGHT-WING EXTREMISM IN THE SECOND DEMOCRACY

BELL, DANIEL, ed. *The Radical Right.* New York: Doubleday, 1963.

BOTT, HERMANN. *Die Volksfeind-Ideologie. Zur Kritik rechtsradikaler Propaganda.* Stuttgart, 1969.

BRACHER, K. D. "Democracy and Right Wing Extremism in West Germany," in *Current History,* May, 1968.

BRÜDIGAM, HEINZ. *Der Schoss ist fruchtbar noch* . . . 2d ed. Frankfurt/M., 1965.

BÜSCH, OTTO, and FURTH, PETER. *Rechtsradikalismus im Nachkriegsdeutschland.* Berlin, 1957.

JENKE, MANFRED. *Verschwörung von rechts?* Berlin, 1961.

KALOW, GERT. *Hitler—Das gesamtdeutsche Trauma.* Munich, 1967.

KNÜTTER, HANS-HELMUTH. *Ideologien des Rechtsradikalismus im Nachkriegsdeutschland.* Bonn, 1961.

KÜHNL, REINHARD. *Das Dritte Reich in der Presse der Bundesrepublik.* Frankfurt/M., 1966.

PROSS, HARRY. *Vor und nach Hitler. Zur deutschen Sozialpathologie.* Olten, 1962.

"Rechtsradikalismus in Deutschland," in *Die neue Gesellschaft,* No. 14 (July, 1967).

ROTH, GUENTHER, and WOLFF, KURT H. *The American Denazification of Germany.* Columbus, Ohio, 1954.

SCHEUCH, ERWIN K., and KLINGEMANN, HANS D. "Materialien zum Phänomen des Rechtsradikalismus in der Bundesrepublik 1966." Unpublished manuscript. Cologne, 1967.

SCHÖNBACH, PETER. *Reaktionen auf die antisemitische Welle im Winter 1959/1960.* Frankfurt/M., 1961.

TAUBER, KURT P. *Beyond Eagle and Swastika: German Nationalism Since 1945.* 2 vols. Middletown, Conn.: Wesleyan University Press, 1967.

THE NPD—A NEW STARTING POINT?

BESSEL-LORCK, SIPPEL, and GÖTZ. *National oder radikal? Der Rechtsradikalismus in der BRD.* Mainz, 1966.

Bundeszentrale für politische Bildung, eds. *Rechtsradikalismus in der BR im Jahre 1967.* Bonn, 1968.

DUVE, FREIMUT. *Die Restauration entlässt ihre Kinder.* Reinbeck, 1968.

FETSCHER, IRING, GREBING, HELGA, et al. *Rechtsradikalismus.* Frankfurt/M., 1967.

JENKE, MANFRED. *Die nationale Rechte.* Berlin, 1967.

KÜHNL, REINHARD. "Der Rechtsextremismus in der BR," in *PVS,* No. 9 (1968).

———. *Die NPD.* Berlin, 1967.

LIEPELT, KLAUS. "Anhänger der neuen Rechtspartei," in *Politische Vierteljahresschrift,* No. 8 (1967).

MEIER, HANS, and BOTT, HERMANN. *Die NPD. Struktur und Ideologie einer "nationalen Rechtspartei."* Munich, 1968.

NIETHAMMER, LUTZ. *Angepasster Faschismus, politische Praxis der NPD.* Frankfurt/M., 1969.

OERTZEN, PETER VON. *Soziologische und psychologische Struktur der Wähler und Mitgliedschaft der NPD.* Hanover, 1967.

SCHMIDT, GISELHER. "Ideologie und Propaganda der NPD," in *Schriften der Bundeszentrale für Politische Bildung.* Bonn, 1968.

WINTER, FRANZ FLORIAN. *Ich glaubte an die NPD.* Mainz, 1968.

Index

Abetz, Otto, 406
Abwehr (Intelligence), 397, 433, 439, 447, 452
Academy for German Law, 214
Action Committee for the Protection of German Labor, 216
Action Française, 12, 13
Adenauer, Konrad, 468, 469, 478, 499–500
Adler, H. G., 427
Adolf Hitler Foundation, 219, 321, 333
Adolf Hitler Schools, 263–64, 265
Agrarian movement and NSDAP, 153, 154, 214, 217, 335
Ahlwardt, Hermann, 40, 41
Air Force, (Luftwaffe), 279, 296, 307, 314, 323, 391, 400, 405, 413, 450, 458
All-German Party, *see* Gesamtdeutsche Partei
Alldeutscher Verband, 43
Allied Control Council, 465
Alsace-Lorraine, 263, 348, 360, 362, 406, 410–11, 419
Amann, Max, 93, 132, 181, 255, 277
Ammon, Otto, 14
Anrich, Ernst, 269, 481
Anti-Comintern Pact, 303, 304, 305, 307, 315, 326
Anti-Semitic People's Party, 41
Anti-Semitism, 10, 12, 13, 16, 22, 32, 34–45, 47, 50, 90, 100, 123, 133, 165, 250, 412, 424; historical German, 5, 20–21, 26, 28, 29, 30–31, 146; Hitler and, 61, 63–64, 83, 86, 99, 128, 247; and NSDAP, 55, 81, 85, 89, 98, 145, 147, 213, 252–53, 258–59, 267, 325, 331, 389, 494
Anti-Slavism, 22, 44, 90, 247, 408, 486

Anti-Socialist Law, 28, 37
Appeasement policy of West, 295, 296–97, 301, 302, 305, 316, 318, 401; and Munich Conference, 313
Arco-Valley, Anton, Count, 117
Arendt, Hannah, 426
Army (Reichswehr), 46, 71, 84, 90, 95, 96, 101, 103–4, 105, 106, 110–14 *passim*, 120, 121, 122, 167, 171, 173–74, 177, 184, 198, 201, 236–47, 249, 292, 309, 354, 408, 418, 430–31, 464; and Hitler, 86, 117, 119, 120, 133, 188, 189, 193, 206, 233, 236, 237, 240, 242–244, 245, 307, 315, 341, 343, 414, 457; and NSDAP takeover, 210, 224, 323; and opposition to Hitler, 371, 375, 391–99, 433, 434, 439, 445–56 *passim*
Arndt, Ernst Moritz, 25
Aron, Raymond, 497
Art and architecture, Nazi policy on, 259, 347
ASTA (student self-government organization), 165, 166
Ataturk, Kemal Pasha, 108, 114
August Wilhelm, Prince of Prussia, 136, 148
Aumeier, Hans, 420
Auschwitz concentration camp, vii, 281, 360, 419, 420, 428, 429, 430
Auslandsorganisation (AO), 322–23, 328, 348
Aussenpolitisches Amt (APA), 325
Austria, 26, 43–45, 55, 68, 80, 87, 136, 165, 263, 279, 348; annexation of, 224, 239, 244, 277, 288, 306, 309–10, 311, 321, 388, 393, 437; Hitler and, 21, 47, 57, 81, 94, 133, 293, 310; National Socialism in, 13, 22, 85, 167, 294, 309, 323, 345, 415; and

535